SINGAPORE: A BIOGRAPHY

'The publishers have outdone themselves with this well-written and eminently readable volume that should find a welcome home on shelves throughout Asia and, one hopes, globally as well ... Frost and Balasingamchow have, through a judicious selection of anecdote and primary sources, tied together with just the right amount of analysis and a judicious application of drama, teased out a narrative that both interests and flows.'

Asian Review of Books

'A tapestry of the sights and sounds and tastes and smells of what Singapore is and who the Singaporeans are ... Frost and Balasingamchow have given Singaporeans a wonderful gift. For non-Singaporeans, the book is also a 3D, Technicolor, Cinemascope account of a colonial outpost in the East and how life unfolded over the nearly 200 years since the British came.'

Chan Heng Wing, *Hong Kong Economic Journal*

'Respected historian Frost and Singaporean educator Balasingamchow show a deep understanding of the subject matter ... well written and engaging ... balanced and thorough ... Highly recommended!'

Sarah Maxim, *Choice: Current Reviews for Academic Libraries*

'A very readable, well crafted work of popular history ... should get wider attention well beyond our shores.'

Wang Gungwu, *University Professor, National University of Singapore and Emeritus Professor, Australian National University*

'Erudite, accessible ... the prose sparkles with varifocal narratives that flit engagingly from anecdotal minutiae of individual life stories to panoramic analyses of the country's most pivotal moments. A compelling read, and a much-needed reminder that Singapore's national memory needn't be singularly owned.'

Time Out (Singapore)

'Something of a Trojan Horse volume. It masquerades as little more than an interesting collection of stories, while shedding light on the deeper historical roots of modern Singapore.'

Ben Bland, *Global Asia*

'There are history books and there are history books. Some focus on dates and battles and the men who won and lost them. Others bring a time and a place to life. *Singapore: A Biography* is one such book ... Beautifully written ... this is a scholarly yet readable work.'

Expat Living (Singapore)

SINGAPORE
A BIOGRAPHY

Curatorial Text in feature sections
Iskander Mydin
Cheryl-Ann Low Mei Gek
Jason Toh
Wong Hong Suen

Editorial Management
Timothy Auger
Francis Dorai

Editor
Ibrahim Tahir

Design
Annie Teo
Norreha Sayuti

Production Manager
Sin Kam Cheong

First published in 2009 by
Editions Didier Millet Pte Ltd
121 Telok Ayer Street, #03-01
Singapore 068590
www.edmbooks.com

and

National Museum of Singapore
93 Stamford Road
Singapore 178897
www.nationalmuseum.sg

Reprinted 2011

For information and updates
visit
www.singaporebiography.com

ISBN: 978-981-4217-62-0

Printed in Singapore

Notes on Usage

For the sake of simplicity, *hanyu pinyin* words are reproduced without diacritical marks.

Copyright Abbreviations

AWM	Australian War Memorial
IWM	Imperial War Museum
KITLV	Royal Netherlands Institute of Southeast Asian and Caribbean Studies
NARA	National Archives and Records Administration, USA
NAS	National Archives of Singapore
NAUK	National Archives, UK
NIOD	Nederlands Instituut voor Oorlogsdocumentatie
NMS	National Museum of Singapore
SLV	State Library of Victoria
SPH	Singapore Press Holdings

Every effort has been made to trace copyright holders for images used. In the event of errors or omissions, appropriate credit will be made in future printings of this work.

SINGAPORE
A BIOGRAPHY

MARK R. FROST
YU-MEI BALASINGAMCHOW

edm EDITIONS DIDIER MILLET

N S M
National Museum
of Singapore

CONTENTS

SINGAPORE

Museum Lahore

FOREWORD

This biography is an outcome of the intellectually exciting four-year process of designing the Singapore History Gallery at the National Museum of Singapore. To animate the history of Singapore with layers of stories and multiple points of view, we created a virtual Companion for our visitors. We strap this multimedia guiding device onto visitors, and so free ourselves from the constraints of a conventional history gallery and from the need to squeeze all the richness of information about historical objects into short text panels.

The Companion was the work of curators, researchers, writers, designers, actors, voice talent and production crew. It would take us another three years of organising, writing and editing to produce this literary elaboration of the Companion, by two of the writers from the original team. *Singapore: A Biography* ensures that the History Gallery's multiple perspectives on the history of Singapore may live outside the atmosphere and designed circumstances of the History Gallery. I am grateful that Frost and Balasingamchow, both talented writers, were willing to tackle the voluminous materials accumulated and to create afresh a multifaceted experience within the linearity of a book. I am also thankful that Editions Didier Millet shares our vision and that it recognises the intellectual potentials which the Museum sees in the history of Singapore.

I hope that *Singapore: A Biography* will always be a great companion to many of us, particularly in our own journeys into the history of this island, city and nation-state. I also hope that it will be read and re-read many times, and each time when we do re-read it, we find poignant moments that connect us to the different facets of Singapore's history.

Lee Chor Lin
Director, National Museum of Singapore

PROLOGUE

An ancient stone and a new history

There was once a stone, and not just any old stone, but what later became known as the 'Singapore Stone'. It was ten feet high, smooth and square-shaped, it stood at the entrance to the Singapore River, and some people claimed that it had been formed by a lightning strike. It was also covered in an ancient, unintelligible script. As Singapore's most famous Malay chronicler recorded:

> Many learned men came and tried to read it. Some brought flour-paste which they pressed on the inscription and took a cast, others rubbed lamp-black on it to make the lettering visible. But for all that they exhausted their ingenuity in trying to find out what language the letters represented they reached no decision.

In 1843, the British blew this stone to pieces. As part of their public works programme they dynamited the area to widen the river mouth and make way for a new fort and living quarters for its commander. Various fragments of the stone were removed from Singapore (those parts that were not ground up into gravel for road works) and eventually one fragment was returned to the care of the Raffles Museum, now the National Museum of Singapore. Other fragments are believed to still lie buried somewhere in an archive in Calcutta, India, but an attempt around 1990 by a team of Singapore scholars to gain access to them came to nothing. Today, the lone surviving fragment is displayed in the National Museum, as the first artefact that visitors encounter when they enter the Singapore History Gallery.

OPPOSITE: A storyteller and his captive audience along the Singapore River.
1960
K.F. Wong/NAS 19990003433-0077

Can anything better represent the difficulties of writing a history of Singapore than the fate of its famous stone? Even for the most gifted multilingual scholar, Singapore's diversity of languages, dialects and written scripts is a challenge to unlock; urban development and other government initiatives have seen to the destruction of a vast amount of the island's physical heritage; and then there's the fact that a fundamental part of its history lies hidden (sometimes buried) overseas, thanks to centuries of trade, migration and colonial rule. We might say that the ghost of the Singapore Stone looms large over every effort to chronicle the island's past – a national monolith reluctant to disclose all its secrets.

Yet when visitors to the Singapore History Gallery at the National Museum of Singapore venture past the Singapore Stone they discover something new. The showpieces in this gallery are not merely the material artefacts by themselves, but rather the historical personalities that such objects – accompanied by liberal use of dramatic lighting, audio and film – attempt to recover. Here, history comes alive through a multiplicity of voices, experiences and memories. Together, these diverse individual parts form an epic drama that, in a country which has seen such remarkable transformation in the last few decades, maintains a line of continuity between the past and the present.

This book sprang from the Singapore History Gallery following its opening in late 2006 as part of the revamped National Museum of Singapore, and it shares its parent's sensibility. The authors are indebted to the Museum's Director, Lee Chor Lin, and to its curatorial staff – Iskander Mydin, Cheryl-Ann Low, Tamilselvi Muthu, Wong Hong Suen and Jason Toh – whose research, advice, patience and support have made this volume possible. We are also grateful to the scholars and other individuals who agreed to be interviewed for the Singapore History Gallery and whose contributions feature in this book, especially John Miksic, Timothy Barnard, Peter Borschberg, Karl Hack, Anthony Reid, Hadijah Rahmat, Geoff Wade, Derek Heng, Wang Gungwu, Tan Tai Yong, Mark Emmanuel, Chua Ai Lin,

Ann Wee, Subbiah Laksmanan, C. C. Chin, Lim Chin Joo, Lim Hock Siew, Tan Jing Quee and Albert Lau. However, the selection of evidence and the historical interpretations that follow are entirely our own – as are any errors (and we hope that there are few).

We have not intended that the multiple stories making up this history be taken as comprehensive or fully representative of Singapore's past. Several works place greater emphasis on economics, foreign relations and policy-making, and in these specific areas they provide greater depth. Instead, *Singapore: A Biography* plots a more personal journey through the continuities and transformations that have shaped this island and its people over several centuries – a course that we hope, for the expert and the newcomer alike, will be both intimate and engaging. Naturally, in writing such a history, some aspects of Singapore's past have been sacrificed so that others might take precedence. Nonetheless, the intention has been consistent throughout: to write history, as the historian Simon Schama once put it, with 'the play of imagination' and to 'bring a world to life, rather than entomb it in erudite discourse'.

Mark Ravinder Frost
Yu-Mei Balasingamchow

Singapore, February 2009

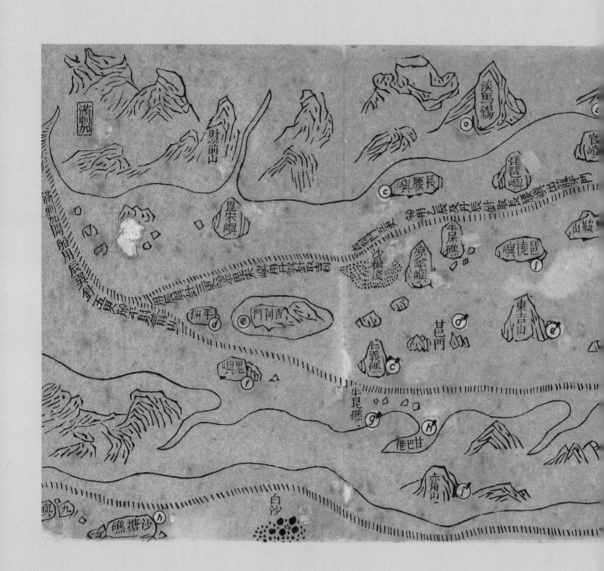

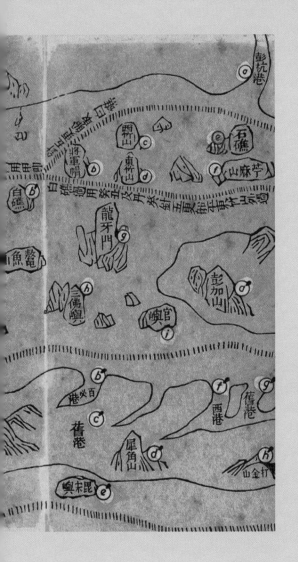

TEMASEK
1300s – 1600s

1. REMNANTS FROM THE FIRE

In the 17th century, sometime around the year 1611, early Singapore was set on fire and razed to the ground. To this day, it's still unclear who was responsible. Historians believe it might have been the Portuguese, or more likely the Acehnese from the northern tip of nearby Sumatra. Why exactly Singapore burned also remains a mystery, although these were turbulent times when wars between regional powers were common, often fought around the island's shores and on occasion across its territory. Perhaps Singapore had become a strategic target in some broader struggle or perhaps its inhabitants had become too much of an annoyance to their powerful neighbours. Or maybe the settlement was razed to the ground merely because that was then the preferred, if somewhat brutal, sport of warriors and conquerors. The major difficulty we face in recovering the island's early history is that very little was written down and what else remains appears broken up into fragments.

In one sense, therefore, the flames which engulfed early Singapore represent the end of a story and not its beginning. Yet they also suggest, rather strongly, that two centuries before the British arrived a settlement existed that was substantial enough for its enemies to bother setting on fire. Moreover, from the scattered historical records that survive, we know that such a settlement had a history dating back to the 14th century and possibly earlier. To place this in perspective, early Singapore (roughly dating from 1300 until around 1611) existed longer than modern Singapore has (founded in 1819) by over a century.

Naming Singapore: some early sources

Some of these historical records (which we'll turn to in more detail later) have to be taken with a pinch of salt. Often, they are not strictly historical in the modern understanding of that word. For example, a Chinese chronicle from the 8th century speaks of a Southeast Asian island-kingdom that stood at the extremity of a peninsula whose inhabitants possessed tails 'five or six inches long' and were 'accustomed to cannibalism'. The peninsula in question might have been the Malay Peninsula, and the island might have been Singapore, but whatever truth lies buried in this account it's difficult to read beyond the fanciful description to find it. Nonetheless, taken together these written sources provide a sketch of the island's early past, a sketch for which the historical detail is now being filled in by archaeological finds recovered from beneath the modern city's foundations.

The first reliable record of early Singapore comes from a 14th-century Chinese text where the island is referred to as Longyamen – 'Dragon Tooth Gate', most likely a reference to the rocky outcrop that once stuck out of the water opposite present-day Fort Siloso on Sentosa (a small island just off Singapore's southern coast). Yet the attention Longyamen initially received owed less to its distinctive

PREVIOUS PAGE:
The Mao Kun map was based on the early 15th-century voyages of Admiral Zheng He through Southeast Asia and across the Indian Ocean as far as the east coast of Africa. The map is included in the *Wubeizhi* (Treatise on Military Preparation), which was presented to the Ming court in 1628. Danmaxi (Temasek) is depicted at the top of the middle section and is labelled 'a', while Longyamen is labelled 'g'. This annotated map was reproduced from photographs of a copy of the *Wubeizhi* and was published by Dr C. A. Gibson-Hill, former Director of the Raffles Museum.
1956
Reproduction
30.5 x 191 cm
NMS XXXX-02140

Gold ornaments.
14th century
Gold
H 0.5 x Dia. 10 cm (armlet)
H 0.5 x Dia. 2 cm (each earring)
NMS A-1570

geology and more to the Chinese emperor's passion for elephants. To the Yuan dynasty that ruled China at this time, elephants were a powerful symbol of royalty and were used in battle to carry the emperor's command post. In 1320, the Yuan court sent a mission to Longyamen (as well as to Vietnam and Cambodia) with a request for such creatures, in return for which the Yuan envoys probably brought along some kind of diplomatic gift in the form of Chinese textiles or precious glass. The Yuan court chroniclers tell us that an embassy from Longyamen repaid the visit by travelling to China a few years later. We don't know if they brought the desired elephants as requested, but they would have certainly prepared a commensurate offering of tribute.

From the mid-14th century, written sources begin to refer not just to Longyamen but to the whole of the island as Temasek, a name that probably originates from old Javanese and simply means 'land surrounded by water'. When the Chinese traveller Wang Dayuan (whom we'll turn to shortly) visited Temasek in the early 1330s, Longyamen was already being used by Chinese junk captains as a navigational landmark. In the same decade, Vietnamese sources tell of the arrival of a Temasek mission to their own country and of a Vietnamese prince who could speak the language of the Temasek ambassadors.

Less amiable is the impression left by Javanese records, which make it clear that to Java's powerful Majapahit Empire (which lasted from the 13th to 16th centuries) Temasek was a place that ought to be conquered and brought to heel. The Majapahit court poem *Desawarnana*, which dates from 1365, appears to confirm that in the end the Javanese got what they wanted. Temasek is described as a vassal state of the Majapahit – a subject kingdom that now owed its southern master allegiance and tribute.

Temasek continues to appear in Chinese maps from the 15th century and in early records of the voyages of the eunuch Admiral Zheng He between 1403 and

The Headless Rider is a Javanese-style lead figurine of a rider on a winged-horse that was discovered at Empress Place, on the banks of Singapore River. It remains the only figurine of its kind discovered on the island.
c. 14th century
Lead
H 5.3 x W 6.2 cm
NMS 2002-00431

15

Chinese bronze coins from the
Parliament House Complex
excavation site.

FROM TOP:

Kai Yuan Tong Bao
Tang Dynasty (618–907 CE)
Dia. 2 cm
NMS

Kai Yuan Tong Bao
Tang Dynasty
Dia. 2 cm
NMS

Tai Ping Tong Bao
Northern Song Dynasty
(960–1127 CE)
Dia. 2 cm
NMS

Huang Song Tong Bao
Northern Song Dynasty
Dia. 2 cm
NMS

Zheng He Tong Bao
Northern Song Dynasty
Dia. 2 cm
NMS

1433. However, Malay chronicles state that at some point after 1300, Temasek underwent another name change, becoming the more grandiose Singapura, the 'Lion City' (from which the British ultimately derived 'Singapore'). The Majapahit from the south and the Siamese from the north were both expanding their dominions at the time, and either might have been responsible for imposing the island's new name. New conquerors have a habit of renaming the territories they have recently vanquished (and devastated), and it would be no surprise if either Siamese or Javanese invaders were in some way responsible for Temasek becoming the new kingdom of Singapura.

By 1400, and by whatever name we call it, early Singapore had drawn regional notice. Even though it was a tiny island, it had diplomatic ties with Vietnam, envious eyes had been cast over it by the Javanese (and probably by the Siamese as well) and it had come to the attention of the Yuan emperor of China – the lord of 'all under heaven' – as a likely place to procure elephants. Who, then, were the people who lived on this island, where did they come from and what did they do?

The river settlement and the 'Forbidden Hill'

The archaeological evidence recovered from sites around the Singapore River and at today's Fort Canning Hill suggests that modern inhabitants of Singapore share more in common with their early predecessors than they might at first assume. To start with, Temasek's early inhabitants appear to have been similarly preoccupied with defence. In the 14th century, the settlement was enclosed by a wall that protected its northern boundary; to the south it was bounded by the Singapore River, to the east by the sea and to the west by a river inlet. The northern wall ran from the present-day Padang, more or less down what is today's Stamford Road, to Fort Canning Hill where it then curved around the hill's northern side. This wall was still standing when the British arrived five centuries later. In 1823, John Crawfurd, the second British Resident of Singapore, described it as 'sixteen feet in breadth at its base, and at present about eight or nine in height'. He concluded that it had not been intended against 'an attack by sea' since 'the inhabitants considered themselves strong in their naval force' and therefore 'thought any other defences in that quarter superfluous'.

Like its present-day successor, 14th-century Singapore was also cosmopolitan. Shards of excavated pottery reveal that the local inhabitants shared a culture in common with people from the Riau-Lingga archipelago (modern-day Batam and Bintan) as well as everybody else in a broad arc which fanned out from Singapore northwards up the Straits of Melaka to Kedah, across to Aceh and along the southern tip of Sumatra, then across to West Java and even West Borneo. But there were other distinctive groups who lived on the island. One prominent group, as revealed by the numerous items they left behind, were Chinese merchants, who had traded in the region since the 11th century at least, bringing with them ceramics, textiles, foodstuffs and coins. In return, they sought out the produce of the Straits, such as sea cucumber and bird's nests, or unique to Temasek, hornbill crests and rare blackwood, which were both used to make precious ornaments.

Other pottery shards indicate the presence of the Javanese, themselves a trading power in the region, while a coin from Sri Lanka and beads and carnelian stones from India point to the arrival of Tamils and Sinhalese. Although the archaeological findings are not yet complete, there is evidence to suggest that Siamese and Vietnamese traders also came to Temasek, sojourned there and maybe even settled. Temasek would have been much like other ports in the region during this time – a vibrant emporium and a cultural melting pot.

Down by the Singapore River, it becomes clear just how commercialised the settlement was. Numerous Chinese coins unearthed from this vicinity indicate a prosperous, cash-based economy not solely dependent on barter and possessing some degree of economic specialisation. It seems that several of these coins were once melted down to make copper items and there is evidence of other manufacturing in the form of fish-hooks, wires, bells, and arrowheads or spearheads made from bronze and other metals. One of the most striking discoveries is a lead statuette of a headless rider and horse that dates from the 14th century. In design, this statuette is similar to Javanese pieces from the same century and hence indicates cultural contact, if not artistic exchange, between early Singapore and Java and Sumatra.

Map showing the major archaeological sites along the Singapore River and Fort Canning Hill. The length of the wall that Crawfurd described is also indicated.

Ceramic and earthenware shards.

FROM TOP:

Interior of an unglazed bowl from the Empress Place site
14th century
Blue & White Porcelain
NMS

Decorated shards from Fort Canning and along the Singapore River
14th century
Earthenware
NMS

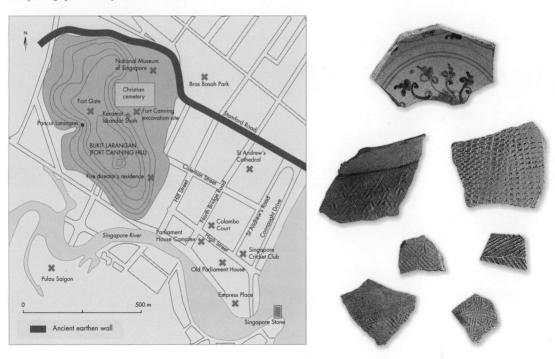

The most common items to have been recovered are shards from stoneware and earthenware jars, pots, dishes and bowls. Many of these pieces are Chinese in origin although some come from Thailand and Vietnam. Certain jars might have transported mercury, which was used to separate gold from its impurities and also as a medicine for royalty and nobility (a remedy which nobody at the time realised was likely to induce madness and eventual death). The plethora of Chinese ceramics indicates a community dependent on external trade, which, all things considered, is not especially surprising. As the British later discovered, the soil in Singapore was unsuitable for extensive agriculture and while some manufacturing of small metal and gold items may have occurred in the pre-colonial period, already the settlement's primary importance lay in what it could offer as an entrepôt.

A different story emerges up on Fort Canning Hill, where the archaeological evidence suggests not so much a bustling emporium as a peaceful retreat for the island's elite. The Chinese ceramics unearthed from this site are of a finer quality than those found by the river; the affluence of the hill-dwellers is also revealed by the discovery of numerous glass beads, decorated vessels and a prize collection of ornaments. These ornaments, discovered in 1928, consist of a pair of gold amulets each inscribed with the grinning head of a *kala* (a mythical lion-like beast), six gold rings, a pale gold ring incised with the figure of a goose, and two other jewelled pieces. Stylistically, they are strongly Javanese, the kind of items that might have been worn by 14th-century Majapahit royalty. The fact that fewer Chinese coins have been found on the hill suggests that its inhabitants depended more on tribute than on cash exchange. Whoever lived on Fort Canning was wealthy, and they stood in every respect above and apart from the riverside hoi polloi.

Indeed, it's very likely that Fort Canning Hill was the royal abode of Singapore's early kings. Across Southeast Asia, hills were traditionally associated with kings, gods and departed spirits. Hindu-Buddhist beliefs that arrived from India held that the holy mountain Mount Meru was the centre of the universe, ruled by the god Indra. Many Southeast Asian rulers borrowed heavily from such beliefs, styling themselves as Indra incarnate and setting up their palaces on hills that overlooked water. In this respect, one of the first Malay palaces in Palembang (on the island of Sumatra) directly mirrors the positioning of the Fort Canning site.

Fort Canning Hill bears few traces of any such settlement today. Even when the first British arrived, they discovered that the hill had been deserted for some time. In true colonial fashion, seemingly ignorant of the hill's prior importance, they designated it their strategic base, the place where they would set up their cannons to fire out to sea and, if necessary, down at the natives in the town. But when the British came to organise the clearing of trees from the hill, they could find no local people willing to set foot on it. In local folklore Fort Canning Hill

Metal artefacts.
14th–15th centuries
Bronze and copper
FROM TOP:
Metal projectile point from Empress Place
NMS
Fishing hook from Empress Place
NMS
Bell fragment from the Parliament House Complex
NMS

Gold ornaments from Fort Canning Hill

The East Javanese style of these gold ornaments are a reminder that in the 14th century, Singapore was under the political and cultural ambit of the East Java-based kingdom of Majapahit. The armlet has extensible chains and bears a repoussé plaque of the Javanese *kala*, which can also be found over the entrances of temples in many parts of Indonesia that date from the 8th to the 14th centuries. The earrings each have a socket joint and wire hinge, and are set with diamonds.

An article about the discovery of these ornaments was published in November 1928 in the *Journal of the Malayan Branch of the Royal Asiatic Society*. This invaluable report recorded that the discovery consisted of 12 gold ornaments. There was another armlet that was almost identical to this, and four other rings. It was noted that one of the armlets had broken strands while

the other displayed better workmanship and was described as 'perfect'. The report also described a ring of pale gold with an incised figure of a goose flapping its wings on the bezel, reminiscent of old Javanese or Sumatran artefacts and architecture. Of the 12 discovered, an elliptical ornament was also recorded. It was set with a pale ruby, with an empty setting for another stone of the same size, and accompanied by 8 small diamonds. Another ornament was a joint or clasp, set with 15 tiny diamonds and one pale ruby, with an empty socket for another ruby.

These were all found at Fort Canning Hill on 7 July 1928 by labourers excavating for a reservoir. The engineer recorded that the ornaments were lying together just beneath the top of the pre-colonial soil strata.

Artefacts have been reported at Fort Canning Hill as early as February 1822. John Crawfurd recorded his observations which were published in 1828 in the

Journal of an Embassy from the Governor-General of India to the Courts and Siam and Cochin China; Exhibiting a View of the Actual State of those Kingdoms. At Fort Canning Hill, he noted the presence of pottery and Chinese copper coins.

Archaeological excavations at Fort Canning Hill from the 1980s would reveal more 14th-century artefacts. Together with these archaeological artefacts and Crawfurd's notes, these gold ornaments attest to the pre-colonial habitation of Fort Canning Hill.

Gold ornaments.

14th century
Gold
H 0.5 x Dia. 10 cm (armlet)
H 0.5 x Dia. 2 cm (each earring)
NMS A-1570

TOP: *Kala* demon head, Chandi Kidal, Java.

1920s
EDM Archives

Beads from Fort Canning.

14th century
Glass
Various dimensions
On loan from National Parks Board

was Bukit Larangan – the 'Forbidden Hill', believed to be the graveyard of old dead kings. Never mind that Bukit Larangan had been deserted for centuries, the names of the once-great rulers who lived on the hill still held sway over Singapore's inhabitants.

Eventually, men from Melaka (by this time a colonial settlement further north) had to be summoned to do the work and as the forest was thinned, the extent of the site became clear. John Crawfurd took a walk around it and described the hill as now forming 'the principal beauty of the new settlement', noting that 'many of the fruit-trees cultivated by the ancient inhabitants of Singapore are still existing'. More significantly: 'The greater part of the west and northern side of the mountain is covered with the remains of the foundations of buildings, some composed of baked brick of good quality. Among these ruins, the most distinguished are those seated on a square terrace, of about forty feet to a side, near the summit of the hill.' Within this square terrace stood 'a circular enclosure, formed of rough sand-stones, in the centre of which is a well, or hollow, which very possibly contained an image; for I look upon the building to have been a place of worship … in all likelihood, a temple of Buddha'. Crawfurd went on to conjecture 'that the other relics of antiquity on the hill, are the remains of monasteries of the priests of this religion'. Local wisdom held that another terrace on the hill, of roughly the same size as the one Crawfurd described, was the burial place of Singapore's last king Iskandar Shah (also known as Parameswara, but more about him later).

This much the archaeological evidence and the corresponding historical texts reveal. To gain further insight into the kind of society that existed in early Singapore we rely on our knowledge of other Southeast Asian kingdoms during this period. Judging by the way these other kingdoms were organised, the people of Temasek were likely to have been divided into three strata.

On top were the aristocracy, the elite who lived up on Bukit Larangan and who would have claimed their status through inheritance and genealogies traceable back hundreds of years. Below them (literally) were the free men, those who inhabited the river settlement and who, as long as they paid the appropriate taxes and tribute to the rulers, could move about and in and out of the port, going about their business as they desired. Finally, there came those at the bottom of the Temasek hierarchy: the bonded servants or slaves. This class of people – who had no freedom of movement, were owned as property by others, and could be bought or sold – probably made up the largest portion of the island's population.

What we know about slaves in 14th-century Southeast Asia does not suggest that all were treated harshly or that their bondage was necessarily onerous. Laws forbade owners from killing their slaves without just cause; in addition, some slaves would have been free men who having fallen into debt took on a life of bondage in order to pay off what they owed and so win back their liberty. Generally, the relationship between slaves and owners was reciprocal. Slaves had to render all kinds of services to their masters, but their masters in turn had to feed and maintain them.

As in many ancient societies, it would have been the slave class that provided the aristocracy with their main source of power, sustaining the kings of early Singapore in royal luxury up on Bukit Larangan, from where they could survey life down by the river, rule their subjects and receive tribute. And just as we began the story of early Singapore with a mysterious fire, so we leave the island's early rulers and their ancient remains with another unsolved riddle. For in spite of all the success and international attention that Temasek had garnered, by the 15th century the king and his followers had fled the scene entirely – evacuating their hill-top palaces and burying some of their precious ornaments. On this fact both the historical records and the archaeological evidence (which on Fort Canning Hill does not date from after 1400) agree. However, exactly why Bukit Larangan was deserted and why Singapore's early kings left is another story – or, to be more precise, another set of stories.

Decorated jar from the Old Parliament House site.

14th century
Stoneware
NMS

2. TRADE WINDS, TALES AND TREACHERY

Call it a happy accident of geography. Singapore sits not just at the southern tip of the Malay Peninsula, which all maritime travellers must pass to get to China, but also at the confluence of even more decisive natural forces: the seasonal monsoons. In the age of sail, travellers who wanted to get from China to Southeast Asia and beyond had to hitch a ride on the northeast monsoon, which blew their ships south from November until around February. To travel in the opposite direction they waited for the southwest monsoon, which started in April and propelled their ships from Southeast Asia either up to China or northwest towards the Bay of Bengal and the Indian subcontinent. The turning point of these monsoons, where the northeast monsoon sputtered out and the southwest one picked up a couple of months later, was in the northeastern corner of the Java Sea – right where Singapore happens to be. In the 14th century, early Singapore was 'discovered' by at least one intrepid voyager blown toward it by these winds; perhaps they were even what brought its mythical founder, Sri Tri Buana, to its shores.

Wang Dayuan's description of 'barbarians'

The key early traveller's account of 14th-century Singapore (or Temasek) is that of the Chinese trader Wang Dayuan. Little is known about Wang except that he was from Nanzhang in Jiangxi province and that in the 1330s he undertook two lengthy sea voyages, later writing up his experiences for a local gazetteer under the title *Dao Yi Zhi Lue* [A Description of the Barbarians of the Isles]. His first trip took him through Southeast Asia and then as far afield as India and Aden (in modern-day Yemen), while on his second voyage he reached north and east Africa. Wang's descriptions of these places are some of the earliest Chinese impressions of far-distant lands, predating the voyages of the eunuch Admiral Zheng He, under China's expansionist Ming Dynasty, by at least 80 years. For his time, Wang was an exceptional fellow whose wanderlust took him to see much more of the world than his contemporaries – and all before he reached the age of 30.

Temasek, or Danmaxi as Wang calls it (this being the Mandarin version of the Chinese characters used to render Temasek in the Hokkien Chinese dialect), is the 50th out of 99 places that he catalogued in his *Description*, which might suggest that it occupied some kind of symbolic position at the centre of what the Chinese then believed to be the world's two oceans (one eastern, one western). However, Wang's details about Temasek are so tantalisingly brief that you could hardly be blamed for thinking it little more than a footnote in his travels. Maybe it was simply not the kind of exotic place he was looking to write about or in which he felt comfortable sojourning, for he depicts Temasek merely as a home for pirates and small-time traders (though the two – logically enough – are said not to inhabit the same parts of the island).

The pirates' domain was Longyamen, named for 'a strait bordered by two hills that looked like dragon's teeth'. Wang relates that the pirates targeted junks on their return journeys to China, launching attacks from Longyamen in fleets of 'some two or three hundred *perahu* [Malay boats]'. Junks that were lucky enough to catch the winds of the southwest monsoon could escape these localised attacks; less fortunate vessels were plundered and their crews butchered. Indeed, the site maintained its reputation as a pirate base for many centuries after. An early 17th-century Portuguese map refers to one side of the strait by the Malay name 'Blakang Mati', which is often translated as 'stabbed in the back'. However, no such natural features are found in the vicinity of what is today's Keppel Harbour – the distinctive teeth-like granite protrusions at its western entrance were demolished by the British in 1848 to widen the strait for modern shipping.

The island's traders lived in a more strategic location further inland. Wang wrote of Banzu, the hill behind Longyamen, as surrounded by 'interconnected terraces' where the people made their homes. The name 'Banzu' might be derived from the Malay word *pancur*, meaning 'spring', which together with the physical description of the hill tallies with modern-day Fort Canning, where a spring once flowed on the hill's southwest side. But here, despite irrigation, the soil was unsuitable for farming so the inhabitants produced goods that could be traded for other necessities. Wang listed occupations that involved the extraction of salt from sea water, the fermentation of rice spirits called *ming-chia*, the production of cotton and the collection of highly valued hornbill casques.

Perhaps it's not surprising, given the limited supply of trade goods at Banzu and the pirates nearby at Longyamen, that Wang makes such brief mention of Temasek. Overall, his *Description*, as archaeologist John Miksic puts it, is not unlike

Longyamen as depicted by an unknown artist.
c. 1848
Photographic reproduction
H 16.3 x W 21.5 cm
NMS PA-0539-A

that of a 'modern travelling salesman'. Wang's main interests were the commercial conditions in the various places he encountered, their climate and their forms of local government. Being a 14th-century Chinese, he was also preoccupied by dress and hairstyles – not because the Chinese of his era were especially slaves to fashion but because they saw the way people presented themselves as revealing much about their status and role in society. Almost like a modern ethnographer, Wang recalled how the people of Longyamen kept their hair long, tied up in buns, and wore short shirts of dark blue cotton. On the other hand, the people of Banzu wore their hair short, under head-pieces made of gold-patterned satin cloth, and their clothes were made from a type of red oiled cloth (perhaps a form of *batik*, some historians have speculated). From what we can gather, these seem to have been two quite separate communities, since Wang makes no mention of any interaction or mutually dependent relationship between them. He does record that there were Chinese living among the locals at Longyamen, but he gives no additional details other than the fact of their existence.

The only further reference Temasek merits in Wang's *Description* is as the location of a Siamese attack some years before he arrived in Southeast Asia. On this occasion, Temasek closed its gates and kept the Siamese at bay for a month, until the fortuitous appearance of a Javanese envoy on his way to China convinced the invaders to break off their attack rather than risk antagonising their powerful regional rival. So Temasek survived to be visited and documented by Wang, who in turn has left us with an intriguing insight into its early commerce and costume.

The Sejarah Melayu

But for a fuller though less historically reliable account of early Singapore, we turn to the most famous indigenous record – the Malay chronicles commonly known as the *Sejarah Melayu* [History of the Malays]. This source tells us that in the 14th century Temasek was 'a great city, to which foreigners resorted in great numbers so that the fame of the city and its greatness spread throughout the world'.

What made it especially great was the bloodline of its kings, who claimed ancient descent from Alexander the Great through his marriage to an Indian princess. The first king from this line to rule Temasek was called Sri Tri Buana (also known as Sang Nila Utama) – the 'lord of the three worlds' of the gods, humans and underworld, but more practically speaking the ruler of Palembang on the island of Sumatra. Travelling northeast in search of a site for a new city, Sri Tri Buana spotted land with 'sand so white that it looked like a sheet of cloth'. 'Temasek', one of his ministers informed him.

There then transpired one of the most famous yet problematic episodes in the *Sejarah*'s account of early Singapore. When Sri Tri Buana landed on the island he spotted a strange animal, 'bigger than a he-goat', with 'a red body

A page from the *Sejarah Melayu*, from which the Christian missionary Dr W. G. Shellabear produced his 1896 edition. A pencilled note on one of the other sheets records that 'Tuan Raffles' requested that the work be transcribed.
1844–52
Ink on paper
NMS XXXX-02325

and a black head', that looked strong and moved with great speed. His chief advisor told him the creature was known in ancient times as a lion, and so Sri Tri Buana dubbed the land Singapura or 'Lion City' – a name that continues to be celebrated in tourism brochures, in the names of local sports teams, and in the icon of a stylised lion's head that has been adopted by the present-day Singapore government as its official emblem. Never mind that lions have never been found in the wild any further east than India, and certainly never in Singapore (although, right up until the mid-20th century, there used to be sightings of the lion's distant relative – the tiger). Sri Tri Buana thought he saw a lion on the island, and so a Lion City it would be.

In truth, by 1300 'Singapura' had become a name common across Asia, since the lion was a symbol closely associated with the Buddhism that spread across the region before the arrival of Islam. Various Singapuras had already existed, in Vietnam, southern Siam, western Java and in India too. Nonetheless, for the island of Temasek the name Singapura stuck – as did Sri Tri Buana's reign, which, according to the Malay chronicles, lasted right through the first half of the 14th century. The problem with these chronicles is just how much of them we can treat as historical fact – a problem that goes well beyond Sri Tri Buana's advisor mistaking something in the bushes for what he imagined to be a lion.

Despite the title *Sejarah Melayu* possessing an authoritative ring (*sejarah* being typically translated as 'history' or 'annals'), the work ought to be more accurately referred to by its formal name: *Penurunan Segala Raja* [Origin and Descent of the Malay Rajas]. Chiefly a genealogy of the Malay rulers of Melaka, its purpose – like any royal genealogy worth its salt – was to legitimise the ruling family's authority, rather than to capture historical events objectively. Scholars have therefore considered the *Sejarah* to be as much a work of literature – with all the dramatic and interpretive features appropriate to a grand epic – as it is a work of history. In its pages we learn of the strong man Badang who could hurl huge rocks great distances like a Malay Hercules and of attacks on the local populace by bloodthirsty garfish (a species similar to swordfish but much smaller). The historian Timothy Barnard has suggested that some of these folk-like tales could have been bedtime stories for 15th-century Melakan children.

However, to Barnard, certain of the *Sejarah*'s more imaginative passages also contain a deeper political significance. For instance, the tale of the ferocious garfish brings to light the failings of Sri Tri Buana's royal descendants. When the Sultan's attempt to thwart the garfish comes to no avail, he is upstaged by a precocious young boy, who suggests building a barricade of banana stems that the garfish snouts will get stuck in, making them easier to kill. The boy's plan works brilliantly, but the Sultan, wary and jealous of the boy's youthful intelligence, puts him to death. From then on, so the *Sejarah* tells us, 'the guilt of his blood was laid on Singapura'.

By the time the text of the *Sejarah* began to be written down in the 1400s – that is, at least one century after the events that it purports to record took place – Melaka was enjoying its heyday as a maritime power. By contrast, Singapura had been relegated to a mere province within Melaka's imperial ambit and its past to the stuff of myth and legend. For the Malay chroniclers the fate of Singapura's kings could be transformed into an object lesson about poor political leadership as well as a warning to the contemporary Melakan court, and to the sons who would succeed the Sultan, of the just deserts that awaited proud and tyrannical rulers.

To this end, the *Sejarah* casts the blame for the ultimate fall of Singapura on the poor judgement of its last king, Sultan Iskandar Shah. After only three years on the throne, the Sultan listened to court gossip and humiliated one of his favourite concubines by publicly exposing her in the market. This act enraged her father, a royal minister, who exacted his revenge by inviting one of Singapura's rivals, the neighbouring Majapahit Empire in Java, to seize and sack

The Singapore Stone

This is the earliest inscription found in Singapore. It is a fragment of a larger boulder that originally stood at the mouth of the Singapore River, near the present-day Fullerton Hotel building. The inscription covered an area 2.1 meters wide and 1.5 meters high on the face of a boulder which had been split into two. The two parts of the boulder reclined opposite each other at an angle of about 40 degrees, with a distance between them, which John Crawfurd noted in 1822, to be 'not more than two and a half feet'.

The full inscription has not been deciphered. Scholars who looked at the script differed in their views on the date and language. It has been variously dated from the 10th to the 14th centuries, and the language is suspected to be ancient Javanese or Sanskrit.

It was noted as early as 1819, and in 1822, John Crawfurd and Munshi Abdullah also saw it on separate occasions and made notes. Munshi Abdullah thought the script looked rather like Arabic, while Crawfurd thought it might have been Pali or a 'religious character used by the followers of Buddha' but could not make any conclusions. Both men noted that some of the inscription had been rendered illegible through weathering over time. Munshi Abdullah reported that crowds of people went to look at the stone inscription and many tried in vain to read it.

The boulder was unfortunately blown up in 1843 during a project to widen the mouth of the river. James Low, then the Assistant Resident of Singapore, managed to salvage at least three fragments which were later sent to Calcutta. Another fragment was later found at the Singapore Treasury where it was being used as a seat by the Sepoy guards. Of the fragments that were sent to Calcutta, one piece was returned to the Raffles Museum in Singapore in 1918 or 1919.

Though the meaning of the inscription remains a mystery, the fragment of the boulder, presently displayed in the National Museum of Singapore, is an important relic of Singapore's pre-colonial history, and has come to be known as 'The Singapore Stone'. It has also become part of local folklore as it is often associated with a legend in the *Sejarah Melayu* where Badang, a war-chief of prodigious strength, lifted a large rock and hurled it to the far bank of the Singapore River. Though the legend does not contain any account of the inscription, it said that the rock Badang threw was located at 'the extremity of the land', thus coinciding with the original position of the boulder.

The Singapore Stone
10th–14th century
Sandstone
H 37 x W 74 x Dia. 15.5 cm
NMS A-1571

the Sultan's kingdom (the father was even there at the gates of the fort to open them for the Javanese army when it landed). The *Sejarah* tells of a fierce battle where 'so many were killed … that blood flowed like a river in spate and flooded the fort of Singapura on the sea shore'. Sultan Iskandar Shah fled north to the Malay Peninsula, where he founded a new settlement of Melaka under the shade of the eponymous *malaka* tree. From here, the Malay chroniclers really hit their stride, describing Melaka's rise and extolling it, as Barnard puts it, as 'an ideal Malay state where every woman was beautiful, every man was handsome and the government worked well'.

From this point, also, Singapura begins to fade from the Malay records. Nonetheless the history of the island continued to play a role in sustaining the Malay ruling house in its claims to royal legitimacy. After Melaka fell to the Portuguese in 1511, the text of the *Sejarah* evolved as it was copied and re-copied by numerous court scribes through the centuries. With their empire in ruins, the remnants of the Melakan sultanate retraced the steps of their founder Iskandar Shah and wound up back at the southern end of the Straits of Melaka, in Johor, in Riau and on the island of Singapore. As the sultanate sought to rebuild its power it was only natural that it used its family history to hark back not only to a once-great Melaka but also beyond that to a kingly line with its power base in Singapura. More important than historical accuracy was substantiating the ruling family's claim to the region, whether it kept its capital at Melaka, Johor, Singapore or elsewhere. So long as the stories in the *Sejarah* circulated, fantastic as some of them might have seemed, what was once Temasek, then Singapura, came to occupy an iconic place in the minds of the Sultan's subjects.

The key fact we can establish from the *Sejarah* without hesitation is that the last king of early Singapore fled the island near the end of the 14th century. This much is clear from the archaeological evidence and from both Chinese and Portuguese sources, which independently confirm that the last ruler of early Singapore was also the founder of Melaka. The Chinese Ming chronicles actually name this last ruler as Iskandar Shah and give a date for his death – the year 1413. Likewise, Portuguese accounts establish the royal lineage of the Melaka sultanate by tracing its origins back to Sumatra via Singapura. However, the Portuguese tell a rather different story when it comes to who this last king was and why he fled the island to establish Melaka – which is perhaps not so surprising since the Portuguese wrote their accounts after they had conquered Melaka and, like all victorious powers, claimed the right to write their own version of history.

The Portuguese account of Afonso D'Albuquerque

The main Portuguese records to mention early Singapore are the voluminous *Commentaries of the Great Afonso D'Albuquerque*, the leader of the Portuguese forces that captured Melaka. The *Commentaries* identify the founder of Melaka as a Hindu king from Palembang named Parimiçura (usually rendered in the Sanskrit form Parameswara). This name stands in direct contrast to the Iskandar Shah mentioned in the *Sejarah Melayu*, a Persian-Arabic name ('Iskandar' being the Arabic version of Alexander and 'Shah' from the Persian for 'king'). The latter name reflects the gradual Islamicisation of the Malay world from the 1400s – a transformation of far more significance to the Muslim scribes, who later revised the *Sejarah*, than to a Catholic emissary such as D'Albuquerque.

Afonso D'Albuquerque.
From Arnold Wright, *Twentieth Century Impressions of British Malaya*, 1908

More fascinating is D'Albuquerque's account of how the Melakan royal line claimed Singapura as part of its patrimony. Where the *Sejarah Melayu* gives us a poetic moment when the ruler espied Singapura's serene white shores from Sumatra and encountered a mythical lion, the *Commentaries* tell a bloodier tale: Parameswara rebelled against his sovereign in Sumatra, sought refuge in Singapura and promptly murdered the local ruler who had welcomed him with open arms. He then took Singapura for himself, turning it into a pirate base for five years. Not exactly what you might consider kingly behaviour; but Parameswara later received his come-uppance. The brother of the murdered ruler, who had his own Siamese power base, eventually drove Parameswara out of Singapura – which was why he ended up heading north and founding Melaka.

Naturally, it was the all-conquering newcomers to the region who pointed the finger at the ruler of Singapura – and by eventual extension, Melaka – as an opportunistic usurper. For the *Sejarah* to impugn anyone associated with the Melaka sultanate would have been unthinkable. Indeed, historian William Linehan has suggested that 'the Malay record was altered to make it appear that Sri Sultan Iskandar Shah [as the founder and first ruler of Melaka] was a direct descendant of the Singapore royal line'.

Nonetheless, we should remember that the Portuguese, as Melaka's new rulers, had no great desire to perpetuate the royal claims of their predecessor. Instead, it would suit the Portuguese to portray the line of rulers they had just supplanted as having as little blood-right to the sultanate as they themselves. This probably accounts for the tendency of other Portuguese chroniclers to unite behind the story of Parameswara the usurper, rather than that of Iskandar Shah the empire-builder. Memories of corrupt and treacherous kings can always be disposed of with greater justification.

Whatever the truth about the first ruler of Melaka, throughout the 15th century the city rose in stature so that – just as Temasek before it – foreigners flocked to it and its fame and greatness 'spread throughout the world'. That this great kingdom should itself fall, at the hands of foreign invaders and through a dramatic act of treachery, and that its rulers should once again be forced to flee, is a case of history repeating itself. Only this time, European forces had entered the fray – forces that would eventually reverse the fortunes of both ports, reinstating Singapore as a great emporium while reducing Melaka to a lesser backwater.

3. MELAKA'S FALL, SINGAPORE'S RETURN

The fall of Melaka in 1511 was one of those momentous occasions rightly considered a turning point in the history of Southeast Asia. For the Portuguese their victory came two decades after Columbus reached America, an event that signalled Europe's entrance into a new age of expansion and conquest that would continue unchallenged until the second half of the 20th century. For the Malay Sultans, the self-styled heirs to Singapura, Melaka's fall terminated a century of independent rule and signalled the end of Melaka's golden age as a maritime empire. During the next three centuries, Melaka's royal successors would be repeatedly on the move, taking their court to Johor, Sumatra and finally to the Riau-Lingga archipelago, as they struggled against European colonisers and rival kingdoms to keep hold of their possessions. For Singapore, the fall of Melaka would lead indirectly to the destruction of its own river settlement around the year 1611, then to its eventual rebirth as a modern possession of the East India Company. To understand what happened to the island during this period – how it transformed from 'early' into 'modern' Singapore – it's vital to understand what happened in Melaka and beyond.

The Europeans at the gates

In 1509, Diego de Sequeira arrived in Melakan waters with a squadron of five galleons, and so set in motion Europe's first major political encounter with the Malay-speaking world. At first, the Malays regarded their new guests with curiosity, referring to them as *Bengali Putih* [white Bengalis]; but then, perhaps

Illustration of Fortaleza de Malaca from Manuel de Faria e Sousa's *Asia Portuguesa*, published 1666.

Drawn before 1640
Engraving
H 27.1 x W 33.1 cm
NMS XXXX-01111

sensing a future threat (the *Sejarah Melayu* claims that de Sequeira wanted to build a Portuguese fort nearby) their ruler Sultan Mahmud gave the order to attack. Most of the Portuguese escaped, but during their retreat they abandoned two ships and 20 of their countrymen.

To exact revenge, in 1511 a force of 18 ships, manned by at least 1,200 Portuguese and South Indian Malabaris, assembled under the leadership of 'the Great' Afonso D'Albuquerque at Goa. The fleet left India on 2 May and two months later it entered Melaka's harbour, its galleons bedecked with flags and its arrival announced by blasts from its trumpets and cannon. These cannon, modern artillery the likes of which had not been seen in the Malay Peninsula before, would prove crucial in the events that unfolded.

In an early instance of 'gun-boat diplomacy', D'Albuquerque exploited his superior firepower from practically the moment he arrived. When the Sultan failed to respond to his requests for the return of de Sequeira's crew, the payment of compensation and the establishment of a Portuguese fort, D'Albuquerque ordered his guns to open up. The first bombardment set several parts of the town alight and destroyed a number of ships in the harbour. Sultan Mahmud, sensing that the odds were mounting against him, agreed to the release of the Portuguese prisoners. But by this time D'Albuquerque had decided Melaka was too great a prize to let pass. After a two-week siege, during which D'Albuquerque waited to see if the Sultan would concede to the rest of his demands (especially the construction of a Portuguese fort at the Sultan's own expense), 'the Great Afonso' ordered his men to take the city. Their attack commenced on 25 July, the day of D'Albuquerque's patron saint the Apostle Saint James.

D'Albuquerque directed the main Portuguese assault against the bridge that ran over the Melaka River and divided the Royal Quarter from the northern part of the city, where most of its inhabitants lived. This attack was intended to split the Melakan forces in half and cut supplies to the Sultan's palace. But the Portuguese appear to have soon encountered a situation not unlike that experienced by modern armies engaged in today's urban warfare.

Though the Portuguese controlled the harbour, which permitted them to rain down fire on the city from all directions, to seize control of the streets against a larger force backed by a hostile population was another matter entirely. Ranged against D'Albuquerque's 1,200 or so men were the Sultan's more than 20,000 soldiers, among them Javanese, Persian and Turkish mercenaries. The Sultan lacked the heavy cannon of the Portuguese but his army had several thousand light artillery pieces, bows and arrows and around 20 war elephants – resources that would prove deadly when the fighting moved to close quarters. More importantly, while the Portuguese enjoyed a clear technological superiority, the people of Melaka were fighting to protect their homes and, given news of Portuguese exploits elsewhere in the Indian Ocean, their religion too. It seems that when D'Albuquerque launched the first Portuguese assault on the bridge and the main road that led to the Sultan's palace, his troops were ambushed from the side-streets and alleyways, then during a second assault beaten back by a charge of war-elephants that must have wreaked havoc in the city's narrow thoroughfares.

The events that turned the battle in D'Albuquerque's favour illuminate the crucial role played by foreign third parties. First, Chinese merchants, who like their Tamil counterparts had cooperated with the Portuguese from the outset, provided D'Albuquerque with a heavily armed Chinese junk, which he ran aground near the bridge and used to send fire down on the defenders for 20 days. Secondly, the leader of the Sultan's Javanese mercenaries, no doubt weary after weeks of naval bombardment with no end in sight, sent gifts to D'Albuquerque with a promise of secret support. When the Portuguese eventually landed the bulk of their soldiers at Melaka, they did so north of the river, in the Javanese quarter of the city.

On 10 August, the Portuguese launched a third attack on the bridge. Under intense fire, the Melakan forces defending it and the stockades that surrounded it, retreated into the Royal Quarter. Here, in his mosque, Sultan Mahmud was ensconced with 3,000 of his shield-bearers. Yet at this point, instead of pressing on, D'Alburqueque sent more envoys to the Sultan to once more demand the construction of a Portuguese fort. The response D'Alburqueque sought never came and after a two-week stalemate he ordered his men to take the mosque, the palace and the entire city. When they did so, they discovered that Melaka's last ruler had vanished, having fled with his family, his entourage and presumably some of his finest treasure.

The Portuguese set fire to the Sultan's palace and demolished the royal mosque stone by stone. After 40 days of bombardment, bloodshed and betrayal, the Melakan Empire was no more.

Colonialism's four 'C's

At one level, the Portuguese conquest of Melaka speaks volumes about the basic impulses that drove European colonialism – namely, gold, god and glory. The Portuguese stormed the Melaka Bridge with the war cry 'St James!', but the city also promised a Sultan's treasure and the glory of a victory that was eventually to be recorded for posterity in D'Albuquerque's *Commentaries*. Fittingly, the fortress the Portuguese built on the site of Sultan Mahmud's demolished palace (using stones that once belonged to the Sultan's mosque) was christened 'A Famosa' – 'to the famous'.

But for a subtler model by which to appreciate the origins of European colonialism in the region we turn to what historian Peter Borschberg calls the 'Four Cs' theory: *curiosity, collaboration, commerce* and *conflict*. Certainly, the Portuguese appeared at the entrance of Melaka's harbour filled with crusading zeal. But they also had a *curiosity* about the world they sought to conquer, and were

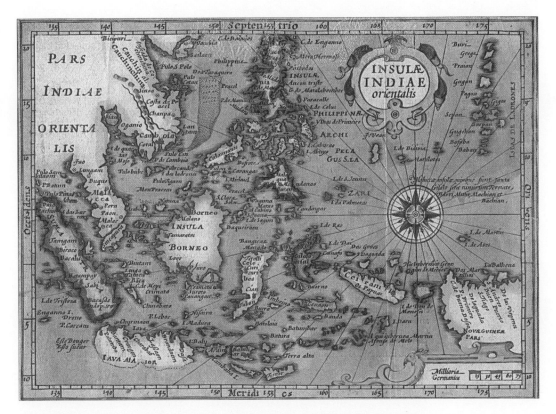

filled with the prevailing Renaissance spirit of enquiry which led adventurers to risk death and disease as they journeyed to the four corners of the earth. A prime example of such curiosity was Ferdinand Magellan, who was with de Sequeira's forces when they first arrived in Melaka back in 1509. Magellan escaped the city and, undeterred, set off a decade later to voyage around the globe. In 1521, after two years of voyaging, having survived storms, sickness and several mutinies, Magellan finally succumbed to a native's cutlass blow in the Philippines.

Magellan's fate reveals how unpopular new European arrivals in the region could be. Yet without the *collaboration* of non-Europeans, the Portuguese would have never made it to Melaka in the first place, let alone overwhelmed it. Iberian mariners navigated their way from the east coast of Africa all the way up to India with the help of local pilots who had plied these stretches long before them. Once the Portuguese established their bases in India at Goa and Bombay, they received additional information from Asian mariners about lands further east. When they arrived in the Straits of Melaka, they gained further contacts with regional merchants, especially the Chinese. In particular, Chinese involvement in the conquest of Melaka was crucial. Chinese merchants offered D'Albuquerque the flat-bottomed junks with which he was able to land his troops on the beaches and they loaned him the tall junk that helped him capture the city's bridge. The support that Chinese merchants gave European colonisers was to be a recurrent feature of the centuries to come – especially in

Map of the East India Archipelago, attributed to Gerard Mercator-Jodocus Hondius, Amsterdam.

c. 1607
Copper engraving
H 17 x W 22.6 cm
NMS XXXX-01963

the establishment of what might be termed the Anglo-Chinese condominiums of Melaka, Penang and modern Singapore.

Naturally, *commerce* – the third of Borschberg's 'Cs' – was fundamental. Before the 19th century, European colonisers in the region did not seem especially concerned with claims to territory but rather with access to maritime trade. When the Portuguese seized Melaka they gained control of the regional gateways to the Spice Islands (known today as the Maluku Islands), from which Europe obtained its supply of cloves, nutmeg, maize and pepper. It's well known that such spices were used to make bland Western food taste better and, in the days before refrigeration, to mask the taste of rotting meat and vegetables. Less well remembered is the fact that all these spices – even pepper – were seen to possess medicinal value, and that it was this medicinal value which sent prices soaring. Profits from the spice trade were such that a few bags of cloves not only covered the costs of Magellan's voyages around the world, they still left a modest profit.

No surprise, then, that in the early 1600s the Dutch and the British followed the Portuguese east for a slice of the action – and thus contributed to the fourth of colonialism's 'Cs': *conflict*. Such conflict not only arose out of existing tensions between European powers, it drew on, and further exacerbated, existing regional rivalries. For instance, in the century after Melaka's fall, the Portuguese fought the Acehnese, the Javanese and the descendants of Melaka's royal line (by then based in Johor-Riau-Lingga), three powers that also regularly fought with each other. Such conflict almost certainly occasioned the raid on early Singapore around the year 1611 which burnt the surviving settlement to the ground. It also led to the eventual expulsion of the Portuguese from Melaka and from most of Southeast Asia. The Sultans of Johor-Riau-Lingga, who never really got over the loss of their empire (if the *Sejarah Melayu* is anything to go by), made an alliance

Illustration of Melaka during the Dutch period, showing VOC ships at the harbour. The work is from Antoine François Prévost's book *Histoire générale des Voyages* published between 1746 and 1759.

Copper engraving
H 18 x W 27.5 cm
NMS 1993-00313

with the Dutch in 1606, and in 1641 joint Dutch-Johor forces laid siege to Melaka and eventually conquered it.

Nor were Europeans the only ones to seek an advantage from the incessant warring between regional powers. After the Portuguese defeat at Melaka, and before the founding of a British settlement on Singapore, the major challenge to Dutch influence in the Malay world came from the mighty Bugis of Sulawesi. In the late 1600s, Bugis warriors, whose *perahu* dominated and often terrorised archipelago trade, offered their services to Malay rulers as mercenaries. Subsequently, they became established as viceroys of Johor-Riau-Lingga and lorded it over their former employers like *dalang* or puppet-masters. To limit their influence, the Sultan of Johore-Riau-Lingga in the mid-18th century moved toward an alliance with the Dutch. The Bugis responded in 1756 with an attempt to crush the Dutch in Melaka. Their persistent attempts failed but the city's suburbs were ravaged. Then, after three decades of outwardly amicable relations, a Dutch blockade of Riau prompted the Bugis and their allies to lay siege to Melaka once again. This time the Dutch felt it was necessary to teach the Bugis a lesson. A powerful fleet sailed from Holland to relieve Melaka and then sack Riau in 1784. Bugis political ambitions in the Straits were thwarted and the Johor-Riau-Lingga sultanate was forced to accept Dutch suzerainty.

The 'sleepy fishing village'?

For history buffs, the battles, dynastic struggles and foreign intrigues that dominate this period will bring to mind the Peloponnesian Wars fought by the maritime city-states of ancient Greece, where alliances constantly shifted and certain kingdoms thought little of inviting powerful foreign empires into the fray. While these struggles largely passed Singapore by, their intensity and proximity belie the popular notion of Singapore at this time as nothing more than a 'sleepy fishing village'. There is little to suggest that Singapore was in any way 'sleepy', even after the river settlement was sacked around the year 1611. For one thing, the Dutch, Portuguese, Acehnese and Johor Malays continued to fight naval engagements around Changi Point. Here, various fleets lay in ambush in the many hidden coves, straits and estuaries, then discharged volumes of cannon-shot likely to wake all but the most comatose fisherman from his afternoon siesta. Indeed, the more we understand about the regional conflicts which plagued these centuries, the more it comes as a surprise that Singapore was not revived as a settlement earlier. The question becomes less why was modern Singapore founded but instead why did it take so long?

According to the *Sejarah Melayu*, in the 15th century Singapura served as a naval base for the Melakan fleet – it was the fiefdom of the *laksamana*, the chief minister who commanded the Sultan's navy. Although the aristocracy had by this time departed the island, its river settlement continued to trade – at least if the

Treasures of the East
– cloves, pepper and nutmeg.

discovery of Ming dynasty porcelain is anything to go by. The Malay records also indicate that at this time Singapore still had the largest number of ships in the Melakan Empire and the largest number of seafaring people. After Melaka's fall, Portuguese sources likewise confirm that Singapore survived as a naval base of the Sultans of Johor-Riau-Lingga and that in 1574 there was still a *shah banda* (harbour master) resident there. In fact, on several occasions the Portuguese considered establishing a fortress on Singapore and 16th-century Portuguese accounts even record the names of villages on the island, such as Tanah Merah, Sungei Bedok and Tanjung Rhu, names still in use today.

However, from the time of the decisive raid that consigned early Singapore to flames around 1611, the historical and archaeological record goes quiet for almost a century. Singapore next reappears in 1703, when there is a record of the Sultan of Johor offering the island to an English private sea captain by the name of Alexander Hamilton. Hamilton, who had good relations with the Sultan, was apparently flattered by the offer but declined it on the grounds that he did not possess the capital to develop a settlement. Instead, he suggested that the island would be a good place for a joint-stock company to take over. Around the same time, the British surveyed the entrance to what would become Keppel Harbour and took soundings of the depths with a view to a possible settlement. But the fact that it took another century for anyone to follow up on Hamilton's suggestion says much about the limited extent of the East India Company's ambitions.

The Dutch, too, had cast an eye on Singapore on more than one occasion. As early as 1609 they explored the possibility of making their principal settlement on the island. Two centuries later, in 1808, a former Dutch governor of Melaka informed his colleagues in Java (on his way out of the Straits) that really Singapore was a much more suitable place for a trading post, much better than Melaka. All of this confirms Borschberg's assertion that 'We would be greatly deluded to take Raffles at his word, that Singapore was for centuries that neglected and abandoned place that he "found" or "discovered"'. Between the early 1600s and 1819, when Sir Stamford Raffles landed and planted the British flag, the island was a bit like an actor standing on the wings of history's stage – an actor who has gone missing for an act but who patiently awaits a cue that will signal his dramatic restoration to the limelight.

What the actual inhabitants of the island made of all these comings and goings, in and around their waters, we can only guess. Perhaps their biggest surprise in 1819 was not so much the arrival of the white man but the arrival of a different white man from the one they had expected. The Dutch, having vanquished the Bugis in Riau, were now the supposed *dalang* of the heirs of the Melakan line and it would have been natural if they had been the ones to make their authority felt on the neglected island of Singapore. But the Dutch were busy with struggles elsewhere in the archipelago, and so it was that another upstart colonial power seized the moment.

Schematic map of a naval confrontation between the Dutch Vice-Admiral Jacob Pietersz van Enkhuisen and the Portuguese Teixeira de Matos, at the Johor River, 6–11 October 1603. A Portuguese armada imposed a blockade of the Johor River to protect Portuguese carracks going through the Straits of Singapore to Melaka.
From de Bry, *Icones seu Gennuinae et Espressae Delineationes Omnium Memorabilium*, 1607

PAINTED by W. J. HUGGINS, MARINE PAINTER TO HIS MAJESTY.

London Published May 1st 1832 by W. J. Huggins, Marine Painter No 105 Leadenhall Street

TO *GEORGE GOOCH, ESQ*.RE One of the Elder Brethren of T

This Plate of the Hon.ble East India Compy. Ship LORD   LOWTH

Leaving the Harbour of   PRINCE

Is most respectfu

VITY HOUSE &c.&c.
ommanded by Charles Steward, Esq.ʳᵉ
ES ISLAND.
ted by his obedient humble Servant W.J. HUGGINS.

SETTLEMENT

1819 – 1824

4. THE YEAR 1819

At the beginning of 1819, Singapore numbered around 1,000 inhabitants. Some were Chinese, trading at the river settlement or working on gambier plantations in the hills, and others were Malay, who like the Chinese had arrived on the island the previous decade and lived by the Singapore River. But the bulk of the population were the nomadic *orang laut*, or 'sea gypsies' as they are sometimes known, the indigenous people of Singapore and the Malay Peninsula who made their living out on the water from fishing, peddling fruit and occasional piracy. These *orang laut* were settled in tribes on the site of the old town of Temasek, at the mouth of the Kallang River, around what would later become Keppel Harbour and on the north side of the island opposite Johor.

Wa Hakim was one of them – an *orang laut* who described himself as 'born in the Singapore waters'. Several decades later, as an old man in his 80s, he decided to share his recollection of a fateful day in Singapore history when he had been just 15 years old:

> I remembered the boat landing in the morning. There were two white men and a Sepoy on it. When they landed they went straight to the Temenggong's house. Tuan Raffles was there, he was a short man … Tuan Farquhar was there; he was taller than Tuan Raffles and he wore a helmet. The Sepoy carried a musket. They were entertained by the Temenggong and he gave them rambutans and all kinds of fruit. … Tuan Raffles went into the centre of the house. About 4 o'clock in the afternoon, they came out and went on board again.

To give these men their full titles, 'Tuan Raffles' was Sir Thomas Stamford Raffles and 'Tuan Farquhar' Major William Farquhar, both servants of the British East India Company. The Temenggong who entertained them was Abdul Rahman, the hereditary prime minister of the Johor-Riau-Lingga sultanate* and a local chief to whom the Sultan had entrusted the island of Singapore and the territory of Johor across the water. Their meeting occurred on 29 January 1819, the day after the Company's small fleet of eight vessels had dropped anchor in Singapore's natural harbour. Such a meeting was, in truth, a risky one, since each man was about to act beyond his given authority and without the full knowledge of his official superiors.

For their collective gamble to pay off, the three men awaited the arrival of a fourth – Tengku Long, eldest son of the late Sultan Mahmud of Johor-Riau-Lingga. He landed in Singapore two days after the British arrived, and a few days later, with Sir Stamford, Major Farquhar and the Temenggong in attendance, he was installed as Sultan Hussein – the island's first Sultan. The

PREVIOUS PAGE:
The East India Company ship, *Lord Lowther*, commanded by Charles Steward, leaving the harbour of Prince of Wales Island (Penang).

1828
Print
H 79 x W 64 cm
NMS 1994-00052

Detail of a painting depicting a merchant at a slave market in Timor.

19th century
Paper
H 14.5 x W 18 cm
NMS 1994-00299

---

* After the fall of the Melaka sultanate (see Chapter 3) the displaced royal family fled south and established the Johor-Riau-Lingga sultanate.

gift of 'rambutans and all kinds of fruit' remembered by Wa Hakim, along with the arrival of sepoys bearing muskets, were the opening exchanges in a drama that within a week transformed the island home of *orang laut* and long-dead ancient Malay kings forever.

The Treaty of 1819

The day of the signing of the Treaty, 6 February 1819, dawned bright and sunny. A small cluster of tents had mushroomed on the Padang – then, as today, a flat, grassy area. Preparations had begun the previous week, during which a hundred Chinese plantation workers had cleared the ground and readied it for the coming formalities. One tent stood out, dressed up with rich scarlet cloth which was used to cover the floor and the five chairs inside, and to line a path from the door and then for about a hundred feet by the side of the river bank. At noon, some 30 officers and soldiers of the East India Company gathered and the hubbub of activity drew local Malay and Chinese bystanders, who squatted by the bedecked tent in anticipation.

About an hour later, a burst of cannon announced the arrival of Tengku Long. Attired in brightly coloured garments of silk and escorted by a military guard, the soon-to-be-Sultan of Singapore was accorded the full royal treatment. As he processed down the red carpet, the Company soldiers who lined the way executed

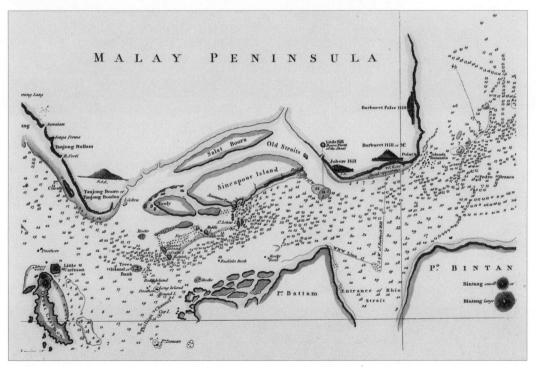

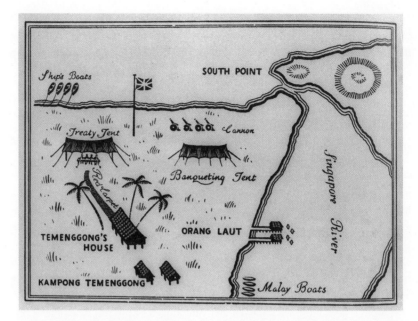

a ceremonial presentation of arms. At the door to the tent, Sir Thomas Stamford
Raffles stood waiting, about to see his long-cherished dream become a reality.

But for some onlookers the Sultan's entrance proved an anti-climax. Captain
Crawford of the survey ship *Investigator* described the new Sultan's dress as
'gaudy' and 'inelegantly put on, his chest was exposed displaying a disgusting
breast and stomach'. With a European prejudice typical of his day, Crawford
went on to record:

> During the whole ceremony the vulgarity of the Sultan's expression, the
> want of expression and the perspiration running down his face ... raised
> in the feelings of the English spectators a horrible and disgusting loathing
> of his person, and several in pretty audible whispers, expressing those
> thoughts on the occasion sufficiently loud for Sir Stamford to hear, and in
> which sensation I suspect he inwardly accorded.

The Sultan's 'want of expression' was perhaps not so surprising; the diplomatic
formalities that established a British foothold on Singapore would probably have
bored even the most enthusiastic lover of official protocol. No sweeping oratory
of grand enterprise or empire-building was to be found here. Instead, a nine-
article 'Treaty of Friendship and Alliance between Sir Thomas Stamford Raffles
and Sultan Hussein and Temenggong Abdul Rahman' was read aloud in English.
In sober language it spoke of an 'English factory [trading settlement]' and 'the
regulation of the British Authorities'.

Likewise, the Treaty's terms were concise and functional: the East India
Company recognised Tengku Long as Sultan Hussein of Singapore, offered him

an annual salary of 5,000 Spanish dollars (then the common currency of the Malay Archipelago), with the Temenggong to receive an annual salary of 3,000 Spanish dollars. Both Malay rulers declared their intention to protect and regulate the port of Singapore, to 'aid and assist [the English] against all enemies' and not to form any alliances with other nations. On the final page, Raffles affixed his signature and the Company seal; Sultan Hussein and the Temenggong added theirs and the deal was done.

Yet the occasion seemed to warrant something extra, at least to show that what had just transpired signified more than the mere signing of a trade agreement. The difficulty for the British was that no formal precedents for Company officials acting as king-makers so far existed. What followed probably forced Raffles and his associates into some hasty improvisation. After the Treaty signing, the Union

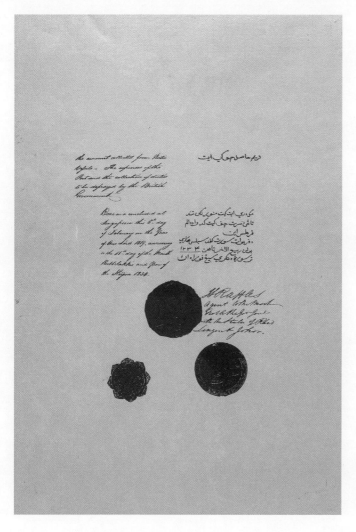

Facsimile of the last page of the Treaty of Friendship and Alliance of 1819, showing the signatures of Raffles, the newly installed Sultan Hussein and Temenggong Abdul Rahman.

6 February 1819
Ink on paper
H 57.5 x 39 cm
NMS XXXX-02869-006

Jack was raised on the beach, to an accompaniment of artillery volleys and salutes. Then the Company officers and Malay leaders celebrated with a banquet.

Captain Crawford, who seems to have been offended by everything that he witnessed the day modern Singapore was established, observed that the Malay chiefs sat down 'promiscuously' with the British, who quaffed 'royal bumpers' undoubtedly filled with some form of alcoholic consolation. Around 4 p.m., once everyone's stomachs had been sated and the minimum diplomatic niceties observed, all parties repaired separately to get on with business – Raffles and Farquhar to consider the practical details of their new settlement, Sultan Hussein and the Temenggong to confer over what this latest turn of events meant in the broader context of regional politics.

Looking back at a date in history that marks the foundation of modern Singapore, it's striking how banal the reality seems to have been. Any sense of momentous occasion was buried under legal formalities and curtailed by the desire of Raffles and the British to get things over and done with as quickly as possible. The day immediately after the Treaty was signed, Raffles left. In the words of Governor John Bannerman of Penang (more of whom shortly), the new settlement's founder was 'like a man who sets a house on fire and then runs away'.

But the day's somewhat hasty and unremarkable proceedings also masked something else: the weeks of careful planning, networking and deal-making that had preceded the Treaty's signing. Indeed, the whole occasion – which if we read Crawford's account brings to mind the visit of a troupe of actors performing with great seriousness in front of a local village crowd – belies the sheer audacity of the intrigue that surrounded it. For some would say that the island of Singapura was not really Sultan Hussein's to give away to the British in the first place.

Rivals and renegades: Hussein, the EIC and the VOC

'[A] Rajah, as if dropped from the clouds, made his appearance in the village, declaring himself the lawful sovereign of the whole territories extending from Lingen [Lingga] and Johore to Mount Muar near Malacca ...' So wrote Crawford of Sultan Hussein's arrival in Singapore on 1 February 1819. He might well have added that the new Sultan arrived with several dark clouds still hanging over his head.

Hussein, since the death of his father Sultan Mahmud in 1812, had been embroiled in a dynastic struggle with his half-brother Tengku Abdul Rahman (not to be confused with the Temenggong, also named Abdul Rahman) over who would inherit the Johor-Riau-Lingga sultanate. As the elder of the two, Hussein's claim was strong and supported by the Temenggong. However, the Bugis Raja Muda, another hereditary minister in the sultanate and the major power behind the Riau throne, preferred Abdul Rahman. In the intrigue that followed, the Temenggong made an effort to remove Abdul Rahman from office and install Hussein in his place. When this attempt failed, the Temenggong relocated to Singapore with his followers. From this time Hussein to all appearances seems to have settled into semi-retirement, biding his time until a Scottish major named William Farquhar decided to pay him a visit.

The exact details of Farquhar's scheming are still not entirely clear. In 1818, the year before he set sail for Singapore, he had already struck a trade agreement with Tengku Abdul Rahman. However, just a few weeks prior to the British landing on the island, Abdul Rahman elected to side with the Dutch and allow them to set up trading posts across the sultanate. Changing tack, Farquhar now went to Hussein, promising him support so long as Britain secured its port at Singapore. Bugis accounts tell us that at a meeting between Farquhar, Hussein and the Temenggong in Riau at the end of 1818 a deal was hammered out. After that, it was simply a matter of getting Hussein across to Singapore to meet Raffles and complete the paperwork.

But by recognising Sultan Hussein as the heir to Johor-Riau-Lingga, then having him sign over a part of Singapore to the British, Raffles and Farquhar were stamping all over Dutch toes. Legally, Dutch officials could claim that 'their' sultan – the 'real' Sultan Abdul Rahman – had granted them the sole right

East India Company coin showing the Company's coat of arms and year of mintage (1804). The motto of the Company, 'Auspicio Regis et Senatus Anglia' (By the Command of the King and Parliament of England), is engraved on a ribbon at the base of the coat of arms.
1804
Copper
Dia. 2.5 cm
NMS 1998-00631

Nederlandsch Oost-Indien.

Goed voor DUIZEND Gulden.

Creatie A°. 1815.

اندیا الند *
اد ﻮﻥ ﺳﻮﺭﺓ این کنان *
سریب کلدن *
کجدین ثد تاهر غضیه *

'INDIA 'OLLAND.

to set up a port in Singapore. In their minds, the fact that the Netherlands had not yet established such a settlement did not entitle Raffles and Farquhar to do so. That Raffles and Farquhar acted in a way so likely to provoke their European rivals shows how desperately they wanted to break the Dutch hold over trade in the Malay Peninsula and Archipelago.

In effect, the arrival of both men in Singapore was part of a high-stakes commercial battle for control of maritime Southeast Asia, a battle that had been waged, on and off, between two global companies for the previous two centuries. From the year 1600, the British East India Company (EIC), the sprawling international enterprise that paid Raffles's and Farquhar's salaries, had tried to give British merchants support and protection overseas. At almost exactly the same time, the Dutch had founded their own company, the Verenigde Oostindische Compagnie (often abbreviated to VOC but sometimes, more confusingly, also known as the Dutch East India Company). In the 17th century, the VOC had victoriously seen off the English from the Malay Archipelago and secured a near monopoly of the extremely profitable spice trade. However, during the 18th century the EIC experienced a revival, largely through the success of its trading posts in India. By 1800, 'the Honourable Company', as the EIC was informally and sometimes ironically known (often the behaviour of its employees was just the opposite), had become not simply a trading concern but also a producer of commodities – particularly Indian cloth and Bengal opium. The EIC was therefore on the lookout for new markets where it could sell these commodities, as well as find supplies of new commodities.

In addition, the EIC, having created its own private army, had come to acquire foreign territory in India. With armed backing, the Company could now send in its troops to protect its interests, or simply to secure them in the first place.

Thousand-guilder note of the Verenigde Oostandische Compagnie. Written in both Dutch and Malay, such notes would have circulated across the Johor-Riau-Lingga Sultanate at the time of the founding of colonial Singapore.

1815
Paper
H 13.9 x W 13.4 cm
NMS 1998-01745

Some people will see strong parallels here between the behaviour of Raffles and Co. and more recent interventions by Western governments in the Middle East to protect their oil interests. During both periods, foreign lands were occupied in the name of liberty and free trade, yet not without some degree of public opposition. Moreover, Raffles and Farquhar embarked on their Singapore adventure without much detailed analysis of the costs and benefits involved, without the explicit permission of their Company Directors (the people who paid their salaries and to whom they were accountable), and definitely without a clear 'exit strategy'. And so it was that both these men landed on Singapore, had a talk with the Temenggong, and immediately arranged for a detachment of Indian sepoys and their guns to come ashore – all in the name of, and for the sake of, free international commerce.

The major reason Raffles and Farquhar chose Singapore was the island's perfect location. By 1819, the lucrative 'China trade', especially in shipments between India and China of Bengal opium, had become essential to the Company's liquidity. The Dutch, however, controlled the seaways in Southeast Asia through which EIC ships had to pass. Raffles summarised the problem a year before he landed at Singapore in a letter to the Company's Directors:

> The Dutch possess the only passes through which ships must sail into the Archipelago, the straits of Sunda and Malacca; and the British have now not an inch of ground to stand upon between the Cape of Good Hope and China, nor a single friendly port at which they can water and obtain refreshment.

So Raffles and Farquhar wanted an alternative port that would break Dutch control, and Singapore stood right at the southern entrance to the Straits of Melaka. Yet Dutch dominance of regional ports was not the only reason for the establishment of a new settlement; the landing at Singapore was also a matter of principle. Philosophically, the EIC and the VOC stood poles apart. Spurred on by Enlightenment ideals, the British believed in free trade; that anyone should be able to come into a port and trade there freely – 'freely' meaning that they were free of encumbrances or restrictions, not that they entered the port free of charge (a nominal duty still had to be paid).

The Dutch, in contrast, were strongly monopolistic and preferred to control the entire flow of key goods in and out of their ports, particularly for such extremely profitable commodities as spices and tin. As Raffles saw it, the struggle to create a new British settlement was about which principle should prevail in the Archipelago. He personally envisioned that 'one free port in the seas must eventually destroy the spell of Dutch monopoly'.

This explains why the British arrived in Singapore, and why they were in such a hurry to complete their business. But why were Sultan Hussein and the Temenggong prepared to meet them there and then go along with their plans?

Dynastic rivalry was one reason, but the terms of the 1819 Treaty did not, in fact, give Hussein all of the territory that he might have considered his birthright. At the same time, the Treaty elevated a less powerful colonial faction in the region and risked perpetuating the conflict that had blighted the rule of Hussein's predecessors for the previous three centuries.

In some ways, Hussein's options were limited. It could be argued that since his half-brother in Riau had already sewn up the support of the Dutch, the choice for Hussein was either to gamble on the British or head back into retirement. He might also have seen the Treaty as his best chance for reviving the grandeur of a sultanate which had somehow outlasted the Portuguese and kept the Dutch at bay until the 1780s. After all, the Treaty merely granted the British permission to set up a trading port – from Tanjong Mallang to Tanjong Katong and inland to the range of a 'cannon shot' – without threatening the Malay rulers' legal authority, and the Temenggong was still entitled to half of all the duties levied on native trading vessels. Historian Mary Turnbull has suggested that the Malay rulers 'envisaged a settlement … where a Malay hierarchy would preside over a cosmopolitan trading community, leasing land, judging lawsuits and exacting dues'.

Was it naive of these Malay rulers to imagine that the British would stay within the Treaty's terms and not seek to expand their influence? In one obvious respect, yes; given the speed of European technological advances, the range of a cannon shot would increase decade by decade. But Hussein and the Temenggong may have also been swayed by Farquhar's intentions and approach, which appeared to ensure them a financial stake in the settlement's future along with the respect to which they were accustomed.

Alternatively, their signing of the Treaty could be seen as a simple act of opportunism, an agreement that they would have gladly rescinded if events had played out badly for them. For three centuries, the rulers of Johor-Riau-Lingga had made similar alliances with foreigners, and then broken them off, in an effort to survive and manoeuvre themselves into positions of greater security. The 1819 Treaty may have been little more than the Sultan's and the Temenggong's short-term bet on a European power yet to prove itself in the region, but willing to pay out nice allowances – a document only binding as long as the British stayed around, which, at the time of their arrival in Singapore, was far from a certainty.

The truth is, soon after the Sultan and the Temenggong signed the Treaty, they informed the Dutch (in dispatches to the Dutch in Riau and Melaka) that they had done so simply to keep the British happy. This could be seen as a simple case of backing both horses; but there are also good reasons why we should take Singapore's Malay rulers (at least partially) at face value. Let's not forget that in the glorious name of free trade, the British had arrived on Singapore with their sepoys and their guns, and with a centuries-long reputation for securing their interests in the region any way they could.

5. THE ADVENTURES OF STAMFORD RAFFLES

Sir Stamford Raffles, the man standing eagerly by the tent on 6 February 1819, was not just one of Britain's most remarkable empire-builders, he was also one of its most complicated. To certain of his contemporaries he was an ambitious schemer, a man willing to take all sorts of irresponsible risks to rise up through the ranks of the EIC. To others, particularly his London high-society friends, he was a more romantic figure: the scholar-adventurer who led an invasion of Java and then wrote a famous book on the island's history. In contrast, most people in Singapore today think of Raffles as the visionary idealist credited as the sole founder of their modern city-state. Few remember the heavy personal price that he paid during the settlement's foundation or that, far from emerging a hero, he eventually returned home to England broken-hearted, penniless and exhausted.

Yet it is the complexity in Raffles's personality that makes him so intriguing. Moreover, it is this complexity which links him to several of the broader tensions of the enlightened yet imperial age in which he lived. To follow the career of Raffles the scholar, idealist and schemer, through the years leading up to the

Sir Thomas Stamford Bingley Raffles. Raffles sat for this portrait in 1817, the year he published *A History of Java* and was knighted.

1817
Oil on canvas
H 140 x W 109 cm
NMS HP-0034

49

founding of modern Singapore and after, helps us understand those powerful and often contradictory forces that would shape European imperialism through much of the 19th century.

Early life and arrival in the Straits

Raffles was born at sea in 1781 and spent his childhood in England in poverty. At the age of 14, and after only a limited education, he joined the London headquarters of the EIC as a junior clerk. Within a decade, during which he pursued his studies largely self-taught, he rose through the Company's ranks and was appointed Assistant Secretary to the newly established settlement at Penang, at that time Britain's chief trading post in Southeast Asia. On the long voyage out he had the foresight to begin learning Malay. When he stepped off the boat, bright-eyed and just 26 years of age, he was one of the few British officials able to communicate with the locals in their own language.

His outlook would not have been that different from many of his equally young colleagues. This was a generation that had begun to enjoy the fruits of the European Enlightenment, when there was a great deal of genuine excitement about new types of knowledge, particularly in the areas of science, economics and philosophy. In addition, the unbridled curiosity of the age had resulted in a florescence in the study of the world beyond Europe and especially of Asian or 'Oriental' (as they were called at the time) cultures. Few British people doubted that Raffles and his peers would bring a better way of life to the foreigners they were about to encounter. In turn, such confidence encouraged a certain chutzpah (the less charitable might call it brash foolishness) in young men who, with no prior training, ventured overseas to administer foreign lands they had previously only read about.

What distinguished Raffles was his genuine concern for the well-being of the governed and his dedication to their improvement – albeit, according to very European ideas of what this 'improvement' actually meant. Raffles was no high-minded ascetic; many of his activities were driven forward by a determination to secure the EIC's commercial position. Nevertheless, he seems to have had little concern for personal wealth, in stark contrast to a previous generation of EIC officials whose private fortunes, amassed through their exploits in India, had brought about a major public scandal. When we consider the poverty of Raffles's upbringing, his lack of materialism stands out. If the ambitious young official had an insatiable longing to achieve greatness, as many of his biographers have noted, then that longing was directed toward high-minded idealism, not to the stockpiling of a small Eastern treasure-house.

While Raffles was stationed in Penang he made two visits to Melaka, which the British had seized from the Dutch in 1795. His sojourns there were not for recreation, but to overcome fever (most likely caused by the malaria that killed

George Town, Penang.
1814
Aquatint
H 14.2 x W 21.7 cm
NMS 1994-00276

so many young EIC servants). It says much for his incessant energy that his reaction to a forced period of convalescence was to throw himself further into his studies. In Melaka, he delved deeper into the Malay language, Malay customs and Malay history. Here, he also met the local British official in charge, Major William Farquhar.

What stands out from both these sojourns is that Raffles was already imagining alternatives to Penang as Britain's main regional trading base. What is more, wherever this base was eventually to be located, he believed it had to be rooted in the local Malay psyche. And so, before Raffles even dreamed of Singapore, he fell briefly in love with Melaka – that once great port, he wrote, whose 'name carries more weight in a Malay ear than any new Settlement, whatever its importance'.

In fact, it appears that wherever Raffles went in Southeast Asia, be it Melaka, Sumatra or finally Singapore, he 'discovered' that place to have once been the ancient centre of the Malay world and thus the best place to establish a new British settlement. Raffles envisioned that such a settlement would restore the greatness of the Malay kingdoms of old and simultaneously serve the EIC's commercial and political interests (though it remains unclear how its second purpose could be reconciled with its first).

Yet while Raffles stayed in Penang he remained the hard working Assistant Secretary with grand ideas about the Company's future but little yet to show for them. The crucial event that got him out of the settlement, and then transformed him into 'Sir' Stamford Raffles 'of the Eastern Isles', as he was later known, occurred in 1811. It was an event that revealed Raffles to be audacious, lucky and filled with such an assured sense of self-importance that at times it bordered on the comical.

The Java Expedition, 1811

Since the early 17th century, the island of Java had played 'host' to the Dutch. However, by 1800 the French Revolutionary and then the Napoleonic Wars had seen the Netherlands occupied by the French. In 1808, Emperor Napoleon ordered Marshall Herman Willem Daendels to Java to administer the colony, and in so doing fuelled British concerns that the French were planning an offensive against British possessions in the East. In a climate full of wartime fear and suspicion, Raffles arrived at the EIC headquarters in Calcutta – in what turned out to be a glorious case of being in just the right place at just the right time.

The irony of Raffles's visit to Calcutta was that at first it seemed he was heading toward an embarrassing humiliation. Raffles had voyaged to Calcutta to see Lord Minto, the Governor General of Bengal, confident that he was about to be given what he believed to be a much-deserved promotion to administer the Spice Islands (today's Maluku Islands). He discovered, on his arrival, that while he had been crossing the Bay of Bengal the appointment had been given to somebody else. Not the kind of man to retreat in disappointment having travelled so far, Raffles went ahead with his meeting with Minto anyway. Raffles recorded that when the interview commenced, he 'drew his Lordship's attention to Java':

> On the mention of Java, his Lordship cast a look of such scrutiny, anticipation and kindness upon me, as I shall never forget. 'Yes', said he, 'Java is an interesting Island; I shall be happy to receive any information you can give me concerning it'.

Straightaway, Minto promoted Raffles and sent him back to Melaka with orders to establish an intelligence network to assess Dutch defences in Java and sound out local opposition in preparation for Britain's proposed annexation of

Boats by the waterfront in Batavia, Java.

Mid-19th century
Lithograph
H 21.5 x W 30.8 cm
NMS XXXX-01158

the island. Clearly, the conquest of a new territory got everyone in and around Melaka excited. The British invasion fleet that gathered in the harbour was one of the most breathtaking ever seen in the region: 57 ships, carrying 11,000 troops, and led by his Lordship Governor General Minto in person. A young Malay scribe by the name of Munshi Abdullah recalled:

> Every day in varying numbers ships came … until the Melaka roads were so full of ships lying at anchor that the masts of the vessels looked like the poles of a fence … At that time no woman dared to move from her house because of the English and Indian soldiers who lay in a drunken stupor along the roads and who engaged in noisy brawls.

In June 1811, the invasion fleet set off for Java and after encountering minimal Dutch resistance (the most lethal threat to the invaders came from illnesses they had picked up in Melaka before they set out) the British secured the island. Raffles was duly appointed Java's first British Lieutenant Governor and at the age of 30 a brilliant future seemed his for the taking.

Yet Raffles the administrator proved to be a very different creature from Raffles the adventurer. What should have been his apotheosis – Java was a larger, richer, more complex island than Singapore and steeped in a much deeper recorded history – turned out to be a disaster. In a letter home he admitted, 'I am here alone, without any advice, in a new country with a large native population of not less than six or seven millions of people.' In particular, his introduction of enlightened schemes to raise the condition of these 'six or seven millions' (which included banning the slave trade, limiting the opium trade, introducing partial self-government and replacing the Dutch forced agriculture system with a more equitable land tenure system) though idealistic, proved ruinously expensive. By the time the Napoleonic Wars came to an end in 1815 and peacetime negotiations between Britain and the Netherlands commenced, the EIC Directors had lost so much money on a colony they had hardly wanted in the first place that they were quite happy to see the Dutch get it back.

Interestingly, when Raffles departed Java for England in March 1816, partly to clear his name with his EIC bosses, he decided to pay Napoleon a visit. The fallen Emperor was then imprisoned on the island of St Helena in the middle of the Atlantic and Raffles' desire to see him tells us much about the Englishman's self-image. To Raffles, Napoleon was the man whose talents 'always demanded my admiration' and whom up till then he obviously regarded as some kind of kindred spirit.

But the great meeting of minds failed to materialise. Napoleon, vanquished and clearly unimpressed at being treated like a caged exhibit for the entertainment of Europe's good, great and would-be great, proved rude and truculent. A disappointed Raffles declared afterwards that his once great hero now generated feelings in him only of 'horror, disgust and alarm'.

Gilbert Elliot,
First Earl of Minto.
From R. Montgomery Martin, *Our Indian Empire*, London, 1860.

In personal terms, the main positive to come out of Raffles's Java experience was his two-volume *A History of Java*, which he published, following his return to Britain, in 1817. This work earned Raffles his knighthood and his election as a Fellow of the Royal Society. During this same interlude back in his homeland he also married his second wife Sophia (herself the daughter of an EIC servant). All in all, this was a happy time for Raffles. Whatever disappointments Java had brought, he now had a devoted new wife and had been welcomed into London high society. Here, his abilities as a scholar-adventurer were lauded, his failings as an administrator politely forgotten.

Of course, these failings were not so easy for the Directors of the EIC to forget; yet Raffles' newfound fame placed them in a predicament. When the man who had lost them so much money last time he journeyed east came looking for a new appointment, such was his status that they could hardly refuse him. Their solution was to send him out to Fort Marlborough in Bencoolen (modern-day Bengkulu), an isolated British outpost on the south coast of Sumatra that had been hopelessly unprofitable since its establishment in 1685. There can be little doubt that Raffles's appointment there was a kind of punishment for his earlier misdemeanours in Java. Perhaps the EIC Directors even hoped to cure the idealistic Raffles of his 'enlightened' excesses.

To Singapore via Bencoolen

Raffles, nonetheless, took the appointment and set sail, accompanied by a pregnant Sophia who, like his own mother, gave birth at sea. What greeted the young family on their arrival in Bencoolen was far from Raffles's previous experience of the region, and probably far also from what Sophia had imagined. Raffles described the tiny settlement that was to be their home for the next six years as 'without exception the most wretched place I ever beheld'. He noted that the locals called it *tana mati* [dead land], a description with which he immediately agreed, little suspecting how true to its name the *tana mati* would be.

Basically, Bencoolen was too obscure, too remote and too small for a man of Raffles's ambitions. He stuck it out for five months, during which time he tried his luck at extending British influence in Sumatra further north to the ports of Padang and Palembang. If supported, Raffles felt, these actions would give Britain greater access to the Straits of Melaka at the expense of the Dutch. However, such support was not forthcoming. When the Dutch discovered what Raffles was up to they protested to his superiors in Calcutta who ordered him to retreat. Calcutta was unwilling to risk a confrontation with a European power with which Britain had only recently sat down at the negotiating table.

Raffles's response was by now typical of the man. Undeterred by his failure to secure a Sumatran port, in September 1818 he set sail for Calcutta to speak with the new Governor General of Bengal, Lord Hastings. The whole trip had a certain

East India Company coin, obverse.
1804
Copper
Dia. 2.0 cm
NMS 1998-00627

quality of déjà vu about it. As on the voyage out from London, Sophia accompanied Raffles and was once more pregnant; Raffles now approached Calcutta once again, with another audacious scheme designed to release him from obscurity.

The question that emerges from his meeting with Hastings is whether anyone apart from Raffles and Farquhar intended there ever to be a new British settlement on Singapore. Hastings's official orders to Raffles in November 1818 reveal how important he felt it was for the EIC to 'secure the free passage of the Straits of Malacca'. Raffles was to go and try and make a treaty with Aceh to this effect. But the more pressing of Hastings's concerns was the 'establishment of a station beyond Malacca, such as may command the entrance of those Straits'. The Governor General felt that Riau was likely to be the best option, if the Dutch had not yet already occupied it.

At the same time, Hastings's letter also contained two warnings. First, Raffles was told that the object of a trading post was 'not the extension of any territorial influence', merely the occupation of an 'advantageous position' to protect British commerce. Second, Raffles was to 'abstain from all negotiation and collision' if the Dutch had already made a reappearance in Riau.

In reality, what did these warnings mean? Was Raffles to avoid all 'negotiation and collision' specifically as regards the island of Riau, or across the entire Johor-Riau-Lingga sultanate? The ambiguity was still there when Hastings sent Raffles further orders to ascertain who controlled Johor, with a view to it becoming an alternative to Riau if the latter had already returned to Dutch hands. Hastings again warned Raffles not to get into a dispute with the Dutch if they claimed authority over Johor, but once more his instructions did not explicitly refer to the island of Singapore or any of the other small territories that in the Sultan's view made up his realm. From the general tone of Hastings's instructions, Raffles

Fort Marlborough, Bencoolen, Sumatra by Joseph C. Stadler, after Andrews.
1799
Aquatint
Courtesy of British Library P326

might have gathered that anywhere the Dutch claimed was officially within their authority was now off limits to the British. However, Hastings's failure to indicate this precisely was one of those important little things that made the establishment of modern Singapore possible.

The cost of founding Singapore

Given the Dutch claim to Singapore, it's not surprising that when news spread that the British flag had been planted on the island angry correspondence flew from Batavia (known today as Jakarta) to Calcutta, and between The Hague and London. Well, not exactly 'flew': in these last decades before steamships replaced sail, letters to London from the Straits frequently took more than six months to reach their destination. As a result, the legality of Raffles's action was not sorted out by the British and Dutch governments until several years later. By that time, the British settlement on Singapore was already up and running, and doing well enough to ensure that the EIC was unlikely to hand it over.

In the interim, however, Raffles was denounced from several quarters. Compared with his later renown, it's remarkable how unpopular he became at this time. Certainly, the European merchants of Calcutta were delighted with the new British base and the commerce it promised. But in the British Parliament, Raffles was labelled 'a mere trade agent who has caused embarrassment to the government'. The last thing the EIC Directors wanted was a confrontation with the Dutch over the acquisition of territory by a 'commercial representative with no authority to make any political arrangements'.

Understandably, Dutch officials were furious. In particular, Baron Godert van der Capellen, the Governor General of Java, appears to have taken Raffles's actions personally. Van der Capellen condemned Raffles as 'untiring in inventing means to prejudice us and to provoke actions which I shall fight as long as possible', and exhorted his superiors in The Hague not to let the Englishman get away with his political sleight-of-hand. At times, Van der Capellen seems to have felt that Raffles was trying to goad him into an open conflict:

> Mr Raffles's way of acting with regard to Singapore surpasses anything which he has done so far. Nothing would please him more than to make us lose our patience with his frantic deeds and fire the first shot.

The tension between the two men dated back to when Raffles had attempted to extend British influence in Sumatra. As Van der Capellen had done then, so he did again in 1819 when news reached him that Raffles had landed on Singapore: he wrote to Calcutta to protest, fully expecting the EIC to rein in their young hothead once more. Van der Capellen's decision to seek a diplomatic solution over Singapore, rather than send in his troops, was another crucial decision that helped ensure the new settlement survived.

The duel between both men eventually saw Raffles emerge as the winner – the dashing hero who would be immortalised through lofty biographies and even loftier statues. The EIC, in spite of both Dutch protests and their own sense of embarrassment, failed to order Raffles off Singapore and Van der Capellen was left to rue the Englishman's superior gall and initiative. His last contact with Raffles occurred in 1823, by which time he blamed his English rival for being 'the sole author of all the disputes which have arisen between us'. In that year, Van der Capellen made his feelings clear to Raffles with a classic case of the diplomatic sulks. Raffles, having departed Singapore for the last time, had been forced to make an unplanned stop at Batavia, partly because Sophia was feverish. However, Van der Capellen refused to give Raffles permission to land, effectively labelling Raffles *persona non grata* 'after all that has happened since 1818'.

If Raffles had outwitted Van der Capellen and the Dutch with the founding of a new British settlement, what kind of victory was it? In Bencoolen, in the years after his successful landing at Singapore, Raffles and Sophia lost three of their four young children to fever; only their daughter survived. Shattered by grief, Raffles's own health deteriorated and he became afflicted by severe headaches that confined him to bed for days. To make matters worse, when he returned to Britain, the EIC decided not to grant him a pension but instead billed him for the expenses of the entire Singapore expedition and the costs relating to the settlement's establishment. Raffles died in 1826, at the age of 45, reportedly of a brain haemorrhage and deeply in debt.

In every way, Singapore cost Raffles dearly. That we even remember him today as the spirited young adventurer presented in his portraits is largely because of

Sophia Raffles, 1817.

from *Sir Thomas Stamford Raffles: Book of Days*, Antiques of the Orient, Singapore,1993.

his widow. In 1830, Sophia published her *Memoir of the Life and Public Services of Sir Thomas Stamford Raffles,* a mammoth biography which became an immediate hit. Posthumously, it established Raffles as one of Britain's greatest empire-builders through what, to more critical minds, remains one of the finest public relations jobs in European colonial history.

Yet we might still find it difficult to grasp why men such as Raffles sacrificed so much – their reputations, their health, even their families – in what were, for them, strange and foreign lands. These were the days before inoculations, penicillin, anti-malarial drugs and modern transport, when colonial outposts in Asia frequently turned into colonial death traps. Singapore was an exception – it was actually considered, in relative terms, an early 19th-century health resort. But a walk through an expatriate graveyard in places such as Madras or Hong Kong quickly makes evident the enormous number of Europeans who, whatever their hopes and ambitions, came out East simply to die, and frequently to die young.

Why, then, did Raffles and his peers come? For some, wealth would have been a lure, though by the time Raffles arrived in the Straits, better accounting practices had made the chance of personal profit through the EIC more uncommon. (Raffles himself felt the hardness of the Company's new regimen when he received the Company's itemised bill for his expenses in founding Singapore.) Likewise, the incomes that Company officials once might have secured for their relatives and friends were becoming harder to obtain. Raffles did manage to set up his brother-in-law, William Flint, with an easy position as Master Attendant of the Singapore harbour, from whence Flint pocketed sizeable profits from hiring out lighters and by collecting anchorage and port clearance fees. However, such irregularities were increasingly frowned upon. Within a few years, and with Raffles back in England, Flint found his privileges as Master Attendant taken away. Like Raffles, he also died in debt.

Another motive, certainly, was to be upwardly mobile. The British Empire continued to be a stage on which a penurious junior clerk could eventually rise to become a knight of the realm and, in an age before mass communications, a celebrity. We should also not forget the religious zeal of men like Raffles, nor their simple enjoyment of power; for even in the case of those idealists who believed that they governed for the betterment of Asian peoples, they never wavered in their belief that Asian peoples still had to be 'governed' – always from above, without representation and by Europeans, who invariably knew better.

However, in the end, perhaps the most powerful reason for the long voyage east was also the simplest: the sheer excitement that 'the Orient' presented Raffles and his enlightened generation. In an age before the vicarious thrills offered by modern technology, when longevity was a blessing but not an expectation, life was there to be lived to the full – something that few people can deny Sir Stamford Raffles managed to achieve.

6. THE RAJA MELAKA: SINGAPORE'S OTHER FOUNDER

'You will immediately embark on the brig *Ganges* and proceed to the Straits of Singapore ...'

So read Raffles's instructions to Major William Farquhar on 16 January 1819. Farquhar at once ordered his prize possessions to be packed and sent along after him. These included a leopard, a porcupine, monkeys and birds, as well as a set of stunning watercolours made by Chinese artists that captured the flora and fauna of the Malay Peninsula. Altogether, it was a fitting collection for a man who had spent almost 30 of his then 49 years in 'the East' and who, by this time, had become deeply attached to the local environment and its people.

Earlier, things had been a little different. Farquhar's relationship with the East, like that of other young men drawn to serve in the EIC in the late 1700s, commenced with violence. In 1790, at the age of 20, he signed on as a cadet with the Royal Madras Engineers and saw military action in campaigns against the Sultan of Mysore and the French in South India. Following this, he joined the British forces that in 1795, with barely a shot being fired, seized Melaka from the Dutch. He stayed on in Melaka and rose through the Company's ranks to become, from 1803, the city's official British Resident – a job that despite its innocuous

William Farquhar. This portrait was completed nine years before his death in 1839.
1830
Oil on canvas
Estate of William Farquhar

title involved full responsibilities for the settlement's administration. However, in 1818 the British promised to return Melaka to the Dutch through a formal treaty. Farquhar turned to pursuing various trade treaties in the region on behalf of the EIC, but practically speaking he was out of a job.

He probably had this in mind when he applied for and was granted leave to return to Britain for three years. But then Raffles's orders arrived, which Farquhar received while in transit at Penang. Suddenly, he found himself launched on an endeavour that would bring him moments of fulfilment, yet ultimately end in a very public and acrimonious spat with his erstwhile colleague. Well after the events of early 1819, Farquhar would be left nursing a deep-seated sense of personal injustice over the founding of the Singapore settlement.

Farquhar and Raffles side by side

Raffles had chosen Farquhar as Singapore's first Resident and Commandant. Unlike the Company's Supreme Government back in London, Farquhar shared Raffles's conviction that a British outpost closer to the Straits of Singapore was a vital necessity. In addition, both men – as students of the Malay world, its peoples, customs and politics – had come to believe that the time was ripe for action.

There, however, the similarities end. In physical terms, Farquhar was Raffles's senior in age and clearly distinguishable by his prominent bald pate with side-fringes of wispy white hair. Farquhar also stood taller than Raffles (the latter being a man of more Napoleonic proportions – that is to say, short). An abiding image of Farquhar from this time is of an amiable, middle-aged Scot who strode about Melaka with his walking stick, forever accompanied by his loyal dogs. Until one of these dogs was devoured by a crocodile, it was almost as if Farquhar had never left the hills outside his native Aberdeen. By contrast, the famous portrait of Raffles from 1817 presents him as young, ambitious and collected, staring out at us with the unmistakable glint of a visionary in his eye.

In temperament, also, the two men appear to have been quite distinct. Raffles, as a rational man of the Enlightenment who had ventured into what he believed to be the still-darkened world of the Malays, was a bundle of ceaseless energy – a 'spirit that will never allow the East to be quiet', as he proudly tells us his contemporaries described him. By comparison, Farquhar was a man more content to go with the flow and accommodate to the local order, an easy-going pragmatist with less of the uncompromising idealism of his ambitious colleague.

Individual experience made this contrast more pronounced. Farquhar had experienced a longer and more successful stint in the region than Raffles, and it's probable that this experience made him less keen on the Englishman's style of enlightened interference. Indeed, Farquhar's relaxed style of administration in Melaka so endeared him to local residents that they affectionately dubbed him the 'Raja Melaka'.

Farquhar's natural history drawings

This collection of 477 natural history drawings was commissioned by William Farquhar when he was British Resident and Commandant of Melaka from 1803 to 1818. He engaged Chinese artists in Melaka to undertake the drawings, and brought the collection to Singapore when he became its first Resident in 1819. He brought the drawings with him when he left Singapore in 1823. As far as is known, Farquhar did not commission any natural history drawings in Singapore. On 17 November 1827, Farquhar donated the collection to the Royal Asiatic Society (RAS) in London. This contributed to the birth of the RAS's own collection of natural history drawings. Over 170 years later, the collection was offered for sale by the RAS on condition that it was acquired in its entirety. G. K. Goh, a Singaporean

stockbroker and philanthropist, purchased the collection in mid-1995 and donated it to the National Museum of Singapore later that year.

In the execution of the drawings, the unidentified Chinese artists in Melaka would have made references to traditional Chinese manuals of painting such as *The Mustard Seed Garden Manual of Painting* and the *Ten Bamboo Studio Album*. The paintings are executed in the *gongbi* style of brushwork with its great attention to detail.

Another characteristic of the drawings is the lack of linear perspective. Many drawings of the animals depict them against a landscape of stylised rocks and wind-swept grass in flat, two-dimensional space, true to traditional Chinese artistic practice. As a result, the animals appear to be 'floating' on

the landscape. The stylised landscape moreover does not resemble the local terrain.

It is clear that the artists, with their training in the traditional Chinese artistic style of drawing, tried to come to terms with the European style of natural history drawings that have a high degree of precise detail and accurate perspective. The Chinese artists' attempts give the Farquhar collection a unique place in the history of British settlement in Melaka as they record a European–Oriental artistic encounter. Farquhar's collection remains a legacy of his career in the East.

FROM LEFT:
Asian Fairy-Bluebird
Watercolour in the *gongbi* style
H 47 x W 30 cm
NMS 1995-3234

Matonia fern
Watercolour in the *gongbi* style
H 39.5 x W 29 cm
NMS 1995-2846

Lesser Mousedeer
Watercolour in the *gongbi* style
H 47 x W 30 cm
NMS 1995-2892

Raffles, on the other hand, had desired to return to the Tropics and make his name with a new enlightened society as fast as he could. Following the Java debacle, Singapore offered the ideal laboratory in which to execute his philosophical principles. Among other things, he hoped that the Malays and Chinese would learn natural history and the Newtonian system of astronomy. Out of the Malay spotlight for too long, Raffles was a man on a mission.

Crucially, each man's attitude to the Malay world, and to Britain's role within it, shaped the character of the early Singapore settlement in distinct ways. Raffles the passionate historian dreamt of a glorious emporium that would succeed the fabled Malay kingdoms of old and become a model Malay society. The flipside to his visionary imagination was a stubbornness and ruthlessness that on occasion rode roughshod over local sensibilities. One of Raffles's most infamous acts in Singapore was the punishment he meted out to Sayid Yasin, a debtor who had run amok. Yasin had stabbed Farquhar and then died in the mêlée that followed this attack, yet Raffles had his corpse placed in a cage and hung from a wooden gibbet for three days to rot. The founder of modern Singapore might have wanted this punishment to serve as an example to the local populace, but his actions contravened Muslim practice for the proper burial of dead bodies and caused deep resentment.

Farquhar, in contrast, seems to have been more sensitive to local practices and attitudes; in fact, in some respects he might be said to have 'gone native'. While Resident of Melaka he had taken a Melakan wife, a half-Malay Eurasian by the name of Nonio Clement, who bore him six children. During the personal dispute that was to erupt between Farquhar and Raffles, Farquhar's domestic arrangements in the Straits would not go unmentioned.

The settlement's early days

In 1819, the open animosity between Farquhar and Raffles was still a few years away. Nonetheless, from the moment they both set foot on Singapore, a clear hierarchy between the two men was evident. The Englishman Raffles immediately went inside to talk politics with the Temenggong in his hut. Meanwhile, the Scot Farquhar went for a walk around the Singapore River where he met with Captain Daniel Ross (another Scot) and set about planning the practicalities of the settlement and its harbour. When Hussein arrived in Singapore a few days later, Raffles invited him onto his ship for a private talk, apparently without Farquhar present (even though Farquhar had only just returned from a mission to Riau to assess the possibility of Dutch intervention). Finally, after both Raffles and Farquhar had signed the treaty with Hussein and the Temenggong, Raffles went back on board to draft Farquhar a series of instructions. As Raffles's ship, the *Indiana*, sailed out of the harbour bound for Bencoolen, Farquhar was left sitting in a tent on the beach to consider the enormity of the task that Raffles had left him.

Raffles Coat of Arms.

From *Sir Thomas Stamford Raffles: Book of Days*, Antiques of the Orient, Singapore, 1993

The most alarming of Raffles's recommendations would most likely have been the one stating that Singapore should remain a free port: 'It is not necessary at present to subject the trade of the port to any duties.' This presented Farquhar with a dilemma. As Java had shown, Raffles had never been the most practical of Company officials and now the grand idealist was at it again, making demands with respect to the formation of Singapore's bureaucracy and the execution of various public works for its defence, with little thought as to where the money would come from. Without resort to duties, how was Farquhar to raise the necessary finance? The simple problem of cash flow was to plague his administration of Singapore from the outset.

Once Raffles had departed, however, Farquhar's immediate concerns were security and provisions. For the initial expedition party there had been little more to eat than fruit and the fish caught by the local *orang laut*. Farquhar therefore sent news to Melaka that he had landed in Singapore and that a new settlement had been founded by the British. What followed amounted to a Melakan 'exodus': on hearing Farquhar's news, Melakan men, especially Indian and local-born Chinese (known as Baba or Peranakan Chinese) packed their boats with provisions and set off south. The newly reinstalled Dutch, seeing the depletion of Melaka's merchant community, attempted to blockade the harbour; yet by 1823, somewhere in the region of 5,000 traders, peddlers, carpenters, labourers and miscellaneous others had escaped Melaka and followed Farquhar to Singapore, a testimony to the Raja Melaka's reputation. Some of those first Chinese who arrived quickly transformed themselves from sellers of chickens and vegetables into powerful *taukeh* (business owners). As Raffles's Malay scribe Munshi Abdullah put it, at a time when Melaka was experiencing 'great drought' Singapore was visited 'with the rain of plenty'.

As for security, the problem was harder to resolve. If Dutch forces in Riau and especially Melaka were to invade Singapore, Farquhar had no more than a hundred Bengal sepoys at his command, many on the verge of mutiny because their home leave had been interrupted by the Singapore expedition. Their light artillery would do little to rebuff a sea-borne bombardment from Dutch men-of-war; on top of this, the one ship Farquhar had left in his command had been ravaged by white ants and was now un-seaworthy. When, on 6 March, Captain Ross returned from Melaka with a mistaken report that the Dutch were making preparations for an invasion, even a quick getaway seemed out of the question.

The situation that developed revealed how far the British landing at Singapore was resented by not just Dutch but other British officials. Unable to contact Raffles, who was on his way back to Bencoolen, Farquhar sent a boat to Penang to request reinforcements. What he received was a near-empty ship carrying 6,000 Spanish dollars and some not-so-friendly advice from the Governor of Penang, Colonel John Bannerman, to get off the island quickly. Bannerman was against any attempt to establish a new settlement in the Straits that might rival

Fort Cornwallis, Prince of
Wales Island (Penang).
1813
Aquatint
H 14.0 x W 23.2 cm
NMS 2000-06696

Fort Cornwallis — Prince of Wales's Island

his own; he also expected that a Dutch invasion of Singapore was imminent. His justification for withholding military support was that this would make it easier for Calcutta to order Farquhar's withdrawal. Moreover, Bannerman believed that in the event of a conflict, the smaller the British force on the island, the fewer the casualties from an inevitable defeat.

Eventually, news reached Raffles of Farquhar's plight and a detachment of 485 troops from Bencoolen arrived in Singapore on 1 April. A few weeks later, another 200 reinforcements were sent from Penang after Calcutta had reprimanded Bannerman and forced him into a volte-face. The immediate danger subsided, yet the possibility of a Dutch invasion had been a real one – so real that (as we discovered earlier in Chapter 4) Sultan Hussein and the Temenggong, after signing the Treaty, had taken the precaution of dispatching letters to the Dutch to explain that the notion of a British settlement on Singapore had not been theirs and that they had agreed to it under duress. Until the British presence on the island increased and it became clear that the Company was not going to abandon it, the 1819 Treaty did not appear to be worth much more than the paper it was written on.

Building the town

Once Raffles left Singapore and returned to Bencoolen, correspondence between himself and Farquhar was rather infrequent. A letter took six to eight weeks to travel between the two settlements, and Farquhar's first report was only submitted to Raffles in September 1819, over six months after Singapore had been founded. Farquhar thus had some breathing space from his energetic superior to set about the establishment of the new settlement as he thought best. Raffles did return in late May 1819, with building materials, bullocks and as writer H. F. Pearson puts it 'enough boxes of stationery for the administration to tie itself up in red tape for years to come' – but after that he was gone for a further three and a half years.

Under Farquhar's guidance, Singapore might not have been the enlightened settlement Raffles had imagined; nonetheless, it was clearly a success. By 1821, the population had grown to around 5,000, and 8 million Spanish dollars' worth of commerce had passed through the harbour. Farquhar's policy was to govern with, and through, the Sultan and the Temenggong, allowing them to retain certain of their traditional rights over duties and slaves and to join him in a three-man council to mete out justice.

However, to solve the problem of revenue Raffles's instructions had been completely ignored. Against his superior's wishes, Farquhar sold licences for gambling and the sale of liquor and opium. Ironically, profits from what Raffles would have considered ill-gotten gains funded Singapore's first steps toward becoming a model European colony. Farquhar's Licence Fund helped pay for a police force, expeditions to put down piracy, street cleaners, and even grass-cutters.

When Raffles returned to Singapore again in October 1822 his first impressions were positive: 'Here is all life and activity; and it would be difficult to name a place on the face of the globe with brighter prospects or more pleasant satisfaction.' However, his opinion changed once it became clear how many of his instructions the Resident had failed to execute. In a heated exchange of correspondence that lasted several months, Raffles faulted Farquhar over his management of the

Singapore Town Plan. This plan, based on Raffles's instructions to the Town Committee formed to assist in the reorganisation of the settlement, was drawn up by Lieutenant Philip Jackson, the settlement's Executive Engineer and Surveyor. As drawn, the plan was not based on an actual survey but was more of an ideal layout proposed by the committee, in line with Raffles's aspirations for the orderly development of the settlement.

1828
Paper
H 10.8 x W 17.5 cm
NMS XXXX-02072-002

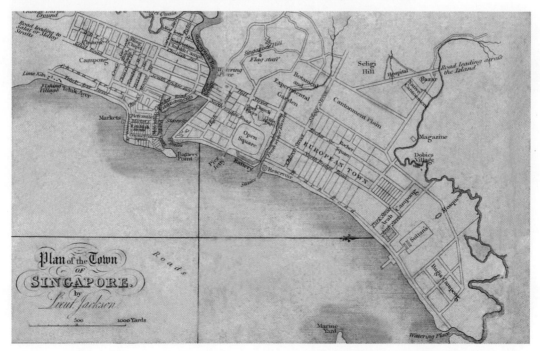

settlement and for its lax condition. In his defence, Farquhar claimed that he had done all that it was in his power to do. Nonetheless, his policy towards licensed vice, especially gambling, was anathema to Raffles, who instead introduced explicit new regulations that banned public gambling and imposed much severer taxes on liquor and opium.

But the key issue that prompted Raffles's dissatisfaction was the manner in which the settlement had been laid out. Among other things, Farquhar had neglected Raffles's wishes by permitting the erection of Chinese godowns[*] and Malay *attap* houses on the Padang and the north bank of the river. Raffles had wanted these areas kept clear for European residents and government buildings, with non-Europeans to settle on the south bank of the river. Farquhar, in his defence, explained that the south bank of the river tended to flood and he had found it impossible to convince new arrivals to build there. To Raffles, this was hardly a valid excuse. Troops and labourers were mustered to make the land habitable; meanwhile, the authorities pulled down the homes of those who had built them in the 'wrong' place and evicted their occupants. According to Munshi Abdullah, all over the settlement men could be seen building houses, looking 'as if they were going to war'.

Raffles next set to work on a reorganisation of the settlement that would remain his enduring legacy, a lasting imprint of his concern for rational, enlightened order. To the north and the south of the river, ethnic neighbourhoods were designated for the Chinese, Malays, Bugis and Indians, and space reserved for government buildings, religious sites and a botanic garden. Regulations governed the width of streets, the size of houses and even the materials to be used in their construction. The new plan was discussed by a Town Committee, sometimes in consultation with local communities, and drawn up by the engineer Lieutenant Philip Jackson in 1822. By the time Raffles left the island he had laid down a blueprint for future generations of urban planners that ensured Singapore, at least within the European Town, would not be left to sprawl and suffocate. Considering Raffles's repeated bouts of illness during the execution of this plan, his achievement was remarkable – a triumph of will over the existing environment and his own frail body.

Farquhar and Raffles fall out

Raffles's other major achievement during his final stay in Singapore was to arrange for Farquhar's removal from office. Within a year of Raffles's return, relations had soured between both men to the extent that not even Farquhar's near-fatal stabbing at the hands of Sayid Yasin could salvage them. In January 1823, Raffles wrote a letter to his EIC superiors in which he felt compelled to tell

---

[*] A local term for a warehouse, derived from the Malay word *gedung*.

Raffles's letter to his cousin

This is probably the first or one of the first letters written by Raffles after he moved into his official residence on Government Hill in January 1823 with his wife, Sophia. The house on the top of the hill was an ideal vantage point, providing them with a commanding view of the port as well as the growing settlement.

The letter, dated 12 January 1823, is addressed to Raffles's cousin, the Reverend Doctor Thomas Raffles. In the letter, Raffles mentions the boom-like conditions that the entrepôt was experiencing. He writes that Singapore 'has already become a great Emporium', and anticipates that it will provide opportunities for British investors, being 'a fine field for European speculation'. The letter also provides a glimpse into Raffles's activities in Singapore which included marking out the town and its roads, and drafting laws and regulations for the protection of person and property. He also mentions that he has selected a spot for his intended College, and would endow the College with lands

from which rent could be collected for its ordinary expenses. This would become the Singapore Institution which was later renamed the Raffles Institution. Raffles also expects a visit by the missionary Dr Robert Morrison in March and hopes to be able to 'make some satisfactory arrangement with him for future labours'.

Besides these extracts, which mention plans and official activities, the letter also tells us that Raffles was not in good health at the time. He feels 'so weak and broken down in constitution' and suffers from headaches for days, which leave him 'distracted and almost unconscious'. He is determined to leave Singapore by the end of the year, and hopes that both he and his wife will regain their health and look forward to a comfortable and quiet retirement.

The letter shows us the two sides of Raffles – one public and one private. We see Raffles as a busy official working to transform the settlement into an orderly, peaceful and prosperous emporium in the limited time that he has on the

island. In his private life, we see Raffles racked by persistent headaches, anxious to return home. At this point, Raffles had lost three young children to illness in Sumatra, while the fourth had been sent off to England to what was believed to be a healthier climate.

Raffles passed away within three and a half years of writing this letter.

TOP: Reverend Dr Thomas Raffles.
From Thomas Stamford Raffles, *Memoirs of the Life and Ministry of Rev Dr Thomas Raffles*, London, 1865

Raffles's letter.
12 January 1823
Paper
H 25 x W 39.8 cm
Anonymous donor
NMS 2005-01281-002

them that he considered Farquhar 'totally unequal to the charge of so important and peculiar a charge as that of Singapore has now become'. He then struck out at Farquhar's undesirably close involvement with the locals. In a thinly veiled reference to Farquhar's Melakan wife Nonio Clement, Raffles argued that the Resident's 'Malay connexion' afforded 'an opening for such an undue combination of peculiar interests as not only to impede the progress of order and regularity but may lay the foundation of future inconvenience which may hereafter be difficult to overcome'.

The growing distaste that Raffles felt towards Farquhar even extended to the Resident's appearance. In March 1823, Raffles reprimanded Farquhar for his 'departure from the usual etiquette in dispensing with the Military Dress of his rank'. The next month, he told Farquhar that he had written to Calcutta on the matter and was awaiting the Company's judgment. Farquhar's response was to claim that he was only required to wear his uniform when he acted in his capacity as military Commandant. Presumably, he felt that when acting as Resident he should be allowed to forego clothes that made him uncomfortable in the local humidity. However, to Raffles, the matter of the Resident's dress was symptomatic of a general lack of discipline. By the end of the month, Raffles had Farquhar informed (by proxy) that he was to be relieved from his official duties.

The way Raffles treated Farquhar certainly invites condemnation. But to be fair to Raffles, he returned to Singapore in 1822 practically a broken man, worn down by his grief and seemingly subject to the onset of brain disease. To find his 'almost only child', as he called Singapore during his final visit, in a less than ideal state, bustling with activity, yet unkempt and vice-ridden – apparently through the decisions of a colleague who seemed to have let himself go a little too 'native' – was an added pressure on an overwrought mind. And in one respect, Raffles was justified in his condemnation of Farquhar. The Scot had chosen to turn a blind eye to slave-trading and thus to a practice outlawed across the British Empire. One slave-trader had been so delighted to carry out his business undisturbed in Farquhar's Singapore that he sent both Raffles and Farquhar the gift of a couple of slaves as a mark of gratitude.

The acrimony between both men continued after they returned to Britain – and in Farquhar's case even went on after Raffles's death. Though the EIC formally decided in Raffles's favour over his assertion that he was the sole founder of the settlement at Singapore, Farquhar continued to fight for equal recognition, publicly criticising Sophia Raffles's *Memoir* for the way it accorded her late husband 'exclusive merit' for Singapore's establishment. Indeed, Farquhar might be said to have literally carried his case to the grave. When he died in Scotland in 1839, his tombstone read:

> During 20 years of his valuable life he was appointed to offices of high
> responsibility under the civil government of India having in addition to his

military duties served as Resident in Melaka and afterwards at Singapore
which latter settlement he founded…

Unfortunately for Farquhar, it took at least another century for historians
to sit up and take notice. Sophia Raffles's heroic narrative, combined with the
prevailing 'great man' theory of history – in which, with his untidy appearance
and Eurasian mistress, Farquhar must have appeared a raggedy misfit – ensured
that Raffles continued to receive the sole credit as modern Singapore's founder.
Today, the island city-state bears no street or place or edifice which remembers
Farquhar, whereas those dedicated to Raffles are numerous. Ironically, the
one street that did bear Farquhar's name used to lie in the Malay suburb of
Kampong Glam, but it was demolished by the inheritors of Raffles's urban legacy
– Singapore's modern town-planners.

Yet, modern scholars have begun to re-appraise Farquhar's contributions. If
Raffles was the founding father of the Singapore settlement then, as historian
Ernest Chew puts it, 'it was really Farquhar who had to play the role of mother
and nurse to the infant during its first four years'. Or as another scholar Karl Hack
has noted, it was Farquhar's knowledge of the Malay rulers and their dynastic
disputes that provided Raffles with his vital 'entry-point'. Though Raffles was
brilliant he was also 'utterly impractical' and it would have been 'a disaster' if he
had set about the establishment of the modern entrepôt by himself. Indeed, the
trust that local people had in the Raja Melaka was what brought many of them to
Singapore in the first place, and ensured the settlement's survival.

We perhaps gain a glimpse into the judgment of the time when we compare
what we know about both men's departures from the island. Munshi Abdullah
tells us that Raffles departed Singapore on 9 June 1823 with tears in his eyes,
sent on his way by 'hundreds'. Farquhar eventually left six months later and in
Abdullah's account was bade adieu with much greater fanfare. Thousands came to
say farewell, bearing different kinds of gifts, including 'some who did not have a
dry eye for the whole of those two days'. As Farquhar's ship pulled out of harbour
'people of all races put out in their boats', gaily decorated with 'flags flying' and
with 'bands playing', trying to follow him as he set sail for the horizon.

Farquhar's Silver Epergne.
Crafted by the London
silversmiths Rundle, Bridge
& Co., the epergne was a gift
presented to William Farquhar
by the Chinese community of
Singapore on his departure
from the island.

1824
Silver
H 40.6 x W 24.8 x Dia. 27.7 cm
NMS 1994-00053

7.   THE DOCTOR, THE SULTAN AND THE SCRIBE

One man who must have felt greatly relieved when Farquhar left Singapore was Dr John Crawfurd, the man Raffles had chosen as Farquhar's replacement. In fact, Crawfurd had taken over his predecessor's official duties as Resident some months before, but Farquhar had elected to remain on the island, lodging his protests over his dismissal with Calcutta. So it was that Singapore's early settlers were given the chance to compare their old and their new Residents side by side. Unfortunately for Crawfurd, the much-loved Raja Melaka was a hard act to follow.

On the face of it, the two men shared much in common. Both were Scots with many years' experience in the East; both had joined the East India Company at the age of 20, though Crawfurd initially served as a doctor rather than as a soldier; and both had been part of Raffles's Java Expedition in 1811, following which Crawfurd became British Resident at the Court of Yogyakarta in central Java. Moreover, in common with Farquhar and Raffles, Crawfurd was a great student of the Malay world, his most impressive work being his three-volume *History of the Indian Archipelago*.

However, Raffles's former scribe Munshi Abdullah (who greatly admired both Farquhar and Raffles) was intensely critical of Crawfurd and his new regime: 'Can ten scattered stars shed the same light as a single moon?' he asked with typical poetic flourish. 'I noticed that Singapore at that time was like a woman whose husband has died, her hair unkempt, her face sad, like one who dwells in sorrow because her glory has gone from her.' In Abdullah's view, though Crawfurd was 'conscientious', 'capable' and 'a man of education', he was also 'tight-fisted' and 'fond of the goods of this world'. 'He gave himself airs' and was 'intolerant of listening to long-winded complaints'. 'Malays and other races which lie in the east', the Munshi tells us, 'enjoy long dissertations and repetition'. Crawfurd, however, was 'inclined to impatience and outbursts of temper'.

Crawfurd's brusque manner might have been a novelty for Singapore, but in other ways he was a natural successor to both the settlement's founders. For one thing, he was a greater realist than even Farquhar and did not hesitate to discard some of Raffles's more utopian plans for the betterment of the island's inhabitants. At the same time, Crawfurd held onto other Enlightenment principles that Raffles held dear and was just as willing to intervene directly in Malay affairs when he felt these principles compromised. On one occasion, Crawfurd is known to have freed 27 female slaves belonging to the Sultan, in the same instant upholding the law of the British Empire and ensuring the new settlement received a much needed influx of eligible young women. If Raffles was the dreamer and the idealist, and Farquhar the locals' friend, then Crawfurd comes across as the stern enforcer – a man for whom all thoughts of the people's love or a place in posterity were a distraction from the immediate goal of making Singapore work.

Crawfurd's Singapore

Naturally, the new authoritarianism of Crawfurd's administration did not go unremarked upon. Once again, Munshi Abdullah provides us with an insider's view of the local response:

> I heard many Malays and Chinese grumbling. They felt aggrieved that things were now being forced on them, instead of being arrived at through their own consent.

But before we make of Crawfurd some kind of ruthless pragmatist, sacrificing the consent of the people at the altar of economic rationality, it's worth emphasising how far the course he plotted for the settlement's future had already been set by those who came before him. Raffles's final regulations before he departed the island in 1823 categorically defined Singapore as a free port 'open to ships and vessels of every nation free of duty, equally and alike to all'. He also banned slavery (as well as gambling and the sale of opium) and instituted a magistracy to administer justice that would follow the principles he had set down for the maintenance of law and the grading of punishments.

What is more, if the Sultan and the Temenggong retained any hopes that they might run Singapore together with the British as a joint enterprise then the additional treaty which Raffles had them sign in June 1823 most likely ended them. The treaty did increase the allowance that the British paid both local chiefs, a gesture intended to compensate them for the loss of their customary rights to taxation. However, it stipulated that, apart from the land granted them for their respective households and retinues, the territory of Singapore and its adjacent islands now passed to the East India Company to dispose of as it wished. Excepting only marriage ceremonies and rules of inheritance, Singapore's inhabitants were henceforth subject to British law, though Raffles assured them that such law would be enforced 'with due consideration to the usages and habits of the people'.

Having secured all this, Raffles left Singapore and returned to Britain. For Crawfurd, the knowledge that the settlement's founder would not be coming back proved a key advantage. Unlike Farquhar, Crawfurd could pick and choose which of Raffles's regulations and recommendations to enforce, and which to ignore, without fear of a backlash from his superior. As a consequence, the new Resident's authority was more like that of a governor – as, indeed, his memorial in St Andrew's Cathedral at the heart of modern Singapore mistakenly describes him.

On assuming his duties, Crawfurd took immediate action to improve the administration's finances, re-introducing licences for opium and spirits and

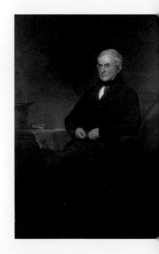

Dr John Crawfurd.
19th century
Oil on canvas
H 210 x W 134 cm
NMS HP-0044

Captain Franklin's map
of Singapore. Franklin, of
the East India Company's
Quarter-Masters Department,
prepared this map in the early
1820s. It is perhaps the first
map to depict the shape of
the island faithfully and it
was commended by British
Resident John Crawfurd for
its usefulness and accuracy.
1820s
Print
H 12 x W 17.4 cm
NMS XXXX-02072-001

bringing in new ones for pawn-broking and the sale of gunpowder. But the greatest refreshment of the government's coffers came through his decision to legalise public gambling, which he described as being to the locals nothing more than a 'mere harmless pastime' and a 'necessary amusement'.

To save money, Crawfurd also ditched some of Raffles's more utopian plans. The most remarkable of these was for the Singapore Institution, whose foundation stone Raffles laid just before his departure. Raffles had imagined a school which would teach Western science, alongside the diverse languages, cultures and histories of Southeast Asia, to the settlement's young elite. Crawfurd, however, felt that primary education was a greater necessity; the expensive enlightenment of the sons of wealthy local settlers would have to wait. When Raffles received news of Crawfurd's attitude to his legacy, he wrote that the new Resident did not 'give as much satisfaction as I could have wished', yet there was now nothing he could do. The Singapore Institution did not become a reality until over a decade later and in 1868 it was renamed the Raffles Institution in honour of its original founder. Today, it still turns out young enlightened elite of the Republic, but through a system and curriculum quite different from what Raffles had originally intended.

Would it be fair to say that Crawfurd was just the kind of chief financial officer that Singapore in the early 1820s needed? As he, himself, recalled: 'For the first three years of its occupation, no attempt was made at an estimate of the amount of trade carried on. I made an effort to remedy this defect in 1823.' Certainly, by reining in public spending, Crawfurd's administration placed British finances in the settlement on a surer footing. Yet the second Resident was also something of a visionary in his own right. By abolishing anchorage and other port fees he fiercely adhered to the principle of free trade; similarly, by encouraging the settlement of more Chinese, he identified those key players whose regional networks would prove so vital to the port's commercial expansion.

It was also under Crawfurd that Singapore took further steps toward attaining the hallmarks of European civilisation. By 1826, the year he departed the island, the first Singapore newspaper had been established, street lighting had been introduced and the town even boasted English street signs. That for much of the 19th century the locals ignored these street signs was one of Singapore's telling little ironies. Most non-Europeans preferred to use their own names for places officially dedicated by and to their colonial masters. So it was that for many decades Commercial Square, later renamed Raffles Place, was more commonly known by local Chinese as 'flower garden corner' or by local Tamils as 'street of the godowns'.

The two treaties of 1824

Besides Abdullah, one man who had much to grumble about with respect to Crawfurd's administration was Sultan Hussein. In August 1824, Crawfurd persuaded Hussein and the Temenggong to sign another 'Treaty of Friendship and Alliance'. However, it would be a mistake to take this treaty's title at face value. Crawfurd's personal view of Hussein was that he was a man 'destitute of energy' who before Raffles's arrival had lived 'in a state of complete indigence'. In reality, the gruff Scot could not wait to rid himself of the Sultan's presence.

Through Crawfurd's Treaty of Friendship and Alliance, Singapore officially became a full British possession, over which the Sultan no longer had authority. To mark this change, the guns of Government Hill (today's Fort Canning Hill) were fired, gongs sounded across the town, and a proclamation was read aloud to the effect that 'full judicial and legal control throughout Singapore had passed to the East India Company and that neither Sultan Hussein nor the Temenggong retains any power'. To drive the message home further, Crawfurd and his party then set sail on the *Malabar* to take formal control of Singapore and its dependencies, stopping off at various outlying islands and at Johor to raise the flag and fire more gun-salutes. An account in the *Singapore Chronicle* noted that the party returned after what was described as 'an interesting trip of ten days', and that while the scenery in the Straits was 'highly imposing', the 'absence of human, and even animal life, give a stillness and tranquillity which are tedious, lonesome and uninteresting'.

No matter how it was dressed up, Crawfurd's 1824 Treaty was essentially a buy-out: to use a phrase of Raffles's, 'filthy lucre' lay at its core. To ensure the Malay chiefs' compliance in the removal of all their former authority, Crawfurd arranged for the Sultan and the Temenggong to be given even more money: a monthly allowance respectively of 1,300 and 700 Spanish dollars and an immediate grant of 30,000 and 15,000 Spanish dollars. Moreover, if the Sultan elected to leave Singapore and live somewhere else, an additional 30,000 Spanish dollars would at once be made available to him.

Once again, we might ask why the Sultan and the Temenggong agreed to this deal? Once again, the answer reveals how limited their options were. To ensure their position and their royal dignity, both the Sultan and the Temenggong had to maintain large retinues of followers. Since the establishment of the British settlement at Singapore, the size of these retinues had grown and both leaders were now short of cash. Territorial control, which by 1824 belonged to the Malay chiefs only in name, was less important than finding the revenue with which to hold onto the external trappings of royal authority.

Contemporary sources do paint Sultan Hussein in a less than positive light, and some historians suggest that his innate weakness of character was what had persuaded the Bugis to back his younger brother as their Sultan in Riau. The British certainly had little faith in Hussein and it's striking that his sons were not allowed to inherit his authority. Instead, the British favoured the descendents of the Temenggong, eventually establishing this line in the new sultanate of Johor. Hussein, fed up with the British failure to grant him sufficient respect, eventually

View from Government Bungalow.

14 November 1828
Watercolour on paper
H 23.5 x W 29.8 cm
NMS 1992-00199

took up Crawfurd's offer to quit Singapore and moved to Melaka, where he lived out the remainder of his days.

However, to lay the blame for European expansion in Singapore at Hussein's feet alone would be to do him an injustice. Not only did the British enjoy a clear military superiority over Hussein and the Temenggong, we shouldn't forget that it had been a long time since any sultan of Johor-Riau-Lingga enjoyed real political independence. If Hussein was a weak pawn in the hands of the British then his younger brother Abdul Rahman was not much better. By most accounts, Abdul Rahman was a recluse and ascetic who spent much of his days in Riau in prayer while the Bugis and the Dutch ran the sultanate in his name.

Furthermore, by 1824 a new imperial order was emerging in Southeast Asia that was to marginalise the Johor-Riau-Lingga sultanate as a political power and in fact split it into two. Early in the same year that saw the signing of Crawfurd's Treaty of Friendship and Alliance, Britain and the Netherlands signed the Treaty of London. Under the terms of this agreement, the issue of Singapore's legality was resolved, and British and Dutch territorial claims in the region settled. The Dutch gave up Melaka and their claims on Singapore; the British handed over Bencoolen and promised no further interference in Sumatra.

And so, after three exhausting centuries of conflicts, intrigues and dynastic disputes, Europe's colonial powers no longer bothered with the pretence of working through the Malay world's local 'authorities'. The Treaty of London ended the Johor-Riau-Lingga sultanate in principle, without there being any consultation over the matter with its rulers or its inhabitants. A new kind of imperialism had arrived in the region, and for at least another 130 years, it was there to stay.

Munshi Abdullah: 'A new world is being created'

As a local, how must it have felt to witness the rapid transformations that characterised the first years of colonial Singapore? As we might expect by now, Munshi Abdullah gives us an invaluable insight:

> I am astonished to see how markedly our world is changing. A new world is being created, the old world destroyed. The very jungle becomes a settled district while elsewhere a settlement reverts to jungle. These things show us how the world and its pleasures are but transitory experiences, like something borrowed which has to be returned whenever the owner comes to demand it.

These lines come from Abdullah's *Hikayat Abdullah* [The Story of Abdullah], which he completed in the early 1840s and which remains the most comprehensive eyewitness account of early 19th-century Singapore by a non-European. As well as being a crucial piece of the historical record, the *Hikayat* is a revolutionary work for its time in terms of its genre. Written as an autobiography, it represents

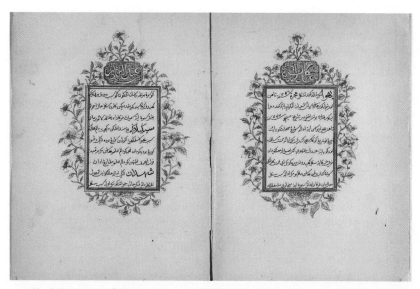

a radical departure from previous Malay writing about the past, which usually
took the form of romanticised court chronicles (such as the *Sejarah Melayu*). By
contrast, the *Hikayat* is filled with Abdullah's personal, sometimes poignant (and
frequently witty) observations, which together with his Malay poetry and other
writings offer a more realistic, even journalistic, account of the world he saw
around him. Not without reason, the *Hikayat Abdullah* has been described as the
first indigenous 'I' of Singapore history.

But what is especially striking about Abdullah's impressions of the young
Singapore settlement is how frequently he is led to dwell on the 'transitory'
nature of life's experiences. His own life – throughout which he played a crucial
part in the new world being created – comes across as a series of repeated
transitions, between a traditional world and a modern, between Melaka and
Singapore, and between different peoples, their languages and beliefs. And
while Abdullah was definitely an advocate of many of the advances brought to
the region by the arrival of Europeans, on more than one occasion the *Hikayat*'s
pages are tinged by the author's regret at the endlessly changing present that he
lived in.

Much of Abdullah's life was spent translating. Well before the events of early
1819, he had made his name in his hometown of Melaka as a pre-eminent Malay
scholar and multilingual scribe (he was familiar with Malay, Arabic, Tamil and
Hindi). There he earned the title of 'Munshi', meaning a teacher of languages.
Even more impressively, he achieved all this by the age of 14.

Yet Abdullah was not what many people today would view as ethnically Malay,
although he himself always regarded himself as such. Strictly speaking he was Jawi
Peranakan – a local-born Muslim of mixed Arab, Indian and Malay ancestry. J. T.
Thomson, an English contemporary and friend of Abdullah's, described him as

having 'the vigour and pride of the Arab, the perseverance and subtility [subtlety] of the Hindoo – in language and national sympathy only was he a Malay'.

In 1811, Abdullah's precocity with languages brought him to the attention of Raffles, who was then in Melaka preparing for the Java Expedition while at the same time looking for scribes to assist him in amassing his personal collection of precious Malay manuscripts. When Raffles departed for Java, he offered to take Abdullah with him, and Abdullah recalled that it was only his tearful mother's protestation that he was too young that prevented him from going. Years later, in 1819, Abdullah – who by this time had added English to his repertoire of languages – joined the exodus from Melaka to pursue his career in Raffles's new 'political child' of Singapore.

Abdullah recalled that he arrived when the new settlement was only 'about four months old' and was immediately confronted by the rough, pioneering, often violent nature of the place. 'Every day without ceasing,' he wrote, 'murders took place along the road to Kampong Gelam [Glam]. There were policemen on duty here and there but they themselves were often murdered' – a situation which continued until the British intervened to restrict the bearing of arms.

Nonetheless, Abdullah stayed and his linguistic skills and previous affiliation with the British served him well. In Singapore, the Munshi taught Malay to colonial officials, merchants and missionaries, and he also earned money,

> [W]riting letters to the Malay rulers from the English merchants, as well as traders' bills and notices of auctions. Many Chinese trading with the Malays dealt with them through letters and notes of hand, all which I wrote myself. Chinese trading with English merchants would call me in as an interpreter …

Abdullah's regular contact with English merchants, as well as colonial officials and missionaries, exposed him to the latest European ideas about trade, politics and progress. In the process, he became one of the first locals from the Straits to experience some of the modern novelties brought by colonisation, 'wonderful things and new changes which our grandparents never saw'. For instance, Abdullah was very likely the first Malay to use a printing press; he also wrote tracts on the camera and the steamship, to explain the scientific advances that lay behind them and prepare his countrymen for their arrival. At times, his zeal in describing such technologies could generate impassioned reactions. In the *Hikayat*, he recalls that when he began to talk about the 'skill and ingenuity of the white men' in inventing steam power his friends became angry, claimed he was a liar and told him forthrightly, 'You always magnify the prowess of the English and tell us the most incredible things.'

That these 'incredible things' mattered so much to Abdullah shows his deep concern that the Malay people should not be left behind by European science and learning. Such was his anxiety that a significant part of the *Hikayat* is devoted to excoriating Malay rulers for their refusal to adapt to the modern world. In a provocative challenge, once again radical for its time, Abdullah directly challenged these leaders:

> Do you really wish to retain your ignorant practices as a heritage for your descendants until the end of time? ... Is it right that hundreds, nay thousands of men should grow up not knowing how to read or write or do simple sums? It makes them look ridiculous in the eyes of the other races who cheat them over measurements and weights and computations, and in general wherever writing is involved.

In this modern Singapore of 'measurements and weights and computations' Abdullah himself profited greatly. The industrious scribe, despite his repeated claim that he had no talent for enterprise and the loss of many of his possessions in a fire in 1830, became a wealthy man. His will reveals that by his death he had amassed many of the trappings of a successful Singapore merchant and was able to pass on a sizeable legacy to his descendants. It would seem that Abdullah was a prime example of an early Singapore success story (the likes of which we will hear more shortly).

Yet despite all Abdullah's achievements, the related themes of loss and regret continue to surface throughout the pages of the *Hikayat*. For a start, and notwithstanding his evident excitement about Singapore, his domestic arrangements there were far from ideal, with the consequence that he never really settled but instead made frequent trips back to his birthplace of Melaka. He had wanted his family to move to Singapore with him but things had not gone according to plan. In the *Hikayat*, he describes the scene in the Abdullah household on the eve of his family's planned departure:

> When everything in my house had been packed, the baggage tied up and my wife was due to sail to Singapore in two day's time many of our relations, men and women, came to us. Some wept, others, gave advice, each according to his mood. They behaved as if grief would kill them, until my wife changed her mind and my heart relented. So it came about that I did not take my wife but sailed by myself.

As for his house in Singapore, which he had built soon after his arrival, it was empty (an emptiness that 'vexed' him), surrounded by jungle and frightening. In the end, Abdullah regretted that he never settled in Singapore permanently; had he done so, he tells us, his life 'would certainly have been different'.

But it was through his association with Raffles and Singapore that Abdullah faced perhaps his greatest personal disappointment and became party to one of the greatest cultural disasters to hit the Malay world. As Raffles prepared to leave the settlement for the final time, he asked Abdullah to pack his collection of manuscripts and cultural artefacts, accumulated over the previous 20 years.

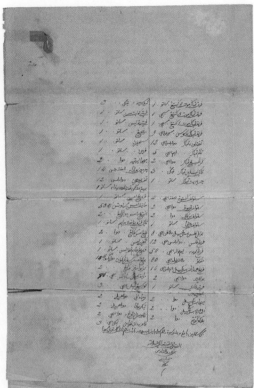

Abdullah records that he packed some three hundred books bound in volumes, many unbound books and loose items in rolls and sheets – not to mention two cases with letters and books, and three or four cases of puppets, pictures and writings on palmyra leaves. Many of those volumes he prepared for Raffles' departure were original manuscripts.

Then, on the Englishman's final voyage out from Bencoolen, the ship carrying Raffles and Sophia caught fire and sank to the bottom. Raffles and Sophia survived; Raffles' prize collection of Malay manuscripts did not. In one of the most poignant passages in the *Hikayat*, Abdullah recalls his reaction:

> [M]y imagination reeled to think of all the works in Malay and other languages, centuries old, which he had collected from many countries, all utterly lost. Not a trace of them was left, for they were all in manuscript … I recalled Mr Raffles' promise that he would write books about the countries of this part of the world and that he would mention my name in them. All his material was lost. The more I thought these things the more depressed I became.

It seems almost a divine joke that the lost ship should have been called the *Fame*. Not only was a major part of the fame of Malay literature rendered

Munshi Abdullah's will.
18 January 1854
Paper
Donated by Mr. John Koh
NMS 2000-05663

extinct for all time, but as a result of his association with Raffles and the British, Abdullah's reputation itself also sank. Instead of being remembered by posterity for his efforts to make Malay literature and the Malay world known amongst the nations, he was labelled by other Malays as a British stooge (*talibarut Ingerris*) or 'Abdullah the Priest' (Abdullah *Patri*), the latter being a pointed reference to his work with missionary presses, translating the Bible and other Christian texts.

However, in the eyes of Malay literary scholar Hadijah Rahmat, though Abdullah was a friend of Europeans and greatly influenced by them, he never turned his back on his Malay cultural heritage or on his religious beliefs as a Muslim. While he was a proponent of many Enlightenment ideals, his adoption of modern innovations was not done unthinkingly and he admitted that he was unable to accept ideas that were at odds with his Islamic faith. As a result, Abdullah's life achieved a synthesis of Western cosmopolitan ideas with traditional Islamic views that was remarkable for its time – one that perhaps even serves as a Singapore example of early Islamic modernism.

Nonetheless, in certain Malay literary circles today, Abdullah, the friend of colonial officials and Christian missionaries, remains a controversial figure. Some of this reaction derives from his extraordinary critique of Malay royalty in the *Hikayat* – which he begins with a salacious account of the reasons for Sultan's Hussein's departure from Singapore, then extends into an attack on local 'tyrants and oppressors' in general (comparing their actions, in the process, with the just government of Queen Victoria). Such is the intensity of this attack that it's perhaps not surprising if some Malay readers have come to view Abdullah as a deracinated 'mimic-man', a man too much in love with all things European.

In reality, Abdullah's views about Malay rulers again reveal his primary concern for the reputation of the Malay people. They also manifest (once more) the *Hikayat's* twin themes of regret and loss. For example, though Hussein's obesity is remarked on at length by Abdullah in the *Hikayat*, it is here a symptom of royal decline rather than something arising from the innate weakness of the

Sultan's character. As opposed to Captain Crawford's eyewitness account, where Hussein is grossly fat from the outset, Abdullah records that Hussein was not always so heavy: 'when he came from Riau to Singapore he was not fat but of average proportions. However, when he had become Sultan his body grew plumper and plumper as time went on.' Never in his life had Abdullah seen 'another man as fat as him', but it was not always so (at least that is what the Munshi would have us believe).

Indeed, much of Abdullah's critique of Malay royalty arises from his strong historical sense of how far the once mighty had fallen:

> Was there not a time when half the world was under Malay dominion and rule? There are many books and records which tell of the rulers of olden times, how great and powerful they were, how rich and full of wisdom. Why have their lands been despoiled by Allah ere now, and passed into foreign bondage? Is it not because of extreme injustice and tyranny that Allah has weakened them and enslaved them under alien rule ...? Ignorant and undiscerning though I may be, it seems clear to me that the very name of the Malays will be lost to the world, for there are many books I have read which say that Allah sets his face against all tyrants.

In this striking passage, we gain a sense of Abdullah's real concern at the present state of the Malay nation and of its rulers, his fear lest in future 'the very name of the Malays will be lost' and even his regret at the arrival of an 'alien rule' that in other parts of the *Hikayat* he has described as so beneficial. And, once again, such ruminations are accompanied by Abdullah's recurring sense of the transitory nature of existence, especially the transitory nature (in a divinely ordered world) of a royal but tyrannical existence:

> [W]hoever incurs the displeasure of Allah must in the course of time be brought low. Even in my own lifetime there have been several Malay principalities which I notice have come to ruin. Some have reverted to jungle where the elephant and the tiger roam, because of the cruel injustices of their rulers and chiefs ... Once they were rich and flourishing states with a large population. Now they are states only in name.

Before Abdullah died in 1854, he took the last of what had been many voyages during his lifetime. He joined the *haj* to Mecca, journeying there from Singapore by steamship. These steamships, which Abdullah so admired, had by this time emerged as a key instrument of European domination. But these same ships had also brought ideas, novelties and a greater population to Singapore, transforming it into an international crossroads of commerce and exchange. In the bustling emporium that Singapore was becoming, some new arrivals would prosper like Abdullah; others would suffer. For in such a transitory place, as the Munshi once put it: 'If you have the luck of a coconut husk you float, if of a stone you sink.'

EMPORIUM

1820s – 1860s

8. A FREE PORT

On 6 February 1833, exactly 24 years to the day after the signing of the 1819 Treaty, English seaman George Windsor Earl arrived in Singapore and beheld a sight that could not have been more different from the unimposing little hamlet that had witnessed Britain's first forays onto the island. Where once there had been a small village of *attap* huts, a bustling emporium had taken shape:

> Ships from all parts of the world are constantly arriving ... and the flags of Great Britain, Holland, France, and America, may often be seen intermingled with the streamers of the Chinese junks, and the fanciful colours of the native *perahus*. ... Singapore contains an epitome of the population of the whole Archipelago, and indeed of Continental India also. Chinese, Malays, Bugis, Javanese, Balinese, natives of Bengal and Madras, Parsees, Arabs, and Caffrees [Africans], are to be found within the circuit of a few miles.

Earl had witnessed the 'picturesque spectacle', as the historian Mary Turnbull has called it, that announced the port's success: the hundreds of different vessels in harbour; Chinese junks moored alongside Malay *perahu*, Bugis *padewakang*, Arab *dhows* and, over time, more square-rigged European sailing ships. Because such a scene was usually a newcomer's first encounter with Singapore, it became the most documented view of the town. From raw pencil sketches to full-blown oil paintings, the many depictions of ships waiting at anchor give us a collective vision of what the harbour must have looked like on any given day between the 1820s and the 1860s.

Once ashore, the sights were just as evocative and became ever more varied as the decades progressed. By the 1850s, shiny white neo-classical monuments marked out the town's European district, minarets and pagodas its Asian quarters. In fact, Singapore's Asian merchants, hand in hand with their commercial success, funded a spate of religious building that seemed to outstrip the efforts of their European counterparts.

BELOW: Singapore Waterfront. This is a panoramic view of the waterfront and town of Singapore by artist W. Gray and engraver A. Arnst. Fort Canning, with its distinctive flagstaff, is on the right. The ships at anchor range from Bugis *perahu*, Chinese junks and European square-rigged, to steamships.
1861
Lithograph
H 46.6 x W 60.5 cm
NMS XXXX-01259

The courtyards and entranceways of their mosques and temples (such as those that lined Chinatown's Telok Ayer Street and still stand there today) were a hubbub of commercial activity – the best place in town to find out what was really going on both in port and overseas. Here, merchants gathered to share news, to gossip and to settle business, before moving inside to seek divine protection for their ventures. In the days before modern market research and risk analysis, the blessings of the heavens were vitally important. In particular, they gave an added insurance against the perils of those sea voyages that any merchant worth his godown was from time to time committed to undertake.

Thus, to a new arrival in port, the steady flow of free commerce, the hustle and bustle of buying and selling, and the growth of new buildings (both secular and sacred) would appear to have been keeping everyone in high and happy spirits. Such, at least, is the impression of early colonial Singapore that European artists and writers have left us with, and perhaps it is no less truthful than the impression made by exotic new places on foreign visitors over a century and a half later. But while early 19th-century depictions capture the excitement that the free port generated, they by no means give a complete picture. Beyond the stories of the town's commercial progress are tales of discontent, exclusion and exploitation, which in the next few chapters we will also try to uncover.

That being said, the success story of the emporium has to come first – not just because it is how Singapore is most remembered in these decades, but because it was news of the free port's success that at the time led so many migrants to arrive in Singapore in the first place.

George Earl's first impressions

Free of taxation and bursting with life, Singapore was a place where almost everything from the region (except slaves and certain weapons) could be had for a price. In 1833, Earl had passed through the port intending to stay just a few days; but the new emporium's vitality was such that he ended up remaining for nine months and devoting three chapters of his book *The Eastern Seas* to trying to describe it. One of the highlights during his sojourn in the 'Queen of the Further East', as he called it, was the arrival of the first junk from China on the northeast monsoon:

> [W]hen its approach is notified by the crew of a Malay *sampan* which has been on the lookout to the eastward, the greatest bustle pervades the Chinese community: some running along the streets to communicate the important intelligence to their friends, come in contact with others rushing from the opposite direction, and many hasten off to the vessel to learn the news from China, everything that will float, from a *sampan* to a cargo-boat, being put in requisition. The first boat reaches the junk when she is still several miles distant, and as she nears the town, she gains an accession of bulk at every fathom, until at last the unwieldy mass slowly

Half-anna East India Company coin.
1835
Copper
Dia. 2.6 cm
NMS N-1275

trails into the roads, surrounded by a dense mass of boats, having the
appearance of a locust which has inadvertently crossed an ant's nest, and
is dragging after it countless myriads of the enraged inhabitants attached
to its legs and feelers.

Given these junks were the only contact that Chinese migrants had with their
relatives, friends, and business partners back home, the excitement their arrival
generated is understandable. Earl likened the impression made by their six-
month stay in harbour to a 'floating fair', and he goes on to tell us that besides
the trade goods they brought from China – porcelain, tea, medicine and silk,
among others – they carried a human cargo of between 5,000 and 8,000 Chinese
labourers per year. The majority then scattered across the Straits and the Malay
Archipelago to work in tin mines and plantations. Earl had witnessed the
beginning of an upsurge in Chinese migration that from the next decade would
transform the region.

The Bugis trading fleet made an equally powerful, if not formidable,
impression. In the early 1800s the Bugis were still the principal small traders
in the Malay Archipelago, with an economic influence that reached well beyond
their home-base in Celebes (south Sulawesi). Their fleet, typically numbering
about 200 vessels in all, brought indigenous produce and goods collected from
Bali, southern Borneo and other ports en route to Singapore from Sulawesi:
coffee, gold dust, pearls, spices and tortoise shell.

Chinese junk sketched by
Louis Le Breton.

c. 1839
Lithograph
H 13.8 x W 18.6 cm
NMS 2000-06667

Malay *perahu* engraved by
Thomas and William Daniel.
c. 1810
Aquatint
H 12.0 x W 18.8 cm
NMS 1993-00396

Unlike the Chinese junks, the Bugis fleet did not bring any labour; however, each ship was manned by about 30 crew-members, which meant an additional influx of around 6,000 men into the town each time the fleet was in port. European accounts invite us to think of the Bugis as a proud, fierce and quick-tempered people, ready to draw arms (which they were not supposed to bring ashore) the moment any dispute developed. Yet to even the harshest observer, the graceful Bugis *padewakang*, moored offshore near Kampong Glam from September till November, when the trade winds changed and the fleet sailed home, remained one of Singapore's most endearing sights.

At the heart of this bustling emporium was the Singapore River. Ships were tethered near the river's mouth, since they were too large to enter it, and their goods loaded onto smaller boats called lighters which brought these goods to quays by the water. Over time, these quays became more built up with the godowns (warehouses) that stored the Straits produce so highly prized in Europe and, increasingly, in China: pepper, nutmeg, gambier, cloves, camphor, birds' nests, sharks' fins, tortoise shell and rattan. In the 1830s, a newcomer in port might have already found such sights and smells intoxicating; a few decades later, as Singapore's trade flourished, bringing more traffic further up its congested river, the atmosphere might have become overwhelming. Nonetheless, most merchants and trading houses were reluctant to move away from the riverside, and so it remained the focal point of commerce in Singapore well into the 1860s.

Earl's *Eastern Seas* depicts much of the excitement of Singapore's burgeoning commercial success; and yet the book itself, following its publication in 1837, was much less of a hit in Singapore than it proved back home in Britain. Perhaps for European readers in the Straits, Earl had merely shown them their own lives and the things that they knew only too well – not so much the exotic as the everyday. Nor did his nine-month stay really permit him to dig beneath the surface of the emporium's seemingly inevitable commercial ascendancy. To what degree, then, was Singapore truly the 'Queen of the Further East', as Earl had described it?

The 'hinge' of maritime Asia

Clearly, trade was Singapore's lifeline and the British brand of free trade was proving to be an exciting novelty. Merchants who had plied their wares in other ports across the region gravitated to Singapore because it acted most effectively as a place of open mediation. By the early 1830s, the island had so leapt ahead of the other British settlements at Penang and Melaka in terms of its commerce that it was made the centre of government for what were now called the Straits Settlements. Singapore had emerged as the crucial 'hinge', as historian Anthony Reid has described it, between trade in the Indian Ocean, the South China Sea and the Java Sea. With free trade, the grand tropical emporium dreamt of by Sir Stamford Raffles was clearly taking shape.

Broader global factors also played their part. Internationally, Britain was riding high following the end of the Napoleonic Wars as the top trading nation in Europe. During the 1820s and 1830s, Singapore extended the possibilities for lucrative British commerce further eastwards, towards China and, to a lesser but still important extent, towards the Bugis-controlled Malay Archipelago. In purely commercial terms, this three-way partnership was what made early colonial Singapore tick. British, Chinese and Bugis traders had all been on the lookout for a place to do business following the return of the Dutch to Riau, the free port which had previously served as their meeting point. Singapore allowed them to come together at a geographically convenient location, removed from Dutch influence. Bugis traders were particularly fond of the cloth the British brought from India and of their guns; the Chinese wanted Indian opium from British-occupied Bengal; the British themselves sought the key commodities that made up the China trade – silk, tea and ceramics – as well as, over time, more and more Straits produce.

But the new settlement was still a long way from being the most comfortable place in which to do business. While not completely lawless, it was definitely rowdy, and a much more rough-and-tumble environment than the older bases that the East India Company had established in India such as Calcutta. In Singapore, males outnumbered females considerably – in 1833, by almost three to one – and

Malay seaman by E. Schlitter.
1858
Watercolour on paper
H 25 x W 19 cm
NMS HP-0064-D

this ratio would get worse as the century progressed (and only start to even out during the 1930s). New arrivals in town were usually young adult men who had left their families back home, and their fortunes would become inextricably entwined with the emporium's unregulated commercial development.

And for many of them, what a fickle destiny Singapore offered! While in hindsight it might seem as if Singapore's prosperity developed unimpeded, the port's commercial rise was punctuated by periods of recession and uncertainty. In the 1840s, the town's European merchants were still unsure whether the free port experiment would work, especially since the Dutch seemed to tirelessly conspire to undermine it (by, for example, imposing heavy duties on trade between Singapore and the Dutch ports in Java). In the same decade, more free ports arose in the region – Hong Kong and the Chinese treaty ports from 1842, Makassar in Sulawesi from 1847 – adding further grounds for concern. 'I think the trade of Singapore has reached its maximum,' wrote merchant G. F. Davidson, 'and that the town has attained its highest point of importance and prosperity'.

Not surprisingly, such uncertainty, when combined with rumours, shortages and an abundance of testosterone, frequently brought the island to the point of major unrest. Yet in the end, the principle of free trade that Singapore had embraced from its foundation held true to its promise. In the 1850s, the port's economic growth catapulted forward to the point where it became the centre of trade in Southeast Asia. In 1856, well over half a million ships arrived in harbour; a year later, the value of the island's commerce was nearly double what it had been 15 years before.

9. TRADING LIVES

Inevitably, the story of Singapore's early success as an emporium is also the story of the town's Chinese. Despite the international shipping that arrived in harbour, the cosmopolitan flavour of the town, and the principle of free trade which meant that (in theory) business was open to anyone and everyone, it was Chinese merchants who came to dominate the city's commerce. In 1866, local Chinese merchants owned two-thirds of all the vessels registered as belonging to Singapore, a figure that corresponded to their physical presence on the island, where by 1867 they made up two-thirds of the population. By this time it was clear that the leading players who would determine Singapore's commercial destiny were the powerful Chinese *taukeh*, the Chinese merchants – literally the 'heads' of the Chinese households.

Yet how these *taukeh* earned their fortunes is only half of our story. How they spent their riches – and so emerged as community leaders, law-enforcers, gentleman-scholars and even spiritual guardians – was equally impressive. Moreover, while the dominance of Chinese *taukeh* in Singapore was clear to most contemporaries, other ethnic groups, although smaller in number, produced at least one or two merchants of similar standing. What is especially interesting about our non-Chinese captains of commerce is how similar to their Chinese counterparts they were in their methods, not just in the way they accumulated their fortunes but also in the uses to which they put them.

The importance of being connected

Success for the Chinese *taukeh* of Singapore was all about networks, certainly of trade, but especially of people. The bulk of the Chinese population in the city consisted of Hokkiens, Teochews, Cantonese and some Hakkas – all from southern China and each group identifiable by its distinctive provincial Chinese

Chartered Bank of India, Australia and China post bill issued in Singapore. Post bills performed the functions of currency notes and, for local merchants, signalled the arrival of a new way of doing business.

1859
Paper
H 12.4 x W 22.8 cm
NMS 2000-03665

91

Rochor River with a Chinese
junk by F. Jagor. The
background shows the raised
attap houses of Rochor's
riverine settlement.

1866
Etching
H 11.5 x W 17.5 cm
NMS XXXX-01270

dialect. The Hokkiens and Teochews produced most of the town's legendary Chinese middlemen – the key intermediaries who moved back and forth between European and Asian traders – most probably because it was these two dialect groups who had been longer established as traders in the region. Earl recalled that the Europeans of Singapore relied heavily on their Chinese go-betweens, 'who have a better acquaintance with the natives, and have patience enough to go into all the necessary details of bargaining and weighing the goods'. Generally, Europeans received trade goods on consignment, which they sold on commission back in Europe, while the Chinese took advances to arrange the sourcing of these goods, often using such advances to speculate on the price of these goods in the period before they were expected to deliver.

Most European contemporaries preferred to do business with the Chinese, rather than with the Bugis and Malays, because they believed them to be inherently more gifted at commerce and to stand at a higher level of civilisation. In reality, the commercial acumen of Chinese merchants had more to do with history than heredity – they simply arrived in Singapore (as they had done earlier in Melaka and Penang) with a longer acquaintance with currency and sophisticated systems of capital. Furthermore, by the time the British arrived in Singapore, Chinese business networks already linked up most parts of Southeast Asia, giving local *taukeh* in the new settlement a major logistical advantage.

These networks became particularly important from the 1840s, after the opening of Hong Kong and the Chinese treaty ports following the First Opium War – which Britain waged successfully against the Qing Empire to open up China to foreign traders and, in particular, to the sale of Bengal opium. Since the main transit-point in Britain's China trade now shifted to Hong Kong, it was feared that Singapore's commerce might be bypassed, even ruined. Instead, Singapore's Chinese merchants utilised their far-flung networks to extend their operations and start selling their goods in their ancestral homeland. A few decades after the First Opium War, such was the extent of China's demand for Straits produce that it allayed any fear that Singapore would become a commercial backwater.

Chinese merchants also found that as more migrants passed through Singapore on their way to work in the plantations and tin mines of the Malay Peninsula, a new market emerged, especially for the opium that had once passed through port largely in transit. In the town and the interior, Teochew merchants dominated the supply of vital necessities to plantation workers such as rice, while the Hokkien – whether local-born 'Baba' or China-born – formed syndicates which dominated the opium 'farms' (not agricultural 'farms', but rather the term given to the government-granted licences to distribute opium, so monopolising its supply and sale).

By the 1860s, many Chinese *taukehs* who had begun their careers as commercial middlemen had diversified into a host of other business ventures that included property, plantations, speculation on commodity prices and even drug peddling. In the process they had amassed spectacular fortunes, fortunes which gave new migrants the notion that Singapore was some kind of El Dorado of the Southern Ocean, or as the Chinese called it, the *Nanyang*. This Chinese success was the outstanding feature of modern Singapore's early commercial history. As Mary Turnbull has observed, though none of the European traders would have been considered poor, none of them appeared to have 'made a fortune to match the most successful Chinese'.

Baba Tan Tock Seng the Chinese guardian

Of all those Chinese whom Singapore made rich and powerful, it was the Straits-born Baba Chinese (later called Straits Chinese and also known as Peranakan [local-born] Chinese) who in the early decades were most conspicuous. A prominent example, often lionised as a 'pioneer of Singapore', was Tan Tock Seng, usually depicted in illustrations as a cheerful moon-faced gentleman wearing small round glasses.

Born in Melaka, Tan came to Singapore as part of Farquhar's Melaka 'exodus' shortly after the British set up shop. His commercial beginnings were humble: he bought vegetables, fruit and chicken from outside the town, and sold them to the townsfolk, whose demand for fresh food always outstripped supply. But once

he had accumulated some capital, he went into business as a middleman and eventually made his fortune through joint investments with English merchants. By the 1840s, he was one of Singapore's most influential Chinese leaders.

Tan benefited from several of the local advantages that Baba merchants at first uniquely enjoyed. Invariably, a successful Baba was an effective multi-linguist; as well as the Malay spoken in his household and in the marketplace he would usually speak the Chinese dialect of his ancestral homeland – not especially well (by most accounts) but well enough to do business with Chinese junk captains. Add a little English to the mix, gleaned in Tan's case from his exposure to the British at Melaka (or in the case of other Baba at Penang), and he was primed to be a locus of communication between all of Singapore's major trading communities. Earl noted that Baba merchants were especially favoured for their familiarity with European ways and manners: 'they have acquired in some measure [the Europeans'] general habits and mode of transacting business, which renders them more agreeable to the latter than those who have not enjoyed similar advantages'.

At the same time, Tan and other successful Baba prospered because in most cases they were tolerant, if not welcoming, of more recent Chinese migrants. Contrary to the common assumption today, early 19th-century Baba Chinese did not isolate themselves from Chinese *sinkeh* (the Chinese term for new arrivals, literally 'new guests') – to do so would have been bad for business. Instead, they sought to maintain ties with their China-born dialect 'cousins' for mutual commercial benefit. In the 1850s, for example, prominent Hokkien Baba befriended and assisted Hokkien families from China who had fled to Singapore during the Taiping Rebellion. Over time, these new arrivals themselves produced sons who became integrated into the local-born Chinese community and, by World War I, had emerged as successful businessmen and community leaders.

When it came to building such relationships, Babas had a key advantage. For Chinese merchants, especially Hokkien traders, it was common practice to extend their business partnerships through marriage, and within an increasingly male-dominated Singapore local Baba possessed the town's main supply of eligible young women: namely, their daughters. The Hokkien Baba Lim Boon Keng (who we'll meet several times in this book) described the scene when the first junks of the season arrived in port. Amongst those who showed 'considerable interest' were Baba Chinese, since in addition to the news and the goods the junks brought with them they also carried 'welcome batches of eligible sons-in-law for the daughters who could not marry the natives of the country'. Tan Tock Seng led the way by marrying one of his own daughters to the China-born merchant Chan Koo Chan, who eventually owned a large estate at Kallang and a gunpowder magazine.

The *sinkeh* who managed to achieve local unions expected to benefit greatly. However, many were at the same time in for an extreme case of culture shock.

Contrary to the practice in most parts of China, where daughters-in-law went to live with their husbands's families, the son-in-law of a Baba merchant usually went to live with his in-laws. His new Baba womenfolk, then, as now, were known as Nonya and in their insular domestic households (in male-dominated 19th-century Singapore, Nonya were rarely allowed out on the streets) they unquestionably ruled.

Today, we might find the traditional Baba household exotic and quaint, its food, fashions and furnishings a charming hybrid of Malay, Chinese, European and even Indian elements. But imagine the situation for a new China-born son-in-law in the 1800s. Many Baba Chinese customs would have seemed alien (and many were, in fact, so archaic that back in China they had been completely forgotten). Then there were the inevitable moments of miscommunication, since the language of Baba households in Singapore was usually Baba Malay (a patois of Malay and Hokkien). Our new arrival's adjustment to the domestic kingdom of the Nonya would likely have involved numerous *faux pas* and much mockery at the hands of his local-born relatives. If he was really unlucky he might have to sit through an evening reading of the 'Story of Zhuang Zixu' – a 19th-century Baba Malay entertainment, translated from the original Chinese, which in six parts told the humiliating tale of a stupid son-in-law.

So while Tan Tock Seng and other Baba prospered from what we might call their 'home advantage', this same advantage also had the potential to distance them culturally from new Chinese arrivals. As Singapore grew, Baba merchants needed to develop their influence within the broader and ever-increasing migrant Chinese community – to show that, despite their domestic arrangements, they were still Chinese.

How then did they bridge the gap between themselves and their 'purer' Chinese cousins who had been born in the ancestral homeland? One particular way was through generous and very public acts of philanthropy, and in this respect Tan Tock Seng provides us with a shining example.

Tan is widely remembered for providing essential social services for the Chinese community at a time when the colonial government in Singapore left most people to fend for themselves. Two of the institutions he was instrumental in building continue to flourish. What is now Singapore's Tan Tock Seng Hospital he originally established in 1844 as a hospital for Chinese paupers. Before this, the plight of this segment of the population had been so ignored by the British authorities that one local newspaper complained of the 'number of diseased Chinese, lepers and others frequent[ing] almost every street in town'. From 1843 until his own death in 1850, Tan also paid for the burial of Chinese paupers – over 1,000 in all – thereby establishing his reputation as their protector and indeed the protector of all Chinese in Singapore.

Furthermore, Tan became a major benefactor of the Thian Hock Keng, the Chinese temple on Telok Ayer Street, providing a hefty part of the finance that was required to build it. Unlike today, when Chinese temples in Singapore are used almost solely for religious purposes, the Thian Hock Keng in the 19th century was a place for socialising, entertainment, education and even job-hunting. Hokkien Chinese *sinkeh*, and some non-Hokkien too, stepped off the boat at Telok Ayer and headed straight for its gates. (The temple was then located right on the water's edge, though thanks to land reclamation in the 1860s it is now situated well inland). Inside the temple's walls, they gave thanks for their safe passage to Singapore then sought contact with members of their dialect group and with other clan members – the Chinese believing that those who shared the same clan name shared an ancestral kinship.

Within the grounds of such temples there sprang up the *kongsi* and the *hui guan*, the Chinese associations organised around dialect, clan or ancestral places of origin. The Thian Hock Keng, for instance, became home to the Hokkien Huay Kuan (*hui guan*) or dialect association, whose first chairman was Tan Tock Seng's son, Tan Kim Ching. Besides employment, such associations provided other essential community services: from dispute mediation to the performance of sacred rites at festivals and burials.

Of course, it would be presumptuous and probably unfair to assume that all Tan's philanthropy was motivated by the prestige it brought him. Nevertheless, for Tan and his fellow Chinese *taukeh*, philanthropic temple activities inevitably reinforced their position as the major players in town, especially among *sinkeh*. In an urban setting that offered little in the way of public entertainment, the grand celebrations at temples such as the Thian Hock Keng became the social highlight of the year, impressing not only the Chinese community for whom they were staged but non-Chinese observers as well. J. D. Vaughan, a 19th-century European resident of Singapore, observed that such events were no different from the political spectacles of 'civilised London' and bore a 'strong resemblance' to the Lord Mayor's Show.

Tan himself was involved in one of the most memorable such spectacles, which occurred in 1840 in celebration of the arrival from China of a statue of Ma Zu, revered as the protector goddess of all those who sailed the high seas, especially by Hokkiens. The goddess was to be housed at the Thian Hock Keng, and since this event also marked the temple's formal opening, Tan and several other Hokkien Baba who made up the temple's management committee spared no effort to make her arrival memorable. All in all they spent more than $6,000 on the festivities (as a point of comparison, Tan gave $7,000 to found his paupers' hospital). As the *Singapore Free Press* reported:

> The procession through town extended nearly a third of a mile, to the usual accompaniment of gongs, and gaudy banners of every colour, form and dimension. ... The chief feature of the procession was the little girls from five to eight years of age, carried aloft in groups on ornamented platforms,

and dressed in every variety of Tartar and Chinese costumes. Ma Zu herself was carried in a very elegant canopy chair, or palanquin, of yellow silk and crape, and was surrounded by a bodyguard of Celestials, wearing tunics of the same colour.

Pageantry such as this no doubt made the colonial authorities sit up and take notice of the community leaders that had footed the bill for it, and in 1844 Tan Tock Seng was appointed as the first Asian Justice of the Peace in the Straits Settlements. Significantly, this was more than an honorary title; as the Chinese population in Singapore grew, the British needed help to govern it, not only because their administration remained impoverished and minimal but because many of their officials could barely muster Malay, let alone speak Chinese dialects. English-speaking Baba such as Tan helped fill this gap; Tan held his office as Justice of the Peace until his death in 1850, at which point it passed to another prominent member of the Tan clan, Tan Kim Seng.

In subsequent decades, the British government formalised the role of Baba Chinese as their loyal go-betweens by making all Chinese born in the Straits Settlements official British subjects. Henceforth, Baba merchants could fly the British flag when trading with China though her treaty ports and thus be protected (in theory) from Chinese taxes and Chinese officialdom. Several Baba merchants did this; however, the protection they received was often not what they had hoped for. This was largely because British officials in China had such great difficulty in determining who was really a Straits-born Chinese, and

Thian Hock Keng by Alfred T. Agate (artist) and J. A. Rolph (engraver).
1842
Engraving
H 25.8 x W 16.9 cm
NMS 2000-06700

therefore a British subject, and who was not (a situation that later in the century led them to request that Straits Chinese dress in European clothes to make their identification easier).

As a final note on Tan Tock Seng, he allegedly once revealed, in a conversation with a European missionary, that he was never really a great believer in the 'idols' venerated at the Thian Hock Keng but went along with such ceremonies because the Chinese expected it of him. Whether this report is true or not, one thing is certain: the growing Chinese population in Singapore demanded of its leaders the kind of lavish displays that Tan and his associates financed. In turn, by involving themselves in such activities, Baba merchants overcame several of the prejudices that they might have otherwise encountered. Despite speaking their ancestral dialects poorly (or with an admixture of local Malay words that new Chinese arrivals found incomprehensible), and despite marrying local women and developing all sorts of unique domestic habits, Baba merchants remained at the top of the pile in Singapore's Chinese community for much of the 19th century.

Seah Eu Chin the 'Gambier King'

The life of Seah Eu Chin, one of Singapore's most famous Teochew merchants, could easily be seen as resembling that of Tan Tock Seng in a variety of ways. Though the two men came from different dialect groups, they knew each other and were associates, if not friends. Like Tan, Seah made his fortune as a Chinese middleman using his superior knowledge of local conditions and the Malay language. Also like Tan, Seah became a major Chinese philanthropist, helping to build the Teochew temple Wak Hai Cheng Bio on Phillip Street, serving on its management committee and jointly establishing (initially within the temple's grounds) the Ngee Ann Kongsi – Singapore's first major Teochew association. Finally, Seah, like Tan, also came to the attention of the British as an influential community leader and so became a useful political intermediary.

But one major difference between Tan Tock Seng and Seah Eu Chin was that Seah was not a Baba. Instead, he was a China-born immigrant who had arrived in Singapore in 1823 at the tender age of 18. This meant that all the advantageous local knowledge that Tan had been born into, Seah had to acquire. Back in his village near Swatow (Shandou) in China, Seah had not even belonged to a merchant family, but was the son of a petty mandarin – which leads us straight to the great unanswered question about his early career. Why did someone from such a relatively privileged background leave his homeland to seek his fortune overseas, in the rough-and-tumble world of early 19th-century Singapore?

Perhaps Seah found the bureaucratic world not to his liking and he yearned for a more adventurous life overseas. Maybe there was some major family incident or dreadful scandal which forced him to flee. Or perhaps he had failed the examinations that would have secured his career as a Qing official like his father and was forced to look elsewhere to support himself. All we can say for sure about Seah's decision is that given his family origins it was not a conventional one. Officially endorsed attitudes that then existed in China placed merchants at the bottom of the social ladder; above them were peasants and artisans, and at the top literati. Naturally, money still bought influence, and many merchants attained positions of power and status. Nonetheless, to truly rid themselves of the stigma of a livelihood made from trade, merchants in China sought to acquire titles and property and to educate their sons to pass their examinations and join the ranks of the literati proper. In setting off for Singapore, Seah was turning his back on an entire social hierarchy.

Seah's advantage from the outset was his ability to read and write. His literacy enabled him to secure his passage on a junk to Singapore by working as the ship's clerk, an employment that he continued with, after his arrival in the port, on other trading vessels that plied the Straits. This period of 'roving sea life', as his biographer Song Ong Siang puts it, took Seah from Penang at the northern end of the Malay Peninsula to Palembang down in Sumatra. It was certainly a risky way to earn a living; the Straits, as we will see shortly, were at that time hardly the safest waters. But Seah's voyages also gave him a wide experience of the workings of regional trade. After five years and armed with an insider's knowledge, he was able to return to Singapore and set himself up in the middleman role of a commission agent. From then onwards, he sold supplies to junks from Riau, Sumatra and the Malay Peninsula in exchange for their indigenous produce, which he then sold on to European and other buyers for a handsome profit.

The major turning point in Seah's career came in 1835. In that year, he decided to take his earnings and invest in real estate, establishing Singapore's first large-scale pepper and gambier plantations, which ran along an impressive eight to ten mile tract from what is now the western end of River Valley Road to Bukit Timah and Thomson Roads. While pepper and gambier plantations had existed in Singapore before the British arrived, the soil had never been fertile enough for these crops to be very profitable. At first, Seah also experienced problems with the soil and was about to give up agriculture altogether when a European friend convinced him to persevere. Eventually his fortunes changed – indeed, when Europe discovered that gambier could be used to tan and preserve leather goods, prices for the crop shot up and he found he was sitting on a pile of it. He made such a killing that he henceforth became known as the island's 'Gambier King'.

Seah's wealth brought him the highest status and respectability that a *sinkeh* in Singapore could hope for. In 1838, he married the daughter of the *kapitan Cina* [Chinese captain] of Perak; two years later, he was elected to the Singapore Chamber of Commerce and then from 1851, he was appointed to serve as a grand juror. In the 1860s, he was so powerful that a popular Chinese saying of the time went: 'the heaven belongs to Tan, the earth to Chua and the emperor is Seah'.

Seah Eu Chin.
19th century
NAS 19980001352-0005

But sadly, whereas gambier made Seah both 'king' and 'emperor' it was for
Singapore as a whole an environmental disaster. By the 1860s, the common slash-
and-burn approach to the crop's cultivation had removed great swathes of jungle
from the island and further damaged its soil, forcing most plantation owners to
eventually move their operations across to Johor. Gambier cultivation had also
played a part in the disappearance of Singapore's tigers, through its destruction
of their natural habitat. Inadvertently, Seah's activities disrupted the island's
once pristine ecosystem.

Of course, most people were ignorant of this reality at the time. Instead, Seah
was best known in Singapore not for starting fires in the interior but for trying
to put them out. During the island-wide Hokkien-Teochew riots of 1854 (which
started following a dispute over rice prices and went on for 12 days), he mediated
on behalf of the British to bring both warring sides together and end the fighting.
Two years later, he again came to the aid of the colonial government when
further violence loomed – this time when rumours swept through the Chinese
community that St Andrew's Cathedral was occupied by evil spirits.

It was said that these evil spirits could only be appeased by a sacrifice of 30
human heads, which the British had instructed Indian convicts building the
church to obtain by murdering passers-by. The story spread throughout the
Chinese community and continued to do so even after the authorities declared
it false and offered a $500 reward for the apprehension of any person found
disseminating it. Seah, as part of the committee of Chinese leaders entrusted
to defuse community tensions, stepped in to denounce those who repeated the
rumour as 'people without reflection' who deserved disgrace and punishment.

Through his intervention, the 'head scare' story was quashed and the government no longer had to fear local retaliation against the European community for its alleged iniquity.

Perhaps, when Seah was in his old age he mused at the way Singapore had transformed him. From a mere ship's clerk, he'd risen to become a respected and extremely powerful Chinese official. Indeed, a well-known portrait shows Seah dressed the part as a Chinese mandarin, decked out in Manchu robes – a fashion adopted by several other Chinese leaders whom the British likewise recognised as their official intermediaries. As a grand juror, Seah had begun to adjudicate cases involving local Chinese referred to him by the Straits courts; the colonial authorities further recognised his authority among local Chinese when in 1867 they made him a Justice of the Peace and in 1872 an honorary police magistrate.

By which time, also, Seah had effectively become one of Singapore's first Chinese literati. In the 1840s, he published two articles – on 'Remittances made by the Chinese to their parents' and on the 'Numbers, tribes and avocations of the Chinese in Singapore' – in the *Journal of the Indian Archipelago*, the first learned periodical to be published in the Straits Settlements. Later, in 1864, Seah retired from commerce to (so his biographer tells us) 'devote the remaining years of his life in the cultivation of Chinese literature'. Looking at his career overall there is a pleasing symmetry to the way that it had come full circle.

Syed Omar Aljunied and the Arab cosmopolitans

Around the same time that Seah Eu Chin arrived in Singapore, the port became home to an Arab called Syed Omar Aljunied. Like Tan and Seah, Aljunied emerged as a wealthy merchant and community leader, who founded the town's first mosque and established its first Islamic burial ground. He proved himself also to be an especially broad-minded philanthropist, at one time donating land for Tan Tock Seng's hospital for Chinese paupers and, on another occasion, for the construction of St Andrew's Cathedral. Given that the Arab community Aljunied belonged to comprised but a small minority in the town, such extra-communal generosity indicates a refreshingly cosmopolitan outlook.

In the Singapore of Aljunied's day, such generosity also made excellent business sense. Good relations with both the dominant Chinese and European communities were vital to the Arab community's commercial success and Aljunied appears to have got on with both groups extremely well. In fact, if any one quality was fundamental to his entrepreneurial rise it was probably his willingness to adjust to new peoples and new conditions, and to seize the opportunities that they presented.

As an Arab, Aljunied belonged to the Hadhrami people, originally from Yemen in the Middle East, who had been trading in Southeast Asia since the middle of the 18th century, and who had set up commercial bases in northern

Java, in Sumatra and then in Singapore. Like the Chinese, Hadhrami traders relied on extensive networks of business contacts that in their case extended west from Southeast Asia across the Indian Ocean to the Persian Gulf and the Red Sea, eventually connecting them back to their ancestral homelands.

Aljunied had already been trading in Palembang in Sumatra when the British free port opened in Singapore. He arrived on the island with his uncle shortly after, bringing his trade networks with him. Quickly he set up a successful business, exporting spices to his homeland and to England, while at the same time importing English cotton goods to sell in Southeast Asia. Aljunied also possessed one local advantage that Chinese merchants rarely enjoyed: because Arab traders were Muslims, the Malay Sultans accorded them a degree of trust and a duty-free status.

It seems that when Raffles drew up his town plan in 1822, he had especially grand expectations of Arab traders such as Aljunied, for he gave them an entire quarter of their own to live in. Over the years that followed, though the Arab community never grew very large, it continued to wield great wealth and social influence. Writing in 1886, Dutch scholar L. W. C. Van den Berg described Singapore as 'the most flourishing, though not the largest, Arab colony in all the Indian Archipelago,' and 'the point by which all Arabs pass who go to seek their fortunes in the Far East'.

For Aljunied, his personal wealth did not grow simply through trade; like local Chinese merchants, he also made shrewd investments in alternative enterprises. One of his crucial gambles was his purchase of property in Singapore town. On a scale as large as, if not larger than, his Chinese counterparts, Aljunied snapped up real estate in strategic locations at attractive prices, then collected rent, and bought and sold properties for many profitable years to come. His purchases included prime plots of land just a stone's throw from the Singapore River in the vicinity of High Street. Today, we might view real estate as a rather unadventurous option for a budding investor, but in 19th-century Singapore, before the days of property insurance, it was an entirely riskier undertaking. In 1847, a major fire razed much of the Muslim neighbourhood of Kampong Glam where Aljunied had several of his properties. Fortunately for him, his business was strong enough by this time to survive such losses and eventually to be rebuilt.

Aljunied was not alone in his willingness to take entrepreneurial risks. Other wealthy Arabs in Singapore were amongst the first traders to seize hold of the new technology that was so changing the face of trade across Southeast Asia. From the mid-19th century, Arab-owned steamships became common sights in Singapore harbour, supplanting traditional craft and obviating the need to rely on trade winds for the movement of goods and people.

Several of these vessels belonged to the wealthy Alsagoffs, another Hadhrami family who in the late 19th century dominated the local steamship business not

only in Singapore and the Malay Peninsula but also across the Archipelago. The main business of their ships was to move consignments of trade goods and produce in and out of Singapore but they also provided transport for pilgrims going to Mecca on the annual *haj*. Each steamship could carry about a thousand *haj* pilgrims at a time, so pilgrims congregated in Singapore for the journey west, some remaining in Singapore for many years to pay off the cost of their passage. By the 1890s, the port was the main departure point for pilgrims from across Southeast Asia, and Bussorah Street in the Arab quarter was bursting with businesses that catered especially to their various needs – from clothing, to accommodation and currency.

Like the Straits Chinese *taukeh* who would eventually come to dominate the steamship business, the Alsagoffs showed a striking open-mindedness when it came to their business partners. In the mid-1870s, Syed Mohamed Alsagoff was Managing Director of the Straits Ships Company, a brief joint-enterprise with local Chinese merchants and one local European shipmaster. (Syed Mohamed was famously the owner of the steamship *Jeddah*, whose abandonment by its crew, following a boiler explosion, was the inspiration for the opening of Joseph Conrad's *Lord Jim*). Then, in 1896, the Alsagoffs became founding members of an even more diverse and expansive shipping syndicate, whose members included British and Dutch shipping companies and the ruler of Mecca.

Inevitably, as the Alsagoffs' steamships plied ever-widening routes across the Indian Ocean, other traders who had once been pivotal players in the entrepôt business faced an eventual decline. It was no longer enough just to sail between regional ports, as the Bugis had done, or to stick to a centuries-old way of life, as the *orang laut* would continue to do – the days of sail were gradually passing.

Mosque in Kampong Glam by John Turnbull Thomson. The existing Sultan Mosque, completed in 1928, stands on the site of this former building.

1846
Watercolour on paper
H 15.3 x W 22.7 cm
Gifted by the Hall-Jones family
Hocken Collections, University
of Otago, Dunedin, New Zealand
92/1155

10. THE MALCONTENTS

So far, our stories of successful merchants are of individuals who worked within 'the system', who kept the peace and even became the local intermediaries of colonial authority – enjoying, in the process, a sudden rise in status they could hardly have contemplated elsewhere. For such men, one of the attractions of the free port was its relative safety as a place of law and order. In Singapore, merchants could get on with their business, away from the vagaries of unreliable officials, unpredictable rulers and their monopolist demands.

Yet, at times, Singapore's spirited, unregulated growth made the new law and order that the British sought to introduce ripe for exploitation. In particular, British laws caused all sorts of problems for those accustomed to a very different way of doing business. The days when a merchant's word was everything, when a 'contract' was a matter of trust and terms were negotiated over some *sirih**, were passing. Transactions now involved binding documents and the settlement of disputes in new colonial courts.

This is not to say that no written laws or formal judiciary had existed in Singapore under its Malay rulers, but rather that following the Treaty of 1824 their authority to define what was legal in Singapore and what was not had passed to the Europeans. With the British now installed as the port's commercial arbitrators, the authorities passed down decisions in a strange language, according to legal principles from an entirely different civilisation. Some traders discovered that while commerce in the emporium was free, justice came at a price.

All of this made for simmering tension. If many merchants were able to work the new system to their advantage – especially those with at least a smattering of English – others became marginalised. Success appeared to depend on how close one was to the newly established authorities. Those who did not enjoy such proximity made their feelings known. Some wrote sardonic poems in protest; others turned to more violent pursuits.

Mr Siami the critic

In the 1820s, Malay-speaking residents of Singapore (who comprised the vast majority in the new settlement) may have come across a poem being recited at street corners or in front of groups gathered by the banks of the river. The poem was entitled *Syair Dagang Berjual Beli*, a poem on 'Trading, Selling and Buying', and it was written by an angry 'Mr Siami'. It began with the lines:

> Oh listen, dear sirs, your ears you may lend
> For such wonders I scarcely understand

---

* Traditionally, chewing *sirih* (betel leaves) had a variety of functions: as an ice-breaker, an act of friendship or as a token of an agreement.

Sikh policeman apprehending
two Chinese pickpockets.
19th century
Engraving
H 25.7 x W 28.7 cm
NMS 2007-00826

Now the merchants are governing the land
A sign that the world has come to an end

The evocative scene that Siami presents would have seemed commonplace in early 19th-century Singapore: 'The boats arrive and everyone clamours / For goods bought and sold, received and given'. Indeed, as Siami depicts Malay, Bugis, Chinese and Indian traders gathering to do business, the atmosphere in the young emporium appears positively buoyant:

All goods are sold with glad release
Nobody settles into any debt
Promises and loyalties are pledged with ease
Until all cash payments are met

However, the poem's opening has warned us already of the deceptive nature of such optimism. No sooner do the boats appear and the merchants gather than Siami hints that trouble lies ahead – for while the Chinese and Indians are 'expert bargainers', the Malays and Bugis are 'foolish and craven'. Sure enough, a dispute between these two groups erupts almost immediately:

When the goods and baubles have all been unloaded
The Chinese and Indians then start with their bluff
Textiles and lustrous goods are paraded
They say, 'Hey, you, shipmaster, come claim your stuff'

Take whatever goods your eyes fancy
The finest textiles from the Dutch obtained
For we are unable to pay with real money
If the shipmaster's cross he can file a complaint

Rather than pay the Bugis shipmaster in cash for the goods that he has brought over to Singapore, the Chinese and Indian merchants force him to barter for goods in exchange. This is not what the shipmaster has previously agreed to:

> The shipmaster asks, 'Could you please explain?
> Was not our agreement made some time ago?
> Now we are told to lodge a complaint
> We are just traders, so how would we know?'

The situation then deteriorates as the Indians and Chinese 'all exclaim / with mouths that snarl and hands that hustle', while the enraged shipmaster simply inflames 'the furious barking and quarrelsome bustle'. Then, at the point where the various parties are about to come to blows, they are all marched off to an Englishman who is made 'referee'. As Siami goes on:

> They finally come to the Englishman's shop
> The Chinese man's words are full of aggression
> People at market all wind to a stop
> To watch as the English tries to lessen the tension:

> 'Go thus and seek the police court's counsel
> Your case will be noted then duly processed
> Three gentlemen are there who sit on the council
> That's where your grievance will best be assessed'

At this point, colonial justice comes into play. The Englishman drafts a letter explaining the dispute for the aggrieved parties to show to the police magistrate. However, the shipmaster does not yet come to enjoy the full process of the law, for at the interview with the magistrate, events suddenly take a different course:

> The Chinese man then shows the Englishman's letter
> To the wise magistrate, a man of respect
> Who reads it through to make sense of the matter
> His frown soon reveals what he's come to suspect

> After reading the letter most thoroughly
> He says, 'Oh, you Chinese are rogues indeed
> Why drag this argument on so craftily
> A fair punishment awaits a foul deed'

> To the shipmaster then he turns and says:
> 'This Chinaman's guilt is painfully obvious
> With his twisted words and shifty ways
> There can be no doubt his motives are devious'

Having publicly affirmed the guilt of the Chinese merchant, the magistrate then passes judgement:

> The magistrate says, 'As God is my witness
> Surely this Chinaman must be in the wrong
> These endless discussions are winding and fruitless
> Let's lock him up and this case not prolong'

But wait, there is a catch, and a major one at that, for as soon as the magistrate has delivered his verdict he goes on to say:

> 'But the shipmaster ought to provide the fee
> If this man is now to be thrown into prison
> This is in accordance with the Raja's decree
> The law of this land and well within reason
>
> 'The daily expense of his prison stay
> It's the shipmaster's duty now to disburse
> And once this Chinaman's debt has been paid
> The shipmaster then we shall full reimburse
>
> 'An agreement like this is both fixed and binding
> Expenses shall be credited every month
> If we find that the shipmaster's payments are lacking
> The Chinaman's guarantee is forfeit at once'

Witnessing this remarkable turnabout in his fortunes, the shipmaster 'feels in his heart a violent churning' and has to resist a 'fainting swoon'. The reality is he has no choice now but to 'let the suit be dismissed!' As Siami has him explain to the court:

> 'Don't wrap up this case and cause me distress
> Forgive me my sins and this awful mistake
> Because of this man I am now powerless
> For his payment I don't know how long he will take
>
> 'I'm confident, Sir, of your most esteemed judgement
> The court will no longer subject me to its wiles
> If there's nothing else I can take for my payment
> I'll just have to take what's due in textiles'

At this, the magistrate is 'terribly pleased' and he even orders all the parties to go away in peace and argue no more. The Chinese merchant, though he now wears a 'mask of sorrow', is likewise 'obviously gladdened', having got exactly what he wanted from the outset. But Mr Siami's sympathies throughout are with the wronged shipmaster, described at the end of the drama as having to force 'a false smile to hide his woe', and it is specifically to an audience who would have shared these sympathies that the poet addresses his parting words:

> Such is the state of us Bugis and Malays
> When to the white man we surrender our fates
> Of their rulings – it's true what they say
> The hand that gives is the hand that confiscates
>
> We often have heard of the white man's wisdom
> Their judgements supposedly fair and just

Now we all know when the court is their kingdom
We are mere jesters performing a farce

Thus is there widespread law and order
But here in Singapore it is all but a show
For those who think this is only a rumour
Visit our port and the truth you will know

Who was Mr Siami? Little is known about him except that he was once, like Munshi Abdullah, a Malay-speaking scribe employed by Raffles. It's also clear from his *Syair Dagang Berjual Beli* that he was no impartial observer. In fact, at times the language he uses to depict the villains of the piece – the Chinese and Indian merchants – more than verges on the obscene. Nonetheless, Mr Siami has left us with a remarkable text that as a contemporary insight into trade and justice in early Singapore stands apart and offsets the rose-coloured picture of trade in the port projected by other accounts (as well as by some works of history). In Siami's emporium, once 'the goods and the baubles have all been unloaded' tensions explode between buyers and sellers, and between those who appear to understand the workings of colonial justice as against those who are 'just traders' and have no idea how to 'lodge a complaint'.

The *Syair Dagang Berjual Beli* is also fascinating because of the new medium it represents. The poem was lithographed, most probably circulated around the Singapore town, where it may have been dropped in prominent public places and recited aloud to non-literate and semi-literate audiences. As an early form of anti-establishment protest it revealed the increasing gap that was emerging within Singapore's trading community between those who for whatever reason seemed favoured by the British and those who felt they were not.

Lastly, the *Syair Dagang Berjual Beli* was to some extent prophetic. By the mid-19th century, many Bugis had quit Singapore, preferring to operate out of the new free port of Makassar in Sulawesi (though their fleets still arrived in Singapore each September). Likewise, many *orang laut* had departed, especially in the 1840s after the British dispersed their floating village on the Singapore River because it obstructed traffic. Meanwhile, those *orang laut* who remained became assimilated into the wider Malay community as boatmen and fishermen. As Mr Siami saw it, a world where Bugis and Malay once ruled the waves was beginning to 'come to an end'.

The pirates of the Straits: rebels or plunderers?

For those who regretted the imposition of British authority in Singapore and its environs, near-anonymous *syair* were one means of protest. Did piracy represent another? Would Malays, Bugis or *orang laut* have seen the pirate fleets that increasingly lay in wait in Singapore waters as the rebellious navies of their dispossessed chiefs who had refused to bow to colonial authority? To put it bluntly, can piracy be seen as a *legitimate* form of resistance against the *illegitimate* expansion of European empires?

Historians have examined this issue and now question the whole colonial definition of piracy in the early 19th century. But before we get into this debate, it's worth recounting a tale from the historical sources of the period. Whatever else may be said, the brutality of piracy in the Straits is hard to ignore. Setting aside the motivations behind a pirate attack – political, commercial or other – it remained a shocking event:

> During the attack Encik Bakak was killed and his *perahu* plundered. Encik Bakak himself was strangled with his shoulder sash and left to rot. His penis was cut off and stuffed in his mouth … Some of Encik Bakak's companions were killed, some were beheaded and some were tied up to be sold. One escaped by jumping overboard in the dark, and he brought back the news.

We might draw back from such an account, assume it to be just the kind of sensationalist report written by Europeans to justify their attempts to suppress Straits pirates – except that this account isn't European at all, but comes from the *Tuhfat Al-Nafis* [The Precious Gift], a 19th-century Bugis chronicle. Both Western and indigenous sources agree that local Malay and Bugis shipping was as much a sought-after bounty for pirates as were Chinese and European vessels, if not more so. One thing we can say for them, the pirates of the Straits did not discriminate according to nationality.

Accounts written by Europeans reveal the extent to which piracy in early colonial Singapore was *the* hot topic of the day. Our traveller-turned-author George Earl declared: 'The Malay pirates absolutely swarm in the neighbourhood of Singapore, the numerous islands in the vicinity, the intersecting channels of which are known only to themselves, affording them a snug retreat, whence they can pounce upon the defenceless native traders, and drag them into their lairs to plunder them at their leisure.' In Earl's view, the local Straits 'system of piracy' was 'perfect in its nature, more so than that which formerly obtained among the Buccaneers of America', and the reason it proliferated rather simple:

> A petty chief of one of the Malay states, who has either been ruined by gambling, or is desirous to improve his fortune, collects under his banner as many restless spirits as he can muster, and sails for one of the most retired islands in the neighbourhood of Singapore. Here he erects a village as a depot for slaves and plunder, and then lies in wait with his armed *perahus*, near the frequented waters, for the native traders, passing to and from the British settlement. Should the chief be eminently successful, he soon gains a large accession to his force, and his village increases to a small town, while his fleet of *perahus* becomes sufficiently numerous to be subdivided into several squadrons, which cruise in the various straits and channels.

Iranun pirate. The Iranun were a maritime people from what are now the southern Philippine islands who by the late 18th century had acquired a fearsome reputation for their attacks on regional shipping.
1840s
Lithograph
H 20.0 x W 13.3 cm
NMS XXXX-01144

Earl's account also reveals the part played by piracy in Singapore's burgeoning economy. Once the vessels which the pirates had captured were brought back to their pirate base, they were plundered and burnt. The goods, however, were taken to be resold in the Singapore bazaars by *perahu* 'fitted up to resemble traders'. Thus, it was quite possible that Singapore merchants discovered goods they had imagined lost reappearing in port a few weeks later in someone else's possession. Unfortunately for the crews and passengers of these captured vessels, no such second lease of life applied. Earl tells us that the survivors of pirate attacks were carried off to the island of Lingga or 'to the opposite coast of Sumatra', where they were 'sold to the Malays, to cultivate the pepper plantations in the interior'.

Earl played down the incidence of pirate attacks on European shipping (when it came to British square-riggers the pirates were 'as cowardly as they are cruel'). However, other writers were struck by the threat they posed. Charles Burton Buckley, the author of *An Anecdotal History of Old Times in Singapore*, recorded one of the first pirate attacks in Singapore waters following the British arrival. In 1826, seven 'Malays or Javanese (one of whom was found afterwards to have been a fisherman in Singapore who left without paying his debts)' went on board the Dutch schooner *Anna* 'saying they were pilgrims returning from Mecca':

> They rose on the crew after leaving Singapore, nearly killing the Captain and driving the crew on deck into the rigging, but some passengers on board and the rest of the crew killed them or drove them into the sea, where it is supposed they were drowned.

Buckley recounted another 'remarkable story of piracy' that involved the ship of one Captain Gravesome. When this vessel was attacked by Borneo pirates, it was carrying 'a valuable cargo of opium and piece-goods', as well as two European passengers, 'a young lady of twenty and a boy of fifteen years of age'. Most of the crew was massacred; however, the European lady and boy were taken prisoner and delivered to the local Sultan, whereupon the Sultan's mother 'interposed on their behalf and took care of them'. Later, a European merchant discovered the whole tale, while he was himself the said Sultan's prisoner, and asked about the young lady's and the boy's whereabouts. The Sultan informed the merchant that both had died of smallpox, but the merchant heard others say 'they had been poisoned, as the Sultan did not feel himself safe as long as they lived'. Looking back from the relative peace of the late 1890s, Buckley felt it 'almost incredible … that such practices should have been so common as to excite only a passing remark, while in these days any similar occurrence would excite universal horror and speedy retribution'.

Indeed, piracy was so endemic that a Singapore newspaper in the early 1830s could remark that 'if fully detailed' the frequency of such attacks 'would furnish matter for a paper to be exclusively devoted to their notice'. Of course, no such paper appeared, so the existing Singapore press was left to detail the pirate menace itself – which it did with some relish. The *Singapore Free Press* reported that pirate *perahu* were usually 50 to 60 feet in length and 'strongly built with a round stern'. They also featured a defensive bulwark made of bamboo 'nearly two feet broad', which 'was made all round the vessel, from the stockade near the bow to the stern'. Through the stockade, 'not far from the bow' pointed an iron four-pounder and 'around all the sides were from three to six guns of the same description, all brass, stuck upon upright pieces of wood'. The pirates themselves carried muskets and spears, 'wore very large bamboo shields covering all the upper part of the body' and 'wore long hair which they let loose in the battle, to give them a savage appearance'. The 'rowers among these pirates were of the lower castes, or slaves captured in their cruises'; hence, the paper warned, 'a strong Chinese became a valuable acquisition to them'.

Most European observers saw the reasons for this upsurge in piracy to be self-evident. Singapore was an ever-growing, increasingly successful emporium: the 'natives' were returning to the dissolute, piratical existence to which they had always tended. Earl, as we have seen, linked piracy with the moral failings of the Malay chiefs and their habit of gambling themselves into heavy debt. Buckley went further, stating that 'the natives on the coasts were barbarous, rapacious, and poor, which tended strongly to beget a piratical character'. Even Raffles described piracy as an 'evil of ancient date, which had struck deep in the Malay habits'.

However, take off the prejudiced spectacles of 19th-century colonials and the issue of piracy becomes suddenly more complex. Today, scholars argue that not only were the causes of piracy various, but the term itself has to be used with caution. Historian Carl Trocki has written of the 'ecological realities' that Malay peoples of the region were forced to contend with: namely that the jungle and the soil of the Malay Peninsula and surrounding islands did not make for good agriculture. Inevitably, this meant that the sea became their main source of power and profit. In contrast with territorial kingdoms, the Malay state's 'lines of control were the sea routes and its authority was strung out from island to island and from one river mouth to another'.

Since Malay sea captains in the employ of local Sultans believed they had a royal sanction that allowed them control over the sea routes and river mouths of the Straits, as well as all that passed upon or through them, maritime patrols to exact tribute were deemed perfectly legitimate – as was any increased resort to such activity when times of necessity demanded it. Malay historical sources make a clear distinction between those bands of seafarers that were licensed to undertake such patrols, through hereditary titles given them by the Sultan, and those that were not. From a local perspective, the real pirates were the *perompak* – wanderers, outlaws and renegades with no royal titles and usually no fixed abodes.

But when the British set up in Singapore everything changed. The maritime authority that the Malay state depended on was immediately challenged. The

Charles Burton Buckley, author of *An Anecdotal History of Old Times in Singapore*.

19th century
Oil on canvas
H 240 x W 147 cm
NMS HP-0018

British, with their belief in free trade and their powerful sense of their own legitimacy, could not accept, or even comprehend, the long historical claim of Sultans and Temenggongs to own the sea routes and all that passed upon them. Indeed, the treaties that the British had these rulers sign ended their traditional rights to tax vessels entering port, making them dependent on colonial allowances.

In a further blow to Malay authority, the British expelled the Temenggong from Singapore town. The Temenggong had long been the Sultan of Johor-Riau-Lingga's hereditary 'sea lord', charged with patrolling the Straits with his fleet and with policing the Sultanate's ports to fix and extract duties. Now, he and his followers were removed to Telok Blangah, away from the port and its population. When the Temenggong died in 1825, the British decided not to permit the appointment of another Malay sea lord of Singapore for another 16 years.

Inevitably, such a sudden change in the fortunes of Singapore's Malay rulers meant that many *orang laut* who had once made their livelihoods patrolling the sea on their Sultan's behalf turned to 'piracy'. But the high incidence of reported pirate attacks in the years after 1824 might also have had something to do with mistaken European perceptions. Historian Nicholas Tarling has argued that the British classed as piratical any business disagreements that emerged between merchants and Malay chiefs who had established outposts at river mouths. We can well imagine how the attitude of some merchants of the time might have led to such disputes: now that the British had arrived advocating free trade, why should they pay the old taxes any longer? When a merchant refused to adhere to a prior agreement, or desired to negotiate a new one, things could easily turn violent.

Finally, conflicts between rival Malay chiefs involved attacks on maritime trade that the British regarded as piracy but which, if judged by Britain's own standards (beginning from the late 16th century) were more akin to privateering. A 'privateer' was an armed vessel owned by private individuals with a government commission for war service, which included attacks on an enemy's merchant shipping. However, European powers did not regard Malay rulers and their subjects as legitimate 'nations' with which they were at war. Rather, they condemned any sea captain and fleet which had not yet accepted their authority as piratical. In the eyes of the Dutch, for instance, the Temenggong – that same authority with whom the British had made their 1819 Treaty – was a buccaneer renegade from the moment he backed Sultan Hussein instead of the Dutch favourite as heir to Johor-Riau-Lingga. Piracy really did seem to depend on the eye of the beholder.

Which brings us to a particularly fine irony, for at one time the Dutch and the British had themselves been the greatest pirates of the Malay world – capable of acts of brutality and savagery, against local populations and against each other, the equal of anything unleashed by 'native' buccaneers. In the 17th century, as Portuguese power waned and the Dutch and British East India Companies battled for control of spices in the Indies, indigenous populations were murdered, uprooted and sold into slavery, and their ships, lands and livelihoods plundered for the European market. After the infamous Ambon massacre of 1623, in which Dutch traders tortured and murdered their British counterparts, such brutality became a scandal across Europe, bringing both these maritime empires to the verge of outright war and providing the inspiration for a play by the Englishman John Dryden. When, centuries later, Raffles, Crawfurd and other Europeans in Singapore called for the suppression of piracy – in the interests of free trade, law and order – they displayed the usual impeccable symptoms of a widespread national amnesia.

The arrival of the pirate hunters

Whatever the complex causes of increased piracy in the Straits, by the mid-1830s one thing was clear: European merchants had had enough. On 23 April 1835, following a public meeting in Singapore, they sent a petition to Calcutta and London requesting government assistance in dealing with the pirate menace. The following year, HMS *Wolf* moored in Singapore harbour, followed soon after by HMS *Andromache* and a third man-of-war, HMS *Raleigh*. The British suppression of piracy had well and truly begun.

The new steamships that had so fascinated Munshi Abdullah also played a pivotal role. The *Diana*, the first East India Company steamship built in India, arrived in the Straits in 1837 and had its initial encounter with pirates soon after. Buckley recorded that the *Diana* was on patrol with HMS *Wolf* when it came across six large *perahu* attacking a Chinese junk. Seeing the smoke pouring from

Pirate attack off Gilolo, in what is now Papua New Guinea.
1848
Lithograph
H 10.5 x W 16 cm
NMS 1994-00302

the *Diana*'s funnels, the pirate *perahu* turned and bore down on her, thinking she was 'a sailing ship on fire' and in clear distress. As they opened up with their cannons, they were in for a rude shock:

> To their horror, the [*Diana*] came close up *against the wind*, and then suddenly stopped opposite each *perahu*, and poured in a destructive fire, turning and backing quite against the wind, stretching the pirates in numbers on their decks. A vessel that was independent of the wind was, of course, a miracle to them.

Buckley also recorded what happened when the same ship appeared in Borneo and some local Malay rulers boarded her for an inspection. The moment the 'machinery was set in motion', the chiefs fled the decks, 'crying out *dia bergrak! dia bergrak!* (it stirs, it stirs) thinking it was a living monster, fed in the hold to move the vessel as it was ordered.'

Whether this particular story is entirely genuine or not, Britain's war against piracy included an element of 'shock and awe' that over the next two decades would prove infamous. The *Tuhfat Al-Nafis* relates the pirate-hunting voyage of HMS *Andromache*, led in person by 'Governor Bonham of Singapore'. When Sultan Muhammad of Riau heard news 'that a warship was scouring the seas', once again 'firing on any Malay *perahu* with matting sails', the Sultan asked, 'How can the English do such a thing? We are already taking steps to eradicate piracy, and they come and act like this.'

The English who increasingly acted like this were Her Majesty's pirate-hunters, a motley cast of adventurers who arrived in Singapore as if having stepped straight from the pages of Robert Louis Stevenson. One of the better known was Henry Chads, the *Andromache*'s captain, who English boys in the port remembered as a hero with one arm. Chad's cunning ruse was to draw pirates to him by disguising his vessel as a Malay trader. More famous still was Captain Henry Keppel, who went by the nickname of 'Raja Laut' – the 'king of the sea'. In the early 1840s, Keppel's naval expeditions from Singapore against Borneo pirates proved instrumental in clearing the way (literally) for a certain James Brooke, at that time on his way to becoming the 'White Raja' of Sarawak.

Malay cannon.
19th century
Brass
L 90.3 x H 29 cm
Donated by Ms. Rita Wong
NMS 1992-00952

By the end of an illustrious career, Captain Keppel had become Sir Henry Keppel, a Royal Navy admiral and a favourite of Queen Victoria. But today – and despite giving his name in Singapore to a road, a harbour and a major company – he comes across as a rather doubtful character. In his account of his expedition to suppress the Borneo pirates (a major hit when it was published back in England in 1846), he happily relates how he blasted his away along the enemy coastline and rivers, wreaking a 'destruction' that 'astonished the whole country beyond description'. Travelling with him were a band of his 'Dyak followers', whose occasional habit it was to collect the heads of their vanquished foes 'as trophies'.

As news of Keppel's exploits spread, public doubts emerged as to how many of his vanquished foes were in fact pirates as opposed to innocent traders. In 1846, the *Singapore Free Press* explicitly blamed the 'warlike operations of our men-of-war in Borneo' for having 'produced a disastrous effect on the native trade between that quarter and Singapore'. After a second expedition in 1849, public concern grew stronger and in 1853 a Commission of Enquiry was held in Singapore to look into the matter. To no one's great surprise, the Commission's proceedings exonerated Keppel, Brooke and the Royal Navy of any wrongdoing. However, one major outcome was that pirate bounties posted in the port thereafter ceased. By the mid-19th century, it seems that the taste of pirate-hunters for brutal destruction had led even the colonial authorities to have misgivings.

The reinvention of Daing Ibrahim

The pirate-hunter who stood apart, and who probably had more to do with the eventual suppression of piracy in the Straits than any Royal Navy captain, was neither an Englishman nor an East India Company servant, nor someone who relied on the superior firepower of British gunships during a campaign of terror against local shipping. He was, instead, Daing Ibrahim, the son of the Temenggong, and his transformation from pirate to pirate-hunter is one of the more remarkable in Singapore's history.

When his father died in 1825, Ibrahim found himself in a precarious situation. Deprived of his hereditary title by the British and forced out of Singapore town, he had only his government pension and the revenue from his *kampong* at Telok Blangah on which to survive. His followers – who during his father's time numbered between 6,000 and 10,000 – were starting to drift away. Just 15 years old, he faced a stark choice: to live out his days as a stooge of the British while his patrimony dissipated, or to become a 'pirate'.

A decade later, it was pretty clear which path the young man had chosen. In 1835, the English press in Singapore claimed that Ibrahim was the mastermind behind a number of pirate attacks in the waters between the island and Riau. British officialdom shared this view and recommended that 'discreet surveillance' be maintained on his

Sir Henry Keppel.
19th century
Oil on canvas
H 194.0 x W 123.0 cm
NMS HP-0016

activities. Typically for his time, Governor George Bonham pronounced there to be evidence of Ibrahim's piratical character in his general manner:

> This young man is ... idle and completely illiterate; indeed, except by his clothes and consequent personal appearance, not a remove higher on the scale of Civilisation than the meaner of his followers. I make these remarks because an opinion exists here that the last is very deeply involved in many of the Piracies which take place in the neighbourhood.

Piracy might well have continued to be what Ibrahim was most famed for, were it not for a piece of arch-pragmatism by Bonham in response to some extraordinary stubbornness on the part of Singapore's European merchants. When the 1835 petition on piracy reached the EIC headquarters in Calcutta, the solution proposed by the government of India was to raise a series of duties and levies in the Straits Settlements to cover the military expenditure that suppression entailed. At once, the merchants of Singapore were in uproar. Anything, even piracy, was preferable to taxation and the loss of Singapore's free port status, so they duly pressured the Company's Directors in London to scuttle the plan.

Bonham was now in a fix. Piracy was on the rampage, the European merchants refused to pay for its suppression and the colonial administration was too impoverished to fund its own naval expeditions. On top of all this, Singapore was experiencing a trade depression that made any resolution of the problem ever more pressing, and yet harder to enforce.

In a major turnabout, Bonham enlisted Ibrahim – the man he had described as 'idle and completely illiterate'. In return for Bonham's assurances that the British would aid his family in recovering their former prestige, Ibrahim the former pirate transformed himself into a key colonial ally, helping the British in their negotiations with other Malay rulers to suppress piratical activities, reining in his own followers from their illegal 'patrols' and, no doubt, providing invaluable intelligence support to the Royal Navy. In 1841, the reinvention of Daing Ibrahim was complete when he was officially recognised by Bonham and the British as the next Temenggong of Johor.

But Ibrahim was more than a compliant puppet, dependent on the colonial regime for his authority and power. As the expeditions of Her Majesty's pirate-hunters laid waste to local shipping, Malay sea captains and traders turned to Ibrahim for protection. In the early 1840s, his position was further strengthened by the discovery in Johor of *gutta percha*, a rubber-like extract from the tree of the same name that was used to insulate telegraph wiring. According to the principles laid down by Raffles, the movement of this valuable commodity out of Johor and into Singapore should have been free and unimpeded. However, nearly all the *gutta percha* for sale in the port soon somehow belonged to the Temenggong. A complaint lodged by the Singapore Chamber of Commerce in 1848 stated that Ibrahim was using his former pirate fleet to establish an illegal

Daing Ibrahim.
19th century
Arkib Negara, Malaysia

monopoly over the trade, intercepting boats arriving in Singapore, intimidating their crews and forcing their captains to hand over their cargoes, on any terms that the Temenggong chose.

In view of the broader significance of Ibrahim's support, the British authorities turned a blind eye to such activities and he continued with his monopoly on *gutta percha*, soon establishing himself as a wealthy entrepreneur. At the same time his family line gained in respectability until finally, in 1855, the British officially recognised Ibrahim as ruler of Johor (forcing Sultan Hussein's descendents to relinquish their claim). Eventually, 30 years later, the British installed Ibrahim's son, Abu Bakar, as Johor's new Sultan.

Nonetheless, it was hard for some European merchants not to see the irony in Ibrahim's transformation. In 1846, in a ceremony held on Singapore's Government Hill (today's Fort Canning), the British publicly thanked Ibrahim for his services in the suppression of piracy and Governor Butterworth conferred on him the Sword of Honour. Among those that attended the ceremony was William Henry Read, a Scottish merchant. Read wryly observed that during these solemn formalities he and his fellow European merchants 'counted several boats stationed outside the island, and manned by the Temenggong's peoples, to seize any *gutta percha* which might be imported from outside places, at arbitrary prices, probably often at no price at all'.

For the likes of Read and his associates, Ibrahim's old piratical habits appeared to die hard.

Governor William John Butterworth conferring the Sword of Honour on Temenggong Daing Ibrahim.

1846
Lithograph
H 13 cm x W 21.8 cm
NMS XXXX-01258

11. A NEW COLONIAL ORDER

Hanging in the National Museum of Singapore's History Gallery is a painting entitled 'The Padang in Singapore', which was painted in 1851 by the government surveyor and self-taught artist John Turnbull Thomson. The scene Thomson presents gives a valuable insight into early colonial life in the settlement for then, as now, the Padang was the centre of the town. Europeans pass by in their carriages, their Asian subjects look on contentedly, a game of cricket goes on in the background and alongside it a local game of *sepak takraw* (a Malay version of football played with a wicker ball). In another part of the picture, Arabs, with their women dressed in burkhas, stroll past, as do a few Chinese, perhaps taking a break from a long day of trading or meeting to negotiate further business. On the horizon, overlooking the Padang's array of colourful, exotic peoples, stand white neo-classical buildings symbolising harmony and progress. Meanwhile, the British watch this happy, peaceful gathering from their superior positions of benign authority, seated on their horses.

All in all, this is an idyllic scene. Of course, it's also a piece of propaganda, one of several romanticised depictions of Singapore produced for a European audience back home – an image of what the British thought their colony ought to be rather than what it actually was.

As we've come to appreciate, the flipside to the successful emporium was an underbelly of piracy, injustice and (as we will discuss later) secret societies, vice

The Padang in Singapore,
John Turnbull Thomson.

1851
Oil on canvas
H 69 x W 89 cm
NMS HP-0054

and opium. At the time when Thomson painted the Padang, Singapore still had only a rudimentary legal system, few public amenities, and it remained a place of wild rumour and potential riot. At eight o'clock each evening, the famous Revere Bell, a gift to the settlement from Maria Revere Balestier (daughter of Paul Revere, the hero of the American Revolution, and wife of the then American Consul in Singapore), rang out to warn inhabitants of the impending curfew. The streets of Singapore were not a safe place to find oneself wandering after dark.

Having said this, between the 1820s and the 1860s things did start to change, especially in Singapore's European district. Here, the frontier character of the town gave way to a new colonial-style order, which manifested itself in two obvious ways. First, the British, as Thomson's picture reveals, imposed themselves architecturally on the town; looming over Singapore's inhabitants by 1851 were shiny new colonial edifices built of stone and brick that seemed to say that the British were here and here to stay. Secondly, European merchants in Singapore became more active in their demands for better government, with the end result that the colony's status as a settlement ruled from the East India Company administration in Calcutta eventually came to an end.

It is to some of the key people involved in these changes – an architect, an industrious class of convicts and a tenacious agitator – that we now turn.

G. D. Coleman: a builder of colonial Singapore

Thomson's painting of the Padang is testimony to the influence of one of Singapore's most important early architects. Of the colonial structures that fill up the picture's horizon, six were designed by the Irishman George Drumgoole Coleman while the rest show the clear imprint of his architectural style. The style in question is Palladian, named after the 16th-century Italian architect Andrea Palladio and characterised by the use of powerful classical motifs: for instance, the use of heavy triangular pediments (à la ancient Roman temple porticos) to designate entrances, an adherence to regimented proportion and a strictly ordered arrangement of façade decoration.

Drawing on Palladianism, Coleman designed several of Singapore's most famous colonial buildings: the Armenian Church of St Gregory the Illuminator, the original Old Parliament House, one of the earliest buildings that came to form the Convent of the Holy Infant Jesus, as well as several European merchant houses that have now been destroyed by redevelopment. Coleman was also responsible for the original design of St Andrew's Cathedral. However, on this occasion his devotion to Andrea Palladio did not go down well. Early Anglican parishioners in Singapore complained that their church looked more like a 'Town Hall', a 'College' or an 'Assembly Room' than a sacred place of worship, with the result that the original plan was modified to incorporate a spire designed by our artist-surveyor John Turnbull Thomson. As an architect Thomson was no Coleman, and

The Revere Bell and Joseph Balestier

The Revere Bell is a symbol of the American connection in Singapore's history. The bell was cast in the Revere foundry in Boston, United States, in the tradition of the Revere bells cast by the famous patriot of the American Revolution, Paul Revere. His daughter, Maria, was married to Joseph Balestier, the first American Consul in Singapore (1837–1852). She presented this bell to St Andrew's Church in 1843 with the condition that it should toll for five minutes every evening at 8 p.m. to signal the start of the curfew. With nightly robberies, thefts and assaults, the town was not a safe place after dark. The tolling of the bell was to remind sailors who were in town to return to their ships and for residents to be watchful. The bell continued to be sounded every evening in the new St Andrew's Church, which replaced the former building that was demolished in 1855. The tolling of the bell was discontinued in 1874.

Balestier outlived his wife and son in Singapore. Maria died in Singapore in August 1847. Joseph Balestier's legacy, among other things, is the road which still bears his name, and his role in the history of the entrepôt in connection with the development of American trade. After Balestier's recognition as Consul by the East India Company's Court of Directors in November 1836, American ships were allowed to trade in the entrepôt with the same opportunities as European trading vessels. As a result, American shipping and trade in Singapore increased greatly. Within a year after his recognition as Consul, some 8,000 tons of American shipping passed through the entrepôt.

Revere Bell
1843
Metal alloy
H 81 x Dia. 89 cm
NMS

in the early 1850s St Andrew's began to collapse, largely as a result of the weight of its spire, whereupon it was demolished and completely redesigned, becoming the neo-Gothic cathedral that stands in the heart of the modern city.

We might wonder why Coleman gave himself so entirely over to Palladianism, making it, as a result, the signature architectural style for Singapore's European Town. Raffles's example earlier at Government House had been to build with wood and *attap* in the traditional Malay manner, which made excellent sense in the sweltering conditions of the time, when, compared with today, there were far fewer trees in built-up areas to offer shade (and certainly no air-conditioning).

To a large extent, the popularity of Palladianism had to do with Singapore's continuing strong ties with India. In its first 50 years, the settlement (along with the other Straits Settlements of Penang and Melaka) was still governed from the East India Company headquarters in Calcutta, where, prior to his arrival in Singapore, Coleman had been in high demand designing homes for European merchants. In Singapore, where many European businesses still had direct dealings with Calcutta, it was natural that Coleman should continue to design buildings in the style to which his clients were accustomed.

Palladianism was, after all, a conservative style, one that a European merchant probably felt comfortable with because if nothing else it clearly displayed his prosperity. But the neo-classical precision of Coleman's buildings also had a moral story to tell. These 'gleaming classical monuments', as the architectural writers Jane Beamish and Jane Ferguson describe them, were 'monuments of rulers, and of a way of life impervious to the riotous and excessive East'. As we are beginning to understand, a major theme of European settler life in Singapore was insulation – against threat and against the local environment, even if this meant (rather perversely) ignoring local wisdom and thereby living in uncomfortable heat and humidity.

The original Palladian building that housed St Andrew's Church (right), with the Padang in the foreground.
1837
Lithograph
H 31.4 x W 48 cm
NMS XXXX-01266

PLAN OF THE TOWN
of
SINGAPORE

Surveyed in the year 1843

BY

J. T. THOMSON

Govt. Surveyor.

NOTE

Allotments coloured thus denote that the
House roots are contiguous

do do are separate

REMARKS.

Population is nearly 50,000.
Value of Imports in 1842 was 13,094,520 and Exports
10,843,312 Spanish Dollars.
Principal products of the Island are Pepper, Gambier,
and Nutmegs.

Prisoner Chetoo and the Indian convicts

A major problem which Coleman and Thomson faced in their efforts to define a new architectural landscape for Singapore was the lack of readily available, affordable labour. For this reason, they turned to Indian convicts whose fundamental importance as builders of early colonial Singapore is sometimes overlooked. On 18 August 1824, the first ship carrying 80 convicts from Madras arrived in port, followed a week later by another ship carrying another 122 convicts from Bengal. Within three decades, Singapore would be home to a convict population of close to 3,000 – a population that the colonial government put to all manner of work which otherwise the administration could not have afforded.

One man who recognised the industrious activities of Indian prisoners – so much so that he wrote a book to record their history – was Major John Frederick Adolphus McNair, Comptroller of Indian Convicts in the Straits Settlements from the 1850s until the 1870s. McNair tells us that in the early years of the colony, Indian convicts helped to fill up marshy ground and construct the roads so vital to the development of the island's interior. In addition, they felled and stacked timber, and made the brick, lime, cement and all else that was necessary for roofing and paving:

> [A]s a matter of fact all material and all labour for the execution of any public work required by the Government were executed by these convicts, from a small timber bridge upon a country road even to the erection of a cathedral and government house.

The shiny white interiors of the European Town were also the work of Indian convicts. Instead of expensive plaster that was, in any case, highly susceptible to tropical humidity, the convicts used a substance called Madras *chunam*, easily manufactured from local ingredients such as shell lime, egg white, *jaggery* (a coarse sugar popular in Indian sweets) and water in which coconut husks had been soaked. Applied to brick walls and then polished, *chunam* shone beautifully, proved especially durable and even kept insects away. Thus, Singapore's first interior decorators were, in fact, hard men from the jails of Madras and Calcutta.

OPPOSITE: Plan of the town of Singapore, surveyed by J. T. Thomson.
1843
Lithograph
H 37.5 x W 30.2 cm
NMS XXXX-02115

Brick made by Indian convict labour.
1850s
H 6.5 x W 23.8 x D 12.4 cm
NMS 2005-01158

Indian labourers at
a work site.
1870s
Albumen print
H 15.7 x W 21.7 cm
NMS 1994-05110

All of which makes it easy to forget that for many Indian convicts their departure for Singapore was likely to have been deeply traumatic. McNair, at least, was aware of what many prisoners went through. Back in the settlement's early decades, he tells us, Indian convicts considered their voyage across the sea as 'worse than death itself, for it carried with it not only expulsion from caste, but "*nuseeb*" as they call it, a dread of pain and anguish in another existence'. The ocean across which they sailed was known to prisoners from Bengal as the '*kala pani*' or 'black water', and the ship that carried them as the '*jet junaza*' or 'living tomb', which, when we consider the conditions that then existed on certain ocean-going vessels, was probably not an inexact description.

What awaited these convicts on their arrival in Singapore was certainly a life of toil and bondage. But in the case of the Straits Settlements it's important not to think in terms of the usual stereotypes of penal servitude. Singapore, especially, provides one of the more progressive examples of 19th-century convict management. Here, Indian prisoners were given a degree of freedom that today seems remarkable, even if this was more a result of economic necessity (the impoverished colonial administration found it hard to act otherwise) than of liberal thinking.

On arrival, the convicts were housed in temporary sheds in the town, a situation that did not change until 1841, the year it was finally decided to construct a jail.

McNair records that before this 'there was little or no prison control over [the prisoners]; only occasionally, an officer of the police came and called the roll in order to report to Government that all were present'. Usually, the prisoners were manacled with light leg fetters, but these came off after a probationary period of three months. In addition, several prisoners were given 'the privilege of going about the town to make their purchases'.

Soon, news of their good behaviour reached the British Resident (later to be Governor) George Bonham. As an added economy, Bonham chose to discharge the prisoners' guards and instead to select men from their own ranks to act as paid overseers (hence providing McNair with the title of his history, *Prisoners Their Own Warders*). By any stretch of the imagination this must have been a surprising situation for those convicted murderers, dacoits and *thugees* among the prisoners in which to find themselves.

Over the decades, the government's treatment of Indian prisoners became more codified. The authorities divided them into six classes, depending on their crimes and their behaviour, and granted them the possibility of moving up the scale to enjoy greater freedoms and privileges. Prisoners of the first class consisted of 'trustworthy convicts allowed out on ticket of leave'. By contrast, prisoners of the fifth class were chained in heavy irons, these being 'convicts degraded from the higher classes, and such as required more than ordinary vigilance to prevent escape, or regarding whom special instructions had been received from India'. Those who arrived with 'special instructions' were usually political prisoners who had resisted the British Raj, while those who required 'more than ordinary vigilance' were the likes of 'Prisoner Chetoo'. Described as 'an incorrigible convict', Chetoo was the only convict of the fifth class whose photograph appears in McNair's book who is explicitly named (probably meaning he was a repeat offender). Incidentally, prisoners in the sixth class were not worse than those in the fifth: rather they were the 'invalids' and those incapable of anything other than 'light work' as sweepers, cleaners and watchmen.

It was the third class that undertook the bulk of the labour involved in the government's public works programmes. Meanwhile, for those in the first and second class, Singapore offered a range of pursuits that went beyond the daily grind of the construction business. McNair tells us that after well-behaved convicts concluded their workday, they might work as a hired servants for residents in the town, 'who, in the scarcity of labour at that time, and the fitness of the convicts for such service, were content to give them a very liberal wage'. Other convicts were hired as 'orderlies and servants' by government officers and thereby assisted the work of the same imperial regime that had incarcerated them. By the time they were old men, some Indian convicts in Singapore were known to have amassed savings sufficient for them to purchase land and live out the remainder of their lives in comfort.

Prisoner Chetoo
From J. F. A McNair, *Prisoners Their Own Warders*, 1899.

125

Furthermore, when 'the presence of a body of men under discipline was required', Indian convicts repeatedly came to Singapore's rescue. In the days before fire engines, Indian convicts served as an ad hoc fire brigade, supplying the human chain and the buckets of water that were then the only means of putting out flames. In the late 1850s, they were also summoned, and then armed, to hunt down tigers menacing the island's interior. During earlier island-wide riots in 1851, they were 'sent out in gangs to follow the rioters into the jungles and disperse them'. McNair felt that such activities in aid of the colonial government 'estranged' the convicts from Singapore's Chinese population, and thus contributed to the St Andrew's 'head scare' two years later (see Chapter 9).

Eventually, what one colonial official described as perhaps the best example of the 'industrial training' of prisoners seen anywhere in the world came to an end – not because of prevailing Chinese sentiments but because of a sudden panic amongst the town's Europeans. In 1857, the Indian Mutiny erupted when Indian troops rose up against their British paymasters. Suddenly, the thought of more Indian convicts being sent out to Singapore led to a flurry of protests from anxious European residents. No less an authority than Governor Blundell of the Straits Settlements wrote:

> [A] large commercial city such as Singapore … is no longer a proper place for the reception of criminals of India and most especially for that of the late sepoys of the Bengal army, men whose hands have been imbrued [sic] with the blood of women and children and whose hearts are full of hatred and revenge.

Three years later, Calcutta halted the transportation of convicts to Singapore and began to send them to the Andaman Islands. However, the last Indian prisoners were taken off Singapore only in 1873, and not before the colonial administration, ever mindful not to waste a precious resource while they still had it, had launched another major programme of public works. Some of the last building projects that Indian convicts worked on included the construction of hospitals, government offices and new roads, as well as Singapore's present Istana, St Andrew's Cathedral and Fort Canning.

W. H. Read: at play and politics

'Fate willed it that my destiny should lead me to Singapore, where I landed on September 12th, 1841', wrote William Henry Read in his memoirs. A few pages later he gave his initial impression of the town: 'I cannot say that Singapore, in my early days, was an amusing place'; his problem, which he believed he shared with the 'younger hands' of his standing 'and even older ones', was the island's dearth of entertainment. Having arrived in Singapore to take up a partnership in his father's trading firm, the young Read discovered that out of office hours, there was: 'No cricket, football, nor golf; no theatre, no library, no race course.'

Read's view of Singapore's then leisure scene is probably exaggerated. Mary Turnbull has written that the 'affluent enjoyed a constant round of dances, suppers and sporting entertainments', many of which were multiracial occasions during which wealthy Europeans and Asians mingled freely. But for Read what the town offered was clearly insufficient. With two other European associates, he started plotting to shake things up.

Read tells us that for their efforts, he and associates were contemptuously branded *'baroe datangs'* ('newcomers') by older members of the European community. Yet within a few years, these same *'baroe datangs'* had 'changed the face of society'. In 1843, Singapore witnessed its first races, held at a course one mile from the town (down what would later become Serangoon Road), and during which Read himself rode a horse called Colonel to victory. The same year he helped establish the first regatta in Singapore harbour. Theatricals soon followed, and then a library, and then even an 'Assembly Room, for balls and meetings'. The essential elements of European social life were now in place and would remain there for decades.

Read, however, was more than an agitator for better leisure facilities. His main claim to fame was as a tireless activist for better governance and for the formal political representation of his class – the town's European merchants. In his first decade in Singapore, he came into conflict with the colonial administration over its public works policy, or rather the lack thereof. The then governor, quoting a local newspaper, accused the fiery Scot of 'making strong assertions without proof, declamation without argument, and censures without dignity or moderation'.

Undaunted, Read continued in this vein, both throughout his career in Singapore and for decades afterwards once he had returned to Britain. The major problem he and other European merchants faced was that Singapore was run from distant Calcutta. As Buckley put it in his *Anecdotal History*, Read and his supporters believed 'that the Supreme Government in Bengal was able to give very little attention to the affairs of a place so far from Calcutta and so different from India in many respects'.

When Calcutta did pay attention, it invariably got things wrong. One of the most vehement rows between Singapore's European merchants and colonial officialdom occurred when the EIC tried to make the Indian rupee the only legal currency in the Straits. Calcutta's repeated attempts to introduce taxes into Singapore, to pay for those public works and better amenities that its European community demanded, likewise aroused rancour. Most European merchants felt that the colonial administration was inefficient, incompetent, even negligent, and totally out of keeping with the port's commercial prosperity (although they were usually against forking out any of their hard-earned cash to make things better).

William Henry Read.
19th century
Oil on canvas
H 208 x W 129 cm
NMS HP-0041

Most of all, they resented the frequency with which decisions affecting the Straits were made from Calcutta without their counsel, and without there being any official avenues through which they could express their views.

How angry they became depended largely on the public relations skills of individual British governors. Governor Bonham was well liked in the 1830s and 1840s because prominent merchants were regular guests at his dining table where he would listen to their grievances. But Bonham's successor, Colonel William John Butterworth, proved much less sociable. Viewed as superior, stiff and pompous, Read and other European merchants nicknamed him 'Butterpot the Great' and during his tenure pushed hard for official municipal representation in what became a bitter wrangle.

But to Read, the situation demanded more than a mere appointment of a more affable, approachable replacement as governor, and so in 1848, at the height of the row with Butterworth, he travelled to Britain to hold discussions with Singapore's former Resident, John Crawfurd. The two men, both tenacious Scots who had become fed up with the Company, quickly formed a plan for full transfer of the government of the Straits Settlements from Calcutta to the Colonial Office in London. Crawfurd, who had already been organising protests against the EIC on behalf of European merchants in Bengal, was to handle things in Westminster; Read would lead the campaign back in Singapore.

Proposal in hand, Read returned to Singapore in 1851 ready for action. However, it took almost two decades for his plan to succeed. Depending on economic conditions, support for his plan varied, sometimes dwindling to the point where he found himself in a tiny minority. What changed things in his favour was the Indian Mutiny of 1857, followed by the dissolution of the EIC and the creation of a new imperial administration across India. This new administration had no great desire to hold onto the Straits Settlements, and when the British Parliament responded favourably to a petition from European merchants requesting a greater say in Singapore's political affairs, it seemed as if the transfer was imminent.

Even then, it took another decade for the transfer to go through – and all because of a problem of accountancy. The Colonial Office in London, concerned about the cost of defending Singapore and unwilling to take on a new colony until assured that it was commercially solvent, asked to see the Straits Settlements' accounts. What it received was a series of conflicting financial estimates from the India Office, Read, Crawfurd and the Singapore Chamber of Commerce, as well as various other old Straits 'hands' now returned to Britain. In the midst of all this confusion, the British Parliament re-affirmed its policy of not taking on additional colonies that were likely to prove a financial burden to the government. As a result, the Treasury decided to halt the transfer negotiations.

That the transfer ever came about was largely thanks to two new developments. In 1863, a new colonial Stamp Act at last made the Straits Settlements'

administration financially self-reliant; around the same time, the British government acknowledged that it needed an alternative military base east of India to Hong Kong, where the number of troops and civilian expatriates falling ill and dying threatened to become a major imperial scandal. When viewed from London, the real reason Singapore became a Crown Colony had little to do with Read and his associates, but instead came down to a matter of administrative revenue and the unhealthy conditions of Singapore's rival British base in China.

Nevertheless, while political decisions that affected the lives of thousands across the British Empire seem often to have been a simple matter of bureaucratic expediency, we shouldn't discount the role of individual activists. It was Read who kept up pressure for the transfer on the colonial government – through repeated letters to the press, public meetings and petitions – and it was Read who continued to demand political representation for Singapore's European merchants. Thus, when the transfer finally went through in 1867, and a Legislative Council was formed to advise the Straits Settlements' administration, Read was duly elected as a member. Like numerous activists in Singapore who would emerge in the years after him, he had become the perpetual irritant – the thorn in the establishment's side – who through stubborn persistence eventually got what he demanded and was simultaneously introduced into government.

What must have disappointed Read was that the new crown colony government of Singapore seemed in its early years not much better than the one it had replaced. Perhaps he wondered if his efforts to secure it had been worth all the trouble. But then again, this new government had far greater problems to wrestle with, for Singapore was now transforming into a larger and more boisterous place – a heavily populated colonial port-city.

Legislative Council of the Straits Settlements. Sir Harry St. George Ord (seated right), as Governor, was the council's President. Hoo Ah Kay (also known as Whampoa, standing second from right) was the council's 'unofficial member' representing the Chinese community.

c. 1870
Albumen print
H 20.2 cm x W 25.3 cm
NMS XXXX-14748-001

PORT-CITY
1860s – 1900s

12. JEWEL OF THE EAST

When did the settlement of Singapore transform into a city?

Some scholars would argue that Singapore was already a city back in the 14th century when it was known as Temasek, since it then functioned as the seat of a royal dynasty and government. We know that certain European writers also described Singapore as a city in the 1830s and 1840s, when its population still numbered in the low tens of thousands. Yet, to our modern eyes neither of these settlements would have seemed more than a lively 'town'. Judged by present-day standards, Singapore truly gained metropolitan status only in the last decades of the 19th century – a period when it became more complex, more globally connected, as well as much more crowded.

In 1871, Singapore numbered around 97,000 inhabitants, the vast majority of whom lived within or just beyond the town limits. By 1897, the island was home to 200,000 people and it would keep on growing up till the outbreak of World War II. Such population pressures forced the town of Singapore to spread out: to the west toward New Harbour (later renamed Keppel Harbour); to the east toward

PREVIOUS PAGE:
A view of Battery Road showing the Hongkong and Shanghai Bank building (left), the Chartered Bank (right) and Tan Kim Seng Fountain (foreground).
1900s
Photogravure
H 14.4 x W 20.8 cm
NMS XXXX-14768-002

Detail of photograph showing a European man on a rickshaw.
1890s
Albumen print
H 33 x W 42.5 cm
NMS 2001-01343

Geylang and Katong along the East Coast Road; to the northwest, along River Valley Road and Orchard Road toward Tanglin; and to the north along Serangoon Road toward the far end of the island. As the municipal limits extended, to the point where by 1891 over 80 per cent of the island's population lived within these boundaries, there came into being that essential feature of any modern city – the suburbs. While the heart of urban Singapore (especially Chinatown) heaved and sweated with the throng of new arrivals, the more prosperous classes, both European and Asian, headed for its greener outskirts.

The port-city that emerged was gentrified and dilapidated, prosperous and poor – European and Asian. In the rest of this chapter and the next, we'll travel through this city to uncover its two faces, first through the eyes of its 'haves' (its colonial visitors and its new Asian bourgeoisie), then through the lives of its 'have-nots' (its coolies, prostitutes, the impoverished and sick). Finally, in the last chapter of this section, we'll discover both faces of Singapore as they stare each other down across a five-foot way, poised (seemingly) for open conflict.

But before we begin, let's first turn to the question of how Singapore grew to become such a lively yet divided city in the first place.

BELOW: Boat Quay panorama by the German photographer Charles Kleingrothe.
1900s
Photogravure
H 9.3 x W 27.4 cm
NMS 2007-50689

The 'Clapham Junction of the East'

The city's expansion was driven by its port. Between 1873 and 1913, the port of Singapore saw an eight-fold increase in the volume of trade that passed through. Such an increase was on the one hand due to that old, even ancient story of Singapore being perfectly located on Asia's main shipping routes; but it also had to do with a more recent revolution in maritime communications. In 1869, the Suez Canal opened to link the Red Sea with the Mediterranean, meaning that ships no longer had to make the lengthier and much riskier voyage round the Cape of Good Hope. East and West had suddenly drawn closer with Singapore providing an ideally situated stopover on the journey either way.

The international status of Singapore's port was further enhanced by advances in steamship technology. The larger, sturdier steamships that increasingly dominated her harbour, at the expense of junks and square-riggers, demanded fuel and maintenance. Well into the 20th century, Singapore remained the primary coaling and refitting station for steamships from across the whole of Southeast Asia, and most ocean-going liners berthed at the port on their way from Europe, via India, to the Far East or to Australia and New Zealand. To the writer Walter Del Mar, a memorable sight for passengers who disembarked at Singapore was 'coolies coaling a big ship':

> Two of them carry, suspended to a short, thick bamboo pole, a large basket containing about a hundred weight of coal, and they go on board by one gang plank, and back by another, keeping up a continued stream that soon fills the bunkers.

Meanwhile, Singapore was developing into an important station in an imperial network of submarine telegraph lines, or, as the poet Rudyard Kipling described them, those 'deep-sea cables' that had 'killed their father Time'. In the

Coolies loading up coal on a
ship at night.

Late 19th century
Wood-block print
H 17 x W 25.5 cm
NMS 2000-06688

Romanticised depiction bearing the title 'The British Enter Singapore' by R. Caton Woodville for *The Illustrated London News*, April 1903.

Hulton Archive / Getty

late 1860s, after several technological hiccups, submarine telegraphy was finally perfected and what later became known as the Cable and Wireless Company began to tie the world together through one of the first examples of global telecommunication. Submarine telegraphy made possible the prompt circulation of market information and the electronic transfer of capital that gave birth to the whole enterprise of modern international banking. By 1900, Singapore was home to several international banks, among them the highly successful Hongkong and Shanghai Banking Corporation.

Globalisation, for in a nutshell that is exactly what it was, had arrived – and with it came a series of clichés by which European writers tried to capture its impact. Just as today, speechwriters in Singapore seem fixated by the idea of their island as a 'hub', so colonial writers over a century ago displayed a parallel talent for literary triteness. By the late 1800s, Singapore was the 'Charing Cross of the East', the 'Clapham Junction of the East', the 'Liverpool of the East' – even the 'Oban of the East' (Oban being a small port in West Scotland, described in tourist brochures as the 'gateway to the Scottish Isles', whose historical similarity to Singapore, save that it was also a port and a naval base, the present authors have yet to uncover). You had only to take some major port or transport junction in Victorian Britain, tack on the words 'of the East' – and there you had a description of late 19th-century Singapore. To some extent, even Chinese writers got in on the act. Temple inscriptions from the mid- to late 19th century refer to Singapore as the 'junction of the seas' – though, to their credit, few if any attempts were made by Chinese literati to draw comparisons with transport 'hubs' back home in the Middle Kingdom.

Clichés aside, the impact of global communications on Singapore inhabitants proved to be epoch-defining. Whereas in the early 1800s it took upwards of six months for a letter or a person departing London to arrive in port, now the journey took just a matter of weeks. Nor was this revolution felt only by the city's wealthy elite. Migrant workers from China and India increasingly depended on steam navigation to bring them to the Straits, and return them home again; they also came to rely on Britain's imperial postal system to send remittance money to their families. An essential element in Singapore's transition to being a modern city was that its inhabitants were now far more 'in touch' with people and places overseas and especially with their lands of origin.

It was a transformation that would have tremendous social, political and intellectual consequences that later chapters in this book will explore in more detail. However, one immediate impact was that a wider social gulf opened up between Singapore's colonial masters and their colonial subjects. For new European arrivals, it was no longer necessary to invest time in adapting to a life in 'exile', and especially in trying to understand local languages and customs, since home was now only a fortnight away. Newspapers kept them in touch with the fashions and foibles of the imperial capital, while their reading and writing of 'home' correspondence became such a frequent ritual that new arrivals complained that older expatriates perpetually excused themselves from basic social niceties with the common refrain 'But it's mail day, you know!' or 'I'm writing for the mail!'

Conversely, safer, speedier voyages from Europe and America brought new, more impatient varieties of European to the Straits: the tourist in search of exotica yet who expected the genteel comforts of home; the colonial *memsahib*, immortalised in numerous novels, who in the tropical heat tried to maintain all

Postcard published by Künzli Frères, Zurich, depicting the Adelphi Hotel, Collyer Quay and a rickshaw puller.

Cancelled in 1898
Paper
H 9 x W 13.9 cm
NMS 1999-01579

Photograph of a European
lady by G. R. Lambert & Co.
1900s
Albumen print
H 16.5 x W 12.1 cm
NMS XXXX-12630

the accoutrements of a civilised European household; and finally, the jingoistic British official, who – dressed all in white, with pith hat and stick in hand – seemed ever more convinced of his racial superiority over the massed 'natives' and of their desperate need to be organised and set to rights. These new 'colonials' transformed European society in the Straits. Gone were the rough-and-tumble days of sea-faring daredevils such as George Earl or Henry Keppel, for whom Singapore had been a place of high adventure that so completely contrasted with home. (Gone, also, were the days when a colonial official might go a bit native and enjoy the domestic pleasures of a local 'connexion'.)

The colonial high life

If we compare the impressions of Westerners who arrived in Singapore around the late 1870s with those who arrived in the decades afterwards, one thing soon becomes apparent: when it came to life's little luxuries, Singapore definitely took a turn for the better.

Consider the experience of the American zoologist William Hornaday, who arrived in 1878. He described entering Singapore through New Harbour as like 'getting into a house through the scullery window': 'One's first impressions of the town are associated with coal-dust, mud, stagnant water, and mean buildings, and I found it required an effort to shake them off.' To get from the docks to the town meant a journey by gharry (a pony-drawn carriage) along a road 'built through a muddy and dismal mangrove swamp', with here and there 'dingy and weather-beaten Malay houses standing on posts over the soft and slimy mud, or perhaps

Panoramas of G. R. Lambert

Singapore's rise as a strategic port city in the later part of the 19th century led to a proliferation of photographic studios being set up around town. Between the 1850s and the 1870s, there were about two dozen different studios operated by Americans, Armenians, Chinese, British, Germans and French, all catering to the growing interest in photography. By the 1880s, stiff competition and the itinerant nature of early photographic businesses led to the closure of several studios. Of the studios which managed to stay afloat, through innovation and diversification, an outstanding one was that of Gustave Richard Lambert.

G.R. Lambert came to Singapore in the late 1860s from Dresden, a city in Germany. Little is known about his first few years in Singapore, but his photography studio was only firmly established in the early 1880s. Business

must have been good: the studio even had branches in Deli (in Sumatra), Kuala Lumpur and Bangkok between the 1890s and the first decade of the 20th century.

A successful studio like Lambert's had to offer more than just studio portraiture. By 1900, the firm advertised the sale of photographs from a collection of 3,000 views. Lambert's photographs could even be bought at John Little's, one of the premier European departmental stores in Singapore.

In the museum's photography collection, there are two photographic panoramas made by Lambert in the early 1880s that deserve special mention. Nineteenth-century photographic panoramas were made by overlapping a series of individual views. Each glass plate had to be prepared, exposed and developed individually and uniform exposures had to be achieved to ensure

consistency of tone and definition. Such technical mastery would not have been possible without the dry-collodion method available since the mid-1850s. The older wet-collodion method necessitated the development of the glass negative immediately after making the exposure. Alignment of the parts was a tricky business requiring extremely dexterous fingers.

Albumen prints, the type of photographic material available from the 1860s, also necessitated a quick mounting onto a secondary support, as the medium curls easily. Photographic panoramas were therefore technically demanding and these ones are thus enduring testimonies to Lambert's skill and expertise. The impressive sharpness of these panorama scenes would have also made them very saleable to Singapore's growing European middle-class in the 19th century.

In the panorama taken from Fort Canning and overlooking the town, the Raffles Library and Museum (completed in October 1887 and to later house the National Museum of Singapore) was yet to be built. It would occupy the space just left of the cross-gabled building on the left of the panorama. The panorama was likely taken between the time Lambert arrived in Singapore and before he left for good in 1885. The identities of both the Malay and European men in the photograph are unknown, but they could be Lambert's assistants. There were three 'Native Malay' and one European assistant listed as being on Lambert's payroll in the *1881 Singapore and Straits Settlements Directory*.

On the right of the Fort Canning view, the tightly packed but ordered rooftops of godowns (warehouses) and shophouses are indicative of the burgeoning

ethnic Chinese immigrant working-class population. Their appearance contrasts sharply with the evenly spaced bungalows and churches of the European part of town on the left.

Another panorama from the 1880s made by Lambert shows the vast expanse of the Padang, the social hub for the ruling elite of the day. Again, conventional (and colonial) rules of photographic aesthetics were employed. Here, the native people are placed as picturesque figures (or perhaps as indicators of scale) against the backdrop of civic institutions such as the Cricket Club, Hotel de l'Europe and St Andrew's Cathedral – all symbols of Western civilisation. This composition is similar to the painting done some 30 years earlier by the Government Surveyor, John Turnbull Thomson in 1851 (see page 118).

FROM TOP:

Panorama taken from Fort Canning Hill by G. R. Lambert & Co.
1880s
Albumen print
H 24 x W 155 cm
NMS 1996-00036

Panorama of the Esplanade in Singapore by G. R. Lambert & Co.
1880s
Albumen print
H 23.5 x W 186 cm
NMS 1996-00035

Gharry and driver
by E. Schlitter.

1858
Watercolour on paper
H 25 x W 19 cm
NMS HP-0064-L

over a thin sheet of murky water'. Another writer describes the heat and the dust of this short three-mile trip as sufficient to turn one's shirt and collar 'pulpy'.

Fast-forward 14 years and the sheer bulk of goods that had to be moved across from the docks to the town's godowns had changed things dramatically. According to the Reverend G. M. Reith, there were now several roads into the town, including one that 'skirted the seashore' along a 'well-kept road, laid with tramway lines' that offered a 'cool breeze from the sea'. First, one passed 'small laterite hills which are being fast quarried away for road-making' (these became the red laterite roads that, by 1900, came to dominate the town and were one of the city's most memorable features). Next, one reached Robinson Quay and then Collyer Quay, the latter comprising 'an imposing terrace of offices with the convexity of the curve fronting the sea'. Here, one could view the fish market at Telok Ayer, Johnston Pier, the Singapore Club and the Exchange (housed in the same building), together with the General Post Office (at the site of today's Fullerton Hotel). Though the Reverend Reith was a domiciled expatriate and so a shade biased, he regarded the journey into town in the early 1890s as pleasant enough to recommend it in his handbook for visitors.

Another sign of improvement was the city's hotels. In the mid-19th century, standards of accommodation in Singapore were by most European accounts dreadful, not just when compared with lodgings back home but when placed alongside hotels found in other Asian cities. According to Charles Walter Kinloch, a visitor from Bengal, the best establishment in town in the 1850s was the London Hotel, but this was not saying much. As Kinloch bemoaned, rooms at the London were uncomfortable, there were no private bathrooms, and to wash oneself one had to journey across to a public bath 'situated in a range of buildings altogether distinct from the hotel'.

Like many Europeans at this time, Kinloch had come to Singapore to recover from illness – Singapore being, until the 1860s, considered a healthy climate in which to recuperate. At the London, however, the good night's sleep so desired by any recuperating invalid proved near-impossible. The French proprietor of the establishment, spotting an opportunity to make some extra cash, had opened a bowling alley in a long tiled building immediately under the hotel's windows. This created a 'pandemonium', Kinloch tells us, that 'is lit up every night, and is filled with the townspeople and others, who play at bowls and drink brandy and water until a late hour in the night'.

In that same decade, the American businessman George Francis Train complained that the London was 'kept in a manner that would disgrace a landlord in the backwoods of Kansas'. Longing for the 'comforts and enjoyments' of the Java Hotel in Batavia (where he had just stayed), Train found himself in an establishment 'where your food looks uninviting … where your boots get mildewed, and your brown leather trunk resembles the skin of a Maltese cat it has become so mouldy'. Even worse, 'the labyrinth of passages, show-cases and rooms, require a man to have a compass, if he does not wish to lose his reckoning, and get out of his proper track'. Train also objected to the London's bowling alley and his dislike of its food was echoed a decade later by another travel writer who denounced the cooking in Singapore hotels generally as 'so filthy, oily and greasy, that a man may starve before he touches a bit that is put before him'.

Yet from the 1870s, as European tourist numbers rose, hotels in Singapore improved to the point where a number became regarded as 'first-class houses'. Chief amongst these were the Hôtel de l'Europe (which took over the premises of the much-castigated London), the Adelphi Hotel and the Raffles Hotel. Though some visitors still complained that the food at the Hôtel de l'Europe was abominable, others wrote of the establishment's pleasant situation 'in the midst of beautiful gardens, facing "the green" [the Padang], and commanding a fine view of the straits'. The American Frank Vincent Junior discovered that the hotel had an 'American bar-room, where Californian mixed drinks are served and there is besides a "regular down east Boston Arctic soda-water fountain"; a billiard room; and a reading room, where one will find papers and journals, in four or five languages'. Meanwhile at the Raffles, the 'hot and inflamed' new arrival, as Colonel R. V. K. Applin put it, could find relief in an 'Indian bath' – which involved a large earthenware jar and a tin bucket, and which the colonel claimed was one of the best he'd ever had.

In addition, as Singapore grew in size after 1870, it began to offer its European arrivals a considerably improved social life. Even by the 1860s, John Cameron, editor of the *Straits Times*, had written of a colonial lifestyle that 'may be set down as luxurious, and this to a degree that could not well be indulged at home on similar means'. The problem with this lifestyle, as Cameron went on to observe, was that it so completely lacked variety. European life in Singapore revolved around an eternal consumption of food and drink: dawn coffee and biscuits;

Entrance to Raffles Hotel
with rickshaw pullers waiting
for fares.
1900s
EDM Archives

the nine o'clock breakfast of curry and rice; tiffin-time around midday and the first glass of beer or claret; then finally more curry, wine or beer, throughout the dinner hour from six o'clock. On the completion of their working day, many younger members of the European community did 'resort to the fives-court or the cricket ground on the esplanade', while on Tuesdays and Friday nights the whole community turned out for Esplanade band nights. Nonetheless, in the 1860s Cameron still yearned for a more sophisticated social intercourse as was 'usual at home, and in most other parts of the world'. It was a source of some regret to him 'that the people of Singapore so determinedly set their faces against every sort of entertainment which does not include a dinner'.

Yet, in a matter of decades, Singapore boasted all the pleasurable amenities of a bustling colonial metropolis. By 1900, the port-city had its numerous clubs, its theatre, its dances, its 'smoking concerts', reading rooms, public library, museum, and botanical gardens. In fact, European 'society' had diversified and become institutionalised, and it was now conducted as much outside the home as within. Cameron, had he lived (he died in 1882) would have found exactly the kind of sophistication he had been craving.

Some things, nevertheless, did not change – and one of them was the great European appetite for consumption. But whereas in the 1860s it was the European community's obsession with elaborate dinners that a writer such as Cameron condemned, by the century's end it was their general dependence on alcohol. William Hornaday (the American we met earlier) denounced the 'appalling' extent to which 'intoxicating liquors of all kinds' were drunk. Hornaday was a teetotaller, and so more than a shade biased; nonetheless, he found the drinking habit 'so universal' that:

> If you say you do not drink, or do not wish anything, you are urged most urgently to 'take something', until it becomes positively disagreeable … Furthermore, when your new acquaintances, or old ones either, for that matter, call upon you at your hotel for half an hour's chat, you are expected to order drinks for the crowd, until the crowd is full of whatever it likes best. To omit this feature is to give positive offence in some cases, and even at the best to send your visitors away saying that you are uncivil and not worthy the acquaintance of gentlemen …

Masters, servants and the 'Western Oriental gentleman'

> The servant question is not so pressing in the Far East because there are always plenty of 'boys', as Chinese domestics are called in pidgin-English …

So wrote Ethel Colquhoun (wife to famous explorer Archibald Ross Colquhoun) of her Singapore sojourn.

A Chinese servant, wearing
a queue, serves a European
sitting under a punkah,
by G. R. Lambert & Co.
1890
Albumen print
H 16.4 x W 12.1 cm
NMS XXXX-12898

She went on to observe:

> John the cook-boy does all the marketing, and arranges all the meals after
> a short morning colloquy with his mistress. John the house-boy looks after
> master's clothes ... John the parlourmaid (or head boy) will arrange the
> flowers, look after guests, concoct cooling drinks, and do anything and
> everything. Every household employs besides a *toucanaya*, often a Malay,
> who does the dirty work of the house, and is a sort of social pariah.

Moreover, as tourist C. D. MacKellar discovered when staying at the Raffles
Hotel, a new arrival's reliance on servants could quickly become an addiction:

> ... I am getting into the way of things here. I could not get on without
> attention, so said to the hotel people I must have boys to wait on me, and
> to 'put them on the bill'. Now I appear to have six. They all look the same
> and I no longer lack attention or attendance ... If I want anything I pull the
> nearest passing bell-rope – I mean pigtail – and point at something. They
> are wonderful, though; they know now even without my pointing. I notice
> too, they have suddenly coiled their pigtails in an elegant coronet around
> their heads. I wonder why?

If only the racism in these two accounts – in the first case implicit and in
the latter quite explicit – was an exception rather than the rule! Unfortunately,

such attitudes were to be found in European hotels, clubs and households across Singapore. The British imperial mindset of the late 19th century ranked the nations of the worlds in terms of a racial league table and naturally Britain stood at the very top, demanding to be waited on by those near the bottom.

But to judge European society in Singapore only by its prevailing attitudes to servants would be to tell just one part of the complex story of colonial encounters during this era, for by the late 19th century Singapore had witnessed a crucial social development. Increasingly, the life of gentrified luxury enjoyed by Europeans was being shared by a new generation of Asian professionals – doctors, lawyers, dentists, clerks, petty officials as well as businessmen and others – many of them educated in English-language schools and some even at universities. More than their middlemen predecessors in the earlier part of the century, this rising Asian bourgeoisie came to appropriate the lifestyle of their colonial masters. In an age of global communication, European trends had arrived in Singapore and young Asian professionals now had the income (and the wherewithal) to afford and obtain them.

So it was that across the city's steadily more urbane and elegant streets, Europeans might observe 'Western Oriental gentlemen', as they became known, coming together to speak in English, dressed in the European fashions of the day and completely at ease in their enjoyment of a European-style high life – the club, the reading room and the luxury hotel, as well as entertainments such as regattas, races, cocktail parties and even that strange game, cricket. European racism still

limited the extent to which the new Asian gentleman about town was welcome in white settler society. Nevertheless, in government departments, in European commercial firms and in colonial law courts, at the theatre, the public lecture and even at certain learned societies, gentlemen from the East and gentlemen from the West increasingly crossed one another's paths.

We'll discuss how this new Asian bourgeoisie emerged and what they achieved in the next section of this book. For now, we'll look only at how they were received among the city's European population. For some Europeans, as we will see, the 'Western Oriental gentleman' represented a great success story for the British Empire – he was Britishness and Western civilisation effectively exported. For others, his imitation of European speech, fashions and habits was a cause of embarrassment, even of unease. Finally, for most colonial officials, no matter how well the 'Western Oriental gentleman' dressed himself or spoke English, he was still a non-European, part of a subject people that was incapable of ruling itself.

B. P. de Silva on display

Hindsight is always an easy vantage point from which to pass down judgement on previous generations and as a result Singapore's new Asian bourgeoisie has received much bad press. Those individuals who fought later against colonial rule (along with those historians who subsequently recorded their freedom-fighting exploits) have frequently treated the English-educated class of this era as mere colonial collaborators – running dogs of the British who helped to keep the Empire under control. The late 19th century in Singapore was not yet an age of impassioned nationalists who would demand of the colonial regime complete freedom, equality and political independence.

Yet, in reality, Singapore's small, privileged Asian elite comprised a wide range of personalities, not all of whom offered the British their unconditional loyalty. On the one hand there was the esteemed community leader Dr Lim Boon Keng, an English-educated Straits Chinese who though lauded by the colonial authorities as a model colonial subject would later end up a committed Chinese patriot. On the other hand there was the Sinhalese jeweller extraordinaire, Balage Porolis de Silva (better known as B. P. de Silva), a man who during his lengthy stay in Singapore remained almost entirely apolitical. De Silva's main concern in life seems to have been to succeed in his business, engage in philanthropy and then return to his home village in Ceylon (today's Sri Lanka) to retire. While he and Lim knew each other well and moved in the same circles, they reflect two extremes of Singapore's then political spectrum. We turn to de Silva first (Dr Lim will be discussed throughought the next few chapters), for his life and business reveal just how far the 'Western Oriental gentleman' could rise socially if he mixed with the right kind of people.

Lim Boon Keng's medal, conferred by the medical school of the University of Edinburgh.
1891
Bronze
Dia. 5.2 cm
Gift of Mrs Ella Toh Guat Kheng
NMS XXXX-08882

The pinnacle of de Silva's career as a jeweller came in 1901, during an occasion that the *Singapore Free Press* deemed 'the greatest Imperial event since the founding of these [Straits] Settlements'. The newspaper was referring to the arrival in Singapore that year of the Duke and Duchess of Cornwall and York – an occasion that became something of a 'B. P. de Silva Show'.

Though their Royal Highnesses spent only three days in the city, the festivities arranged in their honour proved spectacular. Elaborate decorations festooned the trading houses along Collyer Quay and at Raffles Place, near where the Duke and Duchess disembarked at Johnston Pier; reportedly, their route into the town was packed with 'Chinese and natives', many of whom crowded onto temporary platforms down Orchard Road that had been constructed to enable a better view. The city-wide celebrations included a spectacular light-up of Chinatown by night and a torch-light procession, organised by the Malay, Tamil and Chinese communities, from the Esplanade to Government House (today's Istana). All in all it was a display, so the local press claimed, 'that a layman might travel the world for fifty years and never see equalled'.

B. P. de Silva had been invited by the Municipal Commissioners of Singapore to join the Reception Committee that organised this affair – the kind of glitzy international showcase at which Singapore continues to excel over a century later. Indeed, some of the various 'cultural displays' that de Silva and his colleagues arranged might not have seemed out of place in latter-day public demonstrations of Singapore's multiculturalism following independence. As the *Singapore Free Press* reported back in 1901, the torch-light procession through the town featured, amongst other things, a showcase of Chinese women 'with the tiniest of feet, borne aloft … and surrounded by artificial flowers … and lanterns', a gilded Hindu 'religious car of artistic design and finish' and a replica of 'a model Malay house, on wheels, with neat *attap* roof'.

What especially stands out during Singapore's entertainment of the Duke and Duchess is how far prominent Asian elite were given their spot in the limelight. At the Town Hall, the royal couple were received by illustrious Chinese *taukeh* such as Seah Liang Seah (son of Seah Eu Chin), Tan Jiak Kim and Song Ong Siang, the well-established Arab traders Syed Abdulkader Alsagoff and Syed Ali bin Ali Aljunied, as well as by de Silva and by Dr Lim. The wealth and success that these Asian subjects had brought Singapore was something to display and to celebrate. In a colony built on the principle of free trade, wealth could – on occasion – trump racial prejudice.

For British officials it helped that their Asian subjects, at least those invited to officially greet the Duke and Duchess, were so suitably subservient – so 'grateful for the protection of the British flag', as British journalist William Maxwell saw it. Maxwell went on to capture the reverential atmosphere that attended the Town Hall ceremonials in terms that were almost beatific:

They came with tributes of loyalty, and laid them at the feet of the son of their suzerain – tributes of words, and of gold, and silver, and ivory. The deputations filed past with addresses and caskets … a microcosm of East and West, in silk hat and turban, frock coat and burnous. The heap of scrolls and caskets grew larger and larger until it overflowed the table.

B. P. de Silva and Lim Boon Keng did, at least, speak to the Duke and Duchess, having been the only two Asian representatives selected to formally welcome them. De Silva received an additional high esteem for having created the gem-studded caskets that local European and Asian elite presented as their official gifts to the royal couple. However, this was not his first encounter with royalty in Singapore, far from it. As his biographer Richard Boyle has written, during the late 19th century 'Kings, Crown Princes, Dukes, Sultans and Maharajas continually passed through the city' providing a steady stream of business for De Silva's shop on High Street, as well as the illustrious company to which, by 1901, he had become accustomed.

De Silva's royal clientele sealed his reputation as a jeweller of international repute. His first commission by royal appointment arrived in the 1890s from the

Clipping from *The Illustrated London News*. Featured are two caskets made by B. P. de Silva.
1901
Paper
H 21.5 x W 30 cm
NMS 2008-00179

The Royal Visit to Singapore.

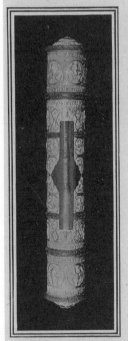

THE CASKET PRESENTED BY THE SINGAPORE CHAMBER OF COMMERCE
The casket, made of silver with gold bands, was of local handiwork, being made by B. P. de Silva. The pictures of the caskets are by Alfred Bean.

THE MIXED CROWD AWAITING THE DUKE'S ARRIVAL AT SINGAPORE
The community at Singapore is more mixed than elsewhere. Eurasians, Malays, and Chinamen in their various garbs made a picture strongly cosmopolitan to the royal party. The picture is by Mr. Wilson of Singapore

The "Ophir" with the Duke and Duchess of Cornwall on board arrived safely at Singapore, the capital of the Straits Settlements, on April 2, and was received by the Governor, members of the British Legislative Council, and the other resident officials and the Sultans of the three tributary states of Perak, Pahang, and Selangor, on the mainland of the Malay peninsula. Singapore town is on Singapore island. Penang is also a small island off the west of the peninsula. The two caskets reproduced here are but two of more than a dozen presented to the Duke on the second day of the visit. The function took place in the Town Hall, deputations of Malays, Chinese, Tamils, Arabs, and other Moslems filing by the dais and presenting their loyal addresses. The scene focussed within a few yards all the types of our Eastern Empire

THE CASKET PRESENTED BY THE MUNICIPAL COMMISSIONERS OF PENANG
The casket is made of polished bamboo with gold fittings. This also was made by De Silva, the Singapore jeweller

B. P. de Silva in Mudaliyar
regalia.
1900s
Albumen print reproduction
H 16 x W 12 cm
B. P. de Silva Holdings

Duke of Connaught, and brought with it the added privilege of permission to display the royal coat-of-arms on his shop façade and business stationery. Soon after, the Governor-General of Siamese Cambodia and Southern Laos became his patron, as did the Sultan of Johor in 1900. In the meantime, de Silva was kept busy creating other pieces for royal recipients, including gifts for the King of Siam and for Queen Victoria on her diamond jubilee in 1897.

De Silva's allegiance to the British is therefore not difficult to understand. Not only had their Empire ensured his commercial success, it had made him socially respectable, even famous, inducting him into a high society of which a previous generation of Asian merchants could only have dreamed.

And as was to be expected, the British Empire rewarded de Silva's unwavering loyalty with official title. Having dissuaded local Sinhalese in Singapore from petitioning the Straits government to have him made a Justice of the Peace (he felt that to be a 'JP' was just not Sinhalese enough), a few months after the Duke and Duchess left Singapore he accepted the title of Mudaliyar (an honorific Sinhalese rank that once signified martial prowess) from the Governor of Ceylon. The only reason he failed to receive the higher rank of Mudaliyar of the Gate, despite lobbying for it, was because the colonial authorities deemed him ineligible on the grounds that he had too long resided outside his homeland, even though he had continued to actively support local charities there while he remained overseas. De Silva's loyalty to the British might have seen him hobnob with royalty, yet it was never sufficient to challenge the implacable logic of the colonial civil service – and so a mere Mudaliyar he remained.

13. THE CITY'S OTHER FACE

Most European arrivals saw Singapore as a port-city clearly divided into two discrete parts: the colonial district, where all the major hotels, banks, department stores and government buildings were situated, and the 'native' quarters, jammed together in Chinatown, down Arab Street into Kampong Glam and (eventually) Serangoon Road through Little India. The colonial district was considered to be ordered, neat, tidy, pretty – even if, to some observers, somewhat dull. By contrast, the 'native' quarters, everyone agreed, overflowed with smells, colours, exotica and people.

However, the Chinese traveller Li Chung Chu, who arrived in Singapore in 1887, saw things somewhat differently. To him, Singapore was divided into a 'Greater' town and a 'Lesser' town. 'Lesser Town', about which he had correspondingly less to say, referred to the 'native' quarters north of the Singapore River and paled into insignificance compared to 'Greater Town', which to Li comprised the colonial district and Chinatown together, and to which no area in Singapore could be compared in terms of prosperity. He was especially drawn to the Kreta Ayer area of Chinatown, a place filled with people, 'restaurants, brothels and theatres' and yet 'where filth and dirt are hidden'.

Li's alternative demarcation of Singapore is interesting because he lumped together the European and Chinese parts of the city, and saw them as incomparable to its other districts. Most Europeans would probably not have viewed Singapore in the same way; certainly they would never have thought of Chinatown as somehow being cleaner and healthier than other 'native' quarters. Nonetheless, Li's account reveals how significant Chinatown was becoming as the commercial engine room of the island's economy. Where he was somewhat biased in his account was in thinking that it was such a salubrious place to live. In reality, Chinatown teemed not just with people but with disease, refuse, gangsters and vice. In such aspects it was no 'greater' than those equally vivacious areas of Bugis Street, Arab Street and Kampong Glam that Li preferred to think of as 'Lesser Town'.

A true Chinatown

The fact that there were so many more people in Singapore, and especially in Chinatown, was a consequence of one of the world's great waves of economic migration. Between 1840 and 1900, about two and a half million people left China, from ports such as Nanking (Nanjing), Canton (Guangdong), Foochow (Fuzhou) and Amoy (Xiamen) to find jobs wherever they could be found: across the Pacific to Hawaii and North America; due south to Australia and New Zealand; and as far afield as the West Indies, South America and Africa. Yet closer to home (in more ways than one) was the *Nanyang*, the 'gateway' to which

Jinriksha Station, Singapore.

Jinriksha (rickshaw) station,
Chinatown.

1900s
EDM Archives

was Singapore. Especially after the opening of the Suez Canal in 1869, tens of thousands of Chinese *sinkeh* (new Chinese immigrants) flooded into the city, and though not all would stay their influx was enough to make Singapore then, as it is now, a heavily Chinese city.

Singapore, by itself, could never have accommodated nor provided work for all these newcomers, but fortunately it didn't have to. From 1870, the British began to expand their political influence beyond the ports of the Straits Settlements to the hinterland of the Malay Peninsula, an area rich in natural resources. When the British and their local Chinese partners moved in they acquired land (not always by the most honourable methods or circumstances) and established tin mines and later rubber plantations. The opening up of China, and the movement of migrant coolie labour out from its treaty ports, could not have been better timed to populate these highly labour-intensive enterprises.

Most Chinese migrants came from just five small regions in the southern provinces of Fujian and Guangdong, and from the island of Hainan. Throughout the 19th century these regions were poor, overpopulated and in a state of constant upheaval – in no small part thanks to the Opium Wars, which had opened the door to Western commercial concessions that were particularly disruptive of the Chinese economy. Civil unrest on the scale of the Taiping Rebellion, which from 1850 to 1864 cut a swathe through central and southern China, added to a general sense of gloom and doom. People were unemployed, sometimes starving and frequently displaced from their villages. Going overseas was a lifeline.

Certain scholars, however, are less convinced that harsh living conditions alone led to such massive Chinese emigration. They point out that Chinese migrants left for greener pastures overseas even when their homes were not threatened by China's many disasters. In fact, they argue, from the mid-19th century working abroad had become such a part of the economic life in many southern Chinese districts that Chinese migrants were not so much 'pushed' out of their homelands by local factors as 'pulled' by better opportunities abroad. Eventually, with a growing demand for Chinese labour overseas on the one hand, and new communications making ocean-going travel so much easier on the other, a global labour system emerged that in reality was far more circulatory than either a 'push' or a 'pull' theory of Chinese migration, by itself, might explain.

In the early decades of the Chinese coolie trade, contractors recruited starry-eyed villagers from southern China with promises of the fortunes that awaited them overseas – then stuffed them into overcrowded vessels and shipped them south to Singapore and other ports of the *Nanyang*, or across the Pacific to far more alien territories in the Americas. A poor Chinese migrant who arrived in Singapore usually couldn't afford the journey himself, so the recruiter profited by paying his fare on his behalf. When the migrant disembarked, his 'credit-ticket', as it was called, was transferred to a local employer, for whom the newcomer was obliged to work till he had paid off his debt. This process might take anything up to three years, even longer if the employer or recruiter were unscrupulous or if the coolie fell into bad ways, bad health or further debt.

Over time, however, the credit-ticket system became less prevalent, partly because of intervention from the colonial authorities and partly because more migrants came out to Singapore on loans provided by relatives, friends or clansmen who were already settled there. Migrants who could afford it worked overseas for a set number of years and then returned to China to see their families, marry or have a child, before journeying abroad once more. Sometimes friends or relatives would replace the original migrant who had sojourned overseas, by a process known today as 'chain migration'.

By the 1890s, the number of these migrants had come to the notice of scholar-officials in Qing China, who began to refer to them as the *huaqiao* or 'the Chinese who sojourn overseas' – a term implying that their overseas stay was temporary and that their sense of affiliation and allegiance lay ultimately with China. In the minds of Qing literati, even if a Chinese sojourner spent decades abroad, with little or no contact with his motherland, his enduring dream remained to return to the hearth and home of his ancestral village.

Yet when we consider the numbers of *huaqiao* who took local wives in the *Nanyang* and made quite a happy and permanent home for themselves overseas, it makes our Qing literati appear guilty of a degree of wishful thinking. Some historians would argue that the *huaqiao* ideal better represented the kind of thing that a Chinese migrant told his relatives and fellow-villagers back home, rather

Chinese coolies arriving by junk.
1900s
NAS 19980006030-009

Sign from an Amoy Street
lodging house for coolies on
transit in Singapore.
Early 20th century
Wood
H 86 x W 106 x D 3 cm
Gift of Min Sing Chan Kim Kee
NMS FL-0037

than the cosmopolitan reality of his new life experience. Not a few successful Chinese migrants in Singapore ended up with two families – one in China and one in their adopted home overseas. As our globe-trotting *huaqiao* shuttled back and forth between both his families, surely, if he was diplomatic, he assured each family that his next journey abroad was but a temporary one and that each represented his one true home.

As for the living a new Chinese migrant might make in Singapore, while it promised greater stability than what was on offer in China, it was still by no means easy. Away from the rarefied atmosphere of Raffles Hotel or the colonial bungalows of Tanglin, most Chinese immigrants faced a daily existence of squalid, overcrowded tenement blocks and poorly paid, backbreaking work under a hot sun, interspersed with meagre meals and scant opportunities for leisure or entertainment. Yet the Chinese came because, as historian James Warren has observed, 'Singapore offered the same hardships as rural China, but with the promise of a future'. At the least there were jobs to be had, even for those who had no special trade or skill.

Rickshaw coolies: people of the streets

In Singapore and the other Straits Settlements many *sinkeh* who stayed, rather than move on to work elsewhere, became rickshaw coolies. It was a job that required little talent or ability beyond physical strength and coordination, while yielding an immediate payment in cash. Rickshaws were plentiful and, because fares were inexpensive, they became the port-city's dominant mode of transport.

Not long after their first appearance in Singapore, in 1880, rickshaws were serving all and sundry, from genteel Europeans and prosperous *taukeh* to market traders, street toughs and school-going children. No other vehicle of the time could be so readily hailed on the street, provide a door-to-door service, and navigate the alleys and by-ways of the inner city as adroitly as they did the proper roads. In the National Museum of Singapore, a rare piece of film footage from the early 1900s shows the sheer proliferation of rickshaws in the city (as they negotiate busy intersections and cross Cavenagh Bridge) with hardly another type of vehicle in sight. Rickshaws even had a starring role in the previously mentioned visit of the Duke and Duchess of Cornwall and York: a procession of rickshaws, their pullers decked out in festive scarlet outfits, brought the royal visitors around Chinatown. Observer Edwin A. Brown remembered a contrast in the royal reactions: 'The Duke looked quite at home in his rickshaw, and the Duchess sat up very stiffly, and seemed most uncomfortable, as if she expected to be thrown out at any moment.'

For most European arrivals, rickshaws and their pullers were part of Singapore's oriental charm, an enjoyable tropical novelty and often the first sight to greet travellers when they disembarked at Johnston Pier. Though a few found the idea of being pulled along by another human being morally reprehensible, the experience of Richard Sydney, as he recalled in his 1920s travelogue, was more typical:

> It is difficult to recapture the early thrill … I have got into a rickshaw somewhere near the top of a hill and have then felt quite thrilled by the fast-moving puller who has made the rickshaw travel at a pace almost equal to that of a smartly stepping horse.

To maintain such a pace exacted a punishing physical toll. It's estimated that each coolie hauled several hundred pounds of weight across the city everyday, working 10–12 hour shifts, with only occasional breaks to get away from the midday sun (or to appease an opium addiction – but more about that later). The puller's main resource was the health and strength of his body, so it's not surprising that there were significantly fewer rickshaw-pullers over the age of 50. The work suited young men in the prime of life, who had to be capable of covering over 11 miles, including a climb up Bukit Timah Hill, in just under an hour. As Sydney marvelled when he wrote of that particular journey: 'Believe me, pullers were pullers in those days.'

Nor was running and pulling the rickshaw coolie's only physical challenge. Traffic in Singapore was an increasing menace. Whereas in the late 19th century, rickshaws had to contend with bullock carts, gharries and then steam trams, by the 1920s they shared the roads with omnibuses, trolley buses, motor cars and lorries – all of which easily outstripped the pace at which the humble rickshaw could safely manoeuvre, while at the same time threatening to smash it to bits. Traffic regulations and signs were nonexistent, and pedestrians swarmed onto the streets from the shophouse five-foot ways, exacerbating the chaos. To quote Warren again: 'The motor vehicles sounded their horns at the pullers, the pullers shouted at the pedestrians, and the pedestrians tended to ignore both.'

A puller's day might take him from the railway station or from Johnston Pier, to the markets of Beach Road, to the red light districts of Bugis Street or Chinatown, during which he was just as likely to ferry goods as people. Hawkers, for example, would use rickshaws to sell their wares in different neighbourhoods

or to take their produce to market. Occasionally, pullers were engaged for longer trips of a more, shall we say, 'recreational', certainly bibulous nature. One Captain A. H. Tilly recalls a four-hour trip that took him to:

> the Rendezvous Tavern, opposite to the Chinese burial ground. Then I went to Smith Street to a spirit shop, as I know a Chinaman who is an interpreter in the Police Court, and had a whiskey and tonic. After finishing the same, I went to the Prince of Wales Hotel and had two glasses of beer there. Then I proceeded home by Tanjong Pagar Road.

As well as scalding heat, the rickshaw coolie faced the choking red dust from Singapore's laterite roads. Hot, dry days meant that the dust got everywhere, into the puller's eyes and as a thick film on his clothes. Hot, wet days might have brought some respite, but the streets then became a muddy, watery mess. Rickshaws could still make their way through floodwaters, and so were eagerly hailed by passengers who did not want to slosh through the mud, but for the puller this was a yet more miserable way to earn a day's living.

For all his trouble, a rickshaw-puller at the turn of the century would generally earn about 6 cents per mile and around 30 to 40 cents in a day. Passengers were supposed to negotiate their fare before getting in, but it was common for them to change their minds on arrival and then start to haggle again. Then there were those passengers who simply refused to pay, behaviour that was not only costly to the puller but could end up lethal. Coroner's Records of the time throw up numerous instances of rickshaw-pullers stabbed or beaten to death not only for protesting against short payment, but for refusing a fare or not moving quickly enough. As solo operators they were easily victimised, especially at remote locations outside the city, and had little redress if they were cheated or abused. With the occupational hazards so great, it was no wonder that the *Straits Times* denounced rickshaw-pulling as 'the deadliest occupation in the East, the most degrading for human beings to pursue'. Unfortunately, the same editorial (almost in the same breath), also revealed the persistent European prejudice of the day when it claimed that only the Chinese would 'serve as beasts of burden and cast away life with almost brutal disregard of its dignity and sanctity'.

Apart from basic economic necessity, the real reason so many Chinese took up rickshaw-pulling was the strong kinship ties that drew them together in foreign surroundings. Rickshaw owners typically hired pullers from their own district or dialect group in China, and given the immigrants' pattern of sojourn-and-return, it became the norm for family members to replace each other, working for the same rickshaw owner for periods of five to seven years at a time (it was rare for anyone to give up the profession entirely). At first, rickshaw-pulling in Singapore was dominated by the Cantonese and Hokkien; by 1900, however, the Hockchew and Hengwah from Fuzhou had begun to take over, largely because they were willing to work for lower wages.

Yet having a family connection did not mean that rickshaw businesses were run as family collectives. Rickshaw owners had anything from one to twenty rickshaws, each rented out to pullers for 8 to 10 cents a day – or roughly a quarter of the puller's daily earnings. Such an arrangement kept owners comfortable, yielding them as much as a 100 per cent return on their yearly capital investment, but for the pullers it was highly restrictive and exploitative. Since rickshaw pullers never took home more than 60 per cent of their daily earnings, even on a good day, it was extremely difficult for them to accumulate enough savings to buy their own rickshaw (a new rickshaw cost about the equivalent of one year's rental fees) and so escape a life of economic bondage. To set up by themselves, or merely to make ends meet, they often had to take on a second job, hiring themselves out as menial labourers or shop coolies.

Moreover, the harshness of their daily existence made rickshaw coolies susceptible to the temptations on offer down some of Singapore's more seedy streets. A melancholy verse by 'G. G. D.' summed up their plight in 1930:

> Life like this, not for men,
> Eating, sleeping in a den.
> Tug and pull, tug and pull,
> Life is short, life is cruel.
> Sob and wheeze, sob and wheeze,
> Finish up, lung disease.
> Nights spent in filthy rooms,
> Dreaming dreams in opium fumes.

'Chasing the dragon': opium highs and lows

The 'opium fumes' of which our poet spoke were considered one of the 'four evils' that plagued the working-class Chinese community in Singapore at this time (the other three were prostitution, drinking and gambling). Rickshaw coolies were hardly the only people tempted by the drug, but from Coroner's Records it's clear that they were the most frequent habitués of the city's opium dens. Opium assuaged the daily aches and pains that came with their job, and it was famous for giving a superb night's sleep.

The ready availability of opium also helped to drive its popularity. Openly sold throughout the city, it was easy for newcomers to procure or simply to stumble upon. Nor were the authorities – while bemoaning the problem of opium addiction – greatly interested in stemming its supply. Beginning with Singapore's first Resident William Farquhar, the colony's administrators had farmed out licenses to sell opium to local *taukeh* in return for their payment of periodic 'rents'. Thus, while opium could be traded freely in the city (like any other goods passing through the port) its local consumption was heavily taxed. For the British government in the Straits, opium was by the late 19th century far too profitable to be given up.

Indeed, without the revenue that the colonial government accrued from opium its administration of the Straits Settlements would barely have functioned. During the first century of colonial rule, opium accounted for between 40 to 60 per cent of all locally derived official revenue. Local merchants likewise benefited, their profits from the trade enabling them to establish new international enterprises that carried the imperial economy forward. Syndicates of Chinese opium farmers (i.e. those who held government licences to sell opium locally) became among the wealthiest and most respected imperial capitalists across Asia, their opium

Chinese men inhaling opium
on a raised bed.

1870s
Albumen print
H 5.8 x W 9.4 cm
NMS 1994-05187

LEFT: Ornate silver opium pipe with *yixing* pipe-bowl and ivory mouthpiece.

Late 19th century
Silver, ceramic and ivory
L 56.7 x W 6.5 x Dia 8.5 cm
NMS S-0840

Opium lamp, designed to heat and vapourise doses of opium into fumes that are then inhaled.

Early 20th century
Glass, metal, wood
H 11.3 x W 8.8 x D 5 cm
NMS 1994-05608

fortunes having provided the capital for them to diversify into the banking, insurance and steamship businesses. No great surprise, then, that some historians have come to think of the British Empire as one of history's most global, successful and resilient drug cartels.

Effects on the local populace, however, were disastrous. The colonial government belatedly acknowledged the problem in 1908, the year the Straits Opium Commission heard evidence that it was the harsh economic conditions facing the *sinkeh* – working too hard, for too long, away from the comforts of home – that drove them into addiction. Not only rickshaw coolies succumbed to the drug, but also plantation workers and tin miners, in short, any labourer whose job entailed gruelling physical exertion. For example, it was common for coolies working in the debilitating tropical heat to refresh themselves with a little opium during their midday break. In their lodging houses, opium lamps were as much a part of the furniture as the sleeping mat or the teapot; alternatively, the neighbourhood opium den or plantation opium shop was never far away. The average coolie was said to consume about 3 *hoon* (35 grams) of *chandu* or refined opium every day; the hard-pressed rickshaw-puller was believed to consume around twice that amount.

Despite such findings, the intimate relationship between opium and colonial power in the Straits Settlements proved hard to break. For years after the 1908 Commission, the opium trade continued, literally with the imprint of the British government plastered all over it. Consider this description by anti-opium activist Ellen La Motte, who visited Singapore in 1916:

> We found these shops established under government auspices, the dealers obtaining their supplies of opium from the government, and then obtaining licenses from the government to retail it. ... We found a thorough and complete establishment of the opium traffic, run by the government, as a monopoly. ... A complete, systematic arrangement, by which the foreign government profited at the expense of the subject peoples under its rule.

Few Europeans saw for themselves the bitter reality of living under the thrall of opium, nor did they grasp the factors that precipitated such addiction. The enduring 19th-century image of the impoverished Chinese was of what historian Carl Trocki has called the 'opium wreck': 'The hollow-eyed, emaciated Oriental

stretched out on his pallet, pipe in hand … the stereotype of Asiatic decadence and indulgence'. La Motte's account of her foray into a Singapore opium den is therefore exceptional. It was still early afternoon, but 'trade was brisk' as each 'grey and emaciated' smoker dutifully purchased a small triangular packet 'containing enough for about six smokes' and lay down on a bench to 'chase the dragon', as the habit was colloquially known in Cantonese. When her Chinese guide pointed out that her presence was making one of the smokers feel ashamed, she retorted, 'The British Government is not ashamed to sell to him, to encourage him to drug himself, to ruin himself. Why should he be ashamed?'

Early efforts to tackle the problem of opium addiction in fact sprang from the Chinese community. Specifically, they were led by the English-educated Straits Chinese leader, Dr Lim Boon Keng. In Lim's view, opium smoking was the gravest of Singapore's four social evils and he spoke out vehemently against it in the *Straits Chinese Magazine* (of which he was the co-founder), as well as campaigning from his position as, variously, Legislative Councillor, Municipal Commissioner and Chinese Advisory Board member. He also started an experimental opium rehabilitation centre in Chinatown, with the support of the Chinese consulate who allowed him to operate the centre out of their premises.

Yet, ultimately, Lim's campaign was thwarted by the combined interests of the opium farmers and the colonial regime. It was not until after 1920, by which time Lim had left Singapore for China, that the British began to view the problem more seriously and to limit opium's sale (no doubt, partly because of strengthening anti-opium movements in the West at this time). Even then, it was not till 1934 that the colonial government banned possession of the drug, except by those who had a medical practitioner's certificate to prove that it was necessary for their health. A complete ban did not come into effect until 1943, during the Japanese Occupation, and even after World War II opium remained popular in certain parts of the city. Some clandestine dens in Chinatown and Tanjong Pagar continued to operate right up until the 1970s, especially in Duxton Street and Amoy Street. In contrast to its users, opium itself had a remarkable longevity.

Karayuki-san: the women who went to the south

If opium was the greatest of the four social evils that blighted Singapore, at least in the eyes of a social reformer such as Dr Lim Boon Keng, then prostitution ran a close second. In 1887, Li Chung Chu (whose description of Singapore's 'Greater' and 'Lesser' Towns we heard earlier) recorded that:

> Along Kreta Ayer, brothels are as many and as close together as the teeth of a comb. It is said that the licensed prostitutes registered at the Chinese Protectorate number three thousand and several hundred. Apart from these, there are countless unlicensed prostitutes and actresses. They are

Lim Boon Keng.
1890s
NAS 19980005828-0095

all Cantonese who were either sold at a young age and sent to *Nanyang*, or
were born and brought up in Singapore.

That prostitution was then so commonplace in Singapore was directly a
consequence of the city's gender imbalance. In 1860, there was only one female
for every fourteen males in the population, a ratio that would not improve till
after World War I. With a constant influx of *sinkeh* and sailors into port, there
was never any lack of custom for houses of ill-repute.

While Li Chung Chu may have observed how ubiquitous such Chinese
establishments were, he failed to register the existence of another type of
prostitute in the city – undoubtedly, the most exoticised and least understood
of all. *Karayuki-san*, or Japanese prostitutes, had begun to show up in Singapore
from the 1850s and had gradually established themselves in the town's eastern
precincts of Bugis, Malay and Malabar Streets, with a few brothels also operating
along Sago, Banda and Spring Streets in Chinatown. Such red-light districts or
suteretsu (a corruption of the English word 'street') possessed their own distinct,
telltale decor, as reported by a Japanese newspaper in 1910:

> Under the verandah hung red gas lanterns with numbers such as one, two,
> or three, and wicker chairs were arranged beneath the lanterns. Hundreds
> and hundreds of young Japanese girls were sitting on the chairs calling out
> to passers-by … Most of them were wearing *yukata* of striking colours. …
> Their hair was arranged in the pompadour style with big ribbons attached.
> Most of them were young girls under twenty years of age.

By 1900, the *karayuki-san* in Singapore numbered around 2,000, most having
arrived from Amakusa Island and Shimabara Peninsula in Japan's southwestern
Kyushu region. These were among the most impoverished regions of the
country, where high rates of taxation, combined with the difficulties of eking
out a living from the area's barren soil, pushed poor farmers into sending their
daughters overseas to support their families. The proximity of the Chinese
mainland and the settlements of the *Nanyo* (Japanese for 'southern seas') meant
that many of them wound up in Singapore and other parts of Southeast Asia
– usually as prostitutes.

Why did these girls fall into the sex trade? To put it bluntly, with so few
occupations open to women at all, a rural farm-girl could earn more working as
prostitute than as domestic servant or female coolie. Like the men from China,
who found the travails of being a rickshaw puller preferable to a still poorer
life at home, women from Japan settled for work that was rough, squalid and
degrading because it paid the bills. A Tokyo newspaper in 1902 quoted one
karayuki-san as saying:

> I have never been happier. I no longer have to plough the land and harvest
> rice with a sickle. I can wear beautiful kimonos and eat white rice rather
> than sweet potatoes. I can even have fish and meat with my meals.

Of course, such an account belies the harsh and often heart-wrenching circumstances that forced most *karayuki-san* from their homelands to their 'new' lives abroad. Theirs was a patriarchal society that placed little value on daughters; indeed, many *karayuki-san* were knowingly sold into prostitution by their own relatives. The rapidly modernising Japanese nation was scarcely less ruthless and looked to the *karayuki-san* to perform a patriotic duty to the fatherland by bringing home foreign currency. Even the *zegen* (Japanese brothel owners or pimps) got in on the act, telling the girls that their bodies belonged to the state and that they constituted an overseas female army. Those nights when the imperial Japanese navy docked in Singapore port were some of the *karayuki-san*'s hardest.

By the end of the 19th century, the traffic in Japanese and Chinese prostitutes across Southeast Asia had become a multi-million dollar business. In 1905, Singapore had 109 Japanese brothels (with 5 to 7 *karayuki-san* per outfit) located in its two main *suteretsu*, in and around Malay Street and in Chinatown (where Banda Street earned the longstanding Cantonese nickname *phan tsai mei* [lane of foreign prostitutes] while Spring Street became known as *yap pun kai* [Japanese street]). Under the hazy red light of gas lanterns painted with the number of the brothel house, the girls waited with painted faces and demure calls of '*kaminsa*' (a corruption of the English 'come in, sir'), '*mush ru*' (an attempt at 'monsieur'), or '*marishini*' (from the Malay *mari sini* – 'come here'). Unlike their Chinese counterparts, *karayuki-san* accepted customers of all races: Chinese artisans,

Japanese ladies,
by G. R. Lambert & Co.

1890s
Albumen print
H 20 x W 27.2 cm
NMS 2006-01793

Malay sailors, Sikh watchmen, Tamil street sweepers, Japanese naval officers, as well as ordinary European soldiers and sailors.

Each *karayuki-san* saw up to eight customers a day, with each man paying two yen a session. An overnight customer would pay ten yen – enough to buy a *sarong* and *kebaya*, or a pair of sandals, a comb and cosmetics. But like rickshaw coolies, *karayuki-san* were from the start indentured to their employers and had first to work off the price of their voyage from Japan, not to mention the cost of their elaborate kimonos, food and lodging. While they might earn up to 300 yen a month, it still took several years – and hundreds, perhaps thousands of customers – for them to cancel their debts. Until that time, the *karayuki-san* stayed the property, in every commodified sense, of their *zegen*.

In such trying circumstances, *karayuki-san* developed quasi-familial relationships with their *okasan* (the female brothel-keeper or 'mother' of such establishments) and with other prostitutes or 'sisters' from the same house. Living together, they shared their chores, gambled to pass the time or accompanied each other out of the house on errands. It wasn't always a happy family that lived together, but it was the only one they had. As for their kin back in Japan, their only contact with them over the long years in Singapore was through sporadic letters, written for them by local professional letter writers (most *karayuki-san* were illiterate), or through photographs they sent home, partly to prove to their relatives that they were well and healthy.

It is from these photographs – taken in the local studios of Chinese, Japanese and European photographers, in pairs or groups so that the cost could be shared among 'sisters' – that the enduring image of Singapore's *karayuki-san* emerges: a noble, elegant figure, wrapped in an exotic kimono, exquisite, distant and untouchable. *Karayuki-san* were also paid to pose for postcards or for images used in tourist advertisements that sold Singapore, so Warren puts it, as 'a centre of romanticism, exoticism, and easy sex'. Colonial police officer René Onraet (whom we will read more about later) observed in his memoirs: 'All that was known about Singapore, in most places of the world before the 1914 war, was contained in four words: "Raffles Hotel" and "Malay Street".'

Yet for all its distinctive colour and allure, the phenomenon of the *karayuki-san* was short-lived. By 1919, Japan's imperial government in Tokyo had grown concerned about the *karayuki-san*'s impact on national prestige and had ordered its consular representatives to start repatriating them. In Singapore, most *karayuki-san* were pressured to leave and 1921 saw the official abolition of licensed Japanese prostitution in the city. Nonetheless, some *karayuki-san* never went home: they simply disappeared from consular records, perhaps becoming private prostitutes, mistresses or finding other employment. Others, thanks to illness, despair and suicide had already made Singapore their final resting place, their names (though not their occupations) today commemorated by their gravestones in the island's Japanese cemetery.

14. BEYOND THE FIVE-FOOT WAY

When we consider how much the British liked to govern, for much of the 19th century their official policy towards an increasingly sprawling and vice-ridden Singapore was surprisingly *laissez-faire*. Public works programmes notwithstanding, problems of sanitation, housing, congestion, disease, crime and general social welfare were left to sort out themselves. Consequently, much of Singapore Town (at least until the 1860s) remained dirty, smelly and surrounded by polluted swamps. Roads were littered with garbage and plagued by stray dogs; there were few if any hospitals, no fire brigade or adequate water supply; and finally there was no sewage system (meaning that night-soil was collected privately to be later deposited in market gardens). Any 'invisible hand' that existed in such matters was to be found in the activities of civic-minded philanthropists and in the numerous local associations, one particular kind of which we will discuss in a moment.

To be fair, a non-interventionist attitude was common among most colonial officials in other Asian port-cities of the British Empire at this time. Hamstrung by a lack of cash, if municipal administrations could put off doing something about their inhabitants' living conditions, they usually did. But in the late 1800s, as Singapore continued to grow, the city's social problems became so acute as to finally force a change of policy.

For one thing, the European population in Singapore became gravely concerned about the threat of disease, especially when in the 1890s bubonic plague re-emerged, having apparently spread from China via Hong Kong to Bombay, Calcutta and Karachi. In the early 20th century, the colonial government in the Straits responded to the problem of public health with a series of new measures (which we'll discuss in a later chapter).

Men waiting to see a Chinese physician at Thong Chai Medical Institution.

1890s
Gretchen Liu/NAS
19980006568-0035

But back in the early 1870s, the issue that caused an equally deep furrow in the brow of colonial officialdom was law and order; in particular, the British administration's failure to secure law and order amongst the city's dominant Chinese community. As an official commission in 1875 reported:

> We believe that the vast majority of Chinamen who come to work in these settlements return to their country not knowing clearly whether there is a government in them or not.

As we've seen, early 19th-century Singapore was a rough place, in which life was periodically punctuated by the outbreak of riots between different Chinese dialect groups. But what must have troubled colonial onlookers in the early 1870s was that the situation appeared to be getting worse. Not only was the Chinese population continuing to grow while remaining largely ungoverned, now when the Chinese decided to riot it seemed that their new target was the colonial government itself.

The battle for Chinatown

In 1876, the colonial government decided it was time to open a Chinese post office, in an effort to ensure safer, more reliable service for Singapore's various Chinese dialect communities, especially to send their money back home. In spite of the authorities' good intentions, all havoc broke loose. Local Teochew *taukeh*, who had previously run the remittance business using Chinese junks, felt aggrieved at their potential loss of earnings. In response to what they saw as a new government monopoly, farmed out to Straits Chinese from Penang, they put up placards around Chinatown announcing their hope that those responsible would have their wives and daughters dressed in their finery and 'placed at the door for men to buy and deride, and for use of every lustful person'. A reward was also posted for any 'virtuous man' who would 'cut off the heads of the post office farmers'. Soon after, a riot broke out. It didn't last long but it saw to the trashing of the Chinese post office, forcing it to relocate to another part of Singapore away from an angry Chinatown.

What is especially striking about this riot was the class-conscious language that its instigators used to incite it. The placards in question, while they avoided attacking the colonial government directly (reserving their ire for the post office farmers from Penang), still spoke in terms such as these:

> Alas for our coolies, with their toil, labour and miserable condition! If, after toiling with their hands or bearing heavy burdens, they have saved a dollar or two, which they wish to send to their family halls to assist in providing fire and water, they cannot get enough to fill the mouth, how much less can they hope to fill the caverns of this vicious and insatiable lust for gain! ... Now we must clearly awake to this vicious and delusive system ...

Coloured postcard of a
Chinese funeral procession.
1900s
Paper
H 8.7 x W 13.8 cm
NMS 2007-50877

Or, as another placard put it:

> We hear that lately one or two rascals … have established a Post Office,
> intending to begin gently and to go on to great depth; they mean to oppress
> the Chinese in their private gains. To the rich this does not matter, but
> truly it is cheating the poor people. We have come to these barbarous
> tribes, is it not because our families are poor and can scarcely pass the day
> for want of food?

Ultimately, 'the system' won out; the Chinese post office eventually reappeared
(without a riot) and flourished, providing a faster and more reliable service for
Chinese migrants than they had experienced previously. However, in 1888 a
government decision to clear the city's five-foot ways of shopkeepers, to ease
congestion and, so it was believed, improve public sanitation, led to another
outbreak of violence. Before a compromise could be reached, what became
known as the 'Verandah Riots' brought traffic and commerce in Singapore to a
standstill.

Colonial officials believed that such riots were caused not by Singapore's
pressing social injustices but by their main rival for control of Chinatown's
streets – the Chinese 'secret societies' or 'sworn brotherhoods', as they were also
known. These organisations had been a feature of Chinese life in Singapore from
almost the time of its inception as a colonial settlement. Through their distinctive
initiation rites and sworn oaths, most traced their origins back to the *Tiandihui*,

Chinese Funeral, Singapore.

or 'heaven and earth' societies that, legend has it, sprang out of the war of the Shaolin monks against China's Manchu invaders in the 17th century. However, British officials believed secret societies in Singapore to have a less honourable, more sinister purpose. Since the island's police force was woefully undermanned throughout most of the 19th century, large-scale riots in the city could frequently go on for days. The authorities suspected that such unrest was incited by the powerful secret society headmen to aid their respective brotherhoods, not just through the wide-scale looting that ensued, but because an atmosphere of general anarchy enabled them to extend their protection rackets.

Calls for the British to deal with secret societies resulted in legislation in 1867 that permitted the government to deport convicted criminals, and in 1869 that demanded all secret societies register with the authorities. However, when it came to the registration process, there was no certainty that those persons who came forward to help the authorities with their effort were not agents sent by the secret societies to throw the police off the scent. In the opinion of one colonial official (who would probably come to know the secret societies better than any other) the entire attempt to register secret societies was a 'mere farce'.

This official was the Englishman William Pickering, known to the Chinese in Singapore as 'Pi-ki-ling'. With striking determination, Pickering tried (literally) to get inside Singapore's sworn brotherhoods, in order to understand them, control them and ultimately govern through them. His attempt remains one of 19th-century Singapore's most intriguing stories, and one that says much about the real way the port-city was governed.

Blood and bagpipes

In 1879, William Pickering read a paper to his scholarly friends in Singapore at the Straits Branch of the Royal Asiatic Society. In it, he described at length a secret society initiation he had attended in the city at which 70 new members were inducted. In entering the world of the sworn brotherhood, Pickering had passed through into a symbolic universe of such intricacy that even those familiar with Victorian Freemasonry would have found it remarkable.

The whole ceremony lasted five hours and the lodge where it was conducted was clearly designed with the elaborate rituals of the initiation in mind. Pickering recorded how would-be society members first entered a main door where they took into their hands a three-foot staff, known as the Red Baton, and recited the password. (Failure to do so correctly, it was said, would result in instant beheading). Next the initiates passed through the Holy Gate, which displayed the Society's red flags and which was guarded by two office bearers, then through the Hall of Sincerity and Justice, into the City of Willows and toward the Red Flowery Pavilion, above which stood the grand altar and the pulpit of the Master of the Lodge.

William Pickering.
1880s
NAS 19

Here the initiates were given the purifying waters of the Three Rivers before they continued across the Two-Plank Bridge, hung with a symbolic number of coins, and into the Red Valley, guarded by a 'malignant though just Spirit' who went by the name of 'Red Youth' (and whose role was played by a sworn brother armed with a spear). Those who passed unharmed arrived at the Market of Universal Peace and the Temple of the Virtues – from whence they were taken to a side room for a wash, a change of clothes and the settlement of their entrance fees.

Only at this point did the central part of the initiation ritual begin, performed by the Master of the Lodge in front of an altar laid out with symbolic numbers of lamps, candles, cups of tea and wine, bowls of rice, chopsticks, as well as sacrificial meats and tobacco, and the various flags that commemorated the society's history and objectives. The climax came when the candidates knelt in pairs before the altar, answered certain key questions, repeated their oaths to the society and to their new 'brothers', and drank from a cup of wine mingled with pin-pricks of their own blood.

The impact of such an occasion on Pickering must have been considerable, as it must have been on the Colonial Secretary and Major Samuel Dunlop (the Straits Settlements Inspector General of Police), who both also attended the ceremony. Plainly, nothing Singapore's colonial government demanded of new Chinese arrivals in Singapore in terms of loyalty came close to the allegiance expected by the sworn brotherhoods. What these three colonial officials had witnessed were the inner workings of a highly sophisticated informal government that dominated the island's Chinese population. While a rich Asian elite might express their loyalty to the British crown and British Empire, for most Chinese immigrants (and increasingly for Straits-born Chinese too) the secret societies remained the only powers in the land that really mattered. Pickering's career would be dominated by his attempt to transform these mysterious organisations into what he hoped would be a powerful new source of local law and order.

In 1872, seven years before he read his paper on secret society rituals, Pickering arrived in Singapore as the first European official able to speak and write Chinese, a skill he had picked up as a commercial agent working in the Fujian province of China and in Formosa (today's Taiwan). His initial work involved the humble duties of a government interpreter, translating official documents into Chinese and interpreting witness testimonies in the law courts. However, Pickering's linguistic abilities soon proved an invaluable asset, for almost immediately he uncovered a practice that when discovered must have made certain eminent colonial authorities blush with embarrassment.

Pickering discovered that local translators, ordered to render the desires, proclamations and verdicts of the British government into good Chinese, had been conducting an extended joke at the expense of their colonial masters. In 'Chinese copies of our own Government proclamations', he reported, 'colonial officials

Illustration of Ghee Hin Kongsi lodge, showing details of the initiation ceremony.
Late 19th century
Watercolour on paper
H 41.8 x W 30.9 cm
NMS 1996-02889

Various secret society chops
from the William Stirling
collection.

Early 20th century
Ink on cloth
H 61.8 x W 50.1 cm
NMS 1996-02855

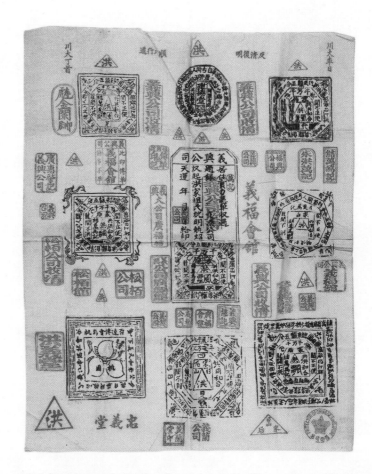

were styled "red-haired barbarians"'– a phrase familiar to many Singaporeans today, who may still refer to Caucasians as *ang moh* (the Hokkien version of this term). Meanwhile in the courts, Pickering complained, 'the judges, magistrates, barristers, and jury were all, by our own paid interpreters, spoken of as "barbarians" or "devils", and the police distinguished by the ironic title of "big dogs"'. There is perhaps no better image of the gulf that existed between the rulers and the ruled in 19th-century Singapore than that of Her Majesty's official representatives being subjected to derogatory name-calling in high places – in full view and hearing of their colonial subjects, yet remaining completely oblivious to it.

Pickering suspected that many of these court interpreters were in fact secret society members, a situation which further undermined the workings of British colonial justice. However, his first clear encounter with the sworn brotherhoods came not in Singapore but in the Malay state of Perak. In 1873, in this rich tin-mining district of the Peninsula, major disputes had erupted between rival Chinese factions for control of the mines, disputes that secret societies were thought to have instigated. Perak's tin mines were particularly important to the economy of Penang and Pickering's handling of the unrest gave birth to a legend that soon spread right across the Straits Settlements and made him, at the age of 33, something of a local celebrity.

As the story goes, Pickering was sent with Major Dunlop to settle disputes between rival secret societies in the town of Larut. Although an Englishman by birth, Pickering took with him a set of bagpipes, which he had discovered during his time in Formosa to intrigue the Chinese and greatly entertain them. When he arrived in Larut he took out his bagpipes and like a tropical pied piper went about the villages playing them. Long-term Singapore resident J. D. Vaughan described what followed:

> He quite won their hearts like Orpheus of old and the result was that the Chinese became most tractable. The rival parties shook hands, peace was restored ...

We'll probably never know how well or even what Pickering played, but according to Vaughan the effect was 'magical':

> When the party was marching up to a stockade and it was not quite certain how they would be received, Mr Pickering would strike up on his pipes. The Chinese would flock out of their strongholds by hundreds and regard the player with wonder, and march along in his wake seemingly delighted with what they doubtless thought was Chinese music.

Back in Singapore a few years later, Pickering became more deeply involved in the city's own Chinese problems. In 1877, he and Major Dunlop heard that angry crowds were gathering at Market Street and set out to investigate. There they found a commotion had erupted over the forcible herding of Chinese *sinkeh* onto vessels bound for Sumatra. Rounding up two of the instigators, Pickering and Dunlop returned to the police station to find 20 more bruised and battered *sinkeh* who had apparently resisted the same attempt at kidnapping. These men told the authorities that they had been promised work and good wages in Singapore, only to discover on their arrival that they were to be immediately shipped out to Sumatran tin mines. On resisting, they had been assaulted and forced toward their designated transport ships by secret society gangs. Further investigations revealed another 15 terrified *sinkeh* already stored below decks on three lighters waiting in the harbour.

The incident took place at a time when the colonial government in the Straits Settlements had finally decided to do something about managing Singapore's growing Chinese population. In May 1877, three months after the attempted mass kidnapping, the British established their Chinese Protectorate (initially at a small office in a Chinese shophouse on North Canal Road). At the age of 37, Pickering was given the job as Protector of Immigrants and Emigrants; more commonly, he became known as the first Protector of Chinese.

The Protector and his plan

The Protectorate began its work by addressing the problem of unregulated Chinese immigration into the Straits Settlements, and within five years achieved considerable success. Recruiters of Chinese labour, and the depots at which *sinkeh* were received, were instructed to register with the Protectorate and any unlicensed operation was deemed illegal. By law, only those migrants who had been engaged as labourers could now be confined to a licensed depot – and then only for a maximum of 10 days, and with access to a plentiful supply of water and good ventilation.

At the same time, Pickering turned the Protectorate's attention to the issue of migrants in transit and to abuses in the credit-ticket system. Protectorate officials now boarded immigrant ships to distribute handbills and advise *sinkeh* of the protection to which they were entitled in a British port. Furthermore, Pickering and his assistants also began to make personal visits to receiving depots to oversee the fair drawing-up of contracts between coolies, labour agents and coolie brokers. When new arrivals left the depots, they were informed by Protectorate officials that they need not join a secret society for protection, since the British government was there to listen to their grievances and to address any unlawful behaviour to which they might find themselves subjected.

Not all these new procedures were implemented smoothly. A number of coolie depots failed to conform to the Protectorate's new licence requirements but were registered anyway so as to avoid driving them underground. Further difficulties arose over regulating the treatment of coolies once they had left port. Some employers in the Dutch East Indies failed to abide by contracts agreed in Singapore, on the grounds that the coolies they received were not healthy enough for the work required of them. Nonetheless, the Protectorate responded speedily to such difficulties. Soon after the abuses in the Dutch East Indies had come to light, it introduced medical examinations for all *sinkeh* who arrived in the Straits Settlements. At the same time, Pickering and his colleagues maintained pressure on plantation and tin-mine owners in Sumatra until the conditions under which migrant labourers paid off their credit-ticket debts were improved. In a matter of years, abuses once suffered by coolies at the hands of ruthless employers and agents had been significantly curtailed.

Yet Pickering's main concern as Protector went beyond regulation of the coolie trade, to the central question of how to govern the Chinese – and it was this concern that once again brought him into direct contact with Singapore's secret societies.

His plan was simple: first, obtain sufficient information about the societies in order to understand them; next, transform the local headmen of these brotherhoods into agents of the colonial government; finally, and with the headmen's help, establish the Protectorate in the minds of the Chinese population as an alternative tribunal for the settlement of disputes. Instead of attempting to

Chinese Protectorate, Singapore.

Postcard depicting the
Chinese Protectorate building
off Havelock Road.
1890s
Paper
H 9.1 x W 14.1 cm
NMS 1999-02530

suppress the secret societies, Pickering's new policy involved trying to work with them and through them.

The first step in his plan was mostly bureaucratic, as it had been in the case of Chinese immigration: all existing sworn brotherhoods were ordered to register with the Protectorate and provide information about their membership so that their individual members could be traced to their headmen and their other 'brothers'. In addition, headmen were now called in to assist the Protectorate in its work and to refer to it any disputes that previously they would have dealt with themselves. Many headmen did so, since those who failed to cooperate or control their followers now faced banishment. Two statistics in particular bear out the Protectorate's early success. In 1879, the number of secret society members registered, and therefore accounted for, totalled 17,900, an improvement on the first registration in 1869, not just in numbers but in the reliability of the new lists. In that same year, Pickering and his colleagues dealt with over 2,600 secret society quarrels, financial disputes and domestic disagreements. In effect the Protectorate had established itself (at least for a while) as the local Chinese population's new centre for community arbitration.

Pickering could thus look back at the Protectorate's rapid achievements with pride – and he did so, commenting that once 'Dangerous' secret societies were now becoming merely 'Friendly' societies. In 1881, he wrote:

> There is no doubt that my Department has become one of the most important in the Colony, and that as far as the largest and most unruly portion of the population is concerned, it is second only to that of the Police.

His plan, however, contained a major flaw: all systems of government, formal or informal and whether they admit to it or not, depend ultimately on the use of force to preserve their authority. Pickering's plan, by taking away their powers of coercion, robbed the secret societies of their capacity to control their members as they had done previously. He had publicly argued that 'strong societies are really a help to the Government', yet his policy toward these societies greatly weakened them. Pickering himself was aware of the paradox at the heart of his plan when he observed that:

> The inferior office-bearers and members, knowing that there is always an appeal from any injustice perpetrated by their chiefs, are apt to obey them only when their orders coincide with their own wishes.

In the 1880s, official reports reveal a growing disquiet as the secret societies reasserted themselves and the Protectorate's success in controlling them began to diminish. Those original secret societies registered from 1879 found it increasingly hard to discipline troublesome members for the reason mentioned above. Friendly societies – those supposedly law-abiding brotherhoods dedicated to social welfare or recreation (and which the authorities had not thought it necessary to register) – began to behave like the secret societies of old. Furthermore, those rebellious societies that the Protectorate had ordered to disband, and to hand over their membership lists and paraphernalia, appeared to be re-forming and continuing to operate underground. The threat of banishment, which the authorities had used to punish non-cooperative headmen, was also losing its impact, since many new headmen were now Straits-born Chinese who, as British subjects, could not be deported. Finally, registered societies that played by the Protectorate's rulebook found that they were attacked by new brotherhoods who did not, and that they had no means of retaliation except to lodge a complaint with the police.

Secret society members.
Early 20th century
NAS 27422

Matters came to a head (in Pickering's case, quite literally) in the year 1887. By this time, it was clear that new secret societies had become deeply involved in illegal gaming houses, a development that Pickering felt threatened to undo all his work in trying to bring the brotherhoods to heel:

> Nothing is more likely to create jealousy and quarrels between the secret societies than the emulation which is aroused to share the great profits accruing from the establishment of gaming houses in the various districts of the Settlements.

Pickering pressed for greater legal powers to tackle the problem of illegal gambling, but before he could do so he almost lost his life. The afternoon edition of the *Straits Times* for 18 July 1887 reported that earlier in the day the Protector had been going about his duties, when:

> A Chinese Tew Chew carpenter, who is supposed to be connected in some way with one of the headmen implicated in gambling matters came into the office ... He went up to Mr Pickering's desk and threw at his face the iron-head of a carpenter's axe, which he carried in his hand.

Fortunately for Pickering, it was the butt end rather than the sharp edge of the axe-head ('which would have split his skull, proving fatal') that struck him 'full on the forehead'. He had reportedly looked up from his desk to ask the carpenter his business and seen the latter 'gnashing his teeth'. A moment later 'the chopper came flying straight at him ... like a cannonball and seemed to take a long time before it struck'.

Bleeding, clutching his hands to his wound, Pickering ran after his assailant, who was eventually held to the ground by half a dozen or so Protectorate staff. However the Protector himself never fully recovered. In 1889, a physician's report claimed that though he was physically mended, the mental scars from the attack were yet to heal: 'He cannot calmly apply his mind to any subject, he becomes excited, loses memory, and, as he describes it, "loses his head".' The following year, and after several periods of extended sick leave, Pickering was permanently retired.

In the interim, the British government in the Straits Settlements, under its newly installed Governor Sir Cecil Clementi Smith, decided that enough was enough. In 1889, and much to Pickering's displeasure, Clementi Smith introduced a Societies Ordinance that abolished all secret societies and made it illegal to belong to one. Yet government efforts to enforce the Ordinance came up against the same old problems: brotherhoods continued to operate by going underground and re-forming, or by using the continued exemption afforded to 'recreational' societies under the ordinance, to continue their illegal activities. By the early 1900s, all the ordinance seemed to have achieved was to make the city's sworn brotherhoods more secretive and more criminalised. Most societies

White censer with joss sticks. One of the items on the initiation altar, this censer bears the slogan '*fanqing fuming*', which means 'Destroy the Qing, Restore the Ming'.
Early 20th century
Porcelain
H 10.4 x Dia. 10.5 cm
NMS 1996-02793

173

五謝宇師傅

405 - Chinese Workmen at Tiffin

had become smaller, operating with looser affiliations between their members and out of small, secretive rooms in coolie lodgings rather than from the larger lodges that had been known to everyone. By banning secret societies outright, the colonial government had done little more than push these organisations further into the gloomy recesses that lay beyond the five-foot way.

This last point brings us round to an interesting question: just how 'secret' were Singapore's secret societies before the British attempted to suppress them? Some scholars argue that the air of mystery surrounding these organisations was mainly a product of the European imagination. For one thing, sworn brotherhoods, in which bonds of fictive kinship were forged through solemn rituals and oaths, were as popular with Singapore's respectable Chinese merchants as with its migrant coolies. A good example is the Keng Teck Whay, a sworn brotherhood of Baba Chinese shopkeepers that was established in the grounds of the Thian Hock Keng. Such an organisation, though exclusive, was hardly secret; in 1919, it even published its elaborate oath of institution in English translation. Indeed, it could well be argued that most 'secret' societies in Chinatown before the Ordinance of 1889 were no great secret to anyone but the British. In any case, following the earlier Ordinance of 1869, most of these lodges had been forced to open their doors to allow in official observers such as Pickering.

Certainly, the British had a problem distinguishing actual criminal brotherhoods from the many other types of associations in which local Chinese participated – associations known in Chinese as *bang*, *hui* and *kongsi*. At one point, for instance, colonial officials even classified the Ngee Ann Kongsi – which today gives its respectable name to important commercial and collegiate landmarks on the island – as a secret society. Another difficulty was that secret societies themselves took on many of the social welfare functions that other Chinese associations provided. For a young *sinkeh* bereft of family and home, arriving in a city where the British administration did little to look after its subjects' welfare, and where the law courts were foreign and the police largely ineffective, the secret society was one of the few places that offered welfare and protection. To many Chinese, its activities would have appeared entirely legitimate.

Yet Singapore's secret societies, whatever their apparent legitimacy in the eyes of their members, were also highly disruptive of Chinese unity. British intervention in Chinese affairs might lead to widespread riots across Chinatown, but the city's sworn brotherhoods were just as likely to oppose each other as their colonial masters. And though the placards that went up on the eve of the Chinese Post Office Riot might speak of a common class, even ethnic interest, Chinatown itself remained deeply divided. For the Chinese of Singapore to engage in a full-blown challenge to colonial authority, first their leaders had to convince them that they belonged to one people who, despite their differences of class and dialect, essentially spoke the same language.

Coolies at mealtime
by G. R. Lambert.
1890s
Albumen print
H 26.1 x W 20.9 cm
NMS 2001-05153

MODERN TIMES
1890s – 1930s

15. An Island on the Move

At first, it might seem mistaken to suggest that Singapore somehow became modern between the 1890s and the late 1930s. Most inhabitants of the island still lived in conditions that by today's standards would be considered under-developed, even primitive. Scholars might well ask what we mean by the term 'modern'. Doesn't every generation try to present itself as such, as having somehow broken with tradition? Didn't Raffles himself try to establish a modern, progressive society in the tropics, where, not long after, his scribe Abdullah wrote of an old world passing and a new world of steamships and printing presses that was coming into being?

For some of us the phrase 'modern times' will recall that classic 1936 film of the same name by Charlie Chaplin, where (in a memorable scene) Chaplin is swallowed up and processed by a heavy piece of machinery – a mechanised monster symbolic of 20th-century industrialisation. However, since Singapore possessed, even by the late 1930s, only a few factories, it would seem that any experience the population at large had of being devoured by machines lay well in the future.

Nonetheless, many people in Singapore, far from being puzzled by the notion that they lived in modern times, would have been absolutely sure of the fact. Chaplin's films were by this time enjoyed at several cinemas across the city (where they were especially popular with rickshaw coolies). Meanwhile, newspapers, magazines, books and advertisements had been defining what being 'modern' meant – in terms of gadgets, fashions, habits, architecture and even haircuts – for decades.

Inevitably, then as now, most of the world considered the West to be at the vanguard of progress and so it contributed heavily to Singapore's new styles, attitudes and technologies. However, on closer inspection, being modern in this city involved more than simple Westernisation. Things modern also arrived from closer to home, from vibrant Asian cities such as Shanghai and Tokyo. Thus,

PREVIOUS PAGE:
Kallang Airport, with its distinctive glass-clad control tower.

1937
Gelatin print
H 8.8 x W 13.8 cm
Donated by Pauline Baron
NMS XXXX-01028

Detail of photograph of a Chinese man in 'Western' attire.

1900s
Paper
NMS XXXX-12141

RIGHT: Wooden case HMV (His Master's Voice) radio.

1940s
Wood, bakelite
L 31.5 x W 20.5 x H 19.3 cm
NMS 1999-01363

'modernity' – the term scholars like to use to describe all things modern – was just as likely to have been 'Asian made'.

More than anything, being modern in Singapore involved a self-conscious embracing of new ideas; ideas that, in the language of the day, were deemed 'progressive'. Such new ideas focused on education, politics and the status of women, and they were spread through schools, reading-rooms and public lectures, as well as the nascent mass media (newspapers, pamphlets, magazines, cinema and later the radio). The upshot: as more people voiced their opinions about being modern, Singapore became a vibrant centre of modernity in its own right. The results were dramatic, and sometimes even explosive.

A faster, safer, slightly healthier city

On the face of it, the arrival of modern times in Singapore was heralded by a series of new and highly visible technologies. In 1896, the first motorcar drove down the city's streets; in 1915, the first aeroplane took off from Farrer Park; and, in that same year, the first wireless station began operation. By 1906, the town centre had been electrified, a development that made possible electric street lights (which made the streets safer) and electric fans (which brought added comfort to the lives of government servants and rich merchants, though they rendered obsolete the once ubiquitous *punkah-wallah*).

None of these novelties brought change overnight – before they became widely accessible, the municipal authorities first had to improve the city's infrastructure to make space for them. However, modern technology eventually created a faster, brighter, more intense urban landscape. When the St James Power Station started operations in 1927, electricity (and all its conveniences) became available for the first time in areas beyond the town centre. By this time, road improvements across the city had enabled motorcars, trolley-buses and omnibuses to start crowding out the gharries and rickshaws. On the outskirts of town, the Seletar Aerodrome (opened in the late 1920s) and then the Kallang Airport (built at the end of the following decade) sprang up to facilitate the arrival of passenger aeroplanes. All of a sudden the island's airwaves became busier too. In 1936, the British Malayan Corporation started radio broadcasts that eventually transformed the wireless set, for many years a strange box of hisses and crackles to all but a few amateur enthusiasts, into an everyday commonplace.

The colonial government's efforts to modernise Singapore had, in fact, begun in the previous century. Between 1857 and 1886, the amount the authorities spent on improvements in the town increased from a paltry $63,000 to half a million Straits dollars. However, since much of this money was spent on building projects in the European district it made little impact on public health and welfare in the city's poorer quarters. In the early years of the new century, the death rate per year in Singapore (of between 44 and 51 per thousand) was well above that

Advertisement for a popular brand of Scotch whisky sold at John Little's.
1926
EDM Archives

of Hong Kong, India or Ceylon. Poor sanitation, malnutrition and overcrowding bred the usual litany of dreadful tropical diseases: beriberi, tuberculosis, enteric fever, dysentery, cholera and malaria.

Things turned around from the year 1900, thanks to a combination of ecomonic growth (which, especially during the 1920s, generated greater public spending) and heightened civic activism. In the 1890s, Dr Lim Boon Keng campaigned against disease in Singapore's poorer quarters and in 1896 he headed a government commission on urban poverty. A wave of public health improvements followed: the first official health survey in 1906, an expansion of the General Hospital the following year, a campaign to deal with malaria in 1911 and the laying of the city's first sewage pipes two years later. In 1921, water supplies to the town increased with the opening of a new reservoir, and in 1927 the government began to tackle overcrowding by forming the Singapore Improvement Trust, a body charged to clear slums and provide alternative housing. To ease Chinatown's problems of hygiene, light and ventilation, the municipal authorities even smashed through the backs of Chinese houses to create new rear alleyways.

The city's emergency services likewise improved. The fire brigade began to use motorised fire engines from 1912, while better training and equipment (especially telephones, motorcars and radios) eventually transformed the police department beyond all recognition. While in the 1920s Singapore had a well-deserved reputation as the 'Chicago of the East' or 'Sin-galore', with street gangs, gunmen, murders and illicit dealings aplenty, by the late 1930s all this had changed: brothels had become illegal, opium dens had been reduced in number and secret societies were under heavy surveillance. By which time also, the daily grind of city life had become punctuated by frequent bursts of a new type of choreography: massed police constabulary emerging from their vans and cars to storm up the

Postcard showing the Chinese Gospel Hall on North Bridge Road with a water cart in front of it. In the days before piped water, the inhabitants of the city relied on these bullock-drawn water carts (*kreta ayer* in Malay).
1911
Collection of Dr Cheah Jin Seng

staircases of old rickety shophouses (or other allegedly 'dubious' premises) before re-emerging (after shouts and curses and perhaps the occasional gunshot) with an array of 'criminal' types in hand. It may have taken over a century, but the British seemed to have at last taken a grip on their prized Eastern possession.

This is not to say that Singapore was by any means a model colony. Malnutrition, slum housing and high infant mortality continued to blight the lives of the urban poor right up to the 1960s. Moreover, while increased demand for living space led to the development of new suburbs such as at Katong along East Coast Road, many rural parts of the island remained completely untouched by the government's modernisation efforts. Before World War II (and for some time after) it was possible to wander through Malay districts such as Kampong Melayu and Geylang Serai, and discover a sedate world of fishing, bullock carts and *attap* houses that had remained largely unaltered.

Yet the city of Singapore definitely became cleaner, faster and more orderly. This, of course, is a story as much about economic development as benign colonialism, save for one crucial factor. To proceed with Singapore's modernisation, the British, as they had done in their other colonial outposts, began to educate, train and employ more of their colonial subjects. It was a change that was to have major long-term repercussions on how the inhabitants of Singapore saw themselves, and perceived their place in the wider world.

The education of Singapore

Compared with other parts of the British Empire, the expansion of modern education in Singapore came late. Raffles had intended the island to be a centre for progressive schooling, but before the 1890s evidence of his good intentions was hard to come by. Partly, this was a consequence of an impoverished administration, but equally it was the result of prevailing colonial attitudes. Singapore was viewed by its rulers as first and foremost a commercial emporium. Unlike colonial administrators in India and Ceylon, the island's officials were noticeably less concerned with improving their subjects along European lines.

In 19th century Singapore, Raffles Institution alone provided secondary education and did so only after 1884, mainly for the sons of local wealthy merchants who saw schooling in English as a ticket to those elevated colonial social circles where their power and influence might be further cultivated. Elsewhere, English instruction was offered at primary level at a handful of mission schools such as St Joseph's Institution, St Andrew's Boys School and the Methodist-run Anglo-Chinese School, all set up in the second half of the 19th century and partially supported by the government.

If you were Chinese, vernacular education amounted to free temple and clan association schools, all of which applied the traditional method of teaching Chinese classics by rote – and thus left most pupils who completed their studies

Rosalind Wong, daughter of the Chairman of the Malaya Tribune Company, on the Singapore end of the first London–Singapore telephone call.
1 December 1935
NAS 19980005826-0115

Chinese school for boys on
Amoy Street.
1905
NAS 19980005095-0096

barely able to muster enough Chinese characters to read more than basic texts. If you were Malay, you might attend one of a few government-aided free primary schools, though the instruction these provided was understood to be pretty deplorable – at least until a new government initiative in the 1880s sought their improvement and expansion. Needless to say, what schooling there existed in Singapore was primarily intended for boys. Apart from Christian missions that took in local orphaned and homeless girls, such as the Convent of the Holy Infant Jesus (established in 1854) and Anglican Zenana Mission School for Girls (founded in 1842, and later called St Margaret's Girls School), female education was notable by its absence.

Towards the end of the 19th century the situation changed, and for a number of reasons. First of all, the government of Singapore – the new Crown Colony – began to take education seriously as its public duty. Following the appointment of the Straits Settlements' first Inspector of Schools in 1872, Malay education was expanded so that by 1901 roughly a quarter of all Malay boys in Singapore under the age of 15 attended classes. Secondly, local businesses and the local colonial bureaucracy were by the 1890s in need of more locally educated English-literate clerks (much cheaper to employ than new appointees despatched from Britain). Thus, in the early 1900s, the government, having established an Education Code and introduced an Education Board, increased the number of schools that offered secondary education in English, as well as greatly increasing its expenditure on education overall.

Furthermore, local ethnic communities in Singapore started to take a more active role providing vernacular education for their younger generations. From the late 1880s, a new crop of Chinese, Tamil and Muslim-Malay institutions appeared, where instruction followed a 'modern' curriculum. For example, at the Madrasah Alsagoff on Jalan Sultan (founded in 1912) it was possible to learn English and Mathematics alongside Arabic and the Qur'an. Not far away, the Yin Sing School on Telok Ayer Street – the first Chinese school, it was said at the time, to be conducted on 'modern lines' – taught 'reading (with explanations), physical drill, drawing, geography, history, arithmetic and singing', and by 1922 had an enrolment of 20 girls alongside its 110 boys. Eventually, the number of pupils at non-English language schools in Singapore outnumbered those at English-language institutions. By 1939, of the 72,000 primary and secondary students, 27,000 attended English-language schools, 30,000 were at Chinese-language schools, 6,000 went to Malay-language schools and 1,000 were placed at Tamil-language schools.

Pupils who received an English-language education might afterwards begin a career as a clerk or a secretary in one of the city's large commercial houses, or in similar employment in government service. As the colonial administration grew it generated new boards, departments and committees to deal with everything from traffic to opium, meaning that there were more lower-ranking positions open to English-educated Asians. Some accomplished students even travelled overseas to complete their further studies, before they returned to Singapore to take up professional work, usually as lawyers, doctors, dentists, veterinarians, teachers and last, but not least, journalists. Such was the case with the respected Straits Chinese leaders Dr Lim Boon Keng and Song Ong Siang, both of whom graduated from Raffles Institution with 'Queen's Scholarships' which allowed them to study for university degrees in Britain. However, with few exceptions, higher positions in such professions, especially those associated with the colonial civil service, were reserved for Europeans. Just to make sure of this fact, in 1912 the British introduced an official 'colour bar' across their Empire which restricted non-Europeans from applying for senior public appointments. Career advancement for the English-educated Asian in Singapore was perpetually blocked by the fact that while he spoke, read and wrote the right language, his skin remained the wrong colour.

Nevertheless, English-educated students in Singapore still had the best prospects for a middle-class existence. For Chinese-educated students there existed opportunities in business, Chinese-language journalism or in teaching, but inevitably the best jobs in the city went to their English-educated counterparts. Though Chinese-educated school-leavers were in greater supply, they remained underappreciated. As we shall see later in this book, had better career prospects been available to them perhaps Singapore's history would have turned out quite different.

A problem for all Singapore's students – the Chinese-educated, the English-educated and those in Malay and Tamil schools – was that, except at a few outstanding institutions (such as those noted above), their so-called 'modern' schooling was extremely narrow. Writing his memoirs in the early 1940s, the

Syed Mohamed bin Ahmed Alsagoff, photographed in Ottoman regalia. Upon Syed Mohamed's demise in 1906, a trust fund was created in his name which made possible the establishment of Madrasah Alsagoff Al-Arabiah in 1912.

Late 19th century
Courtesy of Madrasah Alsagoff Al-Arabiah

BELOW: Song Ong Siang.
1900s
from Arnold Wright and H. A. Cartwright, *Twentieth Century Impressions of British Malaya*, 1908

educational philanthropist Tan Kah Kee observed that for decades government schools failed to teach subjects such as history, geography, chemistry and 'other academic subjects'; their textbooks, he wrote, 'only instructed a person how to be a government clerk, or a secretary'. Tan believed that American Methodists had shown the way forward from 1885 when they established (with the help of local Baba) the Anglo-Chinese Free School on Amoy Street as the first school in Singapore with a truly modern curriculum. However, the colonial government failed to follow this lead. At most government-aided schools, crucial subjects that might have enabled local students to better understand and participate in the modern transformation of the world they lived in continued to go untaught.

As a founder and administrator of Chinese-language schools in Singapore, Tan did his best to ensure that his own institutions provided technical and vocational training. He even donated money to English-language institutions to ensure that subjects such as chemistry and physics were made available. In the early 1930s, with the onset of the Great Depression, others joined his crusade. Faced by sudden unemployment, Asian clerks and secretaries in the city's commercial houses discovered that their liberal arts-style schooling barely equipped them for any other kind of work that did not involve scribbling. As a result, they too lobbied the government for modern education that was geared more towards vocational training.

But in typical fashion, the response of Singapore's colonial rulers was snail-like. True, they set up an official commission to look into the problem, but the commissioners' recommendations were yet to be acted on by the time the island fell to the Japanese in 1942. By that time, Singapore still had no university, even though universities had existed in major Indian port-cities since the 1860s (and in Hong Kong from 1911), and even though prominent Straits Chinese had been calling for a university in Singapore for over two decades. The single tertiary institution that the island did possess was the King Edward VII College of Medicine, originally established in 1905 through the munificence and activism of (who else?) the Straits Chinese. However, the government rebuffed subsequent attempts to convert Raffles College (established in 1928) into a university on the grounds that its educational standards were insufficient. Though Singapore's local philanthropists might have been ready and willing to sponsor tertiary education, they repeatedly came up against an intransigent colonial regime.

Tan Kah Kee: the father of modern Chinese education

Yet the education of Singapore was not merely about about such mundane material concerns as finding a job. From 1900, a change swept across the city's Chinese-language schools that spoke of a much wider intellectual transformation. Mandarin, or as it was called at the time 'Kuan Hua' (guanhua, meaning 'officials' language'), began to replace Chinese dialects as the main medium of instruction.

A movement was emerging within the Chinese community that would take hold of rich and poor alike and unite various dialect groups. It was a movement fuelled by revolutionary new ideas, and if the life of one man were to encapsulate them then that man would have to be Tan Kah Kee.

Born near the treaty port of Amoy (Xiamen) in the Fujian province of China, Tan came to Singapore in 1890 at the age of 16. At first he worked in his father's rice business, but when he was 29 it failed and he decided to strike out on his own. By the outbreak of World War I, he had built a massive commercial empire from rice trading, pineapple canning, real estate, saw mills and, most of all, rubber. By the 1920s, he was known across the world as the 'Henry Ford of Malaya'.

Tan was, by any standard, extremely wealthy. But just as interesting as the way he amassed his fortune was the way he chose to spend it. Quoting from what he said was a 'Western proverb', he once wrote, 'Money is like fertiliser; it is only useful when it is spread around.' He was referring not simply to the diversification of his business interests, but to the large amounts of cash he directed toward philanthropic ventures, especially toward modern education. Right up until World War II, he dedicated himself to establishing new Chinese-language schools in Singapore, including two Chinese girls' schools. His most famous effort was the Chinese High School (founded in 1919), the island's first Chinese secondary institution. Tan claimed in his memoirs that he had given educational institutions in both Southeast Asia and in China over 8 million Straits dollars – an amount which his descendants have subsequently considered to be a major understatement.

According to his principal biographer Yong Ching Fatt, Tan's generosity should be understood in terms of the conservative Confucian values of the Chinese society to which he belonged. These dictated that the pursuit of wealth

Tan Kah Kee.
1900s
from Arnold Wright and H. A. Cartwright, *Twentieth Century Impressions of British Malaya*, 1908

BELOW: Chong Hock Girls' School was established in 1915 by the Hokkien Huay Kuan, of which Tan Kah Kee was a leading member. The school was located beside Thian Hock Keng on Telok Ayer Street.
1930
NAS 20060000782-0002

was not in itself a worthy goal: what was earned must somehow be returned to society. Hard luck for any would-be Chinese millionaire – and yet there was a silver lining, for a wealthy man who fulfilled his social obligations would enhance his social standing. Yong argues that educational philanthropy would have thus appealed to Tan as a means to obtain a 'pre-eminent social status', with all the power and influence that might entail.

But this portrait tends to downplay what was truly modern and radical about Tan. For one thing, if 'pre-eminent social status' was really his heart's desire then he had a funny way of showing it. Compared with a previous generation of Chinese leaders in Singapore (who clearly revelled in their role as local mandarins and even wore fine Manchu robes to display this fact), Tan was famously frugal. Here was a new kind of *taukeh*: a man remembered to have 'given like a prince but to have lived like a pauper', who subsisted on a simple diet of rice, porridge and potatoes, and who carried the same old tatty briefcase and umbrella around with him for decades. To have told him to his face that his philanthropy was motivated by his desire for an increased social standing would undoubtedly have caused him grave offence.

In his memoirs, Tan comes across not so much an arch social-strategist, angling his way to the top through calculated acts of charity, but as a self-improvement enthusiast (he was largely self-taught) with a passion for education that bordered on an obsession. Explaining why he continued to fund various educational projects during the Great Depression (when his entire commercial empire was on the verge of bankruptcy) he wrote:

> supporting education was one social obligation that I would not shirk from. It was a cause I would devote myself to until the end … If my support of education was indeed going to lead to business failure, it would only affect me personally and would not in any way cause harm to society.

Tan's sense of obligation was magnified by the fact that he, like many modern Chinese of his time, held education and patriotism to be inseparable.* As the popular Chinese motto of the 1920s and 1930s went, 'Without Chinese education there can be no overseas Chinese.' Tan maintained his own links with his ancestral lands by spending as much time and effort on educational projects in China as in Singapore. In his home province of Fujian, he financed primary schools and, most famously, a national university at Amoy.

Ironically, though Tan was critical of Chinese students who neglected their studies to embrace nationalist politics, he himself became ever more immersed in them. At one point during the 1930s, he was in the unique position of single-handedly bankrolling the Guomindang (China's Nationalist Party) to the

Advertisement for Tan Kah Kee's products.
1920s
NAS 20060000781-0019

* Other Chinese businessmen in Singapore who also dedicated themselves to education with a similar patriotic fervour included Lim Nee Soon, Tan Lark Lye and Tan Kah Kee's own son-in-law, Lee Kong Chian.

amount of a third of its total finances. Then, during World War II, the Japanese placed him at the top of their 'most wanted' list in Singapore because of his anti-Japanese fund-raising activities, which he had launched following Japan's 1937 invasion of China. Tan fled Singapore and went into hiding in Java for the remainder of the war, following which he arrived at his most extraordinary decision yet. Disillusioned with the corruption of the Guomindang, the man who had been the very epitome of late-imperial capitalism underwent a political conversion and ended his days in China as a respected supporter of Mao Zedong's Communist Party! Whatever Tan's concerns for personal status, he was ultimately swept up by those same powerful forces – capitalism, nationalism and eventually communism – that competed for the minds of Singapore Chinese throughout much of the 20th century.

Divided loyalties: an afterword

Tan's journey through educational philanthropy to Chinese nationalist politics and ultimately communism forms one part of a much wider story to which we'll return shortly. For now, it's simply worth recounting two examples of what lay in store for students enrolled at modern Singapore schools. Both cases highlight that the city's classrooms – once intended merely to inculcate tradition and the basic language skills necessary for commerce – were emerging as the frontline in a series of intense ideological battles.

Less than ten years after the Anglo-Chinese Free School opened on Amoy Street, with a modern curriculum so admired by Tan Kah Kee, it was hit by scandal. In 1894, reports began to circulate that the schools' teachers were, as one contemporary put it, 'doing their best to instill in the minds of their innocent pupils the narrowness and peculiarities of modern occidental Christianity'. Apparently, this breached a promise that the school's authorities had made to their Baba supporters that they would refrain from religious proselytising. As a consequence of the scandal, several prominent Straits Chinese families pulled their sons out of the school.

The scandal also kicked off an extended public debate about sectarian education. In the *Daily Advertiser* newspaper, at that time the first English-language newspaper in Singapore run for Asians by Asians, correspondents discussed whether a religious education was better than none at all. The most interesting contribution came from a self-proclaimed 'non-sectarian' who wrote under the pen name 'Mecca'. 'Mecca' claimed that Straits Chinese boys at the Anglo-Chinese Free School were being encouraged to 'look down on their heathen parents' and were 'losing all respect for Chinese customs and rites'; while 'they may neither accept nor deny the Christian religion as imparted to them', they 'very often scoff at Christianity itself'. Superior yet indifferent, a new generation of English-educated youth in Singapore was emerging.

Lower primary Chinese
textbook featuring a song
in praise of the Chinese
nationalist (Guomindang) flag.
1941
Paper
H 18.2 x W 12.4 cm
NMS 1998-00526

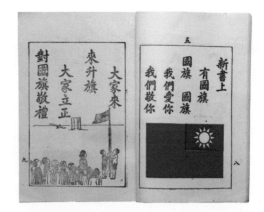

Leap ahead to the 1930s and we find ourselves in an altogether different world. In the city's modern Chinese schools, the issue of indoctrination, far from raising any qualms (let alone discussion), had become an accepted fact of scholastic life. From textbooks and other school publications we learn that Chinese elementary students were being taught to 'welcome local goods' and 'say no to foreign goods'; a message that was repeated verbatim at Tan Kah Kee's Chinese High School. Meanwhile, at the Cheng Fong School, students were left in no doubt as to why they were there: 'The purpose of education is to save the country; to save the country one must be educated.'

Finally, at all these schools, young Chinese were expected to love their flag – that is to say, the national flag of the Chinese Republic. As the 'Song of the Flag' in one school reader declared:

> Clouds hang high on a bright day,
> The sun shines in the East,
> Fresh blood covers the whole land in red
> Oh Sacred Flag, I see you fly spectacularly,
> You witnessed the success of many revolutionaries
> Oh Sacred Flag, I love your imposing grandeur,
> Expressing the righteousness and integrity of our nation,
> Oh Sacred Flag, I wish you would lead us,
> Lead us all in reforming the world

From religion to revolution: the great paradox of modern education in Singapore was that while it brought the city's inhabitants closer together – to the point where they spoke the same language, read the same textbooks and felt they belonged to the same nation – it also opened up tremendous social divides. All the city's schools, be they *madrasahs*, mission schools, government schools or vernacular schools, pulled their pupils toward alternative cultural allegiances. Singapore was an island on the move, no doubt. The direction in which it happened to be moving was far less obvious.

16. RAISING NATIONS

The ripple of modern ideas that began in Singapore's classrooms ended up as a wave that completely transformed the city's public life. In a matter of a few decades, Singapore was replete with societies, clubs, reading rooms, newspapers, magazines and printing presses. Many of these were devoted to pleasurable pursuits – art, literature, music and sports – but others became the setting for a more avid engagement with the key issues of the day. Where once formal debates and letters to the paper had been the preserve of Europeans, now a new generation of Asians began to discover these habits for themselves.

One subject that frequently vexed the minds of educated Asians in Singapore was nationalism: the idea that modern people ought to start thinking and start organising themselves – not as villagers or as provincials, nor as mere colonial subjects, but as citizens of distinct nations. In a place like Singapore, largely populated by sojourning migrants from diverse ethnic backgrounds, the idea of modern nationality raised a series of complex issues: Where did you locate this nation? Who constituted its 'nationals'? Did the term itself refer to a people, geography, culture, or a combination of all three? Finally, was it possible to make a single nation in Singapore and its environs out of so many apparently distinct nations?

From the 1890s, educated Asians in Singapore wrestled with these questions. In the process they discovered a political voice through which they eventually challenged the legitimacy of imperial rule. At first, however, the issue was not so much the making of a new nation at home, but rather how to respond to an ancestral nation – one that had decided to reach out beyond its borders and across the seas, and which now, suddenly, felt closer than ever.

Travel booklet containing sketches and information on tourist sites in Singapore.
1937
Paper
H 18.5 x W 25.2 x D 0.4 cm
NMS 2007-050819

The two faces of Dr Lim and his progressives

In 1900, the *Straits Times* reported an evening's entertainment held at the opulent home of Baba Tan Boon Liat. It was hosted by the Straits Chinese Philomathic Society (known in Mandarin as Hao Xue Hui) which had been founded a few years earlier 'for the regular study of English Literature, Western music and the Chinese language'. On this particular occasion, the Society, which numbered around 50 prominent Straits Chinese (including Dr Lim Boon Keng and Song Ong Siang), let the musical talents of its members take centre stage. Members of the Society played their violins and sang tunes such as the 'Jubilee Polka', before the evening concluded with a stirring rendition of 'God Save the Queen'.

However, the star performance of the night belonged to Mr Song Ong Joo, the brother of Song Ong Siang, who gave a 'particularly successful' impersonation of a 'negro minstrel'. This must have surprised many people in the audience – not least the European guests, who might have expected the entertainments of the Chinese Philomathic Society to have been, well, a little more Chinese. Or perhaps Song's transformation was not such a shock after all. By 1900, Straits Chinese in Singapore had proved themselves remarkably open in their cultural tastes and habits. Indeed, within their diverse social circles, a quick change of costume (literally and figuratively) was now a typical feature of Straits Chinese life.

This was especially the case when it came to their political activities. Unbeknown to the Europeans in the audience, in the very same year the Straits Chinese Philomathic Society put on its Victorian soiree it became a front organisation for the Bao Huang Hui – the 'Emperor Protection Society' of Chinese exile Kang Youwei that sought to restore the Guangxu Emperor to his throne. And with Mr Song Ong Joo wooing his audience as a black minstrel, what a front it turned out to be!

Postcard commemorating the 5th anniversary of the Cornwall Minstrels.
1909
Collection of Dr Cheah Jin Seng

Singapore. The Cornwall Minstrels — (straits chinese amateurs).

How had Lim Boon Keng and his violin-playing Baba associates got themselves involved in a Chinese dynastic conspiracy? The background to this story went as follows.

In 1895, imperial Qing China, ruled by Dowager Empress Cixi, faced a mounting crisis: a humiliating defeat at the hands of the Japanese was followed by loud calls for China's modernisation. These calls culminated in the 'Hundred Days' reform movement of 1898, led by the Confucian official Kang Youwei and his student Liang Qichao, and backed by the young Guangxu Emperor. In fact, to be absolutely precise the 'Hundred Days' reform movement lasted 104 days – at which point the Dowager Empress revoked the reform measures, placed the young Emperor under house arrest in the palace and began executing members of the reformist party. Faced by the prospect of 'death by a thousand cuts', Kang and Liang fled the country.

Before their flight, news of the reform movement in China had filtered through to Singapore. Records of Lim's Philomathic Society tell us that in 1897 he and other younger members felt that 'if reforms were ever to make headway, some decisive step ought at once to be taken so as to mark the difference between the progressive party and the conservatives'. The step Lim and his associates chose was dramatic: they cut off their 'queues', the long Manchu-style pigtails that had been customarily worn by Chinese men since the 17th century. In making such a visible break with tradition, well in advance of most other Chinese across the world, young Singapore Baba revealed how deeply they felt about reform, and how closely they identified with Kang and his reforming movement.

Their condemnation at the hands of older Baba who retained their queues created a split in the community. But already, Lim and his defiant 'progressive party' were mingling with exiled Chinese renegades. In February 1900, Kang arrived in Singapore at the invitation of Lim and Khoo Seok Wan, another Philomathic Society member and a prominent Hokkien Chinese poet. Members of the Society had already signed petitions and sent telegrams of protest to Beijing in support of Kang's reform movement. Now, with Kang in Singapore in person, they set about collecting funds for the young Emperor's rescue and the transformation of China into a constitutional monarchy. According to one source, $100,000 was raised through the Singapore branch of the Bao Huang Hui to fund Kang's failed 1901 uprising in the Chinese city of Hankou. By that time, the Philomathic Society (which now sometimes held its meetings at Khoo's shophouse on Boat Quay) had opened its doors to non-English speaking China-born participants and increased in size from 50 to around 200 members – mostly merchants, doctors, journalists and government servants.

It's easy to understand why China-born patriots attended these meetings; after all, the fate of their homeland lay in the balance. But the political allegiances of the Straits Chinese were far more complex. The same year Kang arrived in Singapore, Lim and other Baba established the Straits Chinese British Association, to assure the colonial government of their political loyalty and to secure their privileges as British subjects. Now these same 'King's Chinese', as they subsequently become known, were throwing their weight (and their money) into the politics of a motherland that several of them had never even visited. Their behaviour seemed inconsistent, to say the least: depending on which night you encountered them, you could either find Lim and his progressives plotting the downfall of the Dowager Empress or happily tapping along to the 'Jubilee Polka'.

For Lim, however, there was no inconsistency. His thoughts about the involvement of overseas Chinese in China are set down in the periodicals he established: the Chinese-language newspapers *Tian Nan Xin Bao* and *Ri Xin Bao*, and the *Straits Chinese Magazine*. His views in the latter journal (which sometimes featured essays on Chinese reform alongside odes to Queen Victoria) make for especially interesting reading since they were directed as his fellow Baba:

> And when the Straits-born Chinese with proper qualifications arrives in China he finds that he is the sort of individual destined by nature to reconcile the great Chinese Nation to the ways of the great world beyond China ... We are more cosmopolitan in our tastes and habits, and in China we can pull along in the same way as the Apostle Paul, a Greek unto the Greeks and a Gentile among Gentiles ... take your fair share of the heritage that belongs to the son of Han ... Moreover, as British subjects you must enjoy all the benefits that accrue from the spread of British influence which unfortunately has not been in evidence for some years in China.

With such pragmatic justifications, we can see why many Baba progressives stayed with the tide of Chinese nationalism even after 1901, when it moved away from Kang's reform movement toward the revolutionary ideas of Sun Yat Sen (the man who would eventually found the Chinese Republic).

Like Kang, Sun visited Singapore several times to muster support and funds for a series of anti-Qing uprisings. Though his initial reception by Singapore's Chinese leaders was not especially warm, certain members of Lim's 'progressive party' rallied to his cause. In particular, three wealthy young Baba, Tan Chor Nam, Lim Nee Soon and Teo Eng Hock, decided to plough their fortunes into setting up Singapore's first revolutionary newspapers and public reading rooms, dedicated to spreading Sun's ideas amongst the city's Chinese working classes – the rickshaw pullers, coolies, hawkers and prostitutes. During Sun's third visit to Singapore in 1906, Tan, Lim and Teo became the founding members of Sun's Revolutionary Alliance, the Tong Meng Hui, which met at Teo's family villa off Balestier Road. 'The motto of the Singapore Revolutionary Alliance,' Sun reportedly told them at their swearing-in ceremony, is to 'expel Tartars [the Manchu Qing], restore China, establish a Republic and equalise land rights'.

After Sun and his followers finally succeeded with their revolution in 1911 they founded the Chinese nationalist party, the Guomindang. In Singapore, Straits Chinese leaders formed a key part of the party's local membership, though

Straits Chinese Magazine.
June 1900

VOL. IV.—No. 14.] [JUNE, 1900.

THE Straits Chinese Magazine.

EDITORS.

Singapore { Lim Boon Keng, M.B., C.M. (Edin.)
Song Ong Siang, B.A., LL.B. (Cantab.)

改憚多則過

"If you have faults, do not fear to abandon them."
Confucius.

CONTENTS.

Singapore :
Printed for the Proprietors by SONG SECK KUM.
No. 114, Amoy Street.

Price 50 cents. Yearly Subscription, $1.50.
(*All Rights Reserved.*)

once more they probably joined up for a variety of reasons. Some would by now have become committed Chinese patriots; others may have still been following Lim's exhortation to reap their just material rewards as both British subjects and 'sons of Han'. Furthermore, it seems that many wealthy overseas Chinese had lost their faith in Kang after it became abundantly clear that he spent an overly large portion of their hard-earned cash on himself and his globe-trotting entourage. Sun presented a more radical solution to China's problems, yet in the end he was a leader of greater integrity, and ultimately a 'winner'.

But the 1911 Revolution presented the Straits Chinese with a dilemma. While China had been ruled by the foreign 'Tartars' (so Lim and friends called them), local-born Chinese patriots could justify their status as loyal British subjects since it afforded them protection from a regime that they did not recognise and sought to change. However, once this regime was removed and the Chinese Republic created, what did they do next: return to being merely interested onlookers, or commit themselves further as citizens of the new Chinese nation? In 1914, this second option became suddenly less attractive when Sun called for further revolutionary struggle to solve China's problems – a move that prompted Lim and other Baba members of Singapore's local Guomindang to walk out of the party in protest.

To remain a loyal British subject was no easy sinecure either. In 1906, Lim had resigned from Singapore's Municipal Council over what he later admitted was his frustration at institutionalised racism. Some years later, he told a public meeting called to protest against the colonial 'colour bar':

> Gentlemen, this is my native country. But I now realise that I must leave it. Because however able my posterity may be, they will never be allowed to be more than the most subordinate servants, clerks and so on, under men who think their white skins are the sole sign of born rulers and administrators.

Educated, patriotic Baba appeared caught between political chaos in China and colonial prejudice back at home. Some decided to leave the Straits to work in their ancestral homeland, others remained as 'loyal' British subjects; several tried their hands at both. From 1911 to 1912, Lim worked as medical advisor to the last Qing and then first republican governments of China before he returned to Singapore to once more lead the Straits Chinese. During World War I, he supported local fund-raising efforts for the Allied military effort and composed lectures and a pamphlet on the 'duty' of the Baba to the British Empire in its time of need. Yet the lure of China remained strong and in 1921 he returned there to take up the Presidency of Amoy University (established, as we saw, through the generosity of Tan Kah Kee). Over the next 16 years, until the Japanese invasion

Dr Sun Yat Sen (seated, fourth from left) with the founding members of the Singapore Tong Meng Hui. Front row: Teo Eng Hock (second from left), Tan Chor Nam (third from left), Lim Nee Soon (extreme right) and Yu Lieh (third from right).

1906
Lim Chong Hsien/NAS
19980005031-0048

of China forced him to return to Singapore once again, Lim laboured at running the university, attempting to groom a new generation that would lead the Chinese Republic into a brilliant future.

By contrast, Lim's old colleague Song Ong Siang arrived at a completely different position with respect to China. In 1923, he published his *One Hundred Years' History of the Chinese in Singapore*, which deliberately played up Straits Chinese loyalty to the British while carefully underplaying their involvement in overseas Chinese nationalism. Following the introduction of the Chinese nationality law in 1929 (which recognised all persons of the Chinese race as subjects of China, regardless of where they had been born), Song then approached the Chinese authorities to have himself de-nationalised. He hoped that by doing this he could assure the British of his and his community's complete allegiance, and so put paid to one of the colonial government's chief arguments for withholding from Straits Chinese senior positions in the civil service. But Song's attempt failed and for the rest of his life the educated Baba remained in a political no-man's land: neither able to divest himself of his Chinese nationality nor gain full recognition as a loyal imperial subject who stood on an equal footing with the European.

Such dilemmas of nationality confronted not just Straits Chinese; local Eurasians, Indians and even Malays shared in them too. But around the same time that Lim and Song assessed the extent of their patriotic feelings toward China, another voice emerged in Singapore that expressed a quite different brand of nationalism. This version had nothing to do with an ancestral homeland across the seas; rather, it was deeply rooted (to borrow Lim's own words) in 'native country'. The voice in question belonged to Mohammed Eunos Abdullah, a man often lauded as one of the founders of modern Malay nationalism.

Eunos Abdullah: an original 'son of the soil'

The son of a Sumatran merchant, Eunos was born in Singapore in 1876 and he became one of a select few Malay boys at that time to attend Raffles Institution. On completion of his studies he entered government service as a harbour master at Muar (in Johor), but then in 1907 he returned to Singapore to edit a new Malay-language newspaper called the *Utusan Melayu* [Malay Messenger]. This marked the start of his flourishing journalistic career and his arrival in public as a man of letters. It also signalled the beginning of a sea change in the leadership of Singapore's Muslim community.

Previously, Muslims in Singapore had been led by wealthy Arab businessmen (among them, the descendants of Syed Omar Aljunied) and by members of the Jawi Peranakan community – local-born Indian Muslims who, like the Baba Chinese, had intermarried with local Malays and adopted many of their customs. In the late 19th century, certain Jawi Peranakan started their own Malay

Mohammed Eunos Abdullah.
c. 1930
NAS 19980005059-0014

periodicals, debating clubs and printing presses, and through these they asserted their intellectual leadership of the island's Muslims. Eunos and his circle of fellow English-educated Malays thus represented a challenge – they were, in a sense, the 'new kids' on the Malay literati 'block'. Their victory over their Jawi Peranakan and Arab rivals came in 1924 when the colonial government appointed Eunos to serve as the first Malay and only Muslim representative on the Straits Settlements Legislative Council.

Entrusted with law-making in the colony, this body was at the time the closest approximation Singapore had to some kind of representative government, since its membership included nominated non-official council members drawn from local Asian communities. However, a parliament of the people it was not. The British governor retained a casting vote and power of assent or veto over any of the council's decisions. Compared to European representatives on the council, Asians remained in a small minority with no real power, although they could air their concerns and grievances.

Nor was the council chamber itself (located in the Empress Place Building which now houses the Asian Civilisations Museum) a particularly inspiring setting for dramatic debates between ruler and ruled. As council member Tan Cheng Lock complained, the chamber was an uncomfortably 'close room' where the sun's afternoon glare came through the windows and blinded the speaker's eyes. The acoustics were 'deplorably bad' and so 'utterly unsuitable for the distinct hearing of oratory' that members seated at the same table were frequently unable to hear what was being said, let alone 'friends and journalists' further back in the audience. On several occasions, the chamber felt woefully empty. Although there were officially over 20 Legislative Council members during the 1920s and 1930s, actual attendance was often just a fraction of that number.

Yet from time to time, the Legislative Council did spring to life. This was especially the case in June 1924 when Eunos Abdullah, in his first public appearance as a councillor, stood up to condemn the government's education policy for the several ways in which it disadvantaged Malay youth.

Eunos complained that the Malay boy in Singapore was the natural product of an 'imperfect education'. He started his English schooling later than his contemporaries, having spent his earlier education at a Malay school; he was forced to compete with other students who had more frequent contact with English speakers; and when he was eventually turfed out of school at the leaving age of 17, he found himself with a school certificate that did not 'carry him far'. 'Being unable to swim,' Eunos concluded, 'he sinks and is lost in the swelling sea of unemployment. Surely, sir, this is not a thing to be desired among the original sons of the soil?'

Five years later, the issue was still on the council's table and Eunos's language had become more forceful. On this occasion he asked the official representatives in the chamber whether they intended to introduce 'Elementary

English' into vernacular schools and whether they would raise the age limit for Malay boys studying at government English schools. The Colonial Secretary replied emphatically that the government was not prepared to do either. It would have been contrary to its 'considered policy', he explained, 'to afford to a community, the great majority of whose members find a congenial livelihood and independence in agricultural pursuits, more extended facilities for learning English which would be likely to have the effect of inducing them to abandon those pursuits'.

Eunos explained that his primary concern was to see that 'present and future generations of Malays are not left too far behind in the great struggle for existence'. If Malay boys, on leaving school, were 'not fit enough to secure appointments which are snatched by others bred and born outside the Colony' then the system of education was 'deplorably faulty':

> I am confident, Sir, that ways and means can be found and introduced
> which will enhance the prospects of boys of the soil and remove for
> ever the penalisation which ousts them from their own markets simply
> because they happen to be the imperfect products of an imperfect system
> of education.

Minutes for the Legislative Council's proceedings record that this, Eunos's final utterance of the session, was followed immediately by applause – presumably from his friends in the audience and from his fellow Asian councillors.

Unfortunately, British officialdom remained blinkered by late-Victorian racial typecasting. Colonial representatives continued in their belief Malays were better left to a 'congenial' existence of fishing and farming. Eunos's campaign over education did have some impact – it was at least partly responsible for the government's introduction in 1929 of Malay trade schools. Yet over the issue of English schooling for Malay boys, the British Empire would continue to have the final say for at least another two decades.

In retrospect, the greatest impact of Eunos's speeches was that they brought to the heart of the Straits Settlements' government a new language that had begun to colour opposition to British rule. In describing Malays as the 'original sons of the soil', Eunos invoked the concept known in Malay as *bumiputra* that would so profoundly shape Malaysian politics after World War II. Meanwhile, in his *Utusan Melayu* newspaper, he had begun to write of his fellow Malays as *bangsa*, the Malay word for 'race' or 'nation'. This might not seem such a radical development today, but at the time it represented a break with the traditional identification of Malays with their local sultans. The ideal of *bangsa* called on all Malays, from whichever lands they originated, to express a new allegiance to a united Malay nation. Historian Mark Emmanuel has noted that such an ideal sprang more easily out of a Singapore context for Eunos had 'no conception of a sultan'; he had always lived under a British administration.

Along with his journalism, Eunos kept himself occupied with social and political activism. In 1924, the same year he became a Legislative Councillor, he helped set up the Singapore Malay Union (Kesatuan Melayu Singapura), the first ever Malay political organisation. Three years later, he persuaded the government to grant him money and land for a Malay settlement. This settlement, known as Kampong Melayu and situated in the east of the island in an area that now bears Eunos's name, was intended as a place where Malays would be 'undisturbed' by the rising rents and costs of living in the town. Eunos never seems to have explicitly rejected colonial rule; throughout his lifetime he worked for his community's interests within the prevailing colonial system and remained a political moderate. Nonetheless, his demands on behalf of the *bumiputra* and his promotion of the ideal of a united *bangsa* were powerful new ideas that would live on in the language of Malay nationalism for many years to come.

Into the Malayan hinterland

If Eunos Abdullah had begun to imagine a united nation of Malays as 'original sons of the soil', where did that leave non-Malays, especially those who had been born and bred in cosmopolitan Singapore?

In the 19th century, local-born Asians had comprised a small minority within a much larger population of transients. However, by the 1930s their number had grown significantly. As more Chinese, Indians and Eurasians settled down to raise families, the only homeland their children grew up knowing was to be found

Malay Girls' School.
Late 19th – early 20th century
NAS 19980006558-0068

immediately around them. Significantly, as the years went by, representatives from these locally settled communities began increasingly to speak of this local homeland as 'Malaya', a country that stretched beyond Singapore's shores and beyond the other Straits Settlements into the heart of the Malay Peninsula.

How had this subtle, almost imperceptible change come about? In one sense, it had a lot to do with two basic items of the modern industrialised world: tin cans and motorcars.

Tin had been exported from Malaya since the time of Temasek, but the invention of the tin can in the 19th century transformed the metal into a globally sought-after commodity. The Malay states of Perak and Selangor witnessed a 'tin rush' in the 1880s, and by 1900 Malaya contributed half the world's tin supply. Singapore served as the metal's main conduit: tin was smelted on the island and exported from its port. The extraction of tin from the interior was also heavily financed by Singapore-based companies.

Likewise, the invention of the motorcar in the late 19th century also drew Singapore and Malaya closer together. Motorcars ran on pneumatic tyres that were best made from rubber, which had been introduced as a crop to the Malay Peninsula by the Director of Singapore's Botanic Gardens, 'Mad' Henry Ridley (nicknamed 'Mad' because of his unwavering faith that rubber trees could be grown commercially in the region). After several failures, Ridley discovered the best way to tap rubber trees and their successful cultivation began in 1895. By 1911, rubber plantations across the Peninsula accounted for over half a million hectares. As with tin, the capital to finance these operations came largely from Singapore-based enterprises and the island became the main point of rubber export and manufacture.

In an administrative sense, too, Singapore's ties with its hinterland strengthened. With tin being such a lucrative industry it was only a matter of time before the British tightened their grip on the Malay Peninsula at the expense of its local Sultans. The British moment came, after decades of negotiation and the occasional assassination, on 1 July 1896, the date that the Federation of the Protected Malay States (otherwise known as the Federated Malay States or FMS) was formally inaugurated, bringing Selangor, Perak, Negeri Sembilan and Pahang under effective British rule. The Straits Settlements still remained politically separate from the Federation, largely thanks to pressure from Singapore and Penang-based merchants who opposed any official efforts to bring them into a more formal union with the Malay States. Nonetheless, the Straits Settlements' governor was, between the wars, vested with dual authority as the Federation's High Commissioner; subsequent administrative reforms created pan-Malayan government departments whose headquarters were in Singapore (although the official capital of the Federation was Kuala Lumpur). Especially for bureaucrats, it became easier to think of Singapore, Melaka, Penang and the Malay States as all forming distinctive parts of a single British colony.

For local people, the crucial development that inspired conceptions of a Malayan homeland was undoubtedly the arrival of overland communications. Tin and rubber extraction stimulated the new colonial administration of the FMS to build railways, roads, bridges, telegraph lines and telephones that connected vast stretches of the Malayan interior. In particular, railways – which no less a personality than Mahatma Gandhi described as the best way to truly experience one's nation – came to traverse the Malay Peninsula, allowing a new generation to explore its length and breadth, right down to Singapore, which became joined by rail to the mainland through the construction of the Johor Causeway in 1923.

Such opportunities for travel across the colony were not available to everyone. Yet those local people who undertook such journeys were likely to play a vital role in expressing a new kind of patriotism. To echo the thoughts of the famous scholar Benedict Anderson, we can imagine our educated Asian itinerant – perhaps a lawyer, doctor or minor official – travelling to and from the outstations where he made his living, no doubt journeying up and down between the administrative capitals of Kuala Lumpur and Singapore as well. Perhaps on each journey he found educated travelling companions with whom he discovered he shared much in common. Perhaps, too, he eventually realised that his mother tongue, his race or his ancestral town or village, though all important, really didn't matter so much in the grander scheme of things – that at most they had started him on his journey, they had not fundamentally determined where he was headed or with whom he travelled. And finally, perhaps, we can imagine that at some point during our traveller's journeys, along routes laid down by his colonial superiors, the idea of a Malayan nation became sealed in his imagination – in all its breadth, colour and remarkable diversity.

We can imagine; but we also have our sources.

The Malaya Tribune

In 1914, the *Malaya Tribune*, a new English-language paper, appeared in Singapore, Penang and Melaka and across the Malay Peninsula. It had been founded by Lim Boon Keng with some other wealthy Straits Chinese, Indians, one Eurasian and one Jew. Unique for its time, the *Tribune*'s staff was mostly Asian and it also appeared in a Malay edition that was edited by Eunos Abdullah. Specifically, the *Tribune* set out to 'express the views and aspirations of the domiciled communities', those communities of Chinese, Malays, Indians, Europeans and Eurasians who had been born in Malaya or settled there and who now made it their home.

The *Tribune*'s release generated tremendous excitement. It was heralded immediately as the 'people's paper' and the 'voice of the Asiatics'. At half the price of its English-language rivals, the *Straits Times* and the *Singapore Free Press*, it soon outstripped them in circulation. By the late 1930s, it was the most-read

English daily in Singapore and the Peninsula, with sales upwards of 15,000 and, through reading clubs and libraries, an actual readership of perhaps twice that figure. Several of its pages were dedicated to Indian, Ceylonese and Chinese news (both from home and abroad), and it also featured a 'Muslim Affairs' column and a special 'Corner' devoted to women (of which more later).

Such varied subject matter corresponded to a broader social reality. With Malaya having received tens of thousands of Chinese and Indian workers destined for its tin mines and rubber plantations, the entire colony, including cosmopolitan Singapore, had become more diverse and complex. A key question on the minds of *Tribune* readers was where in this country, and in what ways, they now took their place in it.

In the early 1930s, discussions in the *Tribune* moved away from the rather abstract question of what a nation was (in terms of language, geography and race) to a debate closer to home. A Chinese lawyer from Singapore put it succinctly when he wrote: 'No matter what their nationality is they [the local-born] should be proud to be called Sons of Malaya as much as Sons of other Countries.' Other contributors took this idea up: the 'New Malayan Community' comprised those 'who had cast off all ties with their countries of origin'. Foreshadowing later political developments in the 1960s, one editorial claimed that 'Malayans' were those 'honest and industrious people who though not Malay by race themselves have no other home than Malaya, in whose development they and their fathers and grandfathers have played a valuable part'.

Inaugural issue of the *Malaya Tribune*.
1914

Of course, there were voices of dissent as well. Several of the *Tribune*'s Malay readers objected to what they felt was a clear challenge to their pre-eminent status as 'legitimate sons of the soil'. One correspondent wrote that 'Malaya is the land of the Malays and not of the fictitious and unrecognised race – Malayan.' Opposition was particularly fierce in the Malay-language press, sometimes inflamed by poor translations of English-language articles that suggested non-Malays were seeking to rob Malays of their national inheritance.

Yet amongst the greater part of the *Tribune*'s readers, the idea of a 'Malaya for Malayans' stuck. Through letters to the paper, English-educated Asians of all backgrounds came together to debate issues that they shared in common and speak to each other on an equal footing. Many discovered, in the process, that they had much in common, not least that their shared sense of belonging to the land in which they were settled was now stronger than any emotional attachment to their ancestral homelands. The pages of the *Tribune* revealed that a new local multicultural nation was being imagined, one that was more inclusive than even the paper's founders, Lim and Eunos, had envisaged.

The question was: would anyone else in Malaya take any notice? Readers of the *Tribune* belonged to a gentlemanly, clubby, heavily Europeanised world that was perhaps the most benign legacy of British colonialism. But as we've also begun to appreciate, public life in Singapore and Malaya did not end there; it encompassed newspapers, night schools, reading rooms and lectures where a much broader non-English speaking public participated. Here, away from the gentrified debates of the English-educated, the atmosphere was less patient, more impassioned and frequently charged with revolutionary fervour – a situation that, from the late 1920s, gravely concerned the British authorities.

But before we go further with this story it's crucial to address one other important change that swept across Singapore in the early 1900s, transforming its appearance, modernising it and even playing a fundamental role in its new feelings of Malayan patriotism. For without the social and economic arrival of women, Singapore would have hardly have become the place it is today.

Postcard depicting the Malaya pavilion at the British Empire Exhibition, Wembley.
1924
Collection of Dr Cheah Jin Seng

17. A WOMAN'S WORLD

In 1930, May Wong, the American-educated wife of a Chinese banker, arrived in Singapore. At once it struck her that 'there were hardly any women in town'. She asked why this was and was told that most women didn't go into the town. 'Don't they want to go into town to shop?' she enquired. 'All their husbands do their shopping for them', came the reply.

Shortly afterwards, May Wong was herself heading into town for lunch. Her options were either the GH Café on Battery Road (which, she was advised, was 'full of men … a businessmen's luncheon place') or the dining room of John Little's department store in Raffles Place (which served as an occasional rendezvous for European women). She chose the latter and was eating her lunch when she saw the waiter 'walking back and forth' looking at her. Finally, she asked him if he wanted something. The waiter explained that he never saw Chinese women come there to eat, let alone by themselves, so he assumed she was a visitor. 'Are you a circus performer?' he asked, since a Chinese circus had just recently arrived in the city. 'A what?' May Wong replied:

> I couldn't believe my ears when he said a circus performer – standing on a
> tight rope. 'I'm sorry I am not a circus performer!'

May Wong.
1920s
Gelatin print
H 24.1 x W 17.6 cm
Donated by Betty Chen
NMS 2006-01748

Samsui women at a
construction site.
1930s
Gelatin print
H 16 x W 11.2 cm
NMS XXXX-12917

The town – that is to say, the European town – had in this respect not really changed much since the early 19th century. It was still a bastion of male commercialism: a world populated by well-tailored bankers and earnest businessmen, who lived by a precious routine of morning newspapers, luncheon with cigars and then later drinks at the club, only occasionally interrupted by the appearance of their wives. However, as May Wong herself would discover, beyond John Little's and Raffles Place, Singapore was changing. Women were emerging out of their homes, and out of their homelands.

Sisterhoods: samsui women, amahs and the Poh Leung Kok

The presence of women in Singapore became more noticeable after 1900 and especially from around the year 1920. In the 19th century, women who lived on the island belonged either to the local Malay community or to wealthy European and Asian families. Otherwise, they were likely to be prostitutes and servants. In the new century, however, many more women, as the men had before them, left an increasingly war-torn, strife-ridden China for a new life in the *Nanyang*.

In the 1930s especially, female migrants surged into Singapore thanks to a confluence of factors. The Great Depression, which began in 1929, created global unemployment and left the Straits Settlements with a population of able-bodied but idle Chinese workers. In response, the colonial authorities implemented unprecedented legislation, enforcing quotas on the number of unskilled labourers from China and India who could enter the colony, as well as imposing landing fees on 'aliens', that is to say migrant Chinese and Indians.

However, the colonial authorities not only left female immigration unrestricted, they positively encouraged it, believing that more women in Singapore would mitigate the social evils that came with a predominantly bachelor population. Official thinking of the time held that a married populace was better behaved and more settled: a married man was less prone to secret societies, vice and gangsterism. So the colonial authorities encouraged more women to come.

Their timing could not have been better. China was itself reeling from the after-effects of the Depression, which had especially damaged the silk industry of the Pearl River Delta in Guangdong. This industry had called upon the labour of an entire generation of Cantonese women who in the process had proved that they could toil as hard as men and earn just as much. When trade slumped, many of these women, now accustomed to working outside the home to support their families, looked for employment abroad.

It's believed that between 1934 and 1938 close to 200,000 of these women arrived in Singapore and Malaya. One group that stood out from the throng were those women who hailed from Guangdong's Samsui county (in Mandarin *Sanshui*, literally 'three rivers'). The image that the Samsui women presented, with their

Amah walking down Holloway Lane, off Victoria Street. In the background is St Joseph's Church.
c. 1938
NAS 154407

starched navy-blue *samfoo*, home-made rubber sandals and unmistakable red headdress (folded into a rectangle into which they tucked their plaited hair), has become a nationalist archetype of pioneering Singapore womanhood.

In reality, the lives of Samsui women were arduous and monotonous. Frequently, they rose before dawn to work in tin mines, on rubber estates and, especially in Singapore, on construction sites. Their meals were sparse and a far cry from what is today offered in restaurants as 'Samsui cuisine': their actual diet was more likely to consist of rice, tofu and pickled vegetables, followed by a cheap cigarette. After a hard day's labour, they returned to cramped lodging houses in Chinatown, which they might share with up to 200 other people. Given the relentless physical pressures on the Samsui women, it's no wonder they earned a reputation for being rude, insular and unapproachable.

Another archetypal image of feminine Singapore, similarly immortalised in period photographs, presents a Chinese woman making her way down streets lined by shophouses. Her long hair is drawn into a tight plait or bun and she is dressed in a white *samfoo* top and baggy black satin trousers. She carries shopping baskets or pulls a trolley in tow, indicating that she has been, or is on her way, to market. She is the Cantonese *amah* or in Mandarin *ma jie* (literally mother-sister), the domestic servant employed by Singapore's wealthier households.

Comb for *sor hei* ceremony.

1930s
Wood
H 9.5 x W 4.5 x D 1.5 cm
Donated by Wong Peng Cheong
NMS XXXX-08646

In Cantonese, the *amah*'s job description was known as *yat geok tek*, literally 'to kick [i.e. take care of] everything with one leg'. Usually, this meant a range of household chores, from cooking and cleaning to looking after the children. Most *amahs* preferred to work in European households where the wages were higher; but here there were also potential difficulties of language and culture. Generally, this seems not to have affected the *amahs*' reputation for hard work and responsibility. The overall impression found in a series of colonial recollections is one of deep fondness. Many *amahs* lavished the same care and affection on their employees' children as they might have done on their own children (had they had any); their charges frequently reciprocated with similar feelings.

Like the Samsui women, the *amah* worked the entire day, typically from before dawn to after the evening meal was cleared away. Some lived in the homes of their employers; others returned to their lodging houses. These lodgings (like those of the Samsui women) were desperately crowded – to the point where *amahs* working for different employers might share a sleeping space and take turns to come back on different days. Yet what the lodging house lacked in space, it made up for as the centre of the *amahs*' social life. This was where they gathered to cook, eat, celebrate holidays and take care of each other, where they shared news and gossip or obtained new work. As former *amah* Leung Ah Hoe recalled: 'There were things to chat about and stories to listen to – how happy it was.'

Ironically, British hopes that female immigration would generate a more settled, married local population were disappointed by both the Samsui women and *amahs* deciding to foreswear marriage. Not all took a formal vow of celibacy, but those who did went through a ritual called *sor hei** in which they combed their hair into a bun to symbolise their new status as independent women who would not marry or have children. They also took an oath before the image of Guanyin, the Goddess of Mercy. The occasion might be celebrated with a new suit of clothes and an intimate celebratory meal with 'sisters' and relatives.

Implicit in this ceremony was a powerful rejection of traditional Chinese notions of family. *Amahs* and Samsui women were not un-filial; throughout their lives most sent money home to their families in China and stayed in contact through letters written for them by professional Chinese letter-writers. Nonetheless, to *sor hei* was to turn away from traditional family expectations and embrace a new freedom, in spite of the stark living conditions that it promised. Former *amah* Wong Ah Yoke explained that from the moment an *amah* did *sor hei*, her family had 'no control over her': 'Her mother also cannot control her. She can decide things for herself, after she has *sor hei*.'

Other female migrants to Singapore had no such freedoms. Trafficking in human beings included girls kidnapped at Chinese ports, or those who left their

---

* *sor hei* meant to literally 'comb hair'

Amah with a European child.
1920
NAS 19980005152-0026

homeland willingly in search of a new life abroad but who were then forced to pay for their passage by working as prostitutes or *mui tsai* (child domestic workers). May Wong encountered this seedier reality through her work as a committee member for the Poh Leung Kok [literally, in Cantonese, the Office to Protect Virtue], a home set up by the Chinese Protectorate for girls rescued from prostitution or slavery. Frequently, girls were brought in from the streets or directly off the ships that had carried them to Singapore. As May Wong recounts, in the 1930s the government employed a Mrs H. P. Winter to inspect the ships and identify the girls or women who were being held against their will:

> [She would] go down the ship and line up the girls. And as they walk out she would know which one was a real friend of a family or a real kinswoman. She could always tell those who were brought in to be sold or to be brought in to be a slave girl.

Not all the residents of the Poh Leung Kok were victims of the slave trade. Some had been given away or sold by their impoverished families into better-off households. Nonetheless, as one Australian missionary remembered, they were 'taken at a very tender age and trained as servants ... and get hard usage all their lives'.

Since rescued girls could not be sent out to school lest they be kidnapped or run away, the Poh Leung Kok put on classes in sewing and cooking, as well as basic lessons in Chinese and English. As May Wong observed, some girls resented what they considered being 'locked up', yet those who were well-behaved might eventually be allowed outside employment, typically as embroiderers, maids and cooks. In addition, some girls found new homes of their own: younger girls were adopted into new families, with government checks in place to ensure that they were not abused or exploited, while older girls might make a marriage-match.

To this end, the Poh Leung Kok itself doubled as a de facto marriage agency, especially for Chinese men who were unable to afford a bride sent out from the homeland or unwilling to go to all the trouble. After the would-be suitor passed a background check he could arrange to meet one of the girls of marriageable age, who had to give her consent before any marriage could be planned. Some girls decided to change their minds upon closer inspection of their potential bridegrooms; others had more than one suitor and chose not to make their decision themselves but to hand it over to the Poh Leung Kok's committee. Even then, the girls had the chance to opt out. According to the society's Malayan records, one girl who had three suitors, having left her choice to the decision of the committee, ultimately decided not to marry any of them.

Yet the reality across much of Singapore was that more and more women were married and were having children. Colonial records reveal that (even taking into account *amahs* and Samsui women) the majority of female migrants after 1900 were wives and mothers, many of whom arrived with their children in tow. Significantly, once these women migrated to Singapore and Malaya they stayed. More settlers were laying down roots and raising families than at any time in the island's history.

The education of Singapore girls

May Wong was herself a mother and a wife; but she also belonged to a new breed of women in Singapore. She was feisty and well-educated (she had studied at the University of California, Berkeley); she spoke both Mandarin and English (the latter with an attractive Californian drawl); she was world-savvy and possessed of an independent spirit. While her privileged upbringing made her unique in many respects, her modern attitudes and expectations were shared by a new generation of educated women in Singapore whose number and voice was growing.

Their modern education had begun in 1887, when an Australian Methodist missionary by the name of Sophia Blackmore opened the Methodist Girls' School in a shophouse on Short Street. Two and a half years later, Blackmore joined forces with the American Methodist Mission to target the Nonya daughters of the Straits Chinese and went door-to-door in Straits Chinese neighbourhoods in person to recruit new students. As she later recalled:

One mother would say, 'We do not want our girls to '*makan gaji*' (earn their livelihood). Another woman told me that if her daughter studied from the same book as her son, the girl would get all the learning out of it; there would be none for the boy, and he would be '*bodoh*' (stupid). The girl might be stupid – that did not matter, but the boy must be clever.

Certain Nonya were even suspicious that Blackmore might be a government spy sent to investigate household gambling (at that time, illegal). Others, once her identity as a missionary had been established, were more concerned with her unmarried status, given she was a woman already in her 30s. Such attitudes were typical of the cloistered, tradition-governed world that Blackmore and other modern educationalists sought to enter and overturn.

Impressed by their efforts, Straits Chinese progressives led a campaign for female education themselves. In 1899, Lim Boon Keng and Song Ong Siang established the Straits Chinese Girls' School (later called the Singapore Chinese Girls' School), to 'encourage and provide every facility for a suitable education for the Chinese girls ... under the direction and control of their own people'. 'Direction' and 'control' were the operative words here since such 'suitable' education had little to do with female empowerment – the objective was to make Straits Chinese girls into better wives and mothers. As an article in the *Straits Chinese Magazine* made clear:

> [The mother's] duty is to see that the children do not play the truant; to help them with their lessons so that they may not lag behind in the class; to instill into them the truths of morality and religion; and to inculcate the duty due to the family, to the State and to mankind. ... As a wife, if she is well educated, the husband will always find in her a delightful companion who is ever ready to give him her advice, persuasion or warning with intelligence and reason ...

Sophia Blackmore (seated, middle) with the students of Methodist Girls' School.
1915
NAS Z45337

Partly, the Straits Chinese Girls' School was founded because of the embarrassment felt by progressive young Baba at the public impression made by their womenfolk. While letters to the *Straits Times* characterised as 'reprehensible' the penchant many Nonya had for popular forms of gambling such as *chap-ji-ki* and *che-ki*, articles in the *Straits Chinese Magazine* castigated them for their general ignorance (even though the latter was largely a result of their domestic confinement). Typical of such criticism was the clearly exasperated outpouring of the colonial Director of Public Instruction in 1906:

> There is no more absolutely ignorant, prejudiced and superstitious class of people in the world than the Straits-born Chinese women. It is about hopeless to expect to be able really satisfactorily to educate the boys while their mothers remain stumbling blocks to real enlightenment.

Lim and Song's remedy for ignorance and superstition was a curriculum that included basic mathematics, reading and writing (in both English and Mandarin), as well as what we would today call 'domestic science': sewing, cooking, hygiene and childcare skills. Lim hoped that the educated Nonya would emerge from school having 'learnt the importance of cleanliness and the proper way to conduct herself in the different spheres of life she will eventually enter – as daughter-in-law, wife and mother'. Echoing the concern of the Director of Public Instruction, he also wanted students at the Straits Chinese Girls' School to raise enlightened Chinese sons who would ultimately (as we saw him exhort earlier) reap their rewards as both 'sons of Han' and British imperial subjects.

Not everyone in the Straits Chinese community was supportive of this new direction. Lim noted that 'with a few honourable exceptions' elder Baba refused to give their patronage to the Straits Chinese Girls' School, and that even the fathers and grandfathers of those girls already enrolled at the school adhered to the same 'conservative and unreasonably prejudiced policy'. Yet a generation later, the efforts of Lim, Song and other female educators had largely vanquished such conservatism. The Methodist Girls' School, the Singapore Chinese Girls' School and a host of other English and Chinese-language girls' schools were all flourishing. In 1935, Sophia Blackmore could affirm that the days when women 'were kept behind closed doors and only saw what was going on outside through a "peep hole"' had well and truly passed.

The 'modern girl' and her modern expectations

Of course, modern feminism in Singapore was still a long way off. The curriculum at most girls' schools was narrow and often (as we've seen) hopelessly domestic. Even if the instruction had been more vocational, job prospects for educated women, apart from in teaching and in nursing, were largely nonexistent. Nonetheless, just as with Singapore's male students, so too for those girls privileged enough to receive an education: modern classrooms opened doors to a world of new ideas.

What kind of ideas depended to a large extent on what type of school. At missionary-run English-language schools, modern ideas were likely to come wrapped up in Western garb and to appear more conservative relative to what was on offer at Chinese-medium schools, where the curriculum became more radical and nationalistic. The simple matter of sports attire provided a telling contrast. That girls in both educational streams received any physical education at all was something novel; yet the differences in their costumes spoke volumes. English-educated girls wore decorous skirts (usually long and pleated); Chinese-educated girls, in their more drill-obsessed schools (at least judging from period photographs) wore daring-for-the-time shorts – these girls, after all, were meant to be the prize physical specimens of a vigorous Chinese nation.

However, in other settings where young Singapore women consumed things modern a strong cultural divide was less in evidence. Films, for instance, provided a vital inspiration for the new styles and attitudes of many young people and appealed across a broad ethnic spectrum. An anecdote from the Anglican Zenana Mission School for Girls tells of a student who went to the local cinema and then turned up to class in sunglasses (much to the fury of her headmistress) having come to assume that this was what all modern young ladies wore. Yet this same story might well have been told of at any girls' school across

Girls of a hockey team,
conservatively attired.
1930
Singapore Girls' Sports Club/NAS
19980005133-0078

Singapore – except that at certain Chinese schools the girl's crime might have been compounded because she had brought Western goods onto the premises of the 'sacred' Chinese nation.

Most strikingly, contemporary discussions of women's issues in both Singapore's English and Chinese periodicals reveal shared concerns that united local women. During the 1920s and 1930s, a series of new Chinese journals in Singapore – echoing the May Fourth Movement that began in China in 1919 – debated female equality and campaigned for 'freedom of male-female social interaction'. Radical young couples even took out advertisements to publicise their unions as modern 'love-matches' not forced on them by their parents. In 1926, the Chinese poetess Li Yumei published an especially poignant plea to her mother to be considered more than just a piece of marriageable property. Her poem concluded:

> Mother, I am not a small dog,
> I am not your little treasure,
> Nor am I father's stash of wealth.
> Mother, I am a person
> I cannot be locked up
> I want to go do the work of a person

Especially in the 'Women's Corner' column of the *Malaya Tribune*, English-educated women repeated these demands for freedom to work, dress, fraternise and marry as they pleased. 'Should a wife obey her husband?' asked one contributor, 'I should expressly say "No".' Male correspondents to the paper also had their opinions on such matters. One announced: 'I would trust woman with absolute liberty. I would treat her as an equal, on a "fifty-fifty" basis, and as a comrade.' Another lamented 'the good old days where the maids were shy and simple, and when a girl could be distinguished from a man'.

These contributions make clear that when the modern girl in Singapore raised her voice she left an emphatic impression. European missionaries, Baba reformers and Chinese nationalist educationalists might have sought to mould her in their different ways; but once she seized hold of the learning they offered there was no certainty she would stick to the paths they had laid out for her. Emboldened by her education, the modern girl emerged from the city's classrooms intelligent, outspoken and demanding of attention. Or, as one grumpy correspondent told readers of the *Tribune*:

> She is rude in her manners and possesses an independent spirit which is
> improper to her, although such a spirit is essential to a man who is to make
> some success in the world. In the modern girl, found in cities, there is a
> lack of modesty and kindness that is usually expected of her. Instead of
> being controlled, she rules others.

Leading ladies: women at the 'Worlds'

The public presence of women in Singapore also re-shaped the island's entertainment scene. Women and their families provided a vital market for Singapore's nascent leisure industry; in turn, women frequently took centre stage, at the very heart of the city's new spectaculars.

The strongest evidence of this transformation was to be found at the 'Worlds' amusement parks. Opened by Chinese businessmen from the early 1920s, New World, Great World and Happy World were giant one-stop entertainment complexes that reached their heyday just before World War II. For a small entrance fee, as a local paper observed of New World, 'a *taukay* may entertain twenty friends to dinner in the "million dollar" private apartment of the expensive restaurants' while at the same time 'the humblest member of the working class may spend his very hard-earned fifty cents or more unostentatiously at the gaming booths, the open-air cinema or the lane-side hawker'. Couples took evening strolls past the rows of refreshment stalls; housewives browsed through the multitude of booths that sold new commodities at the 'exhibition' space

Musicians and dancers at the New World Malay Dance Hall.
c.1940
Gelatin print
H 23.5 x W 28.8 cm
NMS 1998-00219

213

(one popular item was the newfangled thermos flask); families crammed into the cinemas and onto the Ferris wheels and carousels; bachelors could go for a haircut or to one of several nightclubs.

But the most popular attractions were the diverse 'dramatic entertainments' on offer, which showed how cosmopolitan Singapore tastes were becoming. *Bangsawan* (Malay opera) proved as well-attended by a mixed audience as Cantonese opera, while the dance-hall bands of the cabarets played the latest swing tunes from America and Europe alongside *gewutuan* (Chinese revue) melodies. Naturally, the Worlds became a must-see destination for European visitors: Charlie Chaplin was reportedly 'fascinated' by the Malay and Chinese operas on offer when he visited, as was the British novelist and biographer Horace Bleackley.

Bleackley's account of his visit to New World in 1923 draws attention to the commanding allure of several performances which pushed women into the limelight. His evening commenced with a 'Javanese comedy' in which the tragic heroine, 'dressed in black gauze skirt and Turkish trousers', made a 'wonderful play with her arms, while her fingers, which were as flexible as reeds, vibrated like tiny serpents'. He then watched a 'Chinese drama' where the two leading ladies were made-up to look like 'wax dolls', wearing costumes of 'magnificent embroideries worked in gold and silken thread, glittering in all the colours of the rainbow'. In a Malay performance, a man 'dressed like Hamlet, but with a red fez, was having trouble in his harem'. A few scenes later, following a lengthy tête-à-tête which saw 'Hamlet's' favourite wife slimly avoid death by her husband's sword, rickshaws appeared on stage carrying two 'dusky women in Parisian frocks' in what was most likely a parody of local European ladies.

Women also took their places front of stage in the Worlds' more modern entertainments. The new genre of *gewutuan*, for instance, had originated in the dance halls of inter-war Shanghai before arriving in Singapore during the late 1930s. Similar to a variety show, a *gewutuan* performance featured musical numbers, dances, dramatic episodes and sometimes magic acts and acrobatic displays. The highlight of the evening was a drama which ran for and hour to an hour and a half, known either as *gewuju* (which featured music and dance) or *huaju* (spoken drama).

Typically, *gewutuan* performances were fantastic and sensational. Bai Yan and Ye Qing, a husband-and-wife duo who performed with *gewutuan* troupes in Singapore and Penang from the late 1930s, recalled the stir caused by their female members' costumes: 'dancing suits, short pants and brassieres'. Ye remembered her performance in a play called *Persian Nights*, 'a Middle Eastern, Arabian sort of performance' in which she wore a long headdress and shook her head around a lot. 'Showing the thigh was a common thing. We even had hula performances.' An especially provocative number was the *Dance of the Silver Goddess*, during which the lead dancer wore a swimsuit, while the rest of her body was covered in shimmering silver paint.

Bai Yan and Ye Qing in Russian costume.
1950s
Bai Yan/NAS 20060000786-0030

Gewuju and *huaju* might also feature content that was, according to Bai, 'quite forward' as well: 'You wouldn't believe some of the stories we performed – such as *Divorcing the Monk!* With a title like that you know it's strange.' Often written by contemporary Chinese playwrights, some of these dramas provided thinly veiled critiques of traditional male-female relationships. One play called *Little Husband* told the story of a wife who has an affair with a younger man while her husband goes out to gather crops. When she is found out, she introduces her lover to her spouse, claiming that if a man can have a concubine (a 'little wife') then why can't she have a 'little husband'. With such risqué, even subversive, plotlines, along with equally tantalising costumes, *gewutuan* performances became extremely popular. On a good night they might draw audiences in their thousands.

Naturally, sex was one of the Worlds' major appeals; yet before World War II, there seems to have been more titillation on offer than anything else. Bruce Lockhardt, the British journalist and spy, recalled returning to Singapore and visiting New World in 1936. When he passed through the park's main gates, he was greeted by 'alluring posters of Mae West' which revealed 'that *I'm No Angel* had been passed by the Singapore Board of Censors'. He then entered a dance hall, where:

> a crowd of dancers, mostly young Chinese, the men in white European clothes with black patent-leather dancing shoes, the girls in their semi-European dresses slit at the side, filled the dancing floor. Many of the dancers had their own partners. But when the dance was over I noticed a number of girls who left their partner as soon as the music stopped and went to join other girls in a kind of pen ...

These were the famous 'taxi girls' who could be hired for a single dance – the waltz, foxtrot, quickstep, tango and rhumba were à la mode – or 'booked' for an evening of several numbers. Their companionship did not come cheap: hiring a girl for an hour was more expensive than employing an *amah* for an entire month (though, presumably, ten times the fun). But while some girls might spend the night with their regular clients, they were not necessarily prostitutes. Before World War II, which brought with it an influx of rowdy soldiers, the Worlds' dance halls were patronised by couples, families or enthusiastic young men simply there to learn how to dance. Lockhart himself recorded that the 'decorum [...] was unimpeachable and could not have been criticised by even a Wee Free minister in a North of Scotland parish'.

The Worlds were places where, as the *Singapore Free Press* reported, 'can be found laughter and happiness, and the comedies – and tragedies – of life'. This was a modern drama in which women now took centre stage. It was also a drama, especially from the late 1920s – and not just at the Worlds but right across Singapore – where the script became dominated by a radical new politics.

18. CRACKS IN THE EMPIRE

For a Singaporean today – accustomed to a political life that, apart from informal discussions at the coffee shop, is mostly carried out through official government channels – a walk through their city during the inter-war years might have been an alien and confusing experience. Political debate was everywhere – not just in classrooms, in newspapers or in reading rooms, but *everywhere*.

This was a city in which a man could get up at the end of a film at the cinema to harangue the audience into buying Chinese rather than English cigarettes (since these, despite the damage they did to patriotic lungs, would ultimately help the motherland); a city where journalists joined their readers after work to discuss the latest political ideas and happenings; a city where an afternoon stroll through People's Park might bring you to a crowd gathered in front of an animated speaker, who, without prior police permission, might thrust into your hand a leaflet that read: 'Overseas revolutionaries rise up! Support the Northern Expedition.'

This, also, was a city where plays, songs and dances might lead you towards a more radical political consciousness. Yap Pheng Geck, an English-educated Straits Chinese, recalled how 'stirred' he was by the performances of the Wuhan Songsters with their 'patriotic songs about China and China's plight'. Such troupes had toured Singapore from the early 1900s, but following Japan's invasion of China in 1937 they became more conspicuously involved in anti-Japanese fund-raising efforts. In Yap's case, the Wuhan Songsters and the New China Dramatic Group, which dramatised Japanese atrocities in China, converted him

Singapore Overseas Chinese
Relief Fund committee and
volunteers.
1937
NAS 19980005839-0004

from someone once 'unconcerned' into a full-blooded defender of the motherland and a composer of Chinese nationalist verse.

The spirit of radicalism was not just confined to the Chinese population. For Malays, voices urging an immediate end to colonial rule began to be heard in the late 1930s (as we will see a little later). Meanwhile, for certain Indians in the city, such voices had emerged and gone to work several years earlier. So if, as some scholars believe, most people in Singapore were never intensely political in an ideological sense, then it was not for a want of trying. Through the activities of a small but vocal band of agitators, radical politics attempted to gain a foothold in the city's public spaces.

The Singapore Mutiny, 1915

According to a later press report, on the afternoon of 15 February 1915 a group of Europeans were 'out at the park near the golf links' enjoying 'splendid weather'. 'Without warning, there came, it seemed from a dozen places, rifle volleys and several people fell mortally wounded.'

The soldiers of the 5th Indian Light Infantry, stationed at the Alexandra barracks, had mutinied. Having murdered their European officers, they had fanned out in separate groups – some toward the Tanglin barracks, others toward Keppel Harbour and Pasir Panjang – shooting at any Europeans they came across. It was the second day of the Chinese New Year and several witnesses first assumed the sounds of shots to be firecrackers. When the violence ended, around 40 Europeans lay dead, both soldiers and civilians.

Since the Indian 5th was the only regular fighting unit on the island, the government relied on a scratch force of miscellaneous army personnel, police, volunteers and later troops sent by the Sultan of Johor, to put the mutiny down. Of crucial importance were the British, French, Russian and especially Japanese marines whose ships sailed into port in response to Singapore's distress signal. The killing lasted only a few days and the town was quickly secured, but it took weeks for all the mutineers to be caught and for the authorities to restore order to the island as a whole. In the meantime, European women and children were evacuated onto crowded steamers waiting in the harbour.

Coming in the midst of World War I, the Singapore Mutiny created a global sensation. The *New York Times* ran a full-page pictorial entitled 'Vivid Story of Singapore Mutiny – Little Has Leaked Out About the Uprising of Native Troops There Owing to the Censor, but There Was Brisk Fighting'. Earlier, another sensational report had claimed 'Headhunters Chase Singapore Rioters' – in reference to the Dayak trackers employed to flush mutineers out of the jungle. Since 'the headhunters are averse to bringing in their prisoners alive,' the paper went on, 'it is not known how much the number [of mutineers] has been reduced'.

5th Indian Light Infantry.
1915
Gelatin print
H 8.7 x W 13.8 cm
NMS 2007-00866-021

The punishment handed down to the mutiny's ringleaders made an equally forceful impression. Of the 201 Indian soldiers found guilty of participation in the uprising, 47 were sentenced to death by firing squad in the first public executions held in Singapore since the late 19th century. Outside the wall of Outram Prison, spectators, including European women and children, gathered in their thousands. As the crimes of the mutineers were read aloud in English, Malay and Chinese, some of the convicted men broke down: 'One man started to cry out and this affected the others. In a few minutes the line was swaying and praying and shouting.'

A few months earlier, European couples had been serenaded by the band of the Indian 5th during their Christmas Eve dinner and dance at the Sea View Hotel. It turned out to be the regiment's last public engagement in Singapore. Now, the triumphant band of the Singapore Volunteer Force marched through town, to broadcast news of the mutineers' execution.

How had such a tragedy come about? At one level, the Singapore Mutiny can be attributed to the internal problems of morale within the Indian 5th. Before the violence, the regiment was fractious and ill-disciplined, resentful of its superior officers and disgruntled over pay and promotions. Some soldiers had then been posted to guard German prisoners held at the Tanglin barracks, who included Uber Leutenant Lauterbach, a fat and raucous former merchant shipmaster who had worked in Singapore before the war and become a local celebrity. In his biography, Lauterbach claimed to have been the mutiny's prime

instigator, first by convincing his Indian guards that Germany was winning the war, then by persuading them to rise up, having planned with them the details of their insurrection.

Some soldiers of the Indian 5th were certainly influenced by Lauterbach, for as soon as the violence broke out a group of them set off to free the German prisoners. But the official enquiry that followed the mutiny uncovered a web of intrigue, rumour and outright sedition that extended much further. Before the uprising, a middle-aged Muslim coffee-shop owner by the name of Kassim Ali Mansoor had befriended soldiers of the Indian 5th and invited them to his rubber plantation. Kassim Ali Mansoor turned out to be an anti-imperialist revolutionary whom the British eventually hanged for treason. Another shadowy figure connected with the regiment was Nur Alam Shah, the charismatic imam at the Kampong Java mosque that certain soldiers of the Indian 5th attended. The Court of Enquiry heard that the imam had encouraged these soldiers to rise up, with the promise that German warships would sail to their aid.

In addition, both Kassim Ali Mansoor and Nur Alam Shah had links with the Ghadr party, an underground organisation from northern India dedicated to the British Empire's destruction. When World War I broke out, the Ghadr party joined forces with the German government and set about flooding Britain's Asian colonies with anti-imperialist literature. Plans were made for an Empire-wide uprising to break out simultaneously on 19 February 1915 in Indian garrisons from Bombay to Hong Kong.

Although this plot failed (most Indian garrisons remained loyal to the British), in Singapore Ghadr propaganda found an impressionable audience. As a predominantly Muslim regiment, the Indian 5th was especially affected by Turkey's entrance into the war on Germany's side. When its soldiers received news that they were to be shipped out from Singapore to Hong Kong, many believed that in truth they were being sent to Europe, more than likely to fight against their Muslim brothers. This was tantamount to bearing arms against their religion. Adding to these tensions, the Turkish Ottoman Sultan had declared a jihad against Britain and her allies, while Germany busily circulated propaganda that Kaiser Wilhelm II had converted to Islam and intended to marry the Sultan's grand-daughter.

On the eve of the Mutiny, the soldiers of the 5th appear to have been overwhelmed by such stories. Indeed, the Court of Enquiry subsequently found their 'gullibility and credulity' to be 'almost beyond belief'. Their anguished letters home – letters later retrieved, translated, and placed as evidence before the Court of Enquiry – remain some of the most poignant in Singapore's historical record. Many men clearly despaired for their lives and, having heard reports of the 'sometimes twenty thousand, sometimes one hundred thousand, and sometimes two hundred thousand men' that perished on the Western Front on a single day they instructed their brothers and their fellow villagers not to enlist. Some viewed

Commander of the Most
Excellent Order of the British
Empire (CBE) medal awarded
to Major-General Sir Dudley
Ridout for his role in the
suppression of the mutiny.
1915
Enamel, gold and silver
W 6.3 cm
NMS 2000-03669

their departure from Singapore in millenarian terms: 'Believe that the world has died. No one has been saved.' Another soldier confessed to his brother:

> When writing this neither mind nor hand is under control … What is this war? It is resurrection. That who goes there, there is no hope of his returning. It is God's punishment …

For others, the hopes of a Muslim victory raced through their minds. 'Please God that the religion of the Germans (Mohammedanism) may be promoted or raised on high,' wrote Fateh Mohammed to his father. To his mother, Shaikh Mohammed Ali confided:

> You do not be anxious about anything … Germany has become Mohammedan. His name has been given as Haji Mohammed William Kaiser German. And his daughter has been married to the eldest Prince of the Sultan of Turkey who is heir to the throne after the Sultan. Many German subjects and army have become Mohammedans. If God so wishes, it will be the increase of Mohammedan's faith …

While evidence heard at the Court of Enquiry generally confirmed that the regiment's decision to mutiny had been spontaneous, it brought to light the existence of a global network of anti-imperial extremists who had plotted insurrection, in some cases from over a thousand miles away. More than at any time previously, colonial officials in Singapore awoke to the struggle that had commenced for the hearts and minds of their subjects. A new era of surveillance and control dawned: enter René Onraet and the Special Branch.

The surveillance of Singapore

The colonial Special Branch of the Straits Settlements police force was not the kind of department that you simply waltzed into and introduced yourself; more likely, one of its officers would call to ensure that *you* came to see *them*. These officers worked mainly undercover, where they remained largely free from the constraints of normal police procedure. In public, the unit's directors, including its famous second director, the Englishman René Onraet, were introduced under alternative job titles to keep their work a secret.

Special Branch began operations in the Straits Settlements in 1919 and it remained an intimate, close-knit affair for several decades. Before World War II, its personnel consisted of no more than 50 officers (including just six 'Asiatic Inspectors'), concealed within an overall police force of around 4,000. Day to day, its work was much the same as that of any modern internal security agency: surveillance and tracking of political suspects; infiltration of seditious organisations; checking of mails; monitoring of illegal firearms, fake passports and foreigners; and, finally, exchange of political intelligence with other security

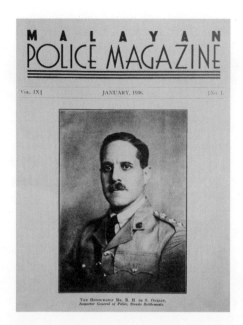

THE MALAYAN POLICE MAGAZINE

Vol. IX]   JANUARY, 1936.   [No. 1.

THE HONOURABLE MR. R. H. DE S. ONRAET,
Inspector General of Police, Straits Settlements.

René Onraet on the cover of
the *Malayan Police Magazine.*
January 1936
Courtesy of the Royal Malaysia
Police Museum

agencies across the then British Empire. Its officers' primary responsibility was to run networks of informants that extended to cover all Singapore's diverse ethnic groups and, in theory, the entire island.

But the unit also had additional roles that reveal how far the British imagined the threat of subversion in Singapore and Malaya to extend. Special Branch was handed the job of censoring publications and films – not just those offerings that were deemed anti-British or overtly nationalistic, but also those believed to encourage the working classes to become unruly. Furthermore, as Onraet himself recorded, the unit maintained surveillance on 'all racial, religious and social activities' since it was believed that any gathering of individuals might turn seditious. Given (as we saw earlier) that a simple gathering of Straits Chinese music and literature aficionados could be used to front an underground Chinese political organisation, this attitude was perhaps not so surprising.

Indeed, it was Chinese nationalists, rather than Indian revolutionaries, who provided the newly formed Special Branch with most of its work. In 1919, the May Fourth Movement erupted in China when students gathered in Beijing to protest against the Allied powers ceding Chinese territory to Japan at the Paris Peace Conference. Hokkien Chinese activists, preaching anti-Westernism and anti-imperialism, arrived in Singapore soon afterwards and mobilised local Chinese students in protests that ended in violence and looting directed at Japanese businesses. The British responded with the Education Ordinance of 1920, which required the registration of all schools, their teachers and managers. However, many Chinese schools simply ignored the Ordinance, forgoing government subsidies to continue with their often politically subversive curriculum.

The Chinese schools' defiance reflected a growing trend across the city. Soon after the Chinese Communist Party was founded in Shanghai in 1921, communist agitators arrived in Singapore. Here, they found a receptive audience at Chinese night schools run for the city's working classes and at newly formed labour organisations. In the same decade, Singapore witnessed a revival of the Guomindang, which had by this time become heavily penetrated by communists and communist sympathisers.

To Onraet, the number of Chinese migrants from Hainan Island who were swayed by leftist revolutionary ideology was especially striking. Onraet declared that the Hainanese (known in Singapore as 'Hailams') had an 'almost complete monopoly' over the 'Early Left Wing movement' in the Straits Settlements and he attributed this to a number of factors: Hailams usually worked as rubber plantation coolies, domestic servants or in the restaurant and lodging-house businesses, and were 'looked down on by the more cultured mainland Chinese'; Hailam women were banned from leaving their homeland, which made the men more likely to band together in subversive brotherhoods; lastly, the entire island of Hainan, as the Englishman put it bluntly, 'had gone Red'.

To halt this 'Red' menace, Special Branch had to innovate and improvise. As an example, the methods of policeman Alec Dixon might be viewed as either counter-subversion at its crude worst or unconventional best. As Singapore's 'first Immigration Officer' (as far as he knew), Dixon was responsible for weeding out 'bandits', 'gunmen' and political subversives from among the thousands of Chinese migrants who sought entry to the port every day. Quickly, he developed a novel, somewhat eccentric approach. As new arrivals filed past to be inspected by the quarantine doctor, Dixon reached out and felt their palms. 'Nine out of ten

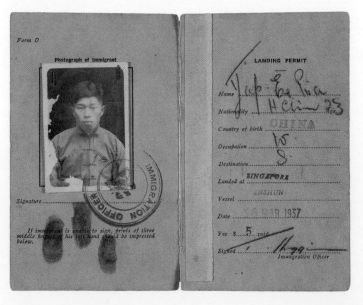

Landing permit of an
immigrant from China.
1937
Paper
H 14.7 x W 18.5 cm
Donated by Yap Hong Gek
NMS 2007-00036

of the hands I touched were hard and calloused. The tenth – a coolie with the soft hands of a cook – was invariably detained for further examination.'

Dixon admitted that his method made it difficult to single out criminal types who had led tough lives and were made of sturdier stuff. However, 'political agents, agitators and teachers were more easily detected, since very few of them were of the muscular coolie type'. Of these 'wandering intellectuals' most were Hailams, who were 'inclined to be foppish in their dress' and to wear what 'an English outfitter would describe as "gents' boaters"'. In these early days of character profiling, Dixon was not sure whether this was 'a coincidence or a psychological discovery'; he stated it 'merely as fact'.

Such weeding-out activities along with deportations and relentless police raids became the core weapons in Special Branch's counter-subversion armoury. Onraet, like most of his colleagues, believed that the threat of subversion was always external: 'no organisation existed within Malaya which was capable of producing such clever political propaganda. All of it came from China.' In 1927, two years into his job as Special Branch director, he faced a crisis that brought home just how explosive this threat could be.

The Kreta Ayer incident, 1927

In many ways, Kreta Ayer was the very heartbeat of Singapore's Chinatown. Thanks to its rowdy nightlife, the area was known in Hokkien as the *buay yeh tien* (the 'sky that is never dark'). Unsurprisingly, the police station here – situated right next to gambling houses, opium dens, as well as the brothels of Smith Street, Sago Street and Spring Street – was endlessly busy.

In 1919, Kreta Ayer was also the site of one of Singapore's first outbreaks of politically motivated violence. It was here that local anti-Japanese protests, inspired by China's May Fourth Movement, had turned ugly and led to clashes with the police that left two rioters dead. In 1927, history was to repeat itself.

This time around the trouble erupted on 12 March, the second anniversary of the death of Sun Yat Sen. To commemorate the founder of the Chinese Republic, various Chinese organisations had asked for permission to hold a public meeting at the Happy Valley amusement park on Anson Road. However, in the lead up to the 12th the authorities sensed that the ground was rumbling. Pamphlets distributed at People's Park called for revolutionary action; Dixon noted that the Hailams (always the authorities' chief political suspects) grew 'bolder every day', going so far as to hang Guomindang flags openly from the windows of their houses.

The authorities, after discussions with local Chinese leaders, gave permission for the observance, on the condition that there would be no speeches, parades or slogan-shouting. However, the Chinese community leaders involved in these negotiations kept the Hailams out of them; no doubt because they thought

Sun Yat Sen's portrait and his
last words encouraging others
to continue his work after
his death.
1925
Paper
H 83.2 x W 56 x D 2 cm
NMS 2000-03683

the Hailams would reject any restrictions placed on their activities in any case. Indeed, to avoid altercations, Hokkien and Teochew leaders went so far as to instruct Hailam representatives to assemble their contingents at the Happy Valley one and a half hours after the time given to everyone else for the observance to begin.

At noon on the 12th, all seemed well. A crowd of around 20,000 Chinese, drawn from clan, dialect and workers associations, as well from just about every Chinese school in the city, gathered at the Happy Valley and began to pay their respects peacefully, shuffling past an image of Sun Yat Sen that had been set up on a dais. Dixon recalled that the police presence was minimal, though Special Branch made its appearance in typical covert fashion. At least one English officer and a handful of Chinese inspectors attended, 'to mix freely with the crowd and to discover, if possible, what the Chinese public thought of communism'.

At 1.30 p.m., roughly 1,000 Hailams, a third of whom were school children, made their entrance, processing through the Happy Valley gates, perhaps only then to discover that the proceedings had started without them. From where he was seated on the verandah of his house, going through paperwork, Dixon witnessed 'several long processions of Hailam schoolchildren pass down the road on their way to the meeting'. The students, who ranged from 'gawky boys of fifteen to tots of five or six', played their drums and trumpets excitedly and looked as if they 'might have been setting out for a picnic'. Their teachers appeared 'grim and purposeful' and every one of them carried a Guomindang flag. Bringing up the rear marched a 'laughing' troop of 'Hailam houseboys and cooks'.

At that moment, Dixon's colleagues were mingling with the crowd at the Happy Valley and later they provided him with their description of what followed. Ignoring the ban on speeches, three Cantonese speakers got up to eulogise Sun Yat Sen. The Hailams 'began to show signs of impatience but there was no disorder until the fourth speaker, a wealthy Cantonese merchant … warned his countrymen against the silver-tongued preachers of communism'. 'One or two' Hailams then 'shouted derisively. Others cried, "Down with Imperialism".' When the Hailam teachers tried to make speeches, scuffles broke out. Other witnesses recorded that at this point several prominent Chinese leaders tried to intervene but were attacked and beaten. The Hailams then streamed out of the Happy Valley where they ran into policemen on traffic duty who attempted to stop them and were also attacked.

From his verandah, Dixon 'saw Hailams hurrying towards Kreta Ayer and heard shouting in the distance'. He immediately set off by car in the direction of the disturbance. As he approached the Kreta Ayer police station 'a mob of white-coated Chinese' came into view 'surging around the entrance', held back by four Indian constables with rifles. When his car stopped outside the station, the crowd retreated and stood in silence. As Dixon got out, he realised why:

> Torn banners, poles, and burst drums littered the road-way in front of the station. Five or six dead Chinese lay in the sun near the pile of debris. Two more were huddled in an abandoned rickshaw near the station door. Their stiff white clothes were spattered with blood, and they appeared to have been shot down only a minute before we arrived on the scene. Turning my head, I watched a wounded Hailam crawl away from those grim reminders of human folly.

The Public Inquest that was subsequently held into the Kreta Ayer incident heard contradictory reports as to exactly how the shooting had started. Witnesses agreed that when the procession reached the junction of South Bridge Road and Kreta Ayer Road, it was held up by a trolley-bus; however, the details of what happened next remain unclear. The trolley-bus driver seems to have at first halted his vehicle to let the procession pass, but then, apparently on the instructions of a European representative of the trolley-bus company riding behind, to have driven through the crowd, knocking down 'one or two of the small boys who were in the procession'. The crowd then attacked the trolley-bus and set upon the policemen who had arrived on the scene. The policemen retreated to the Kreta Ayer police station, where they fought to keep the crowd at bay with batons and bayonets. Finally, someone (it was never discovered who) gave the order to shoot: first a warning-volley over the heads of the crowd, next, a second volley, fired straight into their midst. The second volley killed five and injured eleven.

Newspaper headlines two days after the incident.
14 March 1927
The Straits Times

ATTACK ON POLICE STATION.

Chinese Mob Fired On In Singapore.

SIX KILLED : ELEVEN INJURED.

Sequel to Sun Yat Sen Celebrations.

Cipher Machine

The Special Branch's surveillance and espionage work required officers to communicate secret information, and they did so using encryption and decryption machines such as the Typex that substituted or transposed typed letters according to a predetermined code. With increasing concerns from weapons trafficking, pan-Islamist activities, Indian nationalist movements, the Guomindang and its front organisations, the Special Branch's operational and organisational capabilities grew steadily in the 1920s, with the British Typex first being used by the Malayan Police in 1937.

When an officer received a cipher text, he proceeded to decrypt the message by setting the rotors of the Typex machine to the correct configuration and by typing the cipher text. The typed cipher text and the resulting deciphered text appeared simultaneously on the paper tape. The Typex was able to print at a rate of 50 words per minute. This was an improvement over the German Enigma machines which showed the text by means of letter glow lamps that had to be recorded by the operator's assistant. The Typex also had improved security features over the Enigma, but it was significantly larger, requiring two strong men to carry it.

During World War II, the Combined Cipher Machine (CMM) was developed for inter-Allied communications between Britain and America and was used in the Royal Navy from November 1943. This cipher machine is an example of a Typex that has been modified to be used with the CMM.

An ex-Royal Navy serviceman recalls: 'During World War II, I used the Typex many times and yes it had changeable rotors. Our instructions were to destroy the machine if it was in danger of falling into enemy hands. A heavy mallet was supplied with the machine. When Singapore fell to the Japanese all the rotors from the machine at the signal station were packed into a bag and taken to the evacuating ship. The machine itself was thrown from the top of a fourth storey building (easier than using a hammer) but on examination all it had was a slight dent so it was ditched in the harbour.'

The Typex continued to be used until the early 1970s by the British armed forces as well as in Commonwealth countries such as Canada, New Zealand, Malaya and Singapore.

Typex Mk 23 Cipher Machine
1940s
Courtesy of the Royal Malaysia
Police Museum

The Kreta Ayer incident had two startling effects. First, it triggered an extended period of political unrest such as Singapore had never previously experienced. Dixon recalled that at once handbills appeared in Chinatown giving lurid accounts of the killings and calling on the 'Workers of the World' to unite. (Some featured illustrations of the police shooting down unarmed Chinese outside a 'Cubist' impression of a police station, and one, printed entirely in red, 'showed a colossal trolley-bus bearing down on a group of Chinese schoolchildren'.) Moreover, in the aftermath of the shootings, criticism of the government within the Chinese community was widespread, even from conservative Chinese newspapers and clan and dialect associations, some of which, in their condemnation of the death of the 'Kreta Ayer Martyrs', began to sympathise openly with the Hailam radicals. Enrolments also increased at Chinese night schools and at other political organisations that the British deemed seditious. On 24 March, the Hailams called for a public boycott of trolley-buses and threatened to manhandle anyone who attempted to board them. Attacks on trolley-buses in Chinatown led to more riots, which the police met with blasts from fire hoses and baton charges. At the end of March, the *Straits Times* could report that People's Park appeared 'like a war scene' – such was the heavy police presence.

But at the same time, the Kreta Ayer incident transformed the fortunes of the very unit tasked to pre-empt and suppress such disturbances. Onraet recalled that before the shootings, and despite police warnings, no one in authority took communist subversion 'seriously'. Soon after the incident, the police were promised better pay and buildings, more equipment, improved training facilities and 'sufficient money for secret service'. As Dixon recalled, coverage in the press began discussing the menace of communism 'in such weighty and funereal language that every official of the Colony saw himself as a participant in world-shaking events'.

The police also launched what Dixon termed 'an orgy of raiding': night schools were shut down, printing presses and cyclostyles were confiscated, handbills and posters were seized 'by the dozen' and their contents translated by a police Chinese interpreter forced to work around the clock. Hailams 'of all ages' were rounded up and interrogated, detained and deported. In 1931, four years after the Kreta Ayer incident, police raids peaked at an all time high of 174 (close to one raid every two days); four years later, they had quieted down to on average just one raid per month, a sign that the threat of subversion was beginning to ease.

By that time, not only had the Special Branch put an end to Singapore's first-ever bombing campaign (linked to a strike by Chinese shoemakers in April 1928), but it had practically smashed the Malayan Communist Party (MCP) to pieces. When Onraet later described police operations as having merely kept the strength of the Party 'in check', he was being modest. By the outbreak of World War II, the MCP head, a Vietnamese Chinese by the name of Lai Teck (of whom much more

'The Complete works of Sun Yat Sen'
1927
Paper
H 18.3 x W 13 cm
NMS 2006-00220

Webley .38 police revolver.
1940s
Metal
L 19.5 x W 13.0 cm
Donated by the
Singapore Police Force
NMS 1997-00560

later) was in fact a British agent. It seemed that whenever angry comrades met, Special Branch was there, literally looking over their shoulders.

If Special Branch had one blind spot during the 1930s then it was the threat posed by Japan. Onraet was well aware of Japan's political ambitions in Malaya and Singapore, and in 1934, in one of his last actions as Special Branch head, he redirected its resources to counter Japanese espionage. However, Japanese agents were harder to uncover than radical Chinese leftists, as their mission in Southeast Asia was not to subvert and destabilise but to spy and report back to Tokyo. A Japanese agent in Singapore was more than likely a respectable middle-class professional, someone who treated international espionage as an extra-curricular duty demanded of all loyal subjects by their Emperor.

To combat Japanese espionage, Special Branch continued to rely on its weeding-out operations immediately when a suspect entered port. Journalist Fuji Tatsuki, known to his European colleagues as 'Johnny' Fuji, was one such suspect who arrived in Singapore in April 1939. However, though Fuji was believed to have been a spy, he was never actually caught. In his account of his Singapore sojourn, he recounted how the moment he got off the boat an immigration official greeted him by name and whisked him off for an interview with Special Branch officers that lasted 'more than an hour'. Fuji said little and he was allowed to go free. Inwardly, however, his first impression of Singapore had been revealing and prophetic:

> Finally, I caught a glimpse of the white buildings glinting in the sun. Singapore lay quietly asleep. How characteristic of Britain's fortress this was, I thought to myself.

Change and continuity: a little Indian coda

In the 1930s, Singapore, as it had in the late 19th century, continued to exhibit two faces. On the one hand, it was complacent. Europeans, as newcomers such as Fuji wryly noted, could still enjoy the regattas, the races and the gin fizzes served at the Raffles, while remaining blissfully unaware of anything or anybody else. Yet, at the same time, new forces such as nationalism and communism had emerged and re-ignited the struggle for control of the streets. Both revolutionaries and colonial officials could feel that they were now at the centre of 'world-shaking events'.

The island's split personality was evident in other ways as well. The city, although it had grown considerably, remained surrounded by great tracts of green belt. If you followed one of those arterial roads that led out of the town, such as Bukit Timah Road or Serangoon Road, you soon came to *kampongs* and plantations, swamps, jungle and mangroves. From here Singapore drew its water, vegetables, dairy produce and meat, precious things that continued to sustain the hordes of urban-dwellers packed densely together only a few miles away.

Similarly, while some people experienced Singapore's modern times as a radical upheaval, the lives of many others were marked by continuity. The Great Depression of 1929 afflicted Singapore as it did most parts of the world, but the economy recovered and merchants, traders and moneylenders continued to do business, often in the same traditional manner they had followed for generations. New migrants (mostly female) continued to stream in, as they had done in decades past; yet despite all the nationalist rhetoric that came to punctuate the atmosphere, most stayed loyal to the British – or rather, they did not let politics get in the way of their attempts to earn a living.

By the late 1930s, such a sense of continuity (in spite of upheaval) would probably have been no more evident than if you took a stroll through the city's Indian quarters. As you turned down Serangoon Road, what had been a road flanked by cattle pens, vegetable gardens and swamps was fast evolving into the modern commercial and residential area of 'Little India'. New residences,

R. M. V. Supramanium, a prominent member of the Chettiar community.
1920s
S. Subbiah Lakshmanan/NAS
20050000647-0039

mainly shophouse-style dormitories but also suburban bungalows, were rising; marshy land was being drained to build more streets; and new temples and churches were appearing. Out went the cattle pens and the abattoirs (finally banned within the city limits by a Municipal Ordinance in 1936). In came the astrologers, goldsmiths, *sari* and textile retailers, garland-makers, sundry shops and eating houses.

But walk back to Upper Cross Street in Chinatown, or Chulia and Market streets, near Raffles Place, and you'd discover 'Old Little India'. These were the streets where Indians had first settled in Singapore and where Indian shopkeepers, watchmen, as well as lawyers, bankers and other professionals continued to live and do business.

Especially in Market Street you might come across the Chettiars – the South Indian money-lenders who proved so vital to greasing the wheels of the inter-war colonial economy. To enter their *kittangi*, the shophouse which served as both their business and their lodging place, would transport you into an austere and self-sufficient world steeped in unaltered routine. Here, gambling was outlawed, as were clandestine meetings with women, and all residents had to be inside by 9 p.m. when the front door was locked. Meals were provided by a cook brought over from India and often a *dhoby* (laundry-man) was employed to do the Chettiar's laundry.

Such an existence insulated the Chettiars from the outside world. In their money-lending businesses, Chettiars only hired Chettiars, they did not mix much with other Indians and they certainly didn't marry outside of their caste. Their wives stayed in India, seeing their husbands roughly once every three years (the

An ox-drawn ceremonial cart being led down a street during Thaipusam, a Hindu festival important to the Chettiars.
1930s
NMS Z45623

duration of most Chettiar contracts), and from the age of ten their sons might also be sent overseas, to join the *kittangi* and learn their family trade.

There were certain hints of change. Some younger Chettiars in Singapore eschewed the practice of shaving their heads and instead adopted fashionable 'English' haircuts. Sometimes, they even dressed in modern Western clothes. By the early 1930s the community had also formed its own Chettiar Chamber of Commerce, following a trend set down by its European and Chinese competitors. But generally, Chettiars guarded their traditions zealously. In the mornings they laid out their mats in rows on either side of the *kittangi* and waited for their customers or went through their accounts. Beside them they placed their *peti*, the portable wooden box that contained all the necessary instruments of the money-lending business. Behind them stood their *pettagam*, the large teak cupboards where they kept their records and personal effects. On the walls above hung images of their patron Hindu deities and perhaps a photograph of their company's founder.

In the afternoons, they went out to track down their repayments. Sometimes, when it was payday for the civil service, they lined up outside the government offices at Empress Place and waited for their civil-servant clients to appear so as to immediately collect on their loans. However, by evening the Chettiars would return to their *kittangi*, pack away their boxes, eat, perhaps play a game of *carom* and then lay out their mats to sleep where they had worked. It was a life of almost monastic ritual and simplicity.

And of course most Chettiars, like the Indian community as a whole, remained loyal to the British. Despite the Singapore Mutiny (after which Special Branch registered every Indian resident in Singapore), and despite the rise of Mahatma Gandhi in the 1920s and the surge of Indian anti-colonial feeling, and despite the immigration restrictions of the early 1930s (which directly affected male Indian migrants to Singapore) – the Chettiars did not leave their *kittangi* in search of political change. Whatever their inward thoughts about colonialism, their businesses continued as normal.

The daily lives of Chettiars in Singapore reveal a deeper truth about history. For some people, especially those who had a keen sense of their political destiny, the upheaval of the inter-war era must have felt like a relentless juggernaut, sweeping them ever forward toward an inevitable crisis or dénouement. For others, the period wasn't experienced in that way at all. For the Chettiars, *amahs* and Samsui women (to name just a few), history chugged along like the steady old steamers that had first brought them to the Straits. Sometimes the engine coughed and spluttered, yet these jolts were not in the end more than minor interruptions and the journey continued. But then, occasionally, a sudden storm swept up. At those times, even for people who had led lives relatively insulated from historical change, routine and continuity dissolved and the world turned upside down.

World War II was one of those times.

FORTRESS

December 1941 –
February 1942

THE RT. HON. WINSTON S. CHURCHILL

For Freedom

19. THE SHOCK OF WAR

> The Japanese began a landing in British territory in northern Malaya at about 6 o'clock – that's 1 a.m. local time – yesterday, and they were immediately engaged by our troops, who were there, waiting for them.

The British Prime Minister Winston Churchill made this announcement during a national radio broadcast on 8 December 1941. 'When we think of the insane ambition and insatiable appetite which have caused this vast, melancholy extension of the war,' he went on, 'we can only feel that Hitler's madness has infected the Japanese minds and that the root of the evil and its branch must be extirpated together.' Three days later, he told Parliament: 'It would indeed bring shame upon our generation if we did not teach them [Japan and Germany] a lesson which will not be forgotten in the records for thousands of years.'

Yet it was the British who were about to receive the lesson. Within 70 days of the Japanese landing in Malaya, Singapore would fall in one of Britain's worst and most embarrassing military defeats.

It goes without saying that Churchill and his government never imagined such a disaster. Even after news of the first Japanese attacks filtered through to Whitehall, British newspapers rehearsed decade-old claims that 'Fortress Singapore' was 'impregnable', a 'bastion of British might', 'a new, bigger and better Gibraltar, one of the most formidable concatenations of naval, military and strategic power ever put together anywhere'. Singapore had its naval base, its coastal guns and its new aerodromes; superior air and naval power would drive the Japanese back, if not the three divisions of British Imperial troops (two Indian, one Australian) deployed on the Peninsula.

But for a clue as to why Singapore did fall, Churchill's private reaction to the Japanese attacks is illuminating. On the night when Emperor Hirohito's war machine rolled across the border into British territory, the British Prime Minister was more concerned with a 'supreme world event ... of so startling a nature as to make even those who were near the centre gasp'. This event was Japan's attack on Pearl Harbor, which abruptly brought the United States into the war and, so Churchill believed, immediately turned the conflict in Europe in the Allies' favour. The news thrilled him so much that he later described himself 'saturated and satiated with emotion and sensation':

> England would live; Britain would live; the Commonwealth of Nations and the Empire would live ... No doubt it would take a long time. I expected terrible forfeits in the East; but all this would be merely a passing phase. United we would subdue everybody else in the world.

Churchill went to bed that night and slept (as he put it) 'the sleep of the saved and thankful'.

PREVIOUS PAGE:
Arrival of Australian troops at Singapore.
1941
SLV H98.103/869

Cover detail of *Soldier's Guide to the Japanese Army* issued by the United States War Department depicting a Japanese serviceman.
1940s
Paper
H 13.0 x W 19.8 cm
NMS 2000-00842

ABOVE: Winston Churchill.
1940s
Paper
H 15.2 x W 10.1 cm
NMS 1995-03632-012

Meanwhile, Singapore awoke to the sudden reality of its entrance into World War II. The island would soon confront its fate as one of those 'terrible forfeits in the East' that Churchill had predicted. But far from being a 'passing phase', the experience would transform the consciousness of an entire generation.

Yap Pheng Geck: the bombing of Singapore

Early morning, 8 December: as people slept, the first Japanese bombs fell on Seletar and Tengah airfields, Chinatown and Raffles Place.

Yap Pheng Geck (whom we met briefly in the previous chapter) was patrolling Raffles Place with a fellow officer of the Straits Chinese Volunteers. When the first bombs exploded he rushed back to his command base in the basement of the nearby Ocean Building and telephoned his battalion headquarters. 'A bomb just dropped here', he said. The voice at the other end of the line told him he was talking nonsense. 'Didn't you hear it?' Yap continued. 'Yes, yes, yes,' came the reply, 'but it may be a firing practice somewhere.'

'There was panic among the town-folks', wrote Yap in his memoirs. 'The lights in town were ablaze' and the whole city 'as bright as a fairyland'. No one had bothered to follow air-raid precautions. 'It was near Christmas time and we were told that nothing could be done, and not even the sirens were sounded.' Later it transpired that the head of the Air Raid Precaution Unit had taken the evening off to go to the cinema.

After the smoke cleared, the extent of the damage could be assessed. Japanese bombs had left great craters on the Padang and blown out the windows of

A family mourns the death of a child who became a victim of Japanese bombardment.
1940s
Hulton Archive/Getty

Robinson's department store in Raffles Place. But the worst-hit area was Chinatown, where the largest number of civilians lost their lives. Overall, 61 civilians and military personnel were killed that first night.

Yap recorded that Corporal Raymond Lee, a Volunteer in his company, 'had the dubious honour of being the very first casualty of the Japanese attack on Singapore and was accorded a military funeral'. He had been stationed outside the Chartered Bank and was 'killed on the spot by the very first bomb that dropped'.

Tsuji Masanobu: the Kota Bahru landings

Roughly two hours earlier, the Japanese had launched their assault on Kota Bahru, a coastal town in the northeast of Malaya. Defending the town and its nearby aerodrome were the Indian soldiers of the 8th Brigade, 9th Indian Division, manning a triple line of pillboxes, machine guns and barbed-wire entanglements between the town and the beach. According to Japanese eyewitness accounts, this small stretch of coastline witnessed some of the most intense fighting of the whole Malaya campaign.

The Japanese Chief of Staff Colonel Tsuji Masanobu recorded that the landing commenced with an intense bombardment from the invasion fleet. Immediately, Indian gunners in their pillboxes reacted violently with 'such heavy fire that our men lying on the beach, half in and half out of the water, could not raise their heads'. Supported by fire from the Kota Bahru shore battery, Allied planes swept in and attacked Japanese transports out at sea, causing several ships to catch fire and at least one to sink. As the Japanese launches drifted on the water's surface they were shot through by hails of bullets.

But the Japanese infantry made it ashore. In a darkness punctuated by lurid explosions and tracer fire, the first wave of assault troops formed a line on the beach. 'There,' wrote Tsuji, 'as daylight came,'

> it became impossible to move under the heavy enemy fire at point-blank range. Officers and men instinctively dug with their hands into the sand and hid their heads in the hollows. Then they burrowed until their shoulders, and eventually their whole bodies, were under cover.

Using their steel helmets, the men then dug their way forward like 'moles', piling the sand up in front of them. They now were 'so close to the enemy that they could throw hand grenades into the loopholes in the pillboxes'. Once through the wire, one man 'covered a loophole with his body and a group of the moles sprang to their feet in a spurt of sand and rushed into the enemy's fortified position':

> Hand grenades flew and bayonets flashed and amid the sound of war cries and the calls of distress, in a cloud of black smoke the enemy's front line was captured.

British officers discussing manoeuvres. Second from left is Major General Arthur E. Percival, who in April 1941 would be appointed General Officer Commanding (Malaya). Third from left is Air Chief Marshall Sir Robert Brooke-Popham, Commander-in-Chief of the British Far East Command until December 1941.

January 1941
Time & Life Pictures/Getty

The Japanese landings were a shock and yet they were hardly unexpected. The British had drawn up a secret plan to meet the threat of an attack on Malaya called 'Operation MATADOR', which involved the rapid deployment of troops to head off a seaborne invasion at its most likely landing-points (the points the Japanese in fact used: Singora and Pattani in southern Thailand, as well as Kota Bahru in Malaya). However, any chance of success required immediate, decisive action from British High Command.

Such action never came. After the war, Lieutenant General Arthur Percival, Britain's General Officer Commanding (GOC) in Malaya, wrote: 'The latest time at which MATADOR could have been ordered with any possible prospect of success was when the Japanese convoys were first sighted on 6 December.' But at that time Percival's superiors still hoped that a conflict might be avoided through diplomatic efforts. As would repeatedly become evident over the next three months, war was something for which Singapore and Malaya were never really prepared.

Denis Russell-Roberts: defeat in the air

For Captain Denis Russell-Roberts, 'Dawn on the 8th ushered in the blackest Monday of all time.' His radio told him that Singapore had been bombed during the hours of darkness; the announcer then went on to say that some Japanese bombs had contained gas. The Englishman's wife Ruth and his 11-month-old baby Lynette were both in the city. 'Only ten days earlier Ruth had written to inform me that though she herself had been issued with a gas mask, such things for babies simply weren't available.'

Russell-Roberts was attached to the 5/11 Sikh Regiment, deployed around the coastal town of Kuantan (about 150 miles south of Kota Bahru). His orders were to

British Hawker Hurricane
fighter, depicted on a card.
20th century
Paper
H 10.1 x W 15.2 cm
NMS 1995-03632-026

" HURRICANE " FIGHTERS
RULE THE SKIES

The powerful, fast " Hurricane " fighter
is one of Britain's answers to German
claims of air superiority. It is famous
as both a day and night fighter.

For Freedom

defend the town's strategically important aerodrome 'to the last man and the last
round'. Throughout the day, further signals came 'crowding in' over his radio: at
Kota Bahru the Japanese assault force had fought its way ashore and annihilated
the Indian battalion defending the beaches; more Japanese troopships had been
spotted in the China Sea; across northern Malaya, British airfields had been
'raked with fire'. Then came some additional 'shattering news': Pearl Harbor had
been attacked from the air and the American Pacific Fleet destroyed. 'Only one
scrap of comfort – a denial that Jap bombs on Singapore had contained gas.'

Adding to the gloom that day, the heavens opened up and the monsoon rain
came down, drenching everyone to the skin. At dawn the following morning, a
squadron of Australian Hudson bombers flew off from the aerodrome to intercept
further Japanese transport ships lying off Kota Bahru. They were no match for
the Japanese Zero fighters: five Hudsons were shot down; according to Russell-
Roberts the pilots that made it back looked 'badly shaken'. Later the same
morning, Japanese aircraft attacked Kuantan and for one and a half hours the
aerodrome was bombed and strafed with machine-gun fire.

Following this attack, the Royal Air Force (RAF) Station Commander at
Kuantan received new orders that any aircraft still operational were to return to
Singapore. The greater part of the aerodrome was to be destroyed, leaving just
one runway for Allied use. Russell-Roberts and his men were instructed to stay
behind, to defend a prized asset that their air force would no longer use, merely
to prevent it from falling to the enemy:

> So much for that damned aerodrome we were required to defend to the last
> round and the last man, and which cost the British taxpayer a pretty penny
> to build … Even at this stage the Royal Air Force had practically ceased to
> exist as an effective Service. Although we didn't realise it at the time, the
> Army in Malaya was to fight this war virtually alone.

The sinking of the Repulse and the Prince of Wales

Back in Singapore, the general mood was complacent, over-confident, even disbelieving. On receiving news of the Japanese landings, Governor Shenton Thomas rang up Lieutenant General Percival at 1 a.m. and allegedly told him: 'I suppose you'll shove the little men off.' The city's local newspapers repeated the claim that the island was impregnable. 'Everybody said, "Oh don't worry, Singapore is very well protected,"' remembered schoolteacher Elizabeth Choy. 'And when the bombs dropped, we wouldn't believe it; and some of them said, "Yes, we saw so many dead people and all that." Still we wouldn't believe it.'

Many people assumed that the war would be fought far from Singapore shores. Lee Kip Lin, then a student, recalled:

> The first reaction was that the British Navy would sail out of Singapore and smash the Japanese invading Kota Bahru. And the Americans would of course come and give us a helping hand. And it would be all over soon.

The arrival of the British warships the *Repulse* and the *Prince of Wales* a few days before the invasion had reassured many. On the afternoon of the 8th, both these vessels left Singapore's naval base to intercept the Japanese invasion fleet. But though they were escorted by destroyers, they had received no promise of air cover from the RAF. Force Z, as it was known, would have to rely entirely on stealth.

After just one day at sea, Force Z was sighted by a Japanese submarine and by Japanese aircraft, and forced to turn around and return to base. Force Z probably would have made it, had it not received what later turned out to be a false report of further Japanese landings at Kuantan. Force Z now changed course to intercept the phantom invasion force. On 10 December, just after 11 a.m., Japanese bombers spotted the British warships and swooped down in attack formation.

HMS *Repulse* leaving
Singapore.
December 1941
IWM 119634

Japanese Air Force Pennant belonging to Captain Kameo Sonokawa, Flight Leader in the Genzan Air Corps, 22nd Air Flotilla. The pennant is believed to bear the signatures of some of the pilots who took part in the attack on Force Z.

1941
Cloth
H 79.5 x W 67 cm
NMS 2006-01680

Japanese war correspondents described the ensuing battle in vivid, almost ecstatic terms. One bomb hit the *Repulse* 'beautifully' amidships and caused 'an eruption of brown fire'; next, in went the torpedo bombers, flying low over the water as they delivered their deadly ordnance, following which, several 'colossal columns of water' rose beside both battleships 'showing that we were hitting the mark'. Meanwhile, the anti-aircraft guns of the *Prince of Wales* sent up a 'yellow powder smoke' that filled the sky, the falling projectiles creating a 'lurid spray as if sand was being hurled across the surface of the sea'.

Having discharged their payloads, the torpedo bombers flew back over both ships and raked them with machine-gun fire. As one plane made its pass, 'the sailors of the *Repulse* collapsed on deck before the hail of tracer bullets'; the marines on board 'covered their faces with hands as if to escape the sweeping fire'. 'Shrouded in black smoke', the *Repulse* listed heavily to one side. At the same time, the *Prince of Wales* 'came almost to a standstill'. Another pass from the torpedo bombers resulted in further hits. The *Repulse* and the *Prince of Wales* were now 'bewildered battleships, which were trying to escape'.

The American war correspondent Cecil Brown was on board the *Repulse* as it began to go down. At first there was 'no alarm, no confusion, no panic', he wrote: 'The coolness of everyone' was 'incredible'. He could see the 'torpedo-smashed' *Prince of Wales* ahead, 'low in the water, half shrouded in smoke' as Japanese bombers winged around it 'like vultures'. Those few enemy planes that were shot down appeared as 'bright splotches of burning orange on the blue South China Sea'.

The chaos came moments later. Recalling the scene, Brown wrote in the present tense, as if the details were still before him:

> Men are tossing overboard rafts, lifebelts, benches, pieces of wood, anything that will float … Men are jumping into the sea from the four or five defence control towers that segment the main mast like a series

of ledges. One man misses his distance, dives, hits the side of the *Repulse*, breaks every bone in his body and crumples into the sea like a sack of wet cement. Another misses his direction and dives from one of the towers straight down the smokestack … Twelve Royal Marines run back too far, jump into the water and are sucked into the propeller.

Then it is Brown's turn to jump, a drop of 20 feet. He has 'no vision of what is ahead', no 'concrete thought of how to save himself'. He looks across at the *Wales* and finds it hard to believe that 'these two beautiful, powerful ships are going down. But they are.' He half turns to look back at the 'crazy-angled deck' of his own ship. A padre – 'unconcerned by the fact that the *Repulse* is going down at any moment' – is administering the last rites to a gunner who is dying beside his gun.

Brown jumps and the 'water is warm; it is not water, but thick oil'.

Fifty feet from the ship, 'hardly swimming at all now', he sees the bow of the *Repulse* swing up into the air 'like a church steeple':

> Its red underplates stand out as stark and as gruesome as the blood on the faces of the men around me. Then the tug and draw of the suction of 32,000 tons of steel sliding to the bottom hits me. Something powerful, almost irresistible, snaps at my feet … But I am more fortunate than some others. They are closer to the ships. They are sucked back.

The *Repulse* had vanished beneath the waves in a matter of minutes; the *Prince of Wales* took closer to an hour. For Churchill, the loss of both ships was one of the most devastating events of the entire conflict.

Crew members of the sinking HMS *Prince of Wales* escaping into life boats off the east coast of Malaysia.
December 1941
AWM P02018.055

20. THE MALAYA CAMPAIGN

The advance of the Japanese 25th Army through Malaya was fast and relentless. The soldiers came on foot, packed deep in trucks and, most famously, on bicycles. They raced through the interior, fording rivers and rebuilding bridges along what Churchill and his advisors seemed to forget was one of the British Empire's best inland road systems. They detoured through the jungle, took to the sea in collapsible boats, outflanked their enemy and encircled him; infiltrated behind his lines, cut his communications, donned his uniforms, shouted orders in his language and exploded firecrackers to his rear, sowing panic and confusion. It was what historians have labelled a 'bicycle blitzkrieg'. But the Japanese also had tanks, which their enemy sorely lacked. Moreover, they had superior airpower, military intelligence, battle experience and (especially) leadership.

Most important of all, the Japanese had a cause.

A war for Asia and for oil

As they had sailed towards battle, each Japanese soldier had been given a confidential booklet entitled *Read This Alone – And the War Can Be Won*. It began by explaining the reasons for the coming conflict. For centuries, 'tens of millions of Asian inhabitants' had suffered 'constant exploitation and persecution' at the hands of white men who had 'sailed into the Far East as if it were theirs by natural right'. British, Americans, French and Dutch had all 'terrorised and subjugated the culturally backward natives' who now looked upon Japan as their saviour:

Japanese soldiers crossing a river on an improvised bridge.
December 1941
NAS 20080000052-0007

[T]hey trust and honour the Japanese; and deep in their heart they are hoping that, with the help of the Japanese people, they may themselves achieve national independence and happiness.

Shortly, each Japanese soldier would see, 'only too clearly', what oppression by the white man meant, from the 'imposing, splendid buildings' that looked down from the 'summits of mountains or hills onto the tiny thatched huts of natives', to the money that had been 'squeezed from the blood of Asians' to maintain Malaya's 'small white minorities in their luxurious mode of life', or to disappear 'to the respective home-countries'.

Japan's war was thus a race war, a war of liberation against white oppression led by the one truly independent and modern nation in Asia. At the same time, it was an imperial war: a struggle for natural resources such as rubber, tin and especially oil. The 25th Army's confidential booklet made this second point explicit:

> Britain and America, controlling the greater part of the world's oil and having far more than they can use for their own purposes, have nevertheless forbidden the export of oil to Japan, which is desperately short of it. More than that, they even obstruct Japan from buying oil in South Asia.

If Japan could 'master' this territory not only would she 'gain control of the oil and steel which she needs for herself', but she would 'strike at America where it hurts most'.

Obviously, such war aims – on the one hand to master, and on the other hand to liberate, Asia – were essentially contradictory. However, most Japanese soldiers, if their memoirs and war diaries are anything to go by, seem not to have greatly minded. These sources reveal instead the ordinary Japanese soldier's collective belief, both in Japan's military hierarchy, with their Emperor Hirohito at its top, and in the complete righteousness of their expansionist cause.

By comparison, British and Commonwealth efforts to defend Malaya were bedevilled by an increasing lack of collective belief. As the Japanese drive for Singapore threw the Allies into a seven-week retreat, those further down the military chain of command increasingly doubted the abilities of those

Propaganda artwork on matchboxes distributed by the Japanese in Malaya, Singapore and the Dutch East Indies proclaims the imminent defeat of Britain and the United States by Japanese forces.

1940s
Paper
H 5.6 x W 3.6 cm
H 5.4 x W 3.5 cm
NMS 2000-08416, 2000-08425

above them. Ordinary soldiers began to wonder why they had been sent to a country that was not their own, to fight for a people largely alien to them, under commanders who seemed to have no idea what they were doing. The psychological gulf between senior officers and front-line troops grew wider by the day. Pitched deep in the Malayan mud, lashed by the monsoon rain, Britain's imperial canopy – under which it was claimed millions of loyal subjects had sought shelter – began to collapse.

Yamashita and his driving charge

The commander of the invading 25th Japanese Army was Lieutenant General Yamashita Tomoyuki, the son of a country doctor who had risen to become one of the ablest soldiers in the Japanese Empire. According to Colonel Tsuji, Yamashita bore 'a dignified physique and commanding mien' but was 'quite unlike a hero in appearance'. Certainly, the Chinese in Malaya believed Yamashita was no hero, but rather a war criminal and a plunderer – the man responsible for the massacre of innocent civilians and for making off with a legendary horde of treasure looted from Chinese temples, associations and households.

Yet the 'Tiger of Malaya', as Yamashita became known, had another side. He was a sometime student of calligraphy, had a penchant for making florid public speeches and he was even, on occasion, a poet. On the eve of the invasion, Yamashita penned the following lines:

> The arrow leaves the bow
> It carries my spirit towards the enemy
> With me are one hundred souls
> My people of the East.

With typical flourish, Yamashita told his soldiers mustered on Hainan Island and awaiting their departure for Malaya that they'd be in Singapore by New Year's Day. Once they had landed, he ordered them commence *kiromoni sakuren* – a 'driving charge'.

It began from Singora and Pattani in southern Thailand, where the bulk of the Japanese army had come ashore early morning on the 8th, as well as from the Japanese beachhead at Kota Bahru. Between these forces and Singapore stood approximately 120,000 Allied soldiers, comprising the Indian 9th and 11th Divisions, British regiments and, further south in Johor, the Australian Imperial Forces (AIF). Though the invaders and the defenders were closely matched in number, the Japanese held the advantage of experience. Around two-thirds of Yamashita's front-line troops were battle-hardened veterans who had fought in Manchuria and China. By comparison, most Indian troops had been recruited only after the outbreak of war and had never even seen a tank, let alone combat action; indeed, many were still teenagers.

Lieutenant General Yamashita Tomoyuki.

1940s
Chin Kah Chong/NAS
19980005836-0013

As Yamashita's army crossed the Thai border, they became at once aware of their opponents' shortcomings. Colonel Tsuji dismissed the fighting capabilities of the British and Commonwealth troops with thinly disguised contempt. Having witnessed the enemy 'escaping without even making a sortie … menaced by a small section with a handful of guns', he convinced Yamashita to authorise an audacious – one might say reckless – dash for glory. With just 500 men, two dozen tanks and a few light guns, Tsuji led the charge into Malaya fully a day ahead of the main Japanese landing force at Singora.

The key battle occurred on 11 and 12 December at Jitra, a small village just north of the town of Alor Star and its aerodrome. Here, 14,000 Indian troops, supported by 50 field and 36 anti-tank guns, had dug in to defend positions they had prepared for months. When Tsuji launched his attack at night he seems to have been unaware of the enemy's strength or the extent of their fortifications. However, at Jitra fortune favoured the ignorant as well as the brave. By daylight it was clear that the audacity of Tsuji's lighting strike had sent the defenders into disarray. Though the Japanese vanguard eventually needed reinforcements from the main invasion force to push their advantage home, the 'much bragged about Jitra line' was 'penetrated in about 15 hours by barely 500 men'.

The Allied collapse at Jitra set the pattern for the rest of the Malaya campaign. In 55 days, Tsuji boasted, the 25th Army raced from one end of the Peninsula to

Painting by a Malayan eyewitness to the Malaya campaign.
1942
Pencil drawing and watercolour
H 24.1 x W 34.2 cm
NMS 2000-01454

the other. On average, they 'fought two battles, repaired four or five bridges, and advanced 20 kilometres' every day. A captured enemy brigade commander, when asked why his men surrendered so quickly, is said to have complained:

> When we defend the coast, you come from the dense jungle. When we defend the land, you come from the sea. Is it not war for enemies to face each other? This is not war. There will be no other way than retreat, I assure you.

The story reveals the British and Commonwealth forces' predicament. This was war, but a war of a kind that they were completely ill-equipped for: a war in which the invaders turned the confusion of battle to their advantage, while the defenders, more often than not, simply melted away before them.

Mohan Singh's dark night of the soul

For Captain Mohan Singh, a Sikh officer with the 14th Punjab regiment in Malaya, the defeat at Jitra proved to be the major turning point in his life. In his memoirs, he recalled that on 11 December the heavy Japanese bombardment and the withdrawal of his regiment's transport sowed immediate confusion. 'Some men jumped into the trucks to escape. I lost my temper, got hold of a stick and used it freely on any man trying to slip away.' Shortly afterwards, Japanese tanks burst into sight, tanks which Mohan Singh's British commanding officer had assured him the enemy did not possess. The defenders dispersed 'in utter confusion' in a case of 'everyone for himself'. By the time night fell,

Camouflaged Japanese
Type 97 Tankette in Gemas,
Negeri Sembilan.
January 1942
AWM 127895

Captain Mohan Singh (middle)
with two other officers.
1940s
NAUK WO208/833(251490)

Blind firing had started from all directions. Panic and chaos spread like
wild fire ... The morning of the 12th found British and Japanese troops
terribly mixed up all over the place ... So fell Jitra, the Maginot line of
Malaya ...

Over the next three days, tired and demoralised, Mohan Singh and his men
staggered through jungle, paddy field and leech-infested swamp as they tried
to rejoin the main force of the retreating Allied army. For the Sikh captain
personally, the circumstances of the defeat triggered an additional 'intense inner
struggle'. It was clear that while the Japanese 'had come fully prepared and were
ready to pay the price for their objective, a definite mission to do or die', British-
led forces 'had no patriotic motives to fight with their backs to the wall'. But this
realisation merely brought to mind an even deeper concern:

> Throughout night, a panorama of those four days' fighting was repeatedly
> appearing before my eyes ... The horrible scenes of the drama of death and
> destruction witnessed during those few days deeply distressed my soul. I
> began to ponder over the real worth of life. Within a second or two, one
> could be no more. Like a bubble, the life of an individual could be pricked
> in a moment and it would vanish forever ...
>
> ... If life could be abruptly snapped in a split second, as seen on the
> battlefield, would it not be better to direct and dedicate it to something
> better and nobler?

When Japanese planes dropped leaflets, 'expressing their war aims in
pithy slogans, assuring the coloured races of their immediate liberation and
beseeching them to join hands in that mighty undertaking', Mohan Singh felt
'violently shaken':

> In a normal situation, no one would have given any serious heed to the
> shibboleths [sic] of the invading hordes, but at that moment their effect on
> me was tremendous. I felt as if they were voicing my inner feelings ...

He emerged from three days in the swamp-filled jungle with a mission. He intended to approach the Japanese to obtain their help 'to start a movement for Indian independence', one that would 'cut deep at the roots of the British policy of exploiting Indians for their wars all over the world'. On the 14th, having drawn other Indian stragglers to his cause, he sent a local Indian to make contact with the Japanese on his behalf.

Mohan Singh admitted that his decision was not an easy one: 'It was, indeed, a long drawn-out struggle between two loyalties – one to my own Commission, which meant allegiance to the British Crown, and the other, unwritten yet much more binding – my duty to my beloved country.' In the end he joined the enemy 'simply because, as an Indian, I felt that it was my duty to contribute my humble share to the service of my country'. On 15 December, he met with Japanese military officials at Alor Star and a few days later with Yamashita himself, who assured him that the Japanese had no territorial ambitions in India.

'I was now going to raise an army for India's liberation,' wrote Mohan Singh. 'In the very first week of our joining the Japanese side, I had decided that the name of this force would be THE INDIAN NATIONAL ARMY.'

Mustapha Hussain: between two empires

It was not only demoralised Indian soldiers whom the Japanese targeted with their propaganda. When the Japanese invaded, Mustapha Hussain was a teacher at an agricultural college in the northern Malay state of Perak. He was also the vice-president of the Kesatuan Melayu Muda (KMM or Young Malay Union), a newly formed nationalist organisation that demanded Malay independence from colonial rule.

Towards the end of December, Mustapha was seated on his father's verandah – contemplating, as he put it, his personal fate and that of 'the hapless Malays caught up in the war' – when up drove several cars. A few KMM members emerged escorted by heavily armed Japanese soldiers and together they requested that Mustapha come with them at once. He was unwell, recovering from a nervous complaint that made it hard for him to walk, but the men in uniform were insistent. 'How could I say no?' Mustapha wrote. 'I remember[ed] a Malay adage: *jika tiada senapang, lebih baik beri jalan lapang* (if one has no gun, it is best to give way).'

Whisked away without having time to alert his wife and family, he was taken to the town of Taiping to meet with Major Fujiwara, the head of Japanese military intelligence. He was then moved to Ipoh, where what he already suspected was made explicit: the Japanese wanted him to form a Malay fifth column – a covert force that would operate behind Allied lines under Japanese orders.

Mustapha faced a dilemma. Despite the invader's clarion call of 'Asia for Asians' he was under no illusion that they were anything other than a 'new

Mustapha Hussain with his family in Perak.
1930s
Courtesy of Mustapha Hussain's daughter

Eastern coloniser'. His problem was that the President of the KMM, Ibrahim Yaakob (then languishing in a Singapore jail), appeared to have already begun negotiations with the Japanese without Mustapha's knowledge. As the only KMM leader not at that time incarcerated by the British, Mustapha was being pressed to collaborate with the Japanese without a clear idea of Ibrahim's intentions. Was Ibrahim 'an idealist, opportunist, or mercenary?' wondered Mustapha. 'Only time would tell.'

There was also a further pressing problem. On his way to Ipoh, Mustapha had seen Japanese soldiers looting and destroying local property. Worse, he had witnessed Japanese soldiers taking away local young women 'to satisfy lusts'. How would the collaboration of the Malays be possible while such behaviour continued, frequently in front of their own eyes?

Ultimately, Mustapha acquiesced to Japanese demands, having made an official complaint about the actions of Japanese soldiers. Readers, he declared in his memoirs, could decide for themselves if he was a 'collaborator'. Young Malays were now recruited to the KMM, given military training by Fujiwara's unit and then packed off to the front. But as they clambered into their trucks Mustapha secretly revealed to them his continuing misgivings. If they found themselves in danger, he told them, they were to throw away their weapons. His last advice: 'Should you meet problems, save your own lives first!'

At first, Mustapha's cooperation with the Japanese brought dividends. As he advanced on Kuala Lumpur in the Japanese baggage train, he saw that the KMM had pasted Malay houses with the letter 'F' (for Fujiwara) to indicate that they

should not be looted. In addition, Malay villagers in the way of the Japanese advance had been warned of the approaching conflict and instructed to clear out of their *kampongs*.

But at the Malayan capital, Mustapha's doubts about the Japanese returned and intensified. Although they intended him to merely recruit Malay fifth columnists, he elected to go further. Deciding that it was time for the KMM to make public its desire for Malaya's independence, Mustapha and other KMM members officially presented the Japanese with a song – one that they hoped would become a kind of national anthem. All went well, until it came to the final, climactic stanza:

> Japanese troops have arrived
> Let us assist them
> Japanese troops have arrived
> They came to liberate us

The Japanese officers present had been 'full of smiles'. 'But as soon as the interpreter came to the line 'liberate us', their expressions changed drastically and they blurted "*Nai!*" (cannot).' When Mustapha went on to reveal that the secret name of the KMM was Kesatuan Malaya Merdeka (Independent Malaya Union) there was further surprise. The Japanese believed that the Malays were too backward to aspire to independence – which to Mustapha was a shock in itself, considering that Japan had declared India's independence from colonial rule only a few days after the start of the invasion.

When the Japanese refused to back a proclamation of Malaya's independence, Mustapha decided to found a new covert organisation. At a secret meeting in Kuala Lumpur, he told his followers:

You must all, from now on, keep in mind that KMM has been used by the Japanese for their own interests. Japan is a colonial power. We will now carry on to Singapore, to free our friends from British prisons! After that, we will reorganise as a front to counter the Japanese. In our move south, do be careful. Do not lose your lives in support of the Japanese cause.

From this point on, both Mustapha and Mohan Singh, along with their new recruits, followed in the rear as the Japanese advanced on Singapore. What they encountered there, how far their dreams of liberation and independence were realised, is a story we'll come to shortly. For the moment, it's worth noting that both leaders had few doubts that they would ever get there. The Empire of the Sun appeared to have an unstoppable momentum.

The soldiers' war: Tsuchikane Tominosuke and Russell-Roberts

Yet, not every Japanese soldier was charging helter-skelter forward to victory. Back during the first week of the conflict, the Imperial Guard Corporal Tsuchikane Tominosuke of the Japanese 25th Army was stranded in Alor Star with a bad case of diarrhoea. He was put in charge of 12 other Imperial Guards who were similarly debilitated or suffering from malaria and so unable to stay with their army's advance. Tsuchikane tried to get the men to do bayonet practice to restore their fitness, but they were unimpressed. A week into their convalescence, two men were arrested by the military police for breaking into a home; not long after that, another two were rounded up for looting. Such ill-discipline potentially brought the whole unit a shame that it might never live down. Tsuchikane imagined the reaction of his superiors and comrades: 'While they were fighting a life-and-death struggle, Corporal Tsuchikane was relaxing behind in hospital and having himself a good time looting civilian homes with his band of soldiers.'

Tsuchikane Tominosuke (left) in front of Masjid Baitul Rahman, Sumatra.

1940s
from Tsuchikane Tominosuke, *Shingaporu E No Michi: Aru Kanoe Hei No Kiroku*, 1977

Japanese magazine box.
1940s
Leather
H 9 x W 16.5 cm
NMS 2001-03535

Having personally intervened to have the arrested soldiers released from the custody of the Japanese military police, Tsuchikane sought to get the unit moving. Eventually, they hitched a ride out of Alor Star in an artillery convoy heading south. At Ipoh, they heard that the Imperial Guards had fought there recently; then, at some point around the middle of January, they came across the foul smells and debris that marked the week-old battlefields leading to Slim River (on 7 January the scene of another British debacle). But in other ways the journey was more pleasant. Everywhere they discovered 'Churchill supplies' left by the retreating Allied forces; every night they feasted on brandy, chewing gum, chocolates – even cheese and asparagus. Tsuchikane had never tasted cheese before he came to Malaya, so he set aside a portion of it, and another one of asparagus, to send to his family back home.

After Kuala Lumpur, in which the perfectly intact, whitewashed houses contrasted with the destruction they had earlier passed, their truck became hot like a furnace. Soon they could see the dust made by other vehicles ahead and then the road was suddenly crowded with troops and ambulances. They had almost caught up with the battle.

Russell-Roberts had also waited December out, stranded in Kuantan, 'fighting only a war of nerves'. Japanese aircraft bombed the aerodrome daily, 'sometimes three or four times a day', but repeatedly missed their main target – the aerodrome's oil tanks. All this while, news of further defeats continued to roll in on the English Captain's radio. Just before Christmas, Ruth wrote to tell him that she was sending their daughter Lynette home to her sister in England in an evacuation ship, but that she intended to stay on in Singapore. On New Year's Eve, he imagined her joining the festivities at Raffles Hotel, 'dancing among the maze of streamers and balloons – and in fancy dress'. It was a scene that seemed 'too unreal to contemplate'.

By now, it was clear that the Japanese would attack Kuantan any day. The garrison's only escape route was a road that ran laterally west across the central Malayan highlands. However, if the Japanese advance continued through the west of the Peninsula at the rate it was going, this escape route might fall into enemy hands. Russell-Roberts, the Sikh 5/11, along with the rest of the Kuantan garrison, would then be cut off, their fates sealed.

Shuttling back and forth between the frontlines and his headquarters in Singapore, Lieutenant General Percival decided that this was a risk he could not take. Not long after Japanese patrols were spotted north of the Kuantan River, he ordered Russell-Roberts and the remaining garrison at Kuantan to withdraw. After three weeks of being bombed, the Englishman and his men set off on what would be a month-long retreat.

'Withdraw to prepared positions'

It was the same story for British-led forces across Malaya and an utterly depressing one. Men dug trenches and prepared positions that their high command never intended them to hold. Orders then came to 'fall back', to preserve 'force in strength' because the 'situation elsewhere' demanded it. Major cities, once bastions of colonial authority, were handed to the enemy without a fight.

Wild scenes of disorder accompanied the collapse of civil government. Penang fell on 19 December, the city's population having been left defenceless in the face of horrendous Japanese air attacks, while the European population snuck out three nights earlier. In Kuala Lumpur, the departure of the European population before the arrival of Japanese troops on 11 January sparked off 'fantastic' scenes of looting such as the British war correspondent Ian Morrison 'had never seen before'. Looters were 'carrying every imaginable prize away with them':

> One man with a Singer sewing-machine over his shoulder, there a Chinese with a long roll of linoleum tied on to the back of his bicycle, here two Tamils with a great sack of rice suspended from a pole, there a young Tamil struggling along with a great box of the best Norwegian sardines.

Australian troops alighting from a truck during the Allied retreat to Singapore.
1942
AWM 011303/29

In Singapore, the authorities painted the best picture they could but fooled nobody. 'Every day you read the famous phrase they used to use,' remembered Lee Kip Lin, '"withdraw to prepared positions". That's how they camouflaged their retreat.' The propaganda began to wear thin. Refugees flooded into the city (eventually doubling its size) with firsthand accounts of disastrous defeats. In spite of a press blackout, everyone was soon talking about the shocking events at Penang. Governor Shenton Thomas was forced to make a radio broadcast in which he assured the people that the British would stick by them until the very last.

Meanwhile, Singapore's feuding military and civilian administrators failed to organise proper defences on the island's northern shore. By mid-January, the situation came to the attention of the recently appointed Supreme Commander of Allied forces in the Far East, Field Marshall Archibald Wavell, who in turn informed Churchill. The realisation that Singapore lacked these fundamental fortifications resounded across Whitehall. Churchill demanded a mass conscription of labour, but Percival, ultimately the man on the spot in charge, prevaricated. He preferred to hire civilian labour and to keep any works a secret so as not to panic the civilian population. Civilian labour did not take too kindly to repeated air raids and a lack of sufficient air raid shelters, and ultimately very little was achieved.

Churchill later wrote that the 'possibility of Singapore having no landward defences no more entered into my mind than that of a battleship being launched without a bottom'. Everyone it seemed, even the British Prime Minister, had bought into the myth of the fortress that never was.

Of course, the Japanese had their own propaganda to swallow, but instead of comforting euphemisms and bland assurances it employed a language that was dramatic, even poetic. Chapter nine of the confidential Japanese booklet *Read This Alone* focused on 'The Battle':

> When you encounter the enemy after landing, regard yourself as an avenger come face to face with his father's murderer. The discomforts of the long sea voyage and the rigours of the sweltering march have been but months of watching and waiting for the moment when you may slay this enemy. Here, before you, is the man whose death will lighten your heart of its burden of brooding anger. If you fail to destroy him utterly you may never rest at peace. And the first blow is the vital blow.

Here, in lines most likely penned by Colonel Tsuji, was the imagined instant of reckoning, the compressed split-second of destiny, the moment when enemies came face-to-face and fought for glory, vengeance and even expiation. Yet, as Tsuji must have known, the reality of battle was invariably different. Chance as much as bravery decided the modern soldier's fate. As the earth and the sky churned around him, his life or death came to depend on the random flight of a bullet, a piece of shrapnel or a stray ricochet.

On to Singapore: the soldiers' war continued

After Kuala Lumpur, Tsuchikane and his unit travelled in the same artillery truck to the town of Gemas, where from 14 to 15 January the Australians had ambushed the full might of the Japanese 5th Division. After fierce combat, during which Tsuchikane and his men helped by ferrying artillery shells, Gemas fell. As the convoy continued, it passed the wrecks of Japanese tanks that the Australians had destroyed and the town of Gemas, which Japanese guns had reduced to rubble.

Seated in the back of their vehicle, having not bathed for days, Tsuchikane and his men were by now filthy, smelly and pestered by flies. Dead bodies by the roadside again signalled their approach to the front. When the convoy stopped at a road junction, news came that Melaka had fallen and that the Imperial Guards were at that moment fighting around Batu Pahat and Muar on the western coast. 'You had better get off here and start looking for your own troops,' the artillery commander advised Tsuchikane. 'You can requisition bicycles in this area. We pray for you.'

They rode their bicycles towards Batu Pahat for two days. It was exhausting work. They rode half-standing, half-seated because their saddles were fixed too high from the pedals (the average Japanese soldier being a good few inches shorter than the average Malayan). At last, they caught up with the rest of the Imperial Guard.

After changing into fresh British uniforms, Tsuchikane and his men parted and went to find their respective companies. Since they had last seen their comrades many had died and the ranks of their platoons had been thinned by battle wounds and malaria. The new arrivals made no mention of the real reason why they had become separated. The truth did not seem appropriate.

It was now late January. Artillery shells were thudding ominously in the distance. Tsuchikane and his squad moved forward, up and down hills, advancing through seemingly endless rubber plantations. Suddenly, ahead, dozens of figures streamed out of an entrenched compound. The order was given to shoot.

The first hail of bullets felled a number of those who had tried to run, while those who still could scattered to the left and the right. Tsuchikane ran forward in pursuit. As he passed the bodies on the ground he saw that they were not those of the white enemy. When the shooting stopped and the bodies were checked more carefully, it became clear that the dead were civilians, including women and children. Tsuchikane went straight to speak with his senior corporal.

'We killed civilians. Why did we have to kill them?'

'How can we know they're non-combatants. You still don't know anything!'

Months earlier, Tsuchikane had asked the senior corporal the same question when the Imperial Guards had burnt down local people's houses in China.

The young Guard's encounter with the 'real' enemy came the following day. Again his squad was moving through rubber trees when the order went out to advance. Bullets started flying as Tsuchikane charged forward. An Australian soldier appeared right in front of him and they fought hand-to-hand with bayonets. But Tsuchikane was faster. The Australian let out a strange gurgle and fell to his knees. Tsuchikane pulled out his bayonet and gazed at the blood. The whole macabre dance had seemed like a dream. At first anguish assailed him, but then he felt brave. The deed was done: his first kill in combat. He was now a real soldier.

Later, he watched in disgust as his comrades-in-arms rifled through the pockets of the dead Australians and stole their wristwatches. He wished that his squad would leave the dead in peace, but no one censured their actions. 'Does one become a pilferer on the battleground?' he wondered.

There were only occasional respites in which to consider such questions. Tscuchikane and the Guards were closing in on Singapore, moving relentlessly through the jungle, stumbling along, even sleeping as they marched, ever closer towards the Causeway.

Russell-Roberts and the 5/11 Sikhs were at that time also moving toward the Causeway. In the last week of January, they had joined up with the AIF to take part in the last-ditch defence of the Peninsula, fighting which had seen the Japanese smash through the final line of British defence in Malaya. They had then received their orders to withdraw to Singapore.

By the afternoon of 1 February, they had come to within about 24 kilometres of the Straits of Johor. But the regiment was now just a shadow of its former self. A hundred men had been killed or wounded, with most of the latter having to be left behind to be picked up by the enemy. 'Most of those with us now had reached the limit of their endurance', wrote Russell-Roberts. They had marched, dug and fought without rest for the last ten days, and for the last five they had been without food. Earlier that morning, some men had fallen to their knees and lain on the ground, unable to go further. One of these was a close comrade of Russell-Roberts, a proud Sikh sergeant-major who had broken down and wept openly.

At last, having requisitioned two lorries and a car at pistol-point from fleeing Chinese plantation workers, the remnants of the Sikh 5/11 arrived at a *kampong* facing the western end of Singapore's naval base. As the rain poured down and soaked them to the skin, Russell-Roberts stared across the water. The workshop and the main building of the naval base were completely deserted. 'The scene was one of ghostly silence, with a certain ominous look of desolation.'

They tried to signal the other side by flag and electric torch but received no answer. So Russell-Roberts and another officer procured a *sampan* from local villagers and paddled across, intending to arrange for a patrol boat to collect the rest of their unit. As they reached the steps leading up to the pier of the Naval Base Yacht Club, they were greeted by four smiling Indian sepoys. 'They were washing up dishes following some sort of meal in the club house.'

Russell Roberts had made it out of Malaya alive and unhurt, one of only 63 men from his regiment to do so. 'It was at least comforting', he wrote, 'to find the Island had not been evacuated'; yet it was also clear that the Royal Navy had departed and, so it appeared at that time, that the Royal Air Force had left as well. But what struck Russell-Roberts most forcefully was 'the glaring absence of defences on this northern sector of the coastline on the first day of February' – for on that day the most forward Japanese troops were already in Johor Bahru.

Australian Imperial Force poster encouraging volunteers to draft.
c. 1940
AWM ARTV06715

21. THE SIEGE

Early on 31 January, the last British and Commonwealth troops crossed the Causeway to the sound of bagpipers from the remnants of the Argyll and Sutherland Highlanders playing 'A Hundred Pipers' and 'Highland Laddie'. Indian sappers then blew a 70-foot wide gap in the concrete and stone, severing Singapore from the Malay Peninsula. It was said that the explosion was so loud it could be heard across the island, as far away as Raffles Place.

The Japanese entered Johor Bahru around mid-afternoon on the same day. Soon, the Rising Sun hung from the top of the Sultan of Johor's palace, which Yamashita chose to make his headquarters. 'The Singapore we had once seen in a dream', wrote Tsuji, 'we now saw under our eyes ...'

Tsuji completed his 'final plan for the reduction of Singapore' that same night. The following morning, Yamashita read it aloud to his commanders and senior officers. The veteran warrior's face was 'flushed', recalled Tsuji, 'and on the cheeks of the men listening tears could be seen'. 'The spirits of the seventeen hundred men killed since the landing at Singora were believed by all to be present at this meeting.' Each officer then held out the lid of his canteen and received 'a little of the Imperial gift of *Kikumasumune*' – a type of wine used for ceremonial occasions. They drank a toast to victory in Singapore: 'It is a good place to die. Certainly we shall conquer.'

Thick smoke billowing possibly from the bombed Kallang Airport, as seen from Rochore canal.
1942
AWM P01182.012

Preparations, departures and reunions

Over the next seven days, Japanese forces massed on the Johor side of the Strait. Enemy positions were plotted, boat equipment overhauled, jungle cut back and roads opened to ease the movement of troops and craft from their mustering points inland to the water's edge. Tsuji, the otherwise ruthless head of operations staff, paused once during these preparations to express a moment of regret. The Japanese had forced all local inhabitants within 20 kilometres of the coast to evacuate. This, Tsuji claimed, was for the locals' own safety, as well as because enemy spies might conceal themselves among them. Yet the scene clearly affected him:

> Five- and six-year old girls, with quart bottles of drinking water hanging from their shoulders, pulled along by their mothers' hands, were jostled along in a long line … Seeing them trudging barefoot along the hot asphalt roads, thinking of one's own children left behind in the Fatherland, it was difficult to view this as a matter of military necessity, but there was no alternative but to avert our faces and steel our hearts against compassion …

In that same week, Russell-Roberts was preoccupied with thoughts of his own family. When he reported to his new Divisional Headquarters near the British naval base, an old colleague told him that his daughter Lynette had been evacuated by ship only a few days earlier. It was the friend's impression that Ruth had left with her. But then a chance encounter with another colleague brought different news entirely: Ruth was still in Singapore, staying at a flat near Fort Canning. Immediately, Russell-Roberts arranged for two days' leave and caught a lift into town.

It was night and the road into the city was unlit, slippery and chaotic. His driver, an English artilleryman, chatted away in good spirits, confident that the 'Japs' would 'never set foot on this island' given the recent arrival of equipment and of 'terrific reinforcements'. Indeed, throughout January and into early February fresh troops had arrived in Singapore in preparation for what was expected to be at least a three-month-long siege. Russell-Roberts could think only of the 'complete lack of defences in the Naval Base'. Nonetheless, he chose not to spoil his compatriot's enthusiasm.

He reached the flat after midnight and the house was completely dark:

> I groped my way upstairs to a large living room on the first floor. Still in complete darkness I heard a voice singing softly and then I knew it was Ruth. And suddenly life was good all over again.

That night, husband and wife ignored the air-raid sirens as well as the knock on the door from a concerned housemate who tried to usher them downstairs to the shelter. Instead, they remained in bed, holding each other close and soon falling into a deep, deep sleep. If there were bombs outside they never heard them.

Captain Denis Russell-Roberts with wife and child in happier times.

c. 1940
from Denis Russell-Roberts, *Spotlight on Singapore*, 1965

Air Raid Precaution insignia
worn by wardens who
watched the skies for
Japanese bombers.
c. 1940
Metal
H 3.9 x W 2.6 cm
NMS 2000-05530

Brewster Buffalo fighter
aircraft of the No. 67
Squadron Royal Air Force
being assembled in Kallang.
March 1941
IWM K598

Terence Kelly: death from above

By the beginning of February, Japanese air raids on Singapore had resumed with a ferocious intensity. The Japanese had recommenced high-altitude bombing with often three raids a day and three at night. Adding to the destruction, their long-range guns shelled the city from the Johor heights while Japanese fighters flew low over the streets, dropping anti-personnel fragmentation bombs and machine-gunning civilians.

For the majority of the population, there were no proper air-raid shelters and the crowded streets of the city's Asian quarters – Chinatown especially – became death traps. Civilian casualties in Singapore are estimated to have numbered over 10,000 and perhaps to have risen to twice that figure, with at least 7,000 people dying in the last week of conflict. Dead bodies that lay by the roadside for days became a common sight; there was neither enough manpower nor time between raids to remove them.

Singapore's air defence relied on squadrons of Hurricane fighter planes, 51 of which had arrived on the island in crates during January. Though the pilots of these planes (some of them veterans from the Battle of Britain) fought bravely, the lighter, faster Japanese Zeros proved superior. Moreover, Hurricane squadrons faced severe maintenance problems (they were soon nicknamed 'penguins', so the joke went, because 'only one in a thousand flew'). Added to this, there was the usual confusion at High Command and the ever-present problem of morale.

British Hurricane pilot Terence Kelly flew into Tengah aerodrome in Singapore from Palembang in Sumatra on the evening of 29 January. 'Within ten minutes of ordering a drink in the mess,' he recalled, 'the pall of defeatism was so thick you could have cut it with a knife.' The following day, not only did he discover that his ground crew lacked tools and spare parts, but at one stage he and a fellow airman had to force them back to work at gunpoint: the appearance of a solitary Japanese reconnaissance plane had caused them to down tools and head for the cover of some nearby rubber trees.

In the end, Kelly and his squadron scrambled only once to meet the enemy before Field Marshall Wavell ordered them back to Palembang. From there, without long-range fuel tanks, it seemed to Kelly impossible for the Hurricanes 'to serve any really practical purpose so far as Singapore was concerned'. He and his squadron returned briefly to Singapore on the night of 2 February to accompany a bombing mission up-country in Malaya, only to find that when they went out to their planes their guns had been disassembled and 'contrary orders given although no one knew by whom'. Without fighter support, the bombers suffered severe losses. Kelly and the Hurricanes returned to Palembang 'in shame':

> We had a last look at doomed Singapore we had done nothing to assist. There were oil tanks ablaze and smoke was drifting over the island which was defeated even before it was invaded. I remember raising my hand in a melodramatic gesture – but then it felt a melodramatic moment.

The final honeymoon

The black smoke that engulfed Singapore came mostly from the naval base at Sembawang. In the first days of February, Yamashita had ordered the Japanese artillery in Johor to shell the base's oil tanks, fearing that their contents might be used to create a sea of fire across the Straits of Johor. British and Commonwealth troops then set about finishing the job, destroying the naval base to prevent it falling into Japanese hands. Black clouds billowed south from Sembawang, joining with the smoke rising from fires at the Keppel docks to create a dark, dismal curtain over the city. For many locals, this was the sight that most characterised Singapore in the final week before the Japanese assault – and one that seemed to bode particularly ill for their future.

Yet other eyewitnesses seemed not to have noticed and were instead struck by the week-long almost perfect weather. Russell-Roberts remembered that he and Ruth woke up the morning after their reunion to a Singapore in which the 'sun was shining and life seemed pretty good'. Their next precious days together were like a wartime second honeymoon: a dream-like reverie set against the bombs, the rubble and the persistent air-raid warnings.

After Ruth had reluctantly agreed to have her name placed on the list of evacuees, the couple 'went off to shop'. There was nothing further they could do and Denis Russell-Roberts was badly in need of some new clothes. At Robinsons' department store, they bumped into 'several old friends who had been in action up-country themselves' and who were stockpiling essential supplies. At this

Advertisements for shows at the Alhambra and Cathy alongside appeals for blood donation.
30 January 1942
The Straits Times

Surviving members of a
Chinese family continue to live
in their bomb-shattered home.
1942
NARA/NAS 20060000792-0102

point, the 'usual morning air-raid siren began to wail' and so everyone 'trotted down to some form of shelter in the basement, customers and staff alike'. 'Here the atmosphere was just as it must have been in any air-raid shelter in London.'

It was a surreal scene and yet one that was repeated across the colonial district. Despite the air raids, the Europeans shopped Singapore bare – as if the city were holding its final closing-down sale on a high life that it might never offer them again. In reality, as the siege of Singapore commenced European families had been deserted by their *amahs* and their houseboys, and were forced to go out and fend for themselves. Yet, even in a city cut off and about to be invaded, they continued to pay on credit and many local shop staff continued to accept their signatures, though these no longer held more than a symbolic value.

Meanwhile, notices in the newspapers revealed that Singapore continued to entertain. New World amusement park announced 'Non-stop dancing and cabaret and the usual tiffin dance on Sunday'; the Alhambra cinema offered the Greta Garbo film *Mata Hari*, while the Cathay cinema announced its latest comedy as an opportunity to 'fling away your troubles and have a fling at love and laughter'. These cinemas and the local cabarets were packed, often with Allied soldiers. In the besieged and bombarded city, the queues for light relief stretched well down the street.

But there were other notices that sounded a different note. In the Personal Column of the *Malaya Tribune* 'Lamoon' asked 'Mrs Jennie Lim' to write to her 'as soon as possible' as she was now 'without a home'. Another plea came from 'Mrs Wong Ah Chan' who wrote: 'Can anybody please give news of her husband...' As Japanese air raids intensified, the number of missing persons multiplied. The entertaining diversions of the besieged city were exactly that – a relief and distraction from growing desperation.

The Russell-Roberts spent their precious few days together lunching at the Cricket Club (where the waiters disappeared at the sound of the first air raid warning, leaving them to finish their meal alone and unpaid for). At another club, they swam then enjoyed 'an animated session of highballs in the bar with a number of old friends'. Then it was off to a house party nearby, where earlier in the day a bomb had landed in the garden and blown out the windows and ceiling of the living room.

The next afternoon, they walked down the length of Orchard Road to the Cold Storage building. The air-raid alarm sounded again and hundreds of Chinese and Malays, many of them children, 'could be seen jumping into the deep brick-built drains on either side of the road'. Undeterred, practically the only people still on the street, the Russell-Roberts continued walking. From the drains Chinese and Malays watched them pass, thinking they were evidently crazy.

Eventually, the couple sought shelter in the Cold Storage building, where, seated on high stools at the ice cream bar, they sipped ice cream sodas and counted 'twenty-seven silver-winged bombers' pass directly overhead. Later that night, they looked in at Raffles Hotel. Its open verandah was boarded-up with air-raid blackout screens, yet inside Dan Hopkins and his band were playing dance music just as they had, night after night, for the last three years. 'It seemed fantastic that this should be happening at Singapore's largest hotel', wrote Russell-Roberts, 'within days of invasion and possible extinction.'

Days later, the Japanese did invade. Russell-Roberts bade farewell to Ruth as she was evacuated aboard a steamer bound for Java. He would survive the fall and occupation of Singapore and eventually return to England to be reunited with his four-year-old daughter. But he was to never see his wife again: her ship was captured by the Japanese and she died in a prisoner-of-war camp in Sumatra.

European women and children evacuating Singapore.
1941
SLV H99.200/548

22. THE FALL

Lieutenant General Arthur Percival, the man responsible for the defence of Singapore, has been described in many ways: 'a brilliant blueprint general', 'wholly unsuited for the role fate had suddenly thrust on him', possessed of 'a mind that saw the difficulties to any scheme, before it saw the possibilities' and even as a 'completely negative, colourless personality'. His manner and appearance hardly helped. He was tall, thin and gangly, with prominent buck teeth; shy, sometimes oversensitive in public; and in moments of crisis, a stoic to the point of appearing indifferent. Clearly, he lacked the commanding presence that soldiers admire and which his Japanese counterpart Yamashita reportedly had in abundance.

Given the weight of personal criticism that Percival has received, it's easy to forget that he was once a brave, even ruthless soldier, a man who earned a medal for valour during World War I and who perfected unorthodox tactics against Sinn Fein guerrillas during the Anglo-Irish War of 1919–1921. It's also easy to forget that when it came to the battle for Singapore he was mentally exhausted, having worked around the clock for the previous seven weeks. Nonetheless, one accusation against Singapore's overall commander still stands: Percival was a pedant. This might seem a slight failing, but when the occasion demanded initiative and spontaneity, it quickly revealed itself as a tragic flaw.

Lieutenant General Arthur Percival.

1941
NARA/NAS 20060000793-0039

Percival's 'maintenance of the aim'

As historian Brian Farrell has written, Percival was a stickler for the 'maintenance of the aim', that is to say, the pursuit of a fixed strategic goal in spite of changing circumstances. From the outset, it might be said that such a posture was incompatible with the fluid, unorthodox nature of jungle warfare. In practical terms, it meant that on the eve of a Japanese invasion the island of Singapore still had no proper defences on her northern coastline.

The way Percival saw things, his instructions were not to defend Singapore as a whole but merely to hold her naval base (as his personal memoir repeats at length, to the point where it becomes a kind of *idée fixe*). Singapore's front line of defence thus became Johor, since if the Japanese were to take the whole Peninsula they could shell the naval base from its opposite shore. In Percival's mind, fortifications on the island's northern coast would signal the sacrifice of 'the aim' before the enemy arrived. This would damage the morale of both the troops still fighting in Johor and civilians on the island. Just as significantly, a full coastal defence would be a personal admission on Percival's part that all his efforts towards the 'maintenance of the aim' had been to no avail.

His resolute sense of purpose might have drawn plaudits back at Staff College; but in the reality of conflict, it showed he had a blinkered, almost unreal view of his responsibilities. His failure to ensure an overall contingency plan for Singapore's defence still echoes down through the decades. No wonder historian Mary Turnbull has written that by the time the Japanese landed on the island, Percival seemed 'mesmerised into accepting defeat'. With the naval base already evacuated and then destroyed, what more could be done? In purely military terms, Singapore was already lost.

What Percival did do was spread his forces across Singapore's entire coastline in an effort to cover any attempted Japanese landing, while holding a force in reserve to come to the aid of the defenders when it was clear where the main attack was coming from. He concentrated his largest force in the island's northeast, from east of the Causeway to the now empty naval base at Sembawang. He also deployed a major contingent to guard the south of the island, and another from Changi down Singapore's east coast. Well into the battle these soldiers would still be guarding their positions, awaiting the major seaborne assault that Percival expected but never came.

Notably, an explanation of Percival's reasoning behind this strategy is absent from his memoirs. Allegedly, Wavell warned him that the main Japanese attack was likely to come from the northwest; here, the Straits of Johor narrowed in places to less than half a mile. However, Percival was adamant that the main Japanese force would launch their assault against the naval base around Sembawang and Changi. He was led to this belief partly because of a Japanese feint attack on Pulau Ubin (an island just to the northeast of Singapore) on 7 December, and perhaps also because, as author Colin Smith has put it, he felt a northwest landing was just 'too obvious'.

On the night of 8 February, the Japanese did exactly what was obvious: they crossed the Straits of Johor to land in the northwest of Singapore, at points just east of the Kranji River. But even then, and for crucial days after, Percival baulked at committing his reserve force to meet this threat. As he later explained: 'I had learnt in exercises we had held in England not to commit your reserve until you are quite certain you are dealing with the real thing.' By the time he woke up to the fact that this was the 'real thing' the Japanese were advancing deep into Singapore.

The Australians break: 8–9 February

The night of the 8th had seen chaos descend once more on the troops of the 22nd Australian Brigade deployed in the mangroves of Sarimbun beach at Kranji. Earlier, at 10 a.m., the Japanese had begun an artillery barrage of the whole northern coastline, of such intensity that it reminded some old veterans of World War I. Then, as darkness fell, the shelling began to concentrate on the northwest. About an hour later, the first wave of Japanese troops started to cross the Strait in collapsible boats that they had hidden in the mangroves.

Yamashita had sent his main assault group into this small, 8-kilometre sector to smash a hole through Percival's 'thin green line'. There was a risk in this approach. Concentrating his troops in this manner, Yamashita granted the defenders a potential 'killing zone' – a deadly corridor into which they could pour their concentrated firepower. But the 'killing zone' never materialised. Instead, the unpreparedness and confusion of the 22nd Australians reigned supreme.

First, the Japanese artillery barrage severed the lines of the Australian field telephones. Then, as the first Japanese boats came across, the soldiers manning the searchlights failed to turn them on, either because these were now damaged by shellfire or because of orders not to do so until instructed (for fear of drawing enemy fire). Of course, with their communications knocked out, the 22nd Australian did not receive such orders, nor did their artillery support receive the signal to begin its bombardment. As an alternative signal the Australians relied on green and red flares which they fired high into the night sky. Unfortunately, their artillery observers failed to spot these because they were positioned too far back from the coastline. As the troops at the front got down to their last flares, one exasperated soldier was said to have exclaimed: 'We train and we practice for years and now we get nothing … Can't they hear anything going on up here in front?'

The first wave of Japanese assault troops did sustain heavy losses, just as they had during the first landings at Kota Bahru. But Japanese troops still made it ashore in numbers – where what followed became all too predictable. Japanese soldiers infiltrated and bypassed the defenders' spread-out positions, driving inland at speed. The defenders, overrun and outflanked, fell back in confusion. In the mangroves, advancing Japanese and retreating Australians literally bumped into each other in the dark. By the end of 10 December, the first wave of Japanese assault troops had fulfilled their primary objective to seize Tengah airfield and had taken the Kranji–Jurong line (which was the Australians' pre-arranged fallback position, running from north to south between the two rivers of that name). This 'line', like much else in Fortress Singapore, turned out not to have been prepared properly and consisted of little more than a half-dug anti-tank ditch.

Could things have been any different? Poor morale amongst the defenders was once again endemic. When the Australians took up their positions, they realised that they were spread out too thinly and they lacked proper fortifications. Their spirits sunk further once the fighting began. Although the AIF had fought bravely and with distinction in Johor, many of those who now filled its ranks were newly arrived reinforcements. Young men (often teenagers) and utterly inexperienced, they were faced by an all-conquering army poised for its final kill. A powerful image of the Australian withdrawal across Singapore is of soldiers emerging from the rubber trees, stripped down to just their underwear, helmets and boots (uniforms and weapons had been dispensed with as they crossed rivers and swamps) – an army of stragglers heading back to the town. Such a display earned them for posterity the nickname 'daffodils': 'they looked pretty, but they were yellow through and through'.

However, on the night of the 9th, it seemed that, for a few hours at least, things might have actually been quite different.

The Mandai inferno: 9–10 February

That night, Yamashita ordered the Imperial Guards to launch a second assault across the Straits of Johor to establish a beachhead just east of the Causeway at the mouth of a small river called Mandai Kechil. Again, the defenders' field telephones went down; once more, their searchlights failed; and this time their artillery stayed silent, not only because the signal flares could not be sighted but because several had swollen up in the humidity and could not to be loaded.

But on this occasion the Australians of the 27th Brigade fought, and fought hard. For over six hours, grouped closer together to defend a smaller area, they held their positions and inflicted heavy Japanese casualties. Then, at about 4.30 a.m. the shoreline around Mandai Kechil suddenly burst into a fiery inferno. It was exactly what the Japanese had dreaded, that the defenders might flood the rivers and swamps of the island's northern shoreline with gasoline to create an impenetrable wall of fire. In fact, the Australian sappers who released the valves of the gas tanks at the nearby Woodlands depot, to prevent their contents from falling into enemy hands, had stumbled on this tactic by chance.

Standing in the midst of this inferno was Corporal Tsuchikane. 'It was a picture of hell', he remembered, '*Abikyokan* – Buddhism's worst of all hells.'

Bombed oil tanks at the naval
base.
1942
AWM 012448

Flames blazed through the mangroves and across the surface of the water; mortar shells continued to explode around him; he heard men shouting in the darkness and others moaning from burns or shrapnel wounds. Bewildered, he wandered along the beachhead, calling out, trying to find the rest of his company.

For a few moments during the early hours of the 10th, the outcome of the battle stood on a razor's edge. When the commander of the Imperial Guards, General Nishimura, saw that soldiers from his first wave had fled back across the water to Johor, he held back his second wave, intending to call the assault off if casualties proved as bad as feared. Tsuji recounts that soon afterwards a staff officer rushed into Japanese headquarters – 'steam rising from his bald head' – to bring Yamashita the news. Though the Tiger of Malaya was a man 'not easily perturbed' his face apparently 'changed colour'. But when Nishimura's aide-de-camp arrived a little while later, Yamashita discovered that the Guards' supposed annihilation was yet to be confirmed by a senior officer on the spot. Irritated by this lapse, Yamashita ordered Nishimura (via his aide-de-camp) to 'have another look at the battle, and come back and report the facts'.

For his part, Tsuchikane, along with a few other soldiers from his unit – all of them so black from the oil that only the whites of their eyes were clear in the darkness – had decided to advance. Better to die at the hands of the enemy, they agreed, than to stay on the shore and be burnt alive. Yet when they moved forward they found that their enemy had unaccountably vanished. Brigadier Duncan Maxwell, the Australian section commander, unaware of developments at the front and having misinterpreted orders from Percival, had ordered a withdrawal.

As dawn broke on the 10th, Yamashita came ashore with his tanks at the new beachhead the Imperial Guards had secured. This was the day, writes Farrell, that 'the high command of the defenders lost any real grip on their battle'. Bukit Timah Road, which led to the highest point of the island and straight into the heart of the city, lay wide open. That night, the Japanese seized Bukit Timah Hill and despite a spirited Allied counter-attack the following day, they held onto it. Percival ordered his forces to retreat to a perimeter line that encircled the city. Singapore's fall seemed imminent.

'Battle for Singapore is not going well': 10–11 February

To make matters worse, Percival had by this time received a remarkable signal from Churchill:

> There must at this stage be no thought of saving the troops or sparing the population. The battle must be fought to the bitter end at all costs ... The honour of the British Empire and of the British Army is at stake. I rely on you to show no weakness or mercy in any form.

Wavell had flown into Singapore early on the 10th and passed this signal to Percival, apparently without comment. Already distressed by the Australians' failure to repel the first Japanese assault, Wavell received news later the same day that the Kranji–Jurong line had collapsed. In the evening (before he left Singapore early the following morning), he paid a visit to Governor Sir Shenton Thomas and his wife Daisy. The Governor recalled that the Supreme Commander of Allied forces in the Far East sat in their sitting room, 'thumping his knees with his fists and saying, "It shouldn't have happened" over and over again'.

Wavell's departure from the island must go down as one of the most painfully apt exits in battleground history. Attempting to board his seaplane, he tripped, fell down an embankment, and broke two small bones in his back. From his sickbed in Java he sent Churchill the following missive:

> Battle for Singapore is not going well. Japanese, with usual infiltration tactics, are getting on much more rapidly than they should in the west of the island ... Morale of some troops is not good, and none is high as I should like to see ...

Certainly, there were many individual instances of heroism during the defenders' withdrawal across Singapore. Nor were the Australians the only force to buckle under the Japanese assault. Percival personally witnessed the extraordinary sight of one Indian regiment, deployed in the north of Singapore and ordered to fall back a mere four miles, retreating in panic until it came to the sea on the opposite side of the island. Nonetheless, the fundamental difference in psyche between the two forces goes a long way to explain Singapore's fall. As much as morale, the problem was one of self-reliance. Japanese soldiers were given clear strategic objectives and instructed to keep moving toward them, no

Depiction of the Japanese
invasion of Singapore on a
bubblegum trading card.
1940s
Paper
H 6.3 x W 8 cm
NMS 2000-03808-001

Singapore's Last Hours

© Gum, Inc.

matter what. If they became separated from their comrades or if their lines of communication failed, they were expected to fight on independently, to keep the momentum of the attack going.

The defenders fought a very different battle. They expected to be supported in number. They watched what other units around them were doing and followed rather than led. If they became cut off or lost contact with their commanding officers (who often placed themselves well behind the lines) they usually withdrew. The contrast between both forces is brought out by such a simple item as the luminous plastic wrist compasses that Yamashita had issued to Japanese assault troops. He had ordered his men to keep advancing across Singapore at all costs, to the south or the southeast. They would march to the compass needle and to the sound of guns.

The contrast was also cultural. To not go forward, to break rank and withdraw without orders to do so, brought upon the Japanese soldier a shame that his opponent could barely comprehend. For the defenders, individuals might fight and die for the sake of their comrades, the pride of their regiment or some personal sense of valour; but how many British and Commonwealth troops felt prepared to sacrifice their lives for Churchill's 'honour of the British Empire' – especially on a tiny island, so far away from their own countries, homes and families?

The story of those defenders who did make a stand is thus highly revealing. On 10–11 February, at Bukit Chandu in the island's west, soldiers of the Malay Regiment along with local European volunteers (many of them old residents of Malaya) held up the advance of the Japanese army and took terrible casualties in the process. Earlier, Dalforce – a company of Chinese irregulars named after its founder, Special Branch officer John Daley – proved itself of similar mettle. Known to the local Chinese as the Singapore Overseas Chinese Volunteer Army, Dalforce comprised around 2,000 Chinese students, clerks, released communists (several of whom Daley had himself rounded up and imprisoned), secret society members and even dance hostesses. Armed with only shotguns and shooting rifles (and, according to one account, sometimes merely clubs, knives and axes), decked out in hastily made-up blue uniforms and distinctive white or yellow headbands, and occasionally fired on by their own side who mistook them for Japanese fifth columnists, Dalforce irregulars fought as though they had nothing to lose. As one member, Teo Choon Hong, recalled:

> I didn't think I would be safe behind the line. Since it wasn't safe, I might as well go to the front to resist them, to fight them. If I could kill one Japanese my sacrifice would be rewarded. If I could kill one more, it would be a bonus.

As for the 'sacrifice' Teo spoke of: out of the 150 Dalforce irregulars sent in to support the Australians at Kranji, only one-third came out alive.

Tsuchikane's final advance: 10–15 February

Daylight on the 10th: Tsuchikane and his platoon were once more marching through the rubber trees but dressed oddly. Tsuchikane wore a blue suit; the other men wore shirts of blue, green, yellow and white. They might well have passed for local armed civilians, if not for the rank insignia and military badges that they'd affixed to their new outfits with safety pins.

Earlier, having survived the Mandai inferno, their platoon had come across a simple rural house. Tsuchikane shouted for everyone to come out and before him there appeared a young boy, a young girl and two old grandparents – all of them shaking visibly. Next there emerged the father, the aunt and uncle, and the mother with a baby crying at her breast. It was this family's clothes that Tsuchikane and the other men had taken from the house and were now wearing, having disposed of their oil-soaked uniforms.

Presently, they arrived at the top of a hill. Below, in front of them, the terrain became open for about 800 metres before it turned once more into rubber forest. In the open ground, a sugar plantation stood on one side and a vegetable garden on the other. Cutting through them, from left to right, was a narrow road.

Suddenly, the shout went out that the enemy was in front. Out of the rubber trees opposite marched a group of Australians, recognisable by their khaki shirts and shorts, and their flat tin helmets. Tsuchikane was struck by how careless and noisy they were – sauntering across the open ground, chatting and occasionally laughing 'as if they were out on a field trip'.

Lieutenant Adnan Saidi of the Malay Regiment. Despite fighting bravely at Bukit Chandu, he and his men were overwhelmed by Japanese forces.
c. 1940
NAS 19980001358-0012

271

Japanese invasion routes.
1940s
Paper
H 14 x W 20.2 cm
NMS 2000-06620

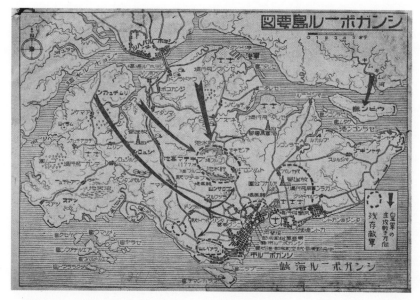

When the Australians reached the road, Tsuchikane's commander gave the order to shoot. Having locked on to one soldier, Tsuchikane pulled the trigger, felt the slight jolt of the recoil and watched as his target fell flat on his face. In the same instant, several other Australians crumpled to the ground. Those who could ran for the cover of the sugar plantation.

A moment later, Tsuchikane's commander cried out. He'd been shot. Soon after the firing stopped, he died. He was the only man in the whole company to take a bullet. It had entered his heart through the right shoulder blade and must have come from behind – most likely a ricochet from of one of his unit's own machine guns.

Over the next four days, Tsuchikane and his company advanced towards the southeast as the great guns from both sides roared in the distance. In the dense rubber forest they charged more Australians, some of whom turned their backs and fled while others simply squatted down and cowered in terror, waiting to be butchered. As they moved on, weaving in and out of the undergrowth, they came across their enemy's trucks, armoured cars and jeeps, lying deserted or destroyed, and often strewn about with more contorted enemy corpses. More metallic grotesques appeared as they passed through abandoned colonial villas – smashed cars and trucks that sat burning or upturned on once picturesque lawns and gardens. Rubber, palm and banana plantations were ablaze; gaping craters made by shells and bombs littered the roads; telephone wires and electric cables lay mangled across the streets.

The ease of their advance, combined with the incessant heat, began to make them careless. On the morning of the 14th, they emerged from the rubber trees and crossed a rice paddy. Filing down a narrow footpath that ran next to a ditch, they now carried their rifles slung over their shoulders and chewed on sugar cane as they marched along. The enemy's machine guns caught them completely by surprise.

Tsuchikane dived for the ditch and felt a sudden jolt as a bullet ripped through his rucksack. Other men landed face-first in the mud beside him. For a moment he couldn't move – it seemed like this was the end. He thought of his family. But he continued to breathe and he remained unhurt.

A comrade set up a light machine gun on the footpath by the ditch and returned fire. Soon Tsuchikane and the other men joined him with their rifles. Quickly, the enemy ambush began to die down.

At that point Tsuchikane heard the groans. Several men in his company had been hit. The soldier at the machine gun was crying out, his hands bloody; other men lay with bullet wounds through their stomachs, through their throats, through their arms, backs and legs. The ditch was awash with blood.

They hid there for nine hours, bleeding – unable to move, their bodies growing cold and purple. Officers called out the names of the rank and file to see who was still alive. The soldiers shouted out to encourage each other to keep going. Finally, as dusk settled, their artillery began to shell the enemy position. When it was completely dark, Tsuchikane and the survivors clambered out.

That night they entered another house. This time, the owners had left in a hurry: hot food still lay in the kitchen pan and an untouched meal on the table, which Tsuchikane and the others devoured immediately. Afterwards, they set about the grisly task of ossifying the hands and the wrists of their dead comrades, taking the bones out from the cooking fire with chopsticks. The dead would enter Singapore with the living – even if it were only as charred remains, kept safe in a British tobacco tin.

But then the great guns opened up and angry fire poured down from the heavens once more. Tsuchikane ran from the house, a moment before the shells came down and blew half of it away. When the barrage stopped, he saw that the

Australian infantryman taking position beside a rubber tree.
1941
SLV H99.200/492-534

mound in the garden where he had just buried his comrades was blown to bits. More dead bodies lay a few yards away, where the garden's air raid shelter had stood. The company's platoon of machine gunners had taken a direct hit and had been completely wiped out. They had survived one attack in a ditch only to perish a few hours later in another.

Tsuchikane's company had been decimated, reduced to a third of its original strength – now, in effect, a platoon commanded by a corporal. Yet the next day they pressed on, and the morning after that they moved to within 800 metres of the enemy's final perimeter line. In the last stage of their march they discovered military vehicles with supplies, uniforms and equipment – all deserted, all untouched. The jeeps and trucks had been driven to the front only to be abandoned.

Tsuchikane's new commander gave the men their orders: they would advance to capture the enemy's positions then keep going straight into the heart of the city. They knew what this meant at once: this would be their final attack, there were too few of them for any other outcome. They straightened their uniforms, readied their bayonets and bade farewell to one another, each promising to carry forward their fallen comrades' ashes into Singapore. Then, no one speaking a word, they advanced through the rubber trees.

But the sounds of battle – the great guns, the rifles and the machine guns – were falling away. In the distance they heard a faint cry. Someone was shouting, '*Banzai! Banzai!*' A few men around Tsuchikane began to shout out the same and to dance about for joy. The commander silenced them, warning them that they had not yet received official word. So they all waited where they were, on the edge of the rubber forest.

It was not long before a messenger returned and confirmed the news: the enemy had surrendered! One soldier immediately burst into tears. Others embraced each other and began to shout '*Banzai! Banzai!*' Then, more men broke down and wept.

It was 15 February. The sun was setting over the rubber trees. Tsuchikane Tominosuke also wept, unable to hold back the tears a moment longer. He was 22 years old – exhausted, relieved, a survivor.

Snapshots of surrender

Percival, with Churchill's tacit permission and citing the deprivation of water supplies, decided to surrender on the morning of the 15th. Before noon, two uniformed British officers and a colonial secretary went to parley with the enemy. When they came forward, white flag in hand, picking their way through the minefield on Bukit Timah Road, they ran into a Japanese patrol. The Japanese soldiers immediately got out their cameras and forced the enemy they had fought for over two months to pose for snapshots.

Japanese infantryman's tin box containing personal religious items
1940s
Metal, wood, paper
L 6.4 x W 4.2 x H 0.6 cm
L 5.3 x W 3 x H 0.3 cm
L 7.2 x W 1.8 cm
L 6.5 x W 2 cm
NMS 2000-00850

A few hours later, Percival and three other officers, all dressed in their khaki shorts and wearing their round tin helmets, walked up to the Ford factory on Bukit Timah Road where Yamashita had established his headquarters. Japanese soldiers walked between them; the Union Jack flew alongside the white flag of surrender. Captured on film, this image would later become the most famous of the entire campaign.

At 8.30 p.m., the ceasefire took official effect. Not long after, Churchill addressed the British people:

> I speak to you all under the shadow of a heavy and far-reaching military defeat. It is a British and imperial defeat. Singapore has fallen.

Historians have pored over the reasons why Singapore fell, debated at length the faulty preparations, the misguided strategy and the failures of leadership in what has been called 'a very British disaster'. Yet Churchill's words on the matter still speak volumes. The fall of Singapore was indeed an 'imperial defeat' – not just for British military pride and British imperial honour, but in terms of the allegiance of those who had expected the Empire to come to their aid. In surrendering Singapore, Churchill had forfeited more than a prized colonial possession; Britain had lost the moral prestige and the moral sanction by which it claimed to rule.

British officers walking towards the Ford factory to sign the surrender documents. 'The Defeat of the British Army at Singapore' by artist Miyamoto Saburo.

c. 1942
Paper
H 9 x W 14 cm
NMS 1995-03519

シンガポール英軍の降伏

宮本三郎筆

SYONAN

1942 – 1945

24. THE FALLEN CITY

During the last days of the battle for Singapore, events passed in a frantic and harrowing sequence that still exhausts the senses to rehearse. Fractured images, by turns shocking and surreal, dissolve one into another in a painful finale of death and defeat. In the streets and public squares, British and Commonwealth troops suddenly appeared, loitered, shouted and sometimes fought in public, disillusioned, often drunk (having looted the town's liquor shops), ending their war on what has been described as an 'unofficial strike'. On the Padang, boozy parties got underway as the cellars of the Singapore Cricket Club were drunk dry before the final hour for destruction of all alcohol in the city – to prevent it passing to the enemy. Meanwhile, behind the elegant façades of St Andrew's Cathedral and the Fullerton Building, makeshift hospitals were awash with blood and blood-soaked water, crowded with wounded who lay unattended because of the dearth of available nursing staff.

Close by, the makeshift air-raid shelter that was the Cathay Building was jammed equally tight, with the privileged elite in its air-conditioned restaurant and the urban poor in its underground basement. As the bombs fell outside, the Cathay's cinema continued to screen blissful scenes from a seemingly happier, unadulterated life. Then, in the very last days, another dreamlike vision: the European children who, while the explosions continued nearby, appeared on Raffles Place dressed in their 'Sunday best', because Robinsons was handing out free outfits to help them prepare for their internment.

There were the inevitable episodes of frenzy and madness: the massacre at Alexandra Hospital over 11 and 12 February, when blood-crazed Japanese soldiers charged through the wards bayoneting staff and patients (even those who lay on the operating table); the chaos at the waterfront as (far too late) crowds waved their evacuation passes in the air and attempted to push their way through the gates to the docks, while Japanese planes bombed them and strafed them with machine-gun fire; the mad cowardice of British and Australian deserters who rushed departing ships, waving their Tommy guns as they tried to force their way onboard (and sometimes succeeded); or the picture of imminent nervous breakdown we have in Major General Henry Gordon Bennet, the Australian commander who told his men to stay at their posts then turned tail in a *sampan* headed for Sumatra. In his boat (we are told), Bennett screamed 'like a young girl', berated his aide-de-camp for standing up in the nude (for fear the Japanese might see) and stirred up such ill-feeling amongst his fellow passengers that it seemed his war might end in a self-induced shoot-out.

Then, there come the scenes of terror in a city left to its fate: a Singapore ablaze, the bombs and high explosive shells of the final Japanese onslaught sending fire coursing through the streets, eating up the car parks full of abandoned vehicles and godowns full of rubber, soya and fireworks, flooding

PREVIOUS PAGE:
Street decorations on Stamford Road for the anniversary of the Japanese victory in Singapore. The Capitol building, at this time still bearing the words 'Namazie Mansions' on its upper façade, housed a cinema which operated under the name Kyo-Ei Gekkyo.

1943
Paper
H 5.6 x W 7.8 cm
NMS 2001-00086

Detail of a propaganda postcard showing a Japanese soldier with East Asian children.

1940s
Paper
H 14.1 x W 8.8 cm
NMS 1999-02042-003

the river with burning oil so that crowds rush down to watch an inferno where it ought not to be. All the while, lines of refugees make their way along roads filled with the acrid smell of burning flesh, out of the city towards what they hope will be the sanctuary of the countryside.

These are the last death throes of 'Fortress Singapore', a devastated landscape of blown-out buildings, burnt-out cars, fires still crackling and smouldering, and corpses that lie bloated and untended where they have fallen. The city's conquerors promptly rename it Syonan-To, 'Light of the South'. In Hokkien, the name could be easily mistaken for the word meaning 'birdcage'; in Mandarin, it sounded ominously like *shou nan dao*, 'island of suffering'.

After the guns: the Japanese enter the city

From chaos and disorder to sudden quiet:

> The inhabitants of Syonan woke up on the morning of the 16th of February, from the first undisturbed sleep that they had for more than a month to a strange and eerie stillness. Those who ventured out into the streets gazed upon a scene of destruction, but a destruction that had taken on a new aspect, an aspect of utter quiet, and the stillness of a grave, after the preceding weeks of nerve-shattering and ceaseless blast of bombs, the explosion of shells and the rat-tat-tat of machine guns. Everything was still. Peace had come to Syonan.

The *Syonan Times* published this account a month after the British surrender. By that time, the Japanese had begun to give Singapore a new history, as well as a new name and a new newspaper. 'Peace had come to Syonan' – and with it some

Japanese troops marching towards Raffles Square.
February 1942
NIOD 55964

feeling of relief. But what civilian eyewitnesses remember more vividly was their deep uncertainty as an inchoate pall of war hung low over their city.

'There was no shelling, there was no bombing, there was no firing, nothing,' recalled Lee Kip Lin. 'And at that moment, during that morning, one felt a bit uneasy ...' When Elizabeth Choy and her family saw Japanese soldiers march past, they 'felt as if that was the end of the world. It's terrible. We didn't know what to do.' Others did know. The night before they had begun to destroy incriminating Chinese books and to sew Japanese flags. 'Next morning', wrote Low Ngiong Ing, 'plasters of a fiery red (the Rising Sun of Japan) sprouted on all front doors.'

Yamashita had decided to hold back his front-line troops from immediately entering the city. The main Japanese army instead spent the day after the surrender burying its dead. Only on the 17th did Japanese trucks and other vehicles drive though the town, all horns blaring, yet even then the victory celebrations were muted. Yamashita and his men attended a solemn commemoration for their comrades lost in battle, at which medals for bravery were handed out. Singapore town was thus spared the ravages of a Nanjing massacre, or (in more recent memory) the drunken sack and rape of Hong Kong that had occurred on Christmas Day 1941.

However, in the city's suburbs and rural outskirts, the more savage consequences of a Japanese victory were apparent at once. There, Japanese soldiers, besides looting property (pens, watches and cars were especially sought after), abused and raped women. Though official war records are silent, anecdotal evidence tells of how families concealed their daughters, disguising them as boys, darkening their skin so that they would pass as Malay (against whom the Japanese soldiers had less animosity), hiding them in *kampongs* and rubber plantations, or even marrying them off in the forlorn hope that their new status might keep them safe. Not every attempt at subterfuge worked: the Japanese might simply become more enraged by what they saw as the audacity and inherent untrustworthiness of the Chinese, and therefore embark on further and more brutal reprisals.

Those Japanese forces who did enter the city on the first day after the surrender were the *kempeitai*, the Japanese military police. Immediately, they set about bringing order to the town by establishing roadblocks to control the movement of people and by firing into crowds of looters. Then came the first acts of arbitrary violence. Malays and Indians caught looting were let off with a warning; Chinese looters were taken away and beheaded, their heads displayed in cages outside the Cathay Building and at bridges that crossed the Singapore River. It was a chilling foretaste of what was to come.

The march to Changi

First, however, the Japanese turned their attention to the colonial presence that they had just supplanted: 85,000 British and Commonwealth troops, and

ABOVE: Lieutenant General Yamashita Tomoyuki on the cover of an issue of *Asahigraph*, a Japanese wartime illustrated magazine.
1940s
Paper
H 36.5 x W 25.7 cm
NMS 2000-05477

Illustration and handwritten note by the artist Ma Jing describing the display of severed heads at Cathay Cinema.
1940s
Paper
H 110 x W 43 x D 2 cm
NMS 1994-05689

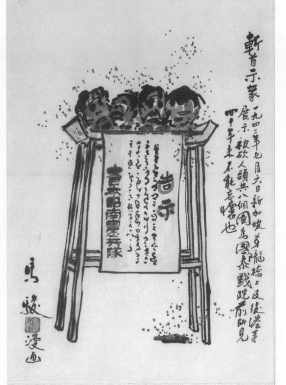

斩首示众 一九四二年七月六日，新加坡九龙桥上及後港畔，被斩人头共八个（图为国泰戏院前所见）四十年来不能忘怀也

马骏 漫画

1982.3.7月6日于北京

40年前的今天，新加坡是个恐怖中最悲惨的一天。1942年7月6日，星期一。日本侵佔新加坡已142天，並已被改名为昭南岛。

日本侵略者南进，其一举虏杀八個，在此晴无天日的海涵两期，第一個7月6日，那天清晨，人们似乎一切如常。我逛在市区中，日本佔领军宪兵队布告示8個斩下未乾之头颅，釘於後港、芽笼时一、九龙桥及国泰戏院对面路旁，尤其后者，一個木架四且未成高案之，故有四個人头（如图）。格前有一指木标志队图显示，会布8個头着之所在，並到，惊到足北彌「罪状」。

肥人围在左右赶走速，脚大围人们为之多，走一看至浑溅无辜内容，原来8個和乾，新营同谋偷窃军火被捕，理當任而被斩首示众。8個无辜，易惧，都受误尽矣人。

人头的鲜血沿白粒粉落染里，人头在中于时刻，安得表若若里，满布海蝇宿饱，满面满布苍蝇蝇的血液上。不當追前细纺望去地罪，南臺地斩首。

在外在画在7月6日。南那大殺人令示血腥人緊迫。原来，日本侵略军有你加的用意時，围此，明天起是「7.7」中国抗日战争5周年纪念，那加坡古时有8萬华人，是海外華人支持中国抗战的中心，最為頻甚有的一部份，故由古日本政府所作的罪恶「1」是震新加坡后天天，与围海江大虐殺。至「7.7」建校街斩的，唯恐華人華地纪念有所難劇明昊動，先殺我围無辜華人及人致示於於中，来個「殺鸡警猴」吧了。

马骏 明 J.146

British prisoners of war
marching towards Changi.
February 1942
David Ng/NAS 19980005712-0090

about 3,000 European civilians. On 17 February, all British, Australians, New Zealanders, Dutch and other Europeans were rounded up at the Padang. Lady Daisy Thomas, wife of the British governor, assumed they had been assembled in order to be killed. A Japanese general appeared to assure the crowd that this was not the case; they were to be taken prisoner, thanks to the 'mercy' of Emperor Hirohito.

Having languished for hours in the morning heat, the Europeans were ordered to march up Beach Road and East Coast Road to Changi, a journey of some 24 kilometres. The troops began in the early afternoon and arrived at the Selarang barracks around midnight; the civilians stayed overnight at Katong and arrived the following day at Changi Gaol. Governor Shenton Thomas and Lady Thomas led the latter procession at its head. In the battle for Singapore and its surrender, both had made good on their promise to remain till the end.

As when British and Commonwealth troops had loitered in Singapore town and refused to return to the front, it was a scene that once more played out in full view of the local populace. Daisy Thomas recalled that 'the Japanese hoped the local population would turn out to jeer at their Governor; but the marchers passed through streets of people with sad and silent faces, who proffered glasses of water when the captives were allowed to stop for the rest'. It was an event 'always spoken of in Camp as one of our greatest hardships and indignities, but when regarded merely as a walk it was not disagreeable.' There were even songs to help lighten the mood: 'We had left Katong singing "Tipperary" and we walked into Changi Gaol singing "There'll Always be an England", while the leaders of the procession, the better to express the unbroken state of their spirits, jumped up and down and laughed.'

Not everyone shared Lady Daisy's high spirits. For Mary Thomas, another female internee (and no relation to the Governor's wife), 'Though the walk was hard on the older and more delicate women, its real sting lay in being thus publicly compelled to do something so foreign to all the ordinary standards of European activity.' Indeed, while Daisy Thomas remembered 'streets of people with sad and silent faces', what she almost certainly witnessed (and either failed to register or to acknowledge) were the looks of complete bemusement and bewilderment. The crowd of Malays and Indians that lined the way were witnessing a remarkable spectacle: the once powerful ruling race being led away like a gang of common criminals.

What greeted the prisoners on their arrival must surely have brought a quiver to even Lady Daisy's stiff upper lip. The civilian prisoners at Changi Gaol, all 2,400 of them (including women, children and men over military age) were to be crammed into premises built to house well under a third of that number. The soldiers at the Selarang barracks fared even worse. Denis Russell-Roberts, now one of those interned, wrote of the 'nightmare' of the camp's early days, during which he and 40,000 other men were 'herded into an area of less than one square mile' built in peace-time to house just 4,000:

> Some of the men ... found themselves sleeping in malaria-ridden sandpits. Some lived in ambulances, some in shacks which they built with *attap* leaves and corrugate iron, and others made themselves a home by up-turning lorries and old motor cars ... The enormity of our defeat had its effect on us all. A miserably ungenerous spirit ran through the camp. Instead of becoming united in adversity, bickering and a frantic search for scapegoats tore us apart.

Such a 'nightmare' had a further cause: 'It was of course our first taste of hunger and that is an unpleasant experience.'

What followed has been well documented. After the relative comfort of the prisoners' first year of captivity, civilians and soldiers alike faced disease, malnutrition and random acts of sadism at the hands of their warders, especially as the war in Asia began to turn in the Allies' favour. Mentally, the prisoners were forced to deal with the crushing despair brought about by their dismal living conditions, and with the temptation simply to succumb. Many survived their stay

Engraved silver case of Sergeant William Neil, who was interred in Changi Gaol.
1940s
Silver
L 5.7 x W 8 x H 2.2 cm
NMS 1999-02769

Australian prisoners of war
at Changi.
1943
AWM 043131

at Changi only to die while building the infamous 'Death Railway', the Japanese
railway line between Thailand and Burma that claimed the lives of over a third
of those prisoners whom the Japanese put to work on it. Others were moved to
much harsher camps elsewhere.

Yet out of this fractious, transitory society, pressed into being by an inglorious
defeat, there grew eventually resilience, ingenuity and camaraderie. Such virtues
would survive Changi to be immortalised in memoirs, art, fiction and film
– works that would collectively define the European experience of the Japanese
Occupation of Singapore within the Western popular imagination.

The Farrer Park round-ups

But on the same day that the Europeans set off for Changi, another drama of
internment was about to commence, and it was one that was equally if not more
harrowing. The Japanese had instructed all Malay and Indian soldiers who
fought with the British to report to Farrer Park. Mustapha Hussain (the Malay
nationalist and KMM leader we last encountered in Kuala Lumpur) immediately
sensed that 'something was amiss':

> Our Malay Union members were told to inform soldiers and volunteers
> to report to Farrer Park. I knew the Japanese were clamouring for revenge
> against [Malays] who fought stubbornly to the end, killing many Japanese.
> Should they assemble at Farrer Park, anything could happen.

Mustapha asked Malay Union members loyal to him to go out and warn
their fellow Malay soldiers to remain in hiding until he gave further orders.

As a consequence, he recalled, 'Many lives … were saved from a most tragic disaster and of the 1,000 Malay soldiers in Singapore only about 400 reported to the Japanese.'

However, Mustapha soon 'heard whispers' that these 400 'might be killed en masse'. Meeting with Japanese officials, he requested the prisoners be released, reasoning that this would symbolise Japanese appreciation of the KMM's assistance 'in the "Asia for Asia" War'. The Japanese relented, on condition that a team from their military political bureau interviewed the prisoners first 'to fathom their hearts and minds'.

When Mustapha arrived at the Farrer Park detention block to see the prisoners for himself, he discovered that Chinese and Eurasian volunteers were being detained on the ground floor while members of the Malay Regiment were kept separately on the floor above. Interrogators from the Japanese political bureau asked the Malays if they appreciated the 'Asia for Asians' slogan, if they would carry arms for Japan, and whether the Eurasian and Chinese soldiers held beneath them would do the same. It seems that most of the 400 Malay prisoners gave the answer the Japanese were looking for, since they were eventually released. However, six senior officers of the Malay Regiment refused to pledge allegiance to Singapore's conquerors. Despite Mustapha's passionate arguments, they remained loyal to the British.

Their end came at Bedok in the last week of February. Here, the Japanese executed the six senior officers, along with another 80 Malay soldiers who had been lured out of hiding by the *kempeitai*'s false promise of 'money and a free ticket home'. Not long after this, Mustapha left Singapore and returned home to Perak. He had seen 'enough war horrors' to haunt him the rest of his life.

British Indian prisoners of war at a prison camp in Johore Bahru.
1942
NIOD Image Bank WW2/2704

In the meantime, the Indian soldiers assembled at Farrer Park watched as three figures climbed up on the rostrum: Major Fujiwara, the head of Japanese military intelligence, Pritam Singh, Secretary General of the Indian Independence League (the civilian arm of the Japanese-backed Indian liberation movement), and Captain Mohan Singh, the founder of the Indian National Army (INA). Unsurprisingly, when the latter came forward, he received the loudest applause and spoke for the greatest length of time. On his way to Singapore, Mohan Singh had recruited 229 soldiers to his cause; now he sought more men from a crowd of over 40,000.

Listening to Mohan Singh was the South Indian soldier John Baptist Crasta:

> He told us that British Imperialism had reduced India to a state of abject poverty, degradation, and humiliation … He wanted Indian soldiers to emulate the Japanese. They were our Asiatic brothers, he said … 'We are going to start a national army which every Indian must join. And with the help of the Japanese, we are going to drive out the British.' He then asked the prisoners to raise their hands if they wished to join the INA …

Crasta recorded in his memoir that after this 'a vigorous propaganda campaign was carried out for enrolment'. Yet out of a total of 65,000 prisoners, only about 25,000 accepted:

> The powers were aghast at the poor response. In what way could the 'Supreme Commander' satisfy the Japanese whom he assured of the support of all Indian troops?

Crasta was one of those who remained unmoved by the 'Supreme Commander' Mohan Singh's words. He and other Indian soldiers who refused to join the INA were branded 'sympathisers with the enemy' and bundled off to what was euphemistically called a 'Separation Camp' near the INA headquarters at Bidadari. It was in fact, as Crasta wrote,

> a concentration camp where the most inhuman atrocities were committed by INA men on their non-volunteer Indian brethren … High ranking officers who refused to have anything to do with the INA were thrown into it without clothing or food, made to carry heavy loads on their heads … They would be caned, beaten and kicked. Various other devices of torture … were introduced. Many people died in that camp.

On 1 October, Crasta and his fellow non-volunteers were ordered to move to Seletar:

Captain Mohan Singh delivering a speech.

c.1942
Courtesy of Netaji Research Bureau, Calcutta, India

> The General Officer Commanding paid a visit to the camp and gave a final warning, saying that the British were our bitterest enemies and this was the time to crush them … The Japanese were going to help us. If we joined

them, we would be treated like brothers. If we refused, God help us. We would be treated as sympathisers of the enemy ... and perhaps taken to some distant places from which we would never return. It would be dying a dog's death...

Confronted with the threat of deportation, more men decided to enlist; those who continued to refuse, such as Crasta, faced an even worse fate. From April 1943, they were sent to the 'distant places' that the Japanese had threatened them with – wretched labour camps on the islands of New Guinea and New Britain. The prisoners were shipped out of Singapore on what Crasta called 'torture ships': 'Heat, suffocation, stench, thirst. Could Inferno be worse?' Those who survived the voyage were then subjected to an ordeal of disease, privation and inhuman cruelty at the hands of their captors, who in some instances (as the war went on and starvation set in) resorted to cannibalism.

Crasta survived the war, and the threat of being 'eaten by the Japanese' (as the title of his memoir put it), to then aid the British in collecting evidence used to prosecute the Japanese for war crimes. However, the full story of the suffering of these Indian POWs remains largely untold. Most official accounts of the units involved have stayed quiet on the matter, recording merely that soldiers were sent to New Guinea, where a great number perished.

Should those Indian soldiers who joined the INA be simply written off as Japanese collaborators? The motivations of the volunteers were highly complex. Some soldiers imagined they had joined an independent army over which the

Propaganda material of the Indian Independence League, an Indian nationalist political party which worked closely with the INA.

1940s
Paper
H 13.2 x W 18.9 cm
NMS 1998-00184

Japanese would exert little control and they continued to justify their actions on such grounds well after the war had finished. Others had grave concerns about cooperating with the Japanese but hoped either to subvert the INA (as Mustapha expected to do to the KMM) or to sabotage it from within. There were also many soldiers who were enlisted under duress by their officers. Some of these officers were certainly supporters of Mohan Singh; others believed that by making their men enlist they were protecting them from a fate far worse. In the crisis of surrender, patriotism might speak out but pragmatism ruled.

In Mohan Singh's case, however, it was clearly patriotism that drove him. Yet as his desire to see the INA turned into a frontline fighting force intensified, so the Japanese attitude toward him cooled. Likewise, his passionate crusade alienated the leaders of the Indian Independence League, who appeared less concerned with raising an army of liberation and more preoccupied with the welfare of locally domiciled Indians. Acting in an increasingly dictatorial fashion, as if he was independent of both the League and the Japanese, Mohan Singh was eventually ostracised by both.

The last straw for the INA's 'Supreme Commander' came in late December 1942, when he discovered that the Japanese had ordered Indian soldiers to Burma without his approval. Just over a year after Mohan Singh had come to his momentous decision to form the INA, he attempted to break it up. His erstwhile allies arrested him when other INA soldiers refused Japanese orders to mobilise, and for the remainder of the war he remained imprisoned, first on Pulau Ubin, then in Sumatra. The rebirth of the INA would have to wait upon the subsequent arrival in Singapore of another charismatic Indian leader – a politician, not a soldier, by the name of Subhas Chandra Bose.

Sook ching: the purge of the Chinese

While it would take several months, even years, for the full repercussions of the events of 17 February to unfold, the Japanese had effectively disposed of all their prisoners of war on that single day. Next, they turned their attention to Singapore's civilian Chinese population. The official intent behind what followed was to root out those individuals who had fought against the Japanese as irregulars and to 'cleanse' Singapore of anti-Japanese elements. Actual events manifested little of this clarity of purpose.

On the afternoon of the 17th, the *kempeitai* circulated orders that all Chinese were to report to specific checkpoints across Singapore the following morning. 'Speculation was rife,' wrote Low Ngiong Ing. 'What was the purpose of this merry wake? None could give an authoritative answer. We guessed and guessed.'

The Japanese were especially after Chinese men aged between 18 and 50. Yap Yan Hong, then 24, had been a member of the Singapore Volunteer unit commanded by Yap Pheng Geck. Completely unaware of what to expect, he presented himself at the Jalan Besar screening centre in his best clothes and a pair of new shoes.

He was held without explanation for three days. On the third day, the Japanese soldiers asked him three questions: 'Where were you working? For whom were you working? What was your work like?'

> Quite a number of people expecting the worse to come either lied or just described something unimportant. And they were just let off. In my case I was silly to say that I was doing mapping work. I do not know how the idea came to me. I said I was just drawing maps. On that information I was detained.

Confused and frightened, Yap was marched with the other detainees to the nearby Victoria School. Here, they were ordered to stand in a long line and tied together, six men to each length of rope. They were then hustled onto lorries:

> We were standing up in the lorry and we were told by three soldiers guarding us to squat down. This was to prevent the civilians from seeing us … It was then that we began to worry as to what would happen. … After we passed Changi Prison and the lorries didn't stop, we began to worry.

Depiction of a *sook ching* screening centre by the artist Ma Jing.

1940s
Paper
H 78.1 x W 107.6 cm
NMS 1994-05687

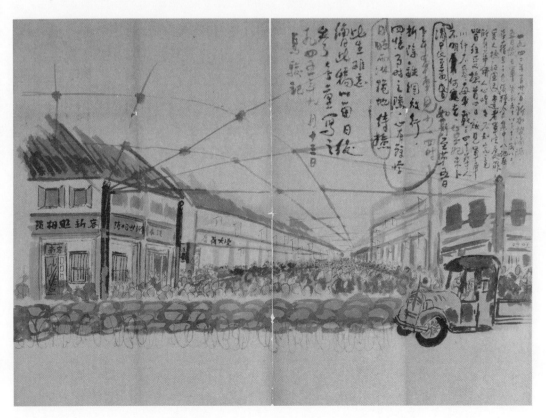

The lorries came to a halt along Changi Beach and the men were told to get out and move towards the water's edge. It was clear what would happen next: a row of corpses already lay on the sand. Yap even recognised one of the dead, the son of a local Chinese Methodist pastor. As the Japanese soldiers mounted machine guns on the concrete parapet along the shore, some of the men began to wade into the sea, hoping to flee or else drown themselves before the Japanese could murder them. Roped together with his group, Yap could only follow them into the water.

He had been praying ever since the trucks had passed Changi Gaol. Suddenly, as his bonds came into contact with the seawater, they came loose. He was able to swim away. But his ordeal was not yet over:

> I swam outwards regardless of what was happening. It was then that I heard a whistle. And after the whistle, the machine gun opened up. I took a deep breath and went underwater and I could hear the bullets ricocheting above me …
>
> When the firing stopped I was telling myself, 'These people will come out to find those who are still wounded to finish them off. They will not leave any wounded.' And I was right. I heard the chug-chug of a motor boat. And then I just swam underwater, not outwards towards the sea but towards my right, towards the Bedok area.
>
> When the sound of the motorboat came nearer to me, I stayed underwater. Immediately after that, the searchlights came on, and it was searching the sea. From the bottom of the sea, I could see rays of searchlights coming along. When the rays moved away from me, I just put my nose up to take a deep breath again.

The Japanese called this purge *dai kensho*, 'the great inspection'. In Chinese it was known as *sook ching*, 'purification through elimination'. Yap miraculously survived and returned to his family, thousands did not. Yet the actual number killed remains unclear. The Japanese army admitted to executing around 6,000 Chinese, but Chief of Staff Colonel Sugita Ichiji subsequently revealed that the total was closer to 25,000. After the war, the Chinese community in Singapore claimed that around 50,000 had perished. Any attempt to arrive at a definitive figure is complicated by the fact that so few bodies of those executed were ever recovered.

What we do know (as Yap's experience at Jalan Besar shows) is that the Japanese screening and killing of Chinese was terrifyingly arbitrary. At some centres men were interviewed; at others, they were detained without explanation and barely questioned before their fates were decided by the Japanese officer present (often with just the flick of an imperial wrist). The process could last a few hours or it could run for up to six days.

Reports later emerged of the presence of black-hooded informants who circulated the centres pointing out those to be executed. Who these spectral figures were remains unclear. They may have been police detectives, captured

Pass issued by the Japanese army certifying that the bearer is a 20 year-old Cantonese male working as an assistant in a store selling dried foodstuff.
1940s
Paper
H 10.5 x W 12.8 cm
NMS XXXX-02446

communists or renegade Taiwanese (whose homeland had been a Japanese colony since 1895); some might have used their position to settle old scores, while others – perhaps in panic – merely picked out faces from the crowd at random. Certain groups were clearly at risk: anyone who had assisted the war effort in China, teachers and journalists, former British employees or those the Japanese thought had pro-British leanings, and members of Dalforce and other volunteer forces. Yet a man's fate might be sealed by something as insignificant as the fact that he spoke the Hainanese dialect (the Japanese assumed all Hainanese were communists), that he bore tattoos (which indicated he was a secret society member), that he wore glasses (which meant he was an intellectual) – even by the fact he wore nice clothes or that he signed his name in English.

The speed at which Japan's military hierarchy demanded the *sook ching* be concluded exacerbated its frightening haphazardness. To complete the screening, the *kempeitai* relied on 1,000 auxiliaries drawn from the 25th Army's infantry. These soldiers went from house to house with their bayonets to flush out Chinese men (and sometimes women and children) who had failed to report to screening centres. These same auxiliaries were then roped in to perform the screening itself. Most were ignorant of the Chinese language and seem to have had imprecise instructions about whom they were looking for and how they were to go about screening them. (Among the categories the soldiers were ordered to look out for were 'rascals and ex-convicts', though there was little indication of how either type were to be identified).

No doubt some soldiers, still fired-up by the battle fury of just a few days earlier, carried a residual hatred for the 'enemy' into their new work. Some, but not necessarily all: Imperial Guard Tsuchikane Tominosuke was one of those seconded to a junior position by the *kempeitai*. Looking back after the war, his role in the *sook ching* and in subsequent brutal *kempeitai* interrogations so horrified him that he felt unable to speak about it for the remainder of his life.

Whatever the *sook ching*'s military objectives, it ended up nothing but a sordid and bloody act of mass retribution. Colonel Tsuji is reported to have toured the screening centres demanding that his soldiers round up more 'suspects', proclaiming his intention 'to cut the entire population of Singapore in half'. To Tsuji, the local Chinese population deserved to be punished en masse, for either they shared in the collective guilt of their mainland brethren, whom they had supplied with men and money in the war against Japan, or they were stooges and puppets of the British. As another senior Japanese officer declared (to a startled delegation of Chinese leaders):

> You are our enemies. You know this. You have fought us for years. Now you know our strength, don't you? Your activities undermined our position here. You helped the scoundrelly British. Now we've got you. We shall have to put you where you'll do no more mischief.

Photograph of Tan Chao Ying. Born in 1929 the daughter of a tailor, she lived on Loke Yew Street during the Occupation. The reverse of this photograph bears an inspection stamp by the Japanese army, probably certifying that the girl has been cleared of any suspicion of anti-Japanese activity.

1940s
Paper
H 8.4 x W 6.2 cm
NMS 2001-05189

Sook Ching Victims: Personal Artefacts

Many thousands of Chinese men were killed during the *sook ching* and their remains were still being discovered in areas such as Changi, Siglap and Bukit Timah even into the 1960s. In February 1962, the Singapore Chinese Chamber of Commerce formed the Remains Disposal Committee to organise the recovery and proper interment of civilian victims of the Japanese Occupation. By 1963, a large piece of land on Beach Road was set aside for the burial of the unidentified remains of not only Chinese victims, but those of all races. The towering Civilian War Memorial was subsequently built on the site.

In 1966, human remains and personal artefacts of *sook ching* victims were recovered in a series of excavations at the Jalan Puay Poon site (in Siglap). The artefacts shown here (c. 1942) range from jewellery to personal effects such as keys and wallets.

Straits Settlements coin, bearing the image of King George VI.
Bronze
W 2.1 cm
NMS 2008-05935-026

Pocket watch.
Gold
L 40.8 x W 4.5 x D 1.1 cm
NMS 2008-05902

Song Heng Hainanese Association badge bearing the Guomindang symbol.
Brass
H 2.8 x W 2.5 x D 0.3 cm
NMS 2008-05924

Crucifix, possibly part of a rosary.
Metal
H 10.1 x W 2.5 x D 0.4 cm
NMS 2008-05897

Set of keys and whistle engraved with the letters 'FMSR' – Federated Malay States Railway.
Metal
H 34.8 x W 4 x D 1.5 cm
NMS 2008-05936

Buddhist swastika medallion.
Metal
H 5.1 x W 3.6 x D 0.1 cm
NMS 2008-05896

Life insurance tag inscribed 'Sye Too Law, Life Insurance Policy, No.26792'.
Brass
H 2.8 x W 2.6 x D 0.1 cm
NMS 2008-05921

Wallet imprinted with the address of its owner: 'Dr. J. C. Chen, 26 Wilkinson Road, Singapore S.S'. 'S.S' stands for Straits Settlements.
Leather, plastic
H 3 x W 11 x D 9 cm
NMS 2008-05907-001

Dr Lim and Shinozaki Mamoru: the price of cooperation

At the venerable age of 73, Dr Lim Boon Keng found himself pulled out of the line at a Japanese screening centre. Various accounts exist of what happened next. In one version, Lim was informed that if he failed to do the Japanese bidding his wife would come to harm. Alternatively, as civilian Japanese administrator Shinozaki Mamoru recalled, it was Lim's son who was in danger. In this version, Shinozaki claimed that he went personally in search of Lim and asked him, 'How can we save your people?':

> I explained to him what was at the back of my mind – the formation of a Chinese organisation to cooperate with the Japanese Imperial Army. That would appear on the surface to be the objective. But the real objective would be to protect the Chinese community.

To some degree, Shinozaki appears as a kind of Japanese Oskar Schindler. He was, at heart, a humanitarian, in stark contrast to the usual stereotype of the sadistic Japanese occupier. He was also charismatic, a lover of the good life and a womaniser, with a particular taste for Western dancing and Western and Eurasian women. Before the war, he had worked as press attaché for the Japanese Consul-General in Singapore until the British jailed him on suspicion of spying (a charge he always denied). After the British surrender, he emerged from Changi Gaol to play a key role in the Syonan administration, eventually becoming its Chief Welfare Officer. During the *sook ching*, Shinozaki gave out thousands of passes bearing his name to protect Eurasians and Chinese who were at risk of being detained:

> I did not bother to find out if those asking for passes were good citizens or bad hats. My only concern was to help as many people as I could in this confusion. The passes read: 'The bearer of this pass is a good citizen. Please look after him and protect him, and let him go about his business without hindrance.'

With Shinozaki's formation of the Overseas Chinese Association (OCA), prominent Chinese business leaders, such as our old friend the banker Yap Pheng Geck, were released from custody. However, Syonan's military establishment soon suspected that Shinozaki was a Chinese sympathiser. For his own protection, he was whisked out of Singapore by the Japanese civilian authorities, acting with the support of the Japanese Navy.

Needless to say, Shinozaki's hard-line successors had quite different ideas about the OCA's function. At a series of dramatic meetings held at *kempeitai* headquarters, Chinese leaders were bawled at, humiliated and threatened. During their first confrontation, these leaders requested the release of their fellow Chinese and were immediately thrown out by a *kempeitai* colonel. Second time around they faced Takasei Toru, a Japanese intelligence officer. As Low

Shinozaki Mamoru.
1940s
NAS 19980005938-8106-3181-8390

Ngiong Ing vividly recalled, when the Chinese leaders offered to 'pledge support to the Japanese Military Administration', Takasei retorted:

> *Bakaro* [Bastard]! Your money, and even your lives are ours to use as we please. Get out! Go home and think how you're going to expiate for the crimes of your community.

Over the next few days, it became clear what the Japanese wanted. Through the OCA, the Chinese community in Singapore and Malaya should offer 'a gesture of submission and a goodwill offer' that amounted to $50 million. This Chinese 'gift', as it became known, was to be recompense for the community's fundraising efforts in Southeast Asia in support of China's war against Japan.

The task was virtually impossible – such an amount was equivalent to about a quarter of all the currency then in local circulation. OCA members devised an elaborate system of assessing wealth and 'taxing' each property owner accordingly, but even with Japanese retribution looming over their heads they could only raise $28 million. At the last minute, the OCA was permitted to borrow the shortfall from a Japanese bank in what was then the largest single bank loan in Malayan history. On the Association's behalf, Dr Lim presented the $50 million cheque to Yamashita at a ceremony on 25 May 1942, along with a short speech that had been approved by the Japanese military the night before:

> In the past we were running-dogs of British imperialism. We wronged the Japanese and helped Chiang Kai-Shek in his criminal resistance to Japan. We now see the error of our ways and heartily repent. We pledge our support to the Military Administration.

Yamashita responded with a speech of his own. In it, he claimed that since the Japanese were the descendants of gods, and since the Europeans, as Darwin had proved, were the descendants of monkeys, the outcome of the war was assured. So ended the Tiger of Malaya's final public appearance in Singapore. Subsequently, he was posted back to Manchuria and then to the Philippines, where he eventually surrendered to the Americans and was later hanged (controversially in some people's eyes) for war crimes.

The ceremony also marked Dr Lim's last appearance in public as the leader of the Singapore Chinese. During the dress rehearsal, the old sage collapsed and had to be revived; throughout the remainder of the Occupation he spent most of his time drunk. The strain of cooperation appeared to have taken its toll, yet behind Lim's insensible state there was also much sense. He confided to Yap:

> If I don't behave like this they will make me do all sorts of things and I can't stand it. The only way I can shake them off is to behave this way. They

can put my name down for anything they like but I am not functioning because I am incapable and drunk most of the time.

For Shinozaki's part, his tense relationship with Syonan's military administration eventually improved and by late 1942 he was restored to the civilian administration and resumed his work with the OCA. After the war, the British released him from internment in response to numerous testimonials from Occupation survivors, and he later aided the Allies with their prosecution of his countrymen for war crimes.

However, the OCA remained controversial. Oral history interviews kept in Singapore's National Archives reveal that while several Chinese acknowledged the organisation's role in shielding the community – in that it prevented a terrible situation becoming worse – others felt nothing but hostility towards it. These interviews recount that most people 'disliked' the OCA, they 'did not look up to it', did not hold it 'in high regard', considered it 'useless', little more than an instrument of Japanese oppression whose leaders were tainted by the stigma of collaboration. Even after the full story of the OCA had emerged, the recollections of some Chinese interviewees suggest that it continued to generate deep resentment.

Nor was the dilemma of whether to cooperate with the Japanese restricted to Singapore's Chinese. The English-educated Ceylonese and Eurasian communities were equally suspect in Japanese eyes because of their employment under the British as clerks and public servants. In the press and at public meetings, the Japanese lambasted the Eurasian community in particular for their supposed sense of superiority, their materialism, and their failure to consider themselves Asians or behave in a manner sufficiently Asiatic. Shinozaki, by establishing a Eurasian Association, attempted to prevent the full excesses of Japanese 'purification' from falling on this community, just as he did with the Chinese.

And once again, collaboration with the Japanese was the source of collective inner turmoil. As Eurasian doctor Dr Farleigh Arthur Charles Oehlers remembered:

> We were all, of course, terribly pro-Allies and all definitely anti-Japanese. But it's a matter of manifesting your feelings. You know, being reasonable about it, being realistic about it and being cautious about it. Some had this feeling of bravado. They thought they were smart by going around and openly condemning the Japanese, which was a wrong thing to do. Some of them suffered the consequences as a result. It was not a thing to do. The thing was to keep quiet about it; keep your feelings pent up. But I did realise it was important to toe the line, though not in an enthusiastic way. You had to do what you were told to do. What else could you do? How could you say no to these masters who had come and occupied Singapore?

Donation receipt issued by the Overseas Chinese Association.
1940s
Paper
H 22.5 x W 11.7 cm
NMS 2000-00443

25. THE RISING SUN

In early September 1942, Indian labourers, under orders from the Japanese authorities, removed the statue of Sir Stamford Raffles from its pedestal in Empress Place in front of the Victoria Memorial Hall. They moved it to the newly renamed Syonan Museum, formerly the Raffles Museum and Library (and today the National Museum of Singapore). The decision to do so was one of the few that warring factions within the Japanese administration could agree upon. It was also a gesture of some political significance. The *Syonan Times* reported that visitors to Syonan would 'no longer see the statue of Raffles, with arms folded across his chest, looking down at them benignly,' as he was now being moved to 'a special place in the Museum for all time'. 'This,' the paper concluded, 'is a generous tribute paid by the conquerors of Singapore to the founder of this settlement.'

When an invading army 'liberates' a subjugated people, statues of that people's former 'oppressors' are usually the first things to topple. But although the Japanese claimed they were in Southeast Asia to free Asians from the bondage of Western imperialism, they elected to preserve the memory of Singapore's first and most famous European coloniser. Raffles may have been taken down from his commanding vantage point (and reduced to the status of a relic inside the institution that had once borne his name), but he remained in one piece. Perhaps the desecration of his memorial would have sent too overt a message to the local populace. Maybe it would have run counter to the Japanese perception of themselves – not so much as the slayers of Western imperialism but as its superior Asian heirs?

Amid the tragic circumstances of a city where tens of thousands had already been imprisoned, tortured or had 'disappeared', and where ordinary civilians had learnt to dip quickly into a low bow to satisfy passing Japanese soldiers (or risk being clubbed with a rifle butt), Japan's 'tribute' to Raffles signalled a further reality. The Japanese had come to Southeast Asia not just to plunder and to master, but to build. Their imperialism contained its own brand of faulty idealism and hypocrisy, and they would impose it on the region with a violent intensity that other empires rarely matched. But the Japanese would also bring about dramatic social change and, for some people, new opportunities. Syonan-To, as its name promised, was to be the radiant 'southern light' in yet another colonial experiment.

Before the Occupation, Raffles's statue stood within a Renaissance colonnade in front of Victoria Memorial Hall. The colonnade was destroyed by the Japanese, while the statue itself was moved to the Syonan Museum.
1926
NAS 19980005492-0054

Singapore's Japanisation

The songs and speeches said it all. In only the first week after the surrender, Yamashita published a lofty declaration of Japan's plans for Southeast Asia in the *Syonan Times*:

> We [the Japanese] ... hope to promote the social development by
> establishing the East Asia Co-prosperity Sphere on which the New Order
> of justice have to be attained under "the Great Spirit of Cosmocracy"
> giving all content to the respect race and individual according to their
> talents and faculties. ... Nippon armies hereby wish Malayan people to
> understand the real intention of Nippon and to co-operate with Nippon
> army toward the prompt establishment of the New Order and the Co-
> prosperity Sphere.

Some while later a Syonan songbook put such thoughts into verse:

> Let Asia greet the Rising Sun
> The herald of a greater day,
> When Asia's people shall like one
> Tread gloriously their destined way

The Greater East Asia Co-prosperity Sphere was Japan's imperial vision
of a self-sufficient dominion stretching from Japan across China to Southeast
Asia, where some territories might be granted political autonomy, while others
(such as Singapore and Malaya) would remain Japanese colonies. The 'Great
Spirit of Cosmocracy' supposed to underpin this project, however, was a little
more complex. It stemmed from the Japanese notion of *Hakkaoichiu* (sometimes
rendered in English as 'Eight Corners of the World under One Roof'), a vague
idea of universal brotherhood and mutual respect for diverse religions, customs
and languages. In practice, it meant unity through 'Japanisation'.

In Syonan, times, dates and place names changed immediately. English signs
came down, Japanese ones went up; streets and buildings were renamed and
rededicated; clocks and other timepieces adopted Tokyo time (which ran one
and a half hours ahead of Singapore time); across the city the Japanese calendar
was introduced. However, Japan's main cultural objectives in their new colony
went much deeper. As the Syonan press described it, the island's new regime
would soon eliminate 'the habits and customs left behind by the haughty and
cunning British'.

To this end, the mass media and the Japanese language were deemed
crucial. Indeed, the Japanese viewed their language as a tool of indoctrination
in itself: learning it would help local people acquire the Japanese spirit, the
qualities of discipline and obedience which had made Japan a great nation,
as well as loyalty to the Emperor. From late February 1942, the *Syonan Times*
(subsequently renamed the *Syonan Shimbun*) began printing *Nippon-go* [Japanese
language] lessons. From April of that same year, the new Radio Syonan began to
broadcast Japanese lessons over the airwaves. Office hours were even shortened
to encourage upstanding Syonan citizens to go home and perfect their mastery
of the language.

For most people in Singapore, this was their first encounter with intense state propaganda. At the newsstands, they were inundated with Japanese-sponsored papers and glossy magazines that featured novel Syonan delights, such as the new fashions worn by the new 'Syonan girl'. At the cinema, they watched Japanese newsreels and documentaries extolling the virtues of Japan's Asian empire and its conquering armies' glorious victories in battle. Initially, audiences could still watch American and British films alongside such offerings; but from November 1943 the Japanese banned all Western films and ordered Singapore's movie houses to show only 'Nippon screen masterpieces'.

A parallel attempt was made to refashion local musical tastes. The Japanese banned some 1,000 American and British popular songs, including love songs and jazz, on the grounds that they undermined Asian identity. A *Syonan Times* article explained that the West used 'the sacred field of music in order to corrupt the minds and souls of the people of Greater East Asia'. Western music had become an 'anaesthetic agent' in American and British attempts to achieve world domination.

In its place, the Syonan authorities offered public concerts that featured Japanese orchestras playing 'Nippon music'. 'Nippon songs' soon dominated the airwaves and were widely used as an aid to learning *Nippon-go*. The repertoire included children's ditties, patriotic anthems and sentimental pieces dedicated to Japan's natural wonders (such as Mount Fuji or the annual cherry blossoms), all intended to stir in the collective local spirit a desire to be Japanese. Ironically, some Western songs such as 'Auld Lang Syne', 'Home Sweet Home' and the 'Last Rose of Summer' escaped the censor's ban because they were already lodged in Japan's national consciousness and deemed to be 'well assimilated with Nippon sentiments'.

Naturally, Japanese attempts to make local people into loyal imperial subjects focused on the new Syonan classrooms. While most Chinese-language institutions remained closed throughout the Occupation, other schools reopened and English-language schools were transformed into *Nippon-go* schools. From July 1942, Japanese became a compulsory subject across Syonan. From this time also, the education of Syonan youth, initially intended just to get children off the streets, became a more systematic attempt at indoctrination. To oust Western ideas and habits, the Japanese dispensed with the liberal-arts-style curriculum of the British and emphasised drill, character building, physical training and vocational studies.

Singaporeans who were students during the Occupation remember spending most of their school day singing, performing exercises (to special music for Japanese callisthenics broadcast over the radio), listening to uplifting propaganda speeches and, as food became scarcer, even gardening. Each day began, as it did in government offices, with the same rituals: the raising of the Japanese flag, the singing of the *Kimigayo* (the Japanese national anthem), followed by deep, low bows in the direction of the Emperor's imperial palace.

Nippon Propaganda Department distributing pamphlets during the *Tentyo-Setu* (Emperor day) celebrations in Syonan.
1942
EDM Archives

OPPOSITE: Chart of routine communal exercises done in synchrony with radio broadcasts.
1940s
Paper
H 43.1 x W 28.3 cm
NMS 1996-01843

健全我們的身體身如馬來人防衛馬來士
JAGA TUBOH KITA SEPERTI MALAI DIKAWAL UMATNYA.

Rajio Taiso
無線電體操

第 一 次
SENAMAN DENGAM RADIO No. 1

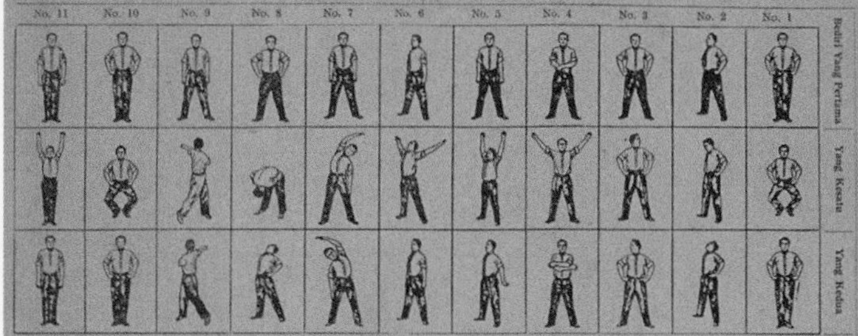

No. 11	No. 10	No. 9	No. 8	No. 7	No. 6	No. 5	No. 4	No. 3	No. 2	No. 1	

Babak Yang Pertama

Yang Kedua

Yang Kedua

無線電體操之歌
Lagu Senaman Radio

1. Odoru asahi no hikari o abite
   Mageyo nobaseyu warera ga kaina,
   Rajio wa sakebu ichi ni san.

2. Kaoru kurotuchi tamatsuyu funde,
   Haneyo odoreyo warera ga suashi,
   Rajio wa sakebu ichi ni san.

3. Kiyoi asagiri surokaze ukete,
   Sueyu idaseyu warera ga taiki
   Rajio wa sakebu ichi ni san.

4. Warera teashi no uchinau tokoro,
   Tsuyoku akaruku tenchi mo odoru,
   Rajio wa sakebu ichi ni san.

第 二 次
SENAMAN DENGAN RADIO No. 2

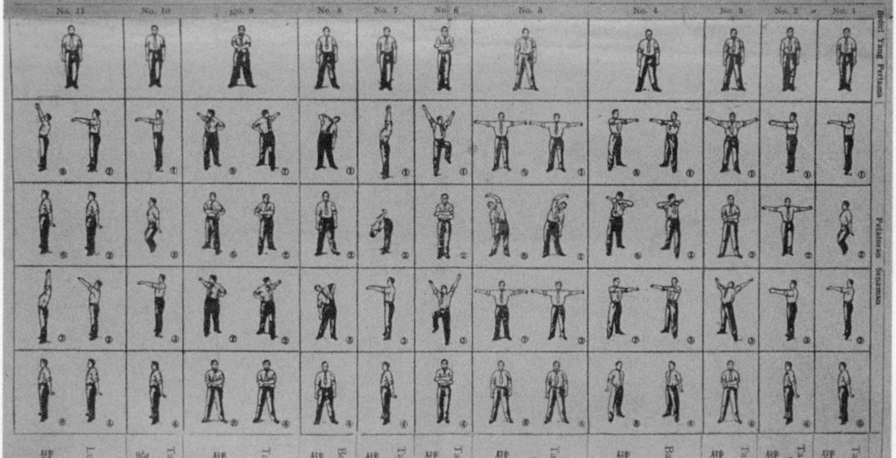

No. 11	No. 10	No. 9	No. 8	No. 7	No. 6	No. 5	No. 4	No. 3	No. 2	No. 1	

Babak Yang Pertama

Pelaksanaan Senaman

Dictionary for *Nippon-Go*
learners.
1940s
Paper
H 15.8 cm x W 13.2 cm
NMS XXXX-02198

These rituals were just one part of a larger transformation in Singapore's public life. Japanese holidays now became Syonan holidays, such that at the appointed time on the Emperor's birthday, lessons, work and transport stopped and all local subjects of the Empire of the Sun faced northwest (in the direction of the imperial palace) to observe a minute's silence. The populace was also expected to commemorate the dates of famous Japanese victories and imperial events, such as the conquest of Singapore, the outbreak of the Sino-Japanese conflict or the beginning of Japan's invasion of Southeast Asia. These commemorations involved mass public parades featuring floats, flag-waving and chanting schoolchildren – a scene not altogether different from Singapore's earlier celebrations of British royal visits, or its future celebrations of national independence.

But the daily ritual that everyone obeyed and remembered most distinctly was bowing to the Japanese. Anyone passing a sentry had to do so because even the lowliest sentry was considered to be a representative of the Emperor. At the hands of a swaggering, self-important Japanese guard, a seemingly harmless cultural rite turned into a galling ordeal. An insufficient display of humility, or just the whim of the Japanese soldier who was passing, could trigger a slapping, a beating or worse.

Aside from the fear, the oppression and the callisthenics, what impact did Japanisation have? At one level, many attempts at Japanisation seem simply to have 'bounced off' their intended targets. Syonan residents would often pay lip service to Tokyo time while at work, but hide watches and clocks that kept Malayan time back at home. Public attendance at imperial ceremonials was not always what the Japanese expected, and government servants, especially, were periodically admonished for their failure to exhibit sufficient imperial spirit. Moreover, Japanese rhetoric about an 'Asia for Asians' had been already undermined by the *sook ching* and other acts of barbarity, so that it left even those who would like to have believed in such ideals cold (and suspicious).

Attempts to make *Nippon-go* an official language in place of English encountered a more practical problem: most people found the language difficult to learn and – what with work, exercises and finding sufficient food for their families – had little time to devote to it. Though at various moments Japanese officials proposed to ban English from schools, from the civil service and even (in early 1943) from postal correspondence and telephone conversations, all such plans were eventually abandoned. If they were to rule effectively, the Japanese would have to work through the very medium that underlay the Westernisation they sought to eradicate.

Nor were Syonan's schools quite the effective centres for indoctrination that their wealth of songbooks and other primary sources might suggest. Compared with the 72,000 students at schools in Singapore in 1939, the number of pupils who attended school during the Occupation was never more than 7,000, and fell dramatically from 1944. Parents kept their children at home for fear of reprisals, disease or because they needed their help in growing vegetables. Perhaps the most telling evidence of the failure of Japanisation is that after the war, while many people in Singapore fondly remembered Japanese music and Japanese films (especially those filled with glorious Nippon scenery), they recollected little of the Japanese language beyond its basic swear words.

Yet, in other ways, the impact of Japanisation on the inhabitants of Syonan was profound. Japan's efforts to establish a tight administrative control over its conquered territories brought the government closer to an average Singapore resident that at any point in the island's previous history. It was Japan that undertook the first ever registration of Singapore and Malaya's entire population, and so announced the birth of the territory's first bureaucratically obsessed state. Japan required its imperial subjects to carry identification cards, permits and badges to prove their residential status, to run vehicles, own radios, trade, work in a range of occupations (even as dance hostesses), purchase food or simply move about.

The regime's need for local administrative personnel also opened up new employment opportunities for groups that had been excluded by the previous colonial system. Clerical positions and office jobs, once the preserve of the English-educated Asian male, began to attract greater numbers of women, who the Japanese deemed to be less tainted with pro-British leanings and who, as a result, often had their first taste of earning a wage. Similarly, Malays benefited from Syonan's new technical schools. Young Malay boys, many of them not yet teenagers, arrived in the city from the countryside to learn an industrial trade and then go to work in a factory. Following the war, these workers formed the basis of a Malay working class that prior to the Occupation had hardly seemed likely (see Chapter 16).

Lastly, as memoirs and oral testimonies underline, the Japanese instilled in the local population a new regard for discipline, drill and even militarism. From 1943, the Japanese administration created units of *heiho* ('subsoldiers' who mainly provided labour support to the Japanese army), *giyugun* (Malay volunteer soldiers) and a local Volunteers Corps (the Malayan equivalent of the British Home Guard). After the Japanese surrender, the experience of such war-time mobilisation would prove fundamental to a new generation of nationalist leaders who demanded an immediate end to colonial rule.

However, in Syonan, well before the British returned, certain young people had already begun to act on such patriotic feeling – and it is to some of their stories that we now turn.

Teenage girl soldiers: Rasamma and Janaki

On 5 July 1943, cries of '*Chalo Delhi*' [to Delhi] could be heard ringing out along Orchard Road. Thousands of Indians, many of them soldiers and labourers, were

Syonan's citizens had to apply for permits for most activities, including fishing and owning radios.

Fishing Licence
1940s
Paper
H 20.2 x W 11.8 cm
NMS 2000-00207

Radio Ownership Badge
1940s
Metal
Dia. 7 cm
NMS 2000-05521

Janaki Thevar in Indian
National Army uniform.
1943
Courtesy of Rasamma Bupalan

on the march, placards in hand. They were on their way to the Padang to hear the famed Bengal revolutionary and one time President of the Indian National Congress, Subhas Chandra Bose. *'Chalo Delhi'* had once been the rebel cry of Indian mutineers back in 1857; now, it became the call to arms of a born-again Indian National Army hastening to meet its much-anticipated saviour.

For Subhas Chandra Bose was a man of extraordinary charisma. Although bespectacled and balding – even in his smart military uniform he looked more the archetypal intellectual than a firebrand warrior – to the crowds who thronged to the Padang he was 'Netaji' [leader]. And in Netaji, the INA had found a living icon of the Indian nationalist struggle to pull it from the morass into which it had fallen since Mohan Singh's imprisonment. Not only did Bose promise to make the INA into a true fighting force again, he intended to transform its charge 'to Delhi' into a genuinely popular movement among Malaya's Indian civilians.

Bose's journey to Singapore was complicated. He arrived after escaping house arrest in Calcutta, fleeing across Afghanistan into Germany, and then getting himself smuggled by German U-boat across the oceans to Japan, from where he eventually flew into Malaya. Nonetheless, his message during his first speech at the Padang was simple: those who genuinely sought to rid India of British domination must face great risks and sacrifice – but the prize was liberation. Addressing another crowd that packed the Padang a few days later, he explained that he wanted a force powerful enough to fight the British government in India from without, and so foment a revolt by the Indian army and the civilian population from within. As part of his plan to rebuild the INA, he demanded: 'a unit of brave Indian women to form a "Death-defying Regiment" who will wield the sword which the brave Rani of Jhansi wielded in India's First War of Independence in 1857'.

The same call went out to rapturous audiences in Malaya when Bose subsequently toured the Peninsula on a fund-raising campaign. Rasamma Bupalan, then only 16 years old, was in the crowd at Kuala Lumpur the day Netaji spoke:

> He offered no sweet talk. There was no cajoling, no persuasion. Stark facts: hunger, suffering, great privation – extreme privation – and even death. This was what he offered to us when we came into the INA. Because we would be soldiers of freedom; and we would be moving to [the] battleground, against the Allies in India.

It didn't seem to matter that Rasamma was of Ceylonese Tamil extraction, an Indian who had thus far never actually set foot on Indian soil; Bose's message was all-inclusive, directed equally at local Indian Muslims (whom Mohan Singh had never managed to win over) and even local Sinhalese (including employees of the jewellery shop B. P. de Silva's). The magnetism of Bose's personality swept Rasamma up, as it did a great number of Malayan Indians in Singapore and across the Malay Peninsula – men, women and children alike. Bose's rallies were often the first time they had attended a mass political event or witnessed a speech by a major Indian politician, let alone a revolutionary hero. Certainly, many Indians in Malaya (including Rasamma's parents) knew all about India's struggle for independence. However, British restrictions after the Singapore Mutiny of 1915 had prevented them from commenting on Indian politics in the press or from making any public expression of anti-British sentiment. Theirs was a silent, suppressed, largely private patriotism – until Bose arrived in town and blew its lid right off.

To Rasamma and other young Indian women, Bose's presence also promised liberation of another kind. The then 17-year-old Janaki Thevar, later the Rani of Jhansi regiment's second-in-command, declared in a Japanese Malayan newspaper:

> We may be the softer and fairer sex but surely I protest against the word 'weaker'. All sorts of epithets have been given to us by man in order to guard his own selfish interests. It is time we shattered this chain of man along with the chain of Indian slavery.

In late 1943, Rasamma and Janaki were two teenage Indian girls among roughly 500 Indian women who enlisted at the Rani of Jhansi's regimental headquarters on Singapore's Waterloo Street. Here, they were placed in the charge of Dr Lakshmi Swaminathan, the daughter of an Indian National Congress politician, who had settled in Singapore shortly before the outbreak of war. The daily drill was tough, the conditions basic and quite unlike the privileged middle-class world to which many of the girls were accustomed. As Janaki explained:

> It was all wooden huts, you know. No beds, nothing … We have to get up very early in the morning. As soon as the gong goes, you have to go. And you see a thousand girls in the camp rushing for bathrooms. It's so cold in the morning. Shower, come out and rush for PT, physical training. That was going on for half an hour. Then we came back. Then we have our breakfast … then started our army training.

Their training included rifle, grenade and machine gun practice, bayonet skills, tactical courses, night marches and assault charges. To Rasamma, the route marches through the town were a particular highlight:

> The people of Singapore – as they watched us marching from Waterloo Street, through Bras Basah, on to Orchard Road, down to the Botanic Gardens – were surprised. Never had they seen Indian women who were normally very demurely attired and very demurely conducting themselves … [at] full blast, singing, shouting. *Inquilab Zindabad, Inquilab Zindabad* – long live the revolution!

In March 1944, their training complete, Rassama, Janaki and the rest of the Rani of Jhansi regiment received instructions to march north and join the INA in Burma. Rasamma recalled the women's deep determination: 'We didn't want to be there for cosmetic value, we were there as real soldiers of freedom.' Indeed, the whole affair, like the rebirth of the INA itself, seemed driven forward by powerful ghosts from the past. Bose had personally asked the regiment's commander Dr Lakshmi to be the new '*Jhansi ki Rani*'; and just as the original Rani of Jhansi had fallen in battle in 1857, so the regiment that had taken her name was expected to go into battle and fight to the last. Their battle cry – '*Rani Lakshmibai*' – was a call to die like her. As Rasamma anticipated, the impact would come when the regiment reached the Bengal border and Indians witnessed 'their sisters and their mothers dying on the battlefield'. It was sure to have an effect 'just like wildfire'.

But after an arduous journey through 'miles of swamps' and 'padi fields', and having braved leeches 'at least six inches, stuck to your jodhpurs, stuck to your feet', Rasamma and Janaki arrived at the front only to find the Japanese army in retreat. By mid-1944, following the decisive Battle for Imphal, Allied forces had begun to push back the Japanese army across Burma. Rather than the victory or martyrdom that Rasamma and the other women expected, they were put to nursing and relief work:

> We waited patiently … And we waited. Then, of course, came the 1945 episode of Maflan, the monsoons … the lack of equipment … and the lack of anybody getting air power: this was really, really critical. And we were given orders to retreat … And we wept.

Subhas Chandra Bose reviews
the Rani of Jhansi at Waterloo
Street.
1943
NAS 19980005770-0051

Oath of loyalty signed by a
member of the Azad Hind
Sangh [Free India Association]
in Syonan.
1944
Card
H 8.4 x W 9.5 cm
NMS 2000-00181

The remnants of the INA limped back into Malaya in 1945. Bose returned to Singapore to try and renew support for the INA, but in defeat the cry '*Chalo Delhi*' had lost much of its former lustre. His war ended in August 1945 when he died in a plane crash in Taiwan.

After the Japanese surrender, Rasamma and Janaki were briefly held by the British for questioning and then released. Following the war, they both became influential figures in Malaysian politics. How much they and the INA actually achieved in the name of Indian independence will probably always be a contested issue. Nevertheless, both women would remain fiercely proud of their efforts as teenage girl soldiers and of what they saw as their fundamental role as overseas participants in India's liberation struggle.

Masuri S. N.: a poet's awakening

For young Malay nationalists in Singapore, any hopes that they might have placed in Japan's 'Asia for Asians' evaporated much earlier. As we have seen, Mustapha Hussein and his fellow KMM members awoke to the reality behind such rhetoric when the Japanese rebutted their demand for political independence. Four months after Singapore's fall, the Japanese banned the KMM outright and in July 1943 they announced their intention to portion off the northern states of Kedah, Perlis, Kelantan and Trengganu to Thailand. Disillusioned, Mustapha had by this time retired from the scene and returned to his home in Perak.

But the story did not end there – at least, not quite. Over the next three years, Malay nationalism underwent its own rebirth. There was little of the drama that accompanied the revival of the INA, but just as certain young Indians in Singapore and Malaya found their nationalism through the heady emotion of Bose's rallies, so too some young Malays were beginning to feel theirs through the emotive power of art. Even if the Japanese restricted Malays from organising themselves politically, they gave a new generation of Malay writers, filmmakers and actors unprecedented access to the media. Japan's demand for propaganda provided the stimulus for a cultural efflorescence that after the war would transform Singapore into a kind of Malay artistic mecca.

Among the new writers was Masuri S. N., set to become one of Singapore's most illustrious post-war poets. Masuri was just 15 years old when Japanese tanks rolled through the city. A few months later, he was one of several young literati to respond to the call from a Japanese-sponsored newspaper, the *Berita Malai* [Malay News], for local Malay contributions.

Like other Malay Syonan periodicals, such as *Fajar Asia* [Asian Dawn] and *Semangat Asia* [Spirit of Asia], *Berita Malai* manifested a split personality. On the one hand it published crude propaganda about Japan's relentless victories and the coming of 'New Asia'; on the other hand, it featured poems, short stories (a relatively new genre in Malay writing) and heavily politicised editorials, all addressed to a Malay audience by their own people. Its circulation of 10,000 gave writers such as Masuri a platform to circulate their thoughts on the spirit of the age, the harshness of wartime conditions and what it meant to belong to the Malay *bangsa* [people]. Anti-Japanese sentiments had to be read between the lines (they relied on a heavy use of literary allusion), but they seem to have been readily understood by the paper's readership, while sailing well over the head of the average Japanese censor.

Masuri wrote 15 poems during the Japanese Occupation, several of which appeared in the *Berita Malai*. His poem '*Rayuan Kelana*' ['The Wanderer's Appeal'] expresses the heartfelt call of one young Malay to his nation. It also stands as testament to the growing suffering in Singapore as the Japanese Occupation wore on.

> I glance at a beggar of my people
> On the five-foot way he sits forlorn
> My heart fills with despair
> A fellow man's fate foregone
>
> Not able to look away
> I feel the agony of his poverty
> Without any friend or family
> No relief for soul or for body
>
> Will no one feel pity
> For this beggar pleading
> Many just laugh
> And delight in demeaning
>
> To the generous of my people
> Give a little of your charity
> That this forsaken one
> Should find purpose in a destiny

The 'Cosmocracy' goes bankrupt

There was, of course, a much darker side to the opportunities that the Japanese Occupation presented. By early 1943, the outer edges of Hirohito's Greater

Eastern Empire had begun to buckle under Allied pressure – first at the Battle of Midway in June 1942, then at Guadalcanal in November. Things were also beginning to fall apart in Japan's Southeast Asian capital. Japanese efforts to kick-start an economy stalled by the loss of its rubber exports failed, and living conditions in Syonan lurched from bad in the latter half of 1942, to worse the following year, and to appalling by the end of 1944.

Increasingly, people depended on alternative sources for their daily necessities. These were the years when rope was made from pineapple fibre; paper from bamboo, pineapple leaves and *lallang* (a kind of grass); soap from coconut shells and palm oil, or from leaves, flowers and cinnamon bark; and when buses and taxis had to run on charcoal, a substance that when finely ground proved a popular substitute for toothpaste.

These were also the years when the black market's covert networks of supply and demand took over. As former middleman Ng Seng Yong described it:

> [E]veryone is a broker. You start trying to sell things for one friend to another. … One has to know a lot of friends. And you just go from a friend to another. … Sometimes you practically walked half a day trying to contact each other.

The Japanese were in on the game as well: certain high-ranking officers were even suspected of being the prime architects of the local underground economy. As they had before the war, Singapore's rural outskirts continued to supply the city, but now in a manner that was fraught with risk. Corrupt Japanese officials and clerks (as well as their Taiwanese and Korean intermediaries) delivered goods and food to remote *kampongs* where local villagers were paid to help conceal the merchandise until the black marketeers appeared to claim it. The punishment for such racketeering was usually severe, but its severity appeared to depend on where you were apprehended. Press notices indicate that racketeers caught in the city faced heavy fines or jail sentences, whereas eyewitness accounts tell of those caught in the countryside being summarily executed by beheading.

Yet even the black market found it hard to cope with increasing shortages. Any habitué of Syonan coffee shops would have witnessed clear signs of the island's economic deterioration. Coffee beans were soon rationed, which meant many shops had to close for sometimes two weeks out of every three; next, white sugar became scarce and had to be replaced by coconut sugar; at around the same time, soft drinks and beer disappeared from the menu, as the factories that produced them halted production; and then, finally, milk supplies ceased. By mid-1944, most coffee shops in the city had shut for good.

In response, Japanese propaganda demanded that the populace be more self-sufficient. Exhibitions demonstrated how various substitute foodstuffs might be manufactured with a little ingenuity – and a large disregard for taste. All forms of mass media encouraged people to plant their own food: 'Grow More Food

Signage of a food ration distribution centre.

1940s
Wood
H 105.7 x W 30.1 x D 2.1 cm
NMS 1998-00847

Food-deprived citizens of
Syonan planting vegetables
on the grounds of St Joseph's
Institution (now the Singapore
Art Museum).

From *Syonan Gaho* magazine, 1942
NMS 1995-01102

Campaign Should Not Be Somebody Else's Affair' ran the headline of the *Syonan Shimbun* in August 1943, employing the seemingly ubiquitous language and tone of government announcements everywhere.

Unfortunately, the soil in Singapore had never been fertile enough for major agricultural undertakings. The notorious Occupation diet of tapioca and sweet potatoes established itself because these foods were easiest to plant and cheapest to buy. But while tapioca contained calories it was low on essential vitamins. As rice became more heavily rationed, malnutrition and associated diseases such as beriberi, tuberculosis, pneumonia and dysentery increased. The total number of officially recorded deaths in Singapore leapt from an average of 15,000 per year before the war, to more than double that number in the Occupation's last two years, peaking at 42,751 in 1944.

As the magnitude of these shortages sank in, the Japanese authorities created two new agricultural settlements across the straits in Malaya, intending that Syonan city-dwellers should relocate there. The first settlement was established at Endau in late 1943 with the cooperation of the OCA and a year later it numbered around 12,000 settlers, and so proved a qualified success. The second settlement was founded at Bahau in Negeri Sembilan and settled by Chinese and (particularly) Eurasian Roman Catholics. The Japanese imagined that they could transform this community's former clerks, teachers and minor administrators into pastoral labourers rooted to the land, but the whole experiment proved disastrous. The soil was poor, the site malarial and the agricultural skills of the settlers limited. Many died (as many as 3,000 by some accounts), including a fearfully high proportion of infants.

Syonan slaves and the 'living corpses'

The 'Great Spirit of Cosmocracy' was also on its way to full-scale moral bankruptcy – if, indeed, given the *sook ching* and the *kempeitai*'s other sadistic endeavours it could be said to have possessed any moral capital to begin with. The tragic stories of women across Malaya who were forced to be the sex slaves of the Japanese army is now well known. In Singapore, the fate of Korean women, in particular, unmasked the sordid reality behind Japan's 'Greater East Asian Co-Prosperity Sphere'. Korea, a Japanese colony since 1910, provided innocent girls who travelled to Syonan on the promise of employment in the city's Japanese restaurants. On arrival, they were taken off to work as 'comfort women' on the island of Sentosa, which the Japanese military had turned into a brothel, or to other 'comfort houses' located elsewhere in the city, at Katong, in Cairnhill Road and even in the former Singapore Chinese Girls' School at Emerald Hill. There, they were enslaved with other women from Taiwan and Indonesia, as well as from Malaya and Singapore.

Another group that was sold promises of new prospects in Syonan only to end up in bondage were the *romusha*, migrant labourers from Java. Chin Sin Chong, a Chinese student employed by the Japanese army, once accompanied a Japanese officer on a visit to a *romusha* camp on Henderson Road:

> [T]here were quite a number of sick patients there. I understand some of them were actually still undergraduates. So they were actually being brought here under the pretext that they would be given a job. There were also quite a number of Indonesian girls ... so they were brought here to entertain the [Japanese] officers. So they, too, had been bluffed.

Chin observed that the *romusha* were fed on rice but 'probably not enough', which led some to escape and forage for themselves. The Japanese at first arrested those who had escaped and returned them to their camps, but then as food shortages in Singapore grew worse they let their prisoners go. The sight of emaciated Javanese youth living out on the streets, begging and scavenging for food, was probably what inspired Masuri to write his poem 'The Wanderer's Appeal'.

The *romusha*'s plight certainly affected another Malay writer who would come to prominence in Singapore after the war. In 1946, Ahmad Luthfi published *Bangkai Bernyawa* [Living Corpses] a novel drawn from real-life incidents he had witnessed as a Syonan journalist. His story centres around the arrival in

Singapore of Pardi and Mas Rahmat, two of perhaps 300,000 *romusha* who left Java on overcrowded and ill-equipped ships, many of whom would never reach their destinations:

> In the train everyone was in their own world. There were those who were lying down because they didn't have enough energy to sit; there were those who squatted; there were also those who seemed like they were waiting for death, because they were severely hungry and none of them looked happy or at ease …

> [Mas Rahmat's thoughts then turn inwards] … a body, thin and withered, that would have separated from my bones, were it not for skin; a face that has changed from being clean to being full of scabs and black from dust; clothes that are torn beyond all mending; perhaps no one will recognise me.

The Japanese Occupation is estimated to have claimed the lives of 19,000 *romusha* in Malaya and Singapore alone. After the war, only 8,500 survived to be repatriated.

But even as Syonan faced escalating shortages and the consequent hunger and misery, the city still managed to throw up a fair display of material excess. Down one street, a newcomer might be presented with distressing scenes of squalor; then, around the corner, an ostentatious display of wealth by Occupation opportunists. This was the time of the 'mushroom millionaires' – of racketeers, pimps, gamblers and tricksters. It was also a time when, as one survivor's memoir puts it, society as a whole turned 'upside down'. 'Old money' hid its wealth or lost it to the OCA's 'donation'; public employees (especially English-educated teachers and clerks) found themselves suddenly unemployed; rickshaw coolies and hawkers emerged as the new middlemen – the vital entrepreneurs who kept the wheels of the black market turning. And while some residents sold their possessions to feed their families, or were forced to go out and beg, money flowed, once again, into the reopened 'Worlds' amusement parks – into drinking, flirting and especially gambling. Singapore was still a city of striking, sometimes shocking contrasts.

26. ENDURANCE, RESISTANCE, VICTORY

The YMCA building, once used by the *kempeitai* as their headquarters.

1940s
Paper
H 5.2 x W 8.2 cm
NMS 1999-02394

As Japan's Asian empire spun towards collapse, as if someone had pressed fast-forward on its inevitable decline and fall, the *kempeitai* in Syonan responded with further erratic violence. The initial massacre of the city's Chinese had shown that the occupiers' nervousness and their brutality went hand in hand. However, a second *sook ching* did not eventuate. Instead, the Japanese unleashed a more focused terror. From mid-1942 the *kempeitai* sharpened the apparatus of the Syonan police state: the tools of choice were now raids, arrests, detentions and sadistic interrogations. Having dealt retribution to an entire community, it was time to turn on individuals.

The atmosphere of menace that the *kempeitai* created could only intensify now that it was clear what they were capable of. Their headquarters – in the 'East District' the former YMCA building along Stamford Road and in the 'West District' a nondescript block on Smith Street in Chinatown – cast shadows across the entire city. Heng Chiang Ki, then a young canteen worker, remembered: 'So once you are in you had it. Nobody leaves the place without being beaten up. It's a question of how serious you are beaten up.'

Yet the Syonan police state still depended on some degree of local compliance. Early in the Occupation, the *kempeitai* sent plain-clothes officers onto the streets to keep tabs on the populace, while at the same time co-opting the former, now 're-educated', colonial police force. But from late 1942, the need for surveillance

over the entire population led to a new system of auxiliary police. This *jikeidan* system, as it was called, operated through a hierarchy of 'starred' local officers. At street level was the 'one-star' man, usually in charge of a neighbourhood of around 30 households; he reported to the 'two-star' man in charge of a district, who in turn informed the 'three-star man', who answered directly to the *kempeitai*. With such a network of local informers in place the cycle of rumour, investigation and arrest (followed by more investigations and then further arrests) took an inevitable toll on neighbourhood life. Storekeeper Soon Kim Seng recalled:

> People would be wondering, 'When is my turn coming …?' All somebody needs to do is spread a false rumour or talk something about somebody and the *kempeitai* would look out for that individual and say, 'Oh, you are pro-British, pro-American or pro-Nationalist China … or you are a communist or you are a black marketeer. They would accuse [you] of anything … just come and take you away for questioning and detain you indefinitely.

Which brings us to what seems almost a paradox: for out of this climate of distrust and suspicion, networks of resistance formed that survived the *kempeitai*'s efforts to crush them and endured until well after the war. Fear, like poverty, seems to have acted on Syonan as a great social leveller. While it pushed some people to throw in their lot with their oppressors, it led others to band together against them – despite their social differences and, literally, 'in spite' of the great dangers that this involved.

Anti-Japanese resistance had its stronghold in the Malayan jungle: this was where the remnants of Dalforce, along with other anti-Japanese elements, had fled after Singapore's fall, and from where a revolutionary army would eventually reach out to the Peninsula's towns and cities. In Singapore, especially, the heroism of individuals, who under extreme and terrifying circumstances refused to give away their friends and their allies, would eventually find a place at the heart of the nation's collective memory.

The torture of Elizabeth Choy

On 27 September 1943, British and Australian commandos raided Keppel Harbour and blew up seven Japanese ships. The *kempeitai* suspected that local POWs were involved and that they had relayed messages from Singapore to Allied forces. On 10 October, in what became known as the infamous 'Double Tenth' incident, the *kempeitai* raided Changi Gaol and seized hidden radio sets. Fifty-seven European prisoners and an unknown number of local civilians were taken away for interrogation. Fifteen of those detained subsequently died during torture.

Elizabeth Choy and her husband were at that time employed as hospital canteen workers at the Miyako Mental Hospital (the predecessor to Woodbridge). Here they had helped smuggle food, medicine and parts for building radio sets to

Allied POWs. Choy's ordeal began at the end of October when her husband was arrested at the hospital canteen, following the *kempeitai*'s initial interrogation of the prisoners from Changi:

> [O]ne day, the soldiers, the *Kempeitai* also came to me. They said, 'You know, you want to see your husband?' I said, 'Yes, of course.' 'All right, we take you to see him.'

Anxious that her husband might be cold, Choy asked permission to bring along a blanket for him. The Japanese officer agreed.

> So I was very happy. So I went. And I was taken to YMCA. And there they questioned me ... and took all my things away, my handbag, my jewellery, everything. Nothing left ... And you know I was taken into the cell with nothing except a blanket.
>
> And in that cell ... about 10 by 12 feet, there's nothing but all these detainees, all squatting there, kneeling there like dumb-bells. Nothing. Couldn't move, couldn't talk, couldn't do anything, not allowed to ... Every night we could hear the agony, crying people, being beaten and crying out. It's heart-breaking.

The cell had no windows, only one narrow air vent, and a hole in the floor with a single tap where the occupants used both to 'do their business' and to drink. Choy shared this cell with 20 other detainees, a mixture of local civil servants, professionals, businessmen and a few Europeans. The stench was suffocating. Food was pushed in through a small hole in the wall:

> [T]hey will feed you with little bit of rice, a small bowl of rice and little bit of meat, little bit of vegetables ... what they called starvation diet. Very effective.

By her own account, Choy's waistline shrank from 25 to 12 inches. But that was not the worst. Almost daily, she was taken away for interrogations. The *kempeitai* could come for their prisoners at any hour of day or night.

> You know when they interrogate you, they would beat you, they would torture you – they would do all kinds of things to you. ... So one day they put some bars of wood on the floor and they tied me up. And I had to kneel on this wood, very rough wood. And they stripped me, the top – topless really, topless. And they tied me to the wood so that I couldn't go forward, I couldn't go backward, I couldn't go sideways. And they applied electric shock to me.
>
> [T]hey brought my husband – I didn't know where he was before. They brought my husband. He was kneeling beside there, watching me being tortured. They said, 'Now, both of you confess, we'll let you go. If not, we'll execute both of you.' My husband said, 'I've nothing to tell you.' They said, 'All right.' They tortured me. Oh, that was terrible! Unless you have gone

Elizabeth Choy.
1955
NAS 19980001106-0019

through it, you don't know what it's like. They're torturing you. Of course, you cry, and then your tears will come, your nose will be running.

After giving you the shock, they questioned you – after giving you the shock, they questioned you! Oh, it's terrible! Absolutely horrible!

Choy was released after almost 200 days. She had given nothing away and implicated no one*.

I went to the office, I crawled into the office. They gave me my handbag, all my things. They said, 'All right, you can go now.'

And I just walked out, looking left and right and everywhere – it's so strange. But for how many years, I never wanted to pass YMCA, never wanted to go that way, never wanted to look at that building. I'm so glad now that building is pulled down. Awful memories. It's like another world. I don't think hell could be worse than that.

Chia Chore Seng and the young devils

As we've begun to see, the Japanese Occupation confronted the majority Chinese population of Singapore with an intense dilemma of loyalty. As the largest local community now under Japanese rule, and the second largest across the whole of Malaya, where did their allegiances lie? With their old colonial masters or with their new ones; with their communities and their families; with one of the two nationalist parties that claimed to represent their ancestral homeland and that were now locked in a bitter war of resistance; or (ultimately) with themselves?

For many young Chinese people such a complex choice was in fact a simple one through which they displayed personal bravery on a par with the likes of Elizabeth Choy. Chew Lee Ngor worked in a shop in Kallang during the day and at Great World amusement park in the evenings. She also gathered donations and passed on confidential communications for the anti-Japanese resistance:

I remember one day I was given some posters, they read: 'Down with the Japanese imperialist!' and 'Down with the traitor!'

The leader asked us to go round pasting posters. We did not know how serious it was. When there were no Japanese soldiers around, we quickly pasted it up and then quickly ran away. The next day, many people went to see the poster. I dared not see it myself. I pasted posters mainly in Jalan Besar area. There were two of us doing this. At that time I was brave. I was running around the streets at midnight. Later I was arrested. We were known as [the] 'Anti-Japanese Unit'. I was always contacted by the same person. She was a woman. She was also arrested and later hanged. She was young.

As for Chia Chore Seng, his decision to join the resistance meant defying his father's express wishes. He had originally come to Singapore to attend the

---

* Elizabeth Choy's husband also survived the interrogation and was relased some time after her.

Presbyterian Boys' School but when the Japanese invaded he returned to Kota Tinggi in Johor to be with his family. There, his father was made head of the local branch of the OCA and Chia and his classmates set up a bookstall to raise funds for the Association's 'gift' to the Japanese. Soon, however, they turned to pasting anti-Japanese handbills and collecting anti-Japanese donations. The news coming out of the jungle was that a Malayan People's Anti-Japanese Army (MPAJA) had been formed to wage a guerrilla war against the occupiers. Chia and his friends decided to enlist:

> It was not a question of whether to or not, because in my class, of the four of us, three had already joined, leaving only me. I was the last to join ...
>
> At that time, I believed that my father would allow me to go, but he was worried that at my age, I did not know the severity of such matters. So that night, he tied me up in the room.
>
> I do not even know what time it was that I left. I remember vaguely that it was dusk, past 4 p.m. Two men came. My clothes were ready. I packed quickly and ran. That's all I remember.

The Malayan Communist Party (MCP) had created the MPAJA from the remnants of Dalforce soon after Singapore's fall. But on 1 September of that same year, disaster struck. Thanks to the duplicity of MCP leader Lai Teck, who had been a British agent but was now a double agent working for the Japanese, almost the entire leadership of the party was ambushed (during a secret meeting near Batu Caves outside Kuala Lumpur) and either arrested or killed.

Nonetheless, the MPAJA survived, recovered and by the end of 1943 had made contact with Force 136, a British-led force of clandestine Special Operations Executive agents. Force 136 provided the MPAJA with arms (usually dropped from Allied planes), training and, at least in theory, overall strategic leadership (though, in reality, for much of the time the MPAJA acted independently of its British advisors). When Chia joined the MPAJA, in the second half of 1944, it was growing towards its eventual strength of 10,000 guerrilla fighters.

The majority of these were Chinese working-class men, but there were also women and units made up solely of youngsters. Chia remembered being assigned to one of these junior divisions, known in Chinese as *xiao gui* [little devils], where no one in his unit was more than 20 years old. While the older, 'rougher' guerrillas would 'carry the light machine gun and the bombs', the training of the *xiao gui* was just as serious and intensive:

> You woke up at 5 a.m. You had to be up by 5.30 a.m. for morning exercise. After morning exercise is your free time ... There's also a rest time in the afternoon ... After that is the military meeting – that is, a discussion of the day's issues, what everyone has done. And after that there is more rest time and then military exercises, like learning how to throw a grenade in

Chia Chore Seng, aged 17, in a studio portrait taken just after the Japanese surrender.
1945
Courtesy of Chia Chore Seng

315

the field, or how to shoot a gun ... After dinner would be the individual learning time, or reading, or talking, or politics class.

Inevitably, a guerrilla army that was backed by the MCP instilled revolutionary leftist doctrine in even its teenagers. Yet Chia recalled that the jungle was also a great teacher. It forced the *xiao gui* to be self-reliant and innovative: to 'use our own brains, use our own circumstances ... utilise the environment'. The soldiers made their beds out of enormous leaves that grew on jungle trees; their food came from the ubiquitous tapioca plant, in the form of tapioca flour and tapioca leaves. Chia remembered such 'revolutionary food' as a particular hardship of jungle life. Yet on the day when better rations finally arrived, he found himself too full of nerves to enjoy them:

> That was my first time. I had just cooked a huge rice ball that morning, had cooked the rice but not the vegetables. Everyone was allowed to take some rice. I took a leaf, and wrapped it up, placed it in a bag, and hence set off. ...
>
> It can be said that this was my first such battle experience. I was very frightened because I didn't know where the Japanese were coming from, from which direction. But frequently, I noticed the rubber plantation that was opposite ... Our commanding officer told the section head that the Japanese would come from that direction. So we all gathered at one place and waited for a day. ...
>
> But I found it difficult, not easy to stand, not easy to sit. I even forgot to eat my rice ball. By the time it came to eat my rice ball it was already stuck within the pockets of my pants. I was so afraid – this was my first experience – so afraid, that my rice ball was never eaten ...
>
> Indeed, close to noon on the second day the Japanese reached the rubber plantation. But once at the rubber plantation, the Japanese seemed to know that we were in the vicinity. It was very odd: they seemed to have discovered that we were in this vicinity. Their commanding officer held up his long sword and split them into two groups ...
>
> We could also see them from our side. But we held our fire, in the hope that they would get nearer before we fired ... The moment I fired, my heart felt more settled, there was no fear or anything at all, because I had fired.

Using hit-and-run tactics like this, lying in ambush and waiting for the enemy to pass, the MPAJA harried the Japanese through late 1944 and with increasing intensity through 1945. Finally, almost at the same moment as the Japanese formally surrendered to the Allies on the Singapore Padang, the British ordered the MPAJA to come out of their jungle hideouts and disband. Force 136 subsequently collected the soldiers' arms and equipment, paid each man a discharge fee and instructed them to return to civilian life.

However, though the British regarded the MPAJA's war as over, for Chia and his comrades life could not so easily return to normal. War had transformed them

Singapore Governor Sir Franklin Gimson (extreme right) inspecting troops made up of representatives of Force 136 and MPAJA at a victory parade in London.
April 1946
Tham Sien Yen Collection/NAS
20080000015-0106

into seasoned resistance fighters who had won a major victory over a foreign occupier and who now understood many new things about the world. Not least of these, as unemployment and recession threatened amidst the post-war wreckage, was that if life under the British failed to improve they could always resort to further armed struggle.

Final surrender

At the beginning of 1945, the *Syonan Shimbun* declared that this was the 'year in which enemy will be driven out of entire East Asia'. Over the next six months, Japanese reports from the front were couched in similar vainglorious terms. But by this time most Syonan inhabitants had come to see through the bluster of their imperial masters. A population that had already experienced the hollow British propaganda of early 1942 sensed that Japan must be nearing defeat.

On 6 August 1945, the Americans dropped their atomic bomb on Hiroshima. Three days later, they dropped another on Nagasaki. Emperor Hirohito formally declared the Japanese surrender on 15 August. Yet the Japanese Occupation of Singapore did not suddenly end; rather, the city remained for over two weeks in a quiet and uneasy limbo. The local press did not publish official notice of the surrender until 20 August. Prior to this, though news of the surrender had spread through back-street radios and word of mouth, the Japanese remained nominally in charge.

On 4 September 1945, British and Japanese representatives met discreetly on a Royal Navy cruiser just outside Keppel Harbour. The British presented the Japanese with their terms of surrender, based largely on the Japanese surrender agreement that had been negotiated in Rangoon the previous week. Its terms treated Japanese soldiers as 'surrendered personnel' rather than as prisoners of war and required them to maintain law and order until Allied forces arrived.

Their additional instructions were to ensure the supply of water and electricity, and to preserve the island's other infrastructure, its inventories of stores and equipment and its war records.

Many Japanese soldiers were not prepared to sit by idly and wait for the shame of captivity. Hundreds committed suicide before the British returned, ending their lives with one last sake party, in which the final toast was followed by a self-detonated explosion of grenades. Other Japanese soldiers deserted and switched allegiance to the nationalist forces that were emerging across Southeast Asia – to anti-Dutch movements in Sumatra or, closer still, to the Malayan Communist Party.

On 5 September, British and Commonwealth forces made landfall unsure of what awaited them, their craft having approached the city in full battle formation. Then, as the war diary of the 5th Indian Division recorded:

> Singapore itself appeared, no longer hidden from view by these Islands
> that cover the approaches. Suddenly, the scene opened up, and the water
> line became visible in its wide semi-circle, a mass of buildings along the
> front showing clearly against a dull and thundery sky. …

In the dock area, only a few civilians were there to witness the British return. But a small number of dockers and coolies gave a cheer and a wave of greeting, and several Chinese shouted from the roofs of the customs sheds.

That evening Singapore clocks showed Malayan time, the Union Jack flew over the Cathay Building and the three Worlds amusement parks once more hopped to the sounds of Western jazz.

A week later, cheering locals turned out again, but in greater number, for the official surrender ceremony. By 10 a.m. that day, the Padang was packed with spectators, as were the rooftops of neighbouring buildings. Across the city, Union Jacks flew alongside Guomindang flags – a sure indication that victory belonged in the popular consciousness as much to China as the British Empire. At the ceremony, Admiral Lord Louis Mountbatten, Supreme Commander of Southeast Asia, inspected the guards of honour, then a small group of seven senior Japanese officers arrived and all parties entered City Hall to sign the official documents. When the Japanese delegation emerged afterwards the air of solemnity had passed. The crowd outside now shouted and hooted, their angry cries of *'Bakaro'* sending the Japanese on their way.

Most Japanese soldiers who remained in Singapore were put to hard labour. At the Padang, angry civilians gathered around their work details to mock and jeer at them. There were similar scenes in the city's main streets, where passing Japanese soldiers were surrounded by crowds of Chinese who beat them and sometimes forced them to kneel and beg for mercy – a copy-cat reprisal for the cruelty that so many had experienced over the previous three and a half years.

Singapore had turned upside down once again and in a sense, with the British reinstalled, regained some of its equilibrium. Yet even among the departing Japanese, whose empire now lay in ruins, there was an understanding that this island colony could never be the same. The final Singapore reminiscence of the sinister Colonel Tsuji conveyed a wider truth:

> The bronze statue of Raffles appeared on its pedestal for the second time; but without anyone knowing the reason, its colour appeared to have faded. Judging from its expression it may be that it had lost confidence in the principle of government by force.

Local Chinese parade a giant Guomindang flag during a celebration following the Japanese surrender.
1945
SLV H98.101/163-185

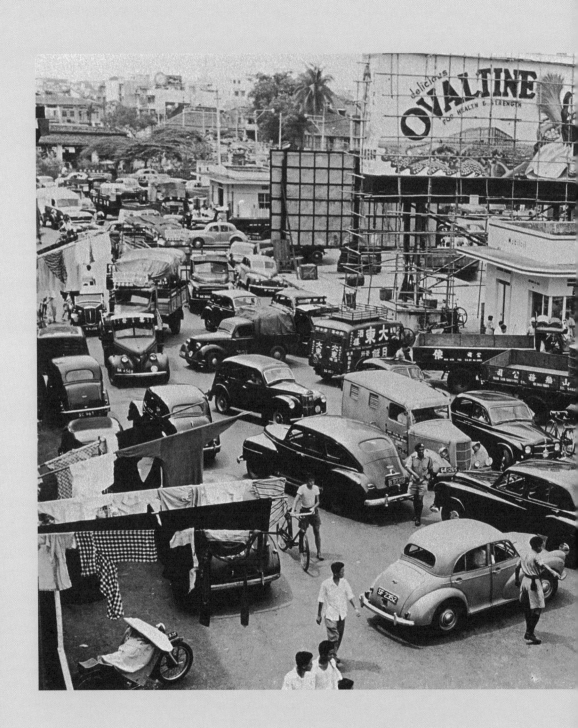

MERDEKA
1945 – 1959

26. A New Beginning

How far did World War II change the course of Singapore history? Was it a major rupture with the past, a drastic change in direction that signalled a new epoch? Or was it more of an interlude, an interruption, after which the same political forces as were at work before the conflict – namely communism, capitalism and colonialism – took up where they had left off, only now more intensely?

The answer is, a bit of both. On the public stage the city witnessed the return of familiar combatants: English-educated lawyers, doctors, journalists and other professionals who once more laid out their case for a greater say in the colony's government; radical leftists who preferred a more revolutionary solution to the colonial predicament; and – facing both these groups – European officials, who held steadfast to their view that Singapore belonged to Britain and that any political change must be gradual, cautious and carefully thought through.

Nonetheless, there were clear signs that Singapore had entered a new era. Now, the English-educated with political ambitions ventured outdoors to speak, the microphone and the radio carried their voices further, and more people gathered to listen to what they had to say (especially when they denounced colonialism and demanded independence). At the same time, communists, unionists and other leftists discovered their ranks swelled by the young, the unemployed and the frustrated. Even the character of colonial officialdom underwent a transformation.

PREVIOUS PAGE:
Traffic jam as petrol pump attendants go on strike.
May 1955
SPH 19990006071-IMG0056

Microphone.
1960s
Metal
H 45 x W 12.5 cm
NMS 2006-00232

RIGHT: 'Missing out on School' by the artist Koeh Sia Yong.
1960s
Woodcut
H 55.9 x W 40.7 cm
NMS 1999-02608

New imperial servants arrived in 'the East' to find the British Empire in retreat. India gained independence in 1947, Burma the following year, and it seemed that while Singapore and Malaya remained crucial to Western strategic interests, their own decolonisation was not far off. All across the region, colonial subjects were throwing off their shackles to demand an immediate transfer of power to the people. World War II had been the catalyst for a sudden run on that priceless commodity called freedom.

In Malay the word for such freedom was '*merdeka*', which soon became an all-encompassing catchword: it turned up as the crowd-pleasing mantra at the public gatherings led by a new generation of charismatic political leaders; it was shouted down city streets by students and workers on the march, and sprayed across their banners and placards; and it was given its own salute, a clenched fist held out at or above shoulder level (not unlike the 'black power' salute that would emerge in the US during the late 1960s). By the end of the 1950s, '*merdeka*' was emblazoned on badges and calendars, and embossed on commemorative plates, cups, clocks and even beer mugs.

What *merdeka* actually meant and how it was to be achieved were issues that would rouse much debate and ultimately political conflict. But this is a story that comes later in our narrative, for in the immediate post-war years the battle lines were not so clearly drawn. Rather, and in spite of all the turbulence and turmoil that subsequently emerged, the early years of Singapore's freedom struggle were a time of enormous excitement and experimentation – and in the short term, at least, of shared and common expectation.

Sudden peace and retribution

Even before the war ended the British government had decided that things in Singapore and Malaya were going to change. In the future, colonial rule would be more direct and efficient, it would provide military security and ultimately it would bring the people closer together as one coherent nation, with a view to them forming a self-governing dominion of the wider British Commonwealth. Tasked with this momentous undertaking was the Malaya Planning Unit (MPU). From mid-1943, from its offices at London's Hyde Park Gate, the MPU drew up plans for a Malayan Union made up of the former Straits Settlements, the Malay States, North Borneo, Brunei and Sarawak – a new territorial entity with a common citizenship to be ruled directly from Britain. Added impetus for the Union came when in 1945 the British people elected a Labour government to replace Churchill and his Conservatives. In a Britain drained by the war, the natural end of colonialism became decolonisation, even though Singapore and Malaya were still seen as having key long-term strategic significance.

In the way of the British plan for Malayan Union stood several, some might say insuperable, hurdles. To start with, the MPU's initial work was conducted thousands of miles away from Singapore and Malaya without much regard for the needs and expectations of the people who actually lived there. Secondly, Singapore proved – not for the last time – to be the fly in the ointment of any grand state-of-Malaya design. Though the Johor royalty, as well as some Chinese and British businessmen (who had escaped Syonan to wait out the war in India), wanted the Malayan Union plan to include Singapore, the British elected to drop the island from the proposal for fear its inclusion might endanger its free-port status and provoke the Malay States with the prospect of Chinese domination. Finally, the MPU was still in the process of drafting Singapore and Malaya's future when the Americans dropped their atom bombs. With no plans finalised yet for the post-war administration of both these territories, control of them passed to the British Military Administration (BMA) with Singapore as its headquarters.

The suddenness of the Japanese surrender likewise caught the MPAJA by surprise. It, however, had the advantage of a three-week period before the British return in which to fill the temporary power vacuum. Suddenly, Guomindang flags (the emblems of nationalist China) were unfurled in Chinese-populated districts to herald the arrival of victorious MPAJA regiments – regiments that emerged from their jungle hideouts to enter the towns and the cities and to immediately appoint themselves judge, jury and executioner over anyone thought to be a Japanese collaborator. After the MPAJA crossed the Causeway and entered Singapore, it unleashed a campaign of what the local Chinese called 'whispering terror' – proceeding on its own intelligence to administer arbitrary justice. Businessmen who had contributed to the Overseas Chinese Association's Japanese 'gift', along with the mistresses of Japanese officers, were singled out for abuse, public humiliation, even murder. Chinatown became almost completely lawless, run by criminal gangs such as the Exterminate Traitor Corps, the Blood and Iron Corps and the Dare to Die Corps. Ordinary bystanders were on the one hand uneasy at the disorder, and on the other not entirely ready to protest or intervene. As Low Ngiong Ing wrote, 'We could not find it in our hearts to condemn this wild justice, which we were too squeamish to mete out ourselves. Indeed, we were thankful to our guttersnipes for doing it for us.'

While the 'guttersnipes' might have used the MPAJA as a cover for their criminality, the organisation overall made great play of its legitimacy. As its soldiers marched in proudly to take control, their leader Lai Teck released his own blueprint for a new Malayan nation. His 'Eight-point Programme', circulated in late August 1945 ahead of the British announcement of their plan for a Malayan Union, committed the MPAJA to the establishment of a democratic government 'with an electorate drawn from all races of each state and the anti-Japanese army'. When just over a week later the British made landfall, they were faced with an unprecedented situation: a rival power had emerged from the jungle, a guerrilla army that in many people's eyes comprised the true heroes and defenders of Singapore and Malaya. Never before had colonial authority in these territories confronted such a real and still-armed alternative to itself. Much would depend on whether the British fulfilled their mandate to restore order and living conditions – and if not win the hearts and minds of the people, then at least convince them that colonialism, not communism, was the lesser of two evils.

The notorious BMA

Instead, the people of Singapore and Malaya got the BMA.

The BMA was given the mammoth task of getting Singapore eating, working and functioning again. But before its officials stood a mutilated landscape of wrecked military installations, tainted water supplies and makeshift 'farms' sitting on any plot of land that would yield tapioca. Looters and then soldiers who dipped into Japanese stockpiles temporarily flooded the market with rations, but such relief dissolved almost as soon as it arrived. Two days after British soldiers made landfall, the British authorities announced that they would not honour Japanese wartime currency (the so-called 'banana notes', named after the pictures they carried of the fruit). Locals who had scrimped, saved and perhaps connived through the Occupation to buy themselves a better future, at once found their savings worthless. As Japanese currency was tossed into the street with the trash, inflation skyrocketed. Rice shot up to 30 to 40 times its pre-war price, while other commodities hovered at ten times their pre-war level. By the end of 1945, the average individual rice ration was still only 4.5 ounces (130 grams) per day.

Not that food scarcity was the sole source of local grievances. To begin reconstruction work the BMA needed labour – and fast. By the end of 1945, it had become the single largest employer in Malaya with 102,000 workers in Singapore alone. Yet, nearly all of its employees were paid at pre-war wage levels and some

Royal Air Force servicemen checking the prices of goods sold by a street trader in an effort to curb opportunistic price increases.
November 1945
IWM CF831

had even been press-ganged into indentured servitude by labour contractors. In addition, as a temporary measure to restore government finances, the BMA decided to restart the import of opium into Malaya. Not only was the British government now the colony's most exploitative employer, it had resumed its place as the island's leading drug dealer.

Such policies might just have been excusable, especially considering the immense task the BMA faced, were it not for the administration's other failings. To begin with, the BMA exhibited the kind of crass racism towards the local population that must have made any reasonable colonial official of the 'old school' (whatever his prejudices) cringe and run for cover clutching his pith hat. Former Force 136 officer Colonel H. T. Pagden complained that the British military behaved 'as if they were in conquered enemy territory'. We get a glimpse of these 'occupiers'' insensitivity through the oversexed British musical (and later movie) *Privates on Parade* and the 1969 film *The Virgin Soldiers*, both of which celebrate the 'humorous antics' of a group of British National Servicemen posted to Singapore and Malaya during the late 1940s and early 1950s. For many of the island's local inhabitants, however, such 'antics' had a much darker side, involving attacks on stallholders and taxi drivers, at least one occasion when soldiers trashed a Chinese clan association, and numerous alleged cases of sexual harassment and even rape.

Then there was the corruption. Not for nothing was the BMA commonly known as the 'Black Market Administration'. Because BMA officers controlled many supplies and stores they were well-placed to grant favours to local businessmen or black-market dealers in exchange for generous kickbacks. As historians Chris Bayly and Tim Harper chronicle in their survey of the end of Britain's Asian empire: 'Military stores and "rehabilitation" goods disappeared en route to Malaya, or were landed in the wrong place; in the docks, goods vanished, invoices never appeared, or when they did, charges were paid three times over.' Scams and logistical sleight-of-hand became so commonplace that

The Malayan dollar, bearing a portrait of King George VI, was re-introduced after the Occupation.
1941
Paper
H 6.5 x W 12.5 cm
NMS NA-0168

an audit report later estimated the losses from these ad hoc 'arrangements' at over $15 million. For many BMA officers – volunteers from the army, planters, lawyers, accountants and businessmen, drafted into service based on their pre-war familiarity with Malaya rather than their experience of government administration – the opportunities for profits of up to 1,000 per cent through the black market were simply too tempting to let pass.

Unsurprisingly, local disillusionment with colonialism reached a new apex. For Lee Kuan Yew, later to become Singapore's first prime minister, the immediate months after the Japanese surrender completed his 'education in the unfairness and absurdities of human existence'. Singapore had become a 'very different place' from his memory of the colonial 1930s:

> The men now in charge – majors, colonels, brigadiers – knew they would be in power only until they were demobilised, when their wartime commissions would vanish like Cinderella's coach. The pumpkin of civilian life to which they would then be reduced was at the back of their minds, and many made the most of their temporary authority.

Lee left Singapore in late 1946 to study law in Britain, but he would return with a burning passion to rid his homeland of the British and in their place effect a Fabian-inspired socialist revolution. Ironically, Britain's return to Singapore and Malaya did stir a nascent nation into being: but as a consequence of her profound administrative failure in the colony rather than her imperial good intentions.

The 'Party' after the peace

It was in this climate of corruption, inequality and continuing post-war shortages that the Malayan Communist Party (MCP) made proverbial hay while the sun shined. In the first three years after the Japanese surrender, MCP members, especially through the 'front' provided by the MPAJA and its offshoots, were still lauded as national war heroes. Not only that: to be a communist was legal. The flags that appeared around Singapore may have belonged to the Guomindang, whose members had formed a part of the MPAJA and which experienced a popular post-war revival; but the real muscle that had fought the Japanese was communist, a fact the British recognised by acknowledging the Party's right to exist. Indeed, the MCP that emerged from the jungle had transformed itself into a new locally rooted entity. Some veterans now spoke and wrote of a Malaya that was their home, the land for which they had spilt their blood – the future site of a revolution that now held as important a place in their proletarian imaginations as China.

Their celebrations began at the Happy Valley amusement park on 2 October 1945 with a commemoration of Gandhi's birthday, during which a crowd of 7,000

FOOD CONTROL
MALAYA B 660652
REGISTRATION
CARD.

Food control card.
May 1948
Paper
H 15 x W 8.3 cm
NMS 1997-00109

chanted slogans that the Mahatma might have found rather disturbing: 'Long live the independence of India! Long live Mr Gandhi! Long live the communists in India! Long live the Malayan Communist Party!' One week later, on China's National Day, communists and Guomindang supporters led a street procession through the city that stretched five miles long. Over the next few months, Communist Party members managed to secure control of 8 of the 18 local relief centres set up under the BMA, often beating local charities and churches to the line. The Party also established its first newspaper, the *New Democracy*, which attacked the BMA and demanded immediate political independence. Though communist recruitment was mainly focused on idealistic Chinese youth who had been too young to join the MPAJA but had heard of its heroic efforts, Malay recruits were targeted too, as part of the Party's effort to be more representative of the Malayan nation. In particular, communist funds were dedicated to establishing a radical Malay nationalist paper, a development which ultimately led to the creation of the leftist Malay National Party (MNP).

Furthermore, the communists sought to woo Singapore's labour movement – then experiencing a powerful post-war resurgence through the revival of old unions and the creation of new ones – and it was here that the Party made its most visible impact on the daily rhythms of Singapore life. On 20 October 1945, Singapore witnessed the first of many post-war stoppages when 7,000 harbour workers walked off the job rather than load British troop ships bound for Indonesia. The BMA responded by drafting in Japanese soldiers as substitute labour, which only brought out more workers – from municipal employees (such as firemen and night-soil collectors) to cabaret girls – in sympathetic protest. Not long after, around 20,000 workers gathered (as was by now customary) at Happy Valley to establish the MCP-linked General Labour Union. Through December the strikes continued and spread to affect hospitals, taxi and bus companies, offices, garages, the telephone exchange and the post office.

It would be a mistake, however, to see the MCP as the sole architect of political protest in Singapore during the immediate post-war years. Much labour unrest at this time was spontaneous, prompted by universal shortages. The BMA's failure to rectify the situation even pushed Singapore's English-educated middle class out on the streets in protest. For this group, the attitude of the British authorities towards expatriate salaries, and the unfairness of an alternative pay-scale based on skin colour, were sources of deep discontent right through the late 1940s and 1950s.

In December 1945, one member of this disaffected class, a 25-year-old Eurasian journalist by the name of Gerald De Cruz, joined a new political organisation. It was called the Malayan Democratic Union (MDU) and its headquarters were in the Liberty Cabaret on North Bridge Road (later the site of the old Odeon Cinema and today's Odeon Towers). The MDU occupied a small office, consisting of a desk and a few chairs, situated on the floor above the dance floor, a space which its members also utilised in the hours before the musicians and taxi girls arrived for their evening shift. It was the kind of spontaneous set-up typical of Singapore's early *merdeka* politics: not particularly grand; in fact, in several people's minds rather seedy. Yet out of this dimly lit cavern of cigarette smoke and beer-fuelled talk about the failings of the government, there emerged something of significance: a political party that was multi-ethnic, led by the English-educated elite yet committed to the working man, and that was perhaps more than a little ahead of its time.

Gerald de Cruz at the Liberty Cabaret

The MDU, so De Cruz remembered, had been started by trainee-lawyer Lee Bee Hong and by William ('Billie') Kuok, the son of a Chinese trader and brother of Robert Kuok (later to become one of the richest businessmen in Southeast Asia). Both men had come up with the idea of the party whilst at the Japanese settlement in Endau and in late 1945 they came to De Cruz's front door to ask him to join them. De Cruz eventually became the Organising Secretary of the MDU, whose other leaders included the British-educated lawyer Philip Hoalim (of mixed European and Chinese descent), John Eber (another Eurasian lawyer) and Eu Chooi Yip (a Chinese journalist).

Their party's objective was to seek 'full democratic self-government for a united Singapore and Malaya as part of the British Commonwealth'. Nothing especially radical here, but the political methods that the MDU employed, especially when compared with those of Lim Boon Keng and Eunos Abdullah a generation earlier, were entirely new. Out went the polite petition, in came mass agitation. On 29 January 1946, the MDU announced its arrival on the political stage by leading a general strike of over 150,000 workers in Singapore and tens of thousands more in Malaya. For a two-month-old party, made up of only about 300 English-educated professionals, civil servants and clerks, it was a stunning achievement.

The MDU of course had help – more specifically, communist help. Some MDU leaders were sympathetic to the goals of communism; others, such as De Cruz himself, became Party members, if they were not so from the outset; all appeared to barely bat an eyelid at the prospect of communist collaboration. 'That shows you the extent to which [...] we were radicalised as a result of the Japanese Occupation,' De Cruz later remarked, 'we admired the communists for standing up to the Japanese while we did not have the organisation, the discipline or the know-how to do so.' Their attitude to working alongside the MCP was captured by the comment of one of De Cruz's non-communist colleagues from the MNP: 'Now we unite. After we have had independence, then we go our own ways and fight for popular support.' As De Cruz himself recalled: 'There was an extraordinary sense of tolerance in that time because what we wanted was [to] all work together in the same direction for self-determination.'

Gerard De Cruz.
1960s
Courtesy of the family of the late
Gerard De Cruz

Malayan Democratic Union
rally at Farrer Park.
Late 1940s
NAS

What is more, it was not always clear who was leading who in this struggle for *merdeka* – the communists or the MDU's non-communist liberals. On the question of civil and democratic rights, which came to a head over the British plan to reintroduce the Societies Ordinance and so control new political organisations, the MDU campaigned against the colonial authorities while the MCP under Lai Teck held back, wary of antagonising its former allies any further. Independently, as De Cruz recalled, Philip Hoalim and the rest of the MDU leadership fought the proposed British plan and won:

> And in this fight, it was the MDU that was the dog, and it was the MCP that was the tail. So we had a vigorous tail. But it was a tail nevertheless. And one of my functions in the MDU Committee was to try and persuade the MDU to follow the communist line. But in practice, in various situations like this, I was doing the reverse. I was being sent by the MDU to the Communist Party to follow the more vigorous MDU line.

Partly, the MDU took the lead on such matters because the MCP was so hamstrung by its cumbersome internal machinery. De Cruz claimed that for the Party to make any key decision on political strategy its Central Committee had first to meet, a major undertaking which usually took about three months to organise since Party members were spread out across the Malay Peninsula. But just as importantly, the communists needed the MDU's leadership because so few of them were at that time able to read and write English. To articulate the 'people's will' for the benefit of the British and the wider world, the MCP relied on De Cruz and his middle-class associates.

The MDU is best remembered for its crucial role in drafting and brokering the 'People's Constitution' (or 'People's Constitutional Proposals'), a document that called for the union of Malaya and Singapore under a democratically elected government which would grant equal citizenship for all races. Over the last four months of 1947, the MDU – as part of a broader coalition eventually called the All-Malaya Council of Joint Action (or AMCJA), which included communist-linked unions and veteran-soldier organisations, along with members of the MNP and the Malayan Indian Congress – helped orchestrate another massive popular agitation.

Once more, MDU leaders stood in the ideological vanguard of the movement, bringing in the support of Singapore's Chinese Chamber of Commerce and persuading the charismatic Tan Cheng Lock (the Straits Chinese leader whom we last heard complaining about the appalling acoustics in Singapore's Legislative Chamber) to act as the campaign's figurehead. Meanwhile, the communists stayed in the background, operating through their front organisations to ensure that busloads of supporters suddenly appeared whenever Joint Action leaders went out to the people to speak.

As De Cruz remembered, communist support even extended to the composition of a People's Constitution Chinese love song:

> [B]oy and girl talking to each other in a garden and then the girl sings to the boy. 'Oh darling', she says, 'Let's stop talking about ourselves and talk about the fate of our country. I have heard something about the People's Constitution. Can you explain to me what it is about?' And then the boy starts explaining in verse what it is about.

On the suggestion of Tan Cheng Lock, the campaign for the People's Constitution culminated on 20 October 1947 with a mass *hartal* (a political boycott of the entire colonial economy first introduced in India by Mahatma Gandhi). On that day, Kuala Lumpur and Singapore were reported to have come to a complete standstill, so that the only people to be seen out on the streets were anxious Council of Joint Action members, scurrying down the five-foot ways to confirm that the *hartal* was actually happening and that it was indeed a success.

Ultimately, however, the MDU's campaign for the 'People's Constitution' proved a great and admirable failure. The problem, as De Cruz saw it, was a simple one:

> It was a demonstration. It aroused the British. But after the *hartal* what do you do? We had no plan. We organised *hartals* but after that everything died down and went back to normal ... People were prepared to stop work and have a holiday for one day and that was a lot from our point of view. But from the government's point of view, it was just one day in the year. Where do you go from there? We didn't know.

When the AMCJA tried to organise further *hartals*, the Chinese Chamber of Commerce, which had provided significant financial support, backed out. Soon, the AMCJA began to fall apart and popular interest in its 'People's Constitution' began to dissipate. Hopes for a common citizenship shared by all Malaya's various ethnic communities were further dashed in January 1948, when, after two years of protests from conservative Malay nationalists, the British agreed to the dissolution of the Malayan Union and the restoration of the Federation of Malaya (along with the sovereignty, in principle, of the Sultans).

By that time also, the MDU was beginning to suffer for its close communist association. First, the MCP persuaded the MDU's leaders, all except the non-communist Philip Hoalim, to boycott the forthcoming elections for the Singapore Legislative Council in 1948, thereby robbing the MDU of its chance to establish its credentials as a legitimate political party dedicated to constitutional methods. Next, and even more crucially, there came that momentous event that sent shock waves across the entire Malay Peninsula: the communists' decision to take to the jungle and fight for an independent Malaya through armed insurrection.

The MDU's position was now untenable. Having decided to dissolve the party before the British did, its leaders went their separate ways: some to flee the country, others to stay on in Singapore and continue the fight for civil rights (and so face imprisonment), and yet others to join the communists in their jungle war of independence. For De Cruz it was a sudden and sad finale, which more than anything revealed the MDU's political innocence:

> I think it was too soon. It was too soon. You know, all of us may have been pro-communist and all that sort of thing. All of us may have at least become politically aware, but we were very green, very green … Events began to move so fast.

But the MDU did have one other important impact. Watching, sometimes participating and always learning, were several key personalities who would later transform Singapore's political landscape: a civil servant in the Social Welfare Department called Goh Keng Swee, who occasionally joined the MDU leaders for beer and discussions about politics after work; a unionist by the name of Devan Nair, who wandered into the Liberty Cabaret one day by accident, heard De Cruz giving a fiery speech against imperialism and found himself joining up; a journalist called Sinnathamby Rajaratnam who shared a bungalow with Eu Chooi Yip in Chancery Lane; and finally the 22-year-old Lee Kuan Yew, who knew Philip Hoalim as an old 'family friend' and had even seen a draft of the MDU's constitution (though he was not involved in its composition). Given the epic rifts and conflicts that would subsequently engulf Singapore post-war politics, it's worth remembering how close a world of mutual friends and associates it was.

27. OTHER MERDEKAS

The exact sequence of events that led to the outbreak of the Malayan Emergency in June 1948 is difficult to trace. Late the previous year, Lai Teck had been finally unmasked as a British agent and communist traitor, by which time the colonial government's decision to evict thousands of Chinese 'squatters' from their rural settlements had pushed relations between it and the MCP to an absolute nadir; by which time, also, violence between communists, Chinese nationalists (Guomindang) and Chinese secret societies vying for control of great tracts of the Malayan interior had risen to a pitch. At some point in early 1948, the MCP chose to depart from the democratic process, and from Malaya's towns and cities, and to launch its armed insurrection. But whether such a course was decided upon as a result of a leadership crisis within the Party that had resulted from Lai Teck's unmasking, as a pre-emptive move ahead of an expected British crackdown, or as a consequence of a change in international communist policy, is still debated by historians over 60 years later.

What is much clearer is the immediate impact of the Emergency on Singapore and Malaya's briefly held political freedoms. In late June 1948, the colonial government's Special Branch leapt back into action, reviving its pre-war security measures (raids, arrests, deportations and the banning of publications and films deemed seditious) and throwing in a few extra ones (in particular, detentions without trial). To the authorities such measures appeared justified in the face of the violence that swept across Malaya as communist insurgents directed their attacks against colonial military and police personnel, and against those civilians (including Indian rubber tappers and Chinese tin miners) whom the Party deemed 'running dogs' of the British. Murders, reprisals and other terrorist outrages increased until October 1951, at which point Chin Peng (the MCP leader) conceded that such tactics had alienated the Party from the very people whose support it sought, and so initiated a re-think of communist strategy.

That Singapore was spared much of this violence was mainly a consequence of Chin Peng's decision to try and secure 'liberated areas' of the countryside rather than cities (a strategy that by 1949 Mao Zedong had successfully used to

Peaked cap with red star worn by members of the military wing of the Communist Party of Malaya.
1950s
Cloth, metal
L 20.5 x W 25 x H 8 cm
NMS 2000-03689

take control of China). Partly, also, the relative calm in Singapore resulted from the success of Special Branch in smashing the Anti-British League – a secret communist-linked organisation which the authorities suspected was planning an island-wide bombing campaign. However, the cost of such security was a drastic change in the island's political climate. As some contemporaries later complained, Singapore under the Emergency Regulations essentially became a 'police state'.

Yet it seems that even before the Emergency erupted, a degree of disillusionment with the confrontational politics of Singapore's immediate post-war years had already set in. By 1948, some workers had come to believe that the MCP, for all its hero status and promises of a new socialist utopia, was more concerned with its own political agenda than with securing practical improvements in their basic living conditions. Continuous labour unrest began to arouse resentment, not least because it frequently involved communist coercion. The British may have given the people back their right to strike but the MCP, especially through the gangster-like tactics of its euphemistically named 'Workers Protection Corps', took away their right not to.

The non-English educated majority in Singapore found that so-called 'constitutional politics' were no great consolation either. Singapore's Legislative and Executive councils remained a distant world whose participants carried out their affairs in a foreign language and who appeared most interested in securing their own commercial prospects or those of their wealthy associates. In 1948, the British allowed more local non-Europeans onto the Legislative Council, and yet more in 1951. But the elections for these seats were notable for low voter registration and even poorer voter turnout. In 1948, a government-commissioned report by two British trade union officials revealed that the main concern of Singapore's workers was rice rather than revolution: 'In all our discussions we

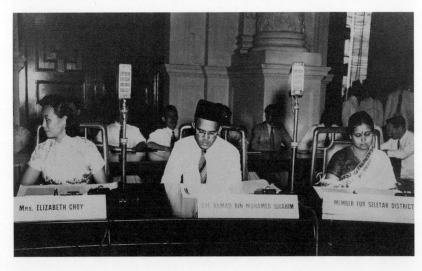

Non-European Legislative
Council members. From left:
Elizabeth Choy, Ahmad bin
Mohamed Ibrahim and
Vilasini Menon.

1951
Bridget Choy Wai Fong/NAS
20080000001-0013

Mrs. ELIZABETH CHOY   CHE AHMAD BIN MOHAMED IBRAHIM   MEMBER FOR SELETAR DISTRICT

got back sooner or later to the same point. "If only", said employers, workers and officials alike, "there was a sufficient supply of rice at a reasonable price, industrial troubles would be solvable.'"

So where do we find a *merdeka* spirit in Singapore following the outbreak of the Emergency? To begin with, amongst that half of the population that frequently finds itself written out of the island's political history but whose experiences of post-war hardships were often most acute: Singapore women – its mothers, daughters and household managers. Though the Emergency Regulations sent the heady politics of mass rallies and *hartals* into abeyance for a while, it was women who took up the mantle of the freedom struggle. Their version of *merdeka* might have been quieter, less macho and more practical, yet it ultimately made an impact that was just as radical.

The quiet revolution: Constance Goh and Mrs Mohamed Siraj

Constance Goh was the sixth daughter in a large Presbyterian Chinese family from Amoy. 'Because I was a girl I was neglected and often sick', she remembered. Her father was a businessman who spent much of his time overseas in the *Nanyang*: 'Naturally he kept other women, and trouble with the concubines led mother to accept a job here in Singapore.' Constance's mother taught at Chong Hock Chinese Girls' School and eventually Constance herself worked as a teacher in Singapore, where she settled and got married.

> It was after the war that we thought of the question of family planning. Seeing the distress and deplorable living conditions in Chinatown [...] led caring people to find ways and means to help. Children were running wild; if parents could not feed those they already had, how could they add more to the family?

These 'deplorable living conditions' were the result of skyrocketing post-war inflation, food scarcity, poor health and severe overcrowding. Counterintuitive as it may sound, Singapore's post-war population stood at one million, double its pre-war figure despite the ravages of the Japanese Occupation (and thanks partly to an influx of new arrivals). Meanwhile, the amount of available housing on the island had declined. Much of the population was crammed into the city area at a density of 300 persons to an acre (most of them living in overcrowded and century-old shophouses) while another 100,000 were squatters living in shanty towns. Poor drainage and sanitation were problems throughout; tuberculosis and other chest diseases were rampant.

After the BMA was disbanded in mid-1946, the colonial government attempted to remedy the situation through its new Social Welfare Department. This body immediately set up People's Restaurants, temporary kitchens and dining areas where anyone could buy a meal for about the price of a newspaper, along with

Crèche on Victoria Street
managed by the Social
Welfare Department.
1950
NAS 19980000912-0018

People's Kitchens, which provided low-cost cooked food in bulk for distribution to factories, offices and schools. Subsequently, the Department also introduced free health centres, inoculations and vaccinations. However, such efforts would have amounted to little were it not for the local volunteers who provided support on the ground and sometimes the pioneering initiative.

Back in 1945, Constance Goh was already at the helm organising the first feeding centre in Singapore, well in advance of official efforts:

> I started the first feeding centre for children in a converted motorshed in Havelock Road. The government gave the food, huge pots of rice, vegetables, fruit and some protein. It was cooked in the General Hospital and delivered to the centre. All we had to do was to organise the children.

The children, however, proved more of a challenge:

> They were like wild animals. They were not orphans, they had families in Chinatown, but they had nothing to eat. By the time we ended the feeding programme there were 32 feeding centres all over Singapore.

Constance received an MBE (Member of the Order of the British Empire) from the British government in acknowledgement of her efforts, but the 'poverty of those post-war months' had convinced her that a much more radical solution was needed. Her solution was unveiled on 25 November 1949 when she opened the first family planning clinic in Singapore, located within the premises of her husband's medical practice along South Bridge Road and manned by volunteers like herself who provided free family planning advice and contraceptives. On that first day, the clinic had just one visitor, a lone woman who found herself the focus of attention of six eager clinic volunteers. Yet within a year, Constance and her co-workers were operating five clinics and seeing so many patients that they could construct a clear profile of a typical mother: on average she would have already had six children, though at one extreme were the women who had about 20 children, some of whom might have been given away because the family was too poor to keep them. A typical working-class family might subsist on a paltry income of not more than $200 a month, and the lower the family income the greater the number of children they were likely to have. A mother's most common refrain: 'I don't know what to do!'

Constance's chutzpah probably had as much to do with the eventual success of these clinics as her immense organisational talents. Undeterred by the dearth of local family planning expertise, she mustered a group of energetic and determined women who contacted their friends in England and other countries to obtain information and, of course, contraceptives. The only contraceptive then available to women was the cap-and-paste (also known as the 'Dutch pessary') which had to be ordered from England. Constance made a trip there in person to convince the contraceptive supplier to lower his price on the product. Revealing her understanding of the male psyche's partiality to playing the heroic lead, she told him: 'The welfare of the people in the East is in your hands.' She came away with a 50 per cent discount on the original price.

Back in Singapore, the most serious hurdle to family planning was potential opposition from conservatives and traditionalists:

> By far our greatest fear was the possible active opposition of religious bodies. To safeguard ourselves, a small committee was assigned to look into the teachings of the Bible, the Koran and the Hindu and Buddhist scriptures in regard to family planning ... Fortunately, there was nothing specific against our immediate objectives. Only the Roman Catholic Church voiced their opposition ... The Catholic Church used to send me to hell twice a month. My friends told me that the priest regularly condemned me to hell for my work in family planning.

Publicity was then 'out of the question' so Constance and her volunteers 'worked quietly undercover'. In particular, they used their broader networks of friends and community workers to spread news of the clinics by word of mouth:

> We sent social workers, church Bible women – in those days there were Bible women who went around urging people to come to church – so we used them to get the news to the community that there was a family planning clinic.

Constance Goh.
1950s

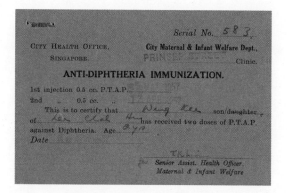

The clinics even advised women how to use their feminine wiles to get their husbands to assent to family planning. A common strategy was to encourage wives to nudge their husbands into thinking that they had come up with the idea of limiting the number of children in the family. In a Singapore of entrenched patriarchal conservatism, women's *merdeka* relied on persistence, subtlety and (in particular) self-reliance. As Constance Goh put it, 'It is for us women to rebel.'

Another rebel whose sheer force of personality left just as indelible a mark on the women's movement in Singapore was Mrs Mohamed Siraj. In the Malay-Muslim community of the early 1950s the problem was not merely the number of children that husbands and wives produced, but the number of wives these husbands married, regardless of whether they could support them. Despite a staggering divorce rate of between 70 to 80 per cent, and the number of abandoned Muslim women and children who ended up reliant on charities (such as St Andrew's Mission Hospital or the Singapore Children's Society), male Muslim leaders preferred to bury the problem and leave it unresolved.

At the age of 27, Mrs Siraj decided to take matters into her own hands. She later recalled putting the issue to her fellow Muslim women in the following terms:

> We've got to do something. If we Muslims don't do anything for these poor women, who's going to do it? Because we are the people who understand the culture, the religion – everything.

Her rallying cry led in 1952 to the formation of the Persatuan Pemudi Islam Singapura (PPIS) or Young Women's Muslim Association – a 'mini-United Nations', Mrs Siraj remembered, made up of Muslim women of different races, both local and foreign-born. Their primary objective was to lobby the government to set up an Islamic family court that would protect the rights of women and children. A major issue was the ease with which a man could get a divorce: 'the man can just say, "I divorce you." That's the end. ... The divorce papers can come by post to the wives and the wives can *pengsan* [faint].' Added to this was the common practice of marrying off Malay-Muslim girls in their mid-teens. As

Mrs Siraj saw it, this was an age when 'the child is supposed to be in school and not in the kitchen cooking for her husband'. Marrying so young meant that by the age of 20 these girls were mothers already, perhaps even divorced. It was also clear that the more children they had themselves, the earlier they sent their own daughters off to get married.

Not everyone saw this as a problem, or as a problem that it was for women to solve. But to her detractors Mrs Siraj had a ready response. To those who justified the practice of polygamy by quoting the Qur'an, she replied: 'The Qur'an says if you can treat all your wives equally well and give them food, clothes, everything equal, you can marry.' Not surprisingly, such a confident riposte, especially from a woman, unsettled members of the local Muslim hierarchy. Some wondered if Mrs Siraj was setting herself up as a *kadi* [religious judge], a role traditionally filled by men. Others reprimanded her for having overstepped the boundaries of modest feminine behaviour:

> I remember one man was scolding me and saying things. So one day I went
> up to him, I said: '... Supposing this happens to your own daughter. Tell
> me what will you do? Will you accept and just say "Oh". Or what would
> you do? Would you be happy that your daughter is being treated like this
> by a man?'

In 1955, Mrs Siraj and the PPIS scored a major victory when the government of Singapore set up a Syariah Court with marriage and family matters under its purview. Muslim men who wanted to marry or divorce their wives now had to go through due process. Those who wanted to marry more than one wife had to come before the Court and obtain their current wife's consent (as well as the consent of the next woman they intended to marry). In addition, the Court could order that men who divorced their wives must pay *nafkah* [alimony].

Marriage counselling session.
1960s
Courtesy of Mrs Mohamed Siraj

It was a first step and in some respects only a minor one. (An indication of the slow pace of reform were the paltry rates of *nafkah* that the Syariah Court initially imposed on divorced husbands, payments that it might only demand they pay for three months or less.) Yet the new system signalled a major change within the Malay-Muslim community – if nothing else because it stimulated a growing consciousness about Muslim women's rights. In the 1960s, Mrs Siraj worked for the Court as its first female social worker, assisting the *kadis* in mandatory conciliation proceedings and in monitoring cases after divorce. No great surprise, then, that as more Muslim women came to see her and were made aware of their entitlements (she sometimes dealt with more than 500 cases in a year), the divorce rate among Malay-Muslims began to spiral down. Whether through their hearts or their pockets, the men were beginning to see the light.

Such successes were part of a much broader social transformation across post-war Singapore. Whereas women in the pre-war decades had raised concerns over their place in the world, and written letters and even poems in the press on the matter, the 1950s and 1960s were the era of action. These were the decades when increasing numbers of Singapore women earned a wage, when they obtained the vote and when they came to demand much more from the society to which they belonged.

Many of their demands became crystallised in the activities of the Singapore Council of Women, which from 1951 sought to promote the 'economic, educational, cultural and social status of women' and to root out 'all the social evils that exist and handicap the progress of women towards their emancipation and their enjoyment of equal rights with men'. In particular, the Council sought to end the practices of polygamy and child marriage. Following Singapore's first general elections in 1959 it submitted its proposed bill on these matters and women's rights in general to the victorious People's Action Party government. This same bill, which had been rejected by the British six years earlier on the grounds that it might stir religious and racial tensions, this time received a better hearing. In 1961, it became ratified as the Women's Charter, one of the most progressive pieces of legislation on women's rights to have ever been enacted across the whole of Southeast Asia. Against the backdrop of turbulence and violence that usually characterises this period (and to which we will return shortly), Constance Goh, Mrs Mohamed Siraj and their numerous 'Singapore sisters' had overseen a quiet revolution.

Creative merdeka: a Singaporean identity?

Before Mrs Siraj set out on her quest to improve the lot of Muslim women in Singapore, she had witnessed what would later become known as the Maria Hertogh riots of 1950. The riots broke out in reaction to the final verdict of the Singapore courts at the end of a highly contentious and complex legal battle for

Maria Hertog and her foster
mother Aminah (second and
third from right) leaving the
court after a hearing.
1950
SPH PCD 001-023

custody of one Maria Hertogh. Born in Java and baptised a Catholic, Maria had
been given by her Eurasian mother to the care of a local Muslim family after her
Dutch father had been interned by the Japanese during World War II. After the
war, Maria and her foster family moved to Malaya. The courts' final decision to
grant Maria's natural parents custody led Muslims in Singapore to riot for three
days, during which 18 people were killed and 173 were injured.

These riots were the first major instance of communal strife on the island
involving Malays against Chinese and Europeans. Moreover, they brought to
many people's minds a fundamental concern about Singapore's post-war future.
Given the island's ethnic diversity (in 1957 its population was just over 75 per
cent Chinese, just under 14 per cent Malay, and exactly 9 per cent Indian), could
its people ever share in a common Singaporean consciousness, let alone be a
harmonious independent nation?

At the end of the 1950s, the same question was still being asked and it
prompted Victor Purcell, Cambridge history don and former colonial official
in Malaya, to pen an article for the *Times* of London entitled 'Singapore seeks a
personality'. Purcell's views are worth recounting because he had left Malaya in
the late 1940s dismayed at its prospects for democratic self-government; yet in
his article he highlights the cultural vitality that came to fruition in Singapore
during the subsequent decade – despite the island's many riots, strikes and
problems of social welfare.

Though Purcell began by summarising the cultural and religious barriers
between the island's various peoples and the cultural 'pulls' that influenced them
from outside, he went on to look at how and where a 'Singapore consciousness'
might emerge or was already emerging. Education was key, it was where he
believed the 'battle for a "Singapore outlook" is being fought'. In particular,
English education was vital since it provided 'the "cement" holding the colony

together'. No doubt, he had in mind recent developments at the University of Malaya which had finally been established in 1949. The first generation of the university's arts graduates included the celebrated poet Edwin Thumboo and the equally well-respected historian Wang Gungwu, both of whose writings at this time encapsulated the hopes of an English-educated elite for a multi-ethnic, cosmopolitan Malayan nation (and whose idealism even extended to their attempted creation of a local Esperanto known as 'EngMalChin').

But Purcell moved on to examine those more populist spaces where 'Singaporeans, irrespective of race, live a life in common'. Besides sport, he highlighted as the 'greatest solvent of communal differences ... the cultural amusements which the people enjoy in common'. Of these, the Worlds amusement parks ('a typically Malayan institution') offered an 'ocular and aural demonstration of the process of cultural exchange at work'. Their various performances were 'primarily intended for either Chinese, Malays or Indians' but there was still often 'a sprinkling of the members of other communities among the audience'. 'Malay music, whether in the form of sentimental folk-song such as the *pantun* and *kronchong*, or the more vigorous dance form of the *joget* with its infectious rhythm' was more 'easily adapted to Western orchestration' and therefore had a 'greater inter-communal appeal'. Above all, the cinema was 'the medium with the greatest appeal, with dubbings in three languages'. Though Purcell conceded that through film 'Singaporeans of all races are subjected to some degree of westernisation (or Americanisation)' and that the medium's 'cultural benefit may be a matter of opinion', he concluded that it at least provided the population with 'some values in common'.

Yet there was more going on than mere westernisation. Today, when people recall Singapore's period of creative *merdeka* during the 1950s (a cultural outpouring which also spread to the island's literary, visual arts and architectural scenes), it is most often the local film industry that takes pride of place. From 1947, posters began to appear across Singapore that – alongside those for American, Shanghainese or Hong Kong films – advertised new releases that were 'locally filmed' and 'shot in Malay'. These films were produced by the island's two main movie studios, Malay Film Productions (owned by the eventually Hong Kong-based Shaw Brothers) and Cathay-Keris Film Productions. What is striking is not just the number of such productions – over 300 were made in Singapore between 1947 and 1972 and at their peak sometimes over 20 a year – but their wide popular appeal.

Certainly, the majority of these films were deeply Malay, embedded in what was then a post-war artistic flowering of Malay national consciousness that integrated Singapore yet further into a wider Malay-speaking world, both across the Causeway and in Indonesia. Malays wrote the scripts, they composed the music, they acted in the lead parts and eventually (after an initial reliance on Indian filmmakers) they directed the action from behind the camera. Likewise, at least in the early years, the plots of local Malay productions drew heavily on Malay folk tales and the conventions of *bangsawan* (Malay opera).

Nonetheless, for many non-Malays, especially those who enjoyed the entertainments on offer at the Worlds, these conventions were familiar. In fact, Singapore's entire film industry during the 1950s was a multi-ethnic affair, featuring Chinese producers and for several years Indian and even Filipino editors and directors. Chinese posters for certain Malay-language productions indicate that a broader 'Malayan' audience existed, and as local films began to explore more contemporary subject-matter their appeal only grew more universal. In viewing a world on celluloid populated by recognisable characters facing recognisable challenges, set against a familiar Singapore or Malayan backdrop, the island's movie-going public was beginning to 'see' its own home, and even its own nation.

The lasting embodiment of Malay cinema's cross-cultural appeal was the Penang-born P. Ramlee – an actor, singer, director and even composer whose films during the 1950s and early 1960s introduced Singaporean audiences to a new European-influenced social realism. Watched and listened to by Malays, Indians, Chinese and Eurasians alike, Ramlee emerged as the home-grown movie star of his generation and as a national Malayan celebrity. In this new era of mass communications the big question was whether any one politician could conjure up the same magic.

Penarek Becha handbill.
1955
Paper
H 39.6 cm x W 27.3 cm
NMS 1999-00890

28. STAGING MERDEKA

On 21 March 1956, a tall, Mediterranean-looking man, who carried a pipe and whose bushy eyebrows seemed to attempt an escape from his forehead each time he emphasised a point, spoke into a microphone in front of a crowd of his supporters. He was standing underneath the 'apple tree' at Empress Place (next to what is today Old Parliament House), from where his words were broadcast live by Radio Malaya. In the present age, in which politicians try hard to appear natural and approachable, his performance serves as something of a master class:

> *Merdeka*! People of Singapore! Last year, this time, in the month of March: a time of agony. I came before you, day after day at lunchtime, to speak to you of the dangers that the future held and to put before you a blueprint for a miracle. I did not dream, I did not dare believe, that you would give us an opportunity to make that miracle possible.

The man was David Marshall, a brilliant lawyer, a Sephardic Jew and one of the most colourful personalities Singapore politics has ever known. Then in his late 30s, Marshall had served for the previous year as the island's first elected Chief Minister. He now appeared before his supporters to declare his government's achievements, to relate the obstacles that it had overcome, and to explain the dangers that it faced in the future:

> I think you know, when I was first elected and appointed Chief Minister, I was told I had no office, no clerk, no *thambi*.* And oh they couldn't give me any office – it took a long time – government offices were extremely overloaded – and there was a lot of difficulty. I had to threaten to bring a desk here and set it up here or in my flat [laughter] before I could get an office!
>
> I was told that, of course, the heaven-born, including the Chief Secretary, was the man who would coordinate government policy; that I was just the, the sort of the – the senior *thambi* among the *thambis*! [more laughter] I made it very clear and very soon that I was either Chief Minister or not. Finally, they accepted the position that I could coordinate policy.

Superior colonial officials were not the only obstacle Marshall and his government faced. Recalling another source of opposition, the Chief Minister seemed clearly in his element:

> To read the English press, we are a group of baboons who are trying to impose independence on you against your will. The *Standard* came out on Sunday with an article – not written by a Malayan, thank god. Well, he said, please don't give us independence: we want Papa and Mama colonialism! [loud laughter, then Marshall imitates a child] Mama colonialism! Mama! A lost boy!

---

* A boy, or male servant, usually tasked with simple errands such as fetching tea.

David Marshall speaking at Empress Place.
21 March 1956
SPH PCD 0132-006

Finally, Marshall laid the jokes aside to conclude with a more serious message:

> The communists are the ultimate danger to this country. And whether it is today or it is tomorrow, whatever the threat to my own personal safety may be and to my friends and to my colleagues, we intend to act with all the firmness possible against those disruptive elements that call themselves communists.
>
> You don't want, I don't want, the people of Singapore don't want a *yanko merdeka*.* We want a Malayan *merdeka*! [Loud applause]. And we will get it!

For all these fine words, three months later Marshall was to resign, his dreams of steering Singapore to independence in tatters. His rapid rise and then equally sudden demise tell us much about the high drama (sometimes high farce) of what was then a new style of politics on the island. But his story is equally important because of the leading players who shared his stage. For it was these other rising stars in the political firmament – the young Hakka Chinese lawyer Lee Kuan Yew

---

* The *yanko* was a type of communist dance performed by Chinese students at this time.

Mace of the City of Singapore

The gold and silver Mace of the City of Singapore was presented by philanthropist Loke Wan Tho to T. P. F. McNeice, President of the Singapore City Council in 1954. It was a symbol of the honourable status conferred upon Singapore as a city by King George VI on 22 September 1951. The mace was designed by Charles d'Orville Pilkington Jackson in consultation with a local committee that included the donor and the staff of the Raffles Museum. It was commissioned to Messrs. Hamilton & Inches, a goldsmith firm in Edinburgh. Before its journey to Singapore, the mace was put on display in Edinburgh and London.

The fate of the mace in Singapore was tied to the changing political landscape in the 1950s. Following the City Council election of 1957, Ong Eng Guan was elected Mayor and one of the first things he did as Mayor was to move a motion to cease the use of the mace in the Council as he considered it a relic of colonialism. The motion was carried and the mace was never used in the Council again. Following the Council's dissolution, the mace passed into the possession of the Public Utilities Board (PUB) and was displayed in the PUB's board room for some time before it was donated to the National Museum of Singapore in 2003. The mace is now considered a national treasure.

Apart from its link to a significant political period of Singapore's history, the mace is also a unique work rich in symbolism. The topmost pinnacle of the mace illustrates the city's crest – a lion passant in front of a coconut palm on a mound which rests on a silver heraldic wreath. The mace is embellished with six silver shields bearing the arms of Queen Elizabeth II (who succeeded George VI in 1953); Sir Stamford Raffles; the East India Company; the Straits Settlements; the Colony of Singapore; and the City of Singapore. A silver

Queen Elizabeth II

Sir Stamford Raffles

Straits Settlements

East India Company

Colony of Singapore

City of Singapore

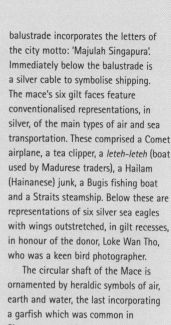

balustrade incorporates the letters of the city motto: 'Majulah Singapura'. Immediately below the balustrade is a silver cable to symbolise shipping. The mace's six gilt faces feature conventionalised representations, in silver, of the main types of air and sea transportation. These comprised a Comet airplane, a tea clipper, a *leteh-leteh* (boat used by Madurese traders), a Hailam (Hainanese) junk, a Bugis fishing boat and a Straits steamship. Below these are representations of six silver sea eagles with wings outstretched, in gilt recesses, in honour of the donor, Loke Wan Tho, who was a keen bird photographer.

The circular shaft of the Mace is ornamented by heraldic symbols of air, earth and water, the last incorporating a garfish which was common in Singapore coastal waters. The shaft also features between its belchered bands, ornamented, engraved gilt panels representing the flora of Singapore. These include yam, pitcher plant, orchid, nutmeg, pepper, sugarcane, rambutan, gambier, and betel-nut. The shaft ends in a gilt band containing nine silver shuttlecocks illustrating badminton, the national game of Malaya then. The hexagonal platform at the shaft's base features the engraved names of the goldsmiths, the principal craftsmen, the designer, and the year of construction. At the bottom of the Mace are silver emblems signifying tin and representations of pineapple fruit and of the leaves and seed-pod of the rubber tree.

Mace of the City of Singapore
1953
Gold, silver
H 125.5 x W 14 cm
Donated by Public Utilities Board
NMS 2003-00230

and the even younger Hokkien Chinese bus worker Lim Chin Siong – who not only matched Marshall for charisma, but who ultimately presented him with a far greater challenge than the British.

The outsider comes in

Looking back over his career in an oral history interview, Marshall claimed that the main motivation that drove him to enter politics was anger: 'Anger at the leprous concept of racial superiority and it had been mounting in my belly since my schooldays.' He was never 'anti-British', he explained; rather, he wanted to 'break through the sonic barrier against Asians and especially Jews'. Nor, he admitted, was he especially ideological. Though he moved in Singapore's socialist circles during the early 1950s he never became especially grounded in socialist dogma. His personal understanding of socialism was that it simply meant 'an effort to create the foundations of the opportunity of all our people to attain conditions of living compatible with human dignity'.

Marshall received his clarion call when in mid-1953 the British governor Sir John Nicoll, in an effort to speed up Singapore's progress towards self-government, announced the formation of a new constitutional commission. The outcome of the 1954 Rendel Commission (named after its chief convener Sir John Rendel) was that popular elections would be held the following year for a newly constituted Legislative Assembly made up of 32 members, 25 of whom would be elected. For Marshall, the political dawn that beckoned was so exciting as to be almost palpable:

> 'Hey we are human beings! Hey, we've got the right to vote! Hey, we've got a right to elect our own representative! We've got a right to a voice in how we are to live.' Now that is something you don't understand today. But that was very, very radical at that time. You know it's like the four-legged animal suddenly finding himself standing straight and looking upwards instead of looking to the ground. It really was a radical change of psychological atmosphere … 'Hey we are standing on two legs!'

Up until this point Marshall had been a rather reluctant politician. When, not long after the end of the Japanese Occupation, Gerald De Cruz had approached him to join the MDU, Marshall had reportedly answered ('slowly' and 'quietly' so De Cruz claimed): 'Gerry, the war is just over. Everything is in a shambles. I've got to build up my career.' Later, Marshall did join the moderate Progressive Party, founded by English-educated lawyers and Straits Chinese businessmen to contest the 1948 Legislative Council elections, yet his commitment was always lukewarm. When further Legislative Council elections were announced in 1951 he declined to stand for the Progressives, eventually leaving them when it became clear to him that they preferred the interests of businessmen and landlords to

City of Singapore coat of arms .

From the commemorative booklet published on the occasion of the presentation of the Mace of the City of Singapore, 1954.

those of the common man, and that their commitment to political *merdeka* was not that strong either.

No such doubts surrounded the Labour Front, a coalition of socialist parties which had been patched together to fight the 1955 elections by the stenographer-turned-union-leader Lim Yew Hock, and so Marshall enlisted. Nonetheless, he behaved from the outset as something of a political lone wolf, single-handedly fighting oppression on behalf of the ordinary man and woman just as he had in the courts. In late 1954, as the election campaign warmed up, Marshall produced not just a Labour Front manifesto but his own personal political credo.

Marshall's 'I Believe' is a remarkable document, unique for its time, which outlines his personal vision of what he called 'dynamic socialism':

> I believe self-government is better for a people than Colonial Government, however enlightened. ... I believe that the future welfare of the inhabitants of the Federation of Malaya and the Colony of Singapore depends upon the grant of immediate self-government for a United Malaya. ... I believe there is urgent need for a drastic re-orientation of our official outlook with the greatest possible emphasis on land distribution, housing, slum clearance, adequate free medical services, unemployment insurance, more technical and elementary education, protection of strikers, strengthening of unions, free legal services. ... All this I believe as a human being seeking justice in peace for all.

This was Marshall the idealist (as well as Marshall the individualist) in the full rhetorical flow that brought him to instant public notice. He followed up with a series of speeches that damned the British presence in Singapore and revealed his instinctive knack for gesture, hyperbole and media-friendly sound-bites. The more the local British-owned press expressed their outrage, the more he upped the ante with his anti-British taunts. Marshall had realised that bad publicity was good publicity and he later candidly admitted that he had set out to court it:

> I was interested in awakening the people. And you awaken them with drama. You don't awaken them with just somnolent sentences. You awaken them with drama. And the drama of David and Goliath is something that would work.

As Marshall also recalled, 'It never entered any of our consideration that we would be the party in office. I thought we would have about two or three [seats].' But win they did. The Labour Front claimed 10 of the 25 seats on offer, and after forming a coalition with two Malayan parties (the United Malays National Organisation and the Malayan Chinese Association, of which more later), it took office. It won partly thanks to the decision of its main rivals, the Progressive Party and the recently established Malayan Democratic Party, to contest the same seats and so split the moderate right-wing vote. The Labour Front's only

David Marshall and Lee Kuan
Yew shake hands after the
results of the polls were
announced.
April 1955
NAS

other significant opposition in the Assembly came from the People's Action
Party (the PAP, of which much more shortly), which having contested four
seats won three. The colonial authorities were no doubt in even greater shock
than Marshall, having expected the British-friendly Progressives to romp home
to victory. After the Labour Front unanimously voted Marshall their Chief
Minister, the British hierarchy found itself sharing its corridors with a potently
charismatic anti-colonialist.

Those first few weeks of the Marshall-led Labour Front government present
us with a series of vivid snapshots, the sheer theatricality of which so contrasts
with the measured and focused politics of Singapore today as to appear sent from
another planet. First, we have Marshall being invested by the British with the
authority of Chief Minister, dressed informally in an open-necked bush jacket.
The British governor is offended, the *Straits Times* screams 'Marshall insults the
Queen' and so Singapore's first elected leader petulantly adopts this uniform
whenever he goes out in public. Next we have Francis Thomas, Marshall's fellow
Labour Front minister, going a sartorial step further by wearing a safari jacket
and sandals to the official opening of the Legislative Assembly. Reportedly, when
Thomas sits down he reveals his sockless feet to members of the gallery who gape
and gasp in astonishment. Finally, we have Marshall attending the first Council
of Ministers meeting with the British governor and getting into a fractious
contretemps about the colour of official ink. The governor warns Marshall that
he alone reserves the right to use 'red ink' and that where it appears his decision
is final. Marshall responds with his own dictate: that he, the people's elected
representative, reserves the right to use an equally symbolic 'green ink' (which
Marshall did for the rest of his life).

But in the Assembly chamber we find that Marshall is not alone in his *merdeka*
antics. Here, day after day, in front of a packed gallery suddenly enthralled by the

new politics being played out in front of them, Marshall faced a rival – the PAP leader Lee Kuan Yew. As Lee recalled:

> After the first two days of that assembly meeting, it was obvious to the reporters in the press gallery and to the members present that the two main players were going to be Marshall and myself. He had the personality, a gift for colourful language, and a histrionic bent that could capture the attention of the House. I had a knack for pricking and deflating his high-flown metaphors and rather enjoyed doing it.

Yet while Lee admitted he enjoyed 'having fun with Marshall in the assembly chamber' he knew all the while that there was 'more serious business at hand'. That business consisted of mass political mobilisation of a kind that had not been seen in Singapore since 1948. Organising and manipulating it were to become Lee's particular forte, not Marshall's.

The talented Mr Lee

Before Marshall and Lee faced each other across the Assembly floor they already had some history between them. In late 1954, in the lead-up to the elections of the following year, Lee and his left-wing colleagues visited Marshall at his home around the time Marshall and Lim Yew Hock were discussing the formation of the Labour Front. 'That had been part of our probing', wrote Lee, 'we wanted to assess what they were capable of.' Obviously Lee did not think they were capable of much. He recalled that when he and his associates burst into laughter at some of Marshall's proposals the future Chief Minister stormed out of his own flat, leaving Lee, his colleagues and Marshall's other guests to make small talk, help themselves to the generous refreshments, thank the maid and go.

Marshall was apparently stung by Lee's brush-off, for in theory the two men shared much in common. Both were talented lawyers and brilliant public speakers, and both, to an extent, outsiders – while Marshall was a Jew, Lee belonged to the minority Chinese dialect group of Hakkas. However, temperamentally the two men were poles apart. Marshall was an emotional, heart-on-his-sleeve idealist; Lee was a pragmatic arch-strategist. Indeed, Marshall and his colleagues later wondered if Lee's 'probing' had been merely intended to delay the Labour Front getting its act together in time for the coming elections so as to give Lee and his colleagues the advantage.

Lee had returned to Singapore in 1951 following the completion of his studies at Cambridge. In Britain he had been a key participant in the Malayan Forum, a gathering of overseas students who met in London to debate their country's political future and whose membership included two men who would become Lee's long-term political allies, Toh Chin Chye and Goh Keng Swee. But now back home, Lee's first priority was to find a job. He joined the legal firm of

Laycock and Ong, owned by John Laycock, the hard-drinking English barrister who had co-founded the Progressive Party and befriended David Marshall. Initially, Lee also worked for the Progressives, assisting Laycock with his 1951 election campaign. However, this experience opened the eyes of the young lawyer to the rather seedy side of local political canvassing. Clearly, Laycock and his Progressives were not the kind of people who would create the corruption-free egalitarian society in Malaya that Lee longed for and which he believed that the Labour Party had started to build in post-war Britain.

For the time being, however, Lee kept his political views to himself and to a few close former Malayan Forum associates who eventually began to meet in the basement dining room of his Oxley Rise home. The turning point in his career came in early 1952. It was an event that in Lee's view not only transformed his personal future but ended up as of pivotal significance in the whole history of Singapore politics.

One afternoon, four men – three Malays, one Indian and all dressed in postmen's uniforms – walked into Lee's offices at Laycock and Ong. They asked if he would act as their legal representative in a pay dispute with their employers, the central cause of which had been the government's award of a higher pay rise for British expatriates. Lee asked Laycock if he should take the case 'given that there would not be much money in it'. Laycock advised Lee 'to carry on for the sake of goodwill'. And so Lee represented the postal workers, forgoing his legal fees: 'Little did I know that I would be guiding union leaders in a strike that in two weeks changed the political climate.'

The postal strike was the first major incident of labour unrest in Singapore since the outbreak of the Emergency in 1948. Lee's essential role was to help build the postal workers' case and when necessary 'reassure them that what they were doing was not illegal'. But his commitment to their cause soon extended to orchestrating their publicity. Through his old friend Goh Keng Swee, Lee was put in touch with S. Rajaratnam, who now worked at the *Singapore Standard* newspaper. Out by the pool of the Chinese Swimming Club, speaking over the blare of loud music, Lee briefed Rajaratnam about the strike. Over the next two weeks, both men met at Lee's Oxley Rise home after midnight to work on the postmen's press campaign.

The strike eventually broke when the government, having agreed to the relatively new concept of arbitration, came to a satisfactory agreement with the workers. Lee's key role in their success, and the persistent press coverage he had received, now catapulted him into the public's consciousness. He had shown that when labour unrest was aimed at achieving dialogue with the government it could achieve tangible results. By the end of the following year, his offices at Laycock and Ong, and his home at Oxley Rise, had witnessed a stream of workers and unionists passing through the doors. 'All the hapless and near hapless cases against the government', Lee observed, 'had been coming to me as a counsel of last resort.'

Trade union badges.
1950s
Metal

FROM TOP:

Singapore Taxi Drivers' Union
H 41 x W 16 cm
NMS 1995-06316

Rubber Tappers' Union
W 2.6 cm
NMS 1995-07323

Singapore Engineering Mechanics Union
H 2.7 x W 2.4 cm
NMS 1995-07297

Singapore General Employees' Union
H 2.8 x W 2.3 cm
NMS 1995-07189

Crucially, the postal strike convinced Lee and his Oxley Rise set that (as he himself phrased it) the unions were the means to achieve 'the mass base and, by extension, the political muscle we had been seeking when discussing our plans for action during all those beer nights spent pub-crawling in London after meeting at Malaya Hall'. Subsequently, Lee's political circle expanded to include many leaders of the unions he had represented, and even anti-colonial extremists such as Devan Nair and Samad Ismail (both of whom had been arrested by the authorities for their involvement with the Anti-British League and then released in 1953). In his basement dining room, Lee invited Nair and Samad to sit with his more moderate political associates, Goh Keng Swee, S. Rajaratnam, Kenny Byrne (then a civil servant) and Toh Chin Chye (then a physiology lecturer at the University of Malaya). It was a scene reminiscent of the MDU at the Liberty Cabaret in the previous decade, except for one crucial difference: when in 1954 the government announced that popular elections for the new Legislative Assembly would be held the following year, Lee and his colleagues decided to contest. Samad and Nair opposed this decision, but unlike the communist-sympathisers in the MDU six years earlier, they found themselves in the minority.

So the momentous choice was made to found a political party. But before the party formally came into being, Lee would first enlist two more remarkable personalities to its ranks. These new recruits came from a quite different world to that of the 'English-educated colonial bourgeoisie', whom Lee freely admitted comprised the majority of his Oxley Rise circle. No doubt because of this, he saw in these two young men the final pieces to complete his party's political jigsaw.

Enter the students

On 13 May 1954, Edwin Thumboo, the University of Malaya student we mentioned in the previous chapter, was heading up Penang Road with some friends after a movie at the Cathay cinema when he ran straight into a riot: 'Tear gas; riot squad with their wicker shields and their batons and so on and so on; and Chinese students were busy chaining themselves to the fence of King George V Park!' The riot had started following a student protest march against the British government's announcement that it would introduce national service in Singapore and co-opt Chinese youths into the armed forces. In reaction to the riots, the British ordered the closure of all Chinese schools across Singapore the following day, but this merely escalated the unrest. Chinese students locked themselves in their classrooms, sang their songs, commenced their own do-it-yourself lessons and went on hunger strike, in protests that lasted right into the second week of June.

Their passion and idealism struck a chord with Thumboo, who later commemorated it in a poem entitled 'May 1954' which features the immortal lines: 'Depart white man ... / ... / Depart Tom, Dick and Harry'. A member of the University of Malaya Socialist Club, Thumboo was also literary editor of the Club's political journal *Fajar* [Dawn], an involvement that soon after the May 13th riots landed him, along with his comrades, in serious trouble. Prior to the riots, *Fajar* had published an article entitled 'Aggression in Asia',

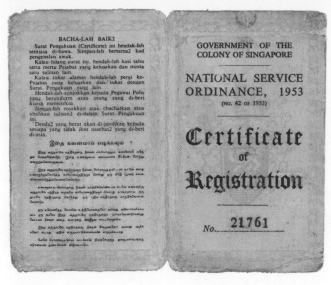

National Service Certificate of Registration.
1953
Paper
H 10.5 x W 12.5 cm
NMS 1992-00457

in which the colonial regime in Singapore was described as operating a 'police state'. Immediately following the riots, Thumboo and eight other Socialist Club members were arrested for sedition.

In Thumboo's recollection, the whole *Fajar* case appeared faintly ridiculous:

> The charge is that you sought to bring Her Majesty's Government into disrepute and contempt. I half-jokingly said, 'Look, you're already disreputable, you're already contemptuous, so why are you charging? We're stating the truth.'
>
> What we were trying to argue was that nothing we had said had not been said before ... a good defence! And most of our sources were British sources, trying to document that most of what we had said wasn't seditious. That, if it were seditious, other people should have been prosecuted.

After a few days in court, the defendants were discharged and released.

Once again, the case and its successful outcome brought Lee Kuan Yew to public notice. Lee had initially acted as the students' legal counsel and then worked with the left-wing barrister D. N. Pritt to fight their case in court. Not long afterwards, as Lee relates in his memoirs, five Chinese students turned up at his doorstep – three ponytailed young women in school uniform and two young men who could speak some English. Having followed the *Fajar* trial, they requested that Lee now represent their fellow Chinese students arrested during the May 13th riots. Impressed by their dedication and their organisation, Lee agreed.

This meeting led a few weeks later to a second, more fateful one. This time, two more young Chinese came to visit Lee, once more accompanied by another student who acted as interpreter. 'Lim and Fong looked the right type', Lee wrote: 'well mannered, earnest and sincere in demeanour, simple in their clothes, Fong to the point of shabbiness. Keenness and dedication were written in every line of their faces and in every gesture.' Lee appears to have decided almost immediately that both men were the 'kind of lieutenants he'd been looking for'.

He was soon explaining his plan to form a political party to represent 'the workers and the dispossessed, especially the Chinese educated'. As Lee recorded, Lim and Fong were at first 'non-committal', but they returned two weeks later and through their interpreter told him: 'Yes, they were prepared to join me, not to seek power but to expose the colonial regime, the inadequacy of the proposed Rendel Constitution, and to demolish the parties that would take office.'

These initial encounters remain extraordinary and today unthinkable: Lim Chin Siong was then only 21 years old, Fong Swee Suan was two years younger. Yet both men had already become powerful leaders of the Chinese student and trade union movements – to such an extent that Lee (himself just 31) saw in them a future for his party. Even more remarkable, these early meetings were carried out by two sides not yet able to converse in each other's favoured language. Lee later described his relationship with Lim as 'an inarticulate, inchoate, indefinable compact'. Goh Keng Swee was more forthright: the whole marriage was 'reckless folly', something he and his colleagues would 'never take on if ever asked to do it again'.

But at the time, Lee's courting of Lim and Fong made perfect political sense. With both leaders onboard, Lee now became, as Toh Chin Chye put it, the man connecting all the 'disconnected bits of the anti-colonial movement', or as Lee described himself: 'the telephone exchange. It was through me that all these lines were established.' But exactly who were Lim and Fong, the final and in many ways most important 'lines' that Lee had secured? This question is still debated in Singapore over 50 years later.

Lim and Fong's world

Back in the 1950s, people's first impressions of Lim Chin Siong and Fong Swee Suan were invariably the same: serious, charismatic and in Lim's case (especially if you were, as Lee Kuan Yew remembered, one of those girls 'in the trade unions') very attractive. Lim, the more dominant of the two, often instilled in new acquaintances a sense that he was possessed of supreme gravitas. Dennis Bloodworth, the Singapore correspondent for the British *Observer* newspaper, wrote of his 'knack at staring fixedly into a speaker's eyes, after he had stopped speaking and then letting the silence drag out dangerously before he caught his breath and broke it himself'. In Bloodworth's eyes, this was an old 'Chinese debating trick', one of several that Lim seemed to have tucked away as one of Singapore's greatest political orators, the man Lee described as having a 'soft baby face, but a ringing voice that flowed in his native Hokkien'.

Nor was Lim, in particular, above resorting to provocative soundbites or populist posturing. During a speech against the registration of Chinese youths under the proposed 1954 National Service bill, he famously observed, 'Look friends, only dogs have licenses and numbers.' He told another adoring crowd, 'The British say you cannot stand on you own two feet. Show them that you

Fong Swee Suan (left) and
Lim Chin Siong.
1950s
SPH

can stand!' – at which point, according to one eyewitness, 40,000 people 'leapt up – shining with sweat, fists in the air – shouting, *Merdeka*'. Both Lim and Fong had what is called the 'common touch' and they were careful to nurture it. Amongst Singapore's new political leaders, they were probably the only who travelled everywhere by bicycle and who slept on their desks at their Middle Road shophouse headquarters, just like their supporters.

But to really get inside the minds of these two men we have to understand where they came from. To be Chinese-speaking or Chinese-educated in early 1950s Singapore was to belong to a marginalised majority that had yet to see much improvement in its prospects. Job opportunities remained poor, Chinese schools were under-funded, overcrowded and neglected, and the qualifications they provided frequently went unrecognised. Further Chinese education after secondary school involved leaving Singapore for China, a prospect which became increasingly difficult following the country's communist revolution of 1949. Meanwhile, the rise of Malay nationalism across the Causeway with its emphasis on Malay as the sole national language brought a sense of foreboding that Chinese culture as a whole was under threat.

Nonetheless, for a young and growing generation (in the mid-1950s around 50 per cent of Singapore's population was under the age of 21) there were also grounds for hope. In 1956, thanks to a massive fundraising effort within the local Chinese community, the first classes commenced at Nanyang University – Singapore's (and for that matter Southeast Asia's) first Chinese university. Moreover, for all their failings, Chinese secondary schools continued to expose their students to a world of vibrant new ideas. As Fong recalled, when in 1950 he and Lim were both pupils at Chinese High School their shared intellectual curiosity was what brought them together:

> He [Chin Siong] liked writing and I liked maths, but we both shared one thing in common: we both loved reading. So we'd discuss about literature and authors, and we realised that we had much in common.

Lim and Fong appear to have read everything and anything, from Russian classics, to Victorian fiction, to Western (deeply critical) accounts of communism – all of which had become available in Chinese translation.

And in addition to world literature, there were new world events to digest. For the vast majority of Chinese in Singapore, China's 1949 communist revolution was greeted as a victory of the people against evil landlords and greedy merchants, and thus a source of great national pride. To Fong, local Chinese interest in the political system in China was therefore 'natural'. Both he and Lim admired Mao Zedong, as did most of their generation. The 1949 Revolution was the culmination, so Lim saw it, of 'a very exciting period throughout Afro-Asia and Latin America ... The success of the Socialist movement at that time came as a great encouragement and excitement to us.'

⑫這情景叫我们怎忘得了！

Finally, to have received any education at all was then regarded in a Chinese context as a great privilege, one that students such as Lim and Fong felt that they were obliged to repay by serving as community leaders. By 1952, both men had been forced to leave Chinese High because of their anti-British sentiments – Lim for his brief involvement with the Anti-British League – and had taken up jobs as bus workers. Within two years they had emerged as strident union leaders, partly through their ability to read and write but equally because of their sheer commitment and charisma.

Fong's first impression of Lee Kuan Yew was 'of someone with a lot of passion, very sharp and determined. After we met and discussed the short- and long-term goals, we felt that we could work together in the PAP.' In November 1954, Lee, his Oxley Rise associates, along with Lim, Fong and several other unionists, came together for the inaugural meeting of their party at the Victoria Memorial Hall. The PAP would dedicate itself to securing *merdeka* for Singapore as part of multicultural Malaya that would see an end to social inequality. But, as with Raffles's signing of the 1819 Treaty with Sultan Hussein, what in hindsight was a momentous occasion was striking at the time for its un-remarkableness. Lee wrote: 'We read set speeches – there was no electricity or magic in the air … no flights of rhetoric, no balloons, no pigeons freed …' A few days later, a sarcastic editorial in the *Straits Times* noted that the newly created PAP had to vacate the Victoria Hall by the early afternoon to make way for a better attended though 'absurd' film which featured 'a Persian princess

Police cracking down on Chinese middle school students protesting against the National Service Ordinance.
1954
Paper
H 8 x W 13 cm
NMS 1994-05493

357

'Visiting the Injured', by artist
Koeh Sia Yong.
1960s
Woodcut
H 15.7 x W 20 cm
NMS 1999-02615

and a shifty barber'. At which performance 'a more intelligent dialogue could be heard', the paper felt unable to say.

However, when the election campaign began in earnest it soon became obvious that the PAP's ability to summon up a groundswell of union and student support made it the party in Singapore to watch. Together on the podium, Lee and Lim made for a formidable double-act. Han Tan Juan, then a student and later a prominent Chinese journalist, vividly remembered Lee as 'one of the idols of the students … In my impression both he and Lim Chin Siong were like the Gemini of the leftist movement.' Few observers were then aware of the emerging tensions that were to engulf these two leaders' 'inarticulate, incohate, indefinable compact'.

So let us pause for a moment, to fully review the situation that greeted David Marshall in his first week as Chief Minister. In the Assembly, Marshall let loose with his brilliant oratory and Lee matched verbal fireworks with equally brilliant put-downs. But there was now another key player in this scene: the young Lim Chin Siong, seated behind Lee, presumably trying to follow the debate with his limited English while relying on Lee to provide him with translations.

Moreover, Marshall's position, despite his flowing rhetoric and his confident delivery, was far more tenuous that it first appeared. While the Chief Minister held forth in the Assembly, the real power in Singapore – the power to mobilise people and get them out on the streets – increasingly lay in the hands of the two men opposite him. Both these leaders had by now publicly professed that their real reason for participating in the Assembly was to 'expose' the colonial regime and to 'demolish' the party that took office.

Marshall, on the other hand, was the elected authority in the government and so obliged to work with the British, which made him risk appearing like a stooge. How to remain true to *merdeka* while co-opted into a not-yet-fully-independent government? Such was Marshall's dilemma, and within a few weeks of him having taken office the problem suddenly exploded into a major political crisis.

The Hock Lee eruption

Down at the Hock Lee Bus Company on Alexandra Road the bus workers were on the verge of a strike. In late April 1955, the company's management, having tried to prevent around two-thirds of their employees from joining a union affiliated with Fong and Lim's Singapore Bus Workers Union (SBWU), decided to fire all those employees who did. The workers retaliated with hunger strikes and by picketing the bus depot, forming a human chain to stop buses from departing. When the police went in to break up the protest, students and other sympathisers flooded into the depot to lend their support. More strikes in solidarity with the bus workers followed and as May Day approached another island-wide stoppage seemed imminent.

Marshall's response was to go directly to the Hock Lee bus depot to try to broker a settlement. He succeeded in getting Lim and Fong, with Lee as their legal representative, to sit on a mediation commission with himself and the Hock Lee management. At this time, Marshall publicly expressed his belief in the worker's right to strike but emphasised that it had to be done responsibly and within the law.

While these negotiations were taking place, Lim, Fong and Lee simultaneously mounted pressure on Marshall and the Hock Lee management by taking to the podium – a perfectly legitimate tactic that had served Lee well during the 1952 postal strike. However, this time Lee was not in complete control of the strikers' public relations campaign. The *Straits Times* reported that on May Day Lee addressed a crowd of 10,000 people crammed into the Oriental Theatre (on New Bridge Road) and mocked Marshall's government for its 'half-past-six democracy', challenging it to push for full *merdeka*. At the same rally, Fong

Hock Lee bus driver badge.
1950s
Metal
H 4.8 x W 2.7 cm
NMS 1999-02730

gave a speech that was allegedly far more inflammatory. According to the Chief Secretary, who related a translation of the union leader's words to the Legislative Assembly, Fong had told the crowd: 'The workers must know that there is bound to be some bloodshed in the course of revolution and they must rise and unite.'

The blood flowed 12 days later. On 12 May, large numbers of workers and students congregated in the Alexandra Road area around the bus depot in preparation for an island-wide protest the following day, timed to commemorate the anti-National Service clashes of the previous year. Official government sources claimed that the rioting began by 7 p.m. when an organised mob with sticks and stones attacked the police stationed near the bus depot. However, Han Tan Juan (the Chinese student so impressed by the Lim and Lee 'Gemini') was in the midst of the chaos and recalled a different scene. He was then only 12 years old:

> The workers participating in the strikes assembled at the gate of the Hock Lee Bus Company. The police wanted them to disperse. They refused. The police then started using high-powered water-cannons on the workers. These were very high-pressure water-cannons, strong enough to send pebbles and glass on the ground flying towards the workers. Some of the workers' bodies and faces were cut and bled from the flying stones and glass. Whenever the water-cannons lulled, the sympathisers would rush to pick up pebbles and glass from the ground. They weren't trying to attack the police, you only have to look at the actions of the people in the photographs and you'll see … The water-cannons were so powerful they could blast a person into a drain. The crowd became very angry, and someone shouted in Hokkien, '*hood!*', which means 'fight'.

Hock Lee crackdown: water-cannons blast striking workers; supporters picking up debris.
May 1955
NAS

By the end of the following day, 14 people had been injured and two killed – a policeman and an American journalist. In response, the government shut down three Chinese schools; in retaliation, all Singapore's bus workers went on strike and further island-wide stoppages threatened. But on 14 May, Marshall announced a breakthrough in the mediation talks. Hock Lee employees would henceforth be allowed to join or form any union that they so desired, and the company's dismissed workers would be reinstated. To resolve the dispute, the Chief Minister, Lee Kuan Yew and the Hock Lee management had worked under extreme pressure up until the final hour. Marshall later recalled feeling 'so lonely in those days – lonely and lost'. But while he had eventually helped settle the strike, his political problems had only just started.

Marshall's report to the people.
1955
Paper
H 18.4 x W 12.4 cm
NMS 1999-02301

The return of Singapore's 'David'

Businessmen, European expatriates and much of the conservative English-educated community in Singapore were furious; the *Straits Times*' headline four days after the riot read, 'UNCONDITIONAL SURRENDER!'. Marshall was accused of going soft on the Hock Lee rioters and failing to show leadership. At a press conference, an English journalist went as far as to call him a 'murderer' for his failure to send in troops to quell the unrest.

Marshall defended his actions in the Legislative Assembly by stating that any resort to the 'bullet and the Emergency Regulations … would have destroyed the concept of democracy and its value in this territory completely'. Meanwhile, Singapore went strike-crazy. Lee Kuan Yew wrote that Fong and his Singapore Bus Workers Union 'now had the full measure of Marshall':

> They knew they had a swing door to push. The way in which the SBWU had fought and won now gave all trade unions – workers and leaders, communists and non-communists – confidence that they had much to gain if they, too, showed fight.

From early April until the end of December 1955, Singapore witnessed a staggering 260 labour stoppages, walk-offs, go-slows and sit-downs – if we exclude Sundays, that means more than one labour protest every working day. All the while support for Lim and Fong's unions grew.

Marshall, stuck between a rock and a hard place, seemed to be losing his grip. To Lee's surprise, when Chief Secretary Sir William Goode pounced on the PAP in the Assembly and accused it of being a front organisation for the communists, Marshall (instead of applying the *coup de grâce*) defended Lee and his party as comprising several 'decent men', many of whom were not communists. Out on the streets, Chinese students ignored the government's official closure of their schools, and in a repeat of the previous year locked themselves into their classrooms, where they established their own revolutionary curriculum. Yet Marshall remained conciliatory. To many people's surprise, he officially recognised Lim and Fong's previously unregistered Chinese Middle School Students' Union and announced an All-Party Committee to address the current problems in Chinese education. In the Assembly he explained: 'our son is as one who is ill. He lies stricken with chicken pox, his body a mass of red spots … This is not the time for the whip or the knife.'

LET THE PEOPLE KNOW

The Chief Minister reports to the people of Singapore on the first six months of Labour Front administration

But a month later the 'whip' and the 'knife' came out. Faced by the prospect of further island-wide labour unrest and further violence, the Chief Minister ordered the detention of five union leaders under the Emergency Regulations. Among those arrested was Fong Swee Suan.

Marshall now found himself applauded by those same segments of the population that had earlier castigated him. But to his political opponents he had given fresh evidence that he was merely the 'puppet' of the colonial authorities. One month after Fong's arrest, Lim Chin Siong taunted Marshall in front of the press: 'I share the same beliefs and the same aims as […] Fong Swee Suan. I therefore challenge the government to arrest me too.' Perhaps Marshall was now haunted by some earlier sage words of Lee Kuan Yew: 'History has shown that those who take office before independence never take office after it.'

With his nationalist credentials ebbing away, his authority openly challenged and Singapore reeling from one strike to another, what could Marshall do? What he chose to do, in the context of the day, proved absolutely stunning. Marshall decided to engineer a constitutional crisis. If the British failed to let his government govern, if they did not provide immediate proof that they were genuinely committed to Singapore's self-government, then the Chief Minister would resign. To put it simply, Marshall gambled on *merdeka* or bust.

Marshall's platform collapses

It was what historian Karl Hack has called 'a moment of madness'. No one had so far imagined Singapore as a self-governing nation – it was surely too small, too complex and too vulnerable to stand by itself? But Marshall's gamble was also a brilliant tactical manoeuvre, a piece of inspired and quite typical individualism (he barely seems to have consulted his fellow Labour Front members) that for nine months transformed his and his party's political fortunes.

Ostensibly, the crisis came about because of bureaucratic obstacles that Marshall believed hindered his government from governing. In early July 1955, the Chief Minister requested the appointment of more ministers of his choosing to the Cabinet and the effective transfer of certain powers still held by the governor. When it seemed as if he might be refused, Marshall threatened to resign. He then went to the Legislative Assembly to get Singapore's elected representatives to support his challenge to the governor's authority and affirm their determination to end colonialism and win self-rule. Marshall now demanded that the Rendel Constitution – that 'scraggy hand of death clutching to the brakes of progress' as he labelled it – be changed, and a new constitution that meant true self-government put in its place. What might have been left as an internal administrative dispute had morphed into a public matter of the highest political significance.

Suddenly, Marshall was thrust back into the political limelight. Pleas came in from around the world for him to remain in office. *Kampong* dwellers appeared outside the Legislative Chamber with placards that read 'We Want Marshall' and 'Marshall Must Stay'. As the Assembly entered the Legislative Chamber to debate Marshall's motion, the gallery was so packed that people had to be turned away. No more the colonial stooge, Singapore's 'David' had returned to slay the colonial 'Goliath'.

The British, for their part, feared that Marshall's resignation would plunge Singapore into further political crisis and so they acceded to his immediate demands and eventually agreed to talks in London over Singapore's constitutional future. Reluctantly (and not without the drama of a complete opposition walk-out led by Lee Kuan Yew over the precise wording of the British promise to enter into constitutional talks), Marshall's political opponents fell into line behind him. Such was the current of popular feeling Marshall had awoken that even the communists dared not run against it. The Party organ *Freedom News* stated: 'The people are willing to give support to any action that is against colonialism; the people will give their support and encouragement even to the dog Marshall barking at his master.'

Over the next few months, Marshall was transformed. In an electrifying session of the Assembly he demanded that Lim Chin Siong declare publicly whether he spoke in the Chamber as a communist or communist sympathiser. Not for the last time, Lee Kuan Yew was forced to make a statement to the press that the PAP stood for an 'independent, democratic, non-communist Malaya' achieved through 'constitutional means'. Chin Siong's own press statement was more ambiguous: 'I am not a communist or a communist sympathiser – but I am also not an anti-communist.'

But while Marshall was on the offensive, clearly revelling in his restored role as anointed *merdeka* hero, more than a few people began to have doubts about his leadership. On his way to London in December 1955 to prepare the ground for the all-party constitutional conference the following year, Marshall met with the prime ministers of Sri Lanka and India, describing himself in Delhi as a 'pilgrim to the land of Gandhi and Nehru'. Nothing wrong here (perhaps apart from a slightly inflated sense of self-importance) but on this same trip, on the eve of sensitive discussions with the British government, the Chief Minister also swore to bring down 'the selfish gods enshrined in the Bank of England and the Colonial Office' along with colonialism in general, threatening (once more) to resign if his mission failed. Our old friend Yap Pheng Geck, who had become leader of the Chinese Chamber of Commerce, described Marshall's performance as 'Marshallism on the rampage'. Lee Kuan Yew remarked (in almost Churchillian cadences): 'Never in the history of the colonial revolution has so much humbug been enacted in so short a time, by so erratic a Chief Minister.'

How far 'Marshallism on the rampage' became a political liability was revealed a few months later. In March 1956, Marshall undertook to organise a 'Merdeka Week' to coincide with the visit by a study mission of British Members of Parliament to assess Singapore's prospects for independence. What particularly concerned his fellow party members was his proposal to hold a 'Merdeka Rally' at Kallang Airport as the culmination of the week's celebrations, at which a massive petition of 170,000 signatures demanding self-government would be presented (in several bound volumes) to the British delegation. Grainy footage in the National Museum of Singapore reveals a huge crowd (estimated to be around 25,000 and many of them PAP supporters) converging on the airport, carrying placards emblazoned with the communist dove of peace and starting to chant, sing and perform the communist *yanko* dance. Marshall arrives in an open-top convertible, standing up and raising his hand in the *merdeka* salute – looking for all-the-world like a Roman emperor, his modern-day chariot carrying him right up to the dais.

The problems started when Marshall, Lee Kuan Yew, Lim Chin Siong and the other leading politicians who were present, climbed up on the stage – a hastily constructed, wooden *wayang* stage. Allegedly, when Marshall gave the *merdeka* salute (other accounts state that it was after the PAP leaders began to speak) the crowd rushed forward, clambered up onto the rickety platform and sent it crashing to the ground. No one was injured but the public address system failed immediately.

Rather tellingly, what followed depends on which eyewitness testimony you consult. Lee Kuan Yew recalled that Marshall tried to speak into a dead microphone while he grabbed one that worked. Lee was unsuccessful in his attempt to calm the crowd, but then so too were Lim Chin Siong and Ong Eng Guan after him. However, the accounts of Lim Chin Siong and his supporters claim that it was Lim who got the crowd to settle by ordering them to sit down. Yet another report from the *Straits Times* provides a further twist. Lim's command to the mob, 'When you leave this place keep calm – don't beat the police', as the

paper's reporter saw it, was interpreted by the crowd as a signal to do exactly that – to attack the police.

Whatever the truth, the British MPs decided that rather than join the Singapore leaders on their collapsed stage, they would stay in the Kallang airport building and greet the people from its balcony. Not long afterwards, bricks started to fly through the same building's windows as clashes between the crowd and the police spread. By that time, the police had whisked the British MPs away to safety. A spectacle to reveal Singapore's readiness for responsible self-government had backfired completely. In the aftermath of the affair, the British governor of the colony informed his superiors in London that Marshall's government was 'a mushroom, all head, thin body and no roots'.

Whether or not the Merdeka Rally single-handedly wrecked Marshall's chances at the constitutional talks in London the following month, it undoubtedly

Crowd at the Merdeka Rally, Kallang.
March 1956
NAS 19980002123-0002

increased concerns about whether Singapore under his leadership should determine its own internal security. As Marshall later admitted, the discussions broke down over this very matter:

> I got the impression they were not confident that I could hold my ground against the communists. And any independence they gave me would merely seep through to strengthen the communist position in Singapore.

At a time when British strategic interests across the world seemed under threat and communism on its relentless march forward, some Western observers came to view Singapore's heady *merdeka* politics and its highly charged Chief Minister as having sprung from the same volcanic source. *TIME* magazine, in explaining the failure of the talks, described Marshall as a 'phenomenon fully representative of volatile, multiracial Singapore' and as a distasteful example of 'the new Asian demagogy'. Marshall was 'vaguely socialistic and violently anti-colonial', a 'flamboyant, pipe-smoking, bush-shirted political campaigner' who 'posed as the prophet of *merdeka*'.

Marshall's painful 'last act' in London, after three weeks of draining and ultimately fruitless negotiations, did nothing to improve his image. When the breakdown of the talks was announced on 15 May he appeared in front of the

Marshall leaving No. 10 Downing Street, official residence of the Prime Minister of the United Kingdom.
May 1956
NAS 19980002123-0017

cameras looking emotionally shattered. Nonetheless, his language proved as unrestrained as ever. Britain's offer of internal self-government while retaining a controlling interest over internal security was a case of 'Christmas pudding with arsenic' – understandable frustration perhaps, but Marshall went on to threaten that if elections were called on his return to Singapore: 'I and my party will boycott them – or we will put forward twenty-five of the most advanced lepers in the island as our candidates.' In a last throw of the dice the following day, Marshall pressed himself on British Prime Minister Anthony Eden and managed to delay his Cabinet meeting for half an hour so that the two men could speak. As Marshall later related, part of their exchange went as follows: Eden told the Chief Minister he had to be 'patient' and 'diplomatic'; Marshall replied: 'I am no diplomat, Mr. Prime Minister, I am ... I am ... I am a missionary of democracy!'

Marshall was by this time a missionary whose followers had begun to desert him. Lee Kuan Yew, Lim Chin Siong, and even one member of Marshall's Labour Front had decided enough was enough and elected to leave London early. Marshall's inability to accept the failure of the talks, and his efforts to single-handedly restart them without properly consulting the rest of the delegation, alienated even his own support. It seemed that having threatened to resign if the talks failed he was now desperately trying to cling onto power. One of Lee's final acts in Britain was to hold a press conference in which he castigated Marshall for his 'political ineptitude'. The British media gave Lee extensive coverage on television, on radio and in the newspapers: a new, more reasonable Singapore leader appeared to have emerged.

Marshall, on his return to Singapore and under some pressure from his own party, eventually did resign as Chief Minister and left the Labour Front and for a brief while Singapore politics. Looking back at his time in office, he described himself in self-sacrificial terms as an 'expendable bridge'. His detractors have been less sympathetic and regarded him as a posturing 'flash in the pan'. It is easy to emphasise the evanescent nature of Marshall's political impact: he was, after all, only in power for 13 months.

But perhaps a fairer verdict would be that Marshall was a flash in the 'wrong' pan. His government may have been hamstrung by civil unrest and colonial obstruction, yet it established real authority for the Chief Minister and set in motion responses to several key issues affecting Singapore that subsequent elected governments would be forced to tackle: citizenship, Chinese education, official multilingualism and the Malayanisation of public services. Most importantly, Marshall's theatrics had a fundamentally serious purpose that ought not to be forgotten. As he put it himself:

> [T]he intangible achievement is [the] awakening of our people to the sense of our own dignity, and the sense of their own rights, and the sense of the constitutional process to achieve a dignified way of life.

馬克思　恩格斯
共 产 党 宣 言

29. The Struggle for Singapore

One night in February 1957, listeners to Radio Malaya might have tuned into a live debate between participants from Britain, Eastern Europe and Southeast Asia, speaking from studios in Singapore and Kuala Lumpur. The global scope of this simulcast was fitting since the topic of the discussion was in many ways *the* debate of the decade. 'Is coexistence possible between communism and democracy?' asked the nice man in Radio Malaya's Singapore studio, and at once his international panellists – a gruff Yorkshire unionist, a Yugoslav intellectual, an Oxford don and a British journalist called Alex Josey – tore into his question.

How long local listeners paid attention probably depended on how much they enjoyed a fiery argument featuring as diverse a variety of accents as of political interests. As the exotic tones of the participants grew more heated, the chance of consensus diminished: 'What kind of capitalism? What kind of communism? Does he mean under communism, the Stalinism in Russia ... I'd say it's impossible for coexistence to come about between communism and democracy as we understand it, because the cause of communism is basically dedicated to the destruction of the latter ... to the destruction of capitalism ... I'd say not only capitalism, but capitalism, socialism, democracy ...' And so on, and so on.

If Marshall had been asked to participate his response to the question would surely have been a loud (very loud) and resounding 'No!' In late December 1955, he had joined Chief Minister Tunku Abdul Rahman of the Federation of Malaya for talks with MCP leader Chin Peng in the tiny northern Malayan town of Baling. On his return to Singapore, he told the Assembly (in a voice that became a powerful screech that set off the microphone feedback):

> [N]either the independence of these territories, nor the welfare of the people, matters in the slightest to the Malayan Communist Party! They don't care a hoot! All they want is to obtain control of the country. All they want is the expansion of their own imperialist communism ...

But as we saw, Marshall left Singapore's political stage the following year and henceforth he would only return periodically as a bit-player. With the possible exception of Lim Chin Siong, the most interesting leader to then pose the same question was Lee Kuan Yew. Whatever Lee's 'on air' response might have been it's probable it would have barely scratched the surface of the dilemma that by 1957 was churning away inside him.

Chinese translation of *The Communist Manifesto* of Karl Marx and Friedrich Engels.
1950s or 1960s
Paper
H 17.4 x W 12.5 cm
NMS 2006-01634

Lee's predicament

The way Goh Keng Swee told the story it went something like this. During the failed constitutional talks of April–May 1956, Lee Kuan Yew visited Goh, then back in London to complete his Ph.D, at his Notting Hill flat. Lee was in 'a mood of despair'. Over an impromptu meal of beers, tinned crab and pickles, he admitted that the PAP 'had been captured by the communists, and that Lim Chin Siong was himself not a free agent but had to take orders from the underground'. The PAP was only a 'very junior partner' in a Communist United Front (CUF) of workers, rural dwellers and students. The whole PAP endeavour, Lee believed, was 'now coming unstuck'.

In a sense, Lee had prophesied his own predicament. 'When social democrats work with communists,' he had earlier told an MCP supporter in London, 'they get eaten up'. However, in the early days of the PAP, Lee had put his personal hostility towards communism to one side. In January 1955, he issued a proposal on behalf of his party for a general amnesty for the MCP if it abandoned armed insurrection. In the same year, just a week before the Hock Lee riots, he made this strikingly candid admission to an Australian journalist:

> Any man in Singapore who wants to carry the Chinese-speaking people with him cannot afford to be anti-communist. The Chinese are very proud of China. If I had to choose between colonialism and communism, I would vote for communism and so would the great majority.

But it was the sudden and shocking violence of the Hock Lee riots – what Lee later described as his 'baptism of fire working with the CUF' – that altered his view entirely. As student lock-ins, hunger strikes and further labour unrest came thick and fast following the night of May 12th, Lee decided 'to get away from this madhouse and go on my annual vacation'. Retreating to Malaya's Cameron Highlands and playing golf every day for three weeks, he 'soaked in the events of

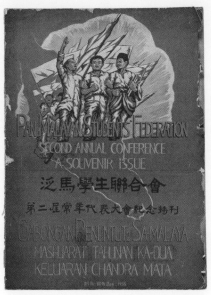

Conference souvenir booklet.
January 1955
Paper
H 26.1 x W 19 cm
NMS 2006-01633

the previous months'. He now felt in his 'bones' that 'to continue on the course Lim Chin Siong and Fong had embarked upon would end in political disaster'. On his return to Singapore, he discussed the matter with his party allies Toh, Rajaratnam and Byrne. It was agreed that Lee should read Lim and Fong 'the riot act' and so he told them that if they failed to change their political methods 'they would have to go it alone'.

These discussions remained internal to the party since Lee could not at that time publicly condemn Lim and Fong lest he risk losing the Chinese workers and breaking up the anti-colonial movement. Lee wrote that Lim and Fong listened to him for a while but that unrest and violence returned to Singapore just a few months later. Once more, Lee was forced to reiterate in public that the PAP abjured violence and stood for a non-communist Malaya. Privately he accepted that there were now 'two PAPs'.

Lim Yew Hock and the battle for the PAP

However, not long after Lee's moment of despair in London, the moderate faction of the PAP received a boost from an unlikely source.

Lim Yew Hock, Singapore's second Chief Minister, is remembered by many people for having been as outrageous a personality as David Marshall as well as an inveterate political joker. To read Lim's own extraordinary memoirs is to have this impression reinforced. This is a man who speaks about himself in the third person, who happily recalls the lewd joke he made at the expense of a female member of his own party in front of the male-dominated Assembly, and who eventually admits that 'whether a politician believes in his own statements is not the moot point; his pervading thought is how to convince his listeners that black is white or white is black or something is not what it is but what it should be'. Yet when it came to what Lim saw as the communist menace threatening to devastate Singapore in the late 1950s, the new Chief Minister revealed a definite sense of purpose: 'My encounter with them was a battle of wits as well as nerves.'

If 1955 had been a bad year in Singapore for civil unrest then the second half of 1956 was the worst on record yet. To have wandered into the city at the end of October must have felt like stumbling into a recent battle zone. Riots late in that month had left 13 dead and 123 injured, the maelstrom of violence once more emanating from Singapore's Chinese schools. Now, the whole of the island was under curfew. Armed troops patrolled the streets, military helicopters swept across the skies and rebel insurgents were rounded up and led away by the dozen. On 18 September, Lim Yew Hock had launched a two-month purge of Singapore's leftists that resulted in 300 people being banished or detained and 12 labour and student organisations being outlawed. Among those arrested were union and PAP leaders Lim Chin Siong, Fong Swee Suan, Devan Nair, James Puthucheary and Sandrasegeram 'Sandra' Woodhull.

Lim's war on the leftists had mixed political consequences. It certainly convinced the British they now had a government in Singapore they could rely on to protect their strategic and economic interests. In 1958, after successful all-party talks the previous year, the Chief Minister returned from London with a finalised deal for Singapore's self-government with general elections to be held in 1959 (pretty much the same agreement that Marshall had previously rejected). But to achieve this, Lim had sacrificed the trust of Singapore's Chinese majority. Chinese protesters along with leftist democrats from all backgrounds denounced him as a 'fascist', a 'dictator', as 'undemocratic', 'anti-socialist' and a 'running dog of the British'. He was even sent a warning letter with a bullet enclosed (remembering which he later remarked, 'Fortunately ... in those days the letter bomb had not been perfected'). Yet while Lim Yew Hock had made himself the source of such hostility, his hard-line attitude also threw Lee Kuan Yew and his moderate faction within the PAP a political lifeline.

Lee had returned to Singapore following his heart-to-heart with Goh in London, determined to ensure that the PAP returned to the original goals that he and his Oxley Rise associates had set out: to be an inclusive, multi-ethnic party committed to a non-communist, democratic Malaya won through peaceful means. However, the party apparatus was then a shambles. The PAP's 'open door' policy to membership meant that many of its branches had fallen into the hands of Lim and Fong's largely Chinese-educated faction. In August 1956, Lee selected Ong Pang Boon, then a Chinese-educated employee at the Federal and Colonial Building Society, as the party's Organising Secretary, the man entrusted with the task of pulling it together. The task was an uphill one from the outset. That same month, the Lim and Fong faction revealed its strength at the PAP's annual conference held at the Badminton Hall in Geylang. Middle Road union members packed the auditorium while Chinese students (wearing red armbands) stood guard at the doors, screening those who entered. Lim, Fong and the more radical leftists won four of the 12 seats on the party executive, with Lim garnering the highest individual number of votes.

But the radical leftists' real challenge for power came the following year. After Lim, Fong, Nair, Puthucheary and Woodhull were incarcerated, their faction found a new leader in Lim's brother, Lim Chin Joo. In the lead-up to the 1957 annual PAP conference in August, Chin Joo led an expression of grievances over the direction in which Lee's leadership had taken the party. A particular gripe was Lee's acceptance of Britain's terms for self-government in which Britain maintained its controlling interest over internal security. Once more, the Badminton Hall was packed with Middle Road union men and when it came to elections for the new party executive, Lim's faction carried away half the offices. Goh Keng Swee later recalled that an air of chaos enveloped the entire proceedings. Admission cards to the conference had been handed out to unionists indiscriminately, so there had been 'no proper checks' and nobody really knew 'who was a party member'.

Lim Yew Hock.
1956
Time & Life Pictures/Getty

Faced by such an outright challenge to their leadership, Lee and his moderate allies refused to take their seats on the party executive. The PAP they had founded, that had been their brainchild, and that the much younger Lim and Fong had merely been invited to join, was in open rebellion against them. Chin Joo tried to smooth things over by offering a deal that would enable Lee and his moderates to remain on the executive in a majority, but this they categorically refused. Thus, the pro-Lim and Fong faction took over the administrative leadership of a party shorn of its founding officers.

It was not long after this that Lim Yew Hock went into action. As he wrote in his memoirs:

> I had reports of what had been going on and I decided that in the interests of Singapore I had to fire a salvo at the communist fellow-travellers. I gave orders to the police and that night six [sic] top communist fellow-travellers in the Party caucus were taken into custody ... I did not care that by this action I could be accused by my Party supporters as having opted for Lee Kuan Yew. This was not so. What I did was done in the best interest of Singapore.

Police riot squad.
1950s
Central Press/Getty

To several PAP members loyal to Lim and Fong, Yew Hock's interventions appeared part of an anti-leftist conspiracy in which Lee Kuan Yew was himself implicated. Lee wrote in his memoirs he 'calculated' that Yew Hock would likely arrest the 'pro-communists' after their bid for the PAP leadership, but he gives little indication of what led him to this calculation. What we can say for sure is that Lee was in the strange situation of feeling some assurance from the British and the Lim Yew Hock government that even as he publicly opposed them they would not let his party fall into the hands of the more radical leftists.

The changes to the PAP that followed the 1957 arrests were dramatic. In October, Lee's men were elected back onto what was now called the party's Central Executive Committee with full authority over party policy. To control party membership and avoid a repeat performance of the 1957 fiasco, a cadre system was introduced which consisted of four probationary levels with only full cadres able to elect the Central Executive Committee. To even qualify at the lowest probationary level one had to be a literate Singapore citizen of over 21 years of age, which immediately excluded many illiterate Chinese workers and under-age Chinese students. From this point, Lee also set about finding Chinese-educated supporters that he could rely on to stand in the coming elections. Sifting through the party's branch membership to find who was loyal to Lee and who retained sympathies with Lim and Fong was a lengthy and time-consuming task, and then there was the question of lurking communist agents. Nonetheless, the PAP was being rebuilt into the slick, controlled and hierarchical machine that it remains to this day.

The striking thing about the months that followed Lim Yew Hock's clampdown is just how soon a PAP victory in Singapore's first-ever general elections began to seem inevitable. The year 1958, recalled Lee Kuan Yew, was one 'when that intense pressure that the communists had been mounting since 1954 subsided'. Matters were helped by the ruling party successfully shooting itself in both feet. If Lim Yew Hock being labelled a 'fascist' and 'colonial stooge' by Chinese workers and students wasn't bad enough, in early 1959 his coalition – by now called the Singapore People's Alliance (SPA) – became embroiled in a major corruption scandal unearthed by one of its former Cabinet ministers. Francis Thomas was the whistle-blower in question and when the scandal broke he dramatically crossed the floor to sit with the opposition. The findings of the public enquiry that followed, released just two days before the general elections, revealed that Lim Yew Hock's ministers had used illegal donations from the US government to help themselves to houses and shares.

Meanwhile, the PAP had found a new Hokkien-speaking hero to substitute for Lim Chin Siong. On 22 December 1957, the PAP had thrashed the Labour Front and Singapore's other political parties to secure control of the newly elected Singapore City Council. Ong Eng Guan, the PAP's candidate for Mayor, was what Lee called 'a crowd puller', with a knack for theatrical political gestures that rivalled David Marshall's. Following his appointment, Ong refused to wear mayoral regalia or stay in the mayoral residence, and in front of a packed City Council chamber (and the rolling cameras) he ordered the public removal of that 'relic of colonialism' – the mayoral mace. He then rushed up to the Town Hall balcony (where, Lee tells us, 'a microphone and loudspeakers had been installed at his request') to speak to his adoring supporters in Chinese for ten minutes, ending with three loud cries of '*Merdeka!*' 'May God protect Singapore' was the *Straits Times* headline the following day.

At the same time, Lee was himself beginning to make an impression on the Chinese majority of Singapore through his own speeches in Chinese, and though his Mandarin might have been halting, the effort he was making to master the language was widely appreciated. Furthermore, Lee had found in Ong Pang Boon and former Chinese journalist Jek Yeun Thong, Chinese-educated lieutenants who spoke on his behalf directly to the people. Moreover, while Lee himself could speak Malay, as could Rajaratnam, his rivals were frequently less comfortable in languages other than English. Lee remembered PAP election rallies as vivid, multicultural affairs that were full of fun and colour, compared with the drab, rather sombre and often poorly attended occasions organised by their opponents. Nor was the PAP merely covering every base in terms of ethnicity. On 25 April 1959 – nomination day – the party fielded candidates in every one of Singapore's 51 electoral wards: 34 Chinese candidates, ten Malays, six Indians and one Eurasian; its closest rival, Lim Yew Hock's SPA, could only muster 39.

And so to polling day: 30 May 1959. It was, as Lee recalled, 'quiet and orderly' compared to the elections of 1955. For the first time voting had been made compulsory and for the first time the vast majority of Singapore's population – the Chinese-speaking and Chinese-educated – had qualified to vote under the new law of citizenship. They were about to make their most important decision thus far in the history of their island.

Riding the elusive tiger

But before we go further to discover what this decision meant, let's pause the action one last time – at the moment when the election results are announced and the victory celebrations begin, as Lee Kuan Yew is garlanded, lifted up on his supporters' shoulders and carried through an ecstatic crowd, while Lim, Fong and the other detainees crowd into a room in Changi Prison to hear the results, as the film cameras move amongst the prisoners capturing their every expression.

In the conventional narrative of Singapore's struggle for *merdeka*, Lee and the moderate faction of the PAP are depicted at the point of their 1959 victory as having ridden the 'tiger' of communist- and pro-communist-orchestrated support into government (following which the beast would have to be tamed). By 1956, the moderates had become convinced that Lim Chin Siong was taking instructions

PAP members canvassing for votes ahead of polling day.
1959
NAS 19980002913-0027

from the communist underground and that a showdown with his radical PAP faction was inevitable. Lee wrote that some time in March 1958 he had the first of a series of secret rendezvous with the 'Plen', the anonymous Communist Party leader in Singapore. Lee's memoirs capture the cloak-and-dagger atmosphere of these meetings and the air of 'stealth and furtiveness' that surrounded his encounter with 'someone truly "underground"'. The Plen offered Lee the cooperation of the MCP; the PAP leader was non-committal, deciding to string his counterpart along for a while to discover the communists' real intentions and potential.

Lee, like Lim Yew Hock and David Marshall, and in common with most British officials, never appears to have doubted the extent of local communist penetration. This was hardly surprising. We are talking about a part of the world that had actually experienced an armed communist insurrection (not one of those more distant countries, such as the US and Australia, whose fears of such an outcome in the same decade turned into mass hysteria). But when we go beyond the recollections and speeches of those local leaders who held authority under the British, or who were on good enough terms with colonial officials (as Lee was)

to have been passed confidential Special Branch reports, the picture becomes at once more complex.

In a recent interview, C. C. Chin, a one-time communist active in the city from the late 1950s, gives his own vivid portrait of an underground revolutionary's life. While a student at Chung Cheng High School, Chin's extracurricular activities included long stints as a Communist Party polemicist:

> I write essays, poetry … critical political essays and so on attacking the government. Sometimes I will continue to write for three days and three nights, only in between I will have a little nap for 20 minutes, half an hour … because at that time everything moves so fast.

Chin recalled the girls who would come over to his place and sometimes stay on after 'a meeting or a study group' (though any romantic intimacy was 'taboo' as it would ruin the collective's effectiveness). There were also the 'student cells' made up of five comrades who would swim, go to the cinema and do just about everything together, building up their 'collectiveness' in preparation for their call to revolutionary action. Not least, there were the famous student picnics, involving games, songs and an 'interesting programme' to 'eventually get some messages across: anti-government or anti-British, to praise [the] socialist system and things like that'.

Yet eventually, Chin makes the following crucial point:

> Now I would say this, during the 1950s and 1960s, the entire struggle, we have to clearly define what is 'Left' and what is really communist activities. There are not really that many communists, okay? ... But in terms of the method of struggle, this is what the communists think: they would use the Left as a front. And the Left is actually leading the struggle in the anti-British movement or anti-whatever the system not to their favour.

Such thoughts are echoed by our Chinese student Han Tan Juan, who like Chin studied at Chung Cheng High School, where his after-school activities consisted of lessons in Chinese history and Marxist dialectics organised by Lim and Fong's Chinese Middle School Students' Union. Han frankly admitted that in the late 1950s he and his fellow students wanted to build a 'socialist Singapore/Malaya' on the 'Chinese model'. But as he looked at the broader situation beyond the Chinese schools, such doctrinal certainty began to dissolve:

> Malaya and Singapore could not establish a new country using the Chinese model. Although the communists could lead, [...] even if they had the power to lead, they could not make Marxism the national ideology. There was the Malay issue. It was unimaginable that most Malays would, one day, give up being a Muslim, convert to Marxism and give up on their Allah.

Apparently, Changi Prison during the late 1950s witnessed a similar realisation take root amongst the PAP detainees. As Devan Nair recalled:

> While we were in prison, the debate began. Where should we be heading? To a Chinese Communist Malaya, or to a multiracial, Democratic Socialist Malaya? What should be the meaning of Malayan nationalism?
>
> We carried on the debate in the prison. And the people who were supporting my stand, vigorously, were James Puthucheary and Sandra Woodhull. I persuaded Fong Swee Suan. And he agreed!

According to Fong's more recent interview, though Lim Chin Siong was for some time detained separately, when he and Fong eventually debated the same issue Lim also agreed: a democratic, multiracial Malaya was the only way forward. It seems that as young revolutionaries got older they also got wiser.

These recollections give us the impression that in the late 1950s radical, anti-colonial leftists were still experimenting, still weighing up the options – in fact not so much 'pro-communist' but rather, as Lim described himself, 'not [yet] anti-communist'. The problem was that such debate and experimentation occurred against a backdrop of political violence that to many people spoke much louder than mere words and ideology. Indeed, with the horrors of the Malayan Emergency still fresh in people's minds, political violence became *the* critical issue that polarised Singapore politics during the late 1950s. These were years when hardworking Singaporeans could read in their morning newspapers of students at Nanyang Girls' School who threw acid in their principal's face, of an American journalist murdered by a mob because of the colour of his skin, and of a young Chinese student shot through the lung by the police – who instead of being taken straight to hospital by his comrades was picked up and paraded around the streets in a lorry as a martyr to the cause (which he became, through no choice of his own, when he eventually bled to death).

And so it didn't really matter to Lee Kuan Yew, his PAP moderates and many other people in Singapore whether Lim Chin Siong and his faction repeatedly denied that they were communists, or whether they were in fact still making up their minds what the best political model for an independent Singapore and Malaya might be. Their supporters' actions spoke for themselves, as did Lim and Fong's repeated failure to explicitly condemn these actions. Moreover, even if Lee Kuan Yew and his moderates saw that not every incident of violent unrest was communist-orchestrated, that on occasion (such as during the Merdeka Rally) it might combust spontaneously, they still believed it ultimately helped the communist cause – by destabilising Singapore and by wrecking its people's chances of securing a peaceful, constitutional solution to their demand for independence.

Which brings us to the crux of the matter, for of course not all revolutions that have relied on force have been communist, nor has every revolutionary. Many people in Singapore would have justified their resort to violent unrest, not in terms of their belief in the ultimate necessity of a future communist state, but simply as a legitimate response to the imposition of an illegitimate colonialism – a colonialism (as they saw it) that was kept in place by its own violence of arbitrary arrests and high-pressure water-cannons that blasted primary school students into drains. These radicals would have argued tht their end was the same as that of the moderates: a free, democratic, Malaya and Singapore. They simply didn't share the same faith in 'constitutional means' as did Lee the lawyer and his British-educated Oxley Rise circle.

Finally, if our snapshot of Singapore's political scene on the eve of self-government has not grown too complex, we have to consider what political analysts often call the 'quiet majority': those Singaporeans who neither considered themselves communist, pro-communist or non-communist, who might not have fully understood what these distinctions meant but who simply wanted a better future for themselves and their children. Such were the many women now compelled to vote en masse in a Singapore election for the first time, perhaps impressed by the efforts of activists such as Constance Goh and Mrs Siraj on their behalf, and even more impressed by the PAP's election slogan of 'one man one wife' and its promise to set up a Women's Affairs Bureau.

Then there were those workers still holding out for the simple matter of a basic improvement in working conditions: the Indian union leader G. Kandasamy who recalled that the struggle was not 'against the white system' but against employers of all colours; or the Chinese bus driver Koh Chung Sian who, barely able to make ends meet, vividly recalled when Lee Kuan Yew got up on stage not to preach *merdeka* but to announce the bus employees' pay rise; or the workers at the Khong Guan biscuit factory who resisted the overtures of Lim and Fong's unions, preferring to trust in their 'brothers' the bosses and refusing to go on strike.

Then, also, there were those parents concerned at their children's involvement in revolutionary unrest, who simply desired (as Fong Swee Suan's own parents did) that their sons and daughters give up politics, get back to their studies and go and find respectable jobs. These were ordinary people forced to struggle in a world that was unfair, unequal and in which a simple matter like catching a bus still often meant having to bribe the bus conductor. By May 1959, it was these people who, unlike many of Singapore's younger student revolutionaries, now had the right to vote.

Revolution on the streets was a young person's game. By 1959 it was becoming – for a generation that had lived through the Occupation, the Emergency, repeated shortages, unemployment and corruption – far too exhausting.

Itinerant seller preparing a bowl of noodles. Everything he needs for his trade can be packed into two large boxes that are suspended from a pole he carries on his shoulder.
1950
NAS 19980005839-0009

NEW NATION

1959 – 1965

30. THE POWER OF ACTION

'It was a victory but I was not jubilant,' wrote Lee Kuan Yew.

In Singapore's first ever general election on 30 May 1959, the PAP had won a landslide victory, securing 43 of 51 seats in the Legislative Assembly. A few days later, 50,000 supporters packed the Padang to celebrate, while the men who would form the new government sat opposite them under brilliant lights on the steps of City Hall. 'At times the scene was more like a carnival than a political rally', wrote the correspondent for the *Times* of London. 'Round the crowd were hundreds of busy mobile food stalls, lit by pressurised paraffin lights, and balloons were on sale. Along the illuminated pillars of the city hall were political banners, and in the centre was a large PAP symbol – a red lightning flash in a blue circle, on a white background.'

That evening Singapore's first elected Prime Minister felt it necessary to 'temper and dampen' his audience's enthusiasm. His party had committed itself to a mammoth undertaking: a 'social revolution through peaceful means' that promised industrial development, workers' welfare, women's emancipation, a streamlined bureaucracy, better health, housing and education, and eventually full independence through a merger with Malaya. Despite the festive mood, Lee warned that 'all the planning and effort on the part of the government will not produce the desired results unless you the people support and sustain the work of your government.'

Lee was not the only person in Singapore in less than jubilant spirits. In the weeks that followed the PAP victory, property prices slumped, foreign capital took flight and several Western companies moved their headquarters to Kuala Lumpur. Expatriates, businessmen and the English-educated were amongst those who believed the PAP to be anti-capitalist, anti-Western, pro-communist and extremist, and there were good grounds for assuming so. During their election campaign PAP candidates had denounced 'white business', decadent Western culture, European clubs and the foreign-owned press, generally playing on working-class resentment against capitalists, colonialists and those seen as their local intermediaries. As Goh Keng Swee put it: 'The fiercer you spoke, the greater the cheers.'

Yet within 18 months, *TIME* magazine observed that a 'startling change' had come over Singapore's 'revolutionary rulers':

> Taking office, they poured out their avenging anti-Western zeal by ripping down Queen Elizabeth's portrait, slashing British bureaucrats' salaries, banning jukeboxes, comic books and other manifestations of what they called the West's 'yellow culture'. Tieless, coatless puritans presiding over the sybaritic center of the old South Seas, they rapidly got a name as Southeast Asia's most honest administrators ... But Prime Minister Lee, a wealthy, Cambridge-schooled Chinese, soon grasped that

Singapore by itself is an island emporium ill suited to revolutionary socialism since, among other things, it lacks any major industries to nationalize. His revised economic policy: 'Teaching the capitalists how to run their system.'

So though the new regime took down pictures of the Queen, it elected to leave Raffles' statue in peace and to retain the city's colonial street and place names. The message this sent was clear: the PAP revolution was going to be unique, on its own terms, neither a slave to inflexible ideology or to populist demands. Ultimately, the government would value political results over political dogma. If the local situation demanded the return of Western capital then that was what would happen – no matter what other post-colonial socialist governments were doing elsewhere in the world, and despite any disgruntlement within Singapore's own left-wing movement.

Men in white

Before this revolution commenced in earnest there were still a few rituals of *merdeka* theatre to complete, at which the new regime proved as attuned to the art of political symbolism as any that had come before. Previously, elected officials were sworn in (in full pomp) by the British governor at Government House, having arrived dressed respectfully in their formal lounge suits (the major exception, of course, being David Marshall). However, on 5 June 1959, Bill Goode, the last British governor, swapped his ceremonial uniform with white plumed hat for a simple suit and tie and went to be received by Singapore's new representatives. The ceremony was held not at Empress Place, where Marshall had spoken under the old 'apple tree', but at City Hall, the new seat of self-government. It was here, so Lee Kuan Yew explained, that Ong Eng Guan 'had given the underprivileged of Singapore the hope that the PAP government would have their interests at heart and would be honest in trying to advance them'.

The actual swearing-in took place in the same chamber where Ong had famously removed the mayoral mace as a relic of colonialism, in what was a conscious effort, so Lee put it, 'to superimpose on that image the imprint of the new Cabinet'. A striking photograph from immediately after the event shows Lee, Toh Chin Chye, Goh Keng Swee and behind them a long line of PAP ministers, leaving City Hall and marching in file towards the Legislative Assembly. All are dressed in the white uniforms the party had adopted since its inception in 1954 as a sign of its impeccable purity. Lee had told the people that their decision to elect the PAP was a 'victory of right over wrong, clean over dirty, righteousness over evil'.

As *TIME* magazine reported, a prevalent evil in the eyes of the PAP was 'yellow culture' (a term translated from the original Malay which referred to

lewd or uncouth behaviour imported from the West). An earlier *TIME* article recorded the kind of minor cultural revolution that marked the PAP's first month in office:

> Lee banned jukeboxes, closed down some 1,200 pinball machines, and ordered the Singapore radio to stop broadcasting rock 'n' roll. Later he ruled that the jukeboxes could stay if they stuck to the classics – Beethoven and Chopin, for example. Meanwhile, police cleared the newsstands of pornography, padlocked eight girlie-magazine publishers and swooped through bars, sending B-girls home.

Subsequently, Lee described his government's 'anti-yellow culture' drive as one of 'several easy populist points to be scored that required no planning': 'It did no harm apart from adding somewhat to unemployment and making Singapore less attractive to tourists.' But the attack on 'yellow culture' was more than just a sop to popular anti-colonial sentiment. In another sign of the new order, police raids quashed several secret societies, along with their protection rackets, prostitution rings, and drug and illicit gambling networks. *TIME* was impressed by the 'immediate, unexpected result' of the crackdown: 'for the first time in memory, a full week went by without a kidnapping, extortion or gangland rumble reported'.

More literally 'down-to-earth' efforts to improve Singapore's international image followed soon after. The government launched a series of clean-up campaigns of the city's streets, its beaches and its parks, in what Lee described as a 'copycat exercise borrowed from the communists – ostentatious mobilisation of everyone including ministers to toil with their hands and soil their clothes in order to serve the people'. But the meaning of these symbolic mass exercises could be read in more than one way. While 'ostentatious mobilisation' brought PAP ministers closer to the people, it also involved English-educated civil servants who were pressed into giving up their Sundays to perform 'voluntary' manual labour. Their participation could be seen as evidence of their new commitment to serve the common people, or, since many civil servants had feared the PAP and voted for other political parties during the election, as a form of punishment – a kind of weekend detention for those the new regime felt needed a lesson in loyalty as well as humility.

These changes tell us much about the mentality of Singapore's new leaders but their impact, as Lee recognised, was largely cosmetic. The more serious work of the government remained elsewhere. Lined up alongside and behind the Prime Minister to take on this challenge (just as when they first processed out from City Hall having been sworn-in) were self-governing Singapore's first Cabinet, a team of ministers whose technocratic expertise as a whole was unrivalled across the whole of Southeast Asia (the only weak link being the island's first Minister for National Development – but we will get to him shortly).

Setting the world to rights

If one word came to mind to describe the PAP government in its early years then surely it was 'zeal'. Few administrators anywhere else in the world could at that time boast the same impassioned and intense work ethic, and the international media were quick to pick up on the fact. *TIME* (as we saw) described the PAP as 'tieless, coatless puritans', and as 'puritans by exertion' who poured out their 'anti-Western zeal'. Even Lee Kuan Yew himself would reflect on the 'puritanical zeal' of his first Minister for Home Affairs Ong Pang Boon, the man who largely orchestrated the government's anti-'yellow culture' crusade. The PAP was out to set Singapore to rights, and perhaps the world if it could.

Inevitably, such zeal (as it always seems to) demanded converts. If civil servants thought their jobs would become more comfortable once Lee, in one of his first acts as Prime Minister, introduced air conditioning to government buildings then they were in for a surprise. Cooler offices were meant to make public employees more efficient, not more relaxed. The arrival of air conditioning was accompanied by a major cut in their salaries, justified by the government as a temporary means to balance its first annual budget. Public sector resentment against the new regime swelled, but the PAP was merely demanding the same

self-sacrifice that it expected from its cohorts. 'Some of the senior officers,' wrote Lee, 'had to give up their maids – too bad, but the country was facing greater hardships and perils, and we had to convince people that this government would govern in the interest of all.'

In material terms, the new regime's impact on the lives of Singaporeans was undeniable. In early 1960, the government replaced the old Singapore Improvement Trust (SIT) with a new Housing and Development Board (HDB) and streamlined what was a previously moribund bureaucracy into a remarkable flat-building machine. In its first three years the HDB built almost as many houses and shops as SIT had in its 32 years: 26,168 units scattered across central Singapore, sometimes put up, according to one government broadcast in 1963, at the rate of 40 units per minute. In 1965, at the end of its first five-year programme, HDB had exceeded expectations and delivered 3,000 flats above its 50,000 target.

Obviously, such zeal came at a price. To maximise available land, the HDB constructed its flats in blocks of ten storeys or more (as compared to SIT blocks of two to seven storeys) with less open space between buildings. Thus, the dominant 'match-box' style of Singaporean public housing was born, superseding the attractive Art Deco aesthetic of many SIT flats (so sought after by Singaporeans decades later). On the other hand, not only were new HDB flats more available than their predecessors, they were more affordable, the government having subsidised their construction costs and pegged their rental rates to 20 per cent of the average wage earner's monthly income.

With similar energy the government set about transforming public health. To fulfil the PAP's election pledge to bring primary healthcare closer to the people, government health expenditure rose from $36.2 million in 1960 (already an increase from the $22.3 million of 1955) to $66.4 million by 1965. In addition to hospitals, much of this money was spent on school, maternal and child clinics and on mass campaigns against diseases such as tuberculosis. Meanwhile, the creation of the Public Utilities Board in 1963 inaugurated a new era for basic amenities – running water, electricity, and gas, improved sanitation and sewage. 'New towns' such as Queenstown sprang up across Singapore from the early 1960s as the HDB built more housing estates, which not only looked cleaner – they smelled much cleaner as well.

Over at the Ministry of Education, the figures were just as impressive. Education Minister Yong Nyuk Lin made good on the PAP's promise to ensure every child a place in school within a year by splitting the existing school day into morning and afternoon sessions (thereby doubling student intake) and by embarking on a crash programme to fast-track senior teachers into higher appointments as headmasters, headmistresses and principals.

Things took longer to get moving at Goh Keng Swee's Ministry of Finance (which had moved into offices at the Fullerton Building) for here the challenges

OPPOSITE: Snapshot of a rapidly changing landscape: Kampong Kuchai, located off Lorong 3 Geylang, is replaced by the HDB flats of Geylang Bahru.
1973
SPH 19980005718-0005

ABOVE: Information booklet, in Malay, by the Ministry of Health.
December 1959
Paper
H 17.4 x W 12.5 cm
NMS 1995-00332

were most intense. Faced with high unemployment and a slowing entrepôt economy, the government launched a five-year plan to transform Singapore into an industrial outpost to rival Hong Kong. In late 1960, Lee announced tax exemptions to attract 'pioneer' industries to Singapore and not long after, the island landed its first major foreign investments. Shipyards and steel mills would soon begin operations, but the most significant new arrivals in terms of Singapore's long-term prosperity were the oil refineries, led by Shell. In October 1960, a team of UN advisers arrived in Singapore to survey the site of a new industrial estate to be built on former swampland at Jurong. The following year, the project was placed under the guidance of a new government agency called the Economic Development Board (EDB).

Those first workers who trickled into Jurong's new industrial facilities remember a brave new world of arduous and ceaseless labour. The landscape itself was a major physical obstacle. 'Mud everywhere', recalled Yip Yue Wai, a young man in his early 20s when he started work at Jurong Shipyard on the island of Pulau Samulun. 'There was no bridge linking the main island and Pulau Samulun. At that time, we used 44-gallon barrels to build rafts, so as to enter and exit Pulau Samulun. Everything was inconvenient.' Furnace-worker Chng Suan Lui remembered a completely alien terrain: 'All I saw in the area were clay mountains and mud tracks. NatSteel [National Iron and Steel Mills Ltd] was

Ship-building in Jurong
Industrial Estate in the days
before covered workshops.
1962
NAS 19980007246-0094

at the furthest end, near the sea.' Safety standards were sometimes low and in some factories workers had to fork out their own money for basic necessities such as gloves. Yet in spite of such challenges, many workers recalled their sense of participation in a major undertaking of national significance. As Jurong pioneer Lim Lak Ee put it so succinctly: 'You are staying in Singapore. You are earning from Singapore. You sure support Singapore.'

Jurong was undoubtedly a risk. Goh later admitted that he had worried, given the island's volatile labour situation, whether the millions of dollars spent on the estate would result in 'several thousand acres of empty wasteland, to be known to posterity as "Goh's Folly"'. But the foundations of Singapore's industrialisation had been laid and Jurong would eventually become its pounding heartbeat – as dramatic a symbol of the island's new order as its modern schools, hospitals and high-rise housing.

Moulding the people

And yet the PAP was not content merely to provide Singaporeans with homes, jobs, health and education. Once in power, the party wanted to prepare the minds of the people for the social revolution it had promised. As self-governing Singapore's first Minister for Culture, Rajaratnam spelled out a key challenge: communal tensions and the tendency of people to only identify with their respective ethnic groups were 'ever present threats' to national unity:

> [W]e must consciously set about inoculating society against such dangers. To sit back and do nothing is to make inevitable the tragedy of racial conflict. … It would be wanton negligence to sit back and do nothing …

From the founding of the PAP in 1954, its vision for Singapore had been one of happy and harmonious multiculturalism. In 1959, the government recognised four official Singaporean languages – English, Chinese, Malay and Tamil – while hoping that Malay would become used by more non-Malays and so become the common national language. Rajaratnam envisaged the growth of a 'Malayan' culture that encompassed elements from every different ethnic group. An early government foray in this respect was the Aneka Ragam Rakyat (People's Cultural Concerts). These were free outdoor shows, held at the Botanic Gardens or on the steps of City Hall, which featured traditional songs and dances from every major ethnic group (Chinese, Malay, Indian and 'Western') – a kind of politically correct version of what had long been on offer at the Worlds amusements parks.

Naturally, such officially orchestrated attempts to manufacture a common Malayan culture were an easy target for criticism. In 1960, the poet and University of Malaya professor D. J. Enright derided the anachronism of 'a sarong culture, complete with *pantun* competitions and so forth'. Nonetheless, the policy had the government's full backing and it was not uncommon to see the Prime

Classical Indian dance
segment during an Aneka
Ragam Rakyat concert on the
steps of City Hall.
June 1962
SPH 211033

Minister and his fellow Cabinet colleagues in attendance at 'People's Cultural Concerts', seated cross-legged on the ground and usually in the front row.

The PAP also wanted a more disciplined national culture, both socially and ideologically. In the early 1960s, the government set up a Political Study Centre to 'teach top-ranking civil servants about the communist threat and our social and economic problems', as Lee wrote. The Centre's workshops, lectures and seminars, partly organised by the now ex-communist expert Gerald De Cruz, eventually expanded to include all government employees, schools and even trade unions. In the same period, the government established a Work Brigade, with its own barracks and uniforms, to provide productive employment for unemployed youths, a group it regarded as the root cause of most social unrest (along with the communists).

Without doubt the PAP's most important new organisation was the People's Association (PA), established on 1 July 1960 as what Lee described as a 'semi-independent, semi-government body'. Tasked by the Prime Minister with the management of community centres and youth clubs that would 'line [people] up on the side of law and order', the PA proved to be one of the government's most successful political tools. PA 'activists and organisers', as Lee called them, were trained in official PAP ideology and in the various workings of government ministries so they could serve as the vital grassroots middlemen (at the outset they were invariably men) linking the party with people. On being assigned to a community centre, a PA activist set about organising adult learning, recreational and cultural activities and annual national festivities with the explicit aim of bringing together people from diverse backgrounds in a productive use of their leisure time. Once he was familiar with his surroundings, he began to function as a local community leader, taking on the functions (as one official booklet noted) of 'marriage counsellor, letter-writer, arbitrator of neighbourhood quarrels, legal adviser, translator of official missives, odd-job man, teacher, job-placement officer, projectionist, sports coach, youth leader and all-round problem-solver' – all the while proudly carrying his affiliation with the PAP government.

To traditional clan and other types of communal associations, the PA's new community centres posed a challenge – not just through their emphasis on multiculturalism but through their sheer number. Having inherited less than 30 community centres from the British in 1959, the PAP pledged to build a new one every month. Between November 1962 and December 1963 (a period of intense political activity, as we will shortly see) the government constructed 121 new community centres across the island, most of them in rural areas. What is more, community centres – with their ubiquitous ping-pong tables and even badminton and basketball courts, their radios and, later, their television sets – were often a lot more fun than traditional social organisations. Indeed, from February 1963, when the first broadcasts by Radio & Television of Singapore commenced, community centres transformed the eating habits of an entire generation, as new addicts bolted down their dinner and then rushed to their local centre for their nightly fix at the flickering box.

For many rural Singaporeans, the community centre was the prism through which they first experienced their new nation. The bare concrete and stark modernist architecture of most centres brought a new aesthetic to *kampong* life that invariably heralded the arrival of electricity and piped water, street lights and proper drainage. Inside, the exhibitions and colourful posters (in four official languages) told of new jobs, new flats, new policies and new political threats – as did those other harbingers of the PAP's social revolution, the radio and the television set.

With the benefit of hindsight, the rise of this new nation appears inevitable. However, two years into self-government its future was far from certain. Singapore was then still not fully independent – Britain controlled her internal security and the power to suspend her constitution – nor was she a part of that wider Malayan nation to which many people felt she ought to belong and which in 1957 had received its own independence. Though the PAP's achievements were already impressive, its social revolution was still in embryo. The government had laid down a comprehensive blueprint for change, but it was a framework yet to be filled in.

At which point, in the middle of 1961, a major political battle broke out for control of the island's future.

31. THE OPPOSITION

If Sir Stamford Raffles set Singapore on her habit of always looking forward to a progressive, visionary utopia, then it was the PAP who handed her the schedule. At the start of 1959, the party published its election manifesto *The Tasks Ahead: PAP's Five-year Plan, 1959–1964*. As we have now seen, this document was merely the preliminary outline for a series of more detailed five-year plans that after the election began to guide the EDB, the HDB, the Ministry of Finance and many other government ministries and agencies besides.

Nothing extraordinary here: socialist and communist governments have had a penchant for five-year plans since Josef Stalin first introduced the practice back in 1928 (the main difference in Singapore being that the government actually tried to stick to its plans by making them realistic). But such long-term thinking revealed another important facet of the PAP regime. The party expected, and intended, to remain in power for many, many years. Given the scale of its 1959 election win, and the state of its parliamentary opposition, we might well ask – and why not?

But from mid-1961 until September 1963, the fate of the PAP and its social revolution stood in the balance. A rebellion from within the party sparked a political struggle that was bitter, ruthless and gripping. The weapons used to wage this struggle would transform Singapore profoundly.

Lim and Fong get out on probation

By the time Lee Kuan Yew stood on the steps of City Hall to give his victorious *merdeka* salute and usher in Singapore's new era of self-government, the PAP detainees – including Lim Chin Siong, Fong Swee Suan, Devan Nair, James Puthucheary and Sandra Woodhull – had languished in jail for over two years. The following day, Lim and the others emerged from Changi Prison freedom-fighter heroes. The *Straits Times* headlines read: 'OUT – and WHAT A WELCOME ... Thousands at jail gate roar "*Merdeka*" ... A volley of crackers greets the former detainees'. Archival footage in the National Museum of Singapore shows Lim, Fong and the other detainees as they are garlanded and embraced by their supporters, and, in a moment of breathtaking poetry, Lim releasing a pair of doves that fly high up into the sky.

Before the detainees stepped out to greet their supporters, one thing about self-governing Singapore was clear. 'In 1957 and during the elections before,' recalled Fong, 'there were two strong contenders [for the PAP leadership]; after 1957, there was only one main player.' Lee, who as their legal representative had been visiting the detainees in prison since that year, carefully orchestrated their release to ram this message home. He had demanded the detainees be freed as a condition of his government taking office; however, he ensured that this did not

Freed detainees outside Changi Prison. From left: Fong Swee Suan, Sandra Woodhull, Lim Chin Siong (holding birdcage) and Devan Nair.
June 1959
SPH 3182549

happen until after the PAP's 3 June victory rally at the Padang. Not only that, Lee ensured that the detainees did not walk free until each of them signed a declaration entitled 'The Ends and Means of Malayan Socialism', a document that committed them to a peaceful, democratic and constitutional struggle for political independence through a merger with Malaya. In a highly symbolic photograph from the time, Lim is shown seated, pen in hand, about to release his declaration to the press, with Lee standing behind him, leaning over him, seemingly pointing to where Lim had to sign.

Free at last, Lim and Fong experienced what one writer has described as 'political quarantine'. Both men, along with Woodhull and Nair, were assigned jobs in the government as political secretaries – Lim at the Ministry of Finance and Fong at the Ministry of Labour – while Puthucheary, being a trained economist, was put in charge of the new Industrial Promotion Board. This decision, like many made by the PAP leadership at this time, could be read in one of two ways: either as punishment for Lim and Fong's challenge to Lee – a clear sign that they were from now on 'out in the cold'; or, as a period of probation – a second chance to show their sincere commitment to the party, its methods and its goals. Either way, Lim, Fong and the other ex-detainees were to have no real influence over government policy. They were not granted PAP cadre status and so could not vote in elections to the party's Central Executive Committee. Nor, since they were banned from standing for election as Assemblymen, had they a constitutional voice in the national legislature.

Of the two comrades, Fong seems initially to have taken better to his role as political secretary. At Goh's Ministry of Finance, in what was becoming a fashionable way to show a newly appointed official that he was unwanted, Lim failed to even merit his own office. Nonetheless, both men still commanded massive union and student support and it wasn't long before they were spending more and more time back at their Middle Road headquarters. During the first half of 1960, the government tried to reorganise various unions into a central trade union congress, which alone could call strikes. The move triggered further labour unrest, especially when the government chose to deregister certain unions that had resisted its earlier policy. Later that year, Fong publicly attacked the PAP leadership for its 'softness on capitalism'. Lee, according to *TIME* magazine, 'retaliated by summarily ordering Fong to "vacate" his post in the Labour Ministry' (he transferred him to Deputy Prime Minister Toh Chin Chye's office).

A split was therefore inevitable. Yet the first open rebellion within the government's ranks originated not with the hard-line leftists but with that charismatic crowd-puller whom Lee once described as Lim Chin Siong's 'substitute'.

Two crises in 1961

Ong Eng Guan was someone Lee Kuan Yew would later claim possessed megalomaniacal tendencies. But at the time of the PAP's election victory such was Ong's public profile that the Prime Minister awarded him the post of Minister for National Development. It wasn't long before Lee and the party leadership concluded that Ong was the wrong man for the job. One of Ong's first decisions was to move his entire ministry out of City Hall, where he had brushed shoulders with Lee Kuan Yew in the corridors, and over to his power base of Hong

Ong Eng Guan encouraging citizens to spring clean the city for National Loyalty Week.
1959
SPH PCD 152-44

Lim (his loyal constituency in the heart of Chinatown). Here, his critics alleged, he ran his Ministry like his own personal fiefdom, behaving tyrannically and unilaterally, and humiliating European bureaucrats in an effort to garner further populist approval. Not only did Ong fail to follow the programme of the PAP in government, which meant dispensing with the disruptive antics of *merdeka* politics, he failed to achieve any positive results with a portfolio absolutely essential to the government's social programme.

When Lee and the Cabinet disciplined Ong by reducing his portfolio – eventually taking away local government, the Harbour Board and public housing from his brief – Ong plotted his revenge. Before the PAP annual conference in July 1960, he drafted a series of resolutions that attacked Lee's leadership and that drew on residual grievances amongst the leftists. Ong demanded that remaining political detainees be released (the government had left 28 of them in prison) and denounced the authorities' deregistration of trade unions. He also opposed the PAP's cadre system and called for the creation of a 'watchdog' committee, drawn from local party branches, to oversee PAP policy-making. Yet Ong never had a chance to present his resolutions. Word got to Lee of Ong's intentions ahead of the conference, and when it convened Ong was immediately expelled from the party and later forced to resign his seat in the Assembly.

His revenge came with the Hong Lim by-election of April the following year – a crisis for the moderate wing of the PAP that revealed how out of touch with some sections of Singapore's Chinese community it remained. The party's election campaign presented Ong as an immoral, self-interested bigamist – a move which backfired badly since, among other things, few people in Hong Lim were overly concerned with their *merdeka* hero's domestic arrangements. Ong, campaigning on his own ticket, demanded immediate political independence for Singapore and won, defeating PAP candidate Jek Yeun Thong (later the party's Minister for Labour) with a massive 73 per cent of the vote. Following this debacle, Lee offered his resignation, which the party rejected, but plenty of soul-searching was underway when a second crisis erupted.

In July 1961, the seat of Anson also came up for by-election and David Marshall reappeared from the wings to contest it, vowing to oppose 'the reign of terror of Emperor Lee Kuan Yew'. Marshall campaigned on an election platform similar to Ong's and won. In his victory speech he taunted the Prime Minister with the words:

> We have had enough of your humbug, hypocrisy and hates, your vanity
> and arrogance and ruthlessness. We are not the blind chicken you think
> we are. Resign!'

Marshall holds up a hammer (symbol of the Workers' Party) in jubilation upon winning the Anson by-election.
July 1961
SPH PCD 105-84

It was especially galling for the PAP moderates that Lim and Fong had withheld their support from the party's candidate and in effect supported Marshall. The rebellion against the Prime Minister was now in full swing. But when the split eventually came it was not over the matter of Lee's leadership, but over the far more complex issue of Singapore's political relationship with her neighbour across the Causeway.

The birth of the Barisan Sosialis

On 27 May 1961, between the PAP's election defeats at Hong Lim and Anson, Tunku Abdul Rahman, the Prime Minister of the Federation of Malaya, dropped a bombshell. In a luncheon speech to foreign journalists held at Singapore's Adelphi Hotel, and with Singapore Cabinet ministers in attendance, he suggested that 'sooner or later' Singapore, the Borneo territories and Malaya ought to be all brought into closer 'political and economic cooperation'. Before this, the Tunku's party UMNO (the United Malays National Organisation and the main party in Malaya's Alliance coalition government) had flatly rejected Singapore's overtures on a possible merger. Now, however, the PAP's Hong Lim election defeat had raised in the Tunku fears that Lee and his moderates might be replaced by a pro-communist government right on Malaya's doorstep – and so he had decided to act.

Six days later, Lee came out in support of the Tunku's suggestion and discussions commenced between the two territories for a proposed Federation of Malaysia in which a federal government would oversee Singapore's defence, external relations and internal security while the island's own Assembly would retain control over education, labour legislation and (eventually it was agreed) a large proportion of its revenue. For Singapore's Cabinet and for Finance Minister Goh in particular, a merger was thought vital to the island's economic progress. A future common market that would ensure the success of Singapore's industrialisation programme now seemed to beckon.

However, for Lim Chin Siong and his supporters, the Cabinet's proposal to hand internal security over to the Federal government was both a threat to their personal freedom (since the Tunku seemed convinced they were dangerous communists who ought to be arrested) and a disaster for democracy in Singapore as a whole (since the merger under discussion continued to allow for detentions without trial). Still mulling over their response to the merger discussions, Lim, Fong, Woodhull and Puthucheary (following a phone call enquiry from the latter) went to see Lord Selkirk, the British Commissioner General for Southeast Asia, at his Eden Hall residence. They asked him point-blank whether the British would arrest them and suspend Singapore's constitution should Lee Kuan Yew be voted out of office. Selkirk replied that the constitution was a free one which the British would respect, as long as any new party stuck to constitutional means and refrained from violence.

The 'Eden Hall Tea Party', as it became known, revealed how deeply conspiratorial were the workings of Singapore's nascent democracy. When Lee first heard of the meeting he imagined that Selkirk was giving the 'nod' to Lim and his supporters to indicate that the British were willing to work with them. He therefore denounced the gathering as a sinister plot by which the British sought to split the PAP and encourage the 'communists' out into the open. If the government then failed to deal with them, so Lee argued, the British would have an excuse to suspend the constitution and pursue the matter themselves. In response, Lee's opponents labelled these claims a 'fairy tale of British lions and communist bears' (as did Selkirk, using much the same language, in colonial dispatches). 'The communist left who are supposed to be arch-conspirators', said Lim, 'have now, we are told, been taken for a ride by the British! How funny can people get? … If meeting Lord Selkirk makes one a plotter, then Mr Lee is the greatest of all plotters for he has dealings with Lord Selkirk more than anyone else in Singapore.'

Any glance through Colonial Office reports from this period will certainly confirm that dealings between the British and Singaporean governments were devious. But whatever the truth about Eden Hall, the parting of ways between Lee and Lim had been so long in coming that Lim's opposition to the merger proposals seemed merely the last farewell. Following the PAP's Anson defeat, Lee called for a vote of confidence in his leadership which he survived by just two votes (24 Assemblymen either abstained or voted against him). Lim, Fong and the other members of their faction were expelled from the PAP and within nine

Barisan Sosialis inauguration
at Happy World.
August 1961
SPH PCD 92-55

days the government had branded Lim a communist. Lim once more denied the allegation, only this time categorically: 'Let me make it clear once and for all that I am not a communist, or a communist front-man or for that matter anybody's front-man.' Then on 13 August, at a mass rally of 10,000 supporters held at the Happy World Stadium, he unveiled his new party: the Barisan Sosialis Singapura [Socialist Front of Singapore].

These days, old Barisan veterans are wont to look back at that first rally with misty eyes and sad thoughts of what might have been. To Tan Jing Quee, Lim Chin Siong had emerged by this time as 'a more engaging, milder, less impatient and thoughtful personality'; he had begun to speak in Mandarin and Malay and to reach out to a wider non-Chinese audience, forsaking the 'flaming raw eloquence which had endeared him to the crowds' when he had earlier restricted himself to Hokkien. So too, Lim's new party claimed to hold to its founder's multi-ethnic idealism. In a direct borrowing from the PAP, the Barisan announced its desire to create a 'democratic, non-communist, socialist Malaya'.

But the Barisan did more than simply pull the ideological rug from under the feet of its old comrades: it ripped the PAP in two. Lim's rebels took with them control of 35 PAP local branches (out of a total of 51), including Lee's own branch at Tanjong Pagar, Toh's branch at Rochor and Rajaratnam's branch at Kampong Glam. Soon after, as Goh Keng Swee recalled, 'The People's Association collapsed at the first blow, and the Work Brigade mutinied' – both organisations launching protests against the government following the Barisan's inauguration. Barisan supporters even hauled away local PAP branch furniture, including sewing machines and typewriters. The government issued a statement that 'those who set

Singapore Work Brigade mutineers being led away by the police. Anti-government writings on the walls of their quarters speak of the overthrow of those in power no matter what the challenges.
December 1961
NAS 19980007263-0079

out to start a political movement on the basis of stolen property cannot be leaders of great stature'. The Barisan retorted that the furniture had belonged to its party members in the first place.

The battle lines were drawn. As well as former PAP branches, Lim and Fong controlled seven out of ten Chinese workers' unions and about 75 per cent of the island's work force, a mass of support they had brought together under an organisation known as SATU (the Singapore Association of Trade Unions). Meanwhile, PAP control of the Legislative Assembly was reduced by death, illness and defections to the slimmest of majorities. Never before had the party's grip on power been so precarious.

The Battle for Merger commences

With the opening shots in what Lee called the 'Battle for Merger', Singapore parted ways with the professed ideals of more liberal democracies and became something quite unique. The relentless purpose with which the PAP conducted its Merger campaign – eventually to be decided by Singapore's first and only referendum – and the methods it used to neutralise its opposition and ensure Merger's peaceful enactment, proved epoch-defining. But such ruthlessness was also a product of the PAP's weakness. Back in 1961, the party was on the ropes, facing an opponent it was convinced was communist and thus far more ruthless than it. As party stalwart Lee Khoon Choy explained: 'Naturally, the government exploited whatever facilities it had.'

These 'facilities' included basic instruments of the state – the law courts and the police – which were employed in a strategy to obstruct, provoke and isolate the Barisan wherever and whenever possible. However, it would be a mistake to imagine that once Lim and his supporters had broken ranks the government simply went out to arrest them. In his memoirs, Lee recorded that that is what the British had wanted during meetings of the joint Internal Security Council (over which Britain still held a controlling influence, and on which Malaya also sat), but he resisted such pressure in order to first win a political fight. In what would be a recurring feature of Singaporean politics over the next two years, political detentions followed a popular vote. Before the government launched a crackdown, it first tested the grassroots for an indication of their implicit approval.

So, during the first 12 months of the PAP's battle for merger the authorities revoked the license of the Barisan's printer (meaning the party had to go out and buy its own press to publish campaign literature), denied it permits for mass rallies (or demanded they be held away from conspicuous central locations), and purged its supporters from the public sector. Singapore was not a place where you held down a government job while being known to have sympathies for the opposition. Perhaps it might have been, but the involvement of public employees in anti-government protests soon put paid to any such hope.

For the Barisan's birth was accompanied by Singapore's immediate slide back into the tumultuous politics of disruption. The mutiny of the Work Brigade involved rough picketing (including, as Lee recorded, the burning of at least one Brigade boss's bicycle); protesting workers from the People's Association vandalised community centres; a strike by public employees (including night-soil collectors, garbage collectors and sewage plant workers) threatened to reduce Singapore to a stinking cesspool – until Lee sent in the troops to man public installations. Young people took to the streets, once more primed for agitation. In November 1961, an exam boycott by Chinese students threatened to trigger further unrest until the government came up with the quite brilliant tactic of holding back the police and sending in the students' parents instead.

For all the Barisan's compelling rhetoric of a full *merdeka* won through peaceful means, hate and conflict still dominated the politics of the street. The graffiti in the offices of a Swiss insurance firm wrecked by its striking employees, and on the walls of the elite Tanglin Club, said it all: near-obscene drawings of white bosses at the first location, Europeans stamping on Chinese workers and drinking their blood at the second. For many observers, whether the Barisan was directly involved in such protests hardly mattered. Their timing confirmed Lee's accusation that the Barisan was the party of 'anarchy and chaos' – it attracted violent elements that it was unable to control.

However, by mid-1962, strikes became less frequent and renewed threats of social unrest died down as the Barisan focused its Merger campaign on house-to-house visits and peaceful rallies. Perhaps the problem for the party at this stage was that it revealed its commitment to a calmer more reasoned type of politics too late in the game. For back in September 1961, the PAP had unleashed another crucial weapon in its struggle: the Prime Minister on Radio Singapore – or as the Barisan preferred to call it: 'Radio PAP'.

The master storyteller

If Singapore had an early taste of 'political stand-up' when David Marshall spoke over the radio, then Lee Kuan Yew was the country's first 'on-air' political confidant. On 13 September 1961, the Prime Minister began the first of 12 radio talks entitled the 'Battle for Merger' intended to give listeners 'the big picture, the background of how the PAP and the communists had formed a united front, why Lim Chin Siong and Fong Swee Suan had broken their undertaking to fight for independence through a merger with Malaysia and why they, the communists, must lose'.

It proved a commanding performance. In Malay, English and Chinese, Lee praised the communists for their sacrifices, bravery and integrity while he revealed how he laboured to win them over to peaceful and democratic socialism. Throughout, he came across as calm and collected – the patriarchal voice of

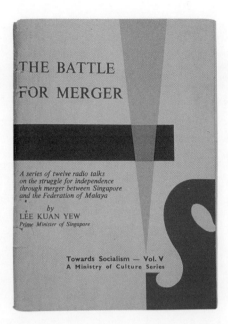

reason in deeply troubled times. To schoolboy Cheong Yip Seng (later editor of the *Straits Times*), the talks were a 'real eye-opener':

> I was struck by their candour, the power of the simple, vivid language, most of all by the inside story of the struggle within the united front against the British colonialists ... Every broadcast ended with the listener in suspense, and anxious for the next instalment, the way ordinary folk at that time lapped up the kung-fu serials broadcast over Rediffusion by Lei Tai Sor in Cantonese. A master storyteller was at work. But this was not fiction. This was life and death for Singaporeans.

Lee himself wrote:

> By the end of the series, I had convinced most people that I had told the truth about the past – the infighting, the betrayals, the Plen – and that I was realistic about the future. I had held their interest. I had told a story that was part of their own recent experience – of riots, strikes, boycotts, all of them fresh reference points in their minds – and I had given them the explanation for mysteries that had puzzled them. It was as if I had gone up on stage where a magician had been performing and exposed his props and accessories by lighting up the darkened areas they had not noticed before.

Barisan leaders were invited to join 12 subsequent radio forums to put their own case across but refused. Lim and Woodhull demanded equal airtime to Lee for 12 talks of their own but were denied. In his memoirs, Lee described when Puthucheary arrived in his office and asked for an autographed copy of the talks. Lee asked him if he would participate in the proposed forums. Puthucheary

Compilation of Lee Kuan Yew's radio addresses.
1960s
Paper
H 17.4 x W 12.5 cm
NMS 1995-00362

reportedly shook his head and said: 'After you have set up the stage props, I would not stand a chance.'

The Barisan's failure to get its message across through the mass media was compounded by the complexity of the Merger issue. In late August 1961, the government asked opposition parties to declare their respective Merger positions. The Barisan responded by demanding 'immediate complete merger with Singapore as the twelfth state in Federation like Penang or Malacca, with proper proportionate representation in Federal Parliament' (which would mean 24 seats for Singapore as against the PAP's proposed 15). Otherwise, the Barisan wanted Singapore to remain an 'autonomous unit within a Confederation (including Borneo Territories if possible)' in which it retained control over certain internal matters, especially internal security.

Some historians have interpreted the Barisan's Merger position as its way of rejecting Merger without appearing to do so; after all, they argue, the Tunku would have never accepted an arrangement in which Singapore had such a strong parliamentary presence in Kuala Lumpur. Old Barisan veterans beg to differ. They cite Lim Chin Siong's speech in front of 10,000 supporters in which he made it clear he and his colleagues knew the risks of 'immediate complete merger' (namely that they would be arrested by the new Federation government as suspected communists) but were willing to sacrifice their freedom for the sake of Singapore and Malaya's reunification. Merger brought to the surface all sorts of impassioned ideals; the public would ultimately decide who was being sincere.

Except that, every time the Barisan was drawn into a face-to-face debate with the PAP, it seemed to eventually come off second best. The party started well. Dr Lee Siew Choh, the Barisan leader in the Assembly, attacked the government's Merger proposal on the grounds that it failed to secure common Malaysian citizenship and would make Singaporeans 'second rate' citizens of the Federation, with no constitutional rights to vote, move or work across the Causeway. Indeed, under the terms of the Merger originally negotiated with the Tunku, Singaporeans were to be defined as Federation 'nationals', not 'citizens', and denied voting rights in Malaysia (Malaysians, meanwhile, would not be allowed to vote in Singapore elections). However, in late September 1961 Dr Lee Siew Choh participated in a Radio Singapore forum which pitted him against Goh Keng Swee. Suddenly, Goh announced that under the Barisan's Merger proposal 'nearly half of the present citizens [in Singapore] will be disenfranchised'. According to Federal law, he explained, only those born in Penang and Melaka qualified automatically for citizenship, the rest had to apply for registration and pass what might easily be an arbitrarily judged Malay language test. Given that so many people in Singapore had been born overseas, Goh described the Barisan's Merger proposal as 'absolute nonsense'.

The Barisan subsequently clarified its position: all new states entering a Federation of Malaysia would have the right to negotiate their terms of citizenship and the party would demand that Singaporeans be granted automatic Federal citizenship on entry; Dr Lee Siew Choh hadn't in fact meant 'like' as in 'exactly the same as' Penang, but 'like' as in 'similar to' Penang. Yet the damage was done. Over the 'like Penang' issue the PAP scored a major rhetorical point to which they pinned their opponents and never let them go. To many people, Lee Kuan Yew triumphed on the issue of citizenship as well when he eventually conviced the Tunku to allow Singaporeans to be constitutionally redefined as 'Citizens of the new Federation (Singapore)' – though the Barisan argued (with some justification) that all this meant was a change in wording not legal status.

In mid-1962, the government announced a referendum on Merger, to be held on 1 September. Instead of a single proposition on which the people voted 'yes' or 'no', voters were given three different Merger options to choose from (the official reasoning was that since no party had objected to Merger on principle, the question was not whether Merger ought to happen but how). Option 'C', that Singapore should enter the Federation on terms no worse then Sabah and Sarawak was the least relevant, since by the time of the referendum these terms had still not been decided upon. Rather, the real decision was between option 'A' and option 'B'. Option 'B', intended by the government to represent the Barisan's Merger proposal, featured the statement: 'I support complete and unconditional merger for Singapore as a state on an equal basis with the other eleven states in accordance with the Constitutional documents of the Federation of Malaya' and appeared next to a flag of Penang. Option 'A', the PAP government's proposal, stood alongside the flag of Singapore.

As polling day drew nearer, Lim Chin Siong told Barisan supporters to submit blank referendum votes in protest at the way their party's position had been

VOTE FOR ALTERNATIVE "A"
ON REFERENDUM DAY

THE SINGAPORE NATIONAL REFERENDUM ORDINANCE 1962
(No. 19 OF 1962)
SECTION 18.

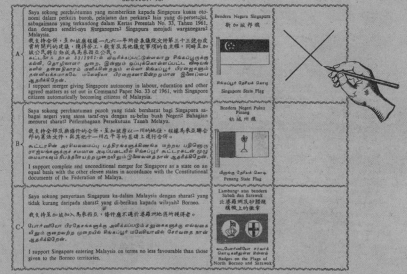

A. Saya sokong perchantuman yang memberikan kapada Singapura kuasa otonomi dalam perkara buroh, pelajaran dan perkara² lain yang di-persetujui, sabagaimana yang terkandong dalam Kertas Perentah No. 33, Tahun 1961, dan dengan sendiri-nya Warganegara² Singapura menjadi warganegara² Malaysia.

我支持合併，呈加坡應根據一九六一年所發表議院文件第三十三號白皮書所開列的建議，獲得勞工，教育及其他議定事項的自主權，同時呈加坡公民將自動成為馬來西亞公民。

I support merger giving Singapore autonomy in labour, education and other agreed matters as set out in Command Paper No. 33 of 1961, with Singapore citizens automatically becoming citizens of Malaysia.

B. Saya sokong perchantuman penoh yang tidak bersharat bagi Singapura sabagai negeri yang sama taraf-nya dengan sa-belas buah Negeri² Bahagian menurut sharat² Perlembagaan Persekutuan Tanah Melayu.

我支持全部及無條件的合併，呈加坡應以一州的地位，根據馬來亞聯合邦的憲法文件，與其他十一州在平等的基礎上進行合併。

I support complete and unconditional merger for Singapore as a state on an equal basis with the other eleven states in accordance with the Constitutional documents of the Federation of Malaya.

C. Saya sokong penyertaan Singapura ka-dalam Malaysia dengan sharat² yang tidak kurang daripada sharat² yang di-berikan kapada wilayah² Borneo.

我支持呈加坡加入馬來西亞，條件應不遜於婆羅洲地區所獲得者。

I support Singapore entering Malaysia on terms no less favourable than those given to the Borneo territories.

Bendera Negara Singapura
新加坡邦旗
Singapore State Flag

Bendera Negeri Pulau Pinang
槟城州旗
Penang State Flag

Lambang² atas bendera Sabah dan Sarawak
北婆羅洲及砂朥越旗幟上的徽章
Badges on the Flags of North Borneo and Sarawak

VOTE FOR OUR OWN SINGAPORE FLAG —
THE SYMBOL OF ALTERNATIVE "A"

VOTE FOR MERGER WITH SPECIAL RIGHTS!

VOTE FOR EQUALITY FOR OUR FOUR LANGUAGES!

VOTE FOR OUR OWN CONTROL OVER EDUCATION!

VOTE FOR OUR OWN LABOUR POLICY!

VOTE FOR A COMMON CITIZENSHIP!

VOTE FOR AUTOMATIC CONVERSION TO MALAYSIAN CITIZENSHIP!

distorted. However, through a late amendment to the referendum's rules, the government stipulated that blank votes were to be treated as 'undecided' and taken as a vote for the ultimate decision of the Legislative Assembly. Barisan speakers now encouraged everyone to cast blank votes – even those in favour of option 'A' – since, they argued, blank votes now meant the same thing: the government's Merger proposal. Prime Minister Lee countered by warning that if option 'B' – the 'Penang' option – tallied the most votes then the Assembly might have to stand by the people's verdict and assign the blank votes to it. To ram home the implications of what this meant, Goh requisitioned 40 trucks carrying loudspeakers to drive around Singapore a week before the referendum, broadcasting the message that anyone not born in Singapore who cast a blank vote stood to lose their citizenship.

In a referendum unlike any other, 71 per cent of the people voted in favour of option 'A', while 26 per cent cast blank votes. The PAP was jubilant, the Barisan dejected. As Goh Keng Swee later put it, his party had fought back from 'a position of total collapse'.

The Barisan's downfall

For Fong Swee Suan, the early morning hours of 2 February 1963 were both life-changing and surreal:

> There was a knock on the door. I opened the door and it was an old neighbour of mine, carrying a rifle. When he saw me he was taken by surprise and exclaimed, 'It's you!' And he apologised. After getting into the car, I was driven across the Causeway and then I realised I was being sent to Malaysia.

Fong was one of over 110 leftists in Singapore taken into custody that night. At 3 a.m., 65 police raiding parties had fanned out across the island intent on arresting 169 suspects but the remainder escaped. Once more, the detained included the core of Singapore's radical left-wing leadership: along with Fong, James Puthucheary, Sandra Woodhull and top of the list Lim Chin Siong were all arrested. Lee Kuan Yew offered Lim permission to leave Singapore for Indonesia or any other country he chose, but he chose to stay and face another incarceration without trial. Fong, being Malayan-born, was handed over to the Federal Government in Kuala Lumpur. At 31 years old, it was his third stint in prison in less than eight years.

'Operation Coldstore', as it was called, had been planned for some time. But for months before it commenced, the Internal Security Council, on which the Malayan government was represented along with Britain and Singapore, argued over the extent of the arrests and their timing. Memoirs and top-secret diplomatic correspondence reveal the mutual suspicions that hung over these meetings.

Referendum Day information flyer promoting 'Alternative A'.
1962
Private collection of Wong Han Min

The Tunku believed Singapore's Prime Minister wanted to use the operation to remove his entire parliamentary opposition; Lee was wary of the Tunku not taking equal responsibility for the arrests; meanwhile, the British wanted the left-wing movement in Singapore smashed but, so as to give their actions at least a semblance of 'fair play', they awaited some clear pretext for doing so.

Lim Chin Siong duly obliged with what amounted to a quiet curry with the wrong type of associate. On 8 December 1962, a leftist rebellion by the self-proclaimed North Borneo National Army broke out in Brunei; two days before, Lim had had lunch in the restaurant of Singapore's aptly named Rendezvous Hotel with Sheik A. M. Azahari, the leading Brunei leftist subsequently accused of masterminding the revolt.

It was enough to satisfy the British; yet such was the continued wrangling on the Internal Security Council that it took nearly two months – during which an initial launch of the operation planned for 16 December had to be aborted the night before – for all parties to commit to action. Immediately following the arrests, the Internal Security Council announced that Special Branch had uncovered a plot to make Singapore a 'Communist Cuba' – full details would follow. But despite weeks of interrogations, strong evidence to substantiate this claim failed to materialise. Toh Chin Chye later described the political detainees who remained in prison after 1959 as 'a sacrifice to Merger'; in early 1963 it appeared that the god of Malaysia still demanded appeasement.

Meanwhile, in late November 1962, Lee began what became a one-man, 11-month election campaign, the likes of which Singaporeans had never before seen. David Marshall might have held 'meet the people' sessions at his Chief Minister's office in Empress Place, but no elected leader had ever taken to the road to visit every one of the island's 51 constituencies (Lee went first to those that had registered the most blank votes in the referendum) nor pushed themselves so far out of their own comfort zone to talk to the people in their own languages. As the Prime Minister toured Singapore, giving speeches in English, Mandarin, Malay and sometimes stumbling Hokkien (occasionally with a few words of Tamil greeting thrown in) he became a kind of Singapore 'everyman'. Invariably, his message was simple and direct:

> The government's got to do the job. Homes must be built, clinics must be built, roads must be made, money must be saved – the people must be taken care of.
>
> You'll get more: better roads, better drains, better schools, and better jobs for your children. But most important of all ... whatever our faults – and I don't say we've got no faults – we have never put our fingers in the kitty and put a few gold coins in the pocket.

Looking back, Lee described these ten months of constituency visits as 'the most hectic' in his life. Sometimes he was heckled, on occasions he was shoved,

many times he was garlanded (especially when he honoured various temples with his presence); always, he made an impression. As Judy Bloodworth, a sound recordist with the TV crew that followed Lee on his visits, remembered:

> [T]he people would cheer and boo and in the middle of all the noise he would be elated, push his way down among them, laugh at the lion dancers around him, careless of the roaring fireworks, never showing fear – he was burned in the face once but took no notice. We really felt like a team, like an army unit; we felt proud of him. You couldn't help it.

Indeed, television, just as radio had been, proved fundamental to Lee's success. He later recalled in a speech: 'People watched on TV the spontaneous response of the crowds to the speeches made. The visits gathered steam;' and in his memoirs he wrote, 'I became a kind of political pop star!' An unscripted, unrehearsed drama of national proportions was taking place and coming soon, to a community centre near you, was its on-screen idol – live in the flesh!

Of course, Lee's televised encounters were not entirely spontaneous. Concerned with how fierce his rabble-rousing *merdeka* persona came across on screen, he sought advice from the famous BBC interviewer Hugh Burnett to help him appear more calm, collected and natural. By contrast, television transformed the Barisan's speakers – still accustomed to projecting themselves from the podium out into the crowd – into demented wild men. When the camera zoomed in

Artwork on a Barisan Sosialis
New Year greeting card
with the message 'A United,
Independent and Democratic
Malaya Will Become Reality!'.
1960s
Private collection of Wong Han Min

for close ups, it picked out their every exaggerated mannerism and contorted facial expression (much as it does today when inexperienced actors bring their theatrical techniques direct from the stage to the screen).

And not long after, those remaining Barisan leaders who had not been detained appeared to live up to their on-screen image. On 22 April 1963, the party and its supporters marched on City Hall to protest against their comrades' detentions. A confrontation with the police ensued, following which 12 more Barisan leaders were arrested. Their court case began in early August and ended on the 29th, just a few days before Lee announced snap elections. Dr Lee Siew Choh, one of those arrested, remembered: 'And, almost immediately ... General Election! You see, we were completely occupied with the trial.'

The *Plebian*, Barisan's newsletter, called these elections 'the most unfair and undemocratic in the history of Singapore'. The party again had trouble obtaining police permits for its rallies. On nomination day, 17 potential Barisan candidates were held for questioning by Special Branch until it was too late for them to file their nomination papers (which then, as now, they had to do in person). Three days earlier, three of the largest unions loyal to the Barisan had their bank accounts frozen to prevent their funds being used for political purposes. Finally, on the eve of the vote, Goh played on electoral anxieties once more by claiming that a Barisan victory would mean Malaysian troops in Singapore the following day.

However both sides played hard, such were the high stakes. Earlier, while canvassing in Hong Lim, Lee Kuan Yew found himself drowned out by music blaring from the offices of a Barisan-loyal trade union located above him. Later, Toh Chin Chye and his colleagues were barracked by opponents who reportedly yelled: 'Don't let them get away. You! The day of your death has arrived!' In areas where Barisan support was strong, PAP canvassers were reportedly insulted, threatened and sometimes physically assaulted.

The imprisonment of the Barisan's 'first team' leadership was not the inevitable death knell for the party as it has sometimes been held to be. As photographs of the Barisan's election campaign reveal, massive portraits of Lim Chin Siong adorned practically every party event. Lim was a hero, a martyr, his unjust incarceration the party's cause célèbre. Even behind bars he remained a major threat to the PAP's hold on power.

In the lead-up to what was without doubt the most important election in Singapore's history thus far, the outcome seemed too close to call. The Australian High Commission told Canberra that the Barisan privately expected to win 35 seats, while the PAP believed it would win 30; British officials in Singapore began to contemplate how to deal with a new Barisan government. However, on 21 September 1963, the PAP won a resounding 37 seats and the Barisan just 13 (the final seat in the Assembly went to the belligerent candidate for Hong Lim, Ong Eng Guan). For the PAP the result was a vindication for its social revolution – the jobs, hospitals, schools and utilities it brought to Singapore – as well its successful negotiation of Merger.

For the Barisan the result was shattering.

Lim Chin Siong – the last word

As the election counts came in, any hopes that Lim Chin Siong had of a repeat walk out into freedom and a hero's welcome must have evaporated. From late September 1963, he looked on helplessly as a succession of police round-ups and detentions decimated his party's membership and ripped through its union and student support. To add insult to his injury, Singapore was now a part of the new Federation of Malaysia and the Singapore government could claim that the responsibility for the crackdown lay with Kuala Lumpur. In prison Lim became depressed and at one point attempted suicide.

In 1969, the PAP government gave Lim permission to leave Singapore and go into exile. By that time, the remnants of the Barisan had boycotted parliament and Singapore's 1968 general elections (leaving the PAP to win every seat), and had taken their political struggle back onto the streets through strikes and protest marches. In a repudiation of the Barisan platform unveiled on that heady night at the Happy World Stadium back in August 1961 (when it had voiced its hopes for

Empty seats: Barisan Sosialis boycotts the first session of parliament.
December 1965
SPH 215319

409

a democratic, socialist and multiethnic Malaya), the party came under the sway of Mao's Zedong's Cultural Revolution. In the Barisan's new Chinese-centric and pro-communist guise, it revealed itself as just what Lee had always claimed it to be. When Lim was released from detention, the Barisan expelled him from the party, denouncing its founder as a traitor for having repudiated its new ideology and its 'extra-parliamentary' struggle.

Renouncing politics, Lim settled in London, where he married his fiancée and worked for a time selling fruit, periodically battling poor health and depression. In 1979, he was permitted to return to Singapore to live with his family, which he did until his death from a heart attack in 1996.

It was a sad end to the career of such a charismatic individual. Unlike many other political stars in Singapore's *merdeka* firmament, Lim did not publish a memoir nor record an oral history. His press statements and speeches aside, our impression of the man comes from other peoples' reminiscences. To his ex-comrades Lim was a hero of Singapore's freedom movement, a martyr to democracy; to his opponents he was a dangerous communist subversive. He remains the great enigma of Singapore history – the man around whom two competing narratives of its post-war struggle for independence cohere, yet whose own personal account is missing from both.

– Except that just a few years before Lim died, the intrepid Singaporean historian Melanie Chew went to interview him. That day, at Lim's family home in the sedate neighbourhood of Serangoon Gardens, the conversation proved intriguing and poignant. When Chew pushed Lim on his role in stirring up political violence, he immediately denied any personal responsibility: 'Riots or big-scale disturbances take place when emotions run high. Such highly charged emotions could only breed under certain social conditions or social psychology.' But a little while later he admitted that he could exert a decisive influence on the crowd's emotions – at least to contain them: 'I could have let the situation go out of hand. I could have released the pent-up frustration, but I did not.' Eventually, Chew asked Lim the perennial question that had dogged him since his early 20s: had he had any connection with the communists? For probably the last time in his life, Lim denied the allegation.

Yet what most resonates from Lim's interview is not his final declaration of innocence, but his deeply personal account of what he had suffered:

> Not knowing when we would be coming out. That, I would say is a torture. A torture. You are detained for years, until such a time that you are willing to humiliate your own integrity. Until you are humiliated publicly. So much so, when you come out, you cannot put your head up, you cannot see your friends …
>
> It is worse than in the Japanese time, when with a knife, they just slaughter you. One shot, you die. But this humiliation will carry on for life. It is very cruel.

Lim Chin Siong (right) with
Barisan associate
Chia Thye Poh.
1962
SPH PCD 0078-064

32. FROM CONFRONTATION TO SEPARATION

On 16 September 1963, the new Federation of Malaysia came into being. To many people from the outset, it was an unlovable child. A sizeable minority within its borders saw it as the product of a troubled union – a 'shotgun marriage' as some Barisan members in Singapore put it. After much wrangling and conflict, even its own parents would come to disown it. But by far the new Federation's fiercest opponent was its powerful neighbour to the south. President Sukarno of Indonesia believed Merger was a neo-colonial plot by which Britain sought to maintain her imperial influence in the region. In July 1963, he announced that he was going to 'Crush Malaysia!' A few months later, his government directed its armed campaign of *Konfrontasi* [Confrontation] against the territory to target Singapore as well.

Thus, life for Singaporeans as part of the Federation would be literally explosive as well as fractious. But beyond the power politics and clashes of leadership that dominate this period, one thing is sometimes overlooked. The story of Merger was also the story of the PAP's bid to make Malaysia more like Singapore – something that the Tunku and his colleagues in Kuala Lumpur took a while to realise.

Eyes on Konfrontasi

Sukarno's campaign against Malaysia involved armed incursions across the border into the territories of Sabah and Sarawak, and even the landing of commandos on the Malay Peninsula. In Singapore, attacks by Indonesian saboteurs commenced not long after the September 1963 general elections with the first of what became a series of bomb blasts, near Katong Park on the east coast. But it was the bombing of Macdonald House on 10 January 1965 – the 29th such attack – that was to have the greatest impact on the island's collective memory.

At around 3 p.m. on that day, Charles Tan Kok Siew, a crime-beat reporter for the Chinese newspaper *Sin Chew Jit Poh*, was with a journalist colleague, dealing with a minor matter at the Orchard Road police station. Suddenly, Tan recalled, they heard the sound of an explosion. 'From inside the police station many policemen rushed out and all of them were fully equipped. So we asked what was happening. Later a police officer told us ...'

MacDonald House was then occupied by the Hongkong and Shanghai Bank. By the time Tan arrived in the vicinity a crowd had gathered and the police had already cordoned off the area. 'Everyone was standing around, exchanging words, discussing how it could have happened ... just speculating. People were guessing and of course some were saying it was carried out by the Indonesians.'

The police cordon was placed so far away from the scene that Tan 'couldn't even see anything inside, what the situation was, what the police were doing, what they were investigating'. His journalist colleague, known for his 'aggressive' tactics, had arrived earlier and tried to force his way through to take a closer look, whereupon an irate Criminal Investigation Department officer intercepted him and manhandled him away. Realising there was no point to hanging around, Tan rushed over to the Singapore General Hospital but here there were no leads for a story either. Eventually, he settled for an interview with one of the victims' family. In addition to injuring more than 30 people, the bombing claimed three lives. Two of those killed were female bank staff, 36 and 23 years old, who both died when rubble from the explosion fell on top of them.

At the time of the bombing, Edward Scully was a Eurasian police inspector attached to Singapore's marine division. When news reached him of the women's deaths, he recalled feeling 'devastated'. In the Coast Guard operations room, he and his colleagues at once discussed how to prevent further Indonesian infiltrators from entering Singapore. Just a few days later, Scully was on duty in the operations room when he received a call from his police boat:

> There were two men on a log, just outside the territory in Singapore territorial waters. So I instructed [the Coast Guard] to intercept these two persons and bring them back. As they were going out to intercept them an Indonesian gunboat approached, so they had to withdraw because [the two men on the log] were in international waters. The British Royal Navy officer in the operations room then contacted a British gunboat to head to the crew, at which the Indonesian gunboat withdrew ...

When the two men were brought in, Scully and two other officers interviewed them:

> They claimed to be barter traders. At that time, we allowed barter traders to come into Singapore to trade. And they said that two days before they were detained, the boat they were travelling in capsized during a storm, and they managed to get on the log and were returning to Indonesia. I was a bit suspicious of them, because both of them were quite strappy and muscular. Whereas actual barter traders, they were a bit thin and appeared emaciated.

Scully checked with the Meteorological Department and discovered that there had been no storms in and around Singapore for the past week. He and his colleagues then re-questioned the two suspects. Under interrogation, both men admitted that they were KKO, Korps Komando Operasi – Indonesian commandos:

> Their instructions were to come into Singapore and bomb any place they liked. They said they came in a few days earlier in a *sampan* and landed somewhere in Changi. They took a bus into town and it dropped

them somewhere – they didn't know where it was. They then timed the
explosives, left it at the staircase of the building, and returned to Changi
to get their boat, but they found it missing …

Scully asked them which building, but not being familiar with Singapore
they were unable tell him. So he drove the two men around town until they
remembered it had been a 'red building' – eventually identified as Macdonald
House.

The two perpetrators, Scully remembered, were young and in their early 20s:
'They did not appear to be frightened. They appeared to be quite, I would say,
normal.' They were eventually tried and sentenced to death for their part in the
bombing and executed in 1968.

In Singapore, as across the rest of the Federation, Merger had plunged the
populace into a major regional conflict. But the experience of *Konfrontasi* also
produced a silver lining. For historian Anthony Reid, who happened to arrive
in Malaysia during the conflict: 'one could feel it – the extent to which the
different ethnic communities in Malaysia, including Singapore, came together in
resistance to Indonesia, to feel that they were being bullied by this huge power on
their doorstep and they had to stick together.'

At the top, however, relations between Singapore and Kuala Lumpur had long
been heading in the opposite direction.

Aftermath of the bomb blast at
Macdonald House.
1965
SPH 107246

Grounds for divorce

Looking back at Merger, Lee Kuan Yew recalled that he was at first unaware of how different UMNO's attitude to Federation politics was: 'I did not understand ... they did not want the Chinese to be represented by a vigorous leadership that propounded a non-communal or a multiracial approach to politics and would not confine its appeal only to the Chinese.' Initially, Lee hoped that UMNO would 'settle' with the PAP and come to some arrangement over how to work in concert. But even if personal differences between himself and the Tunku could have been resolved, any such partnership would require that UMNO drop its existing coalition member in its Alliance government, the Malaysian Chinese Association (MCA). This was something the Tunku never appears to have considered doing.

There was also the not-so-small matter of the two parties' fundamental difference in ideology. Though the Barisan in Singapore might denounce the PAP for having moved to the right (especially in its attitude to foreign capital and civil liberties) it was still in charge of a peaceful revolution that was dramatically transforming Singapore society. UMNO, by contrast, was the party of tradition and entrenched conservative interest, dedicated to protecting Malay rights and led by a Malay king. When Lee gave speeches about bringing Singapore's social revolution to the rest of the Federation, especially to its rural backwaters, UMNO leaders shifted uneasily in their seats. Ultra-nationalists in the party accused him of wanting to wreck traditional Malay society and ultimately get rid of the Sultans.

Tensions erupted into outright hostility when in 1964 the PAP decided to contest nine seats in Malaysia's Federal Elections in April. By this decision, so

UMNO claimed, the PAP broke a 'gentleman's agreement' it had undertaken not to interfere in politics across the Causeway. The PAP responded that UMNO had already broken such a promise by fielding candidates in Singapore's 1963 general elections. To woo the Chinese vote in Malaya, the PAP attacked the MCA and especially its President, Tan Siew Tin, Finance Minister in the Alliance Government, whom it depicted as a 'silver-spoon' millionaire, out of touch with the common people and unable to speak Chinese. What the PAP claimed to offer in the MCA's place was its social revolution; 'the winds of change' – as Lee put it in his opening election speech – that would 'begin to sweep throughout Malaysia'.

Yet despite such sweeping rhetoric, and despite the huge crowds in Kuala Lumpur and other cities who came to hear it, the PAP's only foray into Malaysian politics was disastrous. The party won just a single seat, Devan Nair in the Kuala Lumpur suburb of Bangsar. Lee blamed the defeat on logistics but the most obvious factor, as he also admitted, was the PAP's lack of strong Malaysian grassroots. North of the Causeway, Singapore's social revolution, without the new community centres, factories and flats to back it up, became little more than an idealistic dream – unless the party could somehow manoeuvre itself into an alliance with the ruling party, or else take power from it.

While the PAP was still mulling over what to do next, its social revolution came under threat in its own backyard. Lee wrote afterwards, 'We had jumped out of the frying pan of the communists and into the fire of Malay communalists.'

Othman Wok's march

On 21 July 1964, Othman Wok, the PAP's Minister for Social Affairs, joined a mass celebration of the Prophet Muhammad's birthday on the Padang, at the head of a PAP contingent of Malay-Muslim youth:

> I can never forget that scene, on that day … Just after the road [on the City Hall steps] there was a stage where organisers were seated and there were all around contingents of Malay-Muslim organisations. Twenty thousand people were here, lined up in their own contingents. The PAP contingent […] 70 of us, with our white shirts and white trousers …

The participants were to march in procession from the Padang to the Muslim Missionary Society Headquarters in Geylang Serai, but first they listened to a series of speeches. Othman Wok recalled that during these speeches the crowd became restive: '*Allah–hu Akbar!* God is great! – all around the Padang, in angry mood, you see.' The angry mood intensified when the lawyer and Singapore UMNO representative Esa Almenoar got up to speak and (as was common at such events) chose to take for his text a verse from the Qur'an.

Almenoar told the crowd that Allah did not forbid Muslims from being 'friendly with non-Muslims as long as they do not drive them out of their homes

and disturb their religion'. However, he went on, if it came to the point that 'such people who are non-Muslims' had 'disturbed our religion' and 'driven us from our homes' then Islam said that 'such people are cruel wrong-doers': 'patience and understanding cannot stand the limit when people have come … to disturb our castle, our place to live and our religion. When it comes to such a climax, it is the duty of all Muslims to sacrifice their lives and properties for the sake of the country … This is the teaching of Islam.'

At 2.30 p.m., the procession moved off from the Padang to the beat of Malay drums; about half an hour later, the PAP contingent led by Othman Wok turned from Beach Road into Arab Street:

> And as our contingent passed through these shops, there were people following us in the five-foot way … And somewhere down there, a group of Malay youth, who shouted in Malay when they saw the PAP flags, '*Hidup Cina!*' That means: 'long live the Chinese'. '*Mati Melayu!*': 'death to the Malays'. The idea was to belittle the PAP and the PAP government, to make a division with the Malays on one side and the Chinese on the other side.

The violence started as they came to Kallang Bridge:

> [W]hen I looked back, I saw a couple of participants from other contingents break rank. And there were uniformed policemen following the procession and they stopped them from breaking rank. I think the people, the participants, were quite tired and hot, because it was a very, very hot day. They wanted to find shelter in the five-foot way. So when they were asked to go back, they became very angry. They started chasing the policemen.

It was a public holiday. People brought their families to eat outside, to go to the cinemas, to go to the beach. And when the riot took place, public transport was at a standstill, so people had to walk home. And there, they were attacked by these roving armed Malay youths.

I told my contingent, 'We break rank here.' So I led them into the Kallang Airport, which was empty at that time. There were two metal gates and I closed the gates. Outside we could see people running around, chasing each other – sounds of people trying to help, sounds of people being beaten up. So I told the boys to stay put. By about 6 o'clock, things began to get better and began to be a bit peaceful. And when I thought it was safe for the boys to leave, I told them to leave this place in twos and threes, not in a group. But before that, they have to throw away all the flags – PAP flags, buntings, everything they carry – into the Kallang River. So they did that, and they went off.

I was the last to leave – around about 6.45 p.m. Curfew was only declared around 9 p.m. that night. The next morning it was lifted for one hour, at 8 a.m., so people could go to the market. It started again. And more people were killed that morning.

Syed Jafaar Albar.
1965
SPH 93758

After four days of riots 22 people were killed and 461 injured. Further ethnic violence broke out in late August and early September. Malay families began to depart from Chinese-dominated areas and Chinese families from Malay areas. To Lee Kuan Yew: 'It was terribly disheartening, a negation of everything we had believed in and worked for – gradual integration and the blurring of the racial divide.'

The unwanted revolution

Undoubtedly, the violence of July and August 1964 had been fuelled by the outpourings of Malay ultra-nationalists (such as Esa Almenoar) keen to see UMNO regain the political ground it had lost in Singapore during the 1963 general elections, when all three Malay-dominated constituencies had fallen to the PAP. The spearhead of this campaign was Syed Jafaar Albar, the UMNO Secretary General (and Othman Wok's journalist-colleague before they both became politicians). In the lead-up to the 1964 Federal Elections, Syed Jafaar used the Malay newspaper *Utusan Melayu* to attack the Singapore government over its alleged discrimination against Malays. In fact, once in power the PAP had made a concession to its strictly non-racial approach to policy-making by granting Malays in Singapore special privileges in education. However through Merger, Singapore's minority Malay community had become reconnected with a dominant Malay majority whose representatives now demanded more for the 'sons of the soil'.

But the issue that most inflamed Malay discontent in Singapore was actually a reaction to change rather than a demand for it. In March 1964, the headlines in the *Utusan* read: '1,500 Malays threatened with quit notices – "A private matter",

Lee said – "nothing to do with the Singapore government."' More reports of the evictions followed over the next two months. Lee toured the neighbourhoods in question – Crawfurd, Rochor and Kampong Glam – to explain that the quit notices were sent to everyone, irrespective of race, as part of a UN-sponsored urban renewal plan, and that compensation and temporary re-housing would be provided. The *Utusan* kept up the pressure against the government: 'Do not treat the sons of the soil as step-children' read another headline.

In July, emotions reached boiling point. On the 12th, Albar made a televised speech to a capacity crowd at the New Star cinema in Pasir Panjang, during which his rallying call for Malay unity against the PAP was accompanied by chants of 'Kill him! ... Kill him! ... Othman Wok and Lee Kuan Yew.' Given the tensions of that month, Othman Wok's presence at the Padang on the 21st was a brave act of defiance. Esa Almenoar's use of the Qur'an to justify resistance to government resettlement, was like a match to the tinderbox.

Over the next 12 months, Albar and Lee circled one another in a communal dance of the very wrong sort – their every exchange seeming to deepen the crisis further. Lee's earlier explanation of his government's policy toward the Malay community had been 'blacked out' (as he put it) by the Kuala Lumpur media; Albar's attacks on the Singapore Prime Minister continued to feature unabated. So that the people of Singapore should know what was going on, Radio & Television Singapore broadcast excerpts from inflammatory *Utusan Melayu* articles translated into three languages – as Lee put it, 'to expose to everyone the vicious racist campaign that Jaafar Albar and the *Utusan* were conducting'. At one point, the Tunku intervened to reprimand Lee for speeches that talked of 'strife and strain, of trouble and bloodshed ahead'. Lee's defence was that 'if we faced up to the unpleasant facts of life, we were more likely to resolve them than if we pretended they did not exist'. He had a point; but there's also little doubt that the Singapore government's decision to translate Albar's 'vicious racist campaign' and broadcast it across the mass media gave it an even wider opportunity to stoke communal tensions. The dilemma for Lee was whether to keep people in ignorance, or warn them of the reality of the situation and so increase their fears.

But there were also other signs that Merger was failing. Goh Keng Swee's industrialisation programme appeared to be obstructed by Tan Siew Tin's Finance Ministry in Kuala Lumpur, which now controlled applications for pioneer industry certificates. Then came Tan's Federal budget of November 1964 which promised new taxes that caused an uproar in Singapore, where, not without reason, they were viewed as an attempt by Kuala Lumpur to make Singapore pay for its success. Even at the most mundane level, Malaysia appeared to be changing Singapore rather than (as the PAP had hoped) the other way around. One day, Lee looked out of his office window and noticed cattle on the Esplanade: 'The city looked scruffy ... After the two riots, the place was slovenly, with more litter, more cows and goats meandering on the streets, more stray dogs, more flies, more mosquitoes, more beggars.' For the PAP, Merger was an unpleasant lesson in what it was like to lose control – of the police, of the media, of internal security and economic policy, indeed of many of those things on which its social revolution and the support of the people depended.

By early 1965, both governments in Singapore and Kuala Lumpur realised the situation was unworkable and representatives from either side – especially Goh and his old schoolmate, Malaysian Deputy Prime Minister Abdul Razak – began meetings to sound out the basis for some form of constitutional rearrangement or even disengagement. Yet while such highly sensitive negotiations were underway, Lee, along with his passionately pro-Malaysia colleagues Toh and Rajaratnam, made one last attempt to bring their vision of a more Singapore-like Malaysia into being. In early 1965, discussions began between the PAP and opposition parties in Malaya and Sarawak to create a Malaysian Solidarity Convention – an alternative coalition to the Alliance, one built around the principle of a 'Malaysian Malaysia ... not identified with the supremacy, well-being and interests of any one particular community or race.' On 6 June, the Convention was officially launched at Singapore's National Theatre in front of 3,000 people to embark on, as Toh put it, 'a crusade to preach interracial unity'.

Lee's involvement in the Convention has been the subject of much speculation. British officials concluded that it was an arch piece of brinkmanship – a tactical way for Lee to gain leverage over the Tunku and so pressure him over the terms of Singapore's withdrawal from Malaysia. But such a view perhaps downplays the zealous idealist at the heart of Lee the ruthless strategist. It also implies that he

Chinese-language booklet
outlining the ideals of a
'Malaysian Malaysia'.
1960s
Paper
H 19 x W 13.5 cm
NMS 2000-07933

willingly misled his loyal colleagues Rajaratnam and Toh as to his true intentions. By contrast, Lee's memoirs reveal that he was torn over Merger, unwilling and unable to relinquish his dream of a 'Malaysian Malaysia', fighting for this ideal right up to the last, yet forced to acknowledge the need for contingency plans to secure Singapore's interests. Ten days before Separation, Lee claimed, he 'was still uncertain as to what would happen, whether there would be a rearrangement, a separation or a collision'.

However, from the Alliance government's perspective everything Lee said in public seemed intended to break the Federation up. His talk of a 'Malaysian Malaysia' hinted at Singapore's secession, then Malaysia's partition – with Singapore to perhaps join the old Straits Settlements and Sabah and Sarawak in some sort of 'alternative' arrangement. By this time, Albar was campaigning to have Lee arrested under Malaysia's Internal Security Act for inciting communal hatred. But the 'straw that finally broke the camel's back', as the Tunku put it, had come on 26 May, when Lee had stood up for what proved to be his last speech in the Federal Parliament.

On this occasion, Lee challenged the Alliance government to disown Albar and the Malay extremists and to publicly disclaim that it was working for a Malay-dominated Malaysia rather than a Malaysian Malaysia. Then, switching from English into fluent Malay, he challenged UMNO to show that it really cared for the 'common people' by letting the PAP compete with it to show who had a better programme to improve the standard of living of the Malays:

> They, the Malays, have the right as Malaysian citizens to go up to the level of training and education that the more competitive societies, the non-Malay society, has produced. That is what must be done, isn't it. Not to feed them with this obscurantist doctrine that all they have got to do is to get Malay rights for a few special Malays and their problem has been resolved …

It was a riveting speech, and for the Tunku a deeply disconcerting one. Its aftermath revealed that the decades-old ideological barrier that presented itself at the Causeway had not gone away. Lee's vision of an alternative Malaysia was one that the Alliance government wasn't interested in – certainly not in the form of a blueprint for social revolution supplied from Singapore.

'Singapore is Out!'

In the early morning hours of 7 August 1965, Toh Chin Chye and Rajaratnam received separate telephone calls from Lee Kuan Yew to come to Kuala Lumpur immediately. The two men were driven up in separate cars (Rajaratnam by Othman Wok) to avoid, so Lee put it, arousing 'speculation that something was up'. When they arrived at Kuala Lumpur's Singapore House, Lee and Goh

Proclamation of Singapore.
August 1965
Paper
H 25.1 x W 17.6 cm
NMS XXXX-02677

Telephone No. 88350

~~Deputy~~ Prime Minister,
Malaysia,
Kuala Lumpur

- 5 -

In witness whereof, the undersigned, being duly
authorised thereto, have signed this Agreement.

Done this 7ᵗʰ day of August, 1965, in ~~two~~ copies
of which one shall be deposited with each of the Parties.

For the Government of Malaysia:
    Prime Minister

    Deputy Prime Minister

    Minister of Home Affairs

    Minister of Finance

    Minister of Works, Posts
    & Telecommunications

For the Government of Singapore:
    Prime Minister

    Deputy Prime Minister

    Minister for Finance

    Minister for Law

    Minister for Culture

    Minister for Social Affairs

    Minister for Education

    Minister for Health

    Minister for National
    Development

Minister for Labour

Lee Kuan Yew at a press
conference announcing the
Separation.
9 August 1965
SPH 46646

Keng Swee called them into a meeting and presented them with documents for Singapore's Separation from the Federation, agreed to by the Tunku.

The agreement had been hammered out over the previous few days by Goh and Razak – ex-schoolmates from Raffles College – and then drafted by Eddie Barker, Singapore's Minister for Law (and another old school friend of Razak's) and Kadir Yusof, the Malaysian Attorney General. After both men completed the drafts there was still a long wait past midnight at Razak's house as his stenographer, unaccustomed to legal matters, struggled to type them up and was eventually replaced. At this point, the tension in the air must have been palpable. The whole deal was being kept secret from the British and there was no certainty that the Tunku wouldn't change his mind at the very last minute. Lee recorded that after Barker and Goh eventually returned to Singapore House, Barker told him that at Razak's home 'they had all got drunk while waiting, and when the documents were finally ready, he [Barker] was the only one sober enough to want to read them before he signed'.

For Toh and Rajaratnam, Separation was particularly hard to swallow, not just because of their commitment to the Malaysian Solidarity Convention but because both men still had family across the Causeway. At first Toh and Rajaratnam refused to sign, until a letter was brought from the Tunku in which he acknowledged there was no other solution. The Kuala Lumpur-born Ong Pang Boon, who was then in the Malaysian capital arranging a Malaysian Solidarity Convention event, was similarly distressed and signed, so Lee wrote, 'with the utmost reluctance'. The Separation documents were then flown back to Singapore for the remaining Cabinet Ministers to add their signatures.

On 9 August 1965, radio transmissions in Singapore were interrupted at 10 a.m. by a momentous announcement: Singapore was no longer a part of the

Federation of Malaysia. Two hours later, Lee gave a press interview at the studios of Radio & Television Singapore. As the cameras rolled, he tearfully explained what the reality of independence meant to him – the end of a dream he had worked for the whole of his adult life, the separation of a people bound together by 'geography, economics and ties of kinship'. The following day the headline of the *Straits Times* read: 'SINGAPORE IS OUT!'

For Goh Keng Swee, the challenges that faced the newly independent nation 'loomed in awesome and intimidating proportions'. Singapore had few natural resources, barely an armed forces and even its water had to be imported. Yet there were also several grounds for optimism. By 1965, the PAP's main parliamentary opposition had been vanquished and the country's workforce, thanks to the government's education initiatives and Britain's continuing presence at its naval base, was the best technically trained in the whole of Southeast Asia. Most importantly, with Separation Lee and his colleagues had taken back full control of their social revolution and of the future they had promised the Singapore people.

Separation information booklet.
1965
Private collection of Wong Han Min

EPILOGUE

Rites of the nation

Every 9 August, the people of Singapore commemorate their political independence with a National Day Parade (also known, in a nation that seems to delight in acronyms and abbreviations, as the 'NDP'). The origins of this celebration go back to 3 June 1960, when Singapore first commemorated the day it achieved self-government. But it was from 1966, when 28,000 soldiers, schoolchildren and cultural troupe performers marched past City Hall, that the NDP became embedded in the island's popular consciousness.

Over four decades later, much of the NDP's ritual has remained the same in what is (rare for Singapore) a direct line of continuity between the past and the present. But the changes have also been significant. By the 1990s, the long lines of unionists and party supporters carrying socialist emblems and slogans had given way to colourful floats and a carnival-like atmosphere. Today, the mass displays and militarism that once brought to mind totalitarian states such as China and North Korea are a thing of the past, replaced by song-and-dance, Hollywood-style multimedia spectaculars – all glitz and glamour. Singapore has become a nation that appears to be enjoying its harmony and its prosperity.

The other National Day tradition is the Prime Minister's National Day Rally Speech, an annual briefing on the state of the nation, usually given on a Sunday after 9 August. In 1975, a decade after Separation, Prime Minister Lee Kuan Yew stood up at the old National Theatre to speak. The setting was impressive – the theatre's striking five-pointed façade and fountain represented the five stars and crescent moon of the Singapore flag; the outdoor amphitheatre was open to the sky and intended to symbolise freedom. Yet in the Prime Minister's opening there was no need for symbolism or even hyperbole:

> Friends and fellow-citizens,
> The past decade was probably the most spectacular of all the ten years of
> Singapore's history.

State of the nation

By 1975 tempers in the nation's factories had simmered down and the workers had become more efficient and compliant. Tough new employment legislation in 1968 had put an end to decades of perpetual labour unrest and in the following year there was not a single strike. Trade unions, once the fighting machines of the anti-colonial struggle, now operated in a spirit of tripartite cooperation with the government and employers – or they did not operate at all. In 1969, Singapore's

OPPOSITE: Police contingent marching past City Hall in the republic's first National Day parade.
9 August 1966
SPH 3668830

425

economic growth hit a robust 9 per cent and rose above 10 per cent in the years that followed. As Lee Kuan Yew told his audience at the National Theatre:

> When we borrow from the World Bank or the Asian Development Bank, there are no more soft loans. We are classified as an intermediate country – not developed, not developing, but intermediate – and we pay the going market interest rate.

In the nation's classrooms, things were also calmer. Educators were now tasked with inculcating social discipline and good values in their students, rather than ethnic consciousness and revolutionary ideology. In 1966, the Cabinet had decided to further blur the ethnic divide by making English, not Malay, Singapore's common language. Multiculturalism was kept alive through the compulsory teaching of a second language (or 'mother tongue' – Malay, Mandarin or Tamil) in secondary schools, and that same year the daily flag-raising and pledge-taking ceremony was introduced to promote the ideal of national harmony. In a speech to school principals at this time, Lee was not sure whether such rituals were the 'best solution' but he believed that they were 'a start'. 'The reflexes of group thinking', he went on, 'must be built to ensure the survival of the community, not the survival of the individual.'

Likewise, campus life became more settled at the island's tertiary institutions. Through the mid-1960s, Nanyang University students had been involved in a series of violent confrontations with the police during a remarkable period of student unrest that spread to Ngee Ann Technical College and the University of Singapore. The authorities' response was to introduce the political screening of would-be university entrants through Suitability Certificates. In 1975, Nanyang

'Operation Q': a campaign to encourage commuters to queue up at bus stops.
March 1969
NAS 19980007156-0058

University was forced to introduce English alongside Chinese as a medium of instruction and three years later Southeast Asia's only Chinese-language university was shut down for good when it merged with the new National University of Singapore.

For the nation's young men, before work or further study, there was a new rite of passage. In July 1967, the government introduced national service for all 18-year-olds, a policy that made practical sense given that Singapore at independence had only the barest semblance of a standing army. Moreover, in the light of the previous 13 years of student protests, sit-ins, boycotts and riots, national service made sense as a fundamental tool of social discipline as well. As Minister for Defence, Goh Keng Swee even introduced Singapore's very own 'little red book' – the *Code of Conduct for the Vigilante Corps Members* – to teach new national servicemen correct behaviour as Singapore citizens. Excerpts included: 'Human beings have basic needs. Human beings have basic obligations ... The State provides our basic needs. The Republic of Singapore is our society ... It is through the efforts made by the Government, on our behalf, that we are able to obtain our basic needs ... As an individual: Rule One, Work Hard. Rule Two, Be Fit. Rule Three, Be Clean ... Bathing in hot water is good for bodily cleanliness. Regular moving of the bowels ensures internal cleanliness ...' Although suicide and drug-taking remained problems up until the late 1970s, national service had become one of the government's most important nation-building instruments. As Rajaratnam put it: 'When young Chinese, Malays, Indians and Eurasians train together to defend and die for their country, then they become true blood-brothers.'

Across the nation's coffee shops, the morning papers arrived and the political discussions followed, just as they had done for decades previously. But by the mid-1970s, the channels for news and opinion had narrowed noticeably. Earlier

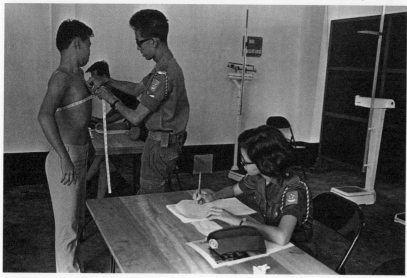

National service enlistment procedures.
1967
NAS 19980005330-0033

427

Mock demonstration at
Singapore Polytechnic in
support of the freedom of
thought and expression.
June 1971
SPH PCD 0390-0091

that decade, the government clamped down on three newspapers, the *Eastern Sun*, the *Singapore Herald* and the venerable *Nanyang Siang Pau*, for conducting 'black operations' – that is, for allegedly being used by foreign parties to foment unrest in Singapore. In late 1974, new legislation was introduced that required all newspaper companies to offer 'management shares' to Singaporean corporations and individuals approved by the government. Though such 'management shares' only comprised 1 per cent of a newspaper company's total shares, on editorial matters they had a voting power that was 200 times stronger than ordinary shares. In this way, every newspaper venture in Singapore came under the scrutiny of government-approved monitors. As Lee told the International Press Institute in Helsinki in 1971: 'Freedom of the press, freedom of the news media, must be subordinated to the overriding needs of Singapore, and to the primacy of purpose of an elected government.'

There was an obvious danger with such a policy. A 'special report' in the *Times* of London in 1971 addressed local criticism in Singapore of the authorities' clampdown on 'the first manifestations of a spirit of responsible dissent'. The *Times*' correspondent concluded: 'the government's real problem is to create a society that is stable without being sterile, loyal and not sycophantic, patriotic but not chauvinist and critical but not irresponsible'. Ever forthright, Goh had complained a year earlier: 'We have in Singapore intellectual conformity in place of intellectual inquisitiveness and the sum total is a depressing climate of intellectual sterility.'

Meanwhile, in the nation's homes the social revolution continued. By 1975 the government's resettlement of residents from *kampongs*, slums and shantytowns into modern HDB estates was fully underway, generating anxiety and excitement in equal measure. Many rituals of rural life were disrupted or discarded; yet the experience of such transformation was entirely mixed. Some people bemoaned the loss of village community life – the daily interactions, family celebrations and annual festivals that brought people closer together. They also resented the loss of their former occupations – such as farming, fishing or boat-building – and found their new jobs and their new homes unfriendly and depressing. Others marvelled at the concrete solidity of their new HDB estates and welcomed the security they provided from fires and floods. For girls and women from rural areas, basic utilities such as electricity and running water were a form of liberation. Instead of having to run to the communal well all hours of the day, or prepare kerosene lights and ovens, they now had time for other pursuits such as going to school. Many adjustments had to be made – some people still lit their lamps and remained fearful of the lifts. Nonetheless, by 1975 a new kind of community was shaping up across the length and breadth of the island.

As Lee told the nation in 1975, 'There had never been such transformation in any ten years. The physical landscape changed with new buildings, new roads, flyovers, traffic jams, homes, new factories.' In the city centre, the low-rise shophouses that had dominated images of Singapore since the early 19th century made way for housing estates, office blocks, car parks and in 1975 the nation's first shopping mall – Plaza Singapura on Orchard Road. A striking new horizon of skyscrapers was taking shape, from Chinatown in the southwest across to

Chinese New Year shopping in Chinatown.
January 1976
SPH 20060000406-0009

where the first Sultan of Singapore had once made his home in Kampong Glam in the southeast. The sounds of the city were changing too – the once ubiquitous calls of itinerant hawkers now drowned out by the horns of cars and scooters, the steady hum of air-conditioning units and the deep rumbles of endless construction work.

– All of which pointed to Singapore's dramatic new prosperity. In 1972, Lee could tell the nation: 'Many people now consider scooters, small cars, TV and refrigerators necessities, not luxuries.' Three years later he observed:

> [W]ith the new standards of incomes, we have got ourselves into a different mood, the younger generation especially – people who were not old enough in 1965 to understand what hardship and unemployment meant. And they are a truly different generation. Expectations have gone up. Unconsciously, we have entered into the free-spending consumer society of the West. Parents spoil their children. There's better clothes, better food, better housing. All the time their expectation goes up and up, believing it is always going to be up the escalator.

But before we conclude the story of Singapore's journey from hardship and unemployment to wealth and consumerism, there is one thing more to add. The great changes the nation experienced during its first decade of independence spoke also of a radically new attitude to its past. In 1966, the government launched its urban renewal programme with the following flourish:

> Urban renewal means no less than the gradual demolition of virtually the whole 1,500 acres of the old city and its replacement by an integrated modern city centre worthy of Singapore's future role as the New York of Malaysia.

The same year, Lee told school principals:

> Even an American whose society is a relatively new one can tell you all about George Washington or Abraham Lincoln. For he has history, and he can say, 'These are the great events in the life of my people.' ... We are not in the same position because our society and its education system was never designed to produce a people capable of cohesive action ...

Two years later, Rajaratnam went further:

> We do not lay undue stress on the past. We do not see nation-building and modernisation as primarily an exercise in reuniting the present generation with a past generation and its values and glories. ... A generation encouraged to bask in the values of the past and hold on to a static future will never be equipped to meet a future predicated on jet travel, atomic power, satellite communication, electronics and computers. For us the task is not one of linking past generations with the present generation, but the present generation with future generations.

Effectively, on 9 August 1965, Singapore's historical clock was set back to zero. From that day on Prime Minister Lee and his colleagues, like many revolutionaries before them, began to make their own history afresh. For the next two decades, their priority would be less to present their nation through its poetry, music, *wayang*, film, or even 'People's Cultural Concerts' – for such things belonged to an old Singapore, a 'Malayan' Singapore, a place that had held such hopes for Merger. Nor would the Prime Minister and his Cabinet prove much concerned with memories of historical personalities long since dead (after all, as Lee saw it, the nation collectively did not actually have any). Instead, the new Singapore, the PAP's Singapore, would make its mark on the world through its prosperity and its modernity – its bright lights and shining concrete monuments a testament to consensus, to stability and to an ideological transformation complete.

This book has mainly been concerned with the 'old' Singapore – the personalities, the relationships and the tensions that made it so unique and so teeming with vitality. For if we fail to comprehend what happened in this 'old' Singapore – fail to understand its passions, dreams, failures and accomplishments – then we can never fully appreciate the extraordinary change that followed. This is not to say that a living history did not characterise Singapore well into its gleaming post-independence future. But rather that, as they say, is another story.

Fishing at sunset: weir stakes in what is now Marina Bay, with the Supreme Court (left) and St Andrew's Cathedral in the background.
1966
National Geographic/Getty

Endnotes

Listed by page number

PROLOGUE

9   *As Singapore's most famous Malay chronicler recorded ... 'they reached no decision'.* Abdullah Abdul Kadir, Munsyi. *The Hikayat Abdullah: The Autobiography of Abdullah bin Abdul Kadir (1797–1854)*, A. H. Hill (trans.), Singapore: Oxford University Press, 1985 (first published in 1955), p. 166.

TEMASEK

14   *For example, a Chinese chronicle ... 'accustomed to cannibalism'.* Tu You, *T'ung Tien*, vol. 187, and Li Fang, *Tai Ping Yu Lan*, vol. 791, cited in Hsu Yun-Ts'iao, 'Singapore in the Remote Past', in *Journal of the Malaysian Branch of the Royal Asiatic Society*, 45(1):6, 1973.

14   *The first reliable record ... 'Dragon Tooth Gate'.* Wang Dayuan, *Dao Yi Zhi Lue* (*Description of the Barbarians of the Isles*), 1349, cited in Paul Wheatley, *The Golden Khersonese: Studies in Historical Geography of the Malay Peninsula before A.D. 1500*, Kuala Lumpur: University of Malaya Press, 1961, p. 82.

15   *In 1320, the Yuan court ... a few years later.* Hsu, 'Singapore in the Remote Past', pp. 3–4.

15   *From the mid-14th century ... 'land surrounded by water'.* John N. Miksic, *Archaeological Research on the 'Forbidden Hill' of Singapore: Excavations at Fort Canning, 1984*, Singapore: National Museum, 1985, p. 16.

15   *In the same decade ... Temasek ambassadors* The Vietnamese Royal Chronicle *Dai Viet Su Ky Toan Thu*, record of 1330, vol. 2, p. 118, Ha Noi edition, 1998, cited in John Miksic, 'Between Two Mandalas: Singapore, Siam and Java', Asia Research Institute Working Paper Series No. 51, 2005, pp. 56–57.

15   *The Majapahit court poem ... allegiance and tribute.* The *Desawarnana* is also known as the *Nagarakertagama*. Cited in R.O. Winstedt, 'Tumasik or Old Singapore', in *Journal of the Malaysian Branch of the Royal Asiatic Society*, 42(1):14, 1969.

15   *Temasek continues to appear ... between 1403 and 1433.* Wheatley, p. 96; Mao Yuanyi, *Wu Bei Zhi*, 1621. Mao cited in 'Sailing Past Singapore', in *Early Singapore, 1300s–1819: Evidence in Maps, Text and Artefacts*, John N. Miksic and Cheryl-Ann Low Mei Gek (eds.), Singapore: Singapore History Museum, 2004, pp. 99–100.

16   *However, Malay chronicles state ... the 'Lion City'.* Sejarah Melayu, or, Malay Annals: An Annotated Translation, C. C. Brown (trans.), Kuala Lumpur: Oxford University Press, 1970 (originally published in 1953), p. 20.

16   *In the 14th century, the settlement ... 'in that quarter superfluous'.* Miksic, *Archaeological Research on the 'Forbidden Hill'*, p. 36; John Crawfurd, *Journal of an Embassy to the Courts of Siam and Cochin China*, Kuala Lumpur: Oxford University Press, 1967 (originally published in London: Henry Colburn, 1828), pp. 44–47.

16   *Shards of excavated pottery ... the riverside hoi polloi.* Cheryl-Ann Low Mei Gek, 'Singapore from the 14th to early 19th century', in *Early Singapore*, pp. 17–34; Miksic, '14th-century Singapore', Ibid., pp. 48–52.

18   *Across Southeast Asia ... that overlooked water.* Low, 'Singapore from the 14th to early 19th century', p. 15.

18   *But when the British ... old dead kings.* John N. Miksic, interview with the National Museum of Singapore, 2006; Miksic, '14th-century Singapore', p. 46.

20   *Eventually, men from Melaka ... more about him later).* Miksic, interview with National Museum; Crawfurd, pp. 44–47. For a little on the site's continuing mystical allure, see also Miksic, '14th-century Singapore', p. 46.

20   *On top were the aristocracy ... receive tribute.* Miksic, interview with National Museum.

22   *Singapore sits not just at ... where Singapore happens to be.* Derek Heng, interview with the National Museum of Singapore, 2006.

22   *Little is known ... north and east Africa. Singapore: The Encyclopaedia*, Tommy Koh, Timothy Auger, Jimmy Yap and Ng Wei Chian (eds.), Singapore: Editions Didier Millet/National Heritage Board, 2006, p. 581. Wang is quoted in Roderich Ptak, 'Notes on the word "Shanhu" and Chinese coral imports from maritime Asia, c. 1250–1600', in *China's Seaborne Trade with South and Southeast Asia (1200–1750)*, Aldershot: Ashgate Publishing Limited, 1998, VIII, p. 70.

22   *Temasek, or Danmaxi ... (one eastern, one western). Singapore: The Encyclopaedia*, p. 582.

23   *The pirates' domain was Longyamen ... and their crews butchered.* Wang Dayuan, cited in Wheatley, p. 82.

23   *An early 17th-century Portuguese map ... 'stabbed in the back'.* Miksic, interview with National Museum; Victor R. Savage and Brenda S.A. Yeoh, *Toponymics: A Study of Singapore Street Names*, Singapore: Eastern Universities Press, 2003, pp. 307–308.

23   *However, no such natural features ... for modern shipping.* Kwa Chong Guan, 'Sailing past Singapore', in *Early Singapore*, p. 105n.

23   *Wang wrote of Banzu ... highly valued hornbill casques.* Wang Dayuan, cited in Wheatley, p. 83.

23   *Overall, his Description ... status and role in society.* Miksic, '14th-century Singapore', p. 43.

24   *Wang recalled how ... the fact of their existence.* Wang Dayuan, cited in Wheatley, pp. 82 and 83.

24   *The only further reference ... powerful regional rival.* Wang Dayuan, cited in Winstedt, p. 14.

24   *This source tells us ... or 'Lion City'. Sejarah Melayu*, pp. 21 and 20.

25   *Various Singapuras ... and in India too.* Miksic, 'Between Two Mandalas', p. 46.

26   *Chiefly a genealogy ... but much smaller). Sejarah Melayu*, pp. 40–41.

26   *The historian Timothy Barnard ... 'was laid on Singapura'.* Timothy Barnard, interview with the National Museum of Singapore, 2006. See also Timothy Barnard, 'Confrontation on a River: Singapore as an 18th-century Battleground in Malay Historiography', in *Early Singapore*, pp. 121–122; *Sejarah Melayu*, pp. 40–41.

26   *After only three years ... the government worked well. Sejarah Melayu*, p. 41. Barnard, interview with National Museum.

28   *After Melaka fell to the Portuguese ... of the Sultan's subjects.* Barnard, interview with National Museum. See also Leonard Y. Andaya, 'The search for the "origins" of Melayu', in *Contesting Malayness: Malay Identity Across Boundaries*, Timothy Barnard (ed.), Singapore: Singapore University Press, 2004, p. 71. For an account of the Sultanate's movements, see Kwa Chong Guan, 'From Temasek to Singapore: Locating a global city-state in the cycles of Melaka Straits history', in *Early Singapore*, p. 132.

28   *The Chinese Ming chronicles ... the year 1413.* Cited in Low, 'Singapore from the 14th to early 19th century', p. 15. See also Geoffrey Wade, 'Melaka in Ming Dynasty Texts', *Journal of the Malaysian Branch of the Royal Asiatic Society*, 70(1):39, 1997.

28   *The main Portuguese records ... Sanskrit form Parameswara).* Afonso D'Albuquerque, *Commentaries of the Great Afonso D'Albuquerque*, Walter de Gray Birch (ed.), London: Hakluyt Society, 1875 (originally published in Lisbon: Barreyra, 1557), p. 73.

29   *Where the Sejarah Melayu gives us ... heading north and founding Melaka.* Ibid., pp. 73–76.

29   *Indeed, historian William Linehan ... the empire-builder.* W. Linehan, 'The Kings of 14th Century Singapore', in *Journal of the Malayan Branch of the Royal Asiatic Society*, 20(2): 62–64, 1947.

31   *In an early instance of 'gun-boat diplomacy' ... the Melakan Empire was no more.* This version of Melaka's fall is based on a synthesis of the Portuguese diplomat and traveller Tomo Pires's account in his *Suma Oriental* and the *Sejarah Melayu*, both of which are reprinted in John Bastin and Robin Winks (eds.), *Malaysia: Selected Historical Readings*, Nendeln, Liechtenstein: KTO Press, 1979, pp. 34–38. It also incorporates the account of the Italian traveller Giovanni da Empoli, *Lettera di Giovanni da Empoli*, Rome: Arti Graphica Scalia, 1970, pp. 136–137 (see also Laurence A. Noonan, *John of Empoli and His Relations with Afonso de Alberquerque*, Lisbon: Ministeria de Educacao, 1989); the fictional account of a repelled invasion of Melaka by the Portuguese in the *Sejarah Melayu*, p. 152; and D'Albuquerque, *Commentaries*, volume 3, pp. 60–70, 90–114 and 119–128. Each of these sources is in its own way biased, but reading between them it appears that the Melakans did put up a strong defence of their city, as the fictional account of Melaka's defence in the *Sejarah Melayu* alludes to (but perhaps for literary and political reasons places at an earlier date before 1511) and as does *The Commentaries* (see pp. 103–104, 107–108 and 122–23).

32   *But for a subtler model ... commerce and conflict.* The following analysis is indebted to Peter Borschberg's interview with the National Museum of Singapore, 2006.

34   *The Sultans of Johor-Riau-Lingga ... conquered it.* Peter Borschberg, 'A Portuguese-Dutch Naval Battle in the Johor River Estuary and the liberation of Johor Lama in 1603', in *Early Singapore*, p. 115.

35   *The Bugis responded in 1756 ... to accept Dutch suzerainty.* Low, 'Singapore from the 14th to early 19th century', p. 38.

35   *For one thing, the Dutch, Portuguese ... around Changi Point.* Ibid., p. 37. Borschberg, 'A Portuguese-Dutch Naval Battle', pp. 109–112; Borschberg, interview with the National Museum of Singapore.

35   *According to the Sejarah Melayu ... seafaring people.* Sejarah Melayu, pp. 117–118, 241 (footnote 625) and 67.

37   *After Melaka's fall ... still in use today.* D'Albuquerque, p. 99; Miksic, interview with National Museum; Manuel Godinho d'Erédia, 'Chorographic Description of the Straits of Sincapura and Sabbam, 1604 A.D.' Reproduced in Kwa, 'Sailing past Singapore', p. 100.

37   *Singapore next reappears ... to a possible settlement.* Alexander Hamilton, *A New Account of the East*, vol. 2, London: C. Hitch and A. Millar, 1744, p. 97; John Thornton, *The English Pilot: The Third Book*, London, J. How, 1703. Thornton cited in Kwa, 'Sailing past Singapore', pp. 97–98.

37   *As early as 1609 ... that he "found" or "discovered".'* C. E. Wurtzburg, *Raffles of the Eastern Isles*, Singapore: Oxford University Press, 1984 (originally published in 1954), pp. 500–501; Borschberg, interview with National Museum.

SETTLEMENT

40   *At the beginning of 1819 ... the island opposite Johor.* C. M. Turnbull, *A History of Singapore, 1819–1988*, Singapore: Oxford University Press, 1989, p. 5.

40   *Wa Hakim was one of them ... 'and went on board again'.* H. T. Haughton, 'The Landing of Raffles in Singapore by an Eye Witness', 1882, in *Singapore 150 Years* (150th Anniversary of the Founding of Singapore Commemorative Reprint), Singapore: Times Books International, 1973, pp. 74–75.

41   *The day of the signing ... 'he inwardly accorded'.* J. G. F. Crawford, *Diary of Captain Crawford*. Cited in Wurtzburg, pp. 490–492.

42   *Instead, a nine-article ... alliances with other nations.* The Treaty has been duplicated in Charles Burton Buckley, *An Anecdotal History of Old Times in Singapore, 1819–1867*, Singapore: Oxford University Press, 1984 (originally published in Singapore: Fraser & Neave Ltd., 1902), p. 38–40.

43   *After the Treaty signing ... broader context of regional politics.* Crawford, cited in Wurtzburg, p. 492.

44   *In the words of Governor John Bannerman ... 'then runs away'.* Wurtzburg, p. 512.

45   *[A] Rajah, as if dropped ... on 1 February'.* Crawford, cited in Wurtzburg, p. 488.

45   *Hussein, since the death ... with his followers.* Turnbull, *History of Singapore*, pp. 8–9.

45   *In 1818, the year before ... the end of 1818.* Wurtzburg, pp. 452 and 470; Raja Ali Haji ibn Ahmad, *The Precious Gift (Tuhfat al-Nafis)*, Virginia Matheson and Barbara Watson Andaya (trans.), Kuala Lumpur: Oxford University Press, 1982, p. 227.

47   *Raffles summarised the problem ... 'and obtain refreshment'.* Raffles's letter to William Brown Ramsay on 14 April 1818, cited in Wurtzburg, p, 433.

47   *Philosophically, the EIC ... as spices and tin.* Anthony Reid, interview with the National Museum of Singapore, 2006.

47   *He personally envisioned ... 'of Dutch monopoly'.* Raffles's letter to Colonel Addenbrooke on 10 June 1819. Reproduced in Sophia Raffles, *Memoir of the Life and Public Services of Sir Thomas Stamford Raffles*, Singapore: Oxford University Press, 1991, pp. 379–380.

48   *Historian Mary Turnbull ... 'and exacting dues'.* Turnbull, *History of Singapore*, p. 16.

48   *The truth is, soon after the Sultan ... keep the British happy.* Ibid., p. 10. For a reproduction (in Jawi and translated into English) of the Temenggong's letter to the Dutch governor of Melaka Adrian Koek, see W. E. Maxwell, 'The Founding of Singapore', in *Singapore 150 Years*, pp. 77–79.

50   *Within a decade, during which he pursued ... in their own language.* Wurtzburg, p. 21.

50   *While Raffles was stationed in Penang ... official in charge, Major William Farquhar.* Ibid., p. 56, 59 and 67. See also pp. 68–79 for the full text of Raffles's report to the Governor and Council at Penang, dated 31 October 1808.

51   *And so, before Raffles even dreamed ... 'whatever its importance'.* Ibid., p. 76.

52   *However, by 1800 the French Revolutionary ... British possessions in the East.* Ibid., p. 96.

52   *Raffles recorded that when the interview ... Governor General Minto in person.* Ibid., pp. 89, 103–108 and 157.

53   *In a letter home he admitted ... 'millions of people'.* Raffles's letter to William Brown Ramsay in October 1812, cited in Wurtzburg, p. 184.

53   *Interestingly, when Raffles departed Java ... 'horror, disgust and alarm'.* Raffles's letter to Alexander Hare on 20 May 1816, reproduced in Wurtzburg, pp. 404–408.

54   *Their solution was to send ... establishment in 1685.* Wurtzburg, pp. 427–428.

54   *Raffles, nonetheless, took the appointment ... tana mati would be.* Ibid., pp. 425 and 429.

54   *He stuck it out ... at the negotiating table.* Ibid., pp. 433–449.

55   *Hastings's official orders ... a reappearance in Riau.* Hastings's letter to Raffles on 28 November 1818, cited in Wurtzburg, pp. 461, 463 and 464.

56   *But in the British Parliament ... 'any political arrangements'.* Noel Barber, *The Singapore Story from Raffles to Lee Kuan Yew*, London: Fontana, 1978, p. 42; Turnbull, *History of Singapore*, p. 9.

56   *Van der Capellen condemned Raffles ... 'fire the first shot'.* Van der Capellen's letter to Anton Reinhard Falck on 19 March 1819, cited in Wurtzburg, p. 514.

57   *His last contact with Raffles ... 'arisen between us'.* Van der Capellen's letter to Calcutta on 16 December 1819, cited in Wurtzburg, p. 555.

57   *Raffles, having departed ... 'has happened since 1818'.* Wurtzburg, pp. 659–661.

57   *In Bencoolen, in the years ... relating to the settlement's establishment.* Turnbull, *History of Singapore*, p. 17; Walter Makepeace, Gilbert E. Brooke and Roland St. J. Braddell (eds.), *One Hundred Years of Singapore*, Singapore: Oxford University Press, 1991 (originally published in London: J. Murray, 1921), vol. 1, p. 67; Demetrius Charles Boulger, *The Life of Sir Stamford Raffles*, Amsterdam: Pepin Press, 1999 (originally published in 1897), p. 370.

58   *Raffles did manage ... died in debt.* Turnbull, *History of Singapore*, pp. 18–19 and 27.

59   *'You will immediately embark ... the Straits of Singapore ...'* Wurtzburg, p. 478.

59   *In 1790, at the age of 20 ... out of a job.* Turnbull, *History of Singapore*, pp. 7–8.

60   *He probably had this in mind ... transit at Penang.* John Bastin, 'William Farquhar: His Life and Interest in Natural History', in *The William Farquhar Collection of Natural History Drawings*, Singapore: Goh Geok Khim, 1999, p. 13.

60   *Until one of these dogs ... his native Aberdeen.* Hikayat Abdullah, A. H. Hill (trans.), p. 168.

60   *Raffles, as a rational man ... his contemporaries described him.* Wurtzburg, p. 448.

60   *Indeed, Farquhar's relaxed style ... the 'Raja Melaka'.* Turnbull, *History of Singapore*, p. 11.

62   *One of Raffles's most infamous acts ... caused deep resentment.* Wurtzburg, pp. 624–625; Turnbull, *History of Singapore*, p. 24.

62   *While Resident of Melaka ... who bore him six children.* Bastin, 'William Farquhar', p. 20.

62   *Nonetheless, from the moment ... a series of instructions.* H. F. Pearson, *Singapore: A Popular History*, Singapore: Times Books International, 1985 (originally published in Singapore: Eastern Universities Press, 1961), pp. 6–7; Wurtzburg, p. 489. For the details of Raffles' instructions, see Wurtzburg, pp. 495–500.

63   *'It is not necessary' … from the outset.* Wurztburg, pp. 497–498; see Turnbull, *History of Singapore*, p. 15: 'Farquhar had to administer the rapidly expanding settlement on a shoestring budget and spent less on salaries in a year than Bencoolen did in a month'.

63   *Farquhar therefore sent news … 'rain of plenty'.* Hikayat Abdullah, A. H. Hill (trans.), p. 150-153; Brian Harrison, *Holding the Fort: Melaka Under Two Flags*, Kuala Lumpur: Malaysian Branch of the Royal Asiatic Society, 1986, p. 99; Turnbull, *History of Singapore*, pp. 13–14.

63   *If Dutch forces in Riau … out of the question.* Turnbull, *History of Singapore*, p. 10; Wurtzburg, p. 508.

63   *Unable to contact Raffles … an inevitable defeat.* Bannerman's minutes and letters (20 February 1819–13 March 1819), cited in Wurtzburg, pp. 510–513.

64   *A few weeks later, another 200 reinforcements … a volte-face.* Turnbull, *History of Singapore*, p. 11.

64   *Farquhar's first report … three and a half years.* Wurtzburg, p. 541; Pearson, p. 11.

65   *By 1821, the population had grown … mete out justice.* Turnbull, *History of Singapore*, pp. 13 and 12.

65   *Against his superior's wishes … even grass-cutters.* Ibid., p. 15; Buckley, p. 63.

65   *When Raffles returned to Singapore again … taxes on liquor and opium.* Wurtzburg, pp. 606, 643 and 645.

66   *But the key issue … 'going to war'.* Ibid., pp. 607–608 and 612–613; Hikayat Abdullah, A. H. Hill (trans.), p. 165.

66   *Raffles next set to work … sprawl and suffocate.* Wurtzburg, pp. 610–612; Turnbull, *History of Singapore*, pp. 20–21.

66   *In January 1823, Raffles wrote … 'be difficult to overcome'.* Raffles's letter to Calcutta on 27 January 1823, cited in Wurtzburg, p. 622.

68   *The growing distaste … his official duties.* Wurtzburg, pp. 637–638.

68   *To find his 'almost only child' … a mark of gratitude.* Ibid., pp. 606 and 613–614.

68   *Though the EIC formally decided … 'exclusive merit' for Singapore's establishment.* Cited in Bastin, 'William Farquhar', p. 19.

68   *'During 20 years of his valuable life … latter settlement he founded …'* Ernest Chew, 'The Man Who Raffles Left Behind: William Farquhar (1774–1839)', in *Raffles Town Club*, 7, 2002. <http://www.postcolonialweb.org/singapore/history/chew/chew6.html> Accessed on 13 March 2009.

69   *Ironically, the one street … modern town-planners.* Savage and Yeoh, p. 125

69   *If Raffles was the founding father … modern entrepôt by himself.* Ernest Chew, 'The Man Who Raffles Left Behind: William Farquhar (1774–1839)', in *Raffles Town Club*, 7, 2002. <http://www.postcolonialweb.org/singapore/history/chew/chew8.html> Accessed on 13 March 2009; Karl Hack, interview with the National Museum of Singapore, 2006.

69   *Farquhar eventually left … for the horizon.* Hikayat Abdullah, G. Shellabear (trans.); Hikayat Abdullah, A. H. Hill (trans.), p. 197. Shellabear cited in Donald Moore and Joanna Moore, *The First 150 Years of Singapore*, Singapore: Donald Moore Press, 1969, p. 109.

70   *Both were Scots …* History of the Indian Archipelago. Turnbull, *History of Singapore*, p. 25; Ernest Chew, 'Dr John Crawfurd (1783-1868): The Scotsman Who Made Singapore British', in *Raffles Town Club*, 8, 2002. <http://www.postcolonialweb.org/singapore/history/chew/chew11.html> Accessed on 13 March 2009.

70   *However, Raffles's former scribe Munshi Abdullah … 'outbursts of temper'.* Hikayat Abdullah, A. H. Hill (trans.), pp. 198–199 and 223–224.

70   *On one occasion … eligible young women.* Ibid., pp. 221–222.

71   *'I heard many Malays … their own consent'.* Ibid., p. 224.

71   *Raffles's final regulations … grading of punishments.* Raffles, *Memoir of the Life and Public Services*, p. 541; Turnbull, *History of Singapore*, pp. 22–23.

71   *The treaty did increase … 'and habits of the people'.* Wurtzburg, pp. 625–653; Turnbull, *History of Singapore*, pp. 21–22.

71   *As a consequence … mistakenly describes him.* Ernest Chew, 'Dr John Crawfurd'.

71   *On assuming his duties … 'necessary amusement'* Turnbull, *History of Singapore*, p. 27; Crawfurd, vol. 2, pp. 394 and 399.

72   *The most remarkable of these … the settlement's young elite.* For details, see Wurtzburg, pp. 630–636 and 648–649.

72   *When Raffles received news … nothing he could do.* Raffles's letter to Mary Anne Raffles on 17 January 1824, cited in Wurtzburg, p. 675.

72   *As he, himself, recalled … the port's commercial expansion.* Crawfurd, vol. 2, p. 357; Turnbull, *History of Singapore*, p. 27.

73   *By 1826, the year he departed … English street signs.* Turnbull, *History of Singapore*, p. 27; Ernest Chew, 'Dr John Crawfurd'.

73   *Crawfurd's personal view … 'of complete indigence'.* Crawfurd's letter to the Governor-General in Calcutta on 10 January 1824, cited in Moore and Moore, p. 127.

73   *Through Crawfurd's Treaty … 'retains any power.'* Hikayat Abdullah, A. H. Hill (trans.), pp. 218–221.

73   *To drive the message home … 'lonesome and uninteresting'.* 'Journal of a voyage round the island of Singapore', in J. H. Moor (ed.), *Notices of the Indian Archipelago and Adjacent Countries*, Singapore: 1837, pp. 260 and 271–273.

74   *To ensure the Malay chiefs' compliance … available to him.* Hikayat Abdullah, A. H. Hill (trans.), p. 219.

74   *The British certainly had little faith … remainder of his days.* Turnbull, *History of Singapore*, p. 50.

75   *By most accounts Abdul Rahman … in his name.* Barnard, interview with the National Museum of Singapore; Ali Haji ibn Ahmad, p. 220.

75   *Early in the same year that saw … interference in Sumatra.* Turnbull, *History of Singapore*, p. 28.

75   *'I am astonished to see … comes to demand it'.* Hikayat Abdullah, A. H. Hill (trans.), p. 162.

75   *As well as being a crucial piece … indigenous 'I' of Singapore history.* Hadijah Rahmat, interview with the National Museum of Singapore, 2006.

76   *Well before the events of early 1819 … the age of 14.* For a detailed account of Abdullah's language learning, see *Hikayat Abdullah*, A. H. Hill (trans.), pp. 39–52.

76   *Strictly speaking … 'was he a Malay'.* Ibid., p. 5.

77   *In 1811 Abdullah's precocity … bearing of arms.* Ibid. pp. 75–76, 101–102, 160 and 177.

77   *In Singapore, the Munshi … 'the most incredible things'.* Ibid., pp. 189, 310 and 234.

78   *'Do you really wish … wherever writing is involved'.* Ibid., pp. 313 and 314.

78   *For a start, and notwithstanding his evident excitement … 'would certainly have been different'.* Ibid., pp. 190 and 165.

78   *As Raffles prepared to leave … 'the more depressed I became'.* Ibid., pp. 192 and 195.

80   *Instead of being remembered by posterity … early Islamic modernism.* Hadijah Rahmat, interview with National Museum.

80   *Some of this reaction derives from … government of Queen Victoria).* Hikayat Abdullah, A. H. Hill (trans.), pp. 264–271.

80   *For example, though Hussein's obesity … would have us believe).* Ibid., pp. 218–219.

81   *'Was there not a time' … 'only in name'.* Ibid., pp. 270–271.

81   *For in such a transitory place… 'of a stone you sink'.* Ibid., p. 163.

EMPORIUM

84   *On 6 February 1833 … 'the circuit of a few miles'.* George Windsor Earl, *The Eastern Seas, or, Voyages and Adventures in the Indian Archipelago, in 1832-33-34*, London: W. H. Allen, 1837, pp. 144, 345 and 360.

85   *Earl had witnessed … European sailing ships.* Turnbull, *History of Singapore*, p. 38.

86   *In 1833, Earl had passed through … Chinese labourers per year.* Earl, pp. 344, 145, 635 and 637.

87   *The Bugis trading fleet … any dispute developed.* Turnbull, *History of Singapore*, pp. 38–39.

89   *Singapore had emerged as the crucial 'hinge' … more Straits produce.* Anthony Reid, interview with the National Museum of Singapore, 2006.

89   *In Singapore, males outnumbered … unregulated commercial development.* Earl, pp. 362 and 369.

90   *In the 1840s, the town's European merchants ... 'of importance and prosperity'.* G. F. Davidson, *Trade and Travel in the Far East*, London: Madden & Malcolm, 1846, p. 69, cited in Turnbull, *History of Singapore*, p. 42.

90   *In the 1850s, the port's economic growth ... 15 years before.* Wong Lin Ken, *The Trade of Singapore, 1819–69*, Singapore: Malayan Branch of the Royal Asiatic Society, 1960, p. 295; Turnbull, *History of Singapore*, p. 15.

91   *In 1866, local Chinese merchants ... two-thirds of the population* Song Ong Siang, *One Hundred Years' History of the Chinese in Singapore*, Singapore: Oxford University Press, 1984 (originally published in London: J. Murray, 1923), p. 119; Turnbull, *History of Singapore*, p. 36.

91   *The bulk of the Chinese population ... 'weighing the goods'.* Turnbull, *History of Singapore*, p. 36; Earl, p. 363.

92   *Generally, Europeans received trade goods ... 'the most successful Chinese'.* Turnbull, *History of Singapore*, pp. 39–40.

93   *Born in Melaka ... 'not enjoyed similar advantages'.* Song, p. 66.

94   *Contrary to the common assumption ... a gunpowder magazine.* Mark Ravinder Frost, 'Transcultural Diaspora: The Straits Chinese in Singapore, 1819–1918', Asia Research Institute Working Paper Series No. 10, 2003, especially pp. 8–9, 9n.

95   *Contrary to the practice in most parts of China ... a stupid son-in-law.* See Ian Proudfoot, *Early Malay Printed Books*, Kuala Lumpur: University of Malaya, 1993, p. 564.

95   *Tan is widely remembered ... all Chinese in Singapore.* Song, p. 63.

96   *J. D. Vaughan ... Lord Mayor's Show.* J. D. Vaughan, *The Manners and Customs of the Chinese of the Straits Settlements*, Singapore: Oxford University Press, 1985 (originally published in 1879), p. 49.

96   *Tan, himself, was involved ... 'of the same colour'.* *Singapore Free Press*, 23 April 1840, cited in Buckley, pp. 345–346.

97   *Pageantry such as this ... Tan Kim Seng.* Song, pp. 46 and 66.

98   *As a final note on Tan Tock Seng ... expected it of him.* See Lee Poh Ping, *Chinese Society in 19th Century Singapore*, Kuala Lumpur: Oxford University Press, 1978, pp. 46–47. Tan is reported to have made these comments in a conversation with the missionary J. Stronach.

98   *The life of Seah Eu Chin ... about his early career.* Song, pp. 19–20.

99   *Seah's advantage from the outset ... the island's 'Gambier King'* Song, p. 20; Buckley, p. 151.

99   *In 1838, he married the daughter ... 'the emperor is Seah'.* Frost, pp. 8–9; David K.Y. Chng, *Heroic Images of Ming Loyalists: A Study of the Spirit Tablets of the Ghee Hin Kongsi Leaders in Singapore*, Singapore: Singapore Society of Asian Studies, 1999, p. 73.

100 *But sadly, whereas gambier ... once pristine ecosystem.* Buckley, pp. 219–221 and 362. For an analysis of colonial attitudes towards animal encounters in Singapore and Malaya, see also Kevin Chua, 'The Tiger and the Theodolite: George Coleman's Dream of Extinction', in *Forum on Contemporary Art & Society*, 6, 2007, pp. 124–149.

100 *During the island-wide Hokkein-Teochew riots ... end the fighting.* Song, p. 21.

100 *Two years later ... for its alleged iniquity.* Buckley, pp. 575–577.

101 *Indeed, a well known portrait ... honorary police magistrate.* Song, p. 17f and pp. 20–21; Frost, p. 15.

101 *By which time ... come full circle.* Song, pp. 20 and 22.

101 *Like Tan and Seah, Aljunied ... Islamic burial ground.* Buckley, p. 563.

101 *As an Arab, Aljunied belonged ... trade networks with him.* William Gervase Clarence-Smith, 'Middle Eastern entrepreneurs in Southeast Asia, c1750-c1940', London: School of Oriental and African Studies, 1998, p. 11. <http://www.eh.net/XIIICongress/cd/papers/10Clarence-Smith301.pdf> Accessed on 16 March 2009; Turnbull, *History of Singapore*, p. 14.

102 *Writing in 1886, Dutch scholar ... 'in the Far East.'* L. W. C. van den Berg, *Le Hadhramout Et Les Colonies Arabes Dans l'Archipel Indien* Batavia: Imprimerie du Gouvemement, 1886, cited in William R. Roff, *The Origins of Malay Nationalism* Kuala Lumpur: Oxford University Press, 1994 (originally published in Singapore: University of Malaya Press, 1967), p. 40.

102 *For Aljunied, his personal wealth ... eventually to be rebuilt.* Clarence-Smith, pp. 7–8; Buckley, pp. 460–461.

102 *From the mid-19th century ... ruler of Mecca.* Clarence-Smith, pp. 11–13.

104 *It began with the lines ... 'Visit our port and the truth you will know'.* This translation is by Alfian Sa'at and Mark Ravinder Frost with the additional assistance of Dr Ian Proudfoot of the Australian National University. The original Malay version of the *Syair Dagang Berjual* has been published in Muhammad Haji Salleh, *Syair Tantagan Singapura Abad Kesembilan Belas*, Kuala Lumpur: Dewan Bahasa dan Pustaka, 1994. Ian Proudfoot has also published an alternative English translation in 'Abdullah vs Siami: Early Malay Edicts on British Justice', in *Journal of the Malaysian Branch of the Royal Asiatic Society*, 80(1):1–16, 2007.

108 *Little is known about him ... scribe employed by Raffles.* For recent research on Siami see John Bastin, 'Abdullah vs Siami', in *Journal of the Malaysian Branch of the Royal Asiatic Society*, 81(1):1–6, 2008.

109 *'During the attack ... brought back the news'.* Ali Haji ibn Ahmad, p. 262.

109 *Our traveller-turned-author George Earl ... 'plantations in the interior'.* Earl, pp. 384–385.

110 *Charles Burton Buckley ... 'and speedy retribution'.* Buckley, pp. 195 and 208–209.

111 *The* Singapore Free Press *reported ... 'a valuable acquisition to them'.* For the full account, Ibid., pp. 278–279.

111 *Buckley went further ... 'the Malay habits'.* Ibid., p. 276; Raffles's letter to Lord Minto on 10 June 1811, cited in Buckley, p. 281. For the full context of the letter, see Wurtzburg, p. 153.

111 *Historian Carl Trocki ... 'one river mouth to another'.* Carl A. Trocki, *Prince of Pirates: The Temenggongs and the development of Johor and Singapore, 1784–1885*, Singapore: Singapore University Press, 1979, pp. xvi–xvii.

111 *Since Malay sea captains ... no fixed abodes.* Ibid., pp. 56–57.

112 *In a further blow ... the port and its population.* Ibid., pp. 58–59.

112 *Historian Nicholas Tarling ... easily turn violent.* Nicholas Tarling, *British Policy in the Malay Peninsula and Archipelago, 1824–1871*, Kuala Lumpur: Oxford University Press, 1969, pp. 14–15, cited in Trocki, pp. 64–65.

112 *In the eyes of the Dutch ... heir to Johor-Riau-Lingga.* Trocki, p. 45.

113 *On 23 April 1835 ... 'move the vessel as it was ordered'.* Buckley, pp. 281 and 282.

114 *The Tuhfat Al-Nafis relates ... 'come and act like this'.* Ali Haji ibn Ahmad, pp. 269–271.

114 *One of the better known ... as a Malay trader.* Buckley, p. 279.

114 *More famous still ... vanquished foes 'as trophies'.* Henry Keppel and James Brooke, *The Expedition to Borneo of H.M.S. Dido*, Singapore: Oxford University Press, 1991 (originally published 1846), vol. 2, pp. 67–68.

115 *In 1846 the* Singapore Free Press *explicitly ... 'that quarter and Singapore'.* *Singapore Free Press*, 4 August 1846, cited in Trocki, p. 87.

115 *After a second expedition ... of any wrongdoing.* Nicholas Tarling, *Piracy and Politics in the Malay World: A Study of British Imperialism in Nineteenth-Century South-East Asia*, Singapore: D. Moore, 1963, pp. 143–144.

115 *When his father died ... become a 'pirate'.* Trocki, pp. 44 and 61.

115 *In 1835, the English press ... be maintained on his activities.* *Singapore Free Press*, 12 November 1835, cited in Trocki, p. 66.

116 *Typically for his time, Governor George Bonham ... 'which take place in the neighbourhood'.* Straits Settlements Records, vol. R3, Bonham to Prinsep, 23 April 1835, cited in Trocki, p. 67.

116 *When the 1835 petition ... to scuttle the plan.* C. M. Turnbull, *The Straits Settlements 1826–1867: Indian Presidency to Crown Colony*, London: The Athlone Press, 1972, p. 191. Cited in Trocki, p. 68.

116 *In return for Bonham's assurances ... on any terms that the Temenggong chose.* Trocki, pp. 69–72 and 76–77.

117 *At the same time his family line ... Johor's new Sultan.* R.O. Winstedt, 'A History of Johore (1365–1895 AD)', in *Journal of the Malayan Branch of the Royal Asiatic Society*, 10(3):92–94, 1932; W. E. Maxwell and W. S. Gibson, *Treaties and Engagements Affecting the Malay States and Borneo*, London: J. Truscott, 1924, p. 125. Both are cited in Trocki, p. 108, 187.

117 *Read wryly observed ... 'at no price at all'.* Quoted in Trocki, p. 87.

119 *Coleman was also responsible ... 'impervious to the riotous and excessive East'.* See Jane Beamish and Jane Ferguson, *History of Singapore Architecture: The Making of a City*, Singapore: Graham Brash, 1985, pp. 19–24, 25–46 and 24.

123 *On 18 August 1824 ... 'of a cathedral and government house'.*
J. F. A. McNair, *Prisoners Their Own Warders,* London: Archibald
Constable and Co., 1899, pp. 38–39, and 91–92.

123 *The shiny white interiors ... even kept insects away.* Beamish and
Ferguson, p. 36.

124 *McNair, at least, was aware ... probably not an inexact description.*
McNair, pp. 8–9 and 157.

124 *On arrival, the convicts were housed ... the title of his history,*
Prisoners Their Own Warders). Ibid., pp. 39–42, 49–53 and 68–70.

125 *The authorities divided them into six classes ... live out the remainder
of their lives in comfort.* Ibid., pp. 84–88.

126 *Furthermore, when 'the presence of a body of men' ... 'head scare'
two years later (see Chapter 9).* Ibid., pp. 43–44.

126 *Eventually, what one colonial official ... 'are full of hatred and
revenge'.* Ibid., p. 10; Blundell is quoted in Anand A. Yang, Indian
Convict Workers in Southeast Asia in the Late Eighteenth and Early
Nineteenth Centuries, in *Journal of World History,* 14(2):206, 2003.

126 *'Fate willed it that my destiny ... 'Assembly Room, for balls and
meetings'.* William H. Read, *Play and Politics: Recollection of Malaya,*
London: Wells, Gardner, Darton and Co, 1900, pp. 1 and 4-6; Turnbull,
History of Singapore, p. 65.

127 *The then governor ... 'without dignity or moderation'.* Quoted in
Read, p. 7.

127 *As Buckley put it ... 'from India in many respects'.* Buckley, p. 754.

128 *Governor Bonham was well liked ... rival British base in China.* See
Turnbull, *History of Singapore,* pp. 67–75; Buckley, pp. 754–780.

PORT–CITY

132 *In 1871, Singapore numbered ... of any modern city – the suburbs.*
Brenda S. A. Yeoh, *Contesting Space in Colonial Singapore: Power
Relations and the Urban Built Environment,* Singapore: Singapore
University Press, 2003, pp. 35, 45–46 and 37.

134 *Well into the 20th century ... Australia and New Zealand.* Turnbull,
History of Singapore, pp. 88 and 91–92.

134 *To the writer Walter Del Mar ... 'that soon fills the bunkers'.* Walter
Del Mar, *Around the World Through Japan,* London: Adam and Charles
Black, 1904, pp. 63–68, reprinted in John Bastin (comp.), *Travellers'
Singapore,* Kuala Lumpur: Oxford University Press, 1994, pp. 155–157.

134 *Meanwhile, Singapore was developing ... Hongkong and Shanghai
Banking Corporation.* Turnbull, *History of Singapore,* p. 90. The lines
from Kipling are from his poem, 'The Deep-Sea Cables' (1896).

135 *'Charing Cross of the East'.* Isabella Bird, 'Sketches in the Malay
Peninsula', in *The Leisure Hour,* London, 1883, pp. 17–19, reprinted in
Bastin (comp.), *Travellers' Singapore,* p. 129.

135 *'Clapham Junction of the East'.* Frank Swettenham, *British Malaya:
An Account of the Origin and Progress of British Influence in Malaya,*
London: G. Allen & Unwin, 1948, p. 342, cited in Turnbull, *History of
Singapore,* p. 123.

135 *'Liverpool of the East'.* Frederick William Burbidge, *The Gardens of
the Sun,* London: John Murray, 1880, pp. 14–19, reprinted in Bastin
(comp.), *Travellers' Singapore,* p. 118.

135 *'Oban of the East'.* Isabella Bird, reprinted in Bastin (comp.),
Travellers' Singapore, p. 129.

136 *Newspapers kept them in touch ... 'I'm writing for the mail!'.* Isabella
L. Bird, *The Golden Chersonese* (1883), reprinted in Michael Wise and
Mun Him Wise (comps.), *Travellers' Tales of Old Singapore,* Singapore:
Times Books International, 1985, pp. 118–119.

137 *Consider the experience ... and collar 'pulpy'.* William T. Hornaday,
Two Years in the Jungle, New York: Charles Scribner's Sons, 1885, pp.
2–9; Frederick William Burbidge, *The Gardens of the Sun,* both are
reprinted in Bastin (comp.), *Travellers' Singapore,* pp. 123 and 119.

140 *According to the Reverend G. M. Reith ... his handbook for visitors.*
G. M. Reith, *Handbook to Singapore,* 1892, reprinted in Wise and Wise
(comps.), p. 137.

140 *According to Charles Walter Kinloch ... 'late hour in the night'.*
Charles Walter Kinloch, *Rambles in Java and the Straits in 1852,*
London: Simpkin, Marshall and Co., 1853, pp. 11–18, reprinted in
Bastin (comp.), *Travellers' Singapore,* p. 71.

140 *In that same decade, the American businessman George Francis
Train ... 'that is put before him'.* George Francis Train, *An American
Merchant in Europe, Asia and Australasia,* New York: G. P. Putnam &
Co., 1857, pp. 66–71; William Walker, *Jottings of an Invalid in Search
of Health,* Bombay: Times of India Office, 1865, pp. 158–161, both are
reprinted in Bastin (comp.), *Travellers' Singapore,* p. 75 and 88.

141 *Though some visitors still complained ... best he'd ever had.* Frank
Vincent, *The Land of the White Elephant,* New York: Harper &
Brothers, 1874; R. V. K. Applin, *Across the Seven Seas,* London:
Chapman & Hall Ltd., 1937, pp. 50–52, both are reprinted in Bastin
(comp.), *Travellers' Singapore,* p. 109 and 144.

141 *Even by the 1860s, John Cameron ... 'does not include a dinner'.*
John Cameron, *Our Tropical Possessions in Malayan India,* London:
Smith, Elder, 1865, pp. 287–303, reprinted in Bastin (comp.), *Travellers'
Singapore,* pp. 90–98.

142 *William Hornaday (the American we met earlier) ... 'acquaintance
of a gentleman ...'* Hornaday reprinted in Bastin (comp.), *Travellers'
Singapore,* pp. 125–126.

142 *'The servant question is not so pressing' ... 'a sort of social pariah'.*
Ethel Colquhoun, *Two on Their Travels,* London: William Heinemann,
1902, pp. 8–16, reprinted in Bastin (comp.), *Travellers' Singapore,* pp.
172–174.

143 *Moreover, as tourist C. D. MacKellar discovered ... 'I wonder why?'*
C. D. MacKellar, *Scented Isles and Coral Gardens,* 1912, reprinted in
Wise and Wise (comps.), pp. 149–150.

146 *The pinnacle of de Silva's career ... 'of these [Straits] Settlements'.*
Singapore Free Press, 20 April 1901.

146 *Though their Royal Highnesses spent only three days ... 'and never
see equalled'.* Ibid., 23 and 24 April 1901.

146 *As the* Singapore Free Press *reported ... 'with neat attap roof'.* Ibid.,
24 April 1901.

146 *At the Town Hall ... de Silva and Dr Lim.* The Straits Times, 23 April
1901.

146 *For British officials it helped ... 'until it overflowed the table'.* William
Maxwell, *With the 'Ophir' round the Empire: An Account of the Tour
of the Prince and Princess of Wales 1901,* London: Cassell and Co.,
1902, p. 61.

147 *B.P. de Silva and Lim Boon Keng did ... formally welcome them.*
Singapore Free Press, 23 April 1901.

147 *As his biographer ... he had become accustomed.* Richard Boyle, *B.P.
de Silva: The Royal Jeweller of South-east Asia,* Singapore: B. P. de
Silva Investments, 1989, p. 43.

147 *His first commission by royal appointment ... her diamond jubilee in
1897.* Ibid., pp. 43–46.

148 *And as was to be expected, the British Empire ... while he remained
overseas.* Ibid., pp. 65–68.

149 *However, the Chinese traveller Li Chung Chu ... 'and dirt are hidden'.*
Li Chung Chu, *A Description of Singapore in 1887,* Chang Chin Chiang
(trans.), 1895, reprinted in Wise and Wise (comps.), p. 134.

149 *Between 1840 and 1900 ... South America and Africa.* Ronald Takaki,
Strangers From a Different Shore: A History of Asian Americans,
Boston: Little, Brown and Company, 1989, p. 32.

150 *Most Chinese migrants came from ... the island of Hainan.* Sucheng
Chan, *Asian Americans: An Interpretive History,* New York: Twayne
Publishers, 1991, p. 5.

150 *Throughout the 19th century ... Going overseas was a lifeline.*
Geoffrey Wade, interview with the National Museum of Singapore,
2006.

151 *Certain scholars, however, are less convinced ... by itself, might
explain.* See especially Adam McKeown, 'Conceptualising Chinese
Diasporas, 1842 to 1949', *Journal of Asian Studies,* 58(2):306–337,
1999.

151 *A poor Chinese migrant who arrived in Singapore ... bad health or
further debt.* James Francis Warren, *Rickshaw Coolie: a people's
history of Singapore, 1880-1940,* Singapore: Oxford University Press,
1986, p. 16.

151 *Migrants who could afford it ... known today as 'chain migration'.*
See Ibid., p. 35.

151 *By the 1890s, the number of these migrants ... represented his one
true home.* Wang Gungwu, interview with the National Museum of
Singapore, 2006.

152 *Yet the Chinese came because ... 'the promise of a future'.* Warren, *Rickshaw Coolie*, p. viii.

152 *In Singapore and the other Straits Settlements ... dominant mode of transport.* Ibid., pp. 14–15.

153 *Rickshaws even had a starring role ... 'thrown out at any moment.'* *Singapore Free Press*, 24 April 1901; Edwin A. Brown, *Indiscreet Memories*, London: Kelly & Walsh, 1935, pp. 55–56, cited in Warren, *Rickshaw Coolie*, p. 71.

153 *For most European arrivals ... at Johnston Pier.* Ibid., p. 159.

153 *'It is difficult to recapture ... a smartly stepping horse.'* Richard John Hamilton Sidney, *Malay land 'Tanah Melayu'; some phases of life in modern British Malaya*, London: C. Palmer, 1926, p. 30, cited in Warren, *Rickshaw Coolie*, p. 158.

153 *To maintain such a pace ... 'pullers in those days.'* Ibid., pp. 25, 26, 39, 144 and 185.

153 *Traffic in Singapore ... 'tended to ignore both.'* Ibid., pp. 62–65.

153 *A puller's day might take him ... 'by Tanjong Pagar Road.'* Ibid., pp. 69–70, 72 and 159.

154 *As well as scalding heat ... earn a day's living* Ibid., pp. 47 and 140.

154 *For all his trouble ... if they were cheated or abused.* Ibid., pp. 318 and 168–170.

155 *With the occupational hazards ... 'dignity and sanctity'.* *The Straits Times* (c.1911), cited in Warren, *Rickshaw Coolie*, p. 53.

155 *Apart from out of basic economic necessity ... work for lower wages.* Ibid., pp. 21, 35 and 36.

155 *Rickshaw owners had anything from ... menial labourers or shop coolies.* Ibid., pp. 21, 22, 28–31, 45 and 47.

155 *'Life like this ... in opium fumes.'* For the full poem, see G.G.D., *The Straits Times Annual* (1938), cited in Warren, *Rickshaw Coolie*, p. xxi.

156 *Rickshaw coolies were hardly ... a superb night's sleep.* Ibid., pp. 240 and 241.

156 *Beginning with Singapore's first Resident ... to be given up.* For a detailed look at the opium trade in Singapore, see Carl A. Trocki, *Opium and Empire: Chinese Society in Colonial Singapore, 1800-1910*, New York: Cornell University Press, 1990.

156 *During the first century of colonial rule ... and steamship businesses.* Ibid., p. 2; Carl A. Trocki, *Opium, Empire and the Global Political Economy: A Study of the Asian Opium Trade 1750-1950*, New York: Routledge, 1999, p. 140.

157 *The colonial government belatedly acknowledged ... twice that amount.* Trocki, *Opium and Empire*, p. 67; Trocki, *Opium, Empire and the Global Political Economy*, pp. 143–144; Warren, *Rickshaw Coolie*, pp. 44, 199, 240–241.

157 *'We found these shops established ... subject peoples under its rule.'* Ellen N. La Motte, *The Opium Monopoly*, New York: Macmillan, 1920, p. xi. <http://www.druglibrary.org/Schaffer/history/om/omintro.htm> Accessed on 31 March 2009.

157 *The enduring 19th-century image ... 'Why should he be ashamed?'* Trocki, *Opium and Empire*, p. 1; La Motte, *The Opium Monopoly*, pp. 19–20.

158 *Specifically, they were led by the English-educated ... operate the centre out of their premises.* Turnbull, *History of Singapore*, p. 114.

158 *It was not until after 1920 ... in certain parts of the city* Carl Trocki, *Opium and Empire*, p. 76, 215.

158 *In 1887, Li Chung Chu ... 'brought up in Singapore.'* Li Chung Chu, reprinted in Wise and Wise (comps.), p. 134.

159 *In 1860, there was only one female ... till after World War I.* James Francis Warren, *Ah Ku and Karayuki-san: Prostitution in Singapore, 1870-1940*, Singapore: Oxford University Press, 1993, p. 34.

159 Karayuki-san, *or Japanese prostitutes ... and Spring Streets in Chinatown.* Ibid., pp. 40 and 46.

159 *'Under the verandah ... twenty years of age.'* *Fukuoka Nichinichi Shimbun*, 25 May 1910, cited in Warren, *Ah Ku and Karayuki-san*, p. 41.

159 *By 1900, the* karayuki-san *in Singapore ... usually as prostitutes.* Warren, *Ah Ku and Karayuki-san*, pp. viii, 3, 27–29 and 32.

159 *To put it bluntly, with so few occupations ... domestic servant or female coolie.* Ibid., p. 35.

159 *'I have never been happier ... meat with my meals.'* *Tokyo Hinode Shimbun*, 22 November 1902, cited in Ibid., p. 240.

160 *Theirs was a patriarchal society ... the* karayuki-san's *hardest.* Ibid., pp. 32, 35, 62 , 85 and 267.

160 *In 1905, Singapore had 109 Japanese brothels ... European soldiers and sailors.* Ibid., pp. 46, 47, 266 and 272.

161 *Each* karayuki-san *saw up to eight ... in every commodified sense, of their zegen.* Ibid., pp. 61, 214, 215 and 275.

161 *In such trying circumstances ... well and healthy.* Ibid., pp. 227–229 and 250.

161 *It is from these photographs ... 'and "Malay Street"'.* Ibid., pp. 252; René Onraet, *Singapore: A Police Background*, London: Dorothy Crisp and Company, 1947, p. 122.

161 *By 1919, Japan's imperial government ... the island's Japanese cemetery.* Cited in Warren, *Ah Ku and Karayuki-san*, pp. 42, 164 and 218. Warren notes that more than 425 women are 'buried there, whose lives spanned the Meiji-Taisho periods, 1868-1925, and whose birthplaces are stated on their headstones, ... mostly from the Kyushu region'.

162 *Consequently, much of Singapore Town... deposited in market gardens).* Turnbull, *History of Singapore*, p. 115. For more details on British and Asian attitudes to sanitation and municipal responsibilities, see Yeoh, pp. 85–89 and 101–123.

163 *As an official commission in 1875 ... 'a government in them or not.'* Turnbull, *History of Singapore*, p. 76.

163 *In 1876, the colonial government decided ... they had experienced previously.* Robert Nicholas Jackson, *Pickering, Protector of Chinese*, Kuala Lumpur: Oxford University Press, 1965, pp. 54–59.

164 *However, in 1888 a government decision ... in Singapore to a standstill.* See Yeoh, pp. 250–253.

164 *Colonial officials believed that such riots ... to extend their protection rackets.* Irene Lim, *Secret Societies in Singapore: Featuring the William Stirling Collection*, Singapore: Singapore History Museum, 1999, pp. 10–13 and 22–23.

165 *Calls for the British ... was a 'mere farce'.* Turnbull, *History of Singapore*, p. 80; Jackson, p. 52.

165 *In 1879, William Pickering read a paper ... pin-pricks of their own blood.* Jackson, pp. 74–76.

166 *In 1872, seven years before ... Formosa (today's Taiwan).* Ibid., p. 18.

166 *Pickering discovered that local translators ... the ironic title of "big dogs".'* Ibid., pp. 18–19.

168 *However, his first clear encounter ... 'what they doubtless thought was Chinese music.'* J. D. Vaughn, *Manners and Customs of the Chinese in the Straits Settlements*, Kuala Lumpur, Oxford University Press, 1971, p. 40, cited in Jackson, p. 28.

169 *In 1877, he and Major Dunlop ... waiting in the harbour.* Ibid., p. 63.

169 *In May 1877, three months after ... the first Protector of Chinese.* Ibid., pp. 64–65.

170 *The Protectorate began its work ... had been significantly curtailed.* Ibid., pp. 68–70.

170 *His plan was simple ... 'coincide with their own wishes'.* Ibid., pp. 77–83.

172 *In the 1880s, official reports reveal ... a complaint with the police.* Ibid., pp. 99–101.

173 *'Nothing is more likely ... various districts of the Settlements.'* Ibid., p. 103.

173 *The afternoon edition of the* Straits Times *... dozen or so Protectorate staff.* Ibid., p. 106.

173 *In 1889, a physician's report ... was permanently retired.* Ibid., p. 111 and 113.

173 *In 1889, and much to Pickering's displeasure ... had been known to everyone.* Turnbull, *History of Singapore*, p. 89; Jackson, p. 112.

MODERN TIMES

178 *Nonetheless, many people in Singapore ... especially popular with rickshaw coolies).* On Chaplin's popularity amongst Singapore's rickshaw coolies see H. Norden, *From Golden Gate to Golden Sun: A Record of Travel and Observation in Siam and Malaya*, London: Witherby, 1923, pp. 61-63. Reprinted in Bastin (comp.), *Travellers' Singapore*, pp. 198–199.

179 *In 1896, the first motorcar ... secret societies were under heavy surveillance.* This survey of the city's modernisation is drawn largely from Turnbull, *History of Singapore*, pp. 111–113, 128–29, 131, 136–38 and 140–41; see also Yeoh, pp. 28–77.

182 *Following the appointment of the Straits Settlements' first Inspector of Schools ... increasing its expenditure on education overall.* See Lim Peng Han, 'Singapore: an Emerging Centre of 19th Century Malay School Book Printing and Publishing in the Straits Settlements, 1819–1899', *Biblioasia*, 4(4):4–11, 2009; Turnbull, *History of Singapore*, pp. 115–18. Lim's research supersedes Turnbull's earlier assertion concerning the lack of Malay education in late 19th-century Singapore.

182 *For example, at the Madrasah Alsagoff ... and 1,000 were placed at Tamil-language schools.* See *Straits Budget*, 24 April 1913; Song, pp. 192–193; Turnbull, *History of Singapore*, p. 141.

183 *Writing in his memoirs in the early 1940s ... chemistry and physics were made available.* A. H. C. Ward, Raymond W. Chu and Janet Salaff (eds.), *The Memoirs of Tan Kah Kee*, Singapore: Singapore University Press, 1994, p. 39; C. F. Yong, *Tan Kah Kee: The Making of an Overseas Chinese Legend*, Singapore: Oxford University Press, 1987, p. 90.

184 *Mandarin, or as it was called ... main medium of instruction.* Kion Chin Eng, 'The Teaching of Kuan Hua in Singapore', *Straits Chinese Magazine* 11(2):105–108, 1907.

185 *Quoting from what he said was a 'Western proverb' ... to be a major understatement.* Ward et al. (eds.), p. 54; see also Yong, p. 87.

185 *According to his principal biographer ... power and influence that might entail.* Yong, pp. 83–88.

186 *Explaining why he continued to fund ... 'cause harm to society.'* Ward et al. (eds.), pp. 334–345.

186 *Tan's sense of obligation ... a national university at Amoy.* Tan Kah Kee provides a detailed account of his educational philanthropy in China in his memoirs.

187 *In 1894, reports began to circulate ... 'very often scoff at Christianity itself.'* See *Daily Advertiser*, 'Can there be such a thing as non-sectarian education?', 2 January 1894; see also, in the same paper, readers' letters from 15, 16, 17 and 24 February 1894.

188 *From textbooks and other school publications we learn ... 'Lead us all in reforming the world'.* 幼稚读本:看图识字 [*Elementary Picture Book*], China: Shanghai Fuzhou Guangyi Shuju, 1937; 南洋华侨小学四适用 [*Nanyang Chinese School Reader*], Hong Kong: The Commercial Press, 1939; 新南洋华侨中学校办工厂1929年毕业 [*Yearbook for The Chinese High School of Singapore*], Singapore: The Chinese High School, 1929; 星洲静方女校筹款建校及概记特刊 [*Cheng Fong School Fund Raising Publication*], Singapore: Cheng Fong School, 1938; 复兴国语教科书 [*Chinese Book Reader*], Hong Kong: The Commercial Press, 1941. These books are in the collection of the National Museum of Singapore.

190 *In 1900, the Straits Times reported an evening's entertainment ... impersonation of a 'negro minstrel'.* *The Straits Times*, 3 March 1900.

191 *Records of Lim's Philomathic Society tell us ... 'between the progressive party and the conservatives'.* *Straits Chinese Magazine*, 1(3):113, 1897.

191 *The step Lim and his associates chose ... mostly merchants, doctors, journalists and government servants.* See Yen Ching Hwang, *Community and Politics: The Chinese in Colonial Singapore and Malaysia*, Singapore: Times Academic Press, 1995, pp. 213–16; Yeap Chong Leng, 'Lim Boon Keng, Khoo Seok Wan and the Chinese Philomathic Society', in *Asian Culture*, 27:121–145, 2003 (in Chinese).

192 *'And when the Straits-born Chinese with proper qualifications ... in evidence for some years in China.'* Lim Boon Keng, 'The Role of the Baba in the Development of China', in *Straits Chinese Magazine*, 7(3):98 and 100, 1903.

192 *'The motto of the Singapore Revolutionary Alliance,' ... joined up for a variety of reasons.* See C. F. Yong and R. B. McKenna, *The Kuomintang Movement in British Malaya*, Singapore: Singapore University Press, 1990, pp. 7–29. Sun's words to his new revolutionary recruits are recorded in Singapore's Sun Yatsen Nanyang Memorial Hall (housed in the former villa belonging to Teo Eng Hock's family off Balestier Road). See <http://www.wanqingyuan.com.sg/english/onceupon/visits.html> Last accessed 31 March 2009.

194 *In 1914, this second option became suddenly less attractive ... to walk out of the party in protest.* See Yong and McKenna, pp. 7–29.

194 *Some years later, he told a public meeting ... 'the sole sign of born rulers and administrators.'* *Straits Echo*, 10 May 1912.

195 *Following the introduction of the Chinese nationality law in 1929 ... an equal footing with the European.* See Chua Ai Lin, 'Negotiating National Identity: The English-Speaking Domiciled Communities in Singapore, 1930-1941', Unpublished M. Phil. Dissertation, 2001, pp. 171–173.

196 *As council member Tan Cheng Lock ... just a fraction of that number.* Proceedings of the Straits Settlements Legislative Council, 3 November 1924, p. 115.

196 *Eunos complained that the Malay boy ... from his fellow Asian councillors.* Proceedings of the Straits Settlements Legislative Council, 30 June 1924, pp. 64–65; 3 July 1929, pp. 73 and 84–85; see also 3 November 1924, pp. 114–115.

197 *In describing Malays as the 'original sons of the soil' ... always lived under a British administration.* Mark Emmanuel, interview with the National Museum of Singapore, 2006; see also Anthony Milner, *The Invention of Politics in Colonial Malaya*, Cambridge: Cambridge University Press, 2002, pp. 90–107.

199 *The Straits Settlements still remained politically separate ... official capital of the Federation was Kuala Lumpur.)* See Turnbull, *History of Singapore*, pp. 156–157.

200 *To echo the thoughts of the famous scholar Benedict Anderson ... in all its breadth, colour and remarkable diversity.* Benedict Anderson, *Imagined Communities: Reflections on the Origin and Spread of Nationalism*, London: Verso, 1991, pp. 114–115 and 121–122.

200 *In 1914, the Malaya Tribune, a new English-language paper ... an actual readership of perhaps twice that figure.* See letters from readers in early editions of the *Malaya Tribune*, especially 2 and 3 January 1914; see also Chua, pp. 51–55.

201 *In the early 1930s, discussions in the Tribune ... to rob Malays of their national inheritance.* See Chua, pp. 58–63, 79–90 and 94–95.

203 *In 1930, May Wong, the American-educated wife ... "I'm sorry I am not a circus performer!"* May Wong, interview with the National Archives of Singapore.

204 *The presence of women in Singapore ... 200,000 of these women arrived in Singapore and Malaya* Ann Wee, interview with the National Museum of Singapore, 2006.

206 *In Cantonese, the amah's job description ... 'how happy it was.'* Leong Ah Hoe, interview with the National Archives of Singapore, translated from the Cantonese by Leow Puay Tin and Hooi Kok Kuang; see also Julian Davison, *One for the Road and Other Stories*, Singapore: Topographica, 2001, pp. 11 and 14.

206 *Former amah Wong Ah Yoke explained ... 'after she has sor hei.'* Wong Ah Yoke, interview with the National Archives of Singapore, translated from the Cantonese by Leow Puay Tin and Hooi Kok Kuang.

207 *May Wong encountered this seedier reality ... 'brought in to be a slave girl.'* May Wong, interview with National Archives.

207 *Nonetheless, as one Australian missionary remembered ... 'get hard usage all their lives.'* Theodore R. Doraisamy (ed.), *Sophia Blackmore in Singapore: Educational and Missionary Pioneer, 1887–1927*, Singapore: Methodist Church of Singapore, 1987, p. 19.

208 *Since rescued girls could not ... older girls might make a marriage match.* May Wong, interview with National Archives.

208 *According to the society's Malayan records ... to Singapore and Malaya they stayed.* Tan Liok Ee, 'Locating Chinese Women in Malaysian History', in Abu Talib Ahmad and Tan Liok Ee (eds.), *New Terrains in Southeast Asian History*, Singapore: Singapore University Press, 2003, pp. 354–384.

208 *Their modern education had begun ... a woman already in her 30s.* Doraisamy (ed.), pp. 16, 21 and 22.

209 *In 1899, Lim Boon Keng and Song Ong Siang ... 'direction and control of their own people.'* 'Singapore Chinese Girls' School', in *Straits Chinese Magazine*, 3(10):70–71, 1899.

209 *As an article in the Straits Chinese Magazine made clear ... 'or warning with intelligence and reason ...'* 'The Singapore Chinese Girls' School (A Historical Sketch)', in *Straits Chinese Magazine*, 11(4):166–167, 1907.

210 *While letters to the Straits Times characterised ... such as chap-ji-ki and che-ki.* Cited in Neo Puak Neo, 'Gambling Amongst Our Nyonyas', *Straits Chinese Magazine*, 11(4):151, 1907.

210 *'There is no more absolutely ignorant ... stumbling blocks to real enlightenment.'* Cited in Lim Boon Keng, 'Female Education for Straits Chinese', in *Straits Chinese Magazine*, 11(2):41–42, 1907.

210 *Lim and Song's remedy for ignorance and superstition ... 'sons of Han' and British imperial subjects.* Lim Boon Keng, 'Female Education for Straits Chinese', p. 41.

210 *Lim noted that 'with a few honourable exceptions' ... 'conservative and unreasonably prejudiced policy'.* Ibid., p. 42.

210 *In 1935, Sophia Blackmore could affirm ... well and truly passed.* Doraisamy (ed.), p. 66.

211 *An anecdote from the Anglican Zenana Mission School for Girls ... modern young ladies did.* Chua Ai Lin, interview with the National Museum of Singapore, 2006.

212 *During the 1920s and 1930s ... 'I want to go do the work of a person'.* See David L. Kenley, *New Culture in a New World: The May Fourth Movement and the Chinese Diaspora in Singapore, 1919–1932*, London; New York: Routledge, 2003, pp. 117–121 and 120; see also Tan Liok Ee.

212 *Especially in the 'Women's Corner' column ... 'Instead of being controlled, she rules others.'* These selections are from the *Malaya Tribune*, 31 December 1930, 28 March 1931, 18 April 1931 and 25 April 1931.

213 *Opened by Chinese businessmen from the early 1920s ... 'the open-air cinema or the lane-side hawker.'* *Singapore Free Press*, 27 April 1937. Cited in Jürgen Rudolph, 'Amusements in the Three "Worlds"', in Sanjay Krishnan (ed.), *Looking at Culture*, Singapore: Artres Design & Communications, 1996, p. 22.

213 *Couples took evening strolls ... a parody of European mems.* See Bleackley's account from his book *A Tour in Southern Asia*, London: Bodley Head, 1928, reprinted in Bastin (comp.), *Travellers' Singapore*, pp. 210–212.

214 *Bai Yan and Ye Qing, a husband-and-wife duo ... draw audiences in their thousands.* Ye Qing and Bai Yan, interview with the National Museum of Singapore, 2006, featured in the National Museum of Singapore's History Gallery film *The Worlds' Cabaret*; Yung Sai Shing and Cahn Kwok Bun, 'Leisure, Pleasure and Consumption: Ways of Entertaining Oneself', in Chan Kwok Bun and Tong Chee Kiong (eds.), *Past Times: A Social History of Singapore*, Singapore: Times Editions, 2003, pp. 167 and 168.

215 *Bruce Lockhardt, the British journalist and spy ... 'and tragedies – of life'.* R. H. Bruce Lockhart, *Return to Malaya*, New York: G. P. Putnam's Sons, 1936, reprinted in Wise and Wise (comps.), pp. 239–240.

216 *This was a city in which a man ... 'Support the Northern Expedition'.* See Ban Kah Choon, *Absent History: The Untold History of Special Branch Operations in Singapore, 1915–1942*, Singapore: SNP Media, 2001, pp. 90–91 and 108; *The Straits Times*, 7 April 1927; Mark Emmanuel, interview with National Museum.

216 *Yap Pheng Geck, an English-educated Straits Chinese doctor ... a composer of Chinese nationalist verse.* Yap Pheng Geck, *Scholar, Banker, Gentleman Soldier*, Singapore: Times Book International, 1982, pp. 40–41.

217 *According to a later press report ... 'several people fell mortally wounded.'* Eyewitness account in *The Rangoon Gazette* (undated), cited in *The Sphere*, 1 May 1915, p. 110.

217 *The New York Times ran a full-page pictorial ... 'the number [of mutineers] has been reduced.'* *The New York Times*, 2 May and 25 April 1915.

218 *Outside the wall of Outram Prison ... news of the mutineers' execution.* See R. W. E. Harper and Harry Miller, *Singapore Mutiny*, Singapore: Oxford University Press, 1984, p. 202; Ban, pp. 54–57.

218 *In his biography, Lauterbach claimed ... 'almost beyond belief'.* See Harper and Miller, pp. 8–12, 17, 23 and 29–39.

219 *Their anguished letters home ... 'the increase of Mohammedan's faith ...'* These letters are published in T. R. Sareen, *Secret Documents on Singapore Mutiny, 1915*, New Delhi: Mounto Publishing House, 1995, pp. 718–732.

220 *Special Branch began operations in the Straits Settlements ... any gathering of individuals might turn seditious.* Ban, pp. 72–75 and 80–88.

222 *To Onraet, the number of Chinese migrants ... put it bluntly, 'had gone Red.'* René Onraet, pp. 109–111.

222 *As an example, the methods of policeman Alec Dixon ... he stated it 'merely as fact'.* Alec Dixon, *Singapore Patrol*, London: Harrap, 1935, pp. 140–143.

223 *Onraet, like most of his colleagues ... 'All of it came from China.'* Onraet, p. 109.

223 *Dixon noted that the Hailams ... The second volley killed five and injured eleven.* This account is taken from Dixon, pp. 126–134 and Ban, pp. 103–106.

226 *An ex-Royal Navy ... 'ditched in the harbour'.* Quoted in <http://www.jproc.ca/crypto/typex.html> accessed 18 March 2008.

227 *Dixon recalled that at once handbills ... duty demanded of all loyal subjects by their Emperor.* See Dixon, pp. 134–135; Ban, pp. 103–113 and 135–166.

228 *Journalist Fuji Tatsuki, known to his European colleagues ... 'I thought to myself'.* Tatsuki Fuji, *Singapore Assignment*, Tokyo: Nippon Times, 1943, pp. 3–8, reprinted in Bastin (comp.), *Travellers' Singapore*, pp. 239–242 and 239.

229 *As you turned down Serangoon Road ... sundry shops and eating houses.* See Sharon Siddique and Nirmala Purushotam, *Singapore's Little India: Past, Present and Future*, Singapore: Institute of Southeast Asian Studies, 1982, p. 42.

230 *To enter their kittangi ... their businesses continued as normal.* This account of Chettiar life is drawn from the interview of Subbiah Laksmanan (a fourth-generation Singapore Chettiar) with the National Museum of Singapore, 2006.

FORTRESS

234 *'The Japanese began a landing' ... 'must be extirpated together.'* Winston Churchill, 'Prime Minister Winston Churchill's Broadcast on War with Japan,' 8 December 1941. <http://www.ibiblio.org/pha/policy/1941/411208e.html> Accessed on 31 March 2009.

234 *Three days later, he told Parliament ... 'in the records for thousands of years.'* Winston Churchill, 'Prime Minister Winston Churchill's Review of the War to the House of Commons', 11 December 1941. <http://www.ibiblio.org/pha/policy/1941/411208f.html> Accessed on 31 March 2009.

234 *Even after news of the first Japanese attacks ... 'ever put together anywhere.'* See Turnbull, *History of Singapore*, p. 159.

234 *On the night when Emperor Hirohito's war machine ... 'sleep of the saved and thankful'.* Winston Churchill, *The Second World War* [abridged], London, 1997, pp. 491–492.

235 *Yap Pheng Geck (whom we met briefly ... 'by the very first bomb that dropped'.* Yap, p. 53; see also Christopher Bayly and Tim Harper, *Forgotten Armies: Britain's Asian Empire and the War with Japan*, London: Penguin, 2005, pp. 117–118.

236 *The Japanese Chief of Staff Colonel Tsuji Masanobu ... 'the enemy's front line was captured.'* Masanobu Tsuji, *Singapore, 1941–1942: The Japanese Version of the Malayan Campaign of World War II*, Singapore: Oxford University Press, 1988, pp. 93–96. Tsuji was not actually present at this landing but culled his account from 'reports of staff personnel, officers and men engaged in the fighting and [...] Press correspondents who were present'.

237 *After the war, Lieutenant General Arthur Percival ... 'first sighted on 6 December.'* Arthur Percival, *The War in Malaya*, London: Eyre and Spottiswoode, 1949, p. 298.

237 *For Captain Denis Russell-Roberts, 'Dawn on the 8th' ... 'was to fight this war virtually alone.'* Denis Russell-Roberts, *Spotlight on Singapore*, Isle of Man: Times Press, 1965, pp. 30–35.

239 *On receiving news of the Japanese landings ... 'And it would be all over soon.'* See Noel Barber, *Sinister Twilight*, London: Arrow Books, 1988 (originally published in London, Collins, 1968), p. 28; Elizabeth Choy, interview with the National Archives of Singapore; Lee Kip Lin, interview with the National Archives of Singapore.

240 *Japanese war correspondents described the ensuing battle ... 'which were trying to escape'.* Japanese newspaper reports summarised in Tsuji, pp. 99–101.

240 *The American war correspondent Cecil Brown ... 'They are sucked back.'* Cecil Brown, *Suez to Singapore*, New York: Random House, 1942, pp. 322–328.

242 *It began by explaining the reasons ... 'strike at America where it hurts most.'* Reprinted in Tsuji, pp. 300–303.

244 *According to Colonel Tsuji, Yamashita bore ... from Chinese temples, associations and households.* Tsuji, p. 35. Legend has it that this hoard of treasure, known as 'Yamashita's gold', was taken out of Singapore and Malaya when Yamashita was posted to the Philippines, where it still lies hidden.

244 *On the eve of the invasion he penned ... kiromoni sakuren – a 'driving charge'.* See Bayly and Harper, *Forgotten Armies*, p. 113–114 and 118.

244 *Between these forces and Singapore ... Australian Imperial Forces (AIF).* Brian Farrell, *The Defence and Fall of Singapore, 1940–1942*, Stroud: Tempus, 2005, pp. 415–417.

245 *Colonel Tsuji dismissed the fighting capabilities ... 'no other way than retreat, I assure you.'* Tsuji, pp. 110–112, 125, 166 and 213. For a detailed account of the Japanese drive into Malaya and the fall of Jitra see Farrell, pp. 140–167.

246 *For Captain Mohan Singh, a Sikh officer ... this force would be THE INDIAN NATIONAL ARMY.* Mohan Singh, *Soldier's Contribution to Indian Independence: The Epic of the Indian National Army*, New Delhi: S. Attar Singh, 1974, pp. 58–72.

248 *Towards the end of December, Mustapha was seated ... 'Do not lose your lives in support of the Japanese cause.'* Mustapha Hussain, *Malay Nationalism Before UMNO: The Memoirs of Mustapha Hussain*, K. S. Jomo (ed.), Insun Sony Mustapha (trans.), Kuala Lumpur: Utusan, 2005, pp. 167–193.

251 *Back during the first week of the conflict ... almost caught up with the battle.* Tsuchikane's account, cited here and throughout, is taken from Henry Frei, *Guns of February: Ordinary Japanese Soldiers' Views of the Fall of Singapore, 1941–42*, Singapore: Singapore University Press, 2004, pp. 49–54 and 60–62. Tsuchikane's memoir is published in Japanese as *Shingaporu E No Michi: Aru Kanoe Hei No Kiroku* [*The Road to Singapore: Diary of an Imperial Guard Soldier*], Tokyo: Sogeisha, 1977.

252 *Russell-Roberts had also waited December out ... a month-long retreat.* Russell-Roberts, pp. 34–44.

253 *Men dug trenches and prepared positions ... 'a great box of the best Norwegian sardines.'* Russell-Roberts, pp. 41–44; Ian Morrison is quoted in John Carey (ed.), *The Faber Book of Reportage*, London: Faber and Faber, 1987, pp. 559–561. See also Bayly and Harper, *Forgotten Armies*, pp. 118–121.

254 *'Every day you read the famous phrase' ... stick by them, until the very last.* Lee Kip Lin, interview with National Archives; see also Turnbull, *History of Singapore*, pp. 173–174.

254 *Meanwhile, Singapore's feuding military ... 'launched without a bottom'.* Quoted in Turnbull, *History of Singapore*, p. 176; see also Bayly and Harper, *Forgotten Armies*, pp. 126–127, Farrell, pp. 316–321.

254 *Chapter nine of the confidential Japanese booklet ... 'And the first blow is the vital blow.'* Tsuji, p. 330.

255 *After Kuala Lumpur, Tsuchikane and his unit ... ever closer towards the Causeway.* Frei, pp. 62–66 and 67.

256 *Russell-Roberts and the 5/11 Sikhs ... already in Johor Bahru.* Russell-Roberts, pp. 109–113.

258 *Early on 31 January ... as far away as Raffles Place.* Colin Smith, *Singapore Burning*, London: Viking, 2005, p. 410; Bayly and Harper, *Forgotten Armies*, p. 130.

258 *The Japanese entered Johor Bahru ... 'Certainly we shall conquer.'* Tsuji, pp. 211 and 222.

259 *Tsuji, the otherwise ruthless head ... 'and steel our hearts against compassion ...'* Tsuji, pp. 230–231.

259 *In that same week Russell-Roberts was preoccupied ... they never heard them.* Russell-Roberts, pp. 119–123.

260 *By the beginning of February ... ever-present problem of morale.* See Turnbull, *History of Singapore*, pp. 178–179; Bayly and Harper, *Forgotten Armies*, pp. 136–137; Malcolm H. Murfett, John N. Miksic, Brian Farrell and Chiang Ming Shun, *Between Two Oceans: A Military History of Singapore from First Settlement to Final British Withdrawal*, Oxford: Oxford University Press, 1999, p. 217.

260 *British Hurricane pilot Terence Kelly ... 'it felt a melodramatic moment.'* Terence Kelly, *Hurricane Over the Jungle*, London: William Kimber, 1977, pp. 54, 65–69 and 80–83. One squadron of Hurricanes remained at Kallang until 9 February (bravely supported by its ground crew), until the aerodrome there was so badly damaged it too was ordered to retreat to Palembang.

261 *In the first days of February, Yamashita ... particularly ill for their future.* Smith, pp. 441–442.

261 *Russell-Roberts remembered that he and Ruth ... 'air-raid shelter in London.'* Russell-Roberts, pp. 123–125.

262 *Despite the air raids, the Europeans shopped ... distraction from growing desperation.* See Bayly and Harper, *Forgotten Armies*, pp. 139–140; Barber, pp. 93–94.

262 *The Russell-Roberts spent their precious few days ... a prisoner-of-war camp in Sumatra.* Russell-Roberts, pp. 125–129.

264 *Lieutenant General Arthur Percival, the man responsible ... to the point of appearing indifferent.* See Turnbull, *History of Singapore*, pp. 175–176; Barber, pp. 116–117.

264 *As historian Brian Farrell has written ... had been to no avail.* Murfett et al., pp. 218–222; Percival, especially p. 254.

265 *No wonder historian Mary Turnbull has written ... 'mesmerised into accepting defeat.'* Turnbull, *History of Singapore*, p. 175.

265 *What Percival did do was spread his forces ... a northwest landing was just 'too obvious'.* Barber, pp. 118–119; Smith, pp. 444–446.

265 *As he later explained: 'I had learnt ... 'dealing with the real thing'.* Percival, p. 272.

265 *The night of the 8th had seen chaos descend ... bumped into each other in the dark.* This account is drawn largely from Smith, pp. 457–471.

267 *Such a display earned them ... 'yellow through and through'.* Bayly and Harper, *Forgotten Armies*, p. 133; see also Smith, pp. 468–471.

267 *Again, the defenders' field telephones went down ... stumbled on this tactic by chance.* See Smith, pp. 475–477.

267 *Standing in the midst of this inferno ... trying to find the rest of his company.* Frei, pp. 87–88.

268 *When the commander of the Imperial Guards, General Nishimura ... 'come back and report the facts'.* Tsuji, pp. 243–245.

268 *For his part, Tsuchikane ... their enemy had unaccountably vanished.* Frei, pp. 89–92.

268 *This was the day, writes Farrell ... 'any real grip on their battle'.* Murfett et al., p. 232.

269 *To make matters worse, Percival had by this time ... 'as I should like to see ...'* Smith, pp. 488 and 497–498; Kelly, p. 65.

269 *Percival personally witnessed the extraordinary sight ... on the opposite side of the island.* Percival, p. 277.

269 *Japanese soldiers were given clear strategic objectives ... to the sound of guns.* See Smith, pp. 466–467, 469 and 486–487; Farrell, pp 322–424.

270 *On 10–11 February, at Bukit Chandu ... only one-third came out alive.* Teo Choon Hong, interview with the National Archives of Singapore, quoted in Tan Beng Luan, *The Japanese Occupation, 1942–1945: A Pictorial Record of Singapore During the War*, Singapore, Times Editions, 1996, p. 42; see also Bayly and Harper, *Forgotten Armies*, pp. 136–138 and Smith, p. 457.

271 *Daylight on the 10th: Tsuchikane and his platoon ... exhausted, relieved, a survivor.* Frei, pp. 91–97 and 131–138.

274 *Before noon, two uniformed British officers ... pose for snapshots.* For a detailed account of this journey see Barber, pp. 223–225.

275 *Not long after, Churchill addressed ... 'Singapore has fallen.'* Winston Churchill, 'Prime Minister Winston Churchill's Broadcast on the State of War', 15 February 1942. <http://www.ibiblio.org/pha/policy/1942/420215a.html> Accessed on 31 March 2009.

275 *Historians have pored over the reasons ... 'a very British disaster'.* As labelled by Tim Harper in *Forgotten Armies*, p. 106. For a comprehensive study of the reasons for Singapore's fall see Farrell, and also Karl Hack and Kevin Blackburn, *Did Singapore Have to Fall?: Churchill and the Impregnable Fortress*, London: Routledge, 2004.

SYONAN

278 *During the last days of the battle ... prepare for their internment.* See Bayly and Harper, *Forgotten Armies*, pp. 138–141 and 149; Barber, *Sinister Twilight*, pp. 211 and 219–220.

278 *There were the inevitable episodes of frenzy ... a self-induced shoot-out.* See Bayly and Harper, *Forgotten Armies*, p. 149 and 209; Barber, *Sinister Twilight*, pp. 206–207 and 197–98; H. R. Oppenheim, quoted in Bayly and Harper, *Forgotten Armies*, p. 151.

278   *Then, there come the scenes of terror ... sanctuary of the countryside.*
      See Bayly and Harper, *Forgotten Armies*, p. 145; Barber, *Sinister
      Twilight*, pp. 193–194 and 213–215.

279   *'The inhabitants of Syonan woke up ... a month after the British
      surrender.'*   Charles Nell, 'A Month in Retrospect', *Syonan Times*, 16
      March 2602 (1942), quoted in Paul Kratoska, *The Japanese Occupation
      of Malaya: A Social and Economic History*, Honolulu: University of
      Hawaii Press, 1997, p. 46.

280   *'There was no shelling' ... 'on all front doors.'*   Lee Kip Lin, interview
      with National Archives; Elizabeth Choy, interview with National
      Archives; Low Ngiong Ing, *When Singapore Was Syonan-To*,
      Singapore: Eastern Universities Press, 1973, p. 2.

280   *There, Japanese soldiers, besides looting property ... chilling foretaste
      of what was to come.*   See Bayly and Harper, *Forgotten Armies*, pp.
      208–210; Lee Geok Boi, *The Syonan Years: Singapore under Japanese
      Rule, 1942–1945*, Singapore: National Archives of Singapore/Epigram,
      2005, pp. 54–56; Turnbull, *History of Singapore*, p. 189.

282   *Lady Daisy Thomas, wife of the British governor ... 'jumped up and
      down and laughed.'*   Brian Montgomery, *Shenton of Singapore:
      Governor and Prisoner of War*, Singapore: Times Books International,
      1984, p. 149; Mary Thomas, *In the Shadow of the Rising Sun*,
      Singapore: Maruzen Asia, 1983, pp. 49 and 51.

282   *For Mary Thomas, another female internee ... 'ordinary standards of
      European activity'.*   Thomas, p. 49.

283   *Denis Russell-Roberts, now one of those interned ... 'and that is an
      unpleasant experience'.*   Russell-Roberts, p. 187.

284   *Mustapha Hussain (the Malay nationalist and KMM leader ... to haunt
      him the rest of his life.*   Mustapha Hussain, pp. 227–232 and 249.

286   *On his way to Singapore, Mohan Singh ... crowd of over 40,000.*
      Bayly and Harper, *Forgotten Armies*, p. 147.

286   *Listening to Mohan Singh ... New Guinea, where a great number
      perished.*   John Baptist Crasta, *Eaten by the Japanese*, Singapore:
      Raffles, 1999, pp. 21–30 and 33.

287   *Some soldiers imagined they had joined ... patriotism might speak out
      but pragmatism ruled.*   See Colonel P. K. Saghal, interview with the
      National Archives of Singapore; Bayly and Harper, *Forgotten Armies*,
      pp. 255–256.

288   *In Mohan Singh's case, however ... first on Pulau Ubin, then in
      Sumatra.*   See ibid., pp. 257–258.

288   *'Speculation was rife' ... 'We guessed and guessed.'*   Low, p. 14.

288   *Yap Yan Hong, then 24 ... 'to take a deep breath again.'*   Yap Yan
      Hong, interview with the National Archives of Singapore.

290   *Yet the actual number killed ... around 50,000 had perished.*
      Shinozaki Mamoru, *Syonan, My Story: The Japanese Occupation
      of Singapore*, Singapore: Times Books International, 1992, p. 24;
      Cheah Boon Kheng, 'Japanese Army Policy toward the Chinese and
      Malay-Chinese Relations in Wartime Malaya', in Paul Kratoska (ed.),
      Southeast Asian Minorities in the Wartime Japanese Empire, London:
      RoutledgeCurzon, 2002, pp. 102–103; Karl Hack and Kevin Blackburn,
      Did Singapore Have To Fall?: Churchill and the Impregnable Fortress,
      London: RoutledgeCurzon, 2004, p. 171. During the post-war claims
      for reparations from the Japanese, the Singapore Chinese Chamber of
      Commerce gave a figure of 40,000 killed (Lee Geok Boi, p. 110).

290   *At some centres men were interviewed ... it could run for up to six
      days.*   See Lee Kip Lin, interview with National Archives; Low, p. 15.

290   *Reports later emerged of the presence ... signed his name in English.*
      Kratoska, *The Japanese Occupation of Malaya*, p. 97; Low, p. 16; Bayly
      and Harper, *Forgotten Armies*, pp. 211–213.

291   *To complete the screening ... 'do no more mischief.'*   See Turnbull,
      History of Singapore, pp. 189–191; Frei, pp. 147–149, 150–151 and
      156–157; Low, p. 47.

293   *Various accounts exist of what happened next ... 'to protect the
      Chinese community.'*   Shinozaki, p. 27; see also Bayly and Harper,
      Forgotten Armies, pp. 214–215.

293   *'I did not bother to find out ... "go about his business without
      hindrance."'*   Shinozaki, p. 19.

293   *As Low Ngiong Ing vividly recalled ... China's war against Japan.*
      Low, p. 50.

294   *'In the past we were running-dogs' ... 'and drunk most of the time.'*
      See Bayly and Harper, *Forgotten Armies*, pp. 215–217; Low, p. 54–55;
      Yap Pheng Geck, p. 67.

295   *Oral history interviews kept in Singapore's National Archives ... to
      generate deep resentment.*   See, *inter alia*, interviews by the National
      Archives of Singapore with Liaw Ching Sing, Lim Soo Gan, Lee Mun Hee.

295   *As Eurasian doctor Dr Farleigh Arthur Charles Oehlers ... 'had come
      and occupied Singapore?'*   Dr F. A. C. Oehlers, interview with the
      National Archives of Singapore, quoted in Tan Beng Luan, p. 94.

296   *In early September 1942, Indian labourers ... 'the founder of this
      settlement.'*   'Raffles Statue Being Removed to Museum', *Syonan
      Times*, 9 September 1942; see also ibid., 13 September 1942.

297   *'We [the Japanese] ... hope to promote ... New Order and the
      Co-prosperity Sphere.'*   *Syonan Times*, 21 February 1942, cited in
      Kratoska, *The Japanese Occupation of Malaya*, p. 45.

297   *'Let Asia greet the Rising Sun ... Tread gloriously their destined way'.*
      This is a loose translation of the Occupation-era song in Malay,
      'Lenkongan Kemamoran Bersama Di-Asia Timor Raya'. The original
      song sheet is on display in the National Museum of Singapore.

297   *As the Syonan press described it ... 'the haughty and cunning British'.*
      Quoted in Turnbull, *History of Singapore*, p. 192.

297   *From late February 1942, the Syonan Times ... 'well assimilated
      with Nippon sentiments'.*   Lee Geok Boi, pp. 177–181 and 192–193;
      Kratoska, *The Japanese Occupation of Malaya*, pp. 141–142; Bayly and
      Harper, *Forgotten Armies*, pp. 319–320.

298   *While most Chinese-language institutions remained closed ... the
      direction of the Emperor's imperial palace.*   Lee Geok Boi, pp. 181 and
      182; Kratoska, *The Japanese Occupation of Malaya*, pp. 136.

300   *Japanese holidays now became Syonan holidays ... future celebrations
      of national independence.*   Lee Geok Boi, p. 189; Kratoska, *The
      Japanese Occupation of Malaya*, pp. 137 and 138.

300   *But the daily ritual that everyone obeyed ... a slapping, a beating or
      worse.*   Kratoska, *The Japanese Occupation of Malaya*, pp. 135.

300   *Compared with the 72,000 students ... fell dramatically from 1944.*
      Turnbull, *History of Singapore*, p. 202; Kratoska, *The Japanese
      Occupation of Malaya*, p. 124.

301   *It was Japan that undertook the first ever registration ... had hardly
      seemed likely.*   See Bayly and Harper, *Forgotten Armies*, pp. 226–229;
      on earlier Malay education see this volume, chapter 17.

302   *Nonetheless, his message during his first speech at the Padang ... 'in
      India's First War of Independence in 1857.'*   Subhas Chandra Bose,
      Chalo Delhi: Writings and Speeches, 1943-45, Delhi: Permanent Black,
      2007, pp. 45–50 and 51–54.

302   *Rasamma Bupalan, then only 16 years old ... any public expression
      of anti-British sentiment.*   Rasamma Bhupalan, interview with the
      National Museum of Singapore, 2006.

303   *The then 17-year-old Janaki Thevar ... 'this chain of Indian slavery.'*
      Penang Shimbun, 22 February 2604 (1944), cited in Kratoska, *The
      Japanese Occupation of Malaya*, pp. 107–108.

303   *As Janaki explained ... an effect 'just like wildfire.'*   Janaki Thevar,
      interview with the National Museum of Singapore, 2006; Rasamma
      Bhupalan, interview with National Museum.

304   *But after an arduous journey ... 'And we wept.'*   Rasamma Bhupalan,
      interview with National Museum.

305   *Japan's demand for propaganda ... a kind of Malay artistic mecca*
      See Bayly and Harper, *Forgotten Armies*, pp. 317–318.

306   *Like other Malay Syonan periodicals ... the average Japanese censor.*
      See John A. Lent, 'Malaysia's National Language Mass Media: History
      and Present Status', in *Southeast Asian Studies*, 15(4):598–612, 1978;
      Bayly and Harper, *Forgotten Armies*, pp. 317–318.

306   *'I glance at a beggar of my people ... Should find purpose in a
      destiny'.*   Masuri S. N., *Awan Putih: Kumpulan Sajak-sajak 1944–1951*
      [*White Cloud: Collection of Poems 1944–1951*] (5th ed.), Singapore:
      Penerbit Pustaka Nasional, 1975 (originally published in 1958), p. 5.
      This English translation is by Ibrahim Tahir and Iskander Mydin.

307   *As former middleman Ng Seng Yong described it ... 'to contact
      each other.'*   Ng Seng Yong, interview with the National Archives
      of Singapore, quoted in Kratoska, *The Japanese Occupation of
      Malaya*, p. 168.

307   *The Japanese were in on the game ... summarily executed by
      beheading.*   Lee Geok Boi, pp. 161–162; Kratoska, *The Japanese
      Occupation of Malaya*, p. 169; Kenneth Chia, interview with the
      National Archives of Singapore, quoted in Tan Beng Luan, p. 131.

307   *Coffee beans were soon rationed ... most coffee shops in the city had shut for good.* Kratoska, *The Japanese Occupation of Malaya*, p. 169; see also coffee shop owner Teong Ah Chin's interview with the National Archives of Singapore, quoted in Tan Beng Luan, p. 128.

307   *In response, Japanese propaganda demanded ... high proportion of infants* Lee Geok Boi, pp. 164–172 and 173; Kratoska, *The Japanese Occupation of Malaya*, pp. 276–282; Bayly and Harper, *Forgotten Armies*, pp. 328–329.

309   *Korea, a Japanese colony since 1910 ... as well as from Malaya and Singapore.* Tan Beng Luan, p. 79; Lee Geok Boi, p. 190.

309   *Chin Sin Chong, a Chinese student employed ... they let their prisoners go.* Chin Sin Chong, interview with the National Archives of Singapore, quoted in Tan Beng Luan, p. 78.

309   *In 1946, Ahmad Luthfi published Bangkai Bernyawa ... 'will recognise me" – he said.'* Ahmad Luthfi, *Bangkai Bernyawa*, Singapore: Qalam, 1949, pp. 10–12. This translation is by Ibrahim Tahir.

310   *The Japanese Occupation is estimated ... only 8,500 survived to be repatriated.* Shigeru Sato, 'Economic Soldiers in Java: Indonesian Labourers Mobilised for Agricultural Projects' (p. 129); Henk Hovinga, 'End of a Forgotten Drama: The Reception and Repatriation of Romusha after the Second World War', (pp. 213–214), both in Paul H. Kratoska (ed.), *Asian Labour in the Wartime Japanese Empire: Unknown Histories*, New York: M.E. Sharpe, 2005.

310   *This was the time of the 'mushroom millionaires' ... drinking, flirting and especially gambling.* Kratoska, *The Japanese Occupation of Malaya*, p. 168, Bayly and Harper, *Forgotten Armies*, pp. 330 and 335.

311   *Heng Chiang Ki, then a young canteen worker ... 'how serious you are beaten up.'* Heng Chiang Ki, interview with the National Archives of Singapore, quoted in Kratoska, *The Japanese Occupation of Malaya*, p. 116.

312   *Storekeeper Soon Kim Seng recalled ... 'and detain you indefinitely.'* Soon Kim Seng, interview with the National Archives of Singapore, quoted in Tan Beng Luan, p. 100.

312   *Elizabeth Choy and her husband ... 'hell could be worse than that.'* Choy, interview with National Archives.

314   *Chew Lee Ngor worked in a shop in Kallang ... 'and later hanged. She was young.'* Chew Lee Ngor, interview with the National Archives of Singapore, cited in Tan Beng Luan, p. 171.

314   *He had originally come to Singapore ... 'That's all I remember.'* Chia Chore Seng, interview with the National Archives of Singapore, translated from Chinese by Leow Puay Tin.

315   *The Malayan Communist Party (MCP) had created ... eventual strength of 10,000 guerrilla fighters.* Kratoska, *The Japanese Occupation of Malaya*, pp. 292–293; Bayly and Harper, *Forgotten Armies*, pp. 262–268.

315   *Chia remembered being assigned ... 'anything at all, because I had fired.'* Chia Chore Seng, interview with National Archives.

317   *At the beginning of 1945, the Syonan Shimbun ... 'out of entire East Asia.'* Kratoska, *The Japanese Occupation of Malaya*, p. 146.

317   *Yet the Japanese Occupation of Singapore did not suddenly end ... remained nominally in charge.* Ibid., pp. 299–300.

317   *The British presented the Japanese ... roofs of the customs sheds* Romen Bose, *The End of the War: Singapore's liberation and the aftermath of the Second World War*, Singapore: Marshall Cavendish Editions, 2005, pp. 12, 85 and 87; Kratoska, *The Japanese Occupation of Malaya*, pp. 300 and 305; Lee Geok Boi, p. 272.

318   *A week later, cheering locals ... previous three and a half years* Lee Geok Boi, pp. 278–281; Romen Bose, p. 116; see also Tan Ah Sang, interview with the National Archives of Singapore.

319   *The final Singapore reminscence of the sinister Colonel Tsuji ... 'the principle of government by force.'* Tsuji, p. 281.

MERDEKA

324   *After the MPAJA crossed the Causeway ... 'guttersnipes for doing it for us.'* Bayly and Harper, *Forgotten Wars: The End of Britain's Asia Empire*, London: Allen Lane, 2007, pp. 42–45; Low, p. 130.

324   *His 'Eight-point Programme' ... was the lesser of two evils.* See Bayly and Harper, *Forgotten Wars*, pp. 37–38.

325   *Rice shot up to thirty to forty times ... still only 4.5 ounces (130 grams) per day.* Bayly and Harper, *Forgotten Wars*, pp. 104 and 106; Turnbull, *History of Singapore*, p. 220.

325   *By the end of 1945 ... the island's leading drug dealer.* Bayly and Harper, *Forgotten Wars*, pp. 105–106.

326   *Former Force 136 officer Colonel H. T. Pagden complained ... 'conquered enemy territory.'* H. T. Pagden, cited in 'Mountbatten versus the Generals: British Military Rule of Singapore, 1945–46', *Journal of Contemporary History*, 36(4):638, 2001, cited in Bayly and Harper, *Forgotten Wars*, p. 110.

326   *As historians Chris Bayly and Tim Harper chronicle ... too tempting to let pass.* Ibid., p. 109.

327   *For Lee Kuan Yew, later to become ... 'the most of their temporary authority.'* Lee Kuan Yew, *The Singapore Story: Memoirs of Lee Kuan Yew*, Singapore: Federal Publications, 2000, pp. 89–90.

327   *Indeed, the MCP that emerged from the jungle... in their proletarian imaginations as China.* Bayly and Harper, *Forgotten Wars*, pp. 197–198.

327   *Their celebrations began at the Happy Valley amusement park ... the telephone exchange and the post office.* See ibid., pp. 117–124 and 197–202.

329   *The MDU, so De Cruz remembered ... 'Events began to move so fast.'* Gerald De Cruz, interview with the National Archives of Singapore; on the MDU in general see also Bayly and Harper, *Forgotten Wars*, pp. 199–207 and 362–367.

332   *Watching, sometimes participating and always learning ... not involved in its composition).* See Dennis Bloodworth, *The Tiger and the Trojan Horse*, Singapore: Times Books International, 1986, pp. 19–22: Lee Kuan Yew, *The Singapore Story*, p. 88.

333   *The exact sequence of events ... debated by historians over sixty years later.* For a detailed account of the Emergency's complex beginnings, see Bayly and Harper, *Forgotten Wars*, pp. 411–435.

334   *By 1948, some workers ... took away their right not to.* Turnbull, *History of Singapore*, pp. 227–229; Lee Kuan Yew, *The Singapore Story*, p. 89.

334   *In the same year, a government-commissioned report ... '"industrial troubles would be solvable."'* Stan S. Awbery and Fred W. Dalley, *Labour and Trade Union Organisation in the Federation of Malaya and Singapore*, Kuala Lumpur: Government Press, 1948, p. 6.

335   *'Because I was a girl' ... 'It is for us women to rebel.'* These extracts are taken from Constance Goh's interview in Perdita Huston, *Motherhood by Choice: Pioneers in Women's Health and Family Planning*, New York: Feminist Press, 1992, pp. 57–64; see also Zhou Mei, *A Point of Light: The Life of Family Planning Pioneer, Constance Goh*, Singapore: Yuyue Enterprise, 1997.

338   *Another rebel whose sheer force of personality ... beginning to see the light.* Mrs Mohamed Siraj, interviews with the National Museum (2006) and the National Archives of Singapore.

340   *Many of their demands became crystallised ... had overseen a quiet revolution.* See Phyllis Chew Ghim Lian, 'The Singapore Council of Women and the Women's Movement', in *Journal of Southeast Asian Studies*, 25(1):112–140, 1994.

341   *(in 1957 its population ... exactly 9 per cent Indian).* P. Arumainathan, *Report on the Census of Population 1970 Singapore – Volume I*, Singapore: Department of Statistics, 1973, p. 54.

341   *Though Purcell began by summarising ... with 'some values in common.'* Victor Purcell, 'Singapore Seek a Personality', *The Times*, 4 June 1959.

342   *From 1947, posters began to appear ... appeal only grew more universal.* See Raphael Millet, *Singapore Cinema*, Singapore: Editions Didier Millet, 2006, pp. 11–12 and 35–38.

344   *'Merdeka! People of Singapore!' ... 'And we will get it!'* Chief Minister David Marshall Under the Apple Tree, 21 March 1956, Singapore Radio Malaya Series.

347   *'Anger at the leprous concept' ... 'compatible with human dignity'.* David Saul Marshall, interview with the National Archives of Singapore.

347   *'Hey we are human beings!' ... 'I've got to build up my career'.* Marshall, interview with National Archives; De Cruz quoted in Chan Heng Chee, *A Sensation of Independence: A Political Biography of David Marshall*, Singapore: Oxford University Press, 1984, p. 56.

348   *Marshall's 'I Believe' is a remarkable document ... 'seeking justice in peace for all.'* See Chan Heng Chee, pp. 78–80.

348   *'I was interested in awakening the people' ... 'have about two or three [seats].'* Marshall, interview with National Archives.

349 *Those first few weeks of the Marshall-led Labour Front government ... Marshall did for the rest of his life).* See Chan Heng Chee, pp. 92–93.

350 *'After the first two days of that assembly meeting' ... 'more serious business at hand'.* Lee Kuan Yew, *The Singapore Story*, pp. 198–99 and 213.

350 *'That had been part of our probing' ... thank the maid and leave.* Ibid., pp. 177–178; see also Chan Heng Chee, pp. 75–76.

350 *Marshall was apparently stung ... Lee and his colleagues the advantage.* See Chan Heng Chee, p. 76.

351 *However, this experience opened the eyes ... to build in post-war Britain.* See Lee Kuan Yew, *The Singapore Story*, pp. 140–141.

351 *One afternoon, four men ... 'after meeting at Malaya Hall'.* See ibid., pp. 146–153.

352 *Subsequently, Lee's political circle expanded to include ... the majority of his Oxley Rise circle.* Ibid., pp. 160–161; Lee Kuan Yew, *From Third World to First: The Singapore Story, 1965–2000*, Singapore: Times Editions, 2000, p. 756.

353 *On 13 May 1954, Edwin Thumboo ... 'to the fence of King George V Park!'* Edwin Thumboo, interview with the National Museum of Singapore, 2006.

353 *Their passion and idealism struck a chord ... 'described as operating a 'police state'.* Thumboo reads his poem in the Singapore History Gallery short film *A Gathering Storm*. The *Fajar* article 'Aggression in Asia' was published in the May 1954 edition of the journal (vol. 7).

354 *'The charge is that you sought to bring ... other people should have been prosecuted'.* Edwin Thumboo, interview with National Museum.

354 *'Lim and Fong looked the right type' ... 'demolish the parties that would take office'.* Lee Kuan Yew, *The Singapore Story*, pp. 177–178.

354 *Lee later described his relationship with Lim ... 'if ever asked to do it again'.* Quoted in Bloodworth, pp. 84 and 87.

355 *With both leaders onboard ... 'all these lines were established'.* Quoted in Bloodworth, pp. 50 and 68.

355 *Back in the 1950s, people's first impressions ... 'that flowed in his native Hokkien'.* See Lee Kuan Yew, *The Singapore Story*, p. 186; Bloodworth, p. 67.

355 *During a speech against the registration ... 'fists in the air – shouting, Merdeka'.* Bloodworth, p. 67; Arthur S. W. Lim, quoted in Tan Jing Quee, 'Lim Chin Siong – a Political Life', in Tan Jing Quee and K.S. Jomo (eds.), *Comet in Our Sky: Lim Chin Siong in History*, Selangor Darul Ehsan : INSAN, 2001, p. 65.

356 *As Fong recalled, when in 1950 he and Lim ... 'we had much in common'.* Fong Swee Suan, interview with the National Museum of Singapore, 2006.

356 *To Fong, local Chinese interest ... 'a great encouragement and excitement to us'.* Ibid.; Lim is quoted in Melanie Chew, *Leaders of Singapore*, Singapore: Resource Press, 1996, p. 113.

357 *Fong's first impression of Lee Kuan Yew ... the paper felt unable to say.* Fong, interview with National Museum; Lee Kuan Yew, *The Singapore Story*, pp. 181–182; *The Straits Times*, 28 November 1954, cited in Hussin Mutalib, *Parties and Politics: A Study of Opposition Parties and the PAP in Singapore*, Singapore: Eastern Universities Press, 2003, p. 46.

358 *Han Tan Juan, then a student ... 'the Gemini of the leftist movement'.* 'Riding the Tide of Idealism: An Interview with Han Tan Juan', Chiang Wai Fong (trans.), in *Tangent*, 6, 2003.

359 *At this time, Marshall publicly expressed ... 'and they must rise and unite'.* See Chan Heng Chee, pp. 98–101, 112n.

360 *'The workers participating in the strikes ... "'hood!", which means "fight".'* 'Riding the Tide of Idealism'.

361 *Marshall later recalled feeling ... '– lonely and lost'.* Marshall, interview with National Archives.

361 *Businessmen, European expatriates and much ... troops to quell the unrest.* See Bloodworth, p. 118; Chan Heng Chee, p. 113; Marshall, interview with National Archives.

361 *Marshall defended his actions ... 'if they, too, showed fight'.* See Chan Heng Chee, p. 113; Lee Kuan Yew, *The Singapore Story*, p. 204.

361 *From early April until the end ... one labour protest every working day.* Lee Kuan Yew, *The Singapore Story*, p. 210.

361 *To Lee's surprise ... 'the whip or the knife'.* Ibid., pp. 207–208; Chan Heng Chee, p. 106.

362 *One month after Fong's arrest ... 'never take office after it'.* See Chan Heng Chee, p. 113; Bloodworth, p. 123.

362 *It was what historian Karl Hack ... to stand by itself?* Hack, interview with National Museum.

363 *He then went to the Legislative Assembly ... true self-government put in its place.* Quoted in Chan Heng Chee, p. 118.

363 *Pleas came in from around the world ... people had to be turned away.* See ibid., pp. 116–117.

363 *The Party organ* Freedom News *... 'barking at his master'.* Quoted in Bloodworth, p. 122.

363 *Not for the last time, Lee Kuan Yew ... 'I am also not an anti-communist'.* See Chan Heng Chee, p. 125.

364 *On his way to London ... 'so erratic a Chief Minister'.* See ibid., p. 153.

364 *Allegedly, when Marshall gave the merdeka salute ... – to attack the police.* See ibid., pp. 160–161; Lee Kuan Yew, *The Singapore Story*, pp. 226–228; Melanie Chew, p. 117.

365 *In the aftermath of the affair ... 'thin body and no roots'.* Quoted in Lee Kuan Yew, *The Singapore Story*, p. 228.

366 *'I got the impression ... communist position in Singapore.'* Marshall, interview with National Archives.

366 TIME *magazine, in explaining ... 'posed as the prophet of merdeka'.* 'A Time of Lepers', *TIME*, 28 May 1956. <http://www.time.com/time/ magazine/article/0,9171,937381,00.html> Accessed on 16 March 2009.

367 *Britain's offer of internal self-government ... 'I am a missionary of democracy!'* Ibid.; Chan Heng Chee, p. 170.

367 *One of Lee's final acts in Britain ... for his 'political ineptitude'.* See Chan Heng Chee, p. 173; Lee Kuan Yew, *The Singapore Story*, p. 238.

367 *Looking back at his time in office ... a posturing 'flash in the pan'.* Marshall, interview with National Archives.

367 *'[T]he intangible achievement is [the] awakening ... a dignified way of life.'* Ibid.

368 *One night in February 1957 ... not only capitalism, but capitalism, socialism, democracy ....'* *Is Co-Existence Possible*, 27 February 1957, Singapore, Radio Malaya Series. The other participants were Victor Feather (Assistant Secretary of the British Trade Unions Congress), Saul Rose (Fellow of St Anthony's College, Oxford), Frank Sullivan (Editor of Radio Malaya Special News Service) and Vladimir Baum (a Yugoslav journalist).

368 *'[N]either the independence of these territories ... of their own imperialist Communism ...'* *Legislative Assembly Sittings*, 8 February 1956, Singapore, Legislative Assembly Debates Series.

368 *The way Goh Keng Swee told the story ... 'now coming unstuck'.* Quoted in Bloodworth, pp. 134–135.

369 *'When social democrats work with communists,' ... 'and so would the great majority'.* Lee Kuan Yew, quoted in Bloodworth, p. 44 and in his own *Singapore Story*, p. 207.

369 *But it was the sudden and shocking violence ... were now 'two PAPs'.* See Lee Kuan Yew, *The Singapore Story*, pp. 205–206; Bloodworth, p. 115.

370 *To read Lim's own extraordinary memoirs ... 'battle of wits as well as nerves'.* Lim Yew Hock, *Reflections*, Kuala Lumpur: Pustaka Antara, 1986, pp. 12, 51, 91 and 77.

371 *Chinese protesters along with leftist democrats ... 'the letter bomb had not been perfected').* Ibid., pp. 78–79 and 83.

371 *Goh Keng Swee later recalled ... 'who was a party member'.* Quoted in Bloodworth, p. 159.

372 *'I had reports of what had been going on ... in the best interest of Singapore.'* Lim Yew Hock, p. 84.

373 *Lee wrote in his memoirs that he 'calculated' ... led him to this calculation.* Lee Kuan Yew, *The Singapore Story*, p. 269.

373 *Ong Eng Guan, the PAP's candidate for Mayor ... headline the following day.* Ibid., pp. 274–275.

374 *Lee remembered PAP election rallies ... compared to the elections of 1955.* Ibid., pp. 296–298 and 300–304.

374 *In the conventional narrative ... PAP faction was inevitable.* See, inter alia, Lee Kuan Yew, *The Singapore Story*; Bloodworth; Edwin Lee, *Singapore: The Unexpected Nation* Singapore: Institute of Southeast Asian Studies, 2008; John Drysdale, *Singapore, Struggle for Success*, Singapore: Times Books International, 1984.

375 *Lee wrote that some time in March 1958 … real intentions and potential.* Lee Kuan Yew, *The Singapore Story*, pp. 278–283.

376 *In a recent interview, C. C. Chin … 'anti-whatever the system not to their favour.'* C. C. Chin, interview with the National Museum of Singapore, 2006.

377 *Han frankly admitted that in the late 1950s … 'give up on their Allah.'* 'Riding the tide of idealism'.

377 *'While we were in prison … And he agreed!'* Melanie Chew, p. 107.

378 *Then there were those workers workers still holding out … go find respectable jobs.* See for instance the transcript of an interview with G. Kandasamy in the collection of the Ong Teng Cheong Labour Leadership Institute; Koh Chung Sian, interview with the National Archives of Singapore; Chew Choo Keng, interview with the National Archives of Singapore; Fong, interview with National Museum.

NEW NATION

382 *'It was a victory but I was not jubilant,' … 'a blue circle, on a white background.'* Lee Kuan Yew, *The Singapore Story*, p. 306; 'Mr Lee Proclaims Goal For Singapore', *The Times*, 4 June 1959.

382 *That evening Singapore's first elected Prime Minister … 'the work of your government.'* Lee Kuan Yew, *The Singapore Story*, p. 308; Lee Kuan Yew, Speech at Victory Rally at the Padang, 3 June 1959.

382 *As Goh Keng Swee put it … 'the greater the cheers'.* Quoted in Bloodworth, p. 192.

382 *Yet within eighteen months … 'how to run their system.'* 'Example for Capitalists', *TIME*, 7 November 1960. <http://www.time.com/time/magazine/article/0,9171,826695,00.html> Accessed on 16 March 2009.

383 *It was here, so Lee Kuan Yew explained … 'righteousness over evil.'* Lee Kuan Yew, *The Singapore Story*, pp. 313–315 and 305.

383 *As TIME magazine reported … 'or gangland rumble reported.'* 'Chophouse Chopin', *TIME*, 29 June 1959. <http://www.time.com/time/magazine/article/0,9171,864665,00.html> Accessed on 16 March 2009; Lee Kuan Yew, *The Singapore Story*, p. 326.

385 *The government launched a series of clean-up campaigns … 'in order to serve the people'.* Lee Kuan Yew, *The Singapore Story*, p. 322.

385 *Even Lee Kuan Yew himself … anti-'yellow culture' crusade.* Ibid., p. 326.

387 *'Some of the senior officers,' … 'in the interest of all.'* Ibid., p. 319.

387 *In its first three years the HDB … above its 50,000 target.* HDB Annual Report 1 April 1976–31 March 1977, 1977, p. 66. *This, Our Singapore (1)*, 14 May 1963, Singapore, Radio And Television Singapore News And Current Affairs Series; *Towards Tomorrow: Essays on Development and Social Transformation in Singapore*, Singapore: Singapore National Trades Union Congress, 1973, pp. 27 and 29. HDB Annual Report cited in Shee Poon Kim, 'The Evolution of the Political System', in Jon S. T. Quah, Chan Heng Chee & Seah Chee Meow (eds.), *Government and Politics of Singapore*, Singapore: Oxford University Press, 1985, p. 20.

387 *To fulfill the PAP's election pledge … diseases such as tuberculosis.* Singapore Annual Reports for 1955 (p. 44), 1960 (pp. 299 and 301) and 1965 (p. 79).

388 *'Mud everywhere', recalled Yip Yue Wai … 'You sure support Singapore.'* Yip Yue Wai, Chng Suan Lei and Lim Lak Ee, interviews with the National Museum of Singapore, 2006.

389 *Goh later admitted that he had worried … 'known to posterity as "Goh's Folly".'* Radio Programme on 'Focus On Industry', 27 April 1964, Singapore, Radio And Television Singapore News And Current Affairs Series.

389 *As self-governing Singapore's first Minister for Culture … 'negligence to sit back and do nothing …'* S. Rajaratnam, 'Malayan Culture in the Making, Part I', in *Petir*, 3(15), 1960, reprinted in S. Rajaratnam, *The Prophetic and the Political*, Chan Heng Chee & Obaid ul Haq (eds.), Singapore: Graham Brash, 1987, p. 121.

389 *In 1960, the poet and University of Malaya professor … 'pantun competitions and so forth'.* D. J. Enright, *Robert Graves and the Decline of Modernism*, Singapore: Craftsman Press, 1960, p. 4.

390 *In the early 1960s, the government set up … 'and economic problems',* as Lee wrote. Lee Kuan Yew, *The Singapore Story*, p. 321.

390 *Without doubt the PAP's most important new organisation … his affiliation with the PAP government.* See ibid., p. 324; Jackie Sam (ed.), *The first twenty years of the People's Association*, Singapore: The Association, 1980, p. 43.

392 *The Straits Times headlines read … fly high up into the sky* 'OUT– and WHAT A WELCOME', *Straits Times*, 5 June 1959, p. 1; the news footage of 4 June 1959 is featured in the National Museum of Singapore's History Gallery film *Lim and Fong: The Opposition*.

392 *'In 1957 and during the elections before,' … 'there was only one main player.'* Fong, interview with National Museum.

393 *Free at last, Lim and Fong … as 'political quarantine'.* Bloodworth, p. 195.

394 *Later that year, Fong publicly attacked the PAP … Deputy Prime Minister Toh Chin Chye's office).* 'Example for Capitalists'.

394 *Ong Eng Guan was someone Lee Kuan Yew … essential to the government's social programme.* See Lee Kuan Yew, *The Singapore Story*, pp. 274–277 and 335; Bloodworth, p. 215.

395 *In July 1961, the seat of Anson … 'you think we are. Resign!'* Quoted in Bloodworth, pp. 229 and 233.

396 *In a luncheon speech to foreign journalists … 'political and economic cooperation'.* See Tan Tai Yong, *Creating Greater Malaysia: Decolonisation and the Politics of Merger*, Singapore: Institute of Southeast Asian Studies, 2008, p. 4.

396 *Still mulling over their response … and refrained from violence.* For a full account of this meeting see 'Note by the office of the UK Commissioner General …', 18 July 1961 (CO 1030/1149, no 127e) in A. J. Stockwell (ed.), *Malaysia: British Documents on the End of Empire*, Series B vol. 8, London: Stationery Office, 2004, pp. 145–147. Often, the second part of this conversation is overlooked. Apparently, Selkirk then told his guests that for Singapore to survive it would need economic stability and he asked Lim and Fong whether they were communists. The Colonial Office report of the meeting reads: 'They [Lim and Fong] seemed to be embarrassed by this question and failed to give a clear reply. Mr Woodhull, on the other hand, stated categorically that he was not a communist'.

396 *The 'Eden Hall Tea Party' … 'anyone else in Singapore.'* See Lee Kuan Yew, *The Singapore Story*, pp. 373–383; Turnbull, *History of Singapore*, p. 271; Bloodworth, pp. 235–238, Stockwell, pp. 146–147.

397 *Any glance through Colonial Office reports … were devious.* For more on such deviousness see the chapters by Tim Harper and Greg Poulgrain in Tan and Jomo (eds.), pp. 3–55 and 114–124; see also Stockwell (ed.).

398 *Lim once more denied the allegation … 'for that matter anybody's front-man'.* Quoted in Lee Kuan Yew, *The Singapore Story*, p. 378.

398 *These days, old Barisan veterans … a 'democratic, non-Communist, socialist Malaya'.* Tan Jing Quee, Lim Hock Siew and Lim Chin Joo, interviews with the National Museum of Singapore, 2007; Tan and Jomo (eds.), pp. 81–82.

398 *Soon after, as Goh Keng Swee recalled … in the first place.* See Bloodworth, pp. 243–244.

399 *As party stalwart Lee Khoon Choy explained … 'whatever facilities it had'.* Quoted in Bloodworth, p. 257.

399 *In his memoirs, Lee recorded … win a political fight.* See Lee Kuan Yew, *The Singapore Story*, p. 390.

399 *So, during the first twelve months … from the public sector.* For a more detailed account of such tactics see Bloodworth, pp. 257–258.

400 *The mutiny of the Work Brigade … sending in the students' parents instead.* See ibid., pp. 243–245 and 254–255; Lee Kuan Yew, *The Singapore Story*, p. 409.

400 *Their timing confirmed Lee's … unable to control.* Bloodworth, p. 255, Lee Kuan Yew quoted in Albert Lau, *A Moment of Anguish: Singapore in Malaysia and the Politics of Disengagement*, Singapore: Times Academic Press, 1998, p. 45.

400 *On 13 September 1961, the Prime Minister … 'they, the communists, must lose'.* Lee Kuan Yew, *The Singapore Story*, p. 394.

401 *To schoolboy Cheong Yip Seng … 'This was life and death for Singaporeans.'* Quoted in ibid., p. 398.

401 *Lee himself wrote: 'By the end' … 'I would not stand a chance'.* Ibid., pp. 398–399.

402 *The Barisan responded by demanding … who was being sincere.* See Tan Tai Yong, pp. 76–77; Lim Hock Siew, interview with National Museum; Lim Chin Siong's speech is quoted in Edwin Lee, pp. 193–194.

402 *Dr Lee Siew Choh, the Barisan leader … Merger proposal as 'absolute nonsense'.* See Bloodworth, pp. 258–259; Tan Tai Yong, pp. 94–95 and 77–78.

403 *The Barisan subsequently clarified ... not legal status.* Dr Lee Siew Choh, quoted in Bloodworth, p. 260; Lim Hock Siew, interview with National Museum; see also Tan Tai Yong, pp. 105–108.

405 *Prime Minister Lee countered ... stood to lose their citizenship.* See Bloodworth, pp. 261–263.

405 *As Goh Keng Swee later put it ... 'a position of total collapse'.* Quoted in Bloodworth, p. 262.

405 *'There was a knock on the door ... I realised I was being sent to Malaysia.'* Fong, interview with National Museum.

406 *The Tunku believed Singapore's Prime Minister ... they awaited some clear pretext for doing so.* See 'Selkirk to Sandys', 5 October 1962 (CO 1030/1036 no 152) and 'Sandys to Selkirk', 12 December 1962 (CO 1030/1160 no 46), in Stockwell (ed.), pp. 396–400 and 407–408; see also Lee Kuan Yew, *The Singapore Story*, pp. 470–472, and Tim Harper, 'Lim Chin Siong and the "Singapore Story"', in Tan and Jomo (eds.) *Comet*, pp. 37–41.

406 *It was enough to satisfy the British ... still demanded appeasement.* See 'Selkirk to Sandys', 14 December 1962 (CO 1030/1160 no 56) and 'The communist conspiracy – paper authorised by the Internal Security Council of Singapore, accounting for operation "Cold Store", 1 February 1963 (CO 1030/1577, no E/99 in Stockwell (ed.), pp. 408–410 and 432–439; see also Harper, 'Lim Chin Siong', pp. 41–45. Toh Chin Chye is quoted in Bloodworth, p. 231.

406 *'The government's got to do the job ... a few gold coins in the pocket.'* Footage of these speeches is featured in the National Museum of Singapore's Singapore History Gallery.

407 *'[T]he people would cheer and boo ... You couldn't help it.'* Quoted in Bloodworth, p. 280. Judy Bloodworth was the Chinese wife of Dennis Bloodworth.

407 *He later recalled in a speech ... 'a kind of political pop star!'* Sam (ed.), p. 11; Lee Kuan Yew, *The Singapore Story*, p. 488.

407 *Concerned with how fierce ... calm, collected and natural.* Lee Kuan Yew, *The Singapore Story*, p. 492. From 1959, Hugh Burnett hosted the groundbreaking television show *Face to Face*.

408 *Remembered Dr Lee Siew Choh ... 'completely occupied with the trial'.* Quoted in Lau, p. 31.

408 *The Plebian, Barisan's newsletter ... and sometimes physically assaulted.* See ibid., pp. 31–32; Bloodworth, pp. 282–284.

409 *The Australian High Commission told Canberra ... a new Barisan government.* See Lau, pp. 45–48.

410 *'Riots or big-scale disturbances take place' ... 'It is very cruel.'* Melanie Chew, pp. 113–119.

411 *A sizeable minority ... Barisan members in Singapore put it.* Lim Hock Siew, interview with the National Museum of Singapore.

411 *At around 3 p.m. on that day ... an interview with one of the victims' family.* Charles Tan Kok Siew, interview with National Museum.

412 *'There were two men on a log' ... 'I would say, normal.'* Edward Scully, interview with the National Museum of Singapore, 2006.

413 *For historian Anthony Reid ... 'they had to stick together'.* Anthony Reid, interview with National Museum.

414 *Looking back at Merger, Lee Kuan Yew recalled ... to work in concert.* Lee Kuan Yew, *The Singapore Story*, pp. 542 and 519.

414 *By this decision, so UMNO claimed ... 'sweep throughout Malaysia'.* Quoted in Lau, p. 110.

415 *Lee blamed the defeat on logistics ... strong Malaysian grassroots.* Lee Kuan Yew, *The Singapore Story*, pp. 546–547.

415 *Lee wrote afterwards ... 'the fire of Malay communalists.'* Ibid., p. 602.

415 *'I can never forget that scene' ... 'in angry mood, you see'.* Othman Wok, interview with the National Museum of Singapore, 2006.

415 *Almenoar told the crowd that Allah ... 'This is the teaching of Islam.'* See Lau, pp. 162–163.

416 *'And as our contingent passed' ... 'more people were killed that morning.'* Othman Wok, interview with National Museum.

417 *To Lee Kuan Yew ... 'the blurring of the racial divide.'* Lee Kuan Yew, *The Singapore Story*, p. 563.

417 *In March 1964 the headlines in the* Utusan *... 'as step children' read another headline.* Quoted in ibid., pp. 551–556.

418 *On the 12th, Albar made ... 'Othman Wok and Lee Kuan Yew.'* See ibid., p. 554; Lau, pp. 146–153.

418 *Lee's earlier explanation ... 'if we pretended they did not exist'.* See Lee Kuan Yew, *The Singapore Story*, pp. 553–556 and 584–585.

418 *One day, Lee looked out of his office window ... 'more mosquitoes, more beggars'.* See ibid., p. 579; see also p. 512.

419 *In early 1965, discussions began ... 'a crusade to preach interracial unity'.* See ibid., pp. 616–620.

419 *Lee's involvement in the Convention ... 'a separation or a collision'.* See Lau, pp. 227–234 and 246; Lee Kuan Yew, *The Singapore Story*, pp. 584–85, 591 and 634.

420 *His talk of a 'Malaysian Malaysia' ... his last speech in the Federal Parliament.* See Lau, pp. 244–248; Lee Kuan Yew, *The Singapore Story*, p. 613.

420 *On this occasion, he challenged ... 'their problem has been resolved ...'* Quoted in Lee Kuan Yew, *The Singapore Story*, pp. 612–613; see also Lau, pp. 246–248.

420 *In the early morning hours of 7 August 1965 ... to add their signatures.* See Lee Kuan Yew, *The Singapore Story*, pp. 638–645.

423 *As the cameras rolled ... 'SINGAPORE IS OUT!'* Press conference given by Lee Kuan Yew at Broadcasting House, Singapore, 9 August 1965. (Footage from this press conference is featured in the National Museum of Singapore's History Gallery film *Point of Separation*); *The Straits Times*, 10 August 1965.

423 *For Goh Keng Swee, the challenges ... water had to be imported.* Quoted in Melanie Chew, p. 142.

EPILOGUE

425 *'Friends and fellow-citizens ... ten years of Singapore's history.'* Lee Kuan Yew, 'Speech at the National Day Rally at the National Theatre', 17 August 1975.

426 *'When we borrow from the World Bank ... we pay the going market interest rate.'* Ibid., 1975.

426 *In a speech to school principals ... 'the survival of the individual'.* Lee Kuan Yew, 'New Bearing in our Education System [an address by the Prime Minister to Principals of Schools of Singapore]', 29 August 1966, p. 9.

427 *Excerpts included: 'Human beings have ... 'ensures internal cleanliness ...'* Quoted in T. J. S. George, *Lee Kuan Yew's Singapore*, London: Deutsch, 1973, p.134.

427 *Although suicide and drug-taking ... 'then they become true blood brothers'.* For a contemporary study of these problems see Leong Choon Cheong, *Youth in the Army*, Singapore: Federal Publications, 1978; Rajaratnam's quote is from his speech at Kampong Glam Community Centre, 1 September 1967, cited in *The Mirror: A Weekly Almanac of Current Affairs*, 37(3), 11 September 1967, p. 4.

428 *As Lee told the International Press Institute ... 'purpose of an elected government'.* Lee Kuan Yew, 'Address to the General Assembly of the International Press Institute at Helsinki', 9 June 1971.

428 *A 'special report' ... 'depressing climate of intellectual sterility'.* James Morgan, 'Singapore – Lessons of press crisis in struggle for balanced society', *The Times*, 9 August, 1971; Goh Keng Swee as quoted in Turnbull, *History of Singapore*, p. 317.

429 *Some people bemoaned ... the length and breadth of the island.* Such diverse reactions are characteristic of numerous oral history interviews held in the National Archives of Singapore, a selection of which are featured in the Singapore History Gallery film *HDB Tales*.

429 *As Lee told the nation in 1975 ... 'traffic jams, homes, new factories'.* Lee Kuan Yew, 'Speech at the National Day Rally', 1975.

430 *In 1972, Lee could tell the nation ... 'is always going to be up the escalator.'* Lee Kuan Yew, 'Prime Minister's Eve of National Day Message', 1972; Lee Kuan Yew, 'Speech at the National Day Rally', 1975.

430 *In 1966, the government launched ... 'the New York of Malaysia.'* Housing and Development Board, *50,000 up: homes for the people*, Singapore: Housing and Development Board, 1966, p. 84, cited in Kwek Mean Luck, 'Singapore: A Skyline of Pragmatism', in Ryan Bishop, John Phillips and Yeo Wei-Wei (eds.), *Beyond Description: Singapore Space Historicity*, London: Routledge, 2004, p. 114.

430 *The same year, Lee told school principals ... 'a people capable of cohesive action ...'* Lee Kuan Yew, 'New Bearing in our Education System', p. 3.

430 *Two years later, Rajaratnam went further ... 'the present generation with future generations.'* S. Rajaratnam, 'Speech at the opening of the 6th Asian Advertising Congress at the Singapore Conference Hall', 1 July 1968.

Bibliography

Abdullah Abdul Kadir, Munsyi. *The Hikayat Abdullah: The Autobiography of Abdullah bin Abdul Kadir (1797–1854)*. A. H. Hill (trans.). Singapore: Oxford University Press, 1985 (first published in 1955). Abu Talib Ahmad and Tan Liok Ee (eds.). *New Terrains in Southeast Asian History*. Singapore: Singapore University Press, 2003.

Afonso D'Albuquerque. *Commentaries of the Great Afonso D'Albuquerque*. Walter de Gray Birch (ed.). London: Hakluyt Society, 1875 (originally published in Lisbon: Barreyra, 1557).

Ahmad Luthfi. *Bangkai Bernyawa*. Singapore: Qalam, 1949.

Ali Haji ibn Ahmad, Raja. *The Precious Gift (Tuhfat al-Nafis)*. Virginia Matheson and Barbara Watson Andaya (trans.). Kuala Lumpur: Oxford University Press, 1982.

Anderson, Benedict. *Imagined Communities: Reflections on the Origin and Spread of Nationalism*. London: Verso, 1991.

Awbery, Stan S. and Dalley, Fred W. *Labour and Trade Union Organisation in the Federation of Malaya and Singapore*. Kuala Lumpur: Government Press, 1948.

Ban Kah Choon. *Absent History: The Untold History of Special Branch Operations in Singapore, 1915–1942*. Singapore: SNP Media, 2001.

Barber, Noel. *Sinister Twilight*. London: Arrow Books, 1988 (originally published in London, Collins, 1968).

Barber, Noel. *The Singapore Story from Raffles to Lee Kuan Yew*. London: Fontana, 1978.

Barnard, Timothy (ed.). *Contesting Malayness: Malay Identity Across Boundaries*. Singapore: Singapore University Press, 2004.

Bastin, John (compiler). *Travellers' Singapore*. Kuala Lumpur: Oxford University Press, 1994.

Bastin, John. 'Abdullah vs Siami'. In *Journal of the Malaysian Branch of the Royal Asiatic Society*, 81(1), 2008.

Bastin, John and Winks, Robin (eds.). *Malaysia: Selected Historical Readings*. Nendeln, Liechtenstein: KTO Press, 1979.

Bayly, Christopher and Harper, Tim. *Forgotten Armies: Britain's Asian Empire and the War with Japan*. London: Penguin, 2005 (originally published by Allen Lane, 2004).

Bayly, Christopher and Harper, Tim. *Forgotten Wars: The End of Britain's Asian Empire*. London: Penguin, 2008 (originally published by Allen Lane, 2007).

Beamish, Jane and Ferguson, Jane. *A History of Singapore Architecture: The Making of a City*. Singapore: Graham Brash, 1985.

Bishop, Ryan; Phillips, John and Yeo Wei-Wei. *Beyond Description: Singapore Space Historicity*. London: Routledge, 2004.

Bloodworth, Dennis. *The Tiger and the Trojan Horse*. Singapore: Times Books International, 1986.

Bose, Romen. *The End of the War: Singapore's liberation and the aftermath of the Second World War*. Singapore: Marshall Cavendish Editions, 2005.

Bose, Subhas Chandra. *Chalo Delhi: Writings and Speeches, 1943–45*. Delhi: Permanent Black, 2007.

Boulger, Demetrius Charles. *The Life of Sir Stamford Raffles*. Amsterdam: Pepin Press, 1999 (originally published in 1897).

Boyle, Richard. *B. P. de Silva: The Royal Jeweller of South-east Asia*. Singapore: B. P. de Silva Investments, 1989.

Brown, C. C. (trans.) *Sejarah Melayu, or, Malay Annals: An Annotated Translation*. Kuala Lumpur: Oxford University Press, 1970 (first published in 1953).

Brown, Cecil. *Suez to Singapore*, New York: Random House, 1942.

Buckley, Charles Burton. *An Anecdotal History of Old Times in Singapore, 1819–1867*. Singapore: Oxford University Press, 1984 (originally published in Singapore: Fraser & Neave Ltd., 1902).

Carey, John (ed.). *The Faber Book of Reportage*. London: Faber and Faber, 1987.

Chan Heng Chee. *A Sensation of Independence: A Political Biography of David Marshall*. Singapore: Oxford University Press, 1984.

Chan Kwok Bun and Tong Chee Kiong (eds.). *Past Times: A Social History of Singapore*. Singapore: Times Editions, 2003.

Chan Sucheng. *Asian Americans: An Interpretive History*. New York: Twayne Publishers, 1991.

Chew, Ernest. 'Dr John Crawfurd (1783–1868): The Scotsman Who Made Singapore British'. In *Raffles Town Club*, 8, 2002. <http://www.postcolonialweb.org/singapore/history/chew/chew10.html>, <http://www.postcolonialweb.org/singapore/history/chew/chew11.html>

Chew, Ernest. 'The Man Who Raffles Left Behind: William Farquhar (1774–1839)'. In *Raffles Town Club*, 7, 2002. <http://www.postcolonialweb.org/singapore/history/chew/chew6.html>, <http://www.postcolonialweb.org/singapore/history/chew/chew8.html>

Chew, Melanie. *Leaders of Singapore*. Singapore: Resource Press, 1996.

Chew, Phyllis Ghim Lian. 'The Singapore Council of Women and the Women's Movement'. In *Journal of Southeast Asian Studies*, 25(1), 1994.

Chng, David K.Y. *Heroic Images of Ming Loyalists: A Study of the Spirit Tablets of the Ghee Hin Kongsi Leaders in Singapore*. Singapore: Singapore Society of Asian Studies, 1999.

Chua Ai Lin. 'Negotiating National Identity: The English-Speaking Domiciled Communities in Singapore, 1930–1941'. Unpublished M. Phil. Dissertation, 2001.

Churchill, Winston. 'Prime Minister Winston Churchill's Broadcast on War with Japan'. 8 December 1941. <http://www.ibiblio.org/pha/policy/1941/411208e.html> Accessed on 31 March 2009.

Churchill, Winston. 'Prime Minister Winston Churchill's Review of the War to the House of Commons'. 11 December 1941. <http://www.ibiblio.org/pha/policy/1941/411208f.html> Accessed on 31 March 2009.

Churchill, Winston. 'Prime Minister Winston Churchill's Broadcast on the State of War'. 15 February 1942. <http://www.ibiblio.org/pha/policy/1942/420215a.html> Accessed on 31 March 2009.

Churchill, Winston. *The Second World War* [abridged]. London, 1997.

Crasta, John Baptist. *Eaten by the Japanese*. Singapore: Raffles, 1999.

Crawfurd, John. *Journal of an Embassy to the Courts of Siam and Cochin China*. Kuala Lumpur: Oxford University Press, 1967 (first published in London: Henry Colburn, 1828).

Da Empoli, Giovanni. Lettera di Giovanni da Empoli. Rome: Arti Graphica Scalia, 1970.

Davison, Julian. *One for the Road and Other Stories*, Singapore: Topographica, 2001.

Dixon, Alec. *Singapore Patrol*. London: Harrap, 1935.

Doraisamy Theodore R. (ed.). *Sophia Blackmore in Singapore: Educational and Missionary Pioneer, 1887–1927*. Singapore: Methodist Church of Singapore, 1987.

Drysdale, John. *Singapore, Struggle for Success*. Singapore: Times Books International, 1984.

Earl, George Windsor. *The Eastern Seas, or, Voyages and Adventures in the Indian Archipelago, in 1832-33-34*. London: W. H. Allen, 1837.

Enright, D. J. *Robert Graves and the Decline of Modernism*. Singapore: Craftsman Press, 1960.

Farrell, Brian. *The Defence and Fall of Singapore, 1940–1942*. Stroud: Tempus, 2005.

Frei, Henry. *Guns of February: Ordinary Japanese Soldiers' Views of the Fall of Singapore, 1941–42*. Singapore: Singapore University Press, 2004.

Frost, Mark Ravinder. 'Transcultural Diaspora: The Straits Chinese in Singapore, 1819–1918'. Asia Research Institute Working Paper Series No. 10, 2003.

George, T. J. S. *Lee Kuan Yew's Singapore*. London: Deutsch, 1973.

Hack, Karl and Blackburn, Kevin. *Did Singapore Have To Fall?: Churchill and the Impregnable Fortress*. London: RoutledgeCurzon, 2004.

Hamilton, Alexander. *A New Account of the East Indies*. London: C. Hitch and A. Millar, 1744.

Harper, R. W. E., and Miller, Harry. *Singapore Mutiny*. Singapore: Oxford University Press, 1984.

Harrison, Brian. *Holding the Fort: Melaka Under Two Flags*, Kuala Lumpur: Malaysian Branch of the Royal Asiatic Society, 1986,

Hsu Yun-Ts'iao. 'Singapore in the Remote Past'. In *Journal of the Malaysian Branch of the Royal Asiatic Society*, 45(1), 1973.

Hussin Mutalib. *Parties and Politics: A Study of Opposition Parties and the PAP in Singapore*. Singapore: Eastern Universities Press, 2003.

Huston, Perdita. *Motherhood by Choice: Pioneers in Women's Health and Family Planning*. New York: Feminist Press, 1992.

Jackson, Robert Nicholas. *Pickering, Protector of Chinese*. Kuala Lumpur: Oxford University Press, 1965.

Kelly, Terence. *Hurricane Over the Jungle*, London: William Kimber, 1977.

Kenley, David L. *New Culture in a New World: The May Fourth Movement and the Chinese Diaspora in Singapore, 1919–1932*. London; New York: Routledge, 2003.

Keppel, Henry and Brooke, James. *The Expedition to Borneo of H.M.S. Dido*. Singapore: Oxford University Press, 1991 (originally published 1846).

Kion Chin Eng. 'The Teaching of Kuan Hua in Singapore'. In *Straits Chinese Magazine*, 11(2), 1907.

Koh, Tommy; Auger, Timothy; Yap, Jimmy and Ng Wei Chian (eds.). *Singapore: The Encyclopaedia*. Singapore: Editions Didier Millet/National Heritage Board, 2006, p. 581.

Kratoska, Paul. *The Japanese Occupation of Malaya: A Social and Economic History*. Honolulu: University of Hawaii Press, 1997.

Kratoska, Paul (ed.). *Southeast Asian Minorities in the Wartime Japanese Empire*. London: RoutledgeCurzon, 2002.

Kratoska, Paul (ed.). *Asian Labour in the Wartime Japanese Empire: Unknown Histories*. New York: M.E. Sharpe, 2005.

La Motte, Ellen N. *The Opium Monopoly*, New York: Macmillan, 1920. <http://www.druglibrary.org/Schaffer/history/om/omintro.htm> Accessed on 31 March 2009.

Lau, Albert. *A Moment of Anguish: Singapore in Malaysia and the Politics of Disengagement*. Singapore: Times Academic Press, 1998.

Lee, Edwin. *Singapore: The Unexpected Nation*. Singapore: Institute of Southeast Asian Studies, 2008.

Lee Geok Boi. *The Syonan Years: Singapore under Japanese Rule, 1942–1945*. Singapore: National Archives of Singapore/Epigram, 2005.

Lee Kuan Yew. 'New Bearing in our Education System [an address by the Prime Minister to Principals of Schools of Singapore]'. 29 August 1966.

Lee Kuan Yew. 'Address to the General Assembly of the International Press Institute at Helsinki'. 9 June 1971.

Lee Kuan Yew. 'Prime Minister's Eve of National Day Message'. 1972.

Lee Kuan Yew. 'Speech at the National Day Rally at the National Theatre'. 17 August 1975.

Lee Kuan Yew. *The Singapore Story: Memoirs of Lee Kuan Yew*, Singapore: Federal Publications, 2000.

Lee Kuan Yew. *From Third World to First: The Singapore Story, 1965–2000*, Singapore: Times Editions, 2000.

Lee Poh Ping. *Chinese Society in 19th Century Singapore*. Kuala Lumpur: Oxford University Press, 1978.

Lent, John A. 'Malaysia's National Language Mass Media: History and Present Status'. In *Southeast Asian Studies*, 15(4), 1978.

Leong Choon Cheong. *Youth in the Army*. Singapore: Federal Publications, 1978.

Lim Boon Keng. 'The Role of the Baba in the Development of China'. In *Straits Chinese Magazine*, 7(3), 1903.

Lim Boon Keng. 'Female Education for Straits Chinese'. In *Straits Chinese Magazine*, 11(2), 1907.

Lim, Irene. *Secret Societies in Singapore: Featuring the William Stirling Collection*. Singapore: Singapore History Museum, 1999.

Lim Peng Han. 'Singapore: an Emerging Centre of 19th Century Malay School Book Printing and Publishing in the Straits Settlements, 1819–1899'. In *Biblioasia*, 4(4), 2009.

Lim Yew Hock. *Reflections*. Kuala Lumpur: Pustaka Antara, 1986.

Linehan, W. 'The Kings of 14th Century Singapore'. In *Journal of the Malayan Branch of the Royal Asiatic Society*, 20(2): 64, 1947.

Low Ngiong Ing. *When Singapore Was Syonan-To*. Singapore: Eastern Universities Press, 1973.

Makepeace, Walter; Brooke, Gilbert E. and Braddell, Roland St. J. (eds.). *One Hundred Years of Singapore*. Singapore: Oxford University Press, 1991 (originally published in London: J. Murray, 1921).

Masuri S. N. *Awan Putih: Kumpulan Sajak-sajak 1944–1951 [White Cloud: Collection of Poems 1944–1951]* (5th ed.). Singapore: Penerbit Pustaka Nasional, 1975 (originally published in 1958).

Maxwell, William. *With the 'Ophir' Round the Empire: An Account of the Tour of the Prince and Princess of Wales 1901*. London: Cassell and Co., 1902.

McKeown, Adam. 'Conceptualising Chinese Diasporas, 1842 to 1949'. In *Journal of Asian Studies*, 58(2), 1999.

McNair, J. F. A. *Prisoners Their Own Warders*. London: Archibald Constable and Co., 1899.

Miksic, John N. *Archaeological Research on the 'Forbidden Hill' of Singapore: Excavations at Fort Canning, 1984*. Singapore: National Museum, 1985.

Miksic, John N. and Low, Cheryl-Ann Mei Gek (eds.). *Early Singapore, 1300s–1819: Evidence in Maps, Text and Artefacts*. Singapore: Singapore History Museum, 2004.

Miksic, John N. 'Between Two Mandalas: Singapore, Siam and Java'. Asia Research Institute Working Paper Series No. 51, 2005.

Millet, Raphael. *Singapore Cinema*. Singapore: Editions Didier Millet, 2006.

Milner, Anthony. *The Invention of Politics in Colonial Malaya*. Cambridge: Cambridge University Press, 2002.

Montgomery, Brian. *Shenton of Singapore: Governor and Prisoner of War*. Singapore: Times Books International, 1984.

Moor, J. H. (ed.). *Notices of the Indian Archipelago and Adjacent Countries*, Singapore: 1837.

Moore, Donald and Moore, Joanna. *The First 150 Years of Singapore*, Singapore: Donald Moore Press, 1969.

Muhammad Haji Salleh. *Syair Tantagan Singapura Abad Kesembilan Belas*. Kuala Lumpur: Dewan Bahasa dan Pustaka, 1994.

Murfett, Malcolm H.; Miksic, John N.; Farrell, Brian and Chiang Ming Shun. *Between Two Oceans: A Military History of Singapore from First Settlement to Final British Withdrawal*. Oxford: Oxford University Press, 1999.

Mustapha Hussain. *Malay Nationalism Before UMNO: The Memoirs of Mustapha Hussain*. K. S. Jomo (ed.), Insun Sony Mustapha (trans.). Kuala Lumpur: Utusan, 2005.

Neo Puak Neo. 'Gambling Amongst Our Nyonyas', In *Straits Chinese Magazine*, 11(4), 1907.

Onraet, Rene. *Singapore: A Police Background*. London: Dorothy Crisp and Company, 1947.

Pearson, H. F. *Singapore: A Popular History*. Singapore: Times Books International, 1985 (originally published in Singapore: Eastern Universities Press, 1961).

Percival, Arthur. *The War in Malaya*. London: Eyre and Spottiswoode, 1949.

Proudfoot, Ian. *Early Malay Printed Books*. Kuala Lumpur: University of Malaya, 1993.

Ptak, Roderich. 'Notes on the word "Shanhu" and Chinese coral imports from maritime Asia, c. 1250–1600'. In *China's Seaborne Trade with South and Southeast Asia (1200-1750)*. Aldershot: Ashgate Publishing Limited, 1998.

Quah, Jon S. T.; Chan Heng Chee and Seah Chee Meow (eds.). *Government and Politics of Singapore*. Singapore: Oxford University Press, 1985.

Raffles, Sophia. *Memoir of the Life and Public Services of Sir Thomas Stamford Raffles*. Singapore: Oxford University Press, 1991.

Rajaratnam, S. 'Speech at the opening of the 6th Asian Advertising Congress at the Singapore Conference Hall'. 1 July 1968.

Rajaratnam, S. *The Prophetic and the Political*. Chan Heng Chee and Obaid ul Haq (eds.). Singapore: Graham Brash, 1987.

Read, William H. *Play and Politics: Recollection of Malaya*. London: Wells, Gardner, Darton and Co, 1900.

'Riding the Tide of Idealism: An Interview with Han Tan Juan'. Chiang Wai Fong (trans.). In *Tangent*, 6, 2003.

Roff, William R. *The Origins of Malay Nationalism*. Kuala Lumpur: Oxford University Press, 1994 (originally published in Singapore: University of Malaya Press, 1967).

Rudolph, Jürgen. 'Amusements in the Three "Worlds"'. In Sanjay Krishnan (ed.). *Looking at Culture*. Singapore: Artres Design & Communications, 1996.

Russell-Roberts, Denis. *Spotlight on Singapore*. Isle of Man: Times Press, 1965.

Sam, Jackie (ed.). *The First Twenty Years of the People's Association*. Singapore: The Association, 1980.

Sareen, T. R. *Secret Documents on Singapore Mutiny, 1915*. New Delhi: Mounto Publishing House, 1995.

Savage, Victor R. and Yeoh, Brenda S. A. *Toponymics: A Study of Singapore Street Names*. Singapore: Eastern Universities Press, 2003.

Shinozaki Mamoru. *Syonan, My Story: The Japanese Occupation of Singapore*. Singapore: Times Books International, 1992.

Siddique, Sharon and Purushotam, Nirmala. *Singapore's Little India: Past, Present and Future*. Singapore: Institute of Southeast Asian Studies, 1982.

Singapore 150 Years (150th Anniversary of the Founding of Singapore Commemorative Reprint). Singapore: Times Books International, 1973.

'Singapore Chinese Girls' School'. In *Straits Chinese Magazine*, 3(10), 1899.

'The Singapore Chinese Girls' School (A Historical Sketch)'. In *Straits Chinese Magazine*, 11(4), 1907.

Singapore Free Press.

Singh, Mohan. *Soldier's Contribution to Indian Independence: The Epic of the Indian National Army*. New Delhi: S. Attar Singh, 1974.

Smith, Colin. *Singapore Burning*, London: Viking, 2005.

Song Ong Siang. *One Hundred Years' History of the Chinese in Singapore*. Singapore: Oxford University Press, 1984 (originally published in London: J. Murray, 1923).

Stockwell, A. J. (ed.). *Malaysia: British Documents on the End of Empire*. London: Stationery Office, 2004.

Straits Budget.

Straits Chinese Magazine, 1(3):113, 1897.

Straits Echo.

Straits Times.

Syonan Times.

Tan Beng Luan. *The Japanese Occupation, 1942–1945: A Pictorial Record of Singapore During the War*. Singapore, Times Editions, 1996.

Tan Jing Quee and Jomo, K. S. (eds.). *Comet in Our Sky: Lim Chin Siong in History*. Selangor Darul Ehsan : INSAN, 2001.

Tan Tai Yong. *Creating Greater Malaysia: Decolonisation and the Politics of Merger*. Singapore: Institute of Southeast Asian Studies, 2008.

Tarling, Nicholas. *Piracy and Politics in the Malay World: A Study of British Imperialism in Nineteenth-Century South-East Asia*. Singapore: D. Moore, 1963.

Takaki, Ronald. *Strangers From a Different Shore: A History of Asian Americans*. Boston: Little, Brown and Company, 1989.

Thomas, Mary. *In the Shadow of the Rising Sun*. Singapore: Maruzen Asia, 1983.

Towards Tomorrow: Essays on Development and Social Transformation in Singapore. Singapore: Singapore National Trades Union Congress, 1973.

Trocki, Carl A. *Prince of Pirates: The Temenggongs and the development of Johor and Singapore, 1784–1885*. Singapore: Singapore University Press, 1979.

Trocki, Carl A. *Opium and Empire: Chinese Society in Colonial Singapore, 1800–1910*. New York: Cornell University Press, 1990.

Trocki, Carl A. *Opium, Empire and the Global Political Economy: A Study of the Asian Opium Trade 1750–1950*. New York: Routledge, 1999.

Tsuji Masanobu. *Singapore, 1941–1942: The Japanese Version of the Malayan Campaign of World War II*. Singapore: Oxford University Press, 1988.

Turnbull, C. M. *A History of Singapore, 1819–1988*. Singapore: Oxford University Press, 1989.

Vaughan, J. D. *The Manners and Customs of the Chinese of the Straits Settlements*. Singapore: Oxford University Press, 1985 (originally published in 1879).

Wade, Geoffrey. 'Melaka in Ming Dynasty Texts'. In *Journal of the Malaysian Branch of the Royal Asiatic Society*, 70(1), 1997.

Ward, A. H. C.; Chu, Raymond W. and Salaff Janet (eds.). *The Memoirs of Tan Kah Kee*. Singapore: Singapore University Press, 1994.

Warren, James Francis. *Rickshaw Coolie: A People's History of Singapore, 1880–1940*. Singapore: Oxford University Press, 1986.

Warren, James Francis. *Ah Ku and Karayuki-san: Prostitution in Singapore, 1870–1940*. Singapore: Oxford University Press, 1993.

Wheatley, Paul. *The Golden Khersonese: Studies in Historical Geography of the Malay Peninsula before A.D. 1500*. Kuala Lumpur: University of Malaya Press, 1961.

The William Farquhar Collection of Natural History Drawings. Singapore: Goh Geok Khim, 1999.

Winstedt, R. O. 'Tumasik or Old Singapore'. In *Journal of the Malaysian Branch of the Royal Asiatic Society*, 42(1), 1969.

Wise, Michael and Wise, Mun Him (compilers). *Travellers' Tales of Old Singapore*. Singapore: Times Books International, 1985.

Wong Lin Ken. *The Trade of Singapore, 1819–69*. Singapore: Malayan Branch of the Royal Asiatic Society, 1960.

Wurtzburg, C. E. *Raffles of the Eastern Isles*. Singapore: Oxford University Press, 1984 (originally published in 1954).

Anand A. Yang. 'Indian Convict Workers in Southeast Asia in the Late Eighteenth and Early Nineteenth Centuries'. In *Journal of World History*, 14(2), 2003.

Yap Pheng Geck. *Scholar, Banker, Gentleman Soldier*. Singapore: Times Book International, 1982.

Yeap Chong Leng. 'Lim Boon Keng, Khoo Seok Wan and the Chinese Philomathic Society'. In *Asian Culture*, 27 2003 (in Chinese).

Yen Ching Hwang. *Community and Politics: The Chinese in Colonial Singapore and Malaysia*. Singapore: Times Academic Press, 1995.

Yeoh, Brenda S. A. *Contesting Space in Colonial Singapore: Power Relations and the Urban Built Environment*. Singapore: Singapore University Press, 2003.

Yong, C. F. *Tan Kah Kee: The Making of an Overseas Chinese Legend*. Singapore: Oxford University Press, 1987.

Yong, C. F. and McKenna, R. B. *The Kuomintang Movement in British Malaya*. Singapore: Singapore University Press, 1990.

Zhou Mei. *A Point of Light: The Life of Family Planning Pioneer, Constance Goh*. Singapore: Yuyue Enterprise, 1997.

INTERVIEWS WITH THE NATIONAL MUSEUM OF SINGAPORE

The following were interviewed in 2006/2007 by the National Museum of Singapore. Audio recordings of the interviews can be accessed at the museum's Resource Centre.

- Timothy Barnard
- Peter Borschberg
- C. C. Chin
- Chua Ai Lin
- Mark Emmanuel
- Karl Hack
- Hadijah Rahmat
- Derek Heng
- John N. Miksic
- Anthony Reid
- Geoffrey Wade
- Wang Gungwu
- Ann Wee

The following were interviewed in 2006/2007 by the National Museum of Singapore. Audio recordings of the interviews are featured in the museum's Singapore History Gallery.

- Rasamma Bhupalan
- Chng Suan Lei
- Fong Swee Suan
- Lim Chin Joo
- Lim Hock Siew
- Lim Lak Ee
- Mrs Mohamed Siraj
- Othman Wok
- Edward Scully
- Subbiah Laksmanan
- Charles Tan Kok Siew
- Tan Jing Quee
- Janaki Thevar
- Edwin Thumboo
- Ye Qing and Bai Yan
- Yip Yue Wai

INTERVIEWS WITH THE NATIONAL ARCHIVES OF SINGAPORE

The following were interviewed by the National Archives of Singapore as part of its Oral History Centre's ongoing efforts to document Singapore history. The interviews can be accessed at the Archives' Reading Room.

- Chew Choo Keng
- Chia Chore Seng
- Elizabeth Choy
- Gerald De Cruz
- Koh Chung Sian
- Lee Kip Lin
- Lee Mun Hee
- Leong Ah Hoe
- Liaw Ching Sing
- Lim Soo Gan
- David Saul Marshall
- Mrs Mohamed Siraj
- Colonel P. K. Saghal
- Wong Ah Yoke
- May Wong
- Yap Yan Hong

OTHER MEDIA SOURCES

The following radio and television broadcasts are accessible at the National Archives of Singapore's Reading Room.

- *Chief Minister David Marshall Under the Apple Tree*, 21 March 1956, Singapore Radio Malaya Series.
- *Is Co-Existence Possible*, 27 February 1957, Singapore, Radio Malaya Series.
- *Legislative Assembly Sittings*, 8 February 1956, Singapore, Legislative Assembly Debates Series.

Index

FRONT COVER

1 Thian Hock Keng *NMS*. **2** British Hawker Hurricane *NMS*. **3** City of Singapore coat of arms *NMS*. **4** Singapore flag, National Loyalty Week poster *NMS*. **5** Postcard showing Supreme Court building *Collection of Dr Cheah Jin Seng*. **6** Japanese fighters *NMS*. **7** Riot police *Central Press/Getty*. **8** HMV radio *NMS*. **9** Straits Settlements 10-cent note *NMS*. **10** Information booklet on Merger *NMS*. **11** Pan-Malayan Students' Federation conference booklet *NMS*. **12** Malayan stamp commemorating the coronation of Queen Elizabeth II *Collection of the late Sng Woo Chwee*. **13** Stamp commemorating the State of Singapore's national day on 3 June *EDM Archives*. **14** East India Company half-anna coin *NMS*. **15** Japanese songbook *NMS*. **16** Badge of the Air Raid Precaution wardens *NMS*. **17** Lee Kuan Yew *SPH*. **18** Iranun pirate *NMS*. **19** Tan Kah Kee *NAS*. **20** Sir Frank Swettenham *NAS*. **21** Elizabeth Choy *NAS*. **22** Goh Keng Swee *SPH*. **23** European lady with parasol *NMS*. **24** Lim Yew Hock *Time & Life Pictures/Getty*. **25** R. M. V. Supramanium *S. Subbiah Lakshmanan/NAS*. **26** Balage Porolis de Silva *B. P. de Silva Holdings*. **27** David Marshall *SPH*. **28** Sophia Raffles *NMS*. **29** Syed Mohamed bin Ahmed Alsagoff *Madrasah Alsagoff Al-Arabiah*. **30** Farquhar's silver epergne *NMS*. **31** Lim Boon Keng *NAS*. **32** Mohammed Eunos Abdullah *NAS*. **33** Lim Chin Siong *SPH*. **34** Sir Shenton Thomas *NMS*. **35** William Farquhar *Estate of William Farquhar*. **36** Young Malay girl *NMS*. **37** Sun Yat Sen *NMS*. **38** Dr John Crawfurd *NMS*. **39** Sir Cecil Clementi Smith *NMS*. **40** Tan Tock Seng *NMS*. **41** Lim Bo Seng *NAS*. **42** Indian woman *NMS*. **43** Mustapha Hussain *Courtesy of Mustapha Hussain's daughter*. **44** William Pickering *NAS*. **45** Sir Henry Keppel *NMS*. **46** European woman *NMS*. **47** Malay man with songkok *EDM Archives*. **48** Malay nobleman *NMS*. **49** Chain belt used by a coolie *NMS*. **50** Major-General Sir Dudley Ridout's Commander of the Most Excellent Order of the British Empire medal *NMS*. **51** Charles Burton Buckley *NMS*. **52** May Wong *NMS*. **53** Sir Harry St. George Ord *NMS*. **54** Chinese man in 'Western' clothing *NMS*. **55** Japanese soldier *NMS*. **56** Janaki Thevar *NMS*. **57** Sir Stamford Raffles *NMS*. **58** Malay seaman *NMS*. **59** European man with pith helmet *NMS*. **60** Postcard showing Collyer Quay *NMS*. **61** Tan Kim Seng fountain, Battery Road *NMS*. **62** Hock Lee Bus Company driver badge *NMS*. **63** Fragment of an unglazed bowl *NMS*. **64** Earthenware shards *NMS*. **65** Decorated stoneware jar *NMS*. **66** Lead figurine of a headless rider *NMS*.

back cover
Chinese Peranakan children *NMS*.

page 5
View of Kampong Glam *NMS*.

page 6
The Raffles Library and Museum, predecessor of the National Museum of Singapore *NMS*.

Printed by Star Standard, Singapore

MAJU-LAH SINGAPURA

SUSUN KATA DAN LAGU
OLEH ZUBIR SAID

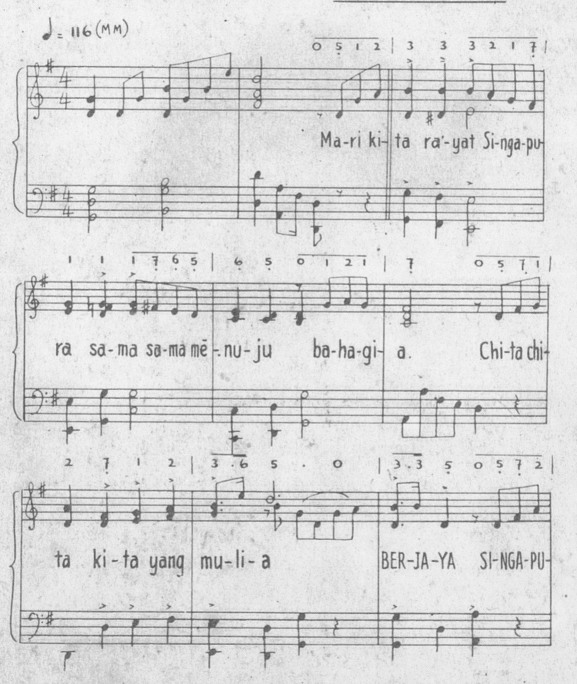